Lecture Notes in Computer Science 6195

Commenced Publication in 1973
Founding and Former Series Editors:
Gerhard Goos, Juris Hartmanis, and Jan van Leeuwen

Lecture Notes in Computer Science 6165

Commenced Publication in 1973
Founding and Former Series Editors:
Gerhard Goos, Juris Hartmanis, and Jan van Leeuwen

Jürgen Münch Ye Yang
Wilhelm Schäfer (Eds.)

New Modeling Concepts for Today's Software Processes

International Conference on Software Process, ICSP 2010
Paderborn, Germany, July 8-9, 2010
Proceedings

Volume Editors

Jürgen Münch
Fraunhofer Institute for
Experimental Software Engineering
Kaiserslautern, Germany
E-mail: juergen.muench@iese.fraunhofer.de

Ye Yang
Institute of Software
Chinese Academy of Sciences
Beijing, China
E-mail: ye@itechs.iscas.ac.cn

Wilhelm Schäfer
Department of Computer Science
University of Paderborn
Paderborn, Germany
E-mail: wilhelm@uni-paderborn.de

Library of Congress Control Number: 2010929804

CR Subject Classification (1998): D.2, F.3, D.3, C.2, D.1, D.2.1

LNCS Sublibrary: SL 2 – Programming and Software Engineering

ISSN 0302-9743
ISBN-10 3-642-14346-6 Springer Berlin Heidelberg New York
ISBN-13 978-3-642-14346-5 Springer Berlin Heidelberg New York

springer.com

Printed in Germany

Typesetting: Camera-ready by author, data conversion by Scientific Publishing Services, Chennai, India
Printed on acid-free paper 06/3180

Preface

2010 was the first time that the International Conference on Software Process was held autonomously and not co-located with a larger conference. This was a special challenge and we are glad that the conference gained a lot of attention, a significant number of contributions and many highly interested participants from industry and academia.

This volume contains the papers presented at ICSP 2010 held in Paderborn, Germany, during July 8-9, 2010. ICSP 2010 was the fourth conference of the ICSP series. The conference provided a forum for researchers and industrial practitioners to exchange new research results, experiences, and findings in the area of software and system process modeling and management.

The increasing distribution of development activities, new development paradigms such as cloud computing, new classes of systems such as cyber-physical systems, and short technology cycles are currently driving forces for the software domain. They require appropriate answers with respect to process models and management, suitable modeling concepts, and an understanding of the effects of the processes in specific environments and domains. Many papers in the proceedings address these issues.

Due to the financial crisis that started in 2008, many software and IT units of organizations have been forced to show their contributions to the business goals of the organization. If software or IT units cannot demonstrate their value with respect to business goals, they are typically seen as cost factors and exposed to risks such as budget cuts or personnel reduction. Therefore, one of the main themes that was addressed at ICSP 2010 was the so-called alignment of processes to an organization's higher-level goals. This includes the strategic alignment of processes to business goals with methods such as GQM+Strategies, but also topics such as the evaluation of processes with respect to their fulfilment of process requirements.

Further trends in the area of software and system processes can be seen with respect to a more careful understanding of planning and re-planning processes, the management of multiple process standards in parallel, the design of process models for large systems of systems, the design of variant-rich processes (also referred to as process lines or process families), the relationship between change management and process improvement, the provision of repositories for reusable simulation model components, and the visualization of software process data. The topics indicate that software process modeling remains a vibrant research discipline of high interest to industry. Emerging technologies and application domains, a paradigm shift to global software and systems engineering in many domains, and the need for a better understanding of the effects of processes are reflected in these papers.

In response to the Call for Papers, 49 submissions were received by authors from Australia, Brazil, Canada, Chile, China, Finland, France, Germany, Ireland, Japan, Mexico, The Netherlands, Spain, Sweden, Switzerland, Turkey, and the USA. Three papers were rejected due to double submissions. The other papers were rigorously reviewed and held to very high quality standards. Due to the high quality of the overall submissions, 31 papers were finally accepted as regular papers for presentation at the conference.

A conference such as this one can only succeed as a team effort. All of this work would not have been possible without the dedication and professional work of many colleagues. We wish to express our gratitude to all contributors for submitting papers. Their work formed the basis for the success of the conference. We would also like to thank the Program Committee members and additional reviewers because their work is the guarantee for the high quality of the conference. Special thanks go to the keynote speakers for giving excellent presentations at the conference. We would also like to thank the members of the Steering Committee, Barry Boehm, Mingshu Lee, Leon Osterweil, David Raffo, and Wilhelm Schäfer, for their advice, encouragement, and support.

We wish to thank the University of Paderborn, the Fraunhofer Institute for Experimental Software Engineering (IESE), the Chinese Academy of Science (ISCAS), and all the other sponsors and supporters for their contributions and for making the event possible. Last but not least many thanks to Jutta Haupt and Jürgen Maniera for the local organization. For further information, please visit the conference website at http://icsp10.upb.de/.

May 2010

Jürgen Münch
Ye Yang
Wilhelm Schäfer

Organization

International Conference on Software Process 2010

Paderborn, Germany
July 8–9, 2010

Steering Committee

Barry Boehm	University of Southern California, USA
Mingshu Li	Institute of Software, Chinese Academy of Sciences, China
Leon J. Osterweil	University of Massachusetts, USA
David M. Raffo	Portland State University, USA
Wilhelm Schäfer	University of Paderborn, Germany

General Chair

Wilhelm Schäfer	University of Paderborn, Germany

Program Co-chairs

Jürgen Münch	Fraunhofer Institute for Experimental Software Engineering, Germany
Ye Yang	Institute of Software, Chinese Academy of Sciences, China

Secretary

Lin Shi	Institute of Software, Chinese Academy of Sciences, China

Program Committee Members

Alexis Ocampo	Ecopetrol, Columbia
Andreas Rausch	Clausthal University of Technology, Germany
Anthony Finkelstein	University College London, UK
Barbara Staudt Lerner	Mount Holyoke College, USA
Barry Boehm	University of Southern California, USA
Casper Lassenius	Helsinki University of Technology, Finland
Cesare Pautasso	University of Lugano, Switzerland
Colette Rolland	University of Paris 1 Pantheon-Sorbonne, France

Dan Houston	The Aerospace Corporation, USA
Dan Port	University of Hawaii, USA
Daniel Rodriguez	University of Alcalá , Spain
Danilo Caivano	University of Bari, Italy
Dennis Goldenson	Carnegie Mellon University, USA
Dewayne E. Perry	University of Texas at Austin, USA
Dietmar Pfahl	Simula Research Laboratory, Norway
Felix Oscar Garcia Rubio	Universidad de La Rioja, Spain
Frank Maurer	University of Calgary, Canada
Guilherme H. Travassos	Federal University of Rio de Janeiro/COPPE, Brazil
Günther Ruhe	University of Calgary, Canada
Hajimu Iida	Nara Institute of Science and Technology, Japan
Jacky Estublier	French National Research Center in Grenoble, France
James Miller	University of Alberta, Canada
Jo Ann Lane	University of Southern California, USA
Juan F. Ramil	The Open University, UK
Jürgen Münch	Fraunhofer Institute for Experimental Software Engineering, Germany
Katsuro Inoue	Osaka University, Japan
Keith Chan	Hong Kong Polytechnic University, Hong Kong
Leon Osterweil	University of Massachusetts, USA
Li Zhang	Beihang University, China
LiGuo Huang	Southern Methodist University, USA
Mercedes Ruiz	University of Cádiz, Spain
Muhammad Ali Babar	IT University of Copenhagen, Denmark
Oscar Dieste	Universidad Politecnica de Madrid, Spain
Paul Grünbacher	Johannes Kepler University Linz, Austria
Paul Wernick	University of Hertfordshire, UK
Pekka Abrahamsson	University of Helsinki, Finland
Qing Wang	Institute of Software, Chinese Academy of Sciences, China
Raymond Madachy	Naval Postgraduate School, USA
Richard W. Selby	University of Southern California, USA
Ross Jeffery	University of New South Wales, Australia
Slinger Jansen	Utrecht University, The Netherlands
Sorana Cimpan	University of Savoie at Annecy, France
Stan Sutton	IBM T.J. Watson Research Center, USA
Stefan Biffl	Technische Universität Wien, Austria
Thomas Birkhölzer	University of Applied Science, Konstanz, Germany
Vahid Garousi	University of Calgary, Canada
Volker Gruhn	University of Leipzig, Germany
Walt Scacchi	University of California, Irvine, USA
Yasha Wang	Peking University, China
Ye Yang	Institute of Software, Chinese Academy of Sciences,China
Yun Yang	Swinburne University of Technology, Australia

External Reviewers

Andrew Tappenden	University of Alberta, Canada
Da Yang	Institute of Software, Chinese Academy of Sciences, China
Gregory Gay	West Virginia University, USA
Juan Li	Institute of Software, Chinese Academy of Sciences, China
Junchao Xiao	Institute of Software, Chinese Academy of Sciences, China
Qiusong Yang	Institute of Software, Chinese Academy of Sciences, China
Jian Zhai	Institute of Software, Chinese Academy of Sciences, China

Table of Contents

Invited Talk

Process Alignment

Process Management

Process Models

Process Representation

Process Analysis and Measurement

Process Simulation Modeling

Experience Reports and Empirical Studies

A Risk-Driven Decision Table for Software Process Selection

Barry W. Boehm

University of Southern California

Abstract. It is becoming increasingly clear that there is no one-size-fits all process for software projects. Requirements-first, top-down waterfall or V-models work well when the requirements can be determined in advance, but are stymied by emergent requirements or bottom-up considerations such as COTS- or legacy-driven projects. Agile methods work well for small projects with emergent requirements, but do not scale well or provide high assurance of critical attributes such as safety or security. Formal methods provide high assurance but are generally expensive in calendar time and effort and do not scale well.

We have developed the Incremental Commitment Model (ICM) to include a set of explicit risk-driven decision points that branch in different ways to cover numerous possible project situations. As with other models trying to address a wide variety of situations, its general form is rather complex. However, its risk-driven nature has enabled us to determine a set of twelve common risk patterns and organize them into a decision table that can help new projects converge on a process that fits well with their particular process drivers. For each of the twelve special cases, the decision table provides top-level guidelines for tailoring the key activities of the ICM, along with suggested lengths between each internal system build and each external system increment delivery. This presentation will provide a summary of the ICM, show how its process decision drivers can generally be determined in the initial ICM Exploration phase, summarize each of the twelve cases, and provide representative examples of their use.

J. Münch, Y. Yang, and W. Schäfer (Eds.): ICSP 2010, LNCS 6195, p. 1, 2010.

Using Process Definitions to Support Reasoning about Satisfaction of Process Requirements

Leon J. Osterweil and Alexander Wise

Department of Computer Science
University of Massachusetts
Amherst MA 01003
{ljo,wise}@cs.umass.edu

Abstract. This paper demonstrates how a precise definition of a software development process can be used to determine whether the process definition satisfies certain of its requirements. The paper presents a definition of a Scrum process written in the Little-JIL process definition language. The definition's details facilitate understanding of this specific Scrum process (while also suggesting the possibility of many variants of the process). The paper also shows how these process details can support the use of analyzers to draw inferences that can then be compared to requirements specifications. Specifically the paper shows how finite state verification can be used to demonstrate that the process protects the team from requirements changes during a sprint, and how analysis of a fault tree derived from the Little-JIL Scrum definition can demonstrate the presence of a single point of failure in the process, suggesting that this particular Scrum process may fail to meet certain process robustness requirements. A new Scrum process variant is then presented and shown to be more robust in that it lacks the single of point failure.

1 Introduction

In earlier work the authors have suggested that software development processes seem to have much in common with application software [1,2]. One similarity was that just as applications are defined using a programming language, so might the processes used to construct such applications also be defined using a *process* programming language. This has led to the development of several such languages, one of which (Little-JIL) is to be described later in this paper [3]. The focus of this paper, however, is on a different similarity, namely that both applications and the processes used to develop them should be designed so as to demonstrably satisfy their requirements. Just as applications must satisfy requirements (e.g. in dimensions such as functionality, speed, responsiveness, robustness, and evolvability), so must development processes also satisfy similar kinds of requirements. For example, software development processes must satisfy speed requirements, namely that they complete within the time limit imposed by customers and users. Development processes also have functional requirements that specify such things as the artifacts they are to produce (i.e. only code, code and design specifications, code and voluminous testing result reports, etc.).

J. Münch, Y. Yang, and W. Schäfer (Eds.): ICSP 2010, LNCS 6195, pp. 2–13, 2010.

This paper suggests the importance of devising a technology that supports the demonstration that software development process implementations meet specified process requirements, and suggests some initial capabilities for supporting that technology. At present the selection of development process approaches to meet process requirements is typically done informally, generally based upon intuition and anecdotal evidence. Thus, for example there is a general understanding that heavyweight processes such as those guided by the application of such approaches as the CMMI [4] can be expected to lead to software products that are relatively more robust, well- documented, and designed for evolvability over a long lifespan. On the other hand such processes seem to be less well-suited to the rapid production of software products, especially those that are not expected to be used for an extended period of time, or evolved in an orderly way. Indeed the popularity of agile approaches [5] seems to have derived largely from a sense that such development processes are more appropriate for the rapid development of software products, especially those that are relatively small, and destined for relatively short lifespans. While there is considerable anecdotal evidence to suggest that these intuitions are well-supported by experience, we suggest that the selection of a software development process should not be left entirely to intuition, and might better be done with at least the support of engineering approaches and technologies.

An essential support for this more disciplined approach to the selection of a software development process would seem to be technology for inferring the properties and characteristics of such processes. This, in turn, would seem to require that these processes be defined with sufficient detail to render them amenable to such analysis. Thus, this paper suggests how to use a process definition as the basis for inferring the properties of a process, so that the inferred properties might be compared to specifications of the requirements that the process is to fulfill.

The example presented in this paper is the use of analyses of a definition of the Scrum software development approach [6] written in the Little-JIL process definition language. Specifically, the paper introduces the Little-JIL language in section 2. In Section 3 Little-JIL is used to define a specific version of the Scrum software development approach. This definition itself is shown to immediately suggest some process properties and characteristics. Section 4 then demonstrates how analysis of the Scrum definition can derive a property that seems suitable for comparison to an expectable type of process requirement. The paper concludes with an evaluation of this process analysis technology in section 6, and a suggestion for future work in section 7.

2 The Little-JIL Process Definition Language

Little-JIL is a process definition language [3] that supports specification of processes involving different agent and non-agent resources. The language is defined through the use of finite state machines, which makes processes defined in Little-JIL amenable to rigorous analysis. Its use of hierarchical decomposition supports the specification of arbitrarily precise process details.

The most immediately noticeable component of a Little-JIL process definition is the visual depiction of the coordination. The coordination specification looks initially somewhat like a task decomposition graph, in which processes are decomposed hierarchically into steps, in which the leaves of the tree represent the smallest specified units of work. The steps are connected to each other with edges that represent both hierarchical decomposition and artifact flow. Each step contains a specification of the type of agent needed in order to perform the task associated with that step. Thus, for example, in the context of a software development process, the agents would be entities such as programmers, testers, managers, the customer, etc. The collection of steps assigned to an agent defines the interface that the agent must satisfy to participate in the process. It is important to note that the coordination specification only includes a description of the external view and observable behavior of such agents. A specification of how the agents themselves perform their tasks (their internal behaviors) is a external to the Little-JIL process definition. Thus, Little-JIL enforces a sharp separation of concerns, separating the internal specification of what a resource is capable of doing and how the agent will do it, from the specification of how agents are to coordinate their work with each other in the context of carrying out the overall process.

While space does not permit a complete description of the language, further explanation of the notation will be provided in the context of the model of the Scrum software development method and interested readers are referred to [3] for a complete description of all of the features of the language.

3 Defining the Scrum Software Development Method

This section describes Scrum, a commonly used approach to the development of software, especially software that must be developed rapidly. Many papers, books, and courses have been developed to explain the Scrum approach, and there have been many additional papers and books written to describe experiences and anecdotes in the use of Scrum[6,7,8,9,10]. The fact that the descriptions of Scrum contained in these many diverse books, papers, and anecdotes are typically informal, and sometimes seem to be inconsistent with each other, has posed problems for those who wish to use Scrum, sometimes leading to uncertainty about whether the process actually being followed can or should be called "Scrum". This lack of rigor and agreement also made it difficult for us to decide just which description of Scrum should form the basis for our own work as described in this paper.

Ultimately, as the goal of this paper is to demonstrate the possibility, and the value, of inferring the properties of a process from the rigorous and precise definition of the process, the specific process definition chosen seemed to be less of an issue than the choosing of some specific process. On the other hand, the work described here does seem to also demonstrate the possibility that our approach of applying a process definition language can also be useful in identifying differences in opinion and interpretation of what is meant by a software development approach such as Scrum, and what the implications of these differences

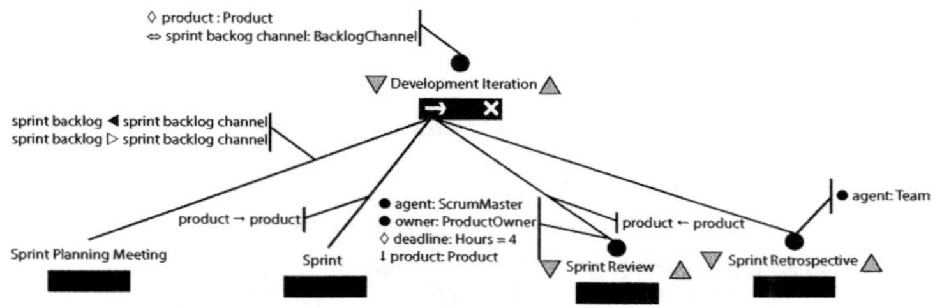

Fig. 1. The Scrum Development Iteration

might be. The Little-JIL definition that is the basis for the work described here is based upon the informal Scrum description provided in [6].

As suggested by the preceding discussion, this process is defined hierarchically. At the highest level, Scrum involves three concurrent activities: the management of the product and release backlogs, and the iterative development of the product. For our example, we elaborate only the heart of the Scrum process: the iterative performance of "sprints." The *Development Iteration* step (Figure 1) specifies how one of these iterations is carried out. An iteration begins with a *Sprint Planning Meeting* to determine the work to be performed during the current iteration. This body of work is represented by the *sprint backlog* artifact and is stored in the *sprint backlog channel* to prevent concurrent updates. The Sprint Planning Meeting step is followed by the *Sprint* step in which the work is actually performed. The iteration concludes with the *Sprint Review* step and the *Sprint Retrospective* step. The Sprint Review step is a time-boxed meeting (note the diamond annotation that specifies a fixed deadline for completion of this step) led by the ScrumMaster agent with the support of the ProductOwner and team as resources. This step takes as an input artifact (note downward arrow annotation) the product artifact that was produced as the output of the Sprint step. The purpose of this Sprint Review step is to enable the team to discuss the results of the preceding sprint, and to close the loop between the product owner and the team. After the Sprint Review step concludes, the Sprint Retrospective is carried out with the team as the agent, indicating that the team meets in private to assess its performance during the last sprint as preparation for the next sprint.

3.1 Sprint

The *Sprint* subprocess (Figure 2) is the activity during which actual development work gets done. To be more precise, the Sprint process consists of 30 (note the 30 annotation on the edge connecting the Sprint parent step to its *Daily Sprint* child step) consecutive (note the right arrow step kind badge in the Sprint step) performances of the Daily Sprint subprocess. As indicated by the = sign badge in the Daily Sprint step, this subprocess is carried out as the parallel performance of its three substeps, *Daily Scrum*, *Work*, and *Revise Sprint Backlog*. Both the

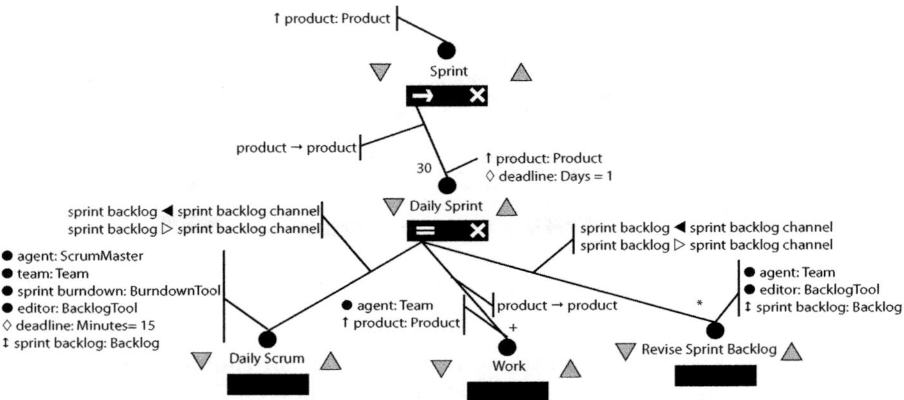

Fig. 2. Elaboration of the Sprint Step

Daily Scrum and the Revise Sprint Backlog steps require both access to, and update capability for, the sprint backlog. These accesses for these two steps are coordinated by using the sprint backlog channel to provide the needed concurrent access permissions.

The Daily Scrum step is a 15 minute (note the specification of this deadline by means of the diamond annotation) progress meeting during which the team meets to assess their progress. Note that the sprint backlog artifact is passed in as a parameter, and then also passed out of this step, after which it is written to the sprint backlog channel so that it is made available to the Revise Sprint Backlog step, which may be executing in parallel.

In addition to the execution of the Daily Scrum step, there are multiple performances of the Work step (note the + sign on the edge connecting the Work step to its parent). Each instance of the Work step produces a new version of the product artifact, presumably being comprised of more completed work items after the execution of this step. The agent for this step is the team.

Concurrently with the performances of the Work step there may be multiple performances of the Revise Sprint Backlog step (note the * on the edge connecting this step to its parent). The agent for this step is also team, and the effect of a performance of this step is to update the sprint backlog to reflect the addition or removal of tasks in the backlog.

4 Using Analysis to Determine Process Robustness

Any of a number of different process definitions could be derived by making different changes to the definition just presented. This paper makes no claim as to which of the resulting processes should still be considered to be Scrum processes. But this paper is intended to suggest that different analyses can be applied to these different processes to yield different characterizations. These different characterizations might then be useful in supporting decisions about which of the different processes seems appropriate for use in meeting different process requirements.

In this section we will demonstrate how analyses can be applied to the process model resulting in a characterization of the process that can be used to determine its adherence to two different process requirements. Additional kinds of analysis are suggested in section 7.

4.1 Applying Fault Tree Analysis

Fault tree analysis (FTA) is an analytic approach that is well known in safety engineering and other engineering disciplines, where it is used to identify the ways in which a specified hazard might arise during the performance of a process. More specifically, in this approach a graph structure, called a Fault Tree (FT), is built using AND and OR gates to indicate how the effect of the incorrect performance of a step can propagate and cause consequent incorrect performance of other steps. The analyst must specify a particular hazard that is of concern, where a hazard is defined to be a condition that creates the possibility of significant loss. Once such a hazard has been specified, FTA can then be used to identify which combinations of incorrect step performances could lead to the occurrence of the specified hazard. Of particular interest are situations in which the incorrect performance of only one step can lead to the creation of a hazard. Such a step, referred to as a single point of failure, creates a particularly worrisome vulnerability, and suggests that processes containing such steps are likely to fail to meet certain critical process robustness requirements. A complete treatment of the way in which an FT is generated from a Little-JIL definition is beyond the scope of this document, but the interested reader is referred to [11].

Identification of a Scrum Method Hazard. One key Scrum process characteristic is that at the end of each sprint the ScrumMaster is always able to present a product that actually runs. Failing to be able to do this could be considered to be a hazard, and identifying a single step leading to such a hazard (a single point of failure) would suggest that such a process contains a robustness vulnerability. By applying FTA, Figure 3 shows that the previously presented Scrum process definition does not preclude the possibility of such a hazard resulting from a single point of failure as "Step 'Work' produces wrong 'product"' is sufficient for "Artifact 'product' from 'Sprint' [to be] wrong." Informally, we suggest that the previously defined process could be performed in a way that could be summarized as "write code for the first 29 days and then only on the 30th day make a first attempt to integrate everything." We hasten to note that this should not be taken as a weakness of the Scrum approach, because the Scrum process description upon which our definition is based explicitly states that it is a management approach that does not incorporate any engineering practices. Any application of Scrum will of course incorporate such practices. What the analysis just presented demonstrates is that it is necessary to incorporate into the Scrum process definition appropriate product integration details that preclude the possibility of the indicated single point of failure.

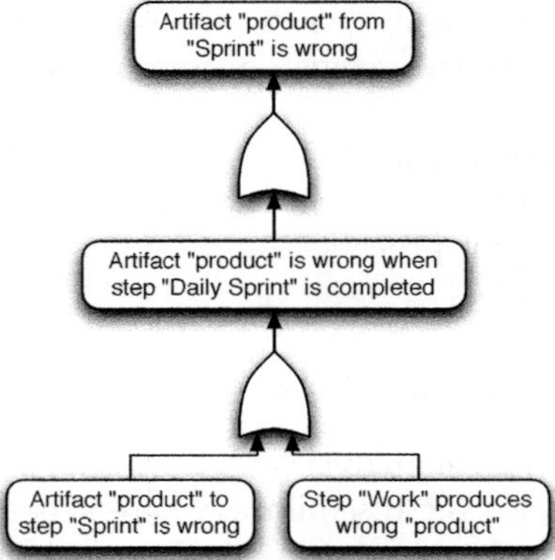

Fig. 3. Fault Tree Showing Single Point of Failure

Modeling Continuous Integration. One way to build such details into the process definition is to integrate the Continuous Integration method into the Scrum method by replacing the step Work in the original Scrum definition, with a sub-process *Checked Work* (Figure 4). In Checked Work, the original Work step is followed by the *Integrate* step, whose purpose is specifically to integrate the work just completed with prior work products. The successful integration of this new work is verified by the performance of a post-requisite(represented by a upward-pointing triangle on the right of a step bar) to the Integrate step that verifies the correctness of the integrated artifact. If the verification does not succeed, then the *Rework* step is performed, to make whatever modifications are necessary in order to ensure that the required modifications are carried out. Details of the Continuous Integration method are not provided here, as the purpose of this section is to indicate how process rigor can support greater assurance about the success of method integration. Details of the Continuous Integration method definition would look very analogous to the details of the Scrum method definition.

As shown in Figure 5, the inclusion of Continuous Integration eliminates the single point of failure step in this definition. For this modified method, if "Step 'Work' produces the wrong 'product' ", then it will still be necessary for "Exception 'BuildFailed' is thrown by step 'integrate' " to fail to be thrown (note that

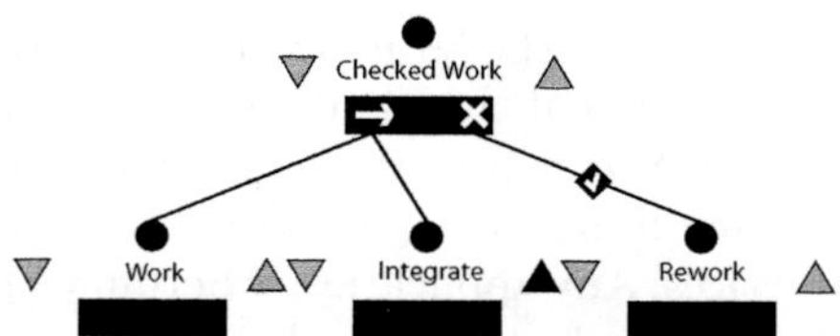

Fig. 4. Integration of Continuous Integration Into the Scrum Process Definition

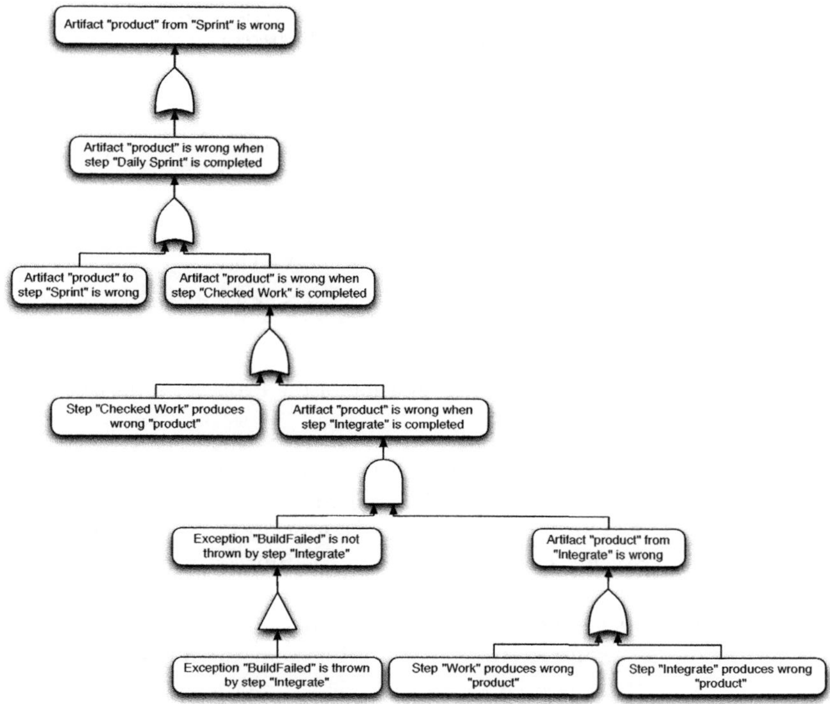

Fig. 5. Fault Tree Showing Fix

the icon connecting "Exception 'BuildFailed' is thrown by step 'integrate' " to its parent is a complementation gate). Thus two steps must fail to be performed correctly in order for the hazard to occur, resulting in a process that meets robustness requirements that were not met by the previously-defined process.

4.2 Applying Finite-State Verification

Finite-state verification techniques are widely used to demonstrate the absence of specified event sequence defects from computer hardware and from software code or designs. In [12], it is shown that Finite-state verification techniques may also be used to check if user defined properties hold in a Little-JIL process model. Finite-state verification is an analysis approach that compares a finite model of a system to a property specification. For example, we might specify an invariant that the development team is protected from requirements "churn" during a sprint, by asserting that the features being implemented cannot be changed except during the Sprint Planning Meeting (shown in Figure 1).

The FLAVERS[13] finite-state verification tool uses finite-state machines to specify properties that are usually created via PROPEL[14], a tool that allows

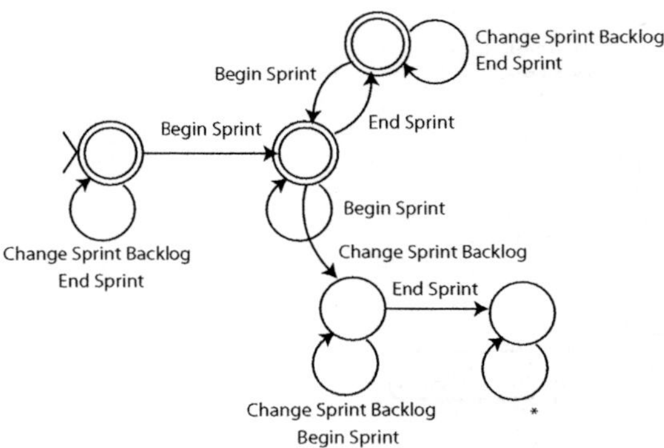

Fig. 6. Finite-State Machine Representation of the Property from PROPEL

the use of guided questions and disciplined natural language to aid the user in the creation of property specification. For our property, we have used PROPEL to specify that "Change Sprint Backlog" may not occur between a "Start Sprint" event and an "End Sprint" event, resulting in the finite-state machine shown in Figure 6.

Checking this property reveals that this property does not in fact hold for Scrum, producing an example trace, which after some preamble indicates that:

1. The step "Sprint" begins.
2. The step "Revise Sprint Backlog" occurs, changing the sprint backlog.

As this trace shows, the team is permitted to make changes to the sprint backlog during the sprint via the Revise Sprint Backlog step shown in Figure 2. Indeed, an anecdote in [6] describes a situation in which the Product Owner was bypassed and individuals were approaching team members and persuading them to make changes during the sprint. If we assume that the team members redirect any direct requests through the Product Owner as they are instructed to, then we can revise our analysis to disregard changes made to the sprint backlog via the "Revise Sprint Backlog" step, and then the property holds, showing that the Scrum process does indeed protect the team since only they themselves are able to make changes to the sprint backlog during the sprint.

5 Related Work

Many authors have addressed the problem of modeling, specifying, and defining various software development processes. Prime venues for this work include the International Conference on the Software Process (ICSP) series[15], and the journal Software Process Improvement and Practice (SPIP). Most of this literature attempts to model processes informally or with pictorial diagrams. In particular the Scrum approach to software development is described mostly in this way. Some examples are [6,7,8,9,10]. There have been a number of noteworthy attempts to create more rigorous notations with which to define processes (e.g. [16,17,18,19]). But these have typically not attempted to define popular software development processes. One notable exception is the Unified Process (UP) [20], which is defined precisely in terms of well-defined formalism. But even the UP definition is not then analyzed in order to infer properties for comparison with requirements. This paper seems unique in demonstrating that this is plausible and desirable.

6 Evaluation

While any clear graphical notation supports better understanding of a process, using a rigorously defined process language allows researchers and practitioners to evaluate, discuss, and improve the process based on analyses that are supported by a rigorous definition. The Little-JIL process definition language semantics are based on finite state machines to provide the precise semantic meanings of each of the language's features, which then serves as the basis for analyses that offer greater insights into such processes, support integration with other methods, and detect defects and vulnerabilities.

In this paper we showed how the Little-JIL Scrum method definition was used successfully for such analyses. First, a fault tree was generated automatically and used to identify a single point of failure in the process, suggesting a lack of process robustness that would presumably be worrisome, and facilitating the removal of that process vulnerability, as verified by analysis of a second automatically generated fault tree that demonstrated greater process robustness. Additionally, finite-state verification was used to show that the model does in fact demonstrate one of the key features of Scrum, namely that the development team is protected from requirements "churn" by the constraint that changes are routed through the Product Owner. We note that the finite- state verification tools and technologies used here have been shown to have low-order polynomial time bounds [13], which suggests that the work described in this paper should scale up from the small example presented here. Other work has demonstrated that these finite-state analyses can be applied to processes having hundreds of Little-JIL steps [21].

7 Future Work

This first demonstration of the use of process definition and analysis suggests that further kinds of analysis might also be successful in supporting additional demonstrations of the adherence of process definitions to additional desired requirements. For example, by attaching time limits to all steps (not just the steps in the example in section 3), and bounding the iterations (also necessary for finite-state verification) analyzers should be able to determine the maximum time required to carry out the specified process and thus determine if the process must always meet speed and responsiveness requirements. Discrete event simulation could also be used to study the adherence of processes to other kinds of requirements.

Finally we note that the application of these analyses to Scrum process definitions was used only as an example. These analysis approaches should be equally applicable to other types of processes to derive various sorts of properties and characteristics. Indeed this approach should be equally applicable to processes defined in other languages, as long as those languages have rigorously defined semantics. It seems particularly interesting to consider the possibility that some set of properties and characteristics might be identified that could be used to define the nature of such types of processes as Scrum. We suggest that a definition of what is quintessentially a "Scrum process" might well best be done by enunciating a set of properties and characteristics, rather than some canonical structure of steps. Analyses of the sorts suggested here might then be used to determine which actual processes are Scrum processes by subjecting them to analyses that determine whether or not the processes adhere to the defining set of properties and characteristics.

Acknowledgments

The authors gratefully acknowledge the many stimulating conversations with Aaron Cass, Bobby Simidchieva, M.S. Raunak, and Junchao Xiao, all of which have helped shape this paper. This work also builds fundamentally on the work of Bin Chen, Lori A. Clarke, and George S. Avrunin who have creating tools and technological approaches that enable the Finite State Verification and Fault Tree Analysis of process definitions. In addition Gordon Anderson's early versions of the Scrum process definition provided an invaluable starting point for this work. Financial support for this work was provided by the National Science Foundation under Award Nos. CCR-0427071 and CCR- 0205575, and a subcontract from Stevens Institute of Technology under the auspices of the DoD-sponsored Systems Engineering Research Center (SERC). The U.S. Government is authorized to reproduce and distribute reprints for Governmental purposes notwithstanding any copyright annotation thereon. The views and conclusions contained herein are those of the authors and should not be interpreted as necessarily representing the official policies or endorsements, either expressed or implied of The National Science Foundation, or the U.S. Government.

References

1. Osterweil, L.J.: Software processes are software too. In: 9th International Conference on Software Engineering (ICSE 1987), Monterey, CA, March 1987, pp. 2–13 (1987)
2. Osterweil, L.J.: Software processes are software too, revisited. In: 19th International Conference on Software Engineering (ICSE 1997), Boston, MA, May 1987, pp. 540–548 (1997)
3. Wise, A.: Little-JIL 1.5 language report. Technical Report UM-CS-2006-51, Department of Computer Science, University of Massachusetts, Amherst, MA (2006)

4. CMMI Product Team: CMMI for development, version 1.2. Technical Report CMU/SEI-2006-TR-008, Software Engineering Institute, Carnegie Mellon University, Pittsburg, PA (August 2006)
5. Highsmith, J., Fowler, M.: The agile manifesto. Software Development Magazine 9(8), 29–30 (2001)
6. Schwaber, K., Beedle, M.: Agile Software Development with Scrum. Prentice Hall, Upper Saddle River (2002)
7. Schwaber, K.: Agile Project Management with Scrum. Microsoft Press, Redmond (2004)
8. Cohn, M.: Succeeding with Agile: Software Development Using Scrum. Pearson Education, Inc., Boston (2010)
9. Scrum Alliance, Inc., `http://www.scrumalliance.org/`
10. Schwaber, K.: `http://www.controlchaos.com/`
11. Chen, B., Avrunin, G.S., Clarke, L.A., Osterweil, L.J.: Automatic fault tree derivation from little-jil process definitions. In: Wang, Q., Pfahl, D., Raffo, D.M., Wernick, P. (eds.) SPW 2006 and ProSim 2006. LNCS, vol. 3966, pp. 150–158. Springer, Heidelberg (2006)
12. Chen, B., Avrunin, G.S., Henneman, E.A., Clarke, L.A., Osterweil, L.J., Henneman, P.L.: Analyzing medical processes. In: ACM SIGSOFT/IEEE 30th International Conference on Software Engineering (ICSE 2008), Leipzig, Germany, May 2008, pp. 623–632 (2008)
13. Dwyer, M.B., Clarke, L.A., Cobleigh, J.M., Naumovich, G.: Flow analysis for verifying properties of concurrent software systems. ACM Transactions on Software Engineering and Methodology (TOSEM) 13(4), 359–430 (2004)
14. Cobleigh, R.L., Avrunin, G.S., Clarke, L.A.: User guidance for creating precise and accessible property specifications. In: ACM SIGSOFT 14th International Symposium on Foundations of Software Engineering (FSE14), Portland, OR, November 2006, pp. 208–218 (2006)
15. International Conference on Software Process, `http://www.icsp-conferences.org/`
16. Dami, S., Estublier, J., Amiour, M.: Apel: A graphical yet executable formalism for process modeling. Automated Software Engineering 5(1) (1998)
17. Katayama, T.: A hierarchical and functional software process description and its enaction. In: Proceedings of the 11th international conference on Software engineering, Pittsburgh, PA, pp. 343–352 (1989)
18. Kaiser, G., Barghouti, N., Sokolsky, M.: Experience with process modeling in the marvel software development environment kernel. In: 23rd Annual Hawaii Internationall Conference on System Sciences, pp. 131–140 (1990)
19. OMG: Software & systems process engineering meta-model specification. Technical Report formal/2008-04-01, Object Management Group (2008)
20. Jacobson, I., Booch, G., Rumbaugh, J.: The Unified Software Development Process. Addison-Wesley Longman, Inc., Reading (1999)
21. Christov, S., Avrunin, G., Clarke, L.A., Osterweil, L.J., Henneman, E.: A benchmark for evaluating software engineering techniques for improving medical processes. In: International Conference on Software Engineering, Workshop on Software Engineering in Health Care (SEHC 2010), Cape Town, South Africa (May 2010)

Early Empirical Assessment of the Practical Value of GQM⁺Strategies

Vladimir Mandić, Lasse Harjumaa, Jouni Markkula, and Markku Oivo

Department of Information Processing Science, University of Oulu, Finland
{vladimir.mandic,lasse.harjumaa,jouni.markkula,markku.oivo}@oulu.fi

Abstract. The success of a measurement initiative in a software company depends on the quality of the links between metrics programs and organizational business goals. GQM$^+$Strategies is a new approach designed to help in establishing links between the organizational business goals and measurement programs. However, there are no reported industrial experiences that demonstrate the practical value of the method. We designed a five-step research approach in order to assess the method's practical value. The approach utilized revised Bloom's taxonomy as a framework for assessing the practitioners' cognition level of the concepts. The results of our study demonstrated that the method has practical value for the case company, and it is capable of addressing real-world problems. In the conducted empirical study, the cognition level of the practitioners was sufficient for a successful implementation of the method.

Keywords: GQM$^+$Strategies, GQM, Software Metrics, Bloom's Taxonomy.

1 Introduction

The success of measurement initiatives in software companies depends on the quality of the links between metrics programs and organizational business goals. According to Hall and Fenton [1] poor goal-metric coupling will lead to frustration between managers and developers that eventually results in reducing and faking measurement practices. Umarji and Seaman [2] observed and noted that the general feeling toward metrics is that it is used for manipulation and control over people; therefore, it is not surprising to find deliberate manipulation of data collection processes done by the very same people who have the fear of being manipulated with metrics data.

In recent years, Basili and his colleagues developed the GQM$^+$Strategies[1] approach [3,4] with the explicit purpose of bridging the gap between business goals and measurement programs at the operational level. The first version of the method was published in 2007 [3]. The foundation concepts are based on sound theoretical groundwork, and the authors' profound experience with software metrics. The method has the potential of addressing important issues and practical problems, but there are no reported experiences with the method's practical use that would uphold this potential. Therefore,

[1] *GQM$^+$Strategies*® is registered mark of Fraunhofer Institute for Experimental Software Engineering, Germany and Fraunhofer USA, Center for Experimental Software Engineering, Maryland.

J. Münch, Y. Yang, and W. Schäfer (Eds.): ICSP 2010, LNCS 6195, pp. 14–25, 2010.

we found it important to address the method's practical value in our research. In our case, *practical value* is defined as a capability of solving relevant practical problems encountered by the case organization.

We carried out a case study of GQM+Strategies applications within the Finnish ICT industry. The main research goal was *to evaluate the practical value of GQM+Strategies as perceived by the company representatives.* Because the method is new and not yet widely adopted by the industry, the only way to get immediate feedback about it is to obtain expert opinions from the practitioners involved using the method. We defined a five-step research approach for our case in order to improve the validity and repeatability of the study.

For a successful adoption of any method or technology transfer in general, the understandability of foundation concepts is a prerequisite [5,6]. Therefore, we designed a questionnaire based on the revised Bloom's taxonomy [7] to evaluate practitioners' cognition level of the foundation concepts of the GQM+Strategies approach.

The rest of the paper is structured as follows: in Section 2, an overview of the GQM+Strategies approach and revised Bloom's taxonomy is given; our research approach is explained in Section 3; Section 4 presents the results of the assessment of method's practical value; validity issues of our research are discussed in Section 5; our final remarks and concluding statements are made in Section 6.

2 Related Work and Background

2.1 GQM+Strategies

GQM+Strategies [8] is an extension of the GQM (Goal Question Metric) approach [9]. The GQM approach provides a method for an organization or project to define goals, refine those goals down to specifications of data to be collected, and analyze and interpret the resulting data with respect to the original goals. However, it does not provide a mechanism for linking high-level business goals to lower-level goals or supporting and integrating *different* goals at different levels of the organization. Such mechanisms are provided by GQM+Strategies.

GQM+Strategies introduced several new concepts: goals, strategies, context & assumptions, and an interpretation model (Figure 1). Discernment is made between the *goal* and the *GQM goal.* The goal is a business goal, and it can be very abstract and difficult to operationalize. Business goals are further derived by *strategies*. The results of applying strategies are less abstract goals. Using this mechanism, abstract business goals are brought to the level where operationalization is possible. Business goals are formalized by using the goal formalization template (Table 1).

The *Goal+Strategies element* represents a single goal and derived strategies, including all context information and assumptions that explain the linkage between the goal and corresponding strategies. The *GQM graph* is a single GQM goal that measures a GQM+Strategies element. *GQM+Strategies grid* is an integrated collection of all GQM+Strategies elements, GQM graphs, and all links. The grid is specified as a result of the *GQM+Strategies grid derivation process.*

GQM+Strategies also introduces the concept of levels. Top-level business goals exist on strategic levels. Further on, the goal derivation process addresses lower levels (e.g.,

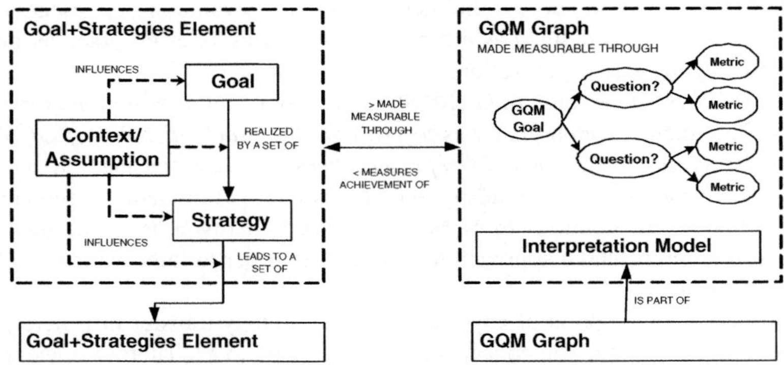

Fig. 1. Components of the GQM+Strategies meta-model

Table 1. GQM+Strategies goal formalization template with an example. The template specifies eight goal elements (dimensions).

Goal template	Example
Activity	Increase
Focus	Net income
Object	ABC Web services
Magnitude	10% per year
Timeframe	Annually, beginning in 2 years
Scope	Development groups assessed at CMMI level 2 or higher
Constraints	Available resources, ability to sustain CMMI levels
Relations	CMMI-related goals

the operational level). The concept of levels is convenient for grouping and organizing GQM+Strategies elements.

The entire process of deriving business goals and GQM graphs is consolidated through the *interpretation model.* During the interpretation process, measured GQM goals and statuses of the context/assumption variables influence assessment of business goal realization.

During the GQM+Strategies grid derivation process, two parallel threads are running: one is related to defining business goals, context/assumption elements, and strategies for addressing goals and the other is related to defining measurable goals and actually deriving the GQM graph. In the following paragraphs we give an overview of the grid derivation process [10].

Elicit General Context and Assumptions. First, the organizational (business) environment is defined by specifying context factors. Second, uncertainties are documented using assumptions, which represent beliefs or estimates regarding relevant business issues.

Define Top-Level Goals. First, an initial set of high-level goals is identified. Second, the goals have to be prioritized and analyzed for potential conflicts. Third, the selected goals are formalized using the GQM+Strategies goal template (Table 1). Potential relationships with other goals are also listed.

Make Strategy Decisions. First, a list of potential strategies for achieving the business goals is identified. Second, the most promising strategy has to be selected, considering such factors as cost and benefit analysis.

Define Goals. First, the implications of the chosen upper-level strategies with respect to lower-level goals have to be determined. Second, potential lower-level goals are identified based on the goal analysis. Third, the most promising goal with respect to feasibility, cost, and benefit is selected. Fourth, the most promising goals are selected and formalized using the goal template.

Define GQM Graphs. The GQM graph derivation process is well documented in the literature[2].

2.2 Revised Bloom's Taxonomy

For the purpose of evaluating the understandability of the GQM+Strategies concepts, we used the revised Bloom's taxonomy as a framework.

The first version of the taxonomy of educational objectives, also known as Bloom's taxonomy, was introduced over 50 years ago. Since then, it has been used to classify curricular objectives on countless occasions. In addition to a measurement framework for educational objectives, the taxonomy provides a common language for defining learning goals [7].

In 2001, a revised version of Bloom's taxonomy was introduced by Anderson et al. [7]. In the new version, the knowledge dimension is defined more precisely and a taxonomy table can be used to categorize the learning objectives within the cognitive and knowledge dimensions. The structure of the refined taxonomy is as follows:

- The first level of the taxonomy concerns **remembering** the learning objective. That involves recognizing relevant concepts and recalling them.
- The second level requires **understanding** the relevant knowledge in different types of communication. The subcategories for this level include: interpreting, exemplifying, classifying, summarizing, inferring, comparing and explaining the material.
- The third level in the taxonomy is **applying** the achieved knowledge in a given situation. It involves executing and implementing the procedure.
- The fourth level requires that the learner can **analyze** the material by breaking it into components and identifying the relationships between the parts, as well as the overall structure. Subcategories at this level are: differentiating, organizing and attributing the knowledge.
- The fifth level assumes that the learner can **evaluate** the subject of learning based on given criteria. This level is further divided into checking and critiquing.

[2] For example, see: van Solingen, R., Berghout, E.: *The Goal/Question/Metric Method.* The McGraw-Hill Company, Maidenhead; England (1999).

– At the sixth level, the learner can **create** the subject. The subcategories for this level are: generating, planning and producing.

The three lowest levels comprise the basic skills, while three upper levels are higher order thinking skills [7].

Bloom's taxonomy is especially useful for defining targets for competence levels. It provides a well-known framework for planning and assessing the knowledge and skills that will be needed to adopt a method in an organization successfully. Pfleeger [11] states that it is important for the practitioners interested in utilizing new technologies to understand clearly the use and benefits of the new approach. Rogers [5] emphasizes that the understandability of a new method is a prerequisite for its successful adoption. Understandability does not mean merely comprehensive guidelines and documentation.

3 Research Approach

The research goal was to evaluate the practical value of the GQM$^+$Strategies method and thus provide initial empirical experiences of using the method in real-life industrial settings. We carried out the research in one Finnish ICT company. Our research approach consists of five steps, which are the following:

Step 1. Analyze practical problems in the case company.
Step 2. Evaluate how the GQM$^+$Strategies can be instrumented to address those problems.
Step 3. Perform a pilot project, for the purpose of transferring basic method knowledge and skills to practitioners.
Step 4. Confirm the success of knowledge transfer by assessing the practitioners level of comprehension of the method.
Step 5. Obtain expert opinions regarding the capability of the method to address practical problems from those practitioners who competently understood the method.

3.1 Step 1: Problem Analysis

The first step involves familiarization with corporate processes. Because the development process is mainly software and system engineering, we have used a semi-structured interview with open questions that were based on the CMMI reference model [12]. In addition, process descriptions of the organization and other written material are beneficial in order to gain understanding of how the company operates.

After familiarization, we interviewed the company representatives in order to find out the most urgent issues that needed to be targeted. By identifying the problems, we were able to make visible what would be the practical value of the method. The practical value should be defined on a case-by-case basis.

3.2 Step 2: Instrumenting GQM$^+$Strategies

In the second step, a set of possible solutions were proposed to solve the problems. The potential benefits of the GQM$^+$Strategies approach were aligned with the results of the problem analysis. This phase was theory-based and done by the researchers. The solution proposals were based on the best practices reported in literature. The main purpose of these first two steps was to identify relevant problems to the organization and to communicate how GQM+Strategies could help in solving them.

3.3 Step 3: Knowledge Transfer

The main purpose of the third step is to provide the practitioners with a familiar exercise to work with the method. Going through a selected problem area within their own domain helps the practitioners to quickly gain adequate skills and knowledge to use the method. This was done in a series of tutorials and workshops. To gain an organization-wide overview, people from all organizational levels should participate. For example in our case, top-level management worked as a one group, and people from the mid-level and operational level worked in the other group. In addition, a joint workshop was arranged as a feedback session.

3.4 Step 4: Confirmation of the Knowledge Transfer

The fourth step aimed at ensuring that practitioners in the case company adequately understood the concepts of the GQM+Strategies method. The method uses the well-known concepts from GQM [9], but it also adds some new concepts. Therefore, the level of cognition of the practitioners was evaluated by the first part of a questionnaire presented to the practitioners (Figure 2). The questions are based on the revised Bloom's taxonomy.

In order to design the questionnaire we had to determine how the taxonomy applies to the GQM+Strategies approach. We took a view as:

Level 1: Remember. Ability to recall or recognize the concepts that represent building blocks in a given grid; for example, a business goal, strategy or GQM graph.

Level 2: Understand. Ability to read the grid, which implies an understanding of the relationships between the building blocks; for example, how the business goals and strategies are related.

Level 3: Apply. Ability to recognize the relationships between the given grid and a real-world situation for which the grid was derived.

Level 4: Analyze. Ability to comprehend how the variations in the given grid would relate to the real-world situation and vice versa.

Level 5: Evaluate. Ability to judge or criticize what are advantages and disadvantages of several given grids derived for the same real-world situation.

Level 6: Create. Ability to derive the best possible grid for a new real-world situation.

Figure 2 illustrates Bloom's taxonomy-related questions. For the remembering level, we listed the GQM+Strategies concepts and asked participants to evaluate how well they remember them on a five point scale from (1)—remember well—to (5)—cannot remember. As the singular result we calculated the median, while for the level 2, we calculated the median of three dimensions of understanding.

Other levels of the taxonomy were probed with one question each (Figure 2). In all questions, we used five-point ordinal scale. The answers where formulated in such way as to recline on the practitioner's experiences with the case study.

My current position in the company is:
[ ]Top level management [ ]Mid level management [ ]Operational level (Developers)

Q1: How well you remember (recall) listed *GQM+Strategies®* concepts?
(1- I remember well, 5- I cannot remember)

Concepts:	*1*	*2*	*3*	*4*	*5*
Business Goal					
Strategy					
Context/Assumptions					

Concepts:	*1*	*2*	*3*	*4*	*5*
GQM Graph					
Interpretation Model					

Q2: If I am given *GQM+Strategies®* grid: (*GQM+Strategies®* grid is the result of derivation process, an overview diagram which links and presents: business goals, strategies, GQM graph, and interpretation model)
(1- I am sure that I would be able; 5- No, I would not be able)

	1	*2*	*3*	*4*	*5*
I would be able to interpret it. (to read the grid)					
I would be able to summarize it. (to extract the most important issues from the grid)					
I would be able to explain it. (to elaborate issues presented in the grid)					

Q3: For the given case of *reducing time to market*, after joint workshops for the exactly same case (same top-level goal and context) I would be able to:

[ ] 1. Go through all steps without any external experts help and produce same results.
[ ] 2. Go through all steps without any external experts help, but final results should be checked by an external expert.
[ ] 3. Go through the steps under supervision of an external expert.
[ ] 4. I would need additional familiarization with the *GQM+Strategies®* method before redoing the case.
[ ] 5. I believe that additional familiarization with *GQM+Strategies®* would not help me to perform steps on my own.

Q4: For the given case of *reducing time to market*, if it is required from me to update *GQM+Strategies®* grid for an alternative strategy.

[ ] 1. I would be able to update entire *GQM+Strategies®* grid without any help.
[ ] 2. I would be able to update entire *GQM+Strategies®* grid, but final results should be checked by an external expert.
[ ] 3. I would be able to perform the update under supervision of an external expert.
[ ] 4. I would need additional familiarization with the *GQM+Strategies®* method before updating the grid.
[ ] 5. I believe that additional familiarization with *GQM+Strategies®* would not help me to perform updates on my own.

Q5: If several *GQM+Strategies®* grids are presented to me, for same case (same top-level goal with same context) and I am asked to evaluate them. (Evaluating how well structure and content of the grids correspond for a given case)

[ ] 1. I **would be** confident in evaluating strengths and weaknesses of the grids.
[ ] 2. I **believe** I would be able to evaluate strengths and weaknesses of the grids.
[ ] 3. I am **not sure** that I would be able to evaluate strengths and weaknesses of the grids.
[ ] 4. I do **not believe** I would be able to evaluate strengths and weaknesses of the grids.
[ ] 5. I would **not be able** to evaluate strengths and weaknesses of the grids.

Q6: If I am asked to derive entire *GQM+Strategies®* grid for another company site.

[ ] 1. I would be able to derive entire *GQM+Strategies®* grid without any help.
[ ] 2. I would be able to derive entire *GQM+Strategies®* grid, but final results should be checked by an external expert.
[ ] 3. I would be able to perform the derivation under supervision of an external expert.
[ ] 4. I would need additional familiarization with the *GQM+Strategies®* method before deriving the grid.
[ ] 5. I believe that additional familiarization with *GQM+Strategies®* would not help me to perform the derivation on my own.

Fig. 2. Questionnaire related to Bloom's taxonomy. The header part of the questionnaire is not given here in its integrated form.

3.5 Step 5: Assessing Expert Opinion

The method's basic skills (the cognition levels from 1 to 3) should be developed through method's tutorial and workshop sessions during the case. Evaluation and creation levels are required for an external expert. Apart from extensive knowledge about the method, levels 5 and 6 also require a solid experience base with different implementations of the GQM+Strategies approach.

Finally, in the last step, those practitioners who gained sufficient knowledge on the method (basic skills), could provide expert opinions on how well the method can address the practical problems identified in the first step. The opinions were collected in the second part of the questionnaire, including two questions about perceived practical value.

For the first question (Q7), about how well the grid represented and documented their context (external and internal environment), the answers were given on five-point scale from 1—context is poorly represented and documented—to 5—all relevant contextual elements are well represented and documented. For the second question (Q8), about if it would be beneficial for the company to invest (effort, training, time, and money) in the GQM+Strategies method, the answers were given on five-point scale from 1—it would not be beneficial at all—to 5—it is worth investing in it.

For the method really to be practical, it is critical that it captures and documents the context of the organization. The more valuable the method is, the more willing the company is to invest in it.

4 Assessment of the Practical Value of GQM+Strategies

We did a case study within a division of a large international ICT company with 24 branches on three continents (North America, Europe, and Asia) with over 4000 employees. The company has been present in the telecommunications market for almost two decades. The primary products of the company are embedded systems used in telecommunications. However, the portion and role of software within the products is growing rapidly and continuously.

The software development unit where this study was carried out in is located in Finland, has about 20 software engineers, and the entire site employs over 100 people. The case-study environment (context) could be characterized as typical for a high-tech enterprise. The product-creation process is human intensive and dependents on the creativity of the people involved with the process.

Overall 12 people participated in the study, from which 3 were representatives of top-management, 4 of mid-level management, and 5 were developers representing the operational level.

4.1 Step 1: Problem Analysis

By analyzing identified issues, we were able to abstract problems as cross-organizational communication, and on-time involvement of the managers.

(1) Cross-Organizational Communication. Requirements for communication practices are far more demanding than just as means to communicate the targets or instructions from the top to the bottom levels and to report on progress. They have to establish simultaneous two-way communication channels in such a way as to enable the top-level managers to "listen" to people from lower-levels when they are defining strategies and business goals, while at same time people from lower-levels have to understand the rationales for the top-level plans and decisions. In that sense, the organizational transparency is important. According to those needs, reporting practices have to be aligned.

(2) On-time Managers' Commitment. Managers have busy schedules that do not allow them to spend enough time reading and analyzing reports. Therefore, they rely on subordinate who have to sign-off the reports. Very often, after a problem emerges, managers make the commitment to solve it. In some cases, that could be avoided by getting the on-time commitment when the problem was on "the paper" (the reports could reveal first indications of the problem).

These two problems are interrelated. Improved organizational transparency and communication practices are contributing to a timely response from managers. At the same time, the prevention of serious problems due to timely managers' commitment is justifying and motivating further improvements in organizational communication practices.

4.2 Step 2: Instrumenting GQM$^+$Strategies

After analyzing the identified issues, we offered our suggestions on how GQM$^+$Strategies method could contribute to mitigating identified problems.

We perceived two components of **cross-organizational communication:** organizational transparency and reporting practices.

Organizational transparency. The GQM$^+$Strategies can be utilized for communicating strategic issues. Furthermore, we have suggested that the process of the grid derivation is a very good communication channel between different organizational levels. The GQM$^+$Strategies grid provides the structure (form), while the grid derivation process mediates the communication between the top-level and operational levels.

Reporting practices. Use of quantitative indicators can significantly increase the readability of the reports. As a part of deriving the GQM graph, GQM goals are used to guide the process of defining relevant metrics. We suggested that reporting practices should include the interpretation model query, which will provide a consolidated view of the strategy implementation status.

On-time managers' commitment. Utilizing quantitative indicators through the interpretation model of GQM$^+$Strategies, which are at same time clearly linked to the business goals and operational activities associated with the operational goals increases the manager's attention. As the overall result, managers can commit themselves before the problems emerge and invoke appropriate actions on time.

4.3 Step 3: Knowledge Transfer

The objective of the pilot project was to implement GQM$^+$Strategies with the purpose of increasing the organizational transparency of how strategic decisions impact operational activities and how operational activities contribute to top-level business goals.

The first workshop was carried out with top-level managers, while the second one was for mid- and operation-level people. Before each workshop a GQM$^+$Strategies tutorial was given. After the workshops, a feedback session was organized for all participants, where the resulting GQM$^+$Strategies grid was presented and discussed.

The company has had defined strategic goals and objectives, which were the starting point to derive the grid and eventually to specify what metrics to collect. The top-level business goal was defined as: activity to *decrease* (focus) the *time-to-market* for (object) *ABC type of products* for the magnitude of *10% of current time-to-market*; within a timeframe of *one year* in the context (scope) of *Finland corporate site* with constraints of *current resources* availability. Relations to the *corporate policy*.

Further context analysis indicated that restructuring the development process could gain a sufficient decrease in time-to-market. The entire grid contained three levels, which reflected the organizational structure (top-level management, mid-level management, and the operational level). The operational level goal made it possible to generate action points, that would be used for planning an internal project to implement the strategy.

4.4 Step 4: Confirmation of the Knowledge Transfer

For each data set, basic *descriptive statistics*[3] were calculated. We extended the five-point number summary with mode, range, and interquartile range (IQR).

The results (Table 2) revealed a trend of decreasing abilities from lower towards higher levels. The majority of participants ($Mode = 2, 3$) responded that they remembered the concepts. In addition, the results showed that the most remembered concepts were business goal and strategy, while the least remembered was the interpretation model. Such results are in consent with time spent on each of the concepts during the workshop sessions.

Table 2. Descriptive statistics for the method's cognition level (Levels 1–6) and expert opinion questions (Q7 and Q8). $N = 12$.

Question	Min.	Mode	Max.	Range	Q_1	Median	Q_3	IQR
Level 1: Remember	2	2, 3	4	2	2	3	3	1
Level 2: Understand	2	3	4	2	2	3	3	1
Level 3: Apply	2	3	4	2	2.5	3	3	0.5
Level 4: Analyze	1	3	5	4	2	3	3.5	1.5
Level 5: Evaluate	2	3, 4	5	3	2.5	3	4	1.5
Level 6: Create	3	3	5	2	3	4	4.5	1.5
Question 7: Environment	2	3, 4	4	2	3	3	4	1
Question 8: Further Investment	2	3, 4	5	3	3	4	4.5	1.5

The most frequent answer for levels 2, 3, and 4 was that participants felt capable of performing steps under the supervision of an expert. However, the distribution of the answers shows an increased confidence in performing steps on level 2 ($Q_1 = 2$ and $Mode = 3$). Further, the confidence was gradually reduced until level 4 where the dispersion of the answers was highest ($IQR = 1.5$).

The ability to perform level 4 steps with almost the same confidence as level 3 steps was a surprise. The probable explanation for this is in the method, which was designed

[3] For example, see: C. J. Wild and G. A. F. Seber: *Chance Encounters*, John Wiely & Sons, Inc., 1999.

to handle relevant context for a particular situation or case. Therefore the participants' natural familiarity with the context made them comfortable with level 4 tasks.

The mode and median statistics indicate that level 5 and 6 responses are clearly shifted for one point on the scale. In general, participants felt that they would not be able to perform evaluation and creation steps.

4.5 Step 5: Assessing Expert Opinion

Table 2 shows results for questions Q7 and Q8. Participants were "neutral positive" towards the method's capability to document relevant context ($Mode = 3, 4$).

Regarding the method's practical benefits, the majority of participants clearly indicated that they found the method beneficial for the company ($Median = 4$). The increased disagreement toward this issue ($IQR = 1.5$) motivated us to look more closely at the data. Further data examination showed that top-managers and mid-managers evaluated the method's benefits with higher marks than operational-level people.

5 Study Validity

Regarding the validity of the study, we identified and addressed following validity issues:

Lack of practical experience. Research work with GQM$^+$Strategies is in the early phase; there are not yet published practical experiences with the method usage. Therefore, we designed a five-step research approach in order to assess experts' opinions. The research approach had twofold purpose: first, to transfer knowledge about the method in the experts' natural environment (analyzing practical problems and suggesting how the method can address those); second, to confirm success of the knowledge transfer with the help of Bloom's taxonomy before assessing experts' opinions.

Expert's self-assessment. Designing a several pages long exam-like questionnaire for Bloom's taxonomy was not acceptable for this type of subjects (top-level managers, chief officers, and so on). Therefore, we limited the length of our questionnaire to two A4 pages. And, presumably we trust subjects in their self-assessments. Under these constraints, we find it important to replicate this study in order to increase the data set and then to perform outlier analysis.

6 Conclusions

This paper provides an early empirical assessment of the practical value of GQM$^+$Strategies method. The empirical study has demonstrated that the method has its practical value for the case company. This inference has been made upon two premises: first, practitioners' opinions that the method can be adequately instrumented to address their problems in a manner beneficial for the company; second, that such opinion has came from the very practitioners who understood the method competently, according to the revised Bloom's taxonomy.

We refer to this study as an early empirical assessment because it was carried out in one case company on a relatively small sample. Our future research will include replications of this study in order to increase the data set.

Our research also has a methodological contribution by demonstrating that Bloom's taxonomy provides a useful framework for assessing the understandability of a new method or tool in the software engineering context.

The results of this study are in favor of future studies on the technology adoption and transfer models. Especially interesting issues for future research might be into grid derivation process in multiple sessions, or in a company that is geographically distributed.

Acknowledgments. Our research was funded by the Finnish Funding Agency for Technology and Innovation (Tekes). We would also like to express special thanks to the GQM+Strategies authors Victor R. Basili, Jens Heidrich, Michael Lindvall, Jürgen Münch, Carolyn B. Seaman, Myrna Regardie, and Adam Trendowicz.

References

1. Hall, T., Fenton, N.: Implementing effective software metrics programs. IEEE Software 2(14), 55–65 (1997)
2. Umarji, M., Seaman, C.: Why do programmers avoid metrics? In: 2nd ACM-IEEE international symposium on Empirical software engineering and measurement (ESEM 2008), Kaiserslautern, Germany, pp. 129–138 (2008)
3. Basili, V., Heidrich, J., Lindvall, M., Münch, J., Regardie, M., Rombach, D., et al.: Bridging the gap between business strategy and software development. In: Twenty Eighth International Conference on Information Systems, Montreal, Canada, pp. 1–16 (2007)
4. Basili, V., Lindvall, M., Regardie, M., Seaman, C., Heidrich, J., Münch, J., et al.: Linking software development and business strategy through measurement. IEEE Computer 43(4), 57–65 (2010)
5. Rogers, E.: Diffusion of Innovations, 3rd edn. The Free Press, New York (1995)
6. Gorman, M.: Types of knowledge and their roles in technology transfer. Journal of Technology Transfer 27(3), 219–231 (2002)
7. Krathwohl, D.: A revision of bloom's taxonomy: An overview. Theory Into Practice 41(4), 212–218 (2002)
8. Basili, V., Heidrich, J., Lindvall, M., Münch, J., Regardie, M., Trendowicz, A.: GQM+Strategies –aligning business strategies with software measurement. In: First International Symposium on Empirical Software Engineering and Measurement, ESEM 2007, Madrid, Spain, pp. 488–490 (2007)
9. Basili, V., Caldiera, G., Rombach, D.: Goal question metric paradigm. In: Marciniak, J. (ed.) Encyclopedia of Software Engineering, vol. 1, pp. 528–532. John Wiley & Sons, Inc., New York (1994)
10. Basili, V., Heidrich, J., Lindvall, M., Münch, J., Seaman, C., Regardie, M., et al.: Determining the impact of business strategies using principles from goal-oriented measurement. In: Internationale Tagung Wirtschaftsinformatik 2009, Wien, Austria, vol. 9, pp. 1–10 (2009)
11. Pfleeger, S.: Understanding and improving technology transfer in software engineering. The Journal of Systems and Software 3(47), 111–124 (1999)
12. Chrissis, M., Konrad, M., Shrum, S.: CMMI: Guidelines for Process Integration and Product Improvement. Addison-Wesley Professional, New York (2006)

Determining Organization-Specific Process Suitability

Ove Armbrust

Fraunhofer IESE, Fraunhofer-Platz 1, 67663 Kaiserslautern, Germany
ove.armbrust@iese.fraunhofer.de

Abstract. Having software processes that fit technological, project, and business demands is one important prerequisite for software-developing organizations to operate successfully in a sustainable way. However, many such organizations suffer from processes that do not fit their demands, either because they do not provide the necessary support, or because they provide features that are no longer necessary. This leads to unnecessary costs during the development cycle, a phenomenon that worsens over time. This paper presents the SCOPE approach for systematically determining the process demands of current and future products and projects, for analyzing existing processes aimed at satisfying these demands, and for subsequently selecting those processes that provide the most benefit for the organization. The validation showed that SCOPE is capable of adjusting an organization's process scope in such a way that the most suitable processes are kept and the least suitable ones can be discarded.

1 Introduction

Many facets of process technology and standards are available in industry and academia, but in practice, significant problems with processes and process management remain. Specifically, an organization's process landscape often does not contain the processes that are required to support its current activities. Typically, a number of outdated processes exist that are not or hardly used any more, yet they still are presented as a possible choice for projects, possibly even maintained. Complementary to this, there are often conditions for which no suitable processes exist within the organization, so whenever such a condition appears, the organization's employees need to improvise due to a lack of guidance. Both cases are aggravated when it comes to future projects: There is often no pro-active preparation of an organization's processes for future demands. This leads to the following question: *How can an organization's processes be managed so that they support all of the organization's activities, current and future, while keeping the maintenance effort on an adequate level?*

This paper presents the SCOPE approach for systematically determining the process demands of current and future products and projects, for analyzing existing processes aimed at satisfying these demands, and for subsequently selecting those processes that provide the most benefit for the organization. The paper is structured as follows: Section 2 presents related work. Section 3 sheds some light on current industrial practice with respect to process scoping. Section 4 presents the SCOPE approach, and Section 5 summarizes the validation results. Finally, Section 6 discusses the approach and gives an outlook on possible future work.

J. Münch, Y. Yang, and W. Schäfer (Eds.): ICSP 2010, LNCS 6195, pp. 26–38, 2010.

2 Related Work

There is a variety of related work connected to identifying suitable processes for an organization. In this section, we distinguish product scoping approaches, technique selection approaches, and process-aware approaches.

Product Scoping Approaches. Schmid [1] describes an approach for systematically determining the scope for a software product line. While this approach explicitly considers future products, it mostly ignores projects and processes. Bayer et al. [2] transfer the concept of software product line scoping to (business) workflows, which are by their very nature somewhat similar to software processes. However, they also only consider products, not projects or processes, and include future development only implicitly.

Quality Function Deployment (QFD) is an approach for directing product capabilities based on customer needs. Cohen [3] defines it as "...a method for structured product planning and development that enables a development team to specify clearly the customer's wants and needs, and then to evaluate each proposed product or service capability systematically in terms of its impact on meeting those needs." This approach explicitly considers the anticipated future of products, but again neglects projects and processes.

To summarize, product scoping approaches assist software engineers in building the product that best supports their customers' requirements. However, the ones reviewed do not consider processes and cannot be transferred easily. For example, while for a product, it is typically clear how to provide a certain functionality, for a process, it is much less known whether a specific process can provide the required features at all.

Technique Selection Approaches. Biffl and Halling [4] provide a framework for supporting Fagan inspections. The approach is very detailed and provides decision models based on a literature survey; however, it does not consider the anticipated future and is limited to Fagan inspections. Schweikhard [5] describes a framework for supporting the decision-making process in inspections. It provides a classification scheme for context and variation factors and uses historic and empirical knowledge; however, it also does not consider the anticipated future and is limited to products.

Vegas and Basili [6] provide a characterization scheme for supporting the selection of testing techniques. They also provide a decision model and integrate existing knowledge; however, they neglect the anticipated future as did the previous two approaches, and support projects only, but no products or processes. Madachy et al. [7] developed a simulation model predicting the impact of quality strategies on defect profiles, cost, and risk, using COCOMO II [8] for cost estimation, as well as inputs on introduced defects. It considers products in a very detailed manner; however, it also does not consider the anticipated future, and is designed for products only, neglecting projects and processes.

In [9], Denger et al. analyze a number of approaches to customizing quality assurance techniques for different parts of the software lifecycle. They provide decision models for quality assurance techniques, but also do not consider the anticipated future, and they neglect projects and processes. Rus and Collofello [10] investigate the use of an expert system for making selection decisions for a reliability engineering strategy. They also provide a decision model for achieving reliability, yet again ignore the anticipated future, products, and processes. In addition to this, they focus on reliability only. In [11], the authors describe a vision for comprehensive software engineering decision support regarding techniques. They provide decision models for individual projects, but do not support products or processes. In addition, they also consider the next project, but do not look any further into the future.

To summarize, the technique selection approaches described support software engineers by providing help for decision-making. Strongly simplified, they assume that a certain quality factor is important (e.g., low defect density in the final product, or reliability of the final product) and assist decision makers in selecting appropriate techniques for achieving this goal. However, they typically investigate only either products or projects, but not both. In general, they also neglect processes. They also largely ignore the anticipated future.

Process-aware Approaches. Becker-Kornstaedt [12] describes an 8-step approach to systematic descriptive process modeling. The approach defines the scope of the process model, but considers the anticipated future use of the process model only implicitly. It does not describe how scoping should be performed.

Avison and Wood-Harper [13] investigated the problem of choosing the right development approach for information systems already very early. In the year 1991, they stated that the number of development methodologies is very large, yet there is no single methodology that is optimal for all contexts. Therefore, for every single context, a suitable methodology (or, as it would be called today, process) has to be chosen. Since an organization cannot excel at every methodology, a reduced set must be provided from which developers can choose. They propose a contingency approach and present Multiview, a framework representing a structure to help developers choose procedures, techniques, and tools from a fixed portfolio. Multiview characterizes techniques based on historical knowledge and provides decision models for some techniques, but it does not consider the anticipated future of an organization beyond the next project. It also does not support products.

Becker et al. [14] discuss the application of Quality Function Deployment (QFD) [3] for strategically planning software process improvement (SPI) programs to support an organization's business goals. Their main idea is to regard SPI as the organization's product that is to be optimized in order to support the business goals. They use the House-of-Quality matrices subset of QFD to operationalize this idea. The approach actively considers the anticipated future through the organization's business goals, yet it does not investigate products or projects, but focuses on business goals and identified problems. The recommendations for the decision model remain on a very high level of abstraction (CMMI process areas).

In summary, the product scoping approaches focus on scoping products, i.e., determining the features a number of products should have. They do not consider processes. However, they typically consider the anticipated future explicitly. The technique selection approaches mostly focus on selecting one out of very few specific techniques. Fagan inspections are a very popular subject in this community. The focus of these approaches is typically very narrow, and adapting them to support other techniques, possibly from other categories (e.g., extending a Fagan variant selection approach to support quality assurance techniques in general) requires enormous effort.

The process-aware approaches consider the processes of an organization in their entirety, instead of focusing on small parts of it. However, the approaches described mostly do not support process engineers when it comes to scoping and selecting processes.

3 Industry Approaches

This section introduces some process management approaches that can be found in today's industrial practice.

Fitzgerald et al. [15] report on an approach to provide a Motorola plant in Cork, Ireland with a software development process. Unfortunately, no information is given on how the process was constructed, apart from the reference to industry standards. In addition, continued management of the process is not detailed. A CMMI Level 5-certified IT supplier from India (2008: <10,000 employees) that the author of this paper has worked with pursues a very strict process management regime. The organization's process design team collects comments, recommendations, and requests for changes from all employees, processes them, and provides new releases of the company standard processes every three months based on the information collected. Every release acknowledges about 100 requests from employees. While process management is very strictly organized and responds systematically to employee feedback, there is no strategic process planning or suitability analysis. All modifications to the organization's processes are based on past experience of the employees and thus retrospective. Anticipated future developments are not used when the processes are adapted. A very similar approach has been taken by Josef Witt GmbH, a medium-sized (2,200 employees) mail order business in the clothing domain within the Otto group (123 companies, 55,000 employees).

ESOC (European Space Operations Centre), the European Space Agency's (ESA) ground segment, provides a ready-to-use implementation of the mandatory ESA process standards (ECSS series [16]) for its suppliers, called SETG (Tailoring of ECSS Software Engineering Standards for Ground Segments in ESA [17]). The main driver for adapting and modifying the SETG standards are changes within the superior ECSS standards. ESOC normally does not modify the SETG standards otherwise, for example to reflect changed project contexts. In particular, ESOC does not utilize their knowledge on the anticipated future when changing the SETG standards.

Except for the Motorola report, industrial case studies and the author's experience do not suggest that the software industry performs systematic strategic process management. Many organizations, for example the Indian IT supplier, are driven by standards such as CMMI or SPICE, which are demanded by their customers. Others, such as Josef Witt GmbH, react to problems or events that occurred in the past, but do not consider the anticipated future in their actions. Organizations with highly safety-critical applications such as ESA, finally, are mostly driven by other standards and not so much by actual problems.

All the case studies have in common that there is no systematic analysis as to whether and how much the application of the individual standards actually contributes to achieving the respective organization's business goals, and how such standards must be adapted to achieve these goals better in the future. The Indian IT supplier example shows that even organizations with high process maturity might not manage their processes strategically, considering the anticipated future.

4 Organization-Specific Process Suitability

This section introduces the SCOPE approach for determining the suitability of an organization's processes and subsequently selecting a subset thereof, thus adjusting their scope. It requires an organization to determine which kinds of products and projects it typically pursues and is likely to pursue in the future. The organization can then identify the support these products and projects demand with respect to processes. For example, one kind of project may require processes that are able to cope with frequently changing requirements, whereas another one may require processes that specifically support distributed development. Process demands can be recorded along such attributes (e.g., "distributed development"), reflecting each individual product's and project's characteristics. The process demands of products and projects are weighted according to the probability of their realization, taking into account that products or projects sketched for the far future have lower probability than those ready to start. Using the same attributes used for product and project analysis, a process analysis determines the suitability of the organization's processes with respect to each attribute.

A more detailed description of the analysis steps can be found in [18] and will not be repeated here due to space restrictions. The result of the product analysis is, for every product *i*, its process demand $P(p_i, a_j)$ with respect to attribute *j*. The project analysis similarly results in a process demand $J(j_i, a_j)$ for every project *i* with respect to attribute *j*. In [18], the values for *P* and *J* range from 1 to 3; however, other (interval or rational) scales may also be used.

In order to determine the process demand *D* for a single attribute across all products *p* (projects *j*), the arithmetic mean of the sum of all *P* (*J*) values is used (Eqn. 1). D_p and D_j here consider how often a specific capability (represented by the appropriate attribute) is required relative to all other capabilities.

$$D_p(a_j) = \frac{1}{n}\sum_{i=1}^{n} P(p_i, a_j)$$
$$D_j(a_j) = \frac{1}{n}\sum_{i=1}^{n} J(j_i, a_j) \qquad (1)$$

The organization-wide process demand *D* across all products *p* and projects *j* is determined by unifying their respective demands (Eqn. 2). *D* thereafter contains, for every attribute, the organization's process demand with respect to this attribute. *D*, like D_p and D_j, considers how often a specific capability (represented by the appropriate attribute) is required relative to all other capabilities.

$$D = D_p \cup D_j \qquad (2)$$

While *D* reflects what an organization needs in terms of processes for its products and projects, our next step is to determine how suitable its processes are with respect to these demands. This suitability of the organization's processes is determined for each demand, i.e., each attribute from the product and project analysis, using expert estimation, empirical knowledge, or a combination of both. The result is a value $S(p_i, a_j)$ for the suitability of each process for each attribute. The sum of the values of all attributes per process indicates its suitability $S(p_i)$ for the organization (Eqn. 3).

$$S(p_i) = \sum_j S(p_i, a_j) \tag{3}$$

Please note that $S(p_i)$ so far only reflects the processes' general suitability for the demands stated by the attributes, but does not consider how much each attribute contributes to the organization's success, and how often the respective capability is actually required for the organization's business. The former can be determined by prioritizing the attributes, e.g., through pair-wise comparison [19]; the latter is considered through the product and project analyses. Prioritizing the attributes orders them by importance. This order can be projected on any scale, reflecting each attribute's relative importance. A projection on 50%...100%, for example, would mean that the least important attribute is considered half as important as the most important attribute.

We reflect the variance in attribute importance by adjusting the generic process suitability through the introduction of an organizational factor. The organizational factor $O(a_j)$ for attribute j is determined by multiplying the process demand D for a specific attribute j with the relative importance I of this attribute for the organization's success, as determined by the attribute prioritization (Eqn. 4).

$$O(a_j) = D(a_j) \cdot I(a_j) \tag{4}$$

The organizational factor $O(a_j)$ is then applied to the process suitability $S(p_i, a_j)$ for process i and attribute j, resulting in an organization-specific process suitability index $S_o(p_i, a_j)$. This adjusts the generic suitability according to the organization's business. The result indicates the suitability of the analyzed processes with respect to the process demands of products and projects and each analysis attribute's contribution to the organization's success (Eqn. 5).

$$S_o(p_i, a_j) = S(p_i, a_j) \cdot O(a_j) \tag{5}$$

Finally, the organization-specific process suitability $S_o(p_i)$ of an individual process i can be determined by summing up the individual organization-specific process suitability values of all attributes j for this process (Eqn. 6).

$$S_o(p_i) = \sum_j S_o(p_i, a_j) \tag{6}$$

The suitability index $S_o(p_i)$ describes how well an organization's processes fit all of its demands, i.e., how well they support the product and project characteristics that were identified in total. Fig. 1 shows a graphical rendition of the suitability index of a (fictional) company for its five requirements processes and four design processes. This information can be used, for instance, to focus training: Teaching the example organization's employees *Delphi* will benefit it more than, for example, *Storyboards,* because the *Delphi* process is far more suitable (i.e., fulfills more and more often requested demands) than the *Storyboards* process.

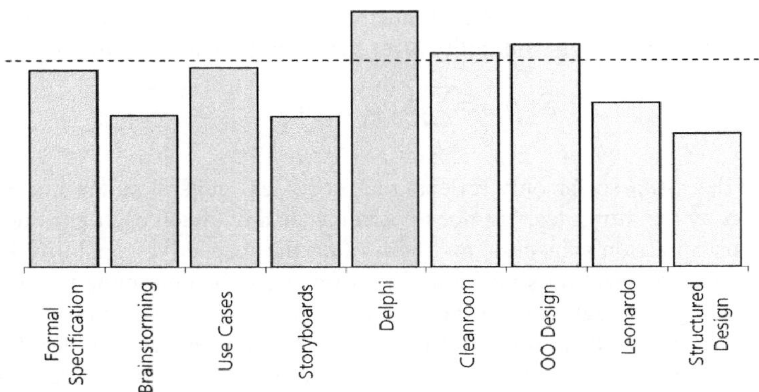

Fig. 1. Example of an organization-specific suitability index (graphical rendition)

Based on the suitability index $S_o(p_i)$, an organization may also adjust the scope of its processes. We will introduce two possible scenarios here: (1) an input-constrained scenario, and (2) an output-constrained scenario.

In the input-constrained scenario, an organization has a limited amount of resources (typically effort or budget) available, and wants to put them to their best use. Using the suitability index $S_o(p_i)$ as an ordering criterion, the processes can be ordered according to their suitability for the organization. Assuming that the organization can provide a budget for maintaining and evolving *n* processes, it can simply choose the first *n* processes from the ordered list, which provide the best support for the entirety of the organization's products and projects. This means that the *globally best* processes are selected. For example, when our example company's budget is sufficient for two processes each for requirements and design, it would choose *Delphi* and *Use Cases* for the former and *OO Design* and *Cleanroom* for the latter.

In the output-constrained scenario, an organization requires processes to achieve a certain minimum suitability in order to be utilized and maintained. Again using the suitability index $S_o(p_i)$, the organization can define thresholds for the requirements and the design processes, based on experience from past projects. Processes with a suitability index below these thresholds will be discarded; only those with equal or higher suitability indices will be kept. The threshold that was set in our example company is depicted by the dashed line in Fig. 1. As can be seen, from the requirements processes, only *Delphi* is accepted, and from the design processes, *Cleanroom* and *OO Design* are accepted. The other processes are deemed unsuitable and should either be discarded or improved in order to reach the threshold.

5 Validation

The SCOPE approach was validated by means of a controlled experiment and an industrial case study. The validation was aimed at showing that SCOPE (a) allows for a greater reduction in unnecessary process variability than ad-hoc selection (hypothesis H1); (b) allows for selecting processes that cover a broader range of demands than ad-hoc selection (H2); (c) allows for reducing process management effort compared to ad-hoc methods (H3); and (d) is fit for industrial application (H4).

The experiment with master students at the University of Kaiserslautern evaluated hypotheses H1 through H4. During the experiment, the students were provided with information describing an organization's projects, its demands with respect to processes, and the processes of the organization itself. They were asked to perform typical process management tasks, e.g., identify suitable and unsuitable processes and identify improvement opportunities.

The application of SCOPE at the Japan Aerospace Exploration Agency (JAXA) tested H1, H3, and H4 in an industrial environment. This included the performance of product and project analyses, attribute prioritization, and a process analysis, and followed the output-constrained scenario, where the goal was to fully support all projects, i.e., to keep all identified processes that were used in the analyzed projects.

5.1 Controlled Experiment

In order to be able to control a higher number of environmental influence factors than is possible in industrial case studies, a controlled experiment was conducted to evaluate hypotheses H1 through H4. The test subjects were students from the master course "Process Modeling" at the University of Kaiserslautern, held during the summer term 2009. The 13 participating students originated from China, Columbia, Germany, India, Indonesia, the Netherlands, Spain, and Thailand. They were randomly divided into two groups A and B, to account for possibly inhomogeneity. The experiment was divided into five sessions (see Table 1). Three sets of experiment materials were distributed throughout the experiment, each describing a total of 9 projects and 16 processes, 6 of which were designed to be suitable for an organization and 10 were not.

The experiment took three hours and 15 minutes and resulted in eleven usable sets of works results. The work results were analyzed in terms of identified processes and the students' assessment of their suitability (true and false positives/negatives) (H1); the students' correct identification of process gaps (i.e., no suitable process exists) (H2); and with respect to the reduction of process management effort, derived from

Table 1. Experiment design: groups and experiment material

	Group A	Group B
Session 0	Familarization	
Session 1	Ad-hoc Data set 1	Ad-hoc Data set 2
Session 2	SCOPE Training Data Set 3	
Session 3	SCOPE Data Set 2	SCOPE Data Set 1
Session 4	Questionnaire	

the number of removed processes (H3). A Shapiro-Wilk test of normality and an analysis of skewness, kurtosis, and variances of the values denied normality; hence, a one-tailed Wilcoxon signed-ranks test [20] was performed for these hypotheses. A significance criterion of $\alpha = 0.1$ was chosen as a compromise between α error (erroneously accept hypothesis) and β error (erroneously reject hypothesis). H4 was tested using an abridged version of Venkatesh's UTAUT questionnaire [21], resulting in six variables. For two of the variables, normality testing allowed for t-tests, whereas for the other four, only a one-tail binomial sign test could be applied. All tests were significant for $\alpha = 0.05$.

Table 2 displays a summary of the statistical test results. Concerning the hypotheses, the experiment indicates that, compared to ad hoc approaches, SCOPE users:

- (a) make a decision (at all, H1.1) significantly more often, and they can spot suitable processes significantly better (H1.2, H1.4); but no significant difference could be proven for unsuitable processes (H1.3, H1.5)
- (b) detect significantly more process gaps (150% improvement, H2)
- (c) remove significantly more unsuitable processes (on average 83% more), promising a proportional reduction in process management effort (H3)
- (d) perceived the approach very positive (averaging 4.09 on a five-point Likert scale, H4).

Table 2. Experiment results

Hypothesis		Significant	Average effect
H1	Process variations		
H1.1	Decisions	yes	32%
H1.2	True positives	yes	28%
H1.3	True negatives	no	31%
H1.4	False negatives	yes	-79%
H1.5	False positives	n/a*	101%
H2	Process gaps	yes	150%
H3	Process management effort	yes	83%
H4	Acceptance	yes	4.09**

*ranks indicate non-applicability of test

**on a scale of 1 ("completely disagree") to 5 ("completely agree")

5.2 JAXA Case Study

The case study evaluated hypotheses H1, H3, and H4 in JAXA's satellite development segment and actually went beyond pure scope determination, also taking the first steps towards a comprehensive software process line [18]. This resulted in sets of common and variable entities, which were used to evaluate the hypotheses. During the course of the case study, JAXA engineers performed product and project analyses, attribute prioritization, and a process analysis, and followed the output-constrained scenario, where the goal was to fully support all projects. For confidentiality reasons, we cannot disclose the detailed process suitability results here, but we can sketch the general conclusions that were drawn.

The results of the scoping activities showed that all identified project types (national/international and scientific/engineering) share 86% of their activities and 77% of their artifacts. This means that only 14% of the activities and 23% of the artifacts *must* vary between the analyzed project types – the rest is unnecessary, yet real variation. So, by using the results of the scoping activity, JAXA could reduce the *potential* variation of their processes across activities and artifacts by an average of 82%: Instead of creating, establishing, and maintaining two completely independent satellite development process standards, they could share all common entities – effectively reducing variation for these entities to zero, which confirms hypothesis H1. By using the scoping results, JAXA also needs to maintain the common elements of the process standards only once, thus reducing management effort for each by half. Assuming that maintenance effort for all activities and artifacts is identical, SCOPE thus enabled a reduction in process management effort by 41%, confirming hypothesis H3. Finally, the feedback collected from JAXA engineers during the application of the SCOPE approach was positive. While the language barrier turned out to be something of an obstacle, product and project as well as process analyses could be performed in the course of the daily work of the JAXA process engineers. The case study results therefore support our assumption that the results from the controlled experiment with respect to hypothesis H4 can be transferred to industrial practice. Table 3 displays an overview of the results of the performed studies.

Table 3. Study results overview

Hypothesis		Controlled experiment	JAXA case study
H1	Process variations	(✓)[1] 46%	✓ 82%
H2	Process gaps	✓ 150%	
H3	Process management effort	✓ 83%	✓ 41%
H4	Acceptance	✓ 4.09 [2]	(✓) [3]

[1] Accepted with respect to making decisions and identifying suitable process variants, but not unsuitable variants

[2] On average, on a scale of 1 ("completely disagree") to 5 ("completely agree")

[3] No comparison value available: based on qualitative data

To summarize, the validation showed that (a) the application of the approach in a controlled experiment led to a 46% reduction in unnecessary process variability compared to ad-hoc approaches and allowed for an 82% reduction in an industrial case study; (b) SCOPE users identified 150% more misalignments between processes and demands in a controlled experiment than when working ad-hoc; (c) the application of the SCOPE approach allowed for a reduction in process management effort of 83% in a controlled experiment and of 41% in an industrial case study; and (d) the SCOPE approach and results were accepted by the controlled experiment participants as well as by the engineers in the industrial case study as a means of providing adequate support for process management.

6 Discussion and Future Work

In our opinion, the greatest advantage of the SCOPE approach is that it makes explicit a number of facts and decisions that are implicit at best otherwise. This way, they can be discussed and evaluated, something that is not possible for implicit knowledge. Another advantage is that the approach makes an organization very flexible within its scope. Setting up a new (or modified) process based on the process landscape can be completed very quickly, as opposed to fully tailoring a standard. For products or projects outside the scope, this is obviously not the case. However, from our experience, this kind of flexibility on a global scale ("we're great at everything") is an illusion anyway. Therefore, SCOPE assists organizations in determining their scope and then achieving process excellence for this scope.

Both product and project analyses encourage an organization's process engineers to think about the product and project future of the organization. This likely leads to identifying information that would otherwise have been neglected. The same applies to process analysis: A thorough analysis of the currently used processes' capabilities with respect to the actual needs of the organization is hardly ever done. The results of this analysis can help to rationalize otherwise sometimes rather emotional discussions regarding advantages and disadvantages of individual processes.

The two scenarios for using the suitability index can help an organization decide about its process future. They reflect two typical industry scenarios, where either an existing budget should be used optimally, or past experience is used as benchmark for process evaluation. From our experience, assistance with these types of questions is often sought, but typical model-based SPI approaches such as CMMI or SPICE do not provide this.

So far, the scenarios support determining what could be called the "global" suitability of an organization's processes. While this helps to determine the "value" of individual processes for the respective organization, there may be scenarios where a process-individual evaluation might not yield the best possible result for an organization. For example, within some organizations, one process may score high for one half of the analysis attributes, while yielding only low scores for the other half. Another process may behave vice versa. In total, these two processes would reach a mediocre suitability index, "losing" against a third process that is slightly better for all

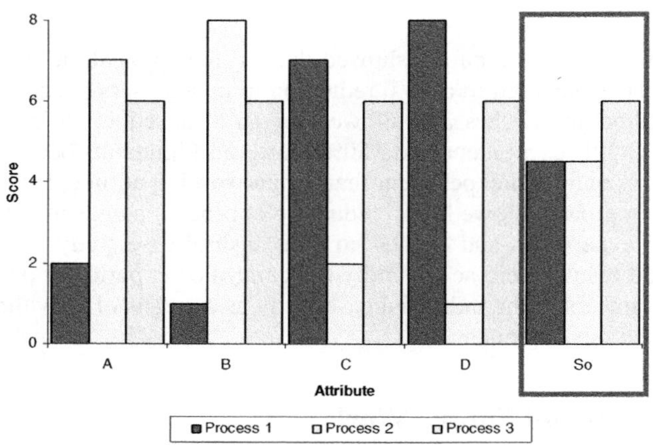

Fig. 2. Combining very different processes

attributes – but not as good as any of the two is for some. Fig. 2 displays this situation. It shows the analysis scores for three processes for four attributes and the resulting suitability index S_o (red box to the right, assuming equal attribute importance). It becomes apparent that process 3 achieves the highest value for S_o, qualifying it for selection. However, a combination of process 1 and process 2 might prove to be more beneficial for the organization if their advantages with respect to the four attributes can be combined. We plan to investigate this interesting possibility in the future.

Acknowledgments

We would like to thank Ms. Sonnhild Namingha from Fraunhofer IESE for reviewing the first version of this article. We also thank the anonymous reviewers for their valuable comments on the first version of this article.

References

1. Schmid, K.: Planning Software Reuse - A Disciplined Scoping Approach for Software Product Lines. PhD Thesis, Department of Computer Science, University of Kaiserslautern, Germany (2003)
2. Bayer, J., Kose, M., Ocampo, A.: Improving the Development of e-Business Systems by Introducing Process-Based Software Product Lines. In: Münch, J., Vierimaa, M. (eds.) PROFES 2006. LNCS, vol. 4034, pp. 348–361. Springer, Heidelberg (2006)
3. Cohen, L.: Quality Function Deployment: How to Make QFD Work for You. Addison-Wesley Longman, Amsterdam (1995)
4. Biffl, S., Halling, M.: Managing Software Inspection Knowledge for Decision Support of Inspection Planning. In: Aurum, A., Jeffery, R., Wohlin, C., Handzic, M. (eds.) Managing Software Engineering Knowledge. Springer, Berlin (2003)
5. Schweikhard, T.: Identification of inspection-variation-factors for a decision-support-tool. Diploma Thesis, Department of Computer Science, University of Kaiserslautern, Germany (2006)
6. Vegas, S., Basili, V.R.: A Characterization Schema for Software Testing Techniques. Empirical Software Engineering 10(4), 437–466 (2005)
7. Madachy, R., Boehm, B.: Assessing Quality Processes with ODC COQUALMO. In: Wang, Q., Pfahl, D., Raffo, D.M. (eds.) ICSP 2008. LNCS, vol. 5007, pp. 198–209. Springer, Heidelberg (2008)
8. Boehm, B.W., Harrowitz, E.: Software Cost Estimation with Cocomo II. Prentice Hall International, Englewood Cliffs (2000)
9. Denger, C., Elberzhager, F.: A Comprehensive Framework for Customizing Quality Assurance Techniques, IESE-Report No. 118.06/E, Fraunhofer Institute for Experimental Software Engineering (ISCE), Kaiserslautern, Germany (2006)
10. Rus, I., Collofello, J.S.: A Decision Support System for Software Reliability Engineering Strategy Selection. In: Proceedings of the 23rd Annual International Computer Software and Applications Conference, Phoenix, AZ, USA, pp. 376–381 (1999)
11. Jedlitschka, A., Pfahl, D.: Towards Comprehensive Experience-based Decision Support. In: Dingsøyr, T. (ed.) EuroSPI 2004. LNCS, vol. 3281, pp. 34–45. Springer, Heidelberg (2004)

12. Becker, U., Hamann, D., Verlage, M.: Descriptive Modeling of Software Processes, ISERN Report 97-10, Fraunhofer Institute for Experimental Software Engineering (IESE), Kaiserslautern, Germany (1997)
13. Avison, D.E., Wood-Harper, A.T.: Information Systems Development Research: An Exploration of Ideas in Practice. The Computer Journal 34(2), 98–112 (1991)
14. Becker, A.L., Prikladnicki, R., Audy, J.L.N.: Strategic Alignment of Software Process Improvement Programs Using QFD. In: Proceedings of the ICSE 2008 Workshop on Business Impact of Process Improvements (BIPI 2008), Leipzig, Germany, May 13 (2008)
15. Fitzgerald, B., Russo, N.L., O'Kane, T.: Software Development Method Tailoring at Motorola. Communications of the ACM 46(4), 65–70 (2003)
16. Collaboration website of the European Cooperation for Space Standardization, `http://www.ecss.nl/` (last visited April 25, 2009)
17. BSSC Guides and Reports, `http://www.esa.int/TEC/Software_engineering_and_standardisation/` (last visited April 24, 2009)
18. Armbrust, O., Katahira, M., Miyamoto, Y., Münch, J., Nakao, H., Ocampo, A.: Scoping Software Process Lines. Software Process: Improvement and Practice 14(3), 181–197 (2008)
19. David, H.A.: The Method of Paired Comparisons. Lubrecht & Cramer, Limited (1988)
20. Sheskin, D.J.: Handbook of Parametric and Nonparametric Statistical Procedures. CRC Press, Boca Raton (1997)
21. Venkatesh, V., Morris, M.G., Davis, G.B., Davis, F.D.: User Acceptance of Information Technology: Toward a Unified View. MIS Quarterly 27(3), 425–478 (2003)

On Scoping Stakeholders and Artifacts in Software Process

Xu Bai[1], LiGuo Huang[1], and He Zhang[2]

[1] Department of Computer Science and Engineering,
Southern Methodist University, Dallas, TX 75205, USA
{bxu,lghuang}@engr.smu.edu
[2] National ICT Australia
University of New South Wales, Sydney, Australia
he.zhang@nicta.com.au

Abstract. Stakeholder and artifact are considered as two important elements in software engineering processes, but they are rarely systematically investigated in software process modeling and simulation. Inspired by the Workshop of Modeling Systems and Software Engineering Processes in 2008 at the University of Southern California and our previous studies on integrating stakeholders' perspectives into software process modeling, we undertook a study on the application of these entities in software engineering, through both a systematic review and a complementary web survey within software process research and practice communities. Our results reveal that the portion of studies on process stakeholders and process artifacts in software engineering is unexpectedly small, and there lacks consistent understanding of process stakeholder roles. By further analysis of stakeholder roles and artifact types based on our results, we define the stakeholder and artifact in the lieu of software process engineering, and differentiate stakeholder and artifact in different application scopes.

1 Introduction

Process modeling and simulation allows individuals (e.g. project manager) or organizations to verify and validate the correctness and to monitor or control the operations of software processes as a generative software system [1]. Identifying the high priority concerns of process stakeholders and process artifacts they depend on are two critical success factors for the selection, integration and design of effective process modeling and simulation techniques. Overlooking them often leads to developing or selecting sub-optimal process modeling and simulation techniques. In software engineering, stakeholders are defined as *individuals or organizations who will be affected by the system and who have a direct or indirect influence on the system requirements* [2] [3], Software artifacts, as *a piece of information that is produced, modified, or used by a process* [4], are associated with these stakeholder roles. Neither definition explicitly explains or identifies stakeholders or artifacts associated with software process modeling itself.

Modeling Systems and Software engineering Processes (MSSP) Workshop[5] held at University of Southern California in 2008 identified an initial set of

J. Münch, Y. Yang, and W. Schäfer (Eds.): ICSP 2010, LNCS 6195, pp. 39–51, 2010.

process modeling stakeholder roles and their top-level modeling goals. Their dependencies on existing process modeling & simulation techniques were also discussed.

While trying to integrate different process modeling techniques based on various process modeling stakeholders' perpectives to address software process trustworthiness [6], we found that the understanding of process stakeholder roles were inconsistent in existing software process related literatures. One typical issue is that process modeling stakeholders and process enactment stakeholders are not clearly scoped or distinguished. For instance, Requirement Engineering (RE) papers often refer project stakeholders involved in RE activities as "requirement process stakeholders" [7]. However, they actually mean project stakeholders involved in RE activities instead of process modeling stakeholders involved in or dependent on process modeling or simulation. Similarly, a majority of artifact-related literature study software product artifacts such as requirement specifications, design documents, source codes, etc. Process artifacts produced from or used by process modeling activities, (e.g. process guidelines, regulations and management plans) are seldom investigated or mentioned.

In response to stakeholder-oriented software process modeling research [5], there is an emergent need to:

- Scope, classify and define stakeholders and artifacts in software process;
- Study and analyze the understanding of proposed process modeling stakeholder roles [5] within software process communities.

To achieve these objectives, we have followed a two step approach. We started with a Systematic Literature Review (SLR) performed on stakeholder and artifact related studies in software process related research. Then we harvested the preliminary results and initially proposed process modeling stakeholder roles in [5] with their associated process artifacts and undertook a questionnaire based web survey to investigate the overall agreement of these two entities in software process research and practice communities.

2 Background and Related Work

2.1 Software Engineering Process

Processes are difficult to identify because their boundaries are often not defined [8]. In software engineering, process (software process) consists of a set of logically ordered tasks or activities in order to deliver or to maintain a software product [9]. Fenton and Pfleeger distinguish three classes of elements in software development: process, product, and resource entities [10].

- Process: collection of software-related activities.
- Product: any artifacts or deliverables that result from a process activity.
- Resource: entities required by a process activity, e.g. tools, roles, and actors.

These three classes also correspond to the entities abstracted in the three dimensions of software development identified in the recent TRISO-Model [11], i.e. actors (SE Human), activities (SE Process), and artifacts (SE Technology).

A software process model is an abstract representation of the software process, that is, it is a collection of recognized patterns of *process enactment* actions and behaviors. Software process can be viewed as a software generative system that comprises both models and enactments [12].

In [13], we divided the software process activities into *process modeling* activities and *process enactment* activities, and the process stakeholders and process artifacts can be also classified corresponding to these two software process concepts (as shown in Fig. 1). The *process modeling* artifacts are generated by the *process modeling* activities but influence the *process enactment* activities, while the *process enactment* artifacts are produced by the *process enactment* activities but influence the *process models.*

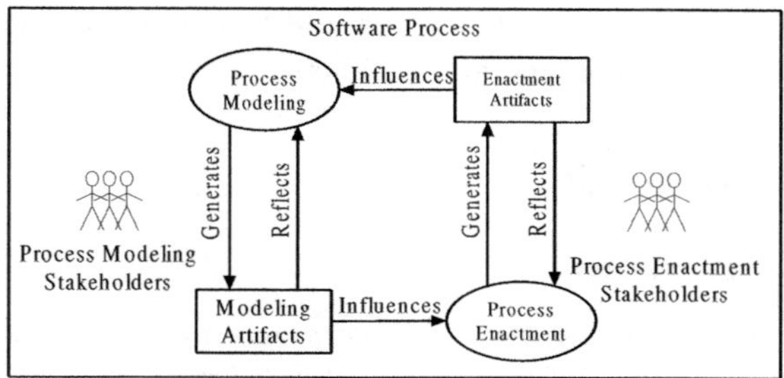

Fig. 1. Software Process as a Generative System: Components and Interactions

2.2 Related Works

VBSE. In 2003, Boehm presents an overview and agenda for Value- Based Software Engineering (VBSE) [14]. The center of VBSE is the stakeholder win-win Theory W, which addresses the questions, like "*which values are important?*" and "*how is success assured?*", for a given software engineering enterprise [14]. VBSE, as a stakeholder-oriented approach, reinforced the stakeholder roles' interactions in the software development process, and its stakeholder WinWin model became a canonical reconciling differing value proposition approach in empirical and evidenced-based software engineering.

MSSP Workshop. Process Modeling Stakeholder roles were initially summarized and discussed in MSSP [5], in which Boehm et al. proposed a list of possible process modeling stakeholders. The major purpose of this proposal is to support the development of process modeling paradigms (e.g. Little-JIL, Petri-Net, System Dynamics), compare and select the appropriate modeling tools, and integrate them, in terms of the identified process modeling stakeholders. The proposed process modeling stakeholders includes *process performer* (PP), *process engineer* (PE), *process manager* (PM), *customer* (CU), *educator* (ED), *tool provider* (TP), *researcher* (RS), *regulator* (RG), *standardizer* (SD) and *domain specific stakeholder* (DS).

This list is generated from a brainstorming session in MSSP Workshop based on the behavior analysis of people involved in software process modeling activities. A set of goals of process modeling and simulation were also identified.

Stakeholder-Oriented Process Modeling. In [6], we integrated multiple process modeling technologies to model software process changes regarding different perspectives of process modeling stakeholders. In the case study, however, we found process enactments activities are limited to process enactment stakeholder roles (e.g. process performer). For example, it is difficult to link the process modeling stakeholders' roles to the process enactment activities. Similarly, most current research on the lower level process enactment may have difficulty in addressing all the process modeling stakeholders' concerns. To leverage future stakeholder-oriented researches in software process, a broader scope of software process scope (than *process enactment*) should be sought to endorse the *process modeling* activities, stakeholders, and artifacts.

3 Research Methods

3.1 Research Questions

Our major objective is to investigate '*how people understand stakeholders and artifacts based on existing software process related research*', which can be specified as following research questions:

RQ1. What is the scope where the stakeholders are identified/studied in software process related research?
RQ2. What are the stakeholder roles in software process?
RQ3. What is the scope where the artifacts are produced or used in software process related research?
RQ4. What are software process artifacts and what is the relationship between these artifacts and software process?
RQ5. How are the proposed process modeling stakeholder roles [5] agreed in software process research and practice communities?
RQ6. How are the proposed process modeling artifacts agreed in software process research and practice communities?

Systematic Literature Review was chosen as our main research method in this study. During the pilot of SLR, however, two questions (RQ5-6) cannot be effectively addressed by the studies. Therefore, questionnaire-based online survey was employed as a complementary method to seek answers to them.

3.2 Systematic Literature Review on Stakeholders and Artifacts

SLR, as an effective method in EBSE, has been adopted in researching a variety of topics in software engineering. Our SLR followed the guidelines proposed by Kitchenham [15]. Three researchers participated in the review process, acting as principal reviewer, checker, and mediator. This subsection briefs the method, more detailed process and results of the SLR are available in [16].

Search Strategy. We combined manual search and automated search in order to maximize the capture of relevant studies on stakeholders and artifacts, which were published prior to 2009. The following major publication channels in software engineering (conferences and journals) were first selected and search issue by issue, paper by paper.

-Journals: TSE, IEEE Software, TOSEM, SPIP, JMSE, JSS, ESE, IST, SPE and IJSI

-Conferences: ICSE, ProSim/SPW, ICSP, PROFES, ISESE/ESEM, MATRICS, EuroSPI, SPICE and PROMISE

The keywords were extracted from the identified studies by the manual search, including '*software*', '*process*', '*project*', '*stakeholder*', '*artifact*'. They were combined to form a group of search strings for automated search. Other relevant keywords, like '*role*' and '*work product*', were excluded because no more relevant studies were retrieved when including them during the trials. Using these search strings, the *title-abstract-keyword* fields were searched through five major digital libraries, i.e. ACM Digital Library, IEEE Xplore, Springer Link, ScienceDirect and Wiley InterScience.

Study Selection. The literature inclusion and exclusion criteria are defined in the SLR protocol [16]. The included primary studies belong to one of the following categories:

• Studies focusing on stakeholder interactions in software engineering;
• Studies which propose and/or apply stakeholder-oriented approaches in software engineering;
• Studies focusing on management of software artifacts;
• Studies which propose new software artifacts in software engineering.

But the studies in following categories are excluded during review:

• Business process related studies;
• Studies focusing on tool implementation;
• Tutorials, editorials, posters, position papers, keynotes, abstract, short papers.

For any duplicate or continued publications, only the latest or the most comprehensive versions were included. We adopt a two-step approach to the study selection process (described in [16]).

Due to the page limit, the quality assessment and data extraction of this SLR are not described in this paper, but is accessible in [16].

3.3 Questionnaire-Based Survey on Process Modeling, Stakeholders and Artifacts

In order to answer the RQ5-6, we conducted a questionnaire-based online survey on process modeling (simulation) stakeholders, their dependencies on two classes of process modeling & simulation techniques (i.e., discrete and continuous) and process artifacts. One of its major objectives is to find out how process stakeholder roles proposed in [5] and the process artifacts they depend on are accepted in software process communities.

By analyzing the proposed process modeling stakeholder roles in [5], we proposed their dependent process artifacts and their entity relation model as shown in Fig. 2. The stakeholder roles and process artifacts are denoted by figurines and eclipse respectively. Each line indicates that a process artifact is generated or used by the corresponding process stakeholder.

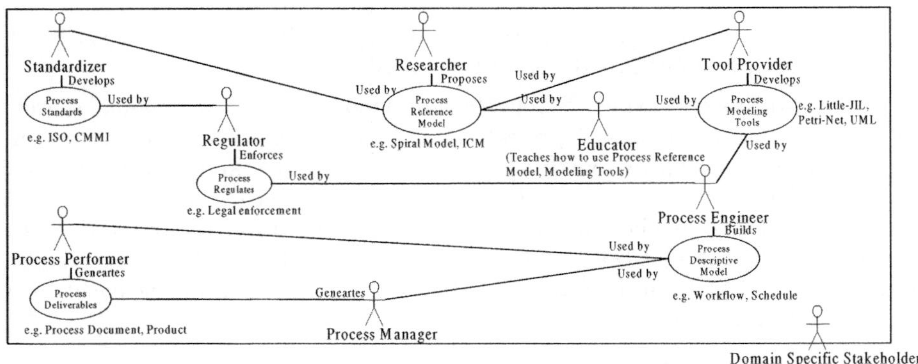

Fig. 2. Process Stakeholders, Process Artifacts and Relationships among them

We have developed 30 questions based on 10 selected process modeling stakeholder roles from [5], 6 process artifacts that these stakeholders usually depend on, and two typical categories of process modeling/simulation techniques.

4 Results

Systematic Literature Review. We selected totally 32 software engineering literatures for the stakeholder study after combining both manual and automatic search results. Among them, 24 pieces are major studies on stakeholders, while the other 8 pieces are minor studies relevant to but not focusing on stakeholders. These studies can be also categorized by sources of their case studies (i.e., from industrial or academic/open source projects). Table 1 shows the statistics.

Totally 25 studies relevant to artifacts were included in our SLR. Table 2 shows 4 different categorizations of these studies. Among the included studies,

Table 1. Two Categorizations of SLR Included Stakeholder-Relevant Studies: Major/Minor Studies and With/Without Case Studies

		Number of Papers	Percentage
Categorization 1	Major Studies	24	75.00%
	Minor Studies	8	25.00%
Categorization 2	With Case Studies from Industry	14	43.75%
	With Case Studies from Academic /Open Source Projects	18	56.25%

Table 2. Four Categorizations of SLR Included Artifact-Relevant Studies:: Major/Minor Studies, With/Without Case Studies and Artifact Types

		Number of Papers	Percentage
Categorization 1	Major Studies	19	76.00%
	Minor Studies	6	24.00%
Categorization 2	With Case Studies from Industry	3	12.00%
	With Case Studies from Academic /Open Source	21	84.00%
	No Case Study	1	4.00%
Categorization 3	Software/Project Artifacts	17	68.00%
	Process Artifacts	8	32.00%
Categorization 4	Specific Artifacts	10	40.00%
	General Artifacts	15	60.00%

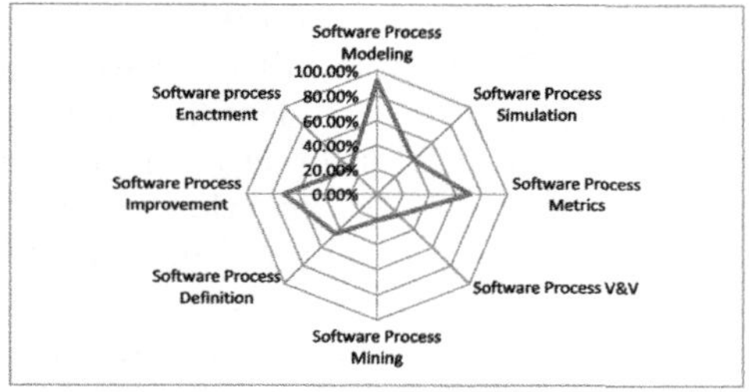

Fig. 3. Process Related Professional Background of 38 of Survey Participants

19 pieces are major studies on artifacts, while the other 6 are minor studies relevant to but not focusing on artifacts. Another categorization shows that 3 of the included studies are enhanced with industrial case studies, and the other 21 either use academic/open source project case studies or lack of case studies. In addition, 40% of the studies discuss specific artifacts, while 60% of them refer to general artifacts used in software development activities.

Web Survey. After sending out 144 invitations among software process research communities (ICSP, ProSIM etc.), we have got 38 responses. The response rate is 26.4%. Fig.3 shows the statistical distribution of all survey takers' professional background with respect to the software process. Most of their professions are related to Software Process Modeling (92.11%), Software Process Metrics (71.05%) and Software Process Improvement (71.05%) with overlap across various areas. Such distribution indicates that our survey results highly represent majority opinions from researchers and/or practitioners in software process modeling communities.

5 Findings and Insights from SLR and Online Survey

Statistics from both SLR and online survey reveal two major issues in existing software engineering process research.

- The portion of studies on process stakeholders and process artifacts is unexpectedly smaller than other studies, such as process modeling and process simulation techniques.
- There lacks consistent understanding on the definition and classification of process stakeholders in existing software process research. Specifically, 6 findings and our insights on stakeholders and artifacts in software process related research are presented below with evidence. Each finding provides at least a partial answer to one research question listed in section 3.1.

5.1 Stakeholders in Software Process Related Research

***Finding 1*: Stakeholders in software process related research were identified/studied more in the project development/maintenance activities but much less in the process modeling activities.**

This is discovered from SLR with regard to research question RQ1. In our selected studies, the stakeholder roles are identified in three different context. 78.13% of the included studies identify or discuss stakeholder roles in the project context (e.g., [17]). 9.38% of the studies mention organizational stakeholders (e.g., [3]), responsible for inter/intra organization project management. Only 12.50% of the studies explicitly identify or discuss "process stakeholder" roles and none of these roles are involved in process modeling but process enactment [12]. For example, "requirement process stakeholders" are identified in [7], which are actually roles in the developing requirement specifications during process enactment (e.g., customer, designer, architect etc.).

Thus, majority of software engineering research refer stakeholder roles in the project scope rather than in the process or organizational scope. Even in the excluded literatures from the SLR, organizational stakeholders are studied or referred more in business or government related research than others. In the SLR, unfortunately we did not find any definition or explicit attention to "process stakeholders" especially in process modeling.

***Finding 2*: Process stakeholder roles in software process related research were not clearly define or classified.**

This is revealed from SLR with regard to research question RQ2. We could not find any definition or classification of process stakeholder roles in our included studies. Thus, a clear definition and classification of Software Process Stakeholders, especially Process Modeling Stakeholders, are needed.

In [17], Project Stakeholders are defined as *people who have a stake or interest in the project.* In [3], the organizational stakeholder is defined as *any group or individual who can affect or is affected by the achievement of the organization's objectives.* We here define the Software Process Stakeholder as following.

***Definition 1*: Software Process Stakeholder is any group or individual who can affect or is affected by the software development and/or maintenance process as a generative system.**

We classify Process Stakeholders into Process Modeling Stakeholders and Process Enactment Stakeholders. Process Modeling Stakeholders can affect or is affected by software process modeling activities and techniques, who depend more on process artifacts (section 5.2 Definition 2). Process Enactment Stakeholders participate in the execution of software process. Process enactment stakeholders may be overlapped with process modeling stakeholders and they show more dependency on project artifacts. A set of process modeling stakeholder roles was initially proposed in [5] including Process Manager, Process Engineer, Process Performer, etc.

Different stakeholder roles in various scopes could be applicable to the same person. Project/organizational stakeholders could also act as process enactment stakeholders during the process execution. In the included studies, when discussing process stakeholders, their roles as project/organizational stakeholder are actually referred to in most cases. We also note that project/organizational stakeholders instantiate process enactment stakeholder roles, e.g. the various enactment roles of Process Performer (a Process Stakeholder role) in a project such as the project manager, developers, designers, etc.

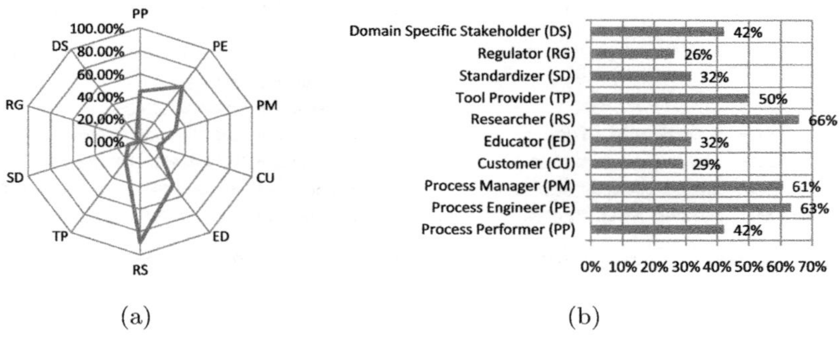

Fig. 4. (a) Process Modeling Stakeholder Roles Played by Survey Participants, and (b) Agreements on Proposed Process Modeling Stakeholder Roles

***Finding 3*: There was a high degree of agreement on the proposed process modeling stakeholder roles except two in software process communities.**

This finding is summarized from our online survey results pertaining to research question RQ5. We asked all survey participants to identify their roles among proposed process modeling stakeholder roles [5], as shown in Fig. 4(a). Except the Regulator role, all proposed roles have been identified with Researchers (89.47%) and Process Engineers (60.53%), the top two roles played in software process community.

We also ask survey participants to rate their acceptance of proposed process modeling stakeholder roles. Fig. 4(b) plots the acceptance rates. PE (63.16%), PM (60.53%) and RS (65.79%) are among the highest agreed process modeling stakeholder roles. CU (28.95%) and RG (26.32%) obtain the lowest agreement.

5.2 Artifacts in Software Process Related Research

***Finding 4*: Software/Project artifacts gained more attention than process modeling artifacts.**

This is concluded from SLR regarding research question RQ3. In Table 2, 68% of included studies look into Software/Project Artifacts (e.g. requirement specifications, code), which are product oriented. 32% discusses Process Modeling Artifacts, e.g. Electrical Process Guide (EPG). Some of project artifacts can be process related artifacts, e.g. budget plan etc. However, the number of studies on this type of artifact is relatively small.

***Finding 5*: Artifacts were mostly studied as work products of various enactment activities in software process but less in modeling activities.**

This is shown from SLR related to research question RQ4. Fig. 5(a) shows related uniform distribution of software development process activities where artifacts are produced or used. Fig. 5(b) shows the frequency of occurrences of specific artifacts in the included studies. Source Code (44%), Design Document (40%) and Requirement Specification (32%) are among the top.

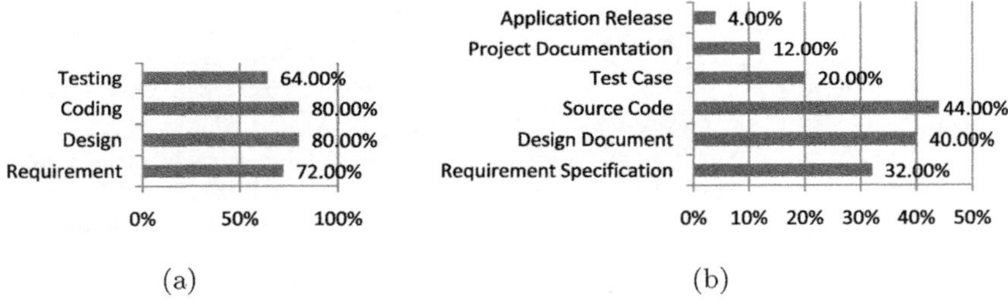

Fig. 5. (a) Software Process Activities Producing or Using artifacts, and (b) Specific Artifacts Discussed in Included Studies

The Artifact is defined as *a piece of information that is produced, modified, or used by a process* [4]. However, the above SLR results (Fig. 5) show that "software artifacts" referred in included studies are artifacts produced or used in software development/maintenance process activities, but there lacks clear understanding of artifacts produced or used in process modeling activities. We define the Process Artifact as following.

***Definition 2*: Process artifacts are information produced or used by process engineering and execution activities.**

Process Modeling Artifacts, as the work products of process engineering related activities, e.g. process models, EPG, process standards, are seldom investigated but gaining more and more attention nowadays. They usually perform as an aid to ensure and improve the quality process enactment.

***Finding 6*: Consistent agreement on proposed Process Modeling Artifacts in software process communities.**

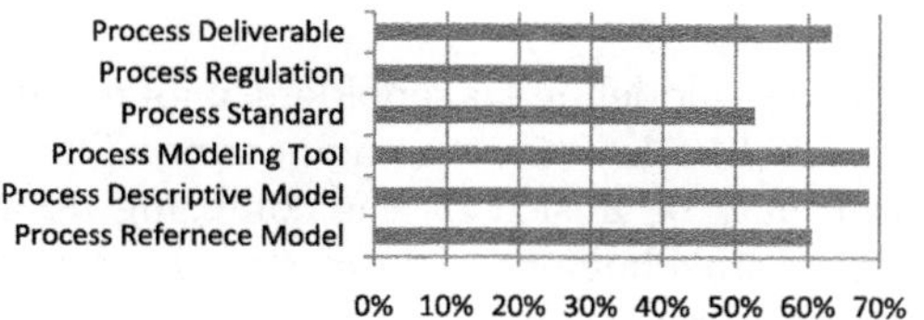

Fig. 6. Process Artifacts Agreement Rates by Survey Participants

This is supported by the online survey results regarding research question RQ6. We initially proposed potential process artifact classes, including Process Reference Models, Process Descriptive Models, Process Modeling Tools, Process Standards, Process Regulations and Process Deliverables. We also denote the relationships among process modeling stakeholders and process artifacts by Fig. 2, without formally defining these terms. Each survey participant was asked to select necessary process artifacts from our proposed list. They were also allowed to propose new process modeling artifacts. Fig. 6 plots the agreement on these process modeling artifacts. Except Process Regulations, the agreement rates of other 5 process artifact classes are all beyond 50%.

6 Discussion

Process Stakeholders. Based on our observations of the available studies, the stakeholder concepts in software engineering are varying between their application context and different research perspectives. Process stakeholders have a very broad coverage because: 1) the *process modeling stakeholders*, who concern more in selecting the appropriate process modeling/simulation techniques, are involved in or affected by the course of activities relating the process model; 2) the *process enactment stakeholders* are involved in executing the activities defined by process models, which generate the software product. They can be further instantiated as more specific project/organization stakeholders depending on their application scenarios.

Threats to Validity. Due to the limited access to the full-text of a small number of papers, our work may miss a few important studies on stakeholder or artifact. This issue may have somewhat impact on out findings. Nevertheless, as most of these studies were published in the early years (before 2000), we believe such impact would not be significant to our conclusions. Another possible limitation is that the respondents to our survey are not uniformly distributed within the proposed process modeling stakeholder roles. For example, no RG in our respondents, and SD, DS and CU are less than 20%. It may also reflects the current composite of the roles in software process research community.

7 Conclusion and Future Work

The introduction of process modeling stakeholders in [5] reshuffled the traditional usage scenarios of stakeholder in software engineering. The research on process modeling & simulation may be misled by the confusing usage descriptions and classifications of process stakeholders, project stakeholders and organizational stakeholders. process modeling & simulation.

In this paper, we revisited and extended the results from [5] to include process artifacts into an entity-relation model among process modeling stakeholders and artifacts. An extensive SLR on stakeholder and artifact related studies and a complimentary online survey enable us to analyze the current status of software process related stakeholder & artifact research. Based on findings and insights from the SLR and survey, we here propose tentative definitions and classifications for process stakeholders and artifacts.

The envision of our next steps are to: 1) perform an extensive SLR focusing on process modeling studies, to find the relationships among process stakeholders, process artifacts and process modeling techniques. 2) improve our analysis and understanding by including studies on stakeholder and artifact in other highly related domains.

Acknowledgements

He Zhang's research is supported by NICTA which is funded by the Australian Government as represented by the Department of Broadband, Communications and the Digital Economy and the Australian Research Council through the ICT Centre of Excellence program, and also supported, in part, by Science Foundation Ireland grant 03/CE2/I303 1 to Lero - the Irish Software Engineering Research Centre (www.lero.ie).

References

1. Osterweil, L.: Software processes are software too. In: ICSE 1987: Proceedings of the 9th international conference on Software Engineering, pp. 2–13. IEEE Computer Society Press, Los Alamitos (1987)
2. Kotonya, G., Sommerville, I.: Requirements engineering. Wiley, Chichester (1998)
3. Freeman, R.: Strategic management: A stakeholder approach. Advances in strategic management 1, 31–60 (1983)
4. Thiel, S.: On the definition of a framework for an architecting process supporting product family development. Lecture notes in computer science, pp. 125–142. Springer, Heidelberg (2002)
5. Madachy, R., Koolmanojwong, S., Osterweil, L., Huang, L., Phongpaibul, M.: Presentations on the workshop of modeling systems and software engineering processes (2008), `http://csse.usc.edu/events/2008/ARR/pages/program.html#mon`
6. Bai, X., Huang, L., Zhang, H., Koolmanojwong, S.: Hybrid Modeling and Simulation for Trustworthy Software Process Management: A Stakeholder-Oriented Approach. SPIP submission (2009)

7. Aranda, G., Vizcaino, A., Cechich, A., Piattini, M.: How to choose groupware tools considering stakeholders' preferences during requirements elicitation? In: Haake, J.M., Ochoa, S.F., Cechich, A. (eds.) CRIWG 2007. LNCS, vol. 4715, p. 319. Springer, Heidelberg (2007)
8. Kiraka, R., Manning, K.: Managing organisations through a process-based perspective: its challenges and benefits. Business Change and Re-engineering 12, 288–298 (2005)
9. Curtis, B., Kellner, M.I., Over, J.: Process modeling. Commun. ACM 35, 75–90 (1992)
10. Fenton, N., Pfleeger, S.: Software metrics: a rigorous and practical approach. PWS Publishing Co., Boston (1997)
11. Li, M.: Triso-model: A new approach to integrated software process assessment and improvement: Research sections. Software Process: Improvement and Practice 12, 387–398 (2007)
12. Cohn, M.L., Sim, S.E., Lee, C.P.: What counts as software process? negotiating the boundary of software work through artifacts and conversation. Comput. Supported Coop. Work 18, 401–443 (2009)
13. Bai, X., Huang, L.: A stakeholder perspective in evaluating process modeling languages and hybrid process simulation (2008) Technocal Report
14. Biffl, S., Aurum, A., Boehm, B., Erdogmus, H., Grnbacher, P.: Value-Based Software Engineering. Springer, Heidelberg (2005)
15. Kitchenham, B., Charters, S.: Guidelines for performing systematic literature reviews in software engineering. Version 2, 2007–01 (2007)
16. Bai, X., Huang, L., Zhang, H.: Software Process Stakeholders and Artifacts: A Systematic Review. Technical Report (2009)
17. Cotterell, M., Hughes, B.: Software project management (1995)

Critical Success Factors for Rapid, Innovative Solutions

Jo Ann Lane[1], Barry Boehm[1], Mark Bolas[1], Azad Madni[1], and Richard Turner[2]

[1] University of Southern California
Los Angeles, California, USA
{jolane,boehm,azad.madni}@usc.edu
bolas@ict.usc.edu
[2] Stevens Institute of Technology
Hoboken, New Jersey, USA
rturner@stevens.edu

Abstract. Many of today's problems are in search of new, innovative solutions. However, the development of new and innovative solutions has been elusive to many, resulting in considerable effort and dollars and no solution or a mediocre solution late to the marketplace or customer. This paper describes the results of research conducted to identify the critical success factors employed by several successful, high-performance organizations in the development of innovative systems. These critical success factors span technical, managerial, people, and cultural aspects of the innovative environment.

Keywords: critical success factors, innovation, systems engineering.

1 Introduction

Most programs start up in situations where there is a high premium on early delivery, or where they are already perceived as "behind schedule". These programs are quickly staffed, then jump into requirements analysis and design, continually trying to "catch up". This leaves little time to explore options and look for innovative solutions. As a result, many organizations tend to minimize risk and protect profits by providing "yesterday's solutions" that use known technologies and approaches. However, there can be limits to how far known technologies and approaches can scale and meet the demand for new capabilities and associated attributes such as performance and security.

Many of today's problems are in search of rapidly-developed, innovative solutions. So, the question is, what do projects need to do to encourage the rapid development of innovative solutions? Over the past few years, efforts have been initiated to explore critical success factors for rapid development [1, 2, 3, 4], or for innovation [5, 6]. However, these generally did not explore how these could be achieved together. We have done a mix of interviews and visits with a set of organizations known for providing innovative solutions while reducing development time, in order to determine these critical success factors and how they were employed. The scope of this effort included technical, managerial, people, and cultural aspects of the innovative environment. This paper discusses the details of these explorations.

J. Münch, Y. Yang, and W. Schäfer (Eds.): ICSP 2010, LNCS 6195, pp. 52–61, 2010.

Section 2 provides background information on recent research that has been done in the area of innovation. Section 3 describes the approach used for the identification and analysis of critical success factors for innovation. Section 4 presents the findings that resulted from the analysis of the data collected from interviews and site visits. Section 5 summarizes the analysis into a set of conclusions.

2 Background

Much has been written about innovation in the commercial product development environment. For example, Brown and Eisenhardt [7] talk about competing on the edge by using structured chaos as a strategy. However, attempts to make software and system development processes repeatable and manageable are based upon concepts such as Max Weber's bureaucratic organizational concepts and Fredrick Taylor's scientific management concepts which focus on compartmentalization and division of labor [8]. Kreitman [8] refers to this as the Weber/Taylor bureaucracy and its influence can be seen in software and system engineering process guidance such as the Software Engineering Institute's Capability Maturity Model [9] and the International Organization for Standardization (ISO) and Electronic Industries Alliance (EIA) systems engineering standards [10, 11]. Those that are focusing on innovation and rapid development of software-intensive systems are writing about working on the edge of chaos [12, 13, 14] (much like Brown and Eisenhardt [7]) and the associated need for flexible, adaptable, agile development processes to deal with rapid change and to facilitate innovative solutions in ultra-large solution spaces [15, 8]. In addition, teams must be able to experiment and have self-adapting processes that don't require process committee approvals and documentation [12, 8].

Chaos theory explains and helps identify underlying order in apparently random data or events. Behaviors thought to be random may have natural boundaries or patterns. Once these boundaries or patterns are determined, the order becomes apparent. This order is sometimes referred to as "emergent order" [16, 17, 12] and can lead to focused innovative solutions. Key principles in this environment include:

- Self-organization as the root of order [16]
- Teams allowed to continually re-organize to deal with new information [17]
- Learning and creative option generation encouraged [18]
- Mission/vision driven [12, 17]
- Technical flexibility with "just enough" process [12]

Faste [19] has shown that problem solving across a group of people exhibits a Gaussian distribution. When a group of people are asked to individually come up with a solution, most will produce an OK solution (within the norm), a few will produce "really good" solutions, and a few will produce "really bad" solutions. It is also interesting that for every solution that someone might rate as "really good", someone else may perceive it as "really bad". Therefore, it can take some additional work (exploration) to determine if something is "really good" or "really bad".

This need to explore before deciding if something is "really good" or "really bad" suggests the use of responsible, leveraged "play" in order to evaluate the feasibility of candidate solutions. It is also well-known that people can't "play" when they are stressed which implies that innovative ideas must be identified before the team becomes stressed over a solution.

To better understand and further elaborate on these concepts, we contacted organizations that have been successful in developing and maturing processes to support the development of innovative technologies and systems that can be rapidly fielded when needed.

3 Identification and Analysis Approach for Critical Success Factors

The organizations targeted for this research are ones that are high-performance United States organizations known for successful and sometimes innovative development in a rapidly changing environment. Most of these organizations are involved in both traditional and rapid response system development. The organizations that provided inputs for this research are:

- The Aerospace Corporation's Concept Design Center (www.aero.org)
- Institute for Creative Technologies, University of Southern California (http://ict.usc.edu/about)
- Lockheed Martin Corporation's Skunk Works (http://www.lockheedmartin.com/aeronautics/skunkworks/SkunkWorksToday.html)
- Northrop Grumman's Futures Lab, a joint venture with Applied Minds (http://appliedminds.com/)
- Commercial rapid-development company that requested anonymity.

Representatives from each of these organizations were contacted and in several cases, visits scheduled to their innovation labs or centers. Questions in several areas were used to guide discussions, but no rigorous attempt was made to obtain a written response from each organization. However, several of the organizations did provide written responses or elaborated on notes captured by the visiting researchers.

The approach used to guide the interviews started with a set of questions shown in Figure 1. These questions were used to define the business domain for innovative projects, how projects are scoped, and the types of products that are developed. Next, the types of processes, methods, and tools employed in the innovation labs or centers were explored as well as the characteristics of typical engineer and engineering teams working in this environment and the characteristics of the associated workplace. Lastly discussions were held to elicit the organization's perspective on critical success factors for rapid innovation, and to validate draft summaries of the results. The following sections describe in more detail the questions used to guide discussions in each category.

Table 1. Critical Success Factors Questions

Category	Question
Scope of Project	1. What is your "home-ground" for projects?
	2. What areas are you most effective/least effective?
	3. What triggers a new project?
	4. How are projects initially defined/scoped?
	5. Do clients participate in the process and if so, how?
Processes	6. How structured is the work environment?
	7. Are formal processes used?
	8. What is the business model for projects?
	9. How are efforts funded (investment vs. outside funding)?
	10. What is the typical duration for a project?
	11. How do you set project time horizons?
	12. How much reuse is there across projects?
	13. Do you support "process improvement initiatives"?
	14. How do you deal with classified or proprietary information?
Methods	15. What methods/methodologies (if any) are used? (e.g., formally defined agile method, quality/evaluation checks)
	16. What percentage of the total process uses these methods/methodologies?
	17. What percentage of projects use these methods/methodologies?
Product	18. What are goals of projects? (potential examples: commercial product, technology to support future system development work, proof of concept for existing project)
	19. What % of a system/system aspect is modeled before proceeding into total system design/development?
	20. How much of model/prototype can be used "as is" vs. re-developed for actual use/integration?
	21. What is the mix of projects in your portfolio? (E.g., commercial, military, space, other government)
Tools	22. What types of development tools support your environment? (Commercial? Internally developed?)
	23. What types of project management tools support your environment?
	24. Do you use any type of prototyping or simulation frameworks?
People	25. What is the typical project size in terms of number of people?
	26. Are these people dedicated full time to each project?
	27. If not full time, how many projects is a typical person supporting?
	28. How would you characterize engineers working in this environment with respect to skills, experiences, work processes?
Work Space	29. How are workspaces organized to support collaboration and innovation?
	30. How controlled is the workspace with respect to clients, potential clients, or other visitors that may participate in collaboration?
Key Success Factors	31. What are critical success factors with respect to people, business practices, intellectual property, and facilities?
	32. What are typical metrics you use to assess the success of your projects?
	33. What aspects of your organization are critical to the success of your projects?
	34. How much of success depends upon innovation? If a significant part, what is done to encourage innovation?

3.1 Scope of Projects

The questions in this category captured information about the business domains or "home-ground" for the organization's innovation-related projects, what triggers a new project, how projects are initially defined/scoped, and how much outside participation there is by actual or potential clients. The goal of these questions was to discern how new innovation projects are selected and how tightly coupled they are to business values and goals.

3.2 Product

These questions probed the types of products that are produced in the innovation environment. They ask about the goals of the projects, whether they are more oriented towards a commercial product, technology to support future system development work, or proof of concepts for existing projects. The questions also probed the role of modeling, simulation, and prototyping; if they are employed, what percentage of the system is typically modeled, simulated, or prototyped; and whether models and prototypes can be used "as is" for an actual system or whether they need to be redeveloped for actual use or integration. The final set of questions asks about the mix of projects in the innovation portfolio.

3.3 Processes

The process questions investigate the business model for innovation projects, the formality of the innovation environment (and if there are formal processes, how are process improvement initiatives managed), how structured the work environment is, as well as funding sources for the projects (internal investment versus outside/sponsor funding). In addition, questions probed typical project duration, how these durations are set, and how classified or proprietary information is handled. Lastly, questions were asked about reuse (components, patterns, etc.) across projects and the role this typically has in innovation projects.

3.4 Methods

Methods can span development methods such as agile to quality methods such as inspections and testing. They can also include "go/no-go" business reviews that monitor results to date to determine where future investments should be made. The questions in this category probed the types of methods used, the percentage of the total process covered by specific methods, and the percentage of projects that use the methods.

3.5 Tools

Typically there are both management and development tools that support project activities. These questions probed the types of development and management tools typically used and whether they were primarily commercial or internally developed tools. Particular attention was paid to any types of prototyping or simulation frameworks that were used.

3.6 People

As pointed out by [12] and others, one can have the greatest development environment, processes, and tools, but it is having the right people that make the most difference. These questions probed both team and individual characteristics. The questions included team size, whether or not individuals worked full time or part time on innovation activities, and if not full time, how many projects each person worked concurrently. Questions were also asked to understand engineer backgrounds with respect to skill types, experience, and personal work processes.

3.7 Workspace

In addition to having the right people, the workspace must be "structured" to support both collaboration and experimentation. In addition, outsiders (clients, potential clients, venture capitalists, etc.) may want to participate in the process or view in-progress activities. This category of questions probed these areas and focused on how the workspaces are organized to support collaboration and innovation as well as the extent of control or access with respect to clients, potential clients, and other visitors. This can be a particular challenge with respect to outsiders since organizations participating in joint ventures may find themselves competitors on related projects.

3.8 Key Success Factors

The final set of questions asked the organization representatives to comment on their perceived critical success factors. These questions covered critical success factors with respect to people, business practices, intellectual property, and facilities. They also probed metrics used to assess success of projects and the aspects of the larger organization that are critical to the success of projects. Finally, the organization was asked to indicate how much of their success depends upon innovation and if a significant part, what is done to encourage innovation.

4 Findings

To encourage candid responses and to protect the proprietary nature of some of the organizations' responses, actual responses captured are not provided. Rather, this section describes critical success factors that were common at several sites, if not all sites, while providing some context in distinguishing classes of solutions.

4.1 Early Concept Exploration and Feasibility Assessment

All of the organizations that provided inputs indicated the importance of early concept exploration and feasibility assessment that often required considerable modeling and prototyping. The level of modeling and prototyping varied, typically based upon perceived risks of the technical approach or the technologies to be integrated into the solution. In order to encourage innovation, organizations think that it is important to establish a supportive culture and environment. The length of the "rapid innovation" period also reflected different balances of the risks of delay versus the risks of system malfunction.

One organization's objectives were to reduce the concept exploration time from 1-2 years to 60 days. This time was used to explore several approaches for major systems with few options for fixes once they were deployed.

The commercial company's strategy was to produce a quick prototype on Day 2, and iterate it into an initial operational capability in 16-24 weeks. This company developed supply-chain domain applications that had lower risks of malfunctioning, as they could be rapidly adjusted in a pilot operation.

4.1.1 Investment in Innovation Environment

Several organizations pointed out the importance in investing in innovation and technology maturation ahead of an identified need, especially when customers may need rapid responses to changing needs, missions, and threats. Innovation is very difficult to achieve in stressful situations. Starting with a clean sheet of paper and designing a solution quickly may produce a useful solution given the right engineering expertise, but it will probably not reach the level of innovation. To enable innovation, organizations:

- **Include Responsible Play:** Organize work to include responsible play with new concepts and ideas in a supported lab environment. Some have found ways to reduce stress and create time for responsible play by promising a customer a solution that is within the "norm", implementing that solution within half the planned time, saving it, then spending the rest of the time trying to build a "really good" solution within the remaining time (reclaimed play time).
- **Focus on Team Rewards:** Set up a collaborative environment that rewards team work rather than individual work. This leads to sharing and collaborating without fear that their personal rewards (e.g., promotions, raises, bonuses) will suffer when someone else gets the credit.
- **Use Both Science and Art:** Learn to balance the engineering focus between science and art. This means that the team looks for ways to make the familiar strange (art) and make the strange familiar (science). Another way to look at this is breaking models (art) and making models (science). This type of exploration follows a basic three-step process: build a model, test the model, reflect and break the model, leading to the building of a new model.
- **Make it OK to Fail:** It is often through failures that people learn and adapt ideas.
- **Leapfrog:** It should also be not-OK to not-fail. Keep teams from trying for 20% improvements. Go for at least a factor-of-2.
- **Multi-sourcing:** If it's OK to fail, you want to have several teams trying different approaches. This also stimulates the competitive juices, often even within a single organization. Some commercial companies have two to four design shops that compete for the next version of their product.

4.1.2 Root Cause Analysis of Customer Problem

Most of the organizations interviewed focused on finding solutions for a specific problem or set of problems. The first step in developing a "solution" is to understand the problem. Spending time up front to investigate the root cause of a customer's problem can result in significant payoffs. Sometimes the best solutions focus on eliminating the root cause of the problem rather than developing something to deal with the problem once it occurs.

4.1.3 Reality Confrontation

Early prototypes are invaluable in both understanding the requirements through iterative feedback from customer and understanding the capabilities and limits of new technologies or existing technologies used in new ways.

Much is learned from taking a design on paper and translating it into a prototype that designers, customers, and potential users can interact with. Have a working prototype on Day 2, and have real users ready to exercise and comment on it. A combination with Leapfrogging is to do a factor-of-1.5 solution, get some quick experience with it, and then try for a factor-of-4 solution. If you have to back off to a factor-of-3, you're still ahead.

4.1.4 Customer or Sponsor Commitment and Participation

For those cases where efforts are applied to a specific customer need, customer/sponsor commitment and participation are extremely important. In fact, at some sites, if the customer/sponsor does not provide the needed level of commitment and participation in developing and assessing the feasibility of the requested solution, work is deferred. The customer/sponsor participation is required to provide insights into the requirements/user needs as well as to interact with models and prototypes to give feedback to the concept developers. Note that innovative design may have no identified customer or sponsor. For example, when the organization is attempting to develop a breakthrough commercial product for a totally new market, they may rely on market surveys and trends rather that a specific customer or sponsor.

4.2 Value-Adding Tools

Tools are required to succeed in this environment. However, the tools must be the right (value-adding) tools and the users must be experienced with those tools. The wrong tool or the right tool with no team expertise is not of value. For those organizations that periodically tap their key corporate resources (i.e. super-stars) to work on special innovative, rapid response projects or to conduct feasibility assessments of concept designs, it is important that the project work environment include the tools that those team members use in their day-to-day work. Another key theme is that tools don't need to be the best or the most sophisticated. Sometimes it is the simple, stable tools that work best.

4.3 The Right People

Most agree that you can have the best tools and the best processes, but without the best people, success is difficult. To achieve the desired results in an innovative, rapid development environment, organizations need to enable the best to achieve the desired task.

4.3.1 Empower the Best

For the rapid response and up-front innovation, prototyping, and feasibility assessment work, the organizations typically focus on their super-stars and experts in the domain(s) of interest. (Some experiences indicate that super-stars can be as much as 10 times more productive than the average performers.) These people work together as a small, lean team, collaborating almost continuously and developing frequent iterations and refinements of concepts until the desired solution is identified and adequately understood.

Managers of these teams typically have full authority and responsibility for them and the technical members are empowered to make the technical decisions. Because of the relatively small size of many of these teams, the project organization is often flat. For larger projects (e.g., new aircraft design and development), teams are still relatively small when compared to the traditional team size, but there are typically not enough super-stars to fully staff the project. However, some super-stars mixed with committed and very experienced team members are still the norm.

4.3.2 Enable Holistic Concurrency

Have experts on tap who cover the key fielding considerations and their tradeoffs (for example performance, reliability, usability, producibility, evolvability, cost), who participate concurrently rather than sequentially, and who pro-actively keep up with the state of the art in their respective domains.

4.3.3 Identify a Keeper of the "Holy Vision" [20]

The strongest successes come when the team has someone with enough range of expertise and experience to understand and synthesize the components of solutions, and to bring the right people together when problems come up (e.g., Kelly Johnson's principles for Boeing's Skunk Works).

4.4 Supportive Work Environment

Whether or not the work is classified or proprietary, the innovative, rapid development teams tend to work in their own large, relatively unstructured open space (sometimes with cubicles) to encourage collaboration and experimentation. When the same key people are being used frequently for intense rapid-response projects, it is important for the organization to provide additional resources and rewards that will help these people with their outside lives (e.g., family, external commitments). If people on the teams are overly stressed, innovation and creativity will suffer. They could easily end up reverting to a 9-to-5 work mode that is counter-productive to the innovation and rapid-response goals.

5 Conclusions

This research work was motivated by the fact that certain organizations are able to innovate consistently. In this paper, we present our investigation of such organizations and our key findings. Successful innovative organizations share certain characteristics. They are all driven by business value and they are all prepared to make the needed investments. They exploit opportunities by taking calculated risks. They follow concurrent engineering practices to accelerate cycle times. They focus on their core business areas and continually look for solution patterns that they can reuse and can reuse in different and novel ways. They have proactive management that believes in small agile teams. As a result, they provide a culture and environment that supports innovation and arrange time for team members to investigate, play with, and learn from candidate solutions. These findings provide considerable guidance to organizations that are striving to rapidly develop innovative solutions and will continue to grow and evolve as more organizations employ these approaches.

References

1. Arthur, L.: Rapid Evolutionary Development. Wiley, Chichester (1991)
2. McConnell, S.: Rapid Development. Microsoft Press, Redmond (1996)
3. Beck, K.: Extreme Programming Explained. Addison-Wesley, Reading (1999)
4. Boehm, B., Turner, R.: Balancing Agility and Discipline. Addison-Wesley, Reading (2004)
5. Christensen, C.: The Innovator's Dilemma. Harper Collins (2000)
6. Chesbrough, H.: Open Innovation. Harvard Business School Press, Boston (2003)
7. Brown, S., Eisenhardt, K.: Competing on the Edge: Strategy as Structured Chaos. Harvard Business School Press, Boston (1998)
8. Kreitman, K.: From the magic gig to reliable organizations: A new paradigm for the control of complex systems. Paper presented at the symposium on complex systems engineering (1996), http://cs.calstatela.edu/wiki/index.php/Symposium_on_Complex_Systems_Engineering (accessed on 1/11/2007)
9. SEI. Capability maturity model integration (CMMI), CMU/SEI-2002-TR-001 (2001)
10. ISO/IEC. ISO/IEC 15288:2002(E) Systems engineering - system life cycle processes (2002)
11. Electronic Industries Alliance, EIA Standard 632: Processes for Engineering a System (January 1999)
12. Highsmith, J.: Adaptive software development: A collaborative approach to managing complex systems. Dorset House Publishing, New York (2000)
13. Markus, M., Majchrzak, A., Gasser, L.: A design theory for systems that support emergent knowledge processes. MIS Quarterly 26(3) (2002)
14. Sheard, S.A.: Practical Applications of Complexity Theory for Systems Engineers. Systems and Software Consortium, Inc. (2005)
15. Boehm, B., Lane, J.: 21st century processes for acquiring 21st century software-intensive systems of systems. CrossTalk - The Journal of Defense Software Engineering 19(5), 4–9 (2006)
16. Kauffman, S.: At Home in the Universe: The Search for the Laws of Self-Organization and Complexity. Oxford University Press, Oxford (1995)
17. Wheatley, M.J.: Leadership and the New Science: Learning about Organization from an Orderly Universe. Berrett-Koehler Publishers (1992)
18. Madni, A.M., Brenner, M.A., Costea, I., MacGregor, D., Meshkinpour, F.: Option Generation: Problems, Principles, and Computer-Based Aiding. In: Proceedings of 1985 IEEE International Conference on Systems, Man, and Cybernetics, Tucson, Arizona, November 1985, pp. 757–760 (1985)
19. Faste, R.: A Visual Essay on Invention and Innovation. Design Management Review 6(2) (1995)
20. Curtis, B., Krasner, H., Iscoe, N.: A Field Study of the Software Design Process for Large Systems. ACM Communications 31(11), 1268–1287 (1988)

Evidence-Based Software Processes

Barry Boehm and Jo Ann Lane

University of Southern California
941 W. 37th Street
Los Angeles, California, 90089 USA
1-213-740-8163
{boehm,jolane}@usc.edu

Abstract. Many software projects fail because they commit to a set of plans and specifications with little evidence that if these are used on the project, they will lead to a feasible system being developed within the project's budget and schedule. An effective way to avoid this is to make the evidence of feasibility a first-class developer deliverable that is reviewed by independent experts and key decision milestones: shortfalls in evidence are risks to be considered in going forward. This further implies that the developer will create and follow processes for evidence development. This paper provides processes for developing and reviewing feasibility evidence, and for using risk to determine how to proceed at major milestones. It also provides quantitative result on "how much investment in evidence is enough," as a function of the project's size, criticality, and volatility.

Keywords: Evidence-based development, feasibility evidence, Incremental Commitment Model, evidence-based reviews, risk assessment, risk management.

1 Introduction

We have found through experience, case study analysis, and cost-benefit analysis that up-front investments in providing evidence that the specifications and plans for a software-intensive system satisfies a set of desired properties produce positive payoffs later. A good way to capture this evidence is in a Feasibility Evidence Description (FED). The FED's evidence, when validated by independent experts, can also be used as a basis for assuring system stakeholders that it is reasonable for the project to proceed into development.

Providing such validated evidence is generally considered to be a good practice, but it generally fails to be done well. This is because of a lack of proof criteria, proof-generation procedures; measures for monitoring proof generation; methods, standards, and contractual provisions that make proof generation optional; and an appreciation of the consequences of proceeding into development with unsubstantiated specifications and plans. The main contributions of this paper are to provide experience-based approaches for dealing with each of these concerns, and to show the consequences of their use via case studies and parametric analysis.

J. Münch, Y. Yang, and W. Schäfer (Eds.): ICSP 2010, LNCS 6195, pp. 62–73, 2010.

2 Evidence Shortfalls in Current Software Practices

Evidence shortfalls can be found in both technical and management practices. The key to success is identifying critical risk elements and focusing engineering efforts to reduce risks through evidence-based methods. The following sections elaborate on the types of technical and management issues that should drive a project to collect further evidence of feasibility.

2.1 Technical Shortfalls

Current software design and development methods focus strongly on the inputs and outputs, preconditions and post-conditions that a software function, object, or service operates by as a product. They generally lack adequate capabilities to support analyses about how well the elements perform, how expensive they will be to develop, or how compatible are their underlying assumptions. In principle, they support reasoning about off-nominal performance, but in practice their descriptions generally focus on sunny-day scenarios. As a result, many software project reviews tend to focus on exhaustive presentations of PowerPoint charts and UML diagrams. They provide little evidence that the system they describe could handle rainy-day scenarios; perform adequately on throughput, response time, safety, security, usability, or other desired quality attributes across a range of representative mission scenarios; be buildable within the available budgets and schedules in the plan; or to generate positive returns on investment for the stakeholders.

Most current versions of model-driven development, for example, strongly focus on expressing product capabilities and relationships, and on reasoning about their combined incompatibilities and incompleteness. However, analyses of failed projects such as the one shown in figure 1 of the Bank of America (BofA) Master Net project [7, 8] find that incompatibilities among product models and other stakeholder value models (process models, property models, success models) are at least as frequent and important as product-product (PD-PD) model clashes.

For example, the MasterNet users specified 3.5 million source lines of code (3.5 MSLOC) worth of wish-list features that were put into the project's requirements specification. Even at an extremely optimistic development cost of $30/SLOC for a project of this size, this would cost $105 million. Thus, the users' product model was in serious conflict with the acquirers' property model of a $22 million budget. Also, many of the wish-list items had no mission effectiveness rationale, conflicting with the acquirers' success model.

Faced with this dilemma, the acquirers searched for a supplier who could reuse a related solution to provide useful features at a low cost. They found one in Premier Systems, who had built similar applications for small banks. However, their product model only worked on Prime computers, which conflicted with the BofA users' and maintainers' product-model value propositions of applications compatibility and ease of maintenance, given that BofA was an IBM mainframe operation. Also, the Prime host could not scale up to BofA's throughput, response time, and reliability needs, causing a property-product evidence shortfall that should have been addressed earlier.

Overall, the implications here, both with the BofA model clashes in red /gray in figure 1 and with further model clashes in black from analyses of other failed projects, is that there are many potential value-proposition conflicts just among the four main stakeholders in a project, and that product-product evidence shortfalls are only a moderate fraction of the total set of issues of concern.

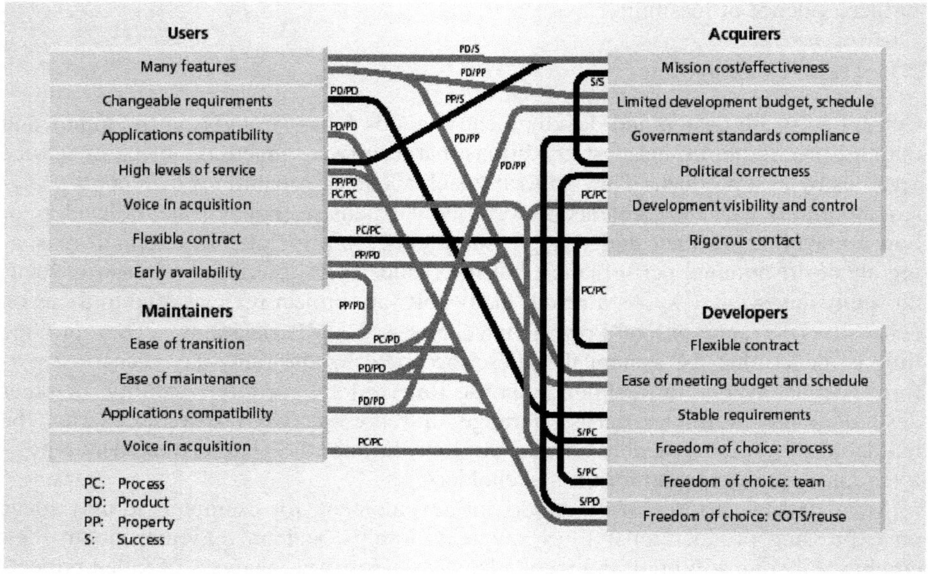

Fig. 1. Stakeholder Value Model Clashes. The red or gray lines show model clashes from the failed MasterNet system.

Al Said's analysis shown in Figure 2 of the risk patterns across 35 electronic-services projects found that product-product model incompatibilities accounted for only 30% of the model clashes and only 24% (ratio of 0.8) of the risk-priority values. [1]

2.2 Management Shortfalls

A major recent step forward in the management of outsourced government projects has been to move from schedule-based reviews to event-based reviews. A schedule-based review says basically that, "The contract specifies that the Preliminary Design Review (PDR) will be held on April 1, 2011, whether we have a design or not."

In general, neither the customer nor the developer wants to fail the PDR, so the project goes into development with the blessing of having passed a PDR, but with numerous undefined interfaces and unresolved risks. As we will show below, these will generally result in major project overruns and incomplete deliveries.

An event-based review says, "Once we have a preliminary design, we will hold the PDR." Such a review will generally consist of exhaustive presentations of sunny-day PowerPoint charts and UML diagrams, and focus on catching the 30% of the project

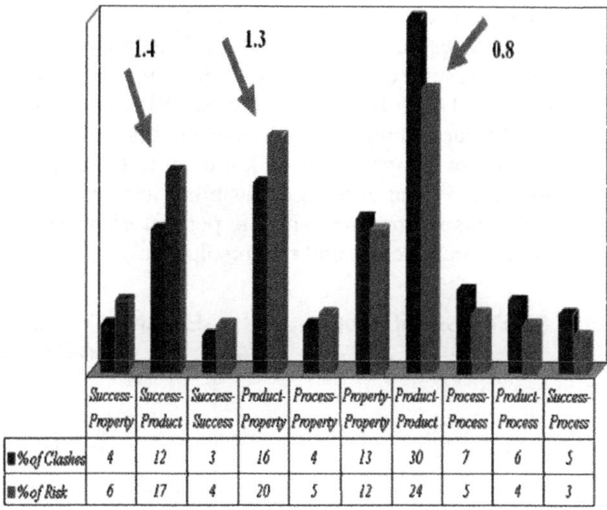

	Success-Property	Success-Product	Success-Success	Product-Property	Process-Property	Property-Property	Product-Product	Process-Process	Product-Process	Success-Process
% of Clashes	4	12	3	16	4	13	30	7	6	5
% of Risk	6	17	4	20	5	12	24	5	4	3

Fig. 2. Frequency of Project Model Clash Types

model clashes of the product-product form. But in general, it will still have numerous other model clashes that are unidentified and will cause extensive project rework, overruns, and incomplete deliveries.

Similarly, most outsourcing contracts focus on product-oriented deliverables and reviews. These reinforce paths toward project disaster, as in the quote from a recent large-project manager, *"I'd like to have some of my systems engineers address those software quality-factor risks, but my contract deliverables and award fees are based on having all of the system's functions defined by the next review."* Similar overfocus on product definition is found in project earned-value management systems for tracking project progress and data item descriptions (DIDs) for deliverables. Most contract DIDs cover function, interface, and infrastructure considerations, but place demonstration of their feasibility in optional appendices where, as with the project manager above, they are the first to go when time and effort are running out.

3 Consequences of Evidence Shortfalls

The biannual Standish Reports consistently identify shortfalls in evidence of feasibility with respect to stakeholder objectives as the major root causes of project failure. For example, the 2009 Standish Report [14] found that only 32% of the 9000 projects reported delivered their full capability within their budget and schedule; 24% were cancelled; and 44% were significantly over budget, over schedule, and/or incompletely delivered. More detail on the top critical success factors distinguishing successful from failed software projects was in the 2005 Standish Report. There, 71% of the sources of failure were primarily due to evidence shortfalls with respect to stakeholder objectives (lack of user involvement, executive support, clear requirements, proper planning, and realistic expectations).

Recent further analyses of the COCOMO II database on the effects of incomplete architecture definition, risk resolution, and resulting feasibility evidence are shown in Figure 3. They show the results of a risk-driven "how much architecting is enough" analysis, based on the COCOMO II Architecture and Risk Resolution (RESL) factor [4]. This factor was calibrated along with 22 other factors to 161 project data points. It relates the amount of extra rework effort on a project to the degree of evidence that the project had demonstrated its architecture feasibility and resolved its technical and management risks. This also correlates with the percent of project effort devoted to software-intensive system architecting and risk resolution.

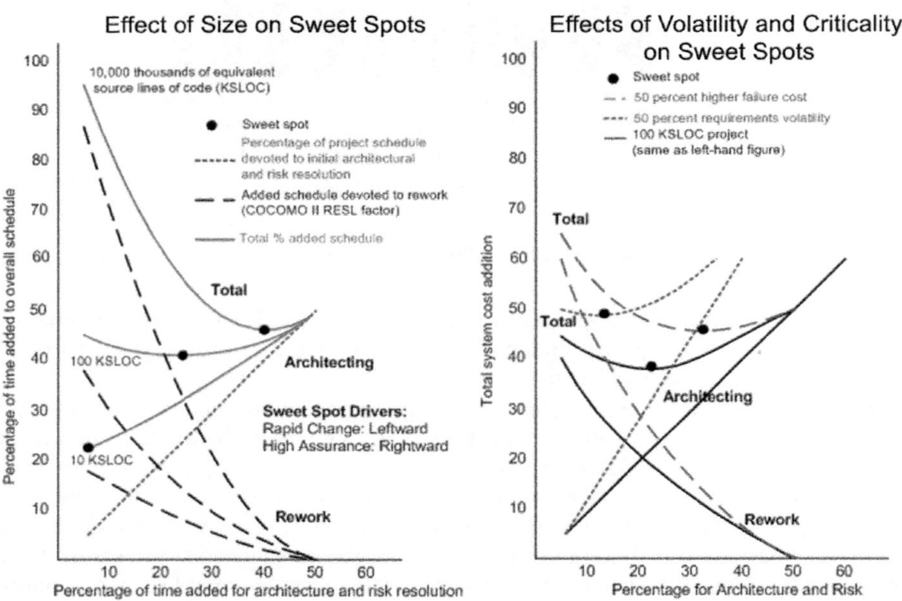

Fig. 3. Architecture Evidence Shortfall Penalties and Resulting Architecting Investment Sweet Spots

The analysis indicated that the amount of rework was an exponential function of project size. A small (10 thousand equivalent source lines of code, or KSLOC) project could fairly easily adapt its architecture to rapid change via refactoring or its equivalent, with a rework penalty of 18% between minimal and extremely thorough architecture and risk resolution.

However, a very large (10,000 KSLOC) project would incur a corresponding rework penalty of 91%, covering such effort sources as integration rework due to undiscovered large-component interface incompatibilities and critical performance shortfalls.

The effects of rapid change (volatility) and high dependability (criticality) on the architecture evidence shortfall penalties and resulting architecting investment sweet spots are shown in the right hand graph. Here, the solid black lines represent the average-case cost of rework, architecting, and total cost for a 100-KSLOC project as shown at the left. The dotted red lines show the effect on the cost of architecting and total cost if rapid change adds 50% to the cost of architecture and risk resolution. Quantitatively, this moves the sweet spot from roughly 20% to 10% of effective architecture investment (but actually 15% due to the 50% cost penalty). Thus, high investments in architecture, feasibility analysis, and other documentation do not have a positive return on investment for very high-volatility projects due to the high costs of documentation rework for rapid-change adaptation.

The dashed blue lines at the right represent a conservative analysis of the external cost effects of system failure due to unidentified architecting shortfalls. It assumes that the costs of architecting shortfalls are not only added development project rework, but also losses to the organization's operational effectiveness and productivity. These are conservatively assumed to add 50% to the project-rework cost of architecture shortfalls to the organization. In most cases for high-assurance systems, the added cost would be considerably higher.

Quantitatively, this moves the sweet spot from roughly 20% to over 30% as the most cost-effective investment in architecting and development of feasibility evidence for a 100-KSLOC project. It is good to note that the "sweet spots" are actually relatively flat "sweet regions" extending 5-10% to the left and right of the "sweet spots." However, moving to the edges of a sweet region increases the risk of significant losses if some project assumptions turn out to be optimistic.

The bottom line for Figure 3 is that the greater the project's size, criticality, and stability are, the greater is the need for validated architecture feasibility evidence (i.e., proof-carrying specifications and plans). However, for very small, low-criticality projects with high volatility, the proof efforts would make little difference and would need to be continuously redone, producing a negative return on investment (the same could be said for proof-carrying code). In such cases, agile methods such as Scrum [15] and eXtreme Programming [2] will be more effective. Overall, evidence-based specifications and plans will not guarantee a successful project, but in general will eliminate many of the software delivery overruns and shortfalls experienced on current software projects.

4 Evidence Criteria and Review Milestone Usage

Having shown that the regions of high payoff for evidence-based specifications and plans are extensive and enterprise-critical, it is now important to define the criteria for the evidence that will be associated with the system development specifications and plans. The criteria are extensions to those for the Anchor Point milestones defined in [3] and adopted by the Rational Unified Process (RUP) [9, 12]. The extensions have been incorporated into the recently-developed Incremental Commitment Model; details of this model can be found in [6, 11].

The evidence criteria are embodied in a Feasibility Evidence Description (FED). It includes *evidence* provided by the developer and validated by independent experts that, *if the system is built to the specified architecture it will:*

1. Satisfy the specified operational concept and requirements, including capability, interfaces, level of service, and evolution
2. Be buildable within the budgets and schedules in the plan

3. Generate a viable return on investment
4. Generate satisfactory outcomes for all of the success-critical stakeholders
5. Identify shortfalls in evidence as risks, and cover them with risk mitigation plans.

A FED does not assess a single sequentially developed system definition element, but the consistency, compatibility, and feasibility of several concurrently-engineered elements. To make this concurrency work, a set of Anchor Point milestone reviews are performed to ensure that the many concurrent activities are synchronized, stabilized, and risk-assessed at the end of each phase. Each of these reviews is focused on developer-produced and expert-validated *evidence*, documented in the FED (or by reference to the results of feasibility analyses), to help the system's success-critical stakeholders determine whether to proceed into the next level of commitment. Hence, they are called Commitment Reviews.

The FED is based on evidence from simulations, models, or experiments with planned technologies and increasingly detailed analysis of development approaches and project productivity rates. The parameters used in the analyses should be based on measured component performance or on historical data showing relevant past performance, cost estimation accuracy, and actual developer productivity rates.

A shortfall in feasibility evidence indicates a level of program execution uncertainty and a source of program risk. It is often not possible to fully resolve all risks at a given point in the development cycle, but known, unresolved risks need to be identified and covered by risk management plans, including the necessary staffing and funding to address them.

The nature of the evidence shortfalls, the strength and affordability of the risk management plans, and the stakeholders' degrees of risk acceptance or avoidance will determine their willingness to commit the necessary resources to proceed. A program with risks is not necessarily bad, particularly if it has strong risk management plans. A program with no risks may be high on achievability, but low on ability to produce a timely payoff or competitive advantage.

A FED needs to be more than just traceability matrices and PowerPoint charts. Evidence can include results of:

- Prototypes: of networks, robots, user interfaces, COTS interoperability
- Benchmarks: for performance, scalability, accuracy
- Exercises: for mission performance, interoperability, security
- Models: for cost, schedule, performance, reliability; tradeoffs
- Simulations: for mission scalability, performance, reliability
- Early working versions: of infrastructure, data fusion, legacy compatibility
- Previous experience
- Combinations of the above.

The type and level of evidence generated depends on perceived risks and their associated levels with no evidence. To determine what feasibility evidence to generate, one must evaluate the expected value of the evidence with respect to lowering risks going forward and the cost and schedule to generate the evidence versus the costs if the perceived risk is realized. If there is significant risk exposure in making the wrong decision and feasibility evidence can be cost-effectively generated, then steps should be initiated to reduce risks early. Feasibility evidence costs can be minimized by focusing on prototypes that can become part of the system or early working versions of key parts of the system. Spending time and money on early feasibility evidence should be viewed as buying information to reduce both risk and the cost of potential rework (assuming that the problem can be resolved later in the project) or to avoid canceling the project altogether after expending considerable resources. Likewise, if risk exposure is low, then comprehensive, detailed feasibility evidence is of less value.

Not only does the evidence need to be produced, but it needs to be validated by independent experts. These experts need to determine the realism of assumptions, the representativeness of scenarios, the thoroughness of analysis, and the coverage of key off-nominal conditions. The risk of validating just nominal-case scenarios is shown in the next section.

The following is a set of criteria that cover the various dimensions of validity for the evidence:

- Data well defined
  a. What is counted
  b. How it is derived (e.g., how measured, calculated, or inferred)
- Representative mission scenarios
  a. Operational environment
  b. Adversaries
  c. Component reliability, scalability, etc.
  d. Nominal and off-nominal scenarios
  e. Treatment of uncertainty
  f. Composability of results; interference effects
  g. Scale
- Parameter values realistic
  a. Based upon measured results
  b. Inferred from representative projects/activities
  c. Derived from relevant scenarios
- Outputs traceable to mission effectiveness
  a. Directly/indirectly
  b. Based on appropriate models, scenarios
- Models verified and validated
  a. Via representative scenarios
  b. Limiting cases, off-nominals realistic

This should be used as a checklist and not as a one-size-fits-all set of criteria, which would generally be overkill.

5 FED Development Process Framework

The most important characteristic of evidence-based software specifications and plans is that *if the evidence does not accompany the specifications and plans, the specifications and plans are incomplete.*

Thus, event-based reviews, where the event is defined as production of the specifications and plans, need to be replaced by *evidence-based reviews*.

This does not mean that the project needs to spend large amounts of effort in documenting evidence of the feasibility of a simple system. As described above, the appropriate level of detail for the contents of the FED is based on the perceived risks and criticality of the system to be developed. It is NOT a "one size fits all" process, but rather a framework to help developers and stakeholders determine the appropriate level of analysis and evaluation. As with reused software, evidence can be appropriately reused. If a more complex system than the one being reviewed has been successfully developed by the same team, a pointer to the previous project's evidence and results will be sufficient. Table 1 outlines a process that can be used for developing feasibility evidence.

The steps are designated by letters rather than numbers, to indicate that they are carried out with considerable concurrency rather than sequentially. The process clearly depends on having the appropriate work products for the phase (Step A). As part of the engineering work, the high-priority feasibility assurance issues are identified that are critical to the success of the system development program (Step B). These are the issues for which options are explored, and potentially viable options further investigated (Step C). Clearly, these and the later steps are not performed sequentially, but concurrently.

Since the preliminary design and plans are incomplete without the FED, it becomes a first-class project deliverable. This implies that it needs a plan for its development, and that each task in the plan needs to be assigned an appropriate earned value. If possible, the earned value should be based on the potential risk exposure costs, not the perceived available budget.

Besides monitoring progress on developing the system, the project needs to monitor progress on developing the feasibility evidence. This implies applying corrective action if progress falls behind the plans, and adapting the feasibility evidence development plans to changes in the project objectives and plans. If evidence generation is going to be complex, it is generally a good idea to perform pilot assessments.

6 Experiences with Evidence-Based Reviews

AT&T and its spinoffs (Telcordia, Lucent, Avaya, and regional Bell companies) have been successfully using versions of evidence-based reviews since 1988. On average, there has been a 10% savings per reviewed project, with substantially larger savings on a few reviewed projects. More detail on their Architecture Review experience is in [10].

The million-line TRW CCPDS-R project summarized in [12] by Walker Royce, and several similar TRW follow-on projects were further successful examples. Evidence-based anchor point milestone reviews are also an integral part of the Rational Software Process, with many successful implementations [13], although a good many RUP applications have been unable to succeed because of the type of contractual constraints discussed in Section 2.

The highly successful Abbott Laboratories' next generation intravenous infusion pump documented in chapter 5 of [11] is a good commercial example of evidence-based specifications and plans.

Table 1. Steps for Developing a FED

Step	Description	Examples/Detail
A	Develop phase work-products/artifacts	For a Development Commitment Review, this would include the system's operational concept, prototypes, requirements, architecture, life cycle plans, and associated assumptions
B	Determine most critical feasibility assurance issues	Issues for which lack of feasibility evidence is program-critical
C	Evaluate feasibility assessment options	Cost-effectiveness; necessary tool, data, scenario availability
D	Select options, develop feasibility assessment plans	The preparation example in Figure 5 below is a good example
E	Prepare FED assessment plans and earned value milestones	The preparation example in Figure 5 below is a good example
F	Begin monitoring progress with respect to plans	Also monitor changes to the project, technology, and objectives, and adapt plans
G	Prepare evidence-generation enablers	Assessment criteria Parametric models, parameter values, bases of estimate COTS assessment criteria and plans Benchmarking candidates, test cases Prototypes/simulations, evaluation plans, subjects, and scenarios Instrumentation, data analysis capabilities
H	Perform pilot assessments; evaluate and iterate plans and enablers	Short bottom-line summaries and pointers to evidence files are generally sufficient
I	Assess readiness for Commitment Review	Shortfalls identified as risks and covered by risk mitigation plans Proceed to Commitment Review if ready
J	Hold Commitment Review when ready; adjust plans based on review outcomes	See Commitment Review process overview below.
NOTE: "Steps" are denoted by letters rather than numbers to indicate that many are done concurrently.		

Lastly, the University of Southern California (USC) has used evidence-based specifications and plans to achieve a 92% on-time, in-budget, satisfied-client success rate on over 50 fixed-schedule local-community e-service projects [6].

7 Conclusions

The most important characteristic of evidence-based software specifications and plans is that *if the evidence does not accompany the specifications and plans, the specifications and plans are incomplete.*

Thus, event-based reviews, where the event is defined as production of the specifications and plans, need to be replaced by *evidence-based reviews*.

The Anchor Point milestones and Feasibility Evidence Descriptions presented in this paper provide an approach for successfully realizing the benefits of proof-carrying software specifications and plans. Further, the Anchor Point milestones enable synchronization and stabilization of concurrent engineering.

The parametric analysis in Section 3 concludes that the greater the project's size, criticality, and stability are, the greater is the need for validated architecture feasibility evidence. However, for very small, low-criticality projects with high volatility, the evidence generation efforts would make little difference and would need to be continuously redone, producing a negative return on investment. In such cases, agile methods such as Scrum and eXtreme Programming will be more effective. Overall, evidence-based specifications and plans will not guarantee a successful project, but in general will eliminate many of the software delivery overruns and shortfalls experienced on current software projects.

Some implications of defining the FED as a "first class" project deliverable are that it needs to be planned (with resources), and made part of the project's earned value management system. Any shortfalls in evidence are sources of uncertainty and risk, and should be covered by risk management plans. The main contributions of this paper are to provide experienced-based approaches for evidence criteria, evidence-generation procedures, and measures for monitoring evidence generation, which support the ability to perform evidence-based software engineering. And finally, evidence-based specifications and plans such as those provided by the FED can and should be added to traditional milestone reviews.

References

1. Al Said, M.: Detecting Model Clashes During Software Systems Development. Doctoral Thesis. Department of Computer Science, University of Southern California (2003)
2. Beck, K.: Extreme Programming Explained. Addison-Wesley, Reading (1999)
3. Boehm, B.: Anchoring the Software Process. IEEE Software, 73–82 (July 1996)
4. Boehm, B., et al.: Software Cost Estimation with COCOMO II. Prentice Hall, Englewood Cliffs (2000)
5. Boehm, B., Lane, J.: Incremental Commitment Model Guide, version 0.5 (2009)
6. Boehm, B., Lane, J.: Using the ICM to Integrate System Acquisition, Systems Engineering, and Software Engineering. CrossTalk, 4–9 (October 2007)
7. Boehm, B., Port, D., Al Said, M.: Avoiding the Software Model-Clash Spiderweb. IEEE Computer, 120–122 (November 2000)
8. Glass, R.: Software Runaways. Prentice Hall, Englewood Cliffs (1998)
9. Kruchten, P.: The Rational Unified Process. Addison-Wesley, Reading (1999)
10. Maranzano, J., et al.: Architecture Reviews: Practice and Experience. IEEE Software (March/April 2005)
11. Pew, R., Mavor, A.: Human-System Integration in the System Development Process: A New Look. National Academy Press, Washington (2007)
12. Royce, W.: Software Project Management. Addison-Wesley, Reading (1998)

13. Royce, W., Bittner, K., Perrow, M.: The Economics of Iterative Software Development. Addison-Wesley, Reading (2009)
14. Standish Group 2009. CHAOS Summary (2009), `http://standishgroup.com`
15. Schwaber, K., Beedle, M.: Agile Software Development with Scrum. Prentice Hall, Englewood Cliffs (2002)

SoS Management Strategy Impacts on SoS Engineering Effort

Jo Ann Lane

University of Southern California,
Los Angeles, California, USA
jolane@usc.com

Abstract. To quickly respond to changing business and mission needs, many organizations are integrating new and existing systems with commercial-off-the-shelf (COTS) products into network-centric, knowledge-based, software-intensive systems of systems (SoS). With this approach, system development processes to define the new architecture, identify sources to either supply or develop the required components, and eventually integrate and test these high level components are evolving and are being referred to as SoS Engineering (SoSE). This research shows that there exist conditions under which investments in SoSE have positive and negative returns on investment, provides the first quantitative determination of these conditions, and points out directions for future research that would strengthen the results.

Keywords: System of systems, system of systems engineering, management processes, process modeling.

1 Introduction

Today's need for more complex, more capable systems in a short timeframe is leading more organizations towards the integration of new and existing systems with commercial-off-the-shelf (COTS) products into network-centric, knowledge-based, software-intensive system of systems (SoS). With this approach, system development processes to define the new architecture, identify sources to either supply or develop the required components, and eventually integrate and test these high level components are evolving and are being referred to as SoS Engineering (SoSE) [1].

In 2007, the United States Department of Defense (DoD) Office of the Secretary of Defense (OSD) Acquisition, Technology, and Logistics (AT&L) Software Engineering and Systems Assurance (SSA) organization sponsored case study investigations to better understand SoSE. The results of these case studies [2] and other reports [3] and [4] have indicated that SoSE activities are considerably different from the more traditional SE activities. These differences are primarily due to adaptations and expansions of traditional SE activities to handle the increased size and scope of SoSs as well as the interactions between the SoS team and the constituent-system (CS) engineering teams.

As a result of other SoS research [5] and [6], four types of SoSE management approaches have been identified: virtual, collaborative, acknowledged, and directed.

J. Münch, Y. Yang, and W. Schäfer (Eds.): ICSP 2010, LNCS 6195, pp. 74–87, 2010.

These categories are primarily based upon the levels of responsibility and authority overseeing the evolution of the SoS and are described in Table 1. Many SoSE teams interviewed as part of the SSA SoSE case studies [2] indicated that their SoS was managed primarily as a collaborative SoS until it reached a point where it was either too important, too complex, or not cost effective to continue managing it in this manner. At this point, an SoSE team was designated to guide the evolution of the SoS CSs. Typically, in this first evolutionary step, the SoSE team has overarching engineering responsibilities and can influence the CSs, but does not have complete authority over the CSs (an acknowledged SoS).

Table 1. SoSE Management Approaches

Type	Description
Virtual [5]	Lacks a central management authority and a clear SoS purpose. Often ad hoc and may use a service-oriented architecture where the CSs are not necessarily known.
Collaborative [5]	CS engineering teams work together more or less voluntarily to fulfill agreed upon central purposes. No SoSE team to guide or manage SoS-related activities of CSs.
Acknowledged [6]	Have recognized objectives, a designated manager, and resources at the SoS level (SoSE team), but not complete authority over constituent-systems. CSs maintain their independent ownership, objectives, funding, and development approaches.
Directed [5]	SoS centrally managed by a government, corporate, or lead system integrator and built to fulfill specific purposes. CSs maintain ability to operate independently, but evolution predominately controlled by SoS management organization.

Of particular interest to SoS sponsors is identifying the point at which a collaborative SoS should be transitioned to an acknowledged SoS. To help answer this question, an SoSE model based on the constructive systems engineering cost model (COSYSMO) [7] was developed. This SoSE model is used to compare the effort required to engineer an SoS capability (or capability modification) using either the collaborative or acknowledged SoSE approach. The model allows one to modify the SoS size, the size and scope of a proposed new SoS capability or capability modification, and the concurrent CS volatility. By varying these parameters and computing the associated SoSE and systems engineering (SE) effort for the collaborative and acknowledged approaches, one can find the point, if any, at which the size and complexity of the SoS or the SoS capability makes it more cost-effective to evolve the SoS using an acknowledged SoSE team. The rest of this paper describes how SoSE was modeled, the model itself, the results of various model executions, and the conclusions developed from the model executions.

2 How SoSE was Modeled

A cost modeling approach was selected to determine the return on investment of an SoSE team. The parametric cost model that most closely estimates SoSE effort is the COSYSMO model. Valerdi developed the COSYSMO model [7] to estimate the effort required to engineer a set of requirements using effort data from over 40 projects from multiple organizations. Valerdi was able to show a predictive capability of PRED(30) = 75% (i.e., the estimated value is within 30% of actual values 75% of the time) when projects from multiple organizations were used to calibrate the model. When projects were limited to a single organization, local calibrations were able to achieve PRED(30) = 85%. By analyzing the differences between traditional systems engineering and SoSE and capturing these differences in an extended COSYSMO model, one can show the differences in total systems engineering effort between the acknowledged and collaborative SoS management strategies.

The DoD SoSE case studies were used to identify the key differences between traditional systems engineering and SoSE. The research team analyzing these case studies identified seven core elements that characterize SoSE and describe how the traditional system engineering activities evolved to support the SoSE. The first step in developing the SoSE model was to ensure that there were COSYSMO cost model parameters that could be used to characterize the SoSE core elements. The results of this analysis are shown in Table 2.

Table 2. Mapping of DoD SoSE Core Elements to COSYSMO Parameters

SoSE Core Element	Related COSYSMO Parameters
Translating capabilities	Requirements understanding
Understanding systems and relationships	Architecture understanding Migration complexity Technology risk Number of recursive levels in the design
Assessing actual performance to capability objectives	Level of service requirements
Developing, evolving, and maintaining an SoS architecture	Architecture understanding Multisite coordination
Monitoring and assessing changes	Level of service requirements Multisite coordination
Addressing new requirements and options	Requirements understanding Architecture understanding Migration complexity Technology risk
Orchestrating upgrades to SoS	Stakeholder team cohesion Personnel/team capability Personnel experience/continuity Process capability Multisite coordination Tool support

The other major differences identified in [2] that must be captured in the SoSE model in order to compare the two management strategies are:

1. *SoS Capability/Requirements*: SoS requirements start with very high level capability need statements that must be analyzed to determine a set of implementable requirements. In the case of an acknowledged SoS, the SoSE performs this activities. In the case of a collaborative SoS, the systems engineering teams from all of the CSs must work together to determine a set of implementable requirements.
2. *SoSE Capability Analysis Support*: When an SoSE team performs the capability analysis and determines an approach for providing the capability, it depends on support from the CS SE teams in conducting the trades and evaluating the feasibility of the various options.
3. *Monitoring of Non-SoS Changes*: In an acknowledged SoS, the SoSE team must also monitor non-SoS changes being implemented in the CSs to ensure that these changes do not adversely affect the SoS. If changes might adversely affect the SoS, the SoSE team negotiates with the CS(s) to determine alternative approaches that better support SoS objectives and performance.

The next modeling step was to determine ways to capture the major differences described above. The SoS capability/requirements issue is modeled using the COSYSMO Requirements Understanding parameter. The SoSE capability analysis support issue is modeled using the work of [8] that provides a distribution of COSYSMO effort across the various systems engineering phases. The SoSE model modifies the system design effort for the single system to account for the additional SoSE support. And lastly, the COSYSMO reuse extension [9] provides a framework for incorporating adjustments related to SoSE monitoring CS non-SoS changes being implemented in parallel with SoS requirements.

One additional problem remained with the COSYSMO model: how to combine models of the SoSE team effort with the multiple system engineering team efforts. The initial COSYSMO model treats the system of interest as a single entity, using a single set of parameters to characterize the system characteristics, the system engineering process, and the system engineering team. In an SoS environment, one needs to be able to characterize SoS and single system characteristics, processes, and system engineering teams differently while capturing the diseconomy of scale as the SoS becomes larger and more complex. The approach used in the SoSE model was the constructive cost model for software (COCOMO) method of integrating different effort multipliers for different parts of the system [10].

The argument that this SOSE process modeling approach is sufficient to compare SoS management approaches for the SoSs described in [2] is based on the following:

- The COSYSMO SoSE characterization is based on the vetted findings in the DoD SoSE guidebook [2] using parameters readily available in COSYSMO 1.0.
- The COSYSMO 1.0 model calibration data set contained several systems that characterized themselves as an SoS and most came from the same domain (DoD) as the SoSE case studies.

- Each of the systems in the COSYSMO calibration data set belonged to one or more SoSs, as indicated by external interfaces to share data and information with other systems.
- Given that there are significant similarities between the COSYSMO 1.0 calibration data set and the DoD SoSE case studies, the accuracy of COSYSMO for SoSE should be somewhere between the values obtained for the COSYSMO 1.0 (PRED(30)=75%) and the local calibrations performed by the COSYSMO industry affiliates (PRED(30)=85%).

However, the major limitation of the SoSE process model is that it is not sufficiently calibrated to estimate actual SOSE effort. This is left for future research.

3 SoSE Model

The SoSE model developed for the analysis of collaborative and acknowledged SoSE management approaches was designed to evaluate the effort required to engineer a single SoS capability in a software-intensive, net-centric SoS. This model uses the SoS capability size expressed in equivalent nominal requirements (the composite COSYSMO size driver used to calculate estimated effort). There are two primary calculations: one to calculate the associated SE effort using an acknowledged SoS management approach and one to calculate the associated SE effort using a collaborative SoS management approach. The acknowledged approach estimates the SE effort at the SoS level and the associated SE effort at the CS level. The collaborative approach estimates the SE effort at only the CS level (since there is no SoSE team in this approach).

The underlying method used to determine the associated effort values (in person-months) is the COSYSMO 1.0 algorithm, $Effort = 38.55*EM*(size)^{1.06}$, where 38.55 and 1.06 are calibration constants for COSYSMO 1.0 [7]. For the SoSE model, effort multiplier (EM) values are calculated for various parts of the engineering process: SoSE for new capability, SoSE for oversight of the non-SoS CS changes, SE at the CS level for the SoS capability (both with and without SoSE support), and SE at the CS level for the non-SoS-requirements being implemented in parallel with the SoS capability. The following sections describe various aspects of the model in more detail.

3.1 SoSE Process Model Assumptions and Constraints

Several assumptions and constraints were used in the development of the SoSE process model. In some cases, these model assumptions and constraints generate more conservative estimates of cost savings for an acknowledged SoSE team and therefore strengthen the resulting findings. The assumptions and constraints are:

1. *All CSs currently exist.* This means that all of the CSs are legacy systems undergoing some level of change (very small to major upgrades). In addition, there are no new "long-lead" CS development activities that may have extraordinarily high levels of internal change and/or may not be fielded within the timeframe of the current SoS capability change. (There could be new systems

under development that may eventually be part of the SoS, but these are not considered as part of the SoSE comparison model.)

2. The model assumes *a relatively mature engineering process at both the CS and SoS levels*. This is primarily because the COSYSMO cost model has been calibrated using SE projects from relatively mature SE organizations. This assumption is also related to the fact that successful system development has been shown to be strongly correlated to relatively "mature engineering processes" [11]. By limiting the CSs to existing systems, as stated in the first assumption above, one can reasonably assume it is appropriate to model the CS engineering processes as "mature." As for the SoSE team processes, they are typically not as mature as the CS due to the fact that these processes are currently evolving to meet the new challenges that SoSs present [2]. However, the SoSE teams typically have a strong foundation upon which to build their processes given that they leverage the processes of the CSs and work with the CS engineers.
3. In general, *each CS has its own evolutionary path based on system-level stakeholder needs/desires*. This is related to the definition of an SoS [5]. The exception for some SoSs is the SoS infrastructure that integrates the CSs together. This is typically identified as an SoS CS, but it does not necessarily have its own evolutionary path outside of the SoS or independent of the SoS.
4. *SoS capabilities are software-intensive*. Most SoSs of interest today are those that are net-centric in nature and the CSs are interfacing each other in order to share data or information.
5. There is *no SoS capability requirements volatility*. The rationale for this is that "no SoS capability requirements volatility" simplifies the initial process model and the impact of this volatility would similarly affect both collaborative and acknowledged SoSs. Intuitively, the presence of an SoSE team would somewhat streamline the configuration management of changes across the CSs and be another "value added" aspect of an acknowledged SoSE team, but this SoSE process dynamic is left for follow-on research. Also note that this assumption is not applicable to the CSs and in fact, the model does assume varying levels of CS volatility.
6. *100% of the SoS capability requirements are allocated to each CS needed to implement the capability*.
7. There is *no focus on schedule or the asynchronous nature of SoS CS upgrades*. The scheduling aspects of SoS capability implementation are typically driven by the asynchronous schedules of the CSs and preliminary reports do not indicate that there are significant differences in the two approaches (collaborative and acknowledged) except for the fact that an acknowledged SoSE team may have some leverage to negotiate different priorities for CS SE changes.
8. *Management of SoS internal interfaces reduces complexity for systems*. This is based on observations [2] and heuristics [12] about the common drivers of complexity within a system or an SoS.
9. *SE effort/information provided to the SoSE team in support of SoSE must be added to SE effort for the subset of the CS upgrade requirements that are at the SoS level*. SoS programs participating in the DoD case studies reported that it is difficult for an SoSE team to make reasonable decisions without input from the CS SEs [2].

These assumptions and constraints (or simplifiers) allowed the model to focus on comparing the two management approaches using the COSYSMO 1.0 calibration to determine when it is cost effective to transition an existing collaborative SoS to an acknowledged SoS. In addition, these assumptions and constraints limit the modeled differences between the collaborative and acknowledged approaches to those key SoSE differences identified in [2] and therefore produce conservative estimates with respect to each approach.

3.2 SoSE Model Effort Calculations

The SoSE model incorporates several effort calculations. As mentioned earlier, each of these calculations is based upon the COSYSMO 1.0 algorithm [7], shown in Equation 1 where *38.55* and *1.06* are calibration constants for COSYSMO 1.0.

$$\text{Effort (in person-months)} = 38.55*\text{EM}*(\text{size})^{1.06}/152\ . \quad (1)$$

In addition, the SoSE model uses the COCOMO II approach for applying different EM factors to different parts of the system that have different cost drivers [10]. The general form of this approach is shown in Equation 2. In Equation 2, *i* ranges from one to the number of components and A and B are the calibration factors.

$$\text{Effort} = \text{A} * \sum \text{EM}_i*(\text{component}_i\ \text{size/total size})*(\text{total size})^{\text{B}}\ . \quad (2)$$

Both the acknowledged and collaborative CS effort calculations include the effort to engineer the non-SoS-requirements being engineered concurrently with the SoS capability. This is to ensure that the SoSE model captures the associated diseconomy of scale that occurs as the number of requirements at the CS level increases (whether they are SoS-related requirements or CS-only requirements). The following sections describe each of the SoSE model calculations using the terms defined in Table 3.

SoSE Effort for Acknowledged SoS. Using the COSYSMO algorithm with different EMs for the SoS capability requirements and the CS "monitored" requirements, the SoSE model calculation for the SoSE team's effort is shown in Equation 3.

$$\text{SoSE Effort} = 38.55*[((\text{SoS}_{\text{CR}} / \text{SoS}_{\text{Treq}})*(\text{SoS}_{\text{Treq}})^{1.06} * \text{EM}_{\text{SOS-CR}})+$$

$$((\text{SoS}_{\text{MR}} / \text{SoS}_{\text{Treq}})*(\text{SoS}_{\text{Treq}})^{1.06} * \text{EM}_{\text{SOS-MR}}*\text{OSF})]\ /152\ . \quad (3)$$

CS Effort with Support from SoSE Team (for Acknowledged SoS). This equation calculates the CS effort for engineering the SoS capability requirements allocated to it plus engineering in parallel the non-SoS-requirements scheduled for the current upgrade cycle. In this case, the SoS requirements engineering is led by the SoSE team with some support from the CS. Therefore, in this calculation, one needs to include the CS engineering effort required to support system design at the SoS level. This SoSE "tax" is based on the findings from the DoD case studies that indicate the SoSE team requires the support of the CSs in the design of the approach for meeting the SoS desired capability.

Table 3. SoSE Model Equation Term Definitions

Term	Definition
CS_{nonSoS}	Number of non-SoS CS requirements planned for upgrade cycle
$CS_{TreqSoSE}$	Total number of requirements planned for CS upgrade cycle with support from an SoSE team and is equal to $SoS_{CSalloc} + CS_{nonSoS}$
$CS_{TreqwoSoSE}$	Total number of CS requirements that must be addressed for the upgrade cycle with no support from an SoSE team
$EM_{SOS\text{-}CR}$	Effort multiplier for SoS capability requirements engineered at the SoS level
$EM_{SOS\text{-}MR}$	Effort multiplier for CS non-SoS-requirements monitored by the SoSE team
$EM_{CS\text{-}CRwSOSE}$	Effort multiplier for CS capability requirements engineering <u>with</u> SoSE team support
$EM_{CS\text{-}CRnSOSE}$	Effort multiplier for CS capability requirements engineering <u>with no</u> SoSE team support
$EM_{CSnonSOS}$	Effort multiplier for CSs engineering for non-SoS-requirements
OSF	Oversight adjustment factor to capture SoSE effort associated with monitoring CS non-SoS changes (Values used include 5%, 10%, and 15%)
SoS_{CR}	Number of SoSE capability requirements (equivalent nominal requirements), based upon the modeled size and complexity of the SoS capability
$SoS_{CSalloc}$	Number of SoS capability requirements allocated to CS
SoS_{MR}	Number of SoSE monitored requirements (equivalent nominal requirements): the sum of all non-SoS-requirements being addressed in parallel with the SoS capability requirements in the upgrade cycle
SoS_{Treq}	Total number of SoSE nominal (weighted) requirements: $SoS_{CR} + (SoS_{MR}*OSF)$

Using the distribution of SE effort for system design in [8], this model approximates the SoSE tax by adding on half of the typical percentage of system design effort (half of 30%) to the CSs for those requirements allocated to the CS from the SoSE team. This factor was based on anecdotal inputs from systems engineers with experience in the SoS environment. Thus the calculation for CS SE effort using an SoSE team is as shown in Equation 4.

$$\text{CS SE Effort with SoSE Team} = 38.55*[1.15*((SoS_{CSalloc} / CS_{TreqSoSE})* (CS_{TreqSoSE})^{1.06} * EM_{CS\text{-}CRwSOSE}) + (CS_{nonSoS} / CS_{TreqSoSE})*(CS_{TreqSoSE})^{1.06}* EM_{CSnonSOS}] /152 . \quad (4)$$

Total Systems Engineering Effort (SoSE and SE) for Acknowledged SoS. The total concurrent systems engineering effort for the acknowledged SoS is the sum of the SoSE effort (Equation 3) and the CS SE effort with the SoSE team support (Equation 4).

CS Effort with No SoSE Team Support (for Collaborative SoS). In the case where there is no SoSE team to support the engineering of the SoS capability requirements, the CSs are responsible for engineering all of the SoS capability requirements (not just an allocated subset) as well as the non-SoS-requirements planned for the system upgrade cycle. Thus the calculation for CS SE effort without SoSE team support is as shown in Equation 5.

$$\text{CS SE Effort without SoSE Team} = 38.55*[((SoS_{CR} / CS_{TreqwoSoSE})*(CS_{TreqwoSoSE})^{1.06}* EM_{CS\text{-}CRnSOSE}) + ((CS_{nonSoS} / CS_{TreqwoSoSE})*(CS_{TreqwoSoSE})^{1.06}* EM_{CSnonSOS})] /152 \,. \quad (5)$$

3.3 SoSE Model Effort Multipliers for Effort Calculations

As indicated above, the SoSE model uses several EMs to calculate the effort associated with the engineering of the SoS capabilities. If all cost drivers are set to nominal, the resulting composite EM is 1.0. If the combined set of EMs is greater than nominal, the resulting composite EM value is greater than 1.0. Likewise, if the combined set of EMs is less than nominal, then the resulting composite EM value is less than 1.0.

Table 4. SoSE EM for SoS Capability Requirements Rationale

Cost Driver	Value	Rationale
Requirements understanding	Low	SoSE team starts with high level capability objectives that must be analyzed and then translated into high-level SoS requirements. This setting is based upon the findings in [2] that the core SoSE activity, translating capability objectives, is typically not performed (not needed) when engineering requirements for a single system.
Level of service requirements	High	Level and complexity of service typically required for performance, interoperability, and/or security in a networked SoS, with the "service" level depending upon the interactions of multiple systems.
# recursive levels in design	High	Added complexity of interdependencies, coordination, and tradeoff analysis required in an SoS versus a single system.
Multisite coordination	Low	A DoD SoS is comprised of multiple systems, each developed/ maintained by one or more organizations, often with time zone impacts and security restrictions.

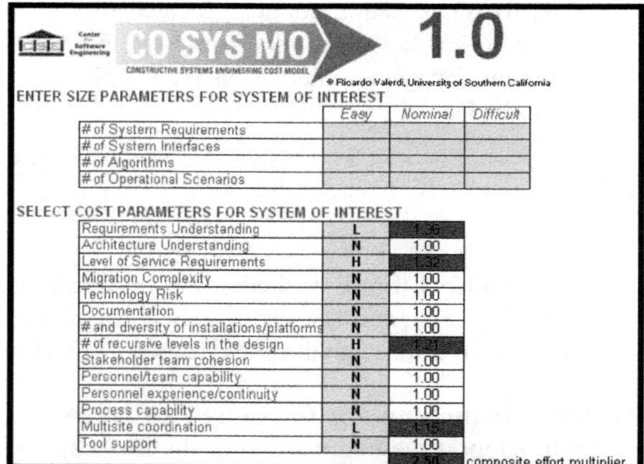

Fig. 1. SoSE EM for SoS requirements

This section presents the COSYSMO-generated EM factors based on cost driver settings and explains the rationale for each of the cost driver settings. In general, each cost driver value is set to "nominal" unless there is some justification within the DoD SoS case studies or CS analysis for adjusting it up or down. Table 4 shows the non-nominal cost driver values for the SoSE SoS capability EM and provides the justification for each one.

Next, these cost driver values are entered into the COSYSMO 1.0 cost parameter section to calculate the composite EM as shown in figure 1. The composite EM value based on the settings described in Table 4 is 2.50, as shown in the lower right corner of figure 1.

Table 5. SoSE Composite EM values and rationales

Category (Value)	Cost Driver	Driver Value	Rationale
SoSE-monitored (0.47)	Technology risk	Very Low	The technology risk for CSs that are characterized as mature legacy systems tends to be nominal and should therefore be even less at the SoS level in those cases where the technology is not directly tied to a new SoS capability.
	Documentation	Very Low	Typically the SoS develops little formal documentation for the CSs.
	Personnel/ team capability	High	The SoSE team is supported by system engineers from the CSs.
CS SoS w/SoSE (1.06)	Architecture understanding	High	In an acknowledged SoS, the SoS architecture is defined and evolved at the SoS level by the SoSE team and not at the CS level.
	Level of service reqs	High	The SoS adds an additional set of service requirements to manage at the CS level and these service levels can be impacted by other CSs within the SoS.
CS SoS w/o SoSE (1.79)	Requirements understanding	Low	SoS requirements addressed at the CS level without the help of an SoSE team are often at a much higher level that the typical CS requirements and therefore requires additional effort. In this case, the CSs must collaborate to accomplish the "Translating Capability Objectives" core activity before they can proceed with the more typical requirements analysis.
	Architecture understanding	Nominal	While more difficult without an SoSE team, there is typically an ad hoc architecture in place for a collaborative SoS and many new capabilities do not require architecture changes, so no additional effect is added to this model parameter.
	Level of service reqs	High	SoS adds an additional set of service requirements to manage at the CS level.
CS non-SoS (0.72)	Architecture understanding	High	The CSs already exist and the SE team should have a good understanding of the existing architecture.
	# recursive levels in design	Low	Non-SoS-requirements tend to only affect the single (existing) CS and that the CS engineers are already familiar with the existing levels.

This same process is used to determine the EM values for each of the other sets of SoSE requirements: a) SoSE "monitored" requirements (SoSE-monitored), b) CS SE for SoS capability with SoSE support (CS SoS w/SoSE), c) CS SE for SoS capability without SoSE support (CS SoS w/o SoSE), and d) CS SE for non-SoS requirements (CS non-SoS). Table 5 explains the rationale for each cost driver that is non-nominal and shows the composite EM as calculated by COSYSMO 1.0.

3.4 SoSE Process Model Execution

To compare the collaborative and acknowledged SoSE management approaches, four SoS characteristics (or parameters) are varied: SoS Size, CS volatility, SoS capability size, and the scope of SoS capability. The range of values for each parameter was determined by the characteristics of the SoSs in the DoD case studies [2] and the associated CSs. Table 6 describes the range of parameters used in the SoSE process model to compare the collaborative and acknowledged SoSE management approaches. These values were used to define a comprehensive set of runs using the boundary values. Additional boundary values were added that focused on areas of interest from the initial set of runs (e.g., around the set of values where the SoSE team goes from "not cost-effective" to "cost-effective" or vice versa).

Table 6. SoSE Model Parameters

Parameter	Description	Range of Values
SoS Size	Number of CSs within the SoS.	2-200
Capability Size	Number of equivalent nominal requirements as defined by COSYSMO.	1-1000
CS Volatility	Number of non-SoS changes being implemented in each CS in parallel with SoS capability changes.	0-2000
Scope of SoS Capability	Number of CSs that must be changed to support capability.	One to SoS Size (total number of CSs within the SoS)
OSF	Oversight adjustment factor to capture SoSE effort associated with monitoring CS non-SoS changes.	5%, 10%, and 15%

Table 7 presents a sample of the data sets used as inputs and a summary of the results of the associated model run.

An evaluation of these results illuminates a set of heuristics that indicate when an SoSE will be cost-effective from an effort perspective:

1. When the SoS capability size is greater than or equal to the non-SoS changes being implemented in parallel with the SoS changes, there is usually an SoS size at which the SoSE team becomes cost effective.
2. For larger SoSs, there are situations where the SoS capability size is smaller than the non-SoS changes and the SoSE team is cost effective.
3. When the SoS size is small (5 or fewer systems) there are few situations where an SoSE team is cost effective. The situation identified in the model executions where an SoSE team would be cost effective for a small SoS is when

Table 7. Sample SoSE Model Runs

Example	Model Inputs				SoSE Team Effectiveness Point		
	SoS Size	SoS Capability Size	CS Volatility	Scope of SoS Capability	OSF 5%	OSF 10%	OSF 15%
1	2-200	100	100	Half of CSs	SoS size 10 or higher	SoS size 11 or higher	SoS size 12 or higher
2	4-200	100	100	Quarter of CSs	SoS size 10 or higher	SoS size 11 or higher	SoS size 12 or higher
3	2-200	100	2000	Half of CSs	Not cost effective for any size	Not cost effective for any size	Not cost effective for any size
4	2-200	100	2000	All CSs	SoS size 28 or higher	Not cost effective	Not cost effective
5	10	1000	1000	1-10	SoS change affects 50% CSs or more	SoS change affects 60% CSs or more	SoS change affects 60% CSs or more
6	100	1000	1000	10% to 100%	SoS change affects 10% or more CSs	SoS change affects 14% or more CSs	SoS change affects 19% or more CSs
7	10	1000	0	1-10	SoS change affects 5 CSs or more	SoS change affects 5 CSs or more	SoS change affects 5 CSs or more
8	10	1	1000	1-10	Not cost effective for any scope	Not cost effective for any scope	Not cost effective for any scope
9	5	1000	1000	1-5	SoS change affects all 5	SoS change affects all 5	SoS change affects all 5
10	5	1	1000	1-10	Notcost effective	Not cost effective	Not cost effective

a. The SoS capability size is greater than or equal to the non-SoS changes being implemented in each CS in parallel with the SoS changes.
b. The SoS capability changes affects all of the CSs within the SoS.

4. When the size of the SoS capability change is extremely small compared to the non-SoS changes being implemented in the CSs, the SoSE team is generally not cost effective.
5. The oversight factor (OSF) which indicates the relative amount of time spent monitoring CS non-SoS changes also impacts the cost effectiveness of the SoS team. This is a parameter that deserves further investigation with respect to a) the level of CS understanding required at the SoS level to adequately engineer SoS changes, b) the potential impacts of CS non-SoS changes, and c) the effects of rework when non-SoS changes adversely impact the goals of the SoS.

It is also important to note that these heuristics are derived from a set of cases that are based upon a set of simplifying assumptions and constraints that are described above.

As was noted, these model assumptions and constraints generate relatively conservative estimates of cost savings for an acknowledged SoSE team and as a result, the actual threshold points for a specific SoS may be lower than indicated by the model. To determine the cost effectiveness for a specific SoS implementing a specific set of SoS changes while the CSs are implementing their specific non-SoS changes, one needs to model those specific characteristics to determine the point where an SoSE team is cost-effective for that SoS.

4 Conclusions and Future Research

The model described in this paper attempted to determine when is it cost-effective to employ an SoSE team to oversee and guide the development and evolution of an SoS. Model executions have shown that there is a "home-ground" for an SoSE team supporting the evolution of a given SoS.

Smaller SoSs and SoSs where the SoS changes are relatively small compared to the CSs changes can generally be managed cost effectively using a collaborative SoS management approach. As the SoS grows in size or as the SoS changes grow in size and scope (for example, the SoS overall architecture needs to change), it will generally be more cost effective to put an SoSE team in place to manage the SoS as an acknowledged SoS. However, these findings were found in the context of evaluating approaches for implementing a single SoS capability or capability change in a single incremental upgrade to the SoS CSs. So, while there is a discernable cost savings in person-months using one approach or the other, it is important to evaluate the cost effectiveness in a much broader context. One must ask the questions such as:

- What is the typical rate of SoS change over time?
- How long will the current rate of change continue?
- Will SoS-level changes or CS (non-SoS) changes predominate over time?

An SoSE team is typically composed of several systems engineers each with different specialty areas. Over time, one must evaluate whether the SoS oversight activities and the rate of SoS capability modifications/changes being implemented are sufficient to keep the SoSE team fully engaged (i.e., little to no slack time). If there is too much slack time for the SoSE team, then the cost benefits may disappear.

Also, this research effort did not address how the quality of the SoS engineering activities are affected by not engineering changes at a level above the CSs and the amount of rework that is generated when changes are not adequately engineered.

These issues lead to future opportunities to expand on this research:

- Incorporate a rework factor to show the rework impacts of not engineering cross-cutting changes at the SoS level.
- Incorporate the evaluation of other measures of SoS effectiveness related to complexity and performance.
- Develop an SoS capability cost model by characterizing the SoSE team and all of the CS engineering teams in COSYMO, then calibrating that model.

References

1. Lane, J., Valerdi, R.: Synthesizing System-of-Systems Concepts for Use in Cost Estimation. Systems Engineering 10(4), 297–307 (2007)
2. Department of Defense: Systems Engineering Guide for System of Systems, Version 1.0 (2008)
3. Northrop, L., Feiler, P., Gabriel, R., Goodenough, J., Linger, R., Longstaff, T., Kazman, R., Klein, M., Schmidt, D., Sullivan, K., Wallnau, K.: Ultra-Large-Scale Systems: The Software Challenge of the Future. Software Engineering Institute, Pittsburgh (2006)
4. United States Air Force (USAF) Scientific Advisory Board (SAB): Report on System-of-Systems Engineering for Air Force Capability Development; Public Release SAB-TR-05-04 (2005)
5. Maier, M.: Architecting Principles for Systems-of-Systems. Systems Engineering 1(4), 267–284 (1998)
6. Dahmann, J., Baldwin, K.: Understanding the Current State of US Defense Systems of Systems and the Implications for Systems Engineering. In: Proceedings of the IEEE Systems Conference, Montreal, Canada, April 7-10 (2008)
7. Valerdi, R.: Constructive Systems Engineering Cost Model. PhD. Dissertation, University of Southern California (2005)
8. Valerdi, R., Wheaton, M.: ANSI/EIA 632 as a Standardized WBS for COSYSMO, AIAA-2005-7373. In: Proceedings of the AIAA 5th Aviation, Technology, Integration, and Operations Conference, Arlington, Virginia (2005)
9. Wang, G., Valerdi, R., Ankrum, A., Millar, C., Roedler, G.: COSYSMO Reuse Extension. In: Proceedings of the 18th Annual International Symposium of INCOSE, The Netherlands (2008)
10. Boehm, B., Abts, C., Brown, A., Chulani, S., Clark, B., Horowitz, E., Madachy, R., Reifer, D., Steece, B.: Software Cost Estimation with COCOMO II. Prentice Hall, Upper Saddle River (2000)
11. SEI: Capability Maturity Model Integration (CMMI), CMU/SEI-2002-TR-001 (2001)
12. Rechtin, E.: Systems Architecting: Creating and Building Complex Systems. Prentice Hall, Upper Saddle River (1991)

Using Project Procedure Diagrams for Milestone Planning

Klaus Bergner[1] and Jan Friedrich[1,2]

[1] 4Soft GmbH, Mittererstraße 3, D-80336 München, Germany
[2] Technische Universität München, Boltzmannstraße 3, D-85748 Garching, Germany

Abstract. This paper presents Project Procedure Diagrams (PPDs) as a technique for specifying and elaborating project milestone plans. The graphical syntax of PPDs is similar to UML activity diagrams. The operational semantics is based on token flow and resembles playing common board games. The base concepts can be easily grasped by project managers and lend themselves to experimentation and simulation.

In spite of their apparent simplicity, PPDs offer support for advanced concepts like parallel subprojects, multi-level iterations, forward and backward planning and for the composition of complex plans from modular process components. Furthermore, PPDs are based on rigorous, formally founded syntax and semantics to ease the development of tools.

1 Motivation: Support for Milestone Planning

Each project is by definition a unique endeavour. Software development projects in particular require flexibility and creativity during their execution. With that in mind, it seems that formal software process models, which try to standardize software development processes, cannot possibly work. Or can they?

A naive transfer of established process modeling techniques is certainly not appropriate. The left side of Fig. 1 shows the typical approach for recurring business processes. Such processes can be formally described by means of established description techniques. People can then enact them routinely, if possible supported by means of a workflow engine. Within the context of software development projects, this approach is only suitable for recurring micro-processes like build and test workflows. In general, it is simply not possible for process designers to consider all possible imponderables of a project in advance.

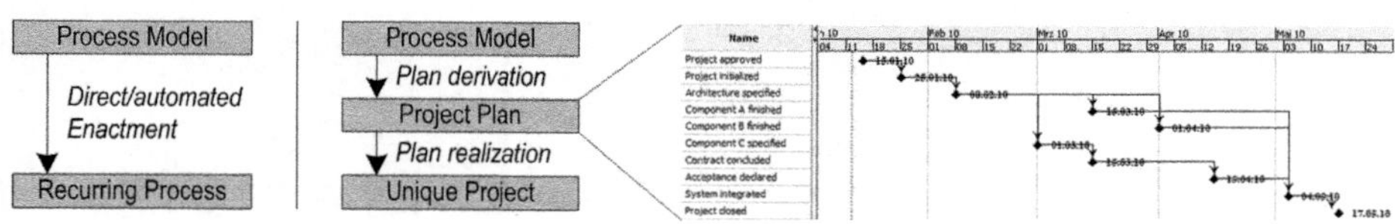

Fig. 1. Direct Enactment versus Plan-Based Enactment

J. Münch, Y. Yang, and W. Schäfer (Eds.): ICSP 2010, LNCS 6195, pp. 88–99, 2010.

Instead of a detailed process description that covers every aspect in advance, a project manager typically relies on a project plan to organize and control the overall project process. Initially, this plan will be rather coarse-grained, covering only the basic milestones. During the project, the project manager will continuously refine, update and often also change the plan based on the current situation. Project process models should thus offer strong support for the initial elaboration as well as the subsequent evolution of suitable project plans.

There are two basic styles of project plans, which can also be mixed. Activity plans strive to identify the activities that have to be performed within the project. Milestone plans instead focus on the major goals and intermediate steps to be reached during the project. From our practical experience, we fully agree with E. S. Anderson's paper titled "Warning: activity planning is hazardous to your project's health". Therein, he argues against the "commonly used practice of activity planning" and claims that "this kind of planning at an early stage is either impossible [...] or gives miserable results" [1]. He strongly votes for milestone plans, as they can be fulfilled "by a wide variety of activities" and are, therefore, much more stable and practical than activity plans.

In this paper, we describe the plan-based process enactment approach of the V-Modell XT [2], the official process model standard of the German public sector. It focuses on the derivation of milestone plans based on a simple yet powerful process description technique named *Project Procedure Diagrams.*

The rest of this paper is structured as follows: Section 2 gives a short overview over the problem domain and lists requirements for a suitable project process description language. Section 3 presents strengths and weaknesses of existing approaches and motivates the need for a novel approach. Section 4 describes the syntax and the operational semantics of Project Procedure Diagrams as a set of rules to be followed by a project manager during the elaboration of a project plan. It also sketches our approach for the mathematical formalization of Project Procedure Diagrams based on Petri nets. A short conclusion ends the paper.

2 Problem Domain and Goals

On the right hand side of Fig. 1 a typical milestone plan is shown as visualized by a project planning tool in the form of a simple Gantt chart. Basically, the plan consists of *milestones*, which are represented as black diamonds, and *milestone relationships*, which are represented as arrows.

A *milestone* is defined as the end of a project stage. Typically, it is marked by the completion of one or more work products at a certain date. An example would be a milestone such as System integrated, marked by the completion of a certain system based on already existing components.

Milestone *relationships* constrain the logical and thereby also the temporal sequence of milestones. In this paper, we only use a simple *After Relationship.* It implies that the date of the predecessor milestone lies before the date of the successor milestone, thereby ensuring that all work products due for the predecessor milestone are finished and thus available as preconditions for the completion of the successor milestone.

Please note that our approach for the support of milestone planning only cares about the logical order of milestones. We explicitely do not address issues like time or resource planning. Nevertheless, when designing PPDs as a process description language, we had to keep other constraints in mind. Each of the following goals is motivated by the fact that the V-Modell XT is a real-life process model with a large number and a wide variety of users:

Ease of Use. The description language must be *understandable* for project managers with no background in process description languages. That means that it should have a *simple, possibly graphical syntax* based on *few, clearly defined concepts* that should lend themselves to hands-on experimentation and simulation. Furthermore, the specification and elaboration of simple plans should be as easy as possible to reduce the acceptance threshold.

Practicability. The description language must support typical activities and *different planning strategies* of project managers, among them forward and backward planning. Furthermore, it must be possible to compose a plan from an extensible library of *reusable project procedure specifications.* This includes support for abstract *procedure types* which can be implemented by a number of different concrete procedure specifications. This feature allows project managers to choose the concrete procedure based on the current project context, and it allows process designers to extend the procedure library without having to change existing procedure specifications. Lastly, the description language should be *formally defined* as a precondition for *tool support.*

Expressivity. The description language must offer support for the generation of milestone plans for *arbitrarily complex projects.* Based on our experience, especially adequate support for arbitrary combinations of *sequential iterations* and *parallel subprocesses* is a critical feature. It must be possible, for example, to derive plans where the development subprocedure of a certain subcomponent is decoupled from the main development flow and spans an arbitrary number of iterations, each based on its own procedure specification.

3 Existing Approaches

As set out in Sect. 1, the approaches for the direct enactment of process models are not appropriate for high-level project processes. FUNSOFT nets as described by [3] are a good example. Although they were once intended to model overall software development processes, they turned out to be better suited for the description of recurring micro-processes and standardized business processes [4].

Other approaches try to provide a formal foundation for project and resource planning [5,6] based on Petri nets. However, these approaches also do not support the derivation of project milestone plans from process models.

Common software development process metamodels are of course aware of the difference of software development projects to recurring business processes. However, their support for plan-based enactment is surprisingly weak. OMG's SPEM 2.0 [7] contains concepts like *Milestone* and *Work Sequence (Kind)*, but states explicitly that it "does not aim to be a generic process modeling language, nor does it even provide its own behavior modeling concepts." Consequently, it only sketches the derivation of project plans. ISO's SEMDM [8] also contains classes like *Milestone* and *MilestoneKind* but states that it "does not include classes to represent a sequence of events". As both standards cannot express the consistency of a milestone plan with a process model, they were not suitable to express our requirements within the V-Modell XT.

SPEM 2.0 refers, amongst others, to UML activity diagrams [9] as a possible description language. Originally, they were intended to specify the behaviour of complex software systems. Activity diagrams thus are a very complex description technique, compromising their understandability especially for project managers without expert knowledge in UML. Furthermore, activity diagrams lack some features that are necessary to fulfill the given requirements. Although they do support the composition of diagrams via the *CallBehaviour* construct, the called behavior is fixed. Thus, the project manager cannot chose it freely during the project without altering the calling activity diagram. This seriously affects the reusability and combinability of process building blocks. Activity diagrams also don't support "inverse token flow" which would be necessary to allow a backward planning strategy. Lastly, the implementation of tools is complicated by the fact that there is no commonly agreed formal foundation [10].

4 Project Procedure Diagrams

This section introduces Project Procedure Diagrams (PPDs) as being used within the V-Modell XT since 2006. They were at first used as a graphical notion only, but then emerged to a comprehensive process description language with formally defined syntax and semantics. As they are an integral part of the V-Modell XT metamodel, they were developed from scratch without any attempt to extent an existing notation (e.g. SPEM 2.0).

The following presentation uses a board game metaphor to explain the graphical syntax (the board) and the operational token flow semantics (the rules for game moves). This approach has been proven to work for non-experts during many training sessions with dozens of attendees from German federal government and German industry. Thus, it demonstrates the *ease of use* and the understandability of the approach. In the course of the presentation, we refer to the remaining goals of Sect. 2 as appropriate to establish the suitability of PPDs for the given task.

4.1 Milestone Plan Derivation

To explain how a project manager may derive a milestone plan from a given set of Project Procedure Diagrams, Fig. 2 introduces some sample Project Procedure Diagrams containing all relevant concepts. Figure 3i shows a corresponding sample milestone plan and its derivation. In the remainder of this section, metamodel concepts are printed *in italics*, whereas instances within the model are

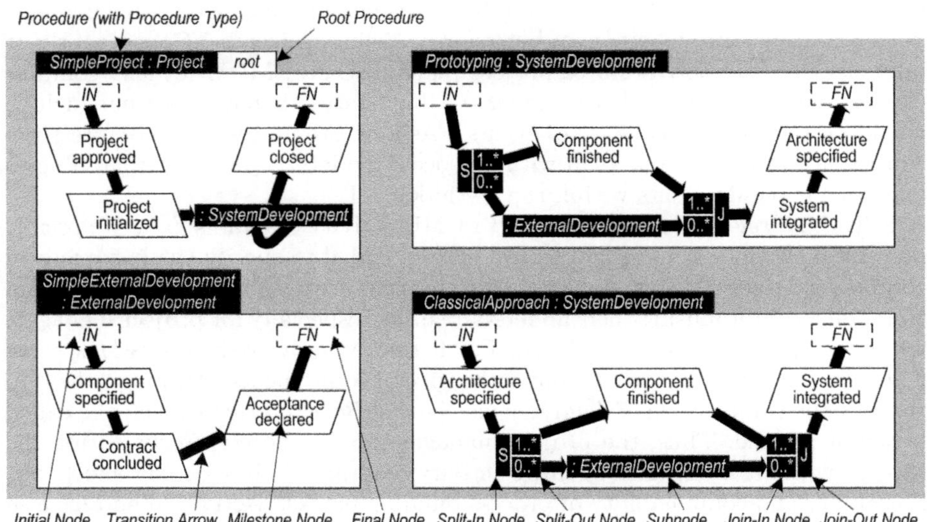

Fig. 2. Sample Procedure Specification denoted in Project Procedure Diagrams

printed in a serifless font. The complete set of rules can be found in table 1; references to certain rules are printed in a **bold font**.

The *Procedure* SimpleProject specifies the top-level procedure for a development project: start the project, develop something, close the project. According to **R1**, the project manager puts a token on the *Initial Node* of the *Root Procedure* as depicted in Fig. 3a on page 94. Each token has a memory, which contains the set of previous milestones. At the beginning, the memory set is empty, as the token is generated afresh.

After following **R1**, **R2** is the only applicable rule. Hence, the project manager moves the token along the outgoing *Transition Arrow*. Consequently, the token arrives at *Milestone Node* Project approved and **R3** must be applied. To do this, the project manager adds the new milestone 1 to the milestone plan and names it "MyProject approved". The token's memory is accordingly set to the milestone set $\{1\}$. Figure 3b illustrates the described course of action.

Again, **R2** is the only applicable rule. The project manager moves the token onto the *Milestone Node* Project initialized and adds milestone 2 to the milestone plan. As the token's memory contained $\{1\}$ when it arrived at the *Milestone Node*, she has to add an *After Relationship*, pointing from milestone 1 to milestone 2 (abbreviated as $1 \rightarrow 2$). At the end of this procedure, the token's memory is reset to $\{2\}$ as shown in Fig. 3c.

According to **R2**, the project manager moves the token onto a *Subnode* labeled with :SystemDevelopment. This triggers the application of **R4**, and the project manager has to decide whether she wants to do Prototyping or to start with a ClassicalApproach, both being procedures of procedure type SystemDevelopment.

Table 1. Rules for Milestone derivation and transformation

No.	Description
Derivation Rules	
R1	At the beginning of the plan derivation phase, a single token with an empty memory is placed on the *Initial Node* of the *Root Procedure*.
R2	A token may be moved along a *Transition Arrow*. During the move, the token's memory remains unmodified.
R3	When a token arrives at a *Milestone Node*, a new milestone has to be added to the milestone plan. The new milestone is labeled with the name of the associated *Milestone Node* (or any modified phrase). Furthermore, from every milestone in the token's memory, an *After Relationship* to the new milestone has to be added. Finally, the token's memory is reset to the set containing only the new milestone.
R4	When a token arrives at a *Subnode*, it must be moved to the *Initial Node* of the *Procedure* that fulfills the *Procedure Type* to which the *Subnode* refers to. If there is more than one adequate *Procedure*, one of them may be chosen at will. The token's memory remains unmodified.
R5	When a token arrives at a *Split-In Node*, it has to be replaced with a number of new tokens (at least one). The new tokens have to be set on the corresponding *Split-Out Nodes*. For each *Split-Out Node*, the number of tokens placed upon must comply with the given cardinality. Other tokens already lying on a *Split-Out Node* are not considered when the rule is applied. The memory of each added token is initialized with the token that has arrived on the *Split-In Node*. After that, this (old) token must be removed. From now on, the new tokens can be moved independently.
R6	One or more tokens lying on the *Join-In Nodes* of a corresponding *Join-Out Node* may be replaced by a single new token, provided that the given cardinalities are respected. The new token must be placed on the *Join-Out Node*. Its memory is set to the union of all memory sets of the removed tokens.
R7	When a token arrives at the *Final Node* of a *Procedure*, it has to be moved to a *Subnode* that references the *Procedure Type* of the *Procedure*. If more than one *Subnode* refers to the type, any of them can be chosen at will. The token's memory remains unmodified. Afterwards, Rule 2 must be applied for the token.
R8	At the end of the plan derivation phase, a single token has to lie on the *Final Node* of the *Root Procedure*, and no other token may exist.
Transformation Rules	
R9	Two temporally independent milestones may be merged to a single milestone. All existing relationships are kept during that operation.
R10	Additional *After Relationships* may be added, as long as they don't lead to cycles in the milestone plan.
R11	Redundant milestone relationships must be removed. A relationship is redundant if it can be derived from other relationships.
R12	Additional (so-called "free") milestones may be added at will.
R13	Milestone relationships have to be added until there is exactly one project start milestone that lies before every other milestone and exactly one project end milestone that lies after every other milestone.

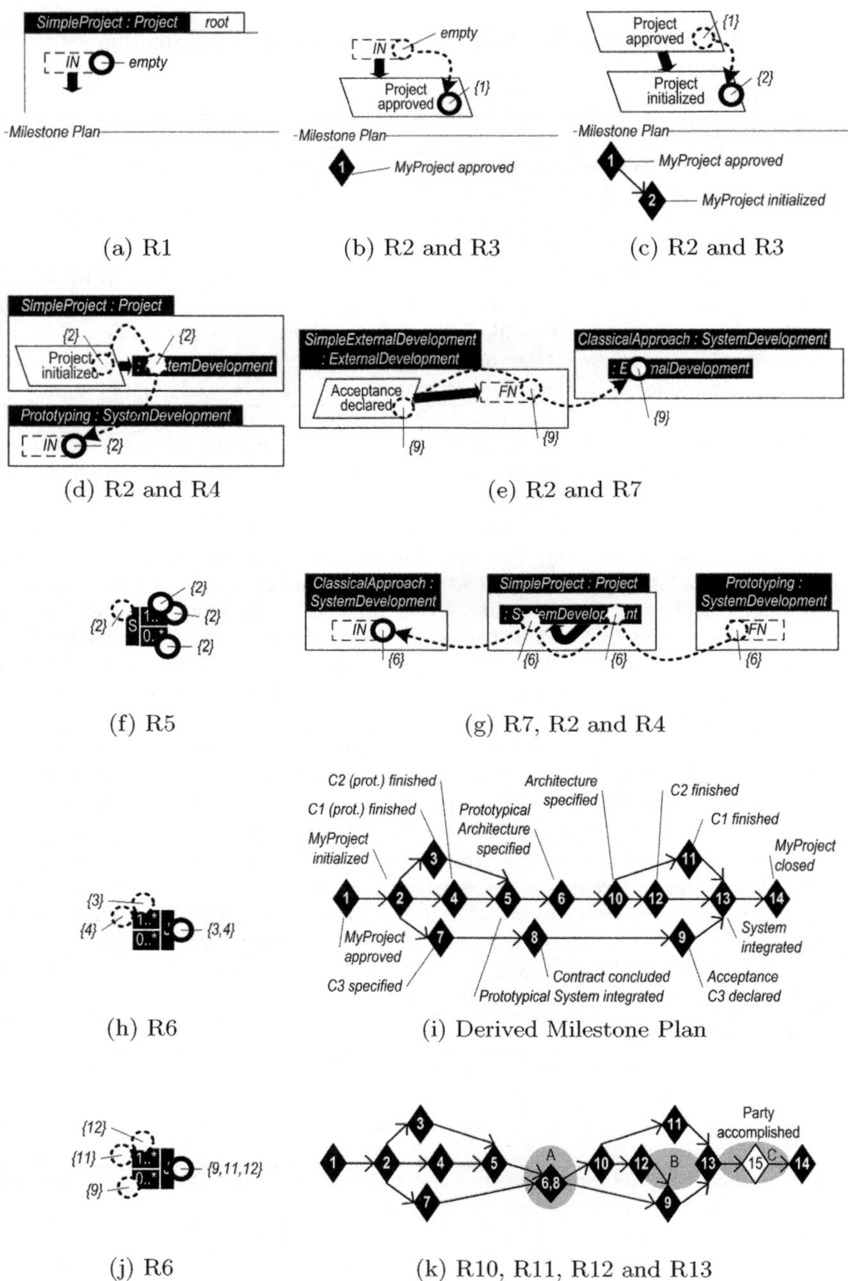

Fig. 3. Token Movement and Development of the Milestone Plan

As the requirements are not yet clear, the project manager decides to move the token to the *Initial Node* of the *Procedure* Prototyping as depicted in Fig. 3d.

Inescapably, the token arrives at a *Split-In Node*. In accordance with **R5** the project manager has to decide whether she needs independent milestone threads or not. She already knows that the system will probably consist of three components $C1, C2, C3$ and that she will commission a sub-contractor with the construction of component $C3$. So she replaces the existing token with three new tokens (each representing the development of one component) as depicted in Fig. 3f. Note that this behavior cannot be easily modeled with a *ForkNode* as provided by UML acticity diagrams, but requires extending the *ForkNode* with other concepts (for example, *ControlFlow.weight* and *MergeNodes*). Afterwards, by applying Rules 2 to 4, the project manager adds the milestones "C1 (prototype) finished" (3), "C2 (prototype) finished" (4) and "C3 specified" (7) as well as the necessary relationships ($2 \rightarrow 3$, $2 \rightarrow 4$, $2 \rightarrow 7$).

In the following, two tokens arrive at the upper *Split-In Node*, as depicted in Fig. 3h. According to **R6**, the project manager has to decide whether she wants to merge the two independent milestone threads. As there is only one prototype system consisting of the two prototype implementations of $C1$ and $C2$ (note that $C3$ is not included in the prototype), she decides to replace both tokens with one and therefore to move only one token onto *Milestone Node* System integrated. As the replaced tokens remember having been at milestones 3 and 4 respectively, the new token's memory is set to $\{3, 4\}$. As consequence, the project manager adds milestone "Prototypical system integrated" (5), which is temporally dependent on milestones 3 and 4, as depicted in Fig. 3i.

After this, the project manager moves the token located in *Procedure* Prototyping onto *Milestone Node* Architecture specified and adds milestone 6 to the milestone plan. Inescapably, the token arrives at the subsequent *Final Node* and **R7** must be applied. As the procedure specification contains only one appropriate *Subnode* (:SystemDevelopment, located in *Procedure* SimpleProject), the token must be moved there. Now, as two outgoing *Transition Arrows* start at the *Subnode*, the project manager can apply **R2** in two different ways: either she moves the token to *Milestone Node* Project closed or she takes the other *Transition Arrow* and moves the token from the *Subnode* to the *Subnode*, leading to the application of **R4**. She chooses the latter, as she wants to re-engineer the prototypical versions of $C1$ and $C2$ in a second iteration. Furthermore, this second iteration is necessary to integrate the externally developed component $C3$ into the system. This time, the ClassicalApproach is used. Figure 3g depicts the described action.

The subsequent moves can be performed according to the already introduced rules. Thus, the project manager moves the tokens and adds milestones 8, 9, 10, 11, 12 as well as the following relations: $7 \rightarrow 8$, $8 \rightarrow 9$, $6 \rightarrow 10$, $10 \rightarrow 11$, $10 \rightarrow 12$. To finish the planning procedure (see **R8**) the project manager has to merge all existing tokens (representing three independent milestone threads) as depicted in Fig. 3j. As a precondition for the merge, she has to move the token lying in *Procedure* ExternalDevelopment to *Procedure* ClassicalApproach as depicted in Fig. 3e. Note that this token came from Prototyping and used the *Procedure* ExternalDevelopment as a kind of "bridge" (or tunnel).

After the merge, the project manager moves the one remaining token to the *Final Node* of SimpleProject and adds milestones 13 and 14 (and relationships 11 → 13, 12 → 13, 9 → 13, 13 → 14) along the way. Now the plan derivation phase is finished according to **R8**. This rule ensures that all parallel subprocesses are finally joined together at some point in time. It also ensures that the token flow game has a clearly defined end. Note that this doesn't follow from rules **R1 to R7**, as the tokens created by a single application of **R5** may be joined by multiple applications of **R6**.

Note also that (in the general case, not in the example) the planning procedure may not be finishable due to a "wrong" move by the project manager during the planning game. Such a move may lead to a situation where some tokens on *Join-In Nodes* cannot be moved anymore. In cases like this, the project manager has to go back and rectify the wrong move.

4.2 Milestone Plan Transformation

The milestone plan derivation phase results in a first version of the project plan, respecting all constraints required by the project process model. In practice, the project manager often wants to add additional constraints between the milestones, making the milestone plan "stricter" than required by the project process model. To do this, the milestone plan transformation rules given in this subsection may be applied.

In our running example, the project manager may note that milestones 6 and 8 are temporally dependent on each other and must be reached simultaneously. According to **R9**, she merges the two milestones, as depicted in Fig. 3k (highlight A). Furthermore, she notes that a finished component $C2$ is required in order to run the tests for $C3$. Therefore, milestone 12 (C2 finished) must be reached before milestone 9 (Acceptance C3 declared). According to **R10**, she adds an additional relationship. Afterwards, according to Rule 11, she removes the relationship between milestone 12 and 13. The result is depicted in Fig. 3k (highlight B).

At the end of the project, the project manager wants to reward her project team for the good work. So she decides to throw a party right before the project is closed, for which she can spend the remaining project budget. As a party like that has to be arranged and planned meticulously, she introduces a new milestone "Party accomplished" (15), adds the necessary relationships and deletes the relationship between milestones 13 and 14 as depicted in Fig. 3k (highlight C). In addition to **R10 and R11**, she needs **R12** to achieve that.

Finally the project manager checks whether the resulting plan is well-formed in the sense of **R13**. If this would not be the case (as could be after adding free milestones or if there is a *Join-Out Node* immediately before the *Final Node* of the *Root*), she would have to add the corresponding milestone relationships.

4.3 Forward and Backward Planning

The token flow game described in Sect. 4.1 corresponds to a forward planning approach. According to that approach, the project manager starts at the beginning of the project and adds new milestones by thinking about the next steps.

Project Procedure Diagrams also support the complementary backward planning strategy, namely, starting at the end of the project and thinking about the previous steps that have to be achieved before. This is due to the symmetry of the given rules R1↔R8, R5↔R6 and R4↔R7. Instead of using "forward tokens", it is, therefore, possible to use "backward tokens" that move backwards in time against the direction of the *Transition Arrows*. The token flow game then starts by placing a single backward token on the *Final Node* of the *Root Procedure* and ends when a single token is lying on the *Initial Node* of the *Root Procedure*.

Furthermore, it is also possible to combine forward and backward planning by starting with a single forward token on the *Initial Node* and a single backward token on the *Final Node* of the *Root Procedure*. For this to work, an additional "pair annihilation" rule is necessary, which allows the removal of a forward token and a backward token meeting at the same node, resulting in relationships between the milestones in the memories of the removed tokens. In this combined playing strategy, the game is finished when there is no token left on the board.

Note that it is even possible to allow the player to place a forward token and a backward token on arbitrary *Milestone Node* at any time during the game! This flexibility makes Project Procedure Diagrams a powerful tool for project managers and allows tool vendors to support many different planning strategies.

4.4 Formalization Approach

The given rules and the derivation of a sample milestone plan are well-suited for the illustration of syntax and semantics of Project Procedure Diagrams. Nevertheless, there are still some open questions concerning special cases or the well-formedness of PPDs that have to be answered in order to remove all ambiguities and to provide a solid foundation for tools.

For that reason, [11] defines syntax and semantics of Project Procedure Diagrams on a formal basis. Figure 4 sketches the formalization approach. To define the consistency between a PPD (Fig. 4a) and a milestone plan (Fig. 4f) a series of intermediate steps are taken.

First, the PPD is transformed to a corresponding place/transition Petri net [12] as shown in Fig. 4b. The Petri net eliminates the "syntactic sugar" by defining where tokens may be placed and how they may be moved or replaced.

The result of the plan derivation phase is then recorded in a trace, as shown in Fig. 4c. As the formalization only defines the consistency between a Petri net and a trace (mathematical semantics) and not sequences of token moves (operational semantics), it therefore supports arbitrary planning strategies. Afterwards, the non-milestone nodes are removed from the trace, so that only relationships between *Milestone Nodes* remain in the reduced trace, as shown in Fig. 4d.

The remaining nodes are mapped to named milestones with the corresponding sets of milestone types (e.g. ":B" may be mapped to "b1:B"). The milestone plan

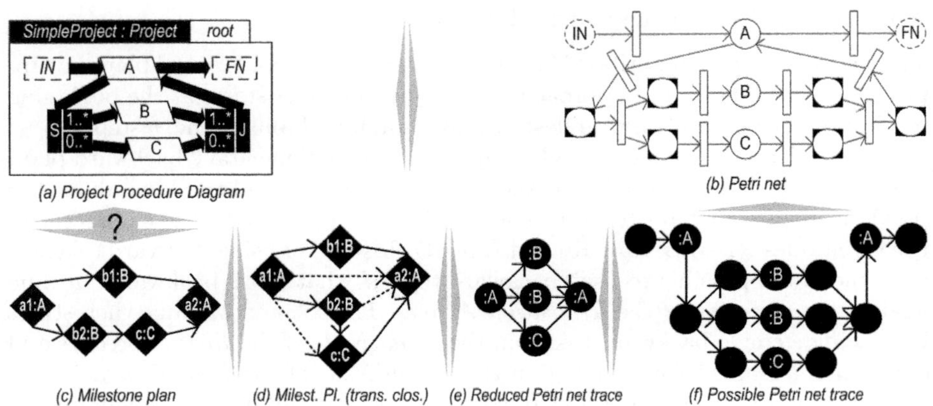

Fig. 4. Sketch of Formalization Approach

(see Fig. 4f) is consistent if and only if every typed milestone is in the image set of the mapping and if the transitive closure of the milestone relationships (see Fig. 4e) is a superset of all relationships induced by the reduced trace. The superset property ensures that the final milestone plan may always be "stricter" than required by the process model.

5 Conclusion and Future Work

In this paper, we have introduced Project Procedure Diagrams as used by the German V-Modell XT. We have demonstrated an operational semantics based on a board game metaphor, thus motivating their practicability for deriving useful milestone plans from graphical process specifications. Furthermore, we have sketched our approach for a rigorous, mathematical semantics.

In the future, we want to build on that foundation and study the integration of other project dimensions, namely, product structures and resources. We feel that the integration of the product model could be particularly valuable as it leads to further constraints on the derived project plans. Without knowledge of the product structure, the plan derivation process may result in milestone plans that try to join parallel subprocesses for unrelated parts of the system. We would also like to encourage others to integrate PPDs with other process metamodels, e.g. SPEM 2.0. Thus, we could collect more data and study the appropriateness of PPDs in other settings outside the public sector.

A further area of research is support for plan refinement, plan evolution and re-planning. It should be possible, for example, to refine an existing, coarse-grained plan during the project. Likewise, a change in a sub area of the plan should be possible without necessitating the re-creation of the whole plan anew.

Finally, we would like to enhance the milestone planning support tool of the V-Modell XT, which is currently restricted to forward planning during the initial plan derivation phase. Extending this tool with support for backward and combined planning strategies (and maybe also with the capability to check the consistency of arbitrary milestone plans with a given set of PPDs) and adding a library of reusable PPDs could ease the job of a project manager considerably.

Acknowledgements

We want to thank Andreas Rausch and Thomas Ternité for stimulating discussions during the definition of PPDs.

References

1. Andersen, E.S.: Warning: activity planning is hazardous to your project's health? International Journal of Project Management 14(2), 89–94 (1996)
2. Friedrich, J., Hammerschall, U., Kuhrmann, M., Sihling, M.: Das V-Modell XT: Für Projektleiter und QS-Verantwortliche kompakt und übersichtlich, 2nd edn. Informatik im Fokus. Springer, Berlin (2009)
3. Deiters, W., Gruhn, V.: Process management in practice: Applying the FUNSOFT Net approach to large-scale processes. Automated Software Engineering 5(1), 7–25 (1998)
4. Graw, G., Gruhn, V., Krumm, H.: Support of cooperating and distributed business processes. In: Proceedings of International Conference on Parallel and Distributed Systems, pp. 22–31 (1996)
5. Kim, J., Desrochers, A.A., Sanderson, A.C.: Task planning and project management using Petri nets. In: Proceedings of the IEEE International Symposium on Assembly and Task Planning, pp. 265–271 (1995)
6. Chen, Y.-L., Hsu, P.-Y., Chang, Y.-B.: A Petri net approach to support resource assignment in project management. IEEE Transactions on Systems, Man and Cybernetics, Part A: Systems and Humans 38(3), 564–574 (2008)
7. Object Management Group (OMG): Software & systems process engineering metamodel specification (SPEM) version 2.0 (2008)
8. International Organization for Standardization (ISO): Software engineering metamodel for development methodologies (SEMDM) (2007)
9. Object Management Group (OMG): Unified modeling language infrastructure (2009)
10. Schattkowsky, T., Forster, A.: On the pitfalls of UML 2 activity modeling. In: MISE 2007: Proceedings of the International Workshop on Modeling in Software Engineering, p. 8. IEEE Computer Society, Los Alamitos (2007)
11. Bergner, K., Friedrich, J.: Modulare Spezifikation von Projektabläufen: Eine formale Fundierung von Syntax und Semantik der Projektdurchführungsstrategien des V-Modell XT 1.3. Technical Report TUM-I0912, Technische Universität München, Institut für Informatik, München (April 2009)
12. Reisig, W.: Petrinetze: Eine Einführung, 2nd edn. Springer, Berlin (1986)

A Framework for the Flexible Instantiation of Large Scale Software Process Tailoring

Peter Killisperger[1,2], Markus Stumptner[1], Georg Peters[3], Georg Grossmann[1], and Thomas Stückl[4]

[1] Advanced Computing Research Centre, University of South Australia
[2] Competence Center Information Systems, University of Applied Sciences - München
[3] Department of Computer Science and Mathematics, University of Applied Sciences - München
[4] Enterprise Processes, Siemens Corporate Technology

Abstract. Due to the variety of concerns affecting software development in large organizations, generic software processes have to be adapted to project specific needs to be effectively applicable in individual projects. We describe the architecture of a tool aiming to provide support for tailoring and instantiation of reference processes. The goal is to minimize the effort for the individualisation of generic software processes to project specific needs. In contrast to existing approaches, our prototype provides flexible support for adaptation decisions made by project managers while adhering to modelling constraints stated by the used modelling language, enterprise policies or business process regulations.

1 Introduction

Traditional process driven software development approaches which are often large, complex and formalized are widely used in industry. Examples are software development within Siemens AG [18] and Motorola [9] with the former having a USD 3 billions annual turnaround in software and 20,000 developers. The tasks which must be conducted during the development are usually defined in so-called *software processes*. They are comparable to reference processes that describe in a generic way which tasks need to be considered in various software development projects across multiple business units within a company. In order to increase their applicability in various projects, they cover a wide range of functionality and are therefore complex and large in size.

The task of adapting a reference process for a project is, apart from size and complexity, further complicated by constraints. Constraints ensure that processes follow certain correctness criteria. We considered two types of constraints in this project, (a) syntax constraints defined by the meta model of the used modelling language and (b) constraints defined by an organization to support the understanding of processes by software developers, e.g., the Siemens Process Framework [18]. Although we investigated only those types of constraints, the presented framework supports constraints on process elements that may originate from other sources, e.g., from legal regulations like the FDA regulations for medial devices [10] or maturity models such as CMMI.

J. Münch, Y. Yang, and W. Schäfer (Eds.): ICSP 2010, LNCS 6195, pp. 100–111, 2010.

The current adaptation process is usually a manual process due to lack of tool support. There are some frameworks available that are discussed in more detail in Section 2 but they provide only limited support for the adaptation of processes and ensuring a correct outcome according to given constraints. They either focus on syntax constraints or small adaptations that are fully automated, a circumstance that is not sufficient for software processes. On the one extreme, a complete manual adaptation of software processes is not desired because it is time consuming and error prone and on the other extreme, a fully automated adaptation is not desired either, because certain adaptation decisions should remain the responsibility of a project manager, e.g., deleting activities in extraordinary circumstances. An approach is therefore required which is balanced between automating certain tasks like constraints checking and providing the opportunity for manual decision making like choosing particular adaptation operators by a project manager.

The contribution of this paper lies in supporting instantiation of software processes on two levels by fulfilling the requirements described above.

First, we provide the idea of using basic instantiation operators which allow instantiation before and during the project. Organizations define the operators they require for instantiation which can be executed step by step or in automated batches. The latter avoids a lengthy instantiation procedure at the start of projects.

Second, we present an algorithm that can automatically identify violations of organisation-specific modelling constraints, resolve them and thus guarantees their adherence. The proposed approach is not restricted to a particular meta-model and scales to large and complex processes.

The paper is structured as follows: Section 2 details related work. A Software Engineering Framework developed for improving the current situation is described in Section 3. Inherent part of the framework is instantiation of software processes including correction of violated modelling restrictions. In Section 4, the approach is evaluated, followed by conclusions.

2 Related Work

The area of project specific composition and adaptation of software processes and methods has attracted significant attention in recent years as in, e.g., Brinkkemper's Method Engineering (ME) proposal [7] as an approach for the creation of situational methods.

However, no existing approach has established itself as a de-facto standard in industry and provides a thorough solution for adapting Siemens processes to project specific needs. For example, ME emphasized bottom-up assembly of project specific methods from fragments but has failed to be widely accepted in industry [9][14]. Contrary to ME, approaches like Little-JIL [8] regard processes as programs, enacted by machines. Here however, we are concerned with flexible method engineering in the large and deal with semi-formal process models offering high level guidance for humans.

An important reason for the lack of acceptance in industry is the variety of meta-models for processes used in practice. For instance, Yoon et al. [20]

developed an approach for adapting processes in the form of Activity-Artefact-Graphs. Since the process is composed of activities and artefacts, only the operations "addition" and "deletion" of activities and artefacts are supported as well as "split" and "merge" of activities. Another example is the V-Modell XT [5], a process model developed for the German public sector. It offers a toolbox of process modules and execution strategies. The approach for developing a project specific software process is to select required process modules and an execution strategy.

In the context of the V-Modell XT, Ternite [19] developed an approach on the basis of software process lines. The software process line concept transfers the idea of software product lines to software processes. Since product creation and processes have a close relationship, a combination of both was already envisioned by Rombach [16]. Process variations can be pre-defined by using feature types. Variability types define the effect of choosing a feature. Ad hoc variability unique to a single project have to be developed from scratch. However, definition of process variations is manual and no tool support for guaranteeing that the resulting process variations are correct and consistent is provided.

Armbrust et al. [2] used the process line approach for defining process variations at the Japanese Space agency. Variant parts of processes depend on project characteristics and are not allowed to depend on each other. The process is adapted by choosing one variant at the start of a project. Although the need for further adaptations during the execution of the process has been identified, no standardization or tool support is provided.

Allerbach et al. [1] developed a similar approach called Provop (Process Variants by Options). Adaptation of processes is limited to the change operations insert, delete, move and modify attributes which are grouped in Options. Options have to be predefined and are used to adapt processes, but they do not guarantee correctness.

Because of the close relationship between Siemens software and business processes, adaptation approaches for the latter are also of interest. Approaches for processes and workflows of higher complexity are often restricted to only a subset of adaptation operations. For instance, Rosemann and van der Aalst [17] developed configurable EPCs (C-EPCs) enabling the customization of reference processes. However, the approach is restricted to processes defined in EPCs and only allows activities to be switched on/off, the replacement of gateways and the definition of dependencies of adaptation decisions.

Contrary to business processes, there are several approaches for guaranteeing automated execution of processes by engines [15,11,6,3]. Processes in this area are defined in a process template (i.e. reference process) and then executed many times with only little adaptations and are executed in short time frames. The focus of these approaches is on ensuring properties like absence of deadlocks, proper process termination and reachability. They solve issues arising due to this nature e.g. assignment of web services to activities or propagation of change made in the process template to currently executed instances. In order to enable this support, complexity of processes is limited.

Contrary to standard workflows, software processes are complex, not fully automatable, applied in only few projects, require substantial adaptation prior to each project they are applied in and projects run months and often years. Constraints on software processes have to accommodate requirements resulting from these characteristics. For ensuring compliance with constraints, flexible and complex correction strategies are required.

In conclusion, none of the existing approaches offer a comprehensive, flexible and tool supported instantiation of software processes required for the diversity of processes and software development encountered in large enterprises.

3 Software Engineering Framework

3.1 Instantiating Software Processes

In order to find out how the current situation can be improved, we conducted interviews with practitioners at Siemens AG which lead to the development of a new Software Engineering Framework [13]. Integral part of the framework is instantiation of processes which comprises (1) tailoring, (2) resource allocation and (3) instantiation of process artefacts.

Since it is unrealistic to completely define a project specific process already at the start of a project [4], processes are instantiated step by step (see Figure 1). Starting with a `reference process`, first `high level instantiation` is conducted, followed by gradual `detailed instantiation`. The result is an `instantiated process`.

`High level instantiation` is a first step towards a project specific software process by adapting the `reference process` on the basis of project characteristics and information that can already be defined at the start of a project and are unlikely to change. Such characteristics can be, e.g., the size of a project (a small project will only use a subset of the process).

`High level instantiation` is followed by `detailed instantiation` in which the process is adapted in detail. `Detailed instantiation` is run frequently during the project for the upcoming process parts.

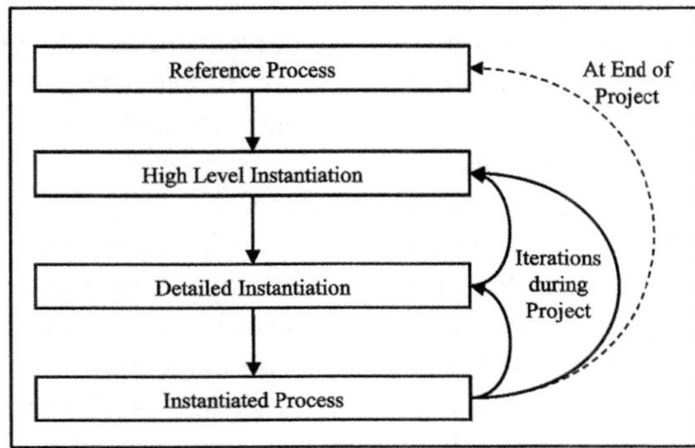

Fig. 1. Instantiation Stages of Software Engineering Framework

The resulting `instantiated process` can be used in projects in different ways including visualization of the process and management of project artefacts.

Although instantiation is split into two distinct stages, both are based on the same principles. Elemental `basic instantiation operators` are used for both stages. By executing them on entities of the process, the process can be instantiated in a predefined way. Examples are: "Deleting an activity", "associating a resource with an activity" or "instantiating a process artefact with a file". Organisations define basic instantiation operators according to their individual needs. From this follows that the definition of operators (i.e. how the process is adapted when executing the operator on its entities) differs depending on the requirements of the organization.

In `high level instantiation`, operators are executed on process elements as batch. That is, execution is predefined, depends on the existence of particular project characteristics (e.g. project type) and is only executed at the beginning of a project. In `detailed instantiation` operators are executed individually. The approach of using the same principles for both instantiation stages fosters reuse and improves flexibility. If for instance a particular adaptation operator is not to be executed on a process entity in `high level instantiation` any more, the execution of the operator on the entity can be easily shifted to detailed instantiation or vice versa.

3.2 Enactment of Instantiation Operators

Execution of operators in high level and detailed instantiation has to result in a process which complies with constraints. Execution of operators is followed by an automated correction stage that reassembles a correct process in case of constraint violations. The approach for checking correctness of processes and their correction is detailed in the following.

In addition to a method `check()` which verifies the adherence, for every constraint a method `correct()` is defined. `correct()` is executed when the constraint is violated and implements the adaptation of the process so that it satisfies the constraint.

However, it cannot be guaranteed that correction of one violation does not cause the violation of a different constraint. Therefore, the procedure of checking constraints and executing `correct()` of violated constraints is continued until there are no remaining violations.

It might be possible to correct a violation not only in one particular way but in a variety of ways. The decision how a violation is corrected influences the further correction procedure (i.e. has an impact on what resulting correct process is generated). The way a violated constraint is corrected also affects what following violations occur and how they can be corrected.

From this follows that as soon as a violation is found, the constraint's `correct()` copies the process for each possible correction and applies the corrections in the individual copies. Each of the resulting processes is checked for violated constraints. As soon as a violation is found, the constraint's `correct()`

copies the process for each possible correction again and applies the corrections in the individual copies.

This procedure is continued until all constraints are satisfied. Processes satisfying all constraints are saved and presented to the user who can decide which variation of the process to adopt after all solutions have been computed. The algorithm for correcting a process is shown in Listing 1.

```
1: controlCorrection(Process original){
2:   Container solutions;
3:   if(original.isValid())
4:     return solutions.add(original);
5:   else{
6:     Stack lifo;
7:     lifo.push(original);
8:     while(lifo.size() != 0){
9:       Process p = lifo.pop();
10:      Constraint vio = p.getViolation();
11:      Container adaptedProcesses = vio.correct();
12:      if(adaptedProcesses != null{
13:        for(Process p2 : adaptedProcesses){
14:          if(p2.isValid())
15:            solutions.add(p2);
16:          else
17:            lifo.push(p2);
18:        }
19:      }
20:    }
21:  }
22:  return solutions;
23:}
```

Listing 1. Correction Algorithm

The algorithm implemented in `controlCorrection()` is executed with process `original` as argument which has been adapted by an operator. After creating a container for correct resulting processes (`solutions`) in line 2, `original` is check for violated constraints (`original.isValid()`) in line 3 and if no constraints are violated `original` is returned since there is no need for further adaptations and `original` can be sent back to the caller as solution (line 4).

If constraints are violated, a stack (`lifo`) for storing the adapted but incorrect process copies is created (line 6) and `original` is pushed in the stack (line 7).

Until there is a process in stack `lifo` (line 8), the next process is taken (line 9) and its violated constraints is retrieved by calling method `p.getViolation()` (line 10). The constraints `correct()` is called returning adapted processes in case the violated constraint can be corrected (line 11). If adapted processes are returned (line 12), each returned process (`p2`) is checked for violated constraints (line 14). If there are no violations, the process is added to `solutions` (line 15). Otherwise the process (p2) is pushed in `lifo` (line 17). Container `solutions` is eventually returned to the caller, if there are no further processes in `lifo` (line 22).

When applying the algorithm as described a mechanism for preventing looping constraints and for avoiding computation of equal resulting correct processes has to be implemented.

Constraints loop when a `correct()` adapts a process leading (not necessarily immediately) to a violation whose `correct()` causes a violation triggering the first `correct()` again.

Duplicates in the resulting process solutions can occur when corrections due to process violations lead to the same adapted process.

A control mechanism for preventing such situations has to find out whether an identical process exists in `lifo` or `solutions` to a newly created and adapted process. This can be expensive since a high number of processes might have to be compared.

However, a loop or equal resulting processes can also be detected when a violation occurs on an entity in the partially corrected process which has already occurred on the same entity in an earlier version of the process during correction (i.e. within `controlCorrection`). However, for it to work, `correct()` must solve a violation entirely (i.e. the constraint is not violated after the execution of this `correct()` any more) otherwise a loop would be detected that does not exist.

The latter approach is less expensive since only violations have to be compared and `correct()` can be defined to satisfy the restriction to correct a violation entirely. For preventing loops and duplicates in solutions we therefore check whether the same violation has already occurred on the same entity during the correction procedure leading to the partially corrected process at hand and if so, the correction is no longer continued.

3.3 Enabling Batch Processing of Operators

For implementing high level instantiation as described in Section 3.1 a number of design decisions have to be made. As described, high level instantiation is batch processing of operators. However, running the correction mechanism in batch processing of high level instantiation as when executing operators individually, can result in (1) increased number of possible correct resulting processes and (2) increased number of necessary corrections.

1. Batch execution of operator will usually result in multiple potential correction outcomes. Consider the example of Figure 2a). Activities A2 and A5 have been deleted as part of a batch, resulting in two control flows with an empty target and two control flows with an empty source 2b). `Correct()` of the violated constraint of control flows with a missing target searches for control flows with a missing source and merges them. `Correct()` of the violated constraint of control flows with a missing source act accordingly, leading to the processes in Figure 2c) and 2d). Syntactically the process in Figure 2c) might be correct, however semantically it is not useful. With sequential execution of two delete operators, each followed by process correction, solution 2c) would not have appeared.

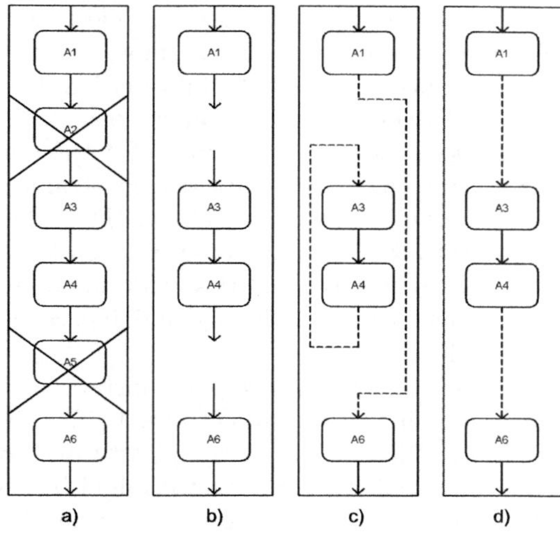

Fig. 2. Increased Number of Process Solutions

From this follows that certain constraints (e.g. on control flows) have to be checked and corrected after execution of each operator of a batch.

2. Batch executions of operators can lead to obviously incorrect interactions between possible correction choices. This is especially inefficient and cumbersome if the correction of the violation requires user input or is expensive regarding computational resources.

   For example, assume an activity A is deleted having an output information flow with a workproduct W (i.e. A creates W), and there is another activity B using W as input information flow, causing a violation because W is input of an activity but never created. If the activities having W as input information flow are deleted in a later stage of the batch, the correction will be unnecessary.

   From this follows that particular constraints (e.g. on information flows) have to be executed after all operators of the batch have been executed.

The issues of an increased number of possible correct resulting processes and increased number of necessary corrections can be resolved by prioritizing constraints at two levels. Constraints with priority (1) are checked and, if necessary, corrected after the execution of each operator, thus limiting the number of possible resulting processes. Constraints with priority (2) are executed after all operators of the batch have been executed thus making the process adaptation more efficient by avoiding unneeded constraint checking and correction.

4 Evaluation

A prototype of a system for instantiating a reference process as described above has been implemented for a particular business unit of Siemens AG. The business unit uses a reference process comprising 23 types of entities including phases (composite activities consisting of a sub process), milestones and control flows. The meta-model of the process comprises furthermore several subtypes of activities, resources, artefacts, splits, joins, events, information-flows and associations of resources with activities (called resource-connections).

135 constraints have been identified on types of entities of the meta-model. `check()` methods which implement verification of constraint adherence and corresponding `correct()` methods have been defined. The reference process used for testing comprises about 3800 instances of entities on two hierarchical levels. The 135 constraints defined on types of entities result in about 15000 constraints on instances of entities which have to be checked and, if necessary, corrected when violated during instantiation.

15 operators defined by experts necessary for instantiation of the reference process of the business unit have been implemented [12]. The operators are as elementary as possible in order to reduce complexity and avoid dependencies with other operators. Because of this simplicity, it might be necessary to execute more than one operator to accomplish a complex adaptation step.

Siemens AG uses ARIS Toolset for modelling their reference processes. In order to avoid limitations due to APIs provided by ARIS, export and import functionality to and from XPDL has been implemented. Process data in XPDL is input for the "Process Tailoring and Instantiation Engine" which implements the instantiation and correction approach described above. It has been implemented as Java application with a graphical user interface for representing processes and for user control. Adapted and corrected processes are graphically presented by the GUI and can be saved in XPDL. Figure 3 gives an overview of the landscape of tool support for process instantiation.

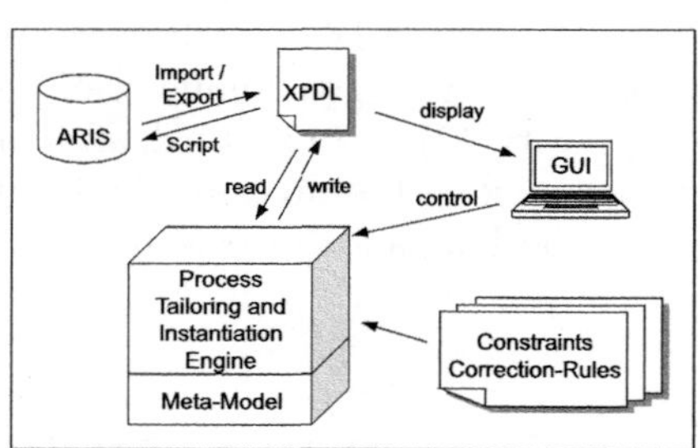

Fig. 3. Landscape of Tools

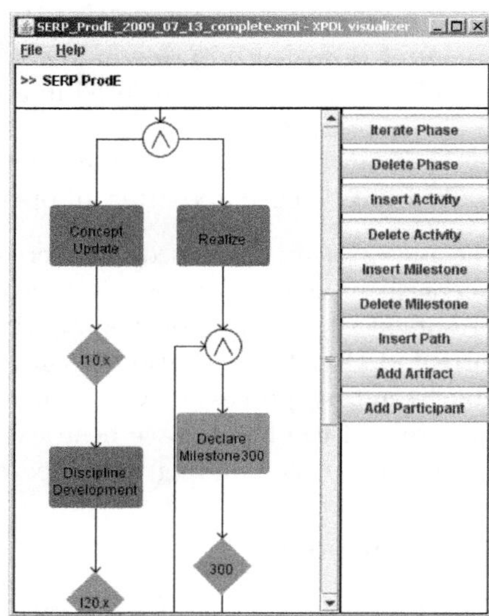

Fig. 4. Graphical User Interface

Figure 4 shows a screenshot of the graphical user interface. Processes can be loaded into the tool which are detailed in the left hand side window. There are views for individual process parts which are linked with each other, e.g. phase view (as shown in the screen shot), activity view, activity detail view (description, associated artefacts and resources), resource view, artefact view etc. Operators are listed in the right hand side window. Only those operators are listed which are applicable in the current view. Necessary user input is entered via message boxes.

Intensive testing proved feasibility of the approach for detailed and high level instantiation.

For the former, the implementation was tested by experts of Siemens AG with representative editing sessions of the business unit's reference process and found viable for interactive use. To give an indication of performance, the unoptimized prototype took less than three seconds in most scenarios to produce the corrected process(es).

The approach's suitability for the latter (i.e. batch processing in high level instantiation) was tested by adapting the given reference process which supports the development of systems (with software, hardware and mechanical components) to a pure software development project. Experts of the business unit defined changes on the process necessary to fit the requirements of a pure software development project. In detail, 108 activities and 41 workproducts had to be deleted. Each deletion required the execution of the corresponding operator. By running the operators additional entities became obsolete which were automatically removed by the corresponding `correct()` methods. Running all operators and subsequently correcting the incorrect resulting process took 3 minutes 41 seconds on a standard PC. Details about changes conducted in the process are shown in Table 1. The left column shows numbers of entities of the given reference process supporting system development. The right column details the number of entities in the process after adaptation for a pure software project.

The prototype has not only been used for testing purposes but has been applied in real world projects.

Table 1. Changes on reference process for software project

Type of Entity	Ref. Process	SW Process
Phase	10	10
Activity	233	125
Artefact	203	111
Resource	72	71
Milestone	11	11
Split	38	27
Join	48	31
Event	24	24
ControlFlow	460	274
InformationFlow	1134	354
ResourceConnection	1557	921
Total	3790	1959

It was used for improving the reference process of the business unit. There had been efforts to make the reference process compliant with constraints but this had not been successful due to the complexity of the task. For example, after manually detecting and correcting of a violation, verification has to be started all over again, since the correction of the violation might have caused other violations. Siemens AG estimates that several man-months of effort were saved due to the application of the approach.

The tool has also been used for creating a variant of the reference process for a pure software system. Manual creation of this variant had not been carried out, due to the effort involved resulting from dependencies of process elements and the necessity of compliance with constraints.

5 Conclusion

We have described a current research effort to improve software process related activities at Siemens AG. Part of these efforts is the development of a system that supports project managers in instantiation of reference processes subject to an explicit constraint representation. The system aims not only to execute decisions but to restore correctness of the resulting process. Since the implementation of such a system is organization-specific and depends on the permitted constructs in the process, a flexible architecture has been developed supporting organization-specific definition of constraints, their correction when violated and instantiation of processes as required by the applying organization. Testing proved feasibility of the approach and thus showed that the approach enables project specific adaptations of Siemens software processes which has not been feasible due to missing tool support until now. Future work includes further testing in real world projects and integration of the approach in a process management tool.

Acknowledgements

This work was partially supported by a DAAD postgraduate scholarship.

References

1. Allerbach, A., Bauer, T., Reichert, M.: Managing Process Variants in the Process Life Cycle. In: Proceedings of the Tenth International Conference on Enterprise Information Systems, vol. ISAS-2, pp. 154–161 (2008)
2. Armbrust, O., Katahira, M., Miyamoto, Y., Münch, J., Nakao, H., Ocampo, A.: Scoping Software Process Models - Initial Concepts and Experience from Defining Space Standards. In: Wang, Q., Pfahl, D., Raffo, D.M. (eds.) ICSP 2008. LNCS, vol. 5007, pp. 160–172. Springer, Heidelberg (2008)
3. Baresi, L., Guinea, S., Pasquale, L.: Self-healing BPEL processes with Dynamo and the JBoss rule engine. In: ESSPE, pp. 11–20 (2007)
4. Becker, U., Hamann, D., Verlage, M.: Descriptive Modeling of Software Processes. In: Proceedings of the Third Conference on Software Process Improvement, SPI 1997 (1997)

5. BMI. The new V-Modell XT - Development Standard for IT Systems of the Federal Republic of Germany (2004), http://www.v-modell-xt.de (accessed 01.12.2008)
6. Boukhebouze, M., Amghar, Y., Benharkat, A.-N., Maamar, Z.: Towards Self-healing Execution of Business Processes Based on Rules. In: ICEIS, pp. 501–512 (2009)
7. Brinkkemper, S.: Method engineering: engineering of information systems development methods and tools. Information & Software Technology 38(4), 275–280 (1996)
8. Cass, A.G., Staudt Lerner, B., McCall, E.K., Osterweil, L.J., Sutton Jr., S.M., Wise, A.: Little-JIL/Juliette: A Process Definition Language and Interpreter. In: International Conference on Software Engineering, vol. 0, p. 754 (2000)
9. Fitzgerald, B., Russo, N., O'Kane, T.: Software development method tailoring at Motorola. Communications of the ACM 46(4), 65–70 (2003)
10. U.S. Food and Drug Administration. Code of Federal Regulations Title 21, Ch. 1, Part 820: Medical Devices Quality System Regulation (2009), http://www.accessdata.fda.gov/scripts/cdrh/cfdocs/cfcfr/CFRSearch.cfm?CFRPart=820&showFR=1 (accessed 11.11.2009)
11. Greiner, U., Müller, R., Rahm, E., Ramsch, J., Heller, B., Löffler, M.: AdaptFlow: Protocol Based Medical Treatment using Adaptive Workflows. Journal of Methods of Information in Medicine (2004)
12. Killisperger, P., Peters, G., Stumptner, M., Stückl, T.: Instantiation of Software Processes: An Industry Approach. In: Information Systems Development - Towards a Service Provision Society, pp. 589–597. Springer, Heidelberg (2009)
13. Killisperger, P., Stumptner, M., Peters, G., Stückl, T.: Challenges in Software Design in Large Corporations - A Case Study at Siemens AG. In: ICEIS (3-2), pp. 123–128 (2008)
14. Niknafs, A., Ramsin, R.: Computer-Aided Method Engineering: An Analysis of Existing Environments. In: Bellahsène, Z., Léonard, M. (eds.) CAiSE 2008. LNCS, vol. 5074, pp. 525–540. Springer, Heidelberg (2008)
15. Reichert, M., Dadam, P.: Enabling Adaptive Process-aware Information Systems with ADEPT2. In: Handbook of Research on Business Process Modeling. Information Science Reference, pp. 173–203. Hershey (2009)
16. Rombach, H.D.: Integrated Software Process and Product Lines. In: ISPW, pp. 83–90 (2005)
17. Rosemann, M., Van der Aalst, W.: A Configurable Reference Modelling Language. Information Systems 32(1), 1–23 (2007)
18. Schmelzer, H.J., Sesselmann, W.: Geschäftsprozessmanagement in der Praxis: Produktivität steigern - Wert erhöhen - Kunden zufrieden stellen, 4th edn. Hanser Verlag (2004)
19. Ternité, T.: Process Lines: A product Line Approach Designed for Process Model Development. In: Proceedings of the 35th EUROMICRO Conference on Software Engineering and Advanced Applications, SPPI Track (2009)
20. Yoon, I.-C., Min, S.-Y., Bae, D.-H.: Tailoring and Verifying Software Process. In: APSEC, pp. 202–209 (2001)

A Methodological Framework and Software Infrastructure for the Construction of Software Production Methods*

Mario Cervera, Manoli Albert, Victoria Torres, and Vicente Pelechano

Centro de Investigación ProS,
46022 Valencia, Spain
{mcervera,malbert,vtorres,pele}@pros.upv.es
http://www.pros.upv.es

Abstract. The theory of Method Engineering becomes increasingly solid, but very few engineering tools have been developed to support the application of its research results. To overcome this limitation, this paper presents a methodological framework based on Model Driven Engineering techniques. The framework provides a method supported by a software platform for the construction of software production methods. This framework covers from the specification of the software production method to the generation of the CASE tool that supports it. This generation process has been semi-automated through model transformations. The CASE tool and the software platform are based on the Eclipse-based MOSKitt tool. The plugin-based architecture and the integrated modelling tools included in the MOSKitt tool turn it into a suitable software platform to support our proposal. To validate the proposal we have applied the framework to a case study.

Keywords: Method Engineering, Model Driven Engineering, CAME Tool, Eclipse Platform.

1 Introduction

Method Engineering (ME) is defined as *the engineering discipline to design, construct and adapt methods, techniques and tools for the development of information systems* [1]. A lot of research work has been developed in this area during the last two decades, especially in the adaptation of Software Production Methods (here after SPM) to a specific situation, area that is known as Situational Method Engineering (SME). Most of the approaches developed in these two areas propose the construction of SPMs by assembling reusable fragments (parts that compose a method). Regarding the fragments assembly we find works focused on the description of these fragments (as it is the case of the MEL language proposed by Brinkkemper in [1]) and on the study of techniques for selecting ([3], [7]) and assembling ([2], [14], [15]) efficiently the fragments stored in a repository. Nevertheless, these approaches are difficult to

* This work has been developed with the support of MEC under the project SESAMO TIN2007-62894 and cofinanced by FEDER.

J. Münch, Y. Yang, and W. Schäfer (Eds.): ICSP 2010, LNCS 6195, pp. 112–125, 2010.

put into practice, mainly because they are neither supported by software tools nor complete solutions for the design and implementation of SPMs (generation of CASE tool support for the designed SPM). This software support is usually provided in the shape of CAME environments (CAME stands for Computer-Aided Method Engineering and refers to the tools supporting ME approaches) which combine theoretical proposals with tool support for the construction of SPMs. However, to our knowledge, the existing environments constitute incomplete prototypes that only cover some parts of the ME process. This fact hinders the expected industrial adoption and success considering the benefits that this type of tools would provide to industry.

In this paper, we provide a methodological framework that allows designing and implementing SPMs. This is possible since the framework includes a set of engineering tools that assist during the development of the SPM. To build this framework we apply the main ideas of the most relevant approaches developed in ME (SPM construction through fragment assembly, usage of a reusable fragments repository, process enactment, etc.). The proposed framework has been designed following the Model Driven Engineering (MDE) principles. These principles advocate for the intensive use of models and model transformations to perform system development. So, the SPM design is done by specifying the model of the SPM which describes the process of the SPM. The key concepts of this model are *tasks* (work done during the process) and *products* (input and/or output of tasks). The construction of this model has been defined in two steps. During the first step, the method engineer creates a generic SPM model that does not include details such as how tasks have to be performed. Then, in the second step, the method engineer instantiates the generic model by providing information about the languages, notations or techniques used in each task or product. This approach allows the method engineer to make different configurations of the same generic description of the SPM according to special features of the different projects or development teams. Once the SPM model is completed, model transformations are used to automate the generation of the CASE tool supporting the SPM. The generated CASE tool includes: (1) all the software components that provide support to the tasks and products of the SPM and (2) the software component that provides support to the process of the SPM. The last component allows the software engineer to keep the state of a SPM instance and to guide him/her during its execution. These two aspects of the CASE tool correspond to the two parts in which a SPM is divided (the *product* part and the *process* part).

The process followed to build the proposed framework has applied a bottom-up strategy. It implies that the process begins by identifying the characteristics of the CASE tools that our framework should obtain. In order to determine these characteristics we have developed a CASE tool that supports a specific SPM. Once these characteristics have been identified, they have been used to determine the concepts required to specify SPM and further on to define the framework. The CASE tool has been built using the MOSKitt tool [12], an Eclipse-based tool which includes (1) a plugin-based architecture and (2) a set of integrated modeling tools (e.g. EMF [5]). The characteristics of the MOSKitt tool turn it into a suitable software platform to support our proposal, i.e. to build on it the CAME and CASE tools.

The main contribution of this work is to provide a methodological framework to help and assist method engineers not only in the definition of SPM but also in deriving CASE tools to support them. Among the characteristics of the framework we highlight

(1) the intensive use of standards, (2) its integrated design being all the process carried out with the same technology (the MOSKitt tool), (3) the automation degree achieved thanks to the application of MDE techniques, (4) the reusability degree of the SPM models (specifying generic SPM that can be configured to suit it to a specific context of use), and (5) the generation of CASE tools that support process enactment.

The remainder of the paper is structured as follows. Section 2 briefly presents the state of the art of the ME and SME making emphasis in the limitations found in the existing proposals. Then, section 3 introduces an overview of our proposal. Section 4 presents in detail the methodological framework designed to cover the limitations found in ME/SME areas. Section 5 presents a case study where we apply the proposed methodological framework. Finally, section 6 provides some conclusions and outlines further work.

2 State of the Art

Kumar and Welke developed the first research work in the area of the ME during the early nineties [10]. Since then, many authors have contributed to this area, in particular to the most theoretical part of the engineering. Among these contributions we find (1) new concepts and terms that were also applied to the SME [1], [9], (2) different techniques to specify methods, for instance by assembling existing fragments [11], [14], [15] or (3) different techniques to specify methods for specific projects [8]. All these works constitute a good proof of the amount of theoretical work developed in this area. However, the existing proposals have not been successfully exploited in industry, being relegated just to educational environments. The main cause of this reality is the unbalanced effort made between the research devoted just to the specification of SPM and the research devoted to the construction of software tools for the support of SPM (this is, for the construction of CASE tools). Surveys such as the one presented in [13] put in evidence this reality, and demonstrate that most of the support is provided as prototype tools that just cover part of the corresponding SPMs.

Fig. 1 presents the components of a CAME environment[1]. Checking the literature, we noticed that none of the existing proposals (1) is accompanied with a CAME environment that provide these components (2) or provides an automated process to generate the CASE tool and the Process Support Environment. This can be due to the fact that all these proposals have been designed following a top-down approach, where the development process begins defining the concepts for specifying SPM and then the generation of tool support is tackled. However, this is a very difficult task, and actually none of the proposals has been successfully developed. Therefore, to improve this situation we have proceeded the other way round, this is, following a bottom-up strategy. We have developed a CASE tool for a specific case study SPM and have identified the characteristics of this tool. These characteristics have been abstracted to determine the concepts required to specify a SPM and further on to build the framework. The CASE tool has been developed using the Eclipse-based tool MOSKitt which has demonstrated us the feasibility of the Eclipse platform, and the plugin architecture in which it is based on, for the support of our ME proposal.

---

[1] In this figure, the CAME environment has been divided in two parts, the CAME part, which provides facilities for ME, and the CASE part, which offers means for the generation of CASE tools and process support environment.

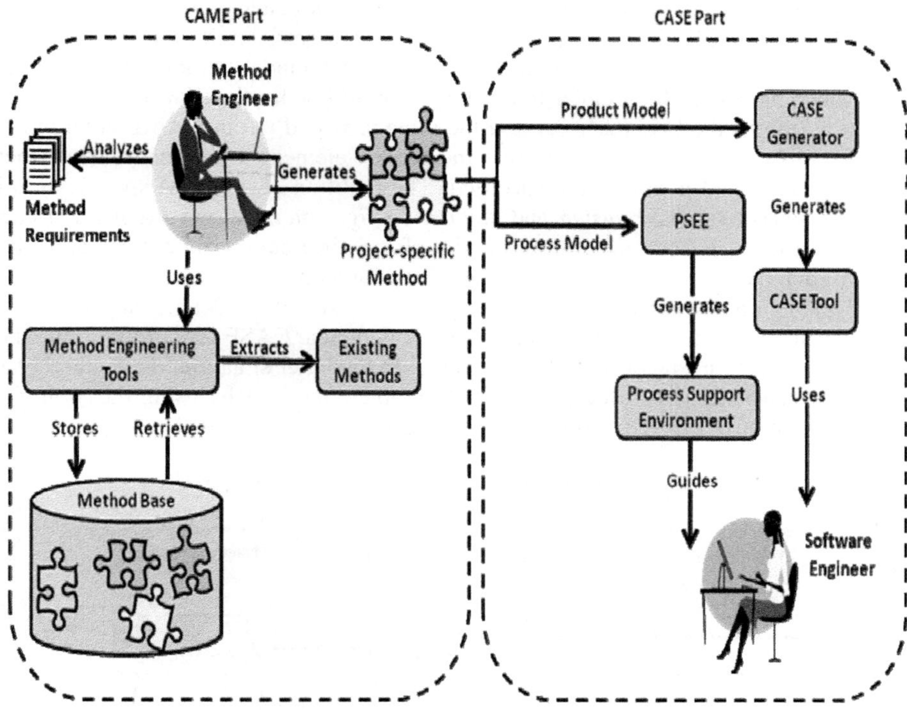

Fig. 1. General architecture of CAME environments from [13]

Trying to solve the limitations found in ME context, this work proposes a methodological framework that, applying the techniques developed in the MDE area, helps and assists the method engineer in both, the specification of SPM and the construction of CASE tools for the support of such methods.

3 Overview of the proposal

The developed framework provides a methodology together with a software infrastructure (CAME environment) aimed at supporting the design and implementation of SPMs. The methodological framework has been organized in three parts, which are *method design*, *method configuration* and *method implementation* (see Fig. 2). These parts constitute the phases that have to be sequentially performed to build a SPM:

- *Method design*: The method engineer builds the *Method Model* by identifying all the elements (tasks, products, etc.) involved in the process of the SPM. These elements can be defined from scratch or selected from a *method base* repository, which contains reusable elements that were specified in other SPM. This first version of the model constitutes a *generic description* where no specific languages or notations are specified for the elements of the model.

- *Method configuration*: The method engineer associates the elements of the *Method Model* built in the previous phase with assets stored in an *asset base* repository. This repository contains models, metamodels, transformations, etc., which have been built either in other SPM or ad-hoc for the SPM under construction (the method engineer can use the tools provided in our CAME environment for this purpose). These assets turn the generic elements into specific ones where languages and notations are specified. The partition of the SPM specification in two phases (*method design* and *method configuration*) allows the method engineer to take generic descriptions and perform different configurations according to each particular target project or development team.
- *Method implementation*: During this phase a set of model transformations is executed to automatically obtain either the complete CASE tool or part of it when the generation cannot be fully automated. In the latter situation, the method engineer can take part in the process and complete the tool by using the tools provided in our CAME environment for this purpose.

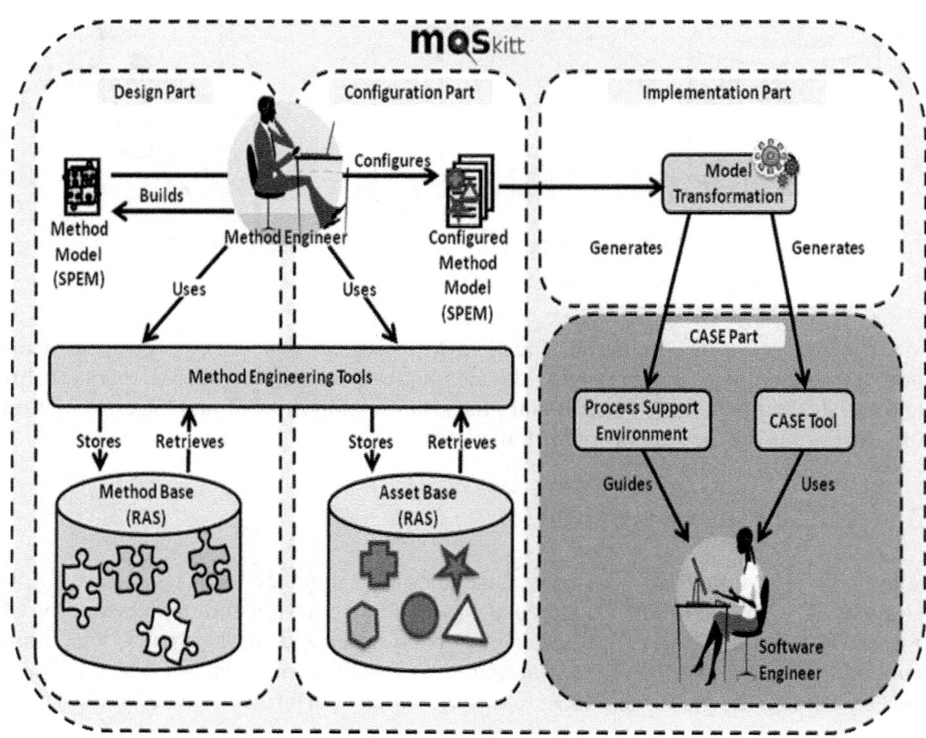

Fig. 2. Methodological Framework

To perform these three phases, we use as much as possible the available standards. To specify SPM we use SPEM 2.0 [17], which is the standard developed by the OMG to define software process methods, and to define both repositories we use RAS [16], the

OMG specification that provides a standard way to assembly, organize, store and document reusable software assets.

We provide a software infrastructure, which is a set of method engineering tools, to support the three phases of the framework. This infrastructure assists the method engineer during the method design and method configuration phases, and automates a large part of the method implementation phase. The tools provided in the software infrastructure are editors, repositories and guides, which are detailed in the next section.

4 A Methodological Framework for the Construction of Software Production Methods

This section presents in detail the three phases that compose the methodological framework. Each phase is described first by introducing its goal and the procedure to achieve it and then by introducing the software infrastructure supporting each phase.

4.1 Method Design Phase

This phase corresponds to the *design part* of Fig. 2. During this phase, the method engineer builds the *method model*, which can either be built from scratch or by reusing method fragments from the *method base* repository. This model describes the process of the SPM by using concepts such as:

- **Task:** It represents an activity performed during the execution of a SPM instance (e.g. *business process analysis, web specification,* etc.).
- **Product:** It represents an artefact that is either consumed or generated in a task (e.g. *business process model, structural model,* etc.).
- **Role:** It represents an agent that participates in a SPM performing different tasks. This can refer to a human being agent (e.g. *analyst, developer,* etc.) or to an automated system.
- **Flow Connector:** It represents the order in which two associated tasks (each one in a different end) are executed.
- **Gateways:** It represents points within the SPM where the flow is diverged or converged depending on the gateway type.
- **Guide:** It is a document that provides some assistance to perform a task or to manipulate a specific product.

All these concepts specify *who* (Role), *when* (Flow Connector and Gateways) and *how* (Task, Product and Guide) the process of the SPM is performed. In this work, to specify the *method model* according to these concepts we have used SPEM 2.0, the standard developed by the OMG for the definition of SPM.

As a result of this phase we obtain the *method model* which is a SPM description that does not include specific techniques or languages/notations associated to its elements (e.g. we can specify the product *business process model* which does not refer to any technique or notation). These details will be provided in the next phase (*method configuration*). The main benefits of this separation are that: (1) we keep generic definitions of SPM (which means that we can take this generic definition and perform different method configurations according to each particular target project or team) and (2) it stresses the importance of reusability.

4.1.1 Software Infrastructure

We provide support to the Method Design phase by means of the following tools:

- *An editor to build the method model*: We use the EPF Composer editor (EPFC), a SPEM 2.0 editor provided in the EPF project [6], which has been integrated in MOSKitt. By using this editor we can build SPM models according to the SPEM metamodel. These models describe the process of the SPM, which can be described associating UML Activity Diagrams to the own model, and the products involved in the process.
- *A method base repository*: Method fragments are stored in a *method base* repository following the RAS standard (which implies that the fragments have to be packaged using this specification). To reuse the fragments of this repository in the *method model,* it is necessary to extend the EPFC editor. This extension allows the user to retrieve fragments from the repository during the specification of the *method model.* To retrieve the fragments in an efficient way, we make use of some of the ideas proposed in [15]. According to these ideas, our method fragments are characterized by (1) a *descriptor,* which provides information about origin, objective and type of the fragment and, (2) an *interface* which is a couple <situation, intention> that characterises the situation that is the input of the fragment and the intention (goal) that the fragment achieves.
- *A guide to build the method model*: A wizard is provided to guide the method engineer through the performance of the *method design* phase.

4.2 Method Configuration Phase

Once the *method design* phase has been finished, the method engineer should add to the *method model* some information related to its execution (*configuration part* of Fig. 2). This is necessary since no information regarding the technique or language/notation was given during the previous phase. Therefore, some of the products and tasks included in the *method model* have to be associated with assets that support them. These assets are contained in the *asset base repository,* which stores metamodels, transformations, editors, etc. With this association, the method engineer instantiates the generic model into a specific one. For example, a *business process model* product identified during the *method design* phase refers to a generic model, which could be built in any language or notation. Later on, during the *method configuration* phase, this product is associated to the BPMN metamodel (which is an asset stored in the *asset base* repository). Thus the method engineer instantiates the generic *business process model* into a concrete notation, which is in this case the BPMN notation.

It is possible that the asset required by the method engineer is not stored in the *asset base repository*. In this case, the flexibility of the plugin-based architecture in which Eclipse relies on allows the method engineer to build this asset. Then, this asset is stored in the repository so that the method engineer can use it in the configuration of the *method model.*

4.2.1 Software Infrastructure

This phase is supported by the following tools:

- *An asset base repository*: To build the assets contained in this repository, we use again the ideas proposed in [15]. To link these assets with the elements of the *method model* (tasks and products), we have extended the SPEM class *ReusableAsset* so its instances can reference the assets from the repository.
- *A guide to configure the method model*: A wizard is provided to guide the method engineer through the performance of the *method model* configuration.

4.3 Method Implementation Phase

The *method implementation* phase corresponds to the *implementation part* of Fig. 2. During this phase the *configured method model* is used to systematically generate the CASE tool that supports the method. This support is twofold:

- A *CASE tool* that contains all the necessary components to support the product part of the SPM.
- A *process support environment* that provides support to the process of the SPM. This support turn the *CASE tool* into a real project environment where users can launch new SPM instances or execute existing ones. The environment allows launching guides that assist during the execution of a specific task, checking the dependences between products or tasks, etc.

4.3.1 Software Infrastructure

This phase is supported by the following tool:

- A *model-to-text (M2T) transformation*: a M2T transformation integrated in MOSKitt. This transformation takes as input the *configured method model* built in the previous phases and obtains an Eclipse *product configuration file*. This file contains all the necessary information to build a MOSKitt reconfiguration containing all the support for the SPM (*the CASE tool* and *process support environment*). The transformation has been implemented using the XPand language [19].

Fig. 3 depicts the steps that the transformation automatically performs to obtain from the *configured method model* its corresponding CASE tool support. The details of the steps are the following:

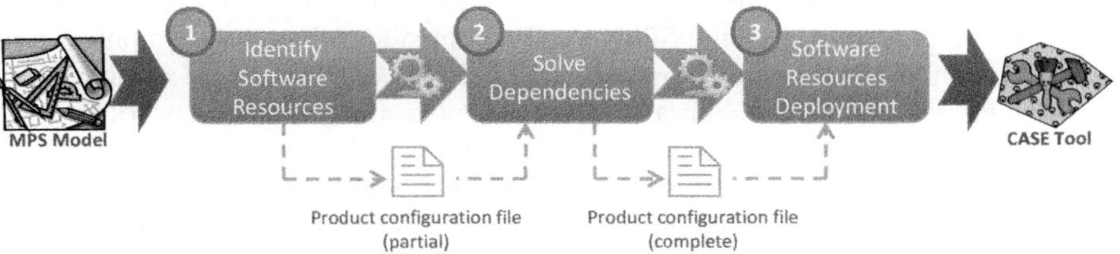

Fig. 3. Case Tool Generation Process

Identify Software Resources: Identifying the software resources that have to be deployed upon the MOSKitt platform to support the products and tasks involved in the SPM. This set of resources is included in a *product configuration file*, which is the result of this step.

Solve Dependencies: Solving the potential conflicts that can arise due to software dependencies. Therefore, all the software resources required by the resources identified in the previous step are also included in the product configuration file.

Software Resources Deployment: Generating the CASE tool from the product configuration file by using the Eclipse Plugin Development Environment (PDE).This tool is a MOSKitt reconfiguration that just includes the plugins strictly necessary to provide support to the SPM definition.

The use of MDE techniques and technologies enables the automation of part of the Method Implementation phase. As SPMs are described in terms of models according to a particular metamodel (in our case SPEM 2.0), model-to-text transformations can be applied to produce the *configuration file* that allows us to reconfigure MOSKitt to support a specific SPM.

5 The Methodological Framework in Practice

In this section the methodological framework is applied to a SPM that is introduced in [18], which proposes the steps for the construction of web applications to support a set of business processes. We present the *method model* specification and its implementation using the CAME environment supporting our methodological framework.

5.1 Method Model specification

The specification of the SPM of the case study is done by building the *method model*. In a first step the *method model* is specified without detailing techniques, languages or notations (*method design* phase). So, we define the tasks (*Business process analysis, system specification,* etc.), products (*Business process model, services model*, etc.) and roles (*Analyst, Developer,* etc.), together with the workflow (process part) of the SPM. To do so, we use the tools provided in our approach to build the *method model* (the EPFC editor, the *method base* repository and the guide to perform the method design).

The *method model* specification of the case study is shown in Fig. 4[2] (which contains a screenshot of the EPFC editor integrated in MOSKitt). In this figure the "Library" view is displayed on the left. This view contains all the elements of the SPM in a tree viewer. Specifically, this view shows all the different roles, tasks and the I/O resources consumed and produced by the different tasks. These I/O resources correspond to the product part of the SPM. On the right side of Fig. 4 the graphical representation of the SPM is shown as an UML activity diagram, where roles appear as *Activity Partition* elements and tasks are distributed along the SPM workflow. This workflow corresponds to the process part of the SPM. Furthermore, aside from what is shown in the figure, the EPFC editor provides other kind of views and editors (graphical and form-based) for the creation and deletion of SPM elements and the edition of its properties.

---

[2] Available also at www.dsic.upv.es/~vtorres/icsp2010

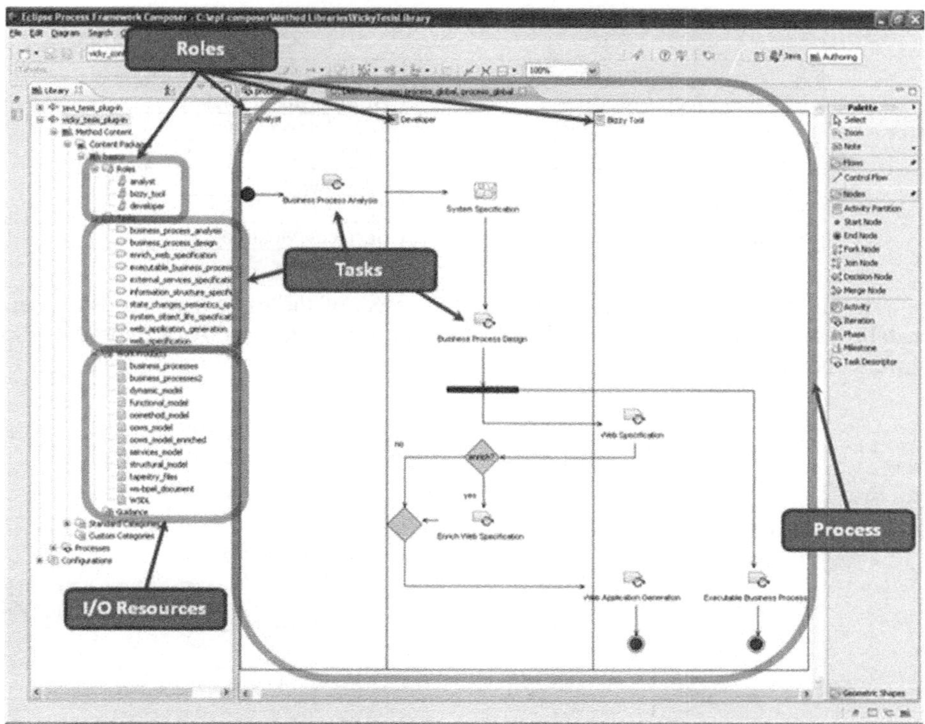

Fig. 4. Case study specification with EPF Composer

Once the *method model* has been built (i.e., the *method design* phase is finished), we configure it (*method configuration* phase). To do so, we define the links between the elements of the model (tasks and products) and the assets that support them, which are stored in the *asset base repository*. Table 1 and Table 2 show the links between the tasks and products specified in the *method model* of the case study and the assets of the *asset base repository*. The symbol * points out that the asset was initially available in the repository, whereas the symbol ** points out that the asset is defined by the method engineer.

Table 1. Tasks and Assets of the SPM

Task	Asset
Business Process Analysis	Guide with the steps of the task *
System Specification	Guide with the steps of the task *
Business Process Design	Guide with the steps of the task **
Web specification	M2M Transformation **
Enrich Web Specification	Guide with the steps of the task **
Web Application Generation	M2T Transformation **
Executable Business Process	M2M Transformation **

Table 2. Products and Assets of the SPM

Product	Asset
Business Process Model	BPMN Metamodel *
Conceptual Model	OO-Method Metamodel *
Navigational and Presentation Models	OOWS Metamodel *
Tapestry Code	Text Editor *
WS-BPEL Document	Text Editor *
Services Model	Services Metamodel **

The links between SPM elements and the assets of the *asset base* repository are established through instances of the SPEM class *ReusableAsset.* An example of this link is shown in Fig. 5.

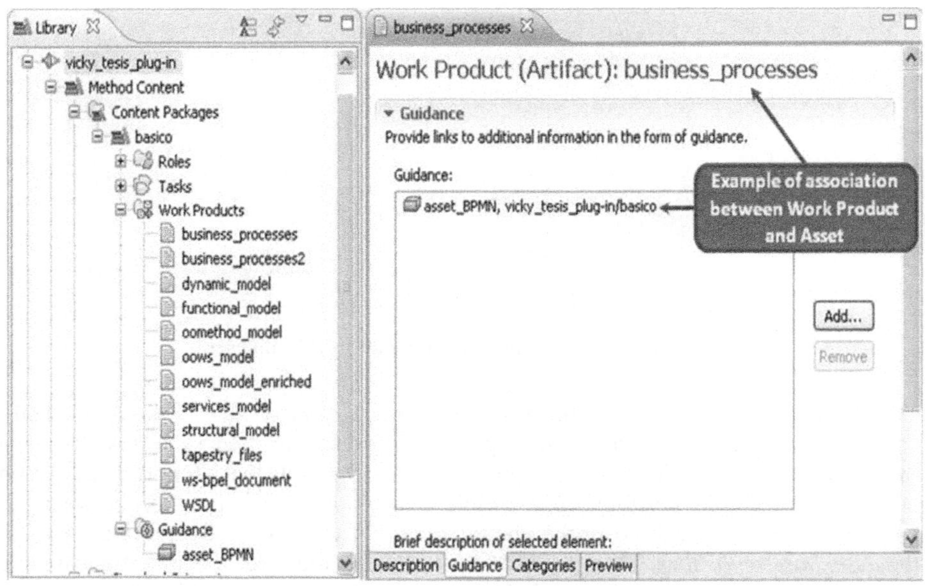

Fig. 5. Association between a product and an asset

5.2 Generated Case Tool support

An Eclipse application (Rich Client Application) is obtained from the *method model* specification. This application represents the CASE tool support (*the CASE tool* and *process support environment*) for the SPM. The CASE tool is a MOSKitt reconfiguration that includes all the plugins supporting the product and process parts of the SPM. A screenshot of this tool is shown in Fig. 6. Several views can be observed in the figure. These views are the following:

- **Product Explorer:** shows in a tree viewer the products consumed/produced/ modified by the ongoing tasks and the tasks that have already been executed.

This view can be filtered by role so the user only see the products he/she is responsible for. By selecting the product element, the associated software resource is opened to edit the product.

- **Process:** shows in a tree viewer the different tasks that can be executed in the current moment. This view can be filtered in a similar way as the Product Explorer so the user only see the tasks he/she is responsible for. When a task is selected in this view:
  - o If this task generates a product, then this product is created and added to the "Product explorer".
  - o If this task consumes a product and this has not been generatead previously in the process, the user has to specify its file system location. On the contrary, if the product has already been created in the process, the user has to indicate which product from the available ones (those appearing in the Product Explorer view) is consumed in the task.

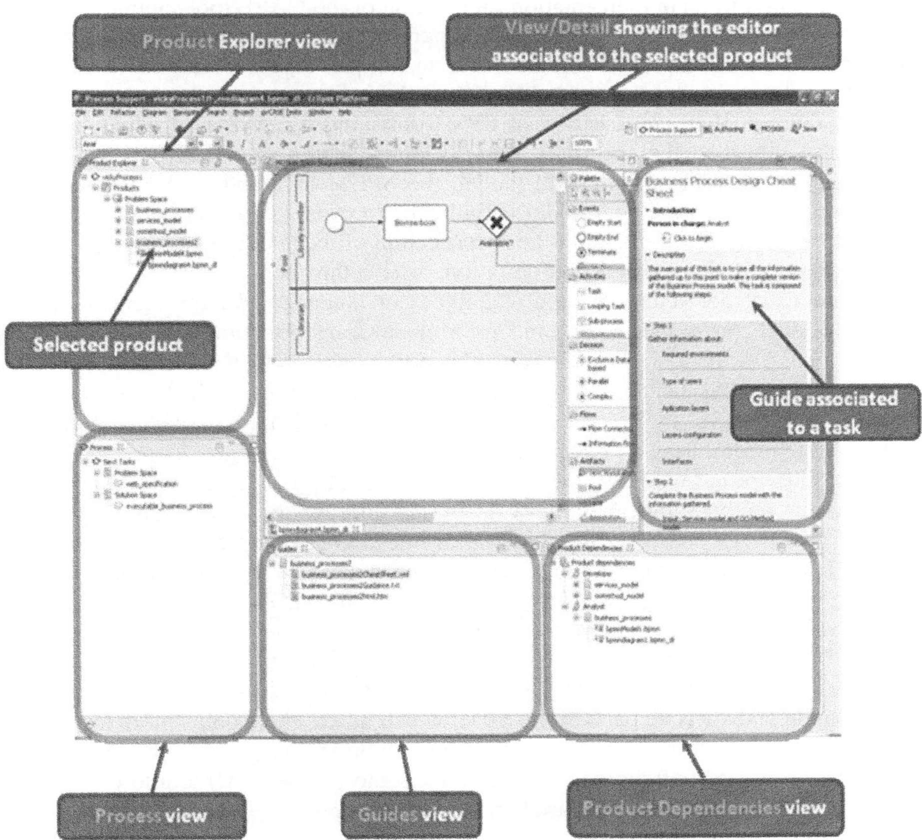

Fig. 6. Final CASE tool

- **Guides:** shows the list of the guides associated to the product or task selected in the corresponding view. The main goal of these guides is to assist the user during the manipulation of the product or the execution of the associated task. There may be more than one guide associated to a product/task as shown in Fig. 6 and even different types of guides (i.e. Eclipse cheat sheets, text files, hyper-text files, etc.). When a guide is selected, it is opened with the corresponding editor.
- **Product Dependencies:** shows the list of dependencies of the product or task selected in the corresponding view. These dependencies are grouped by role allowing the user to know the existing dependencies between the products manipulated by him and also by other roles.

6 Conclusions and Further Work

In this paper a methodological framework for the construction of SPM covering from its specification to its implementation (generation of the CASE tool support) has been presented. The framework includes tool support that has been built on the MOSKitt platform. The combination of ME and MDE techniques together with the flexibility of the plugin-based architecture of MOSKitt allows us to obtain a framework that enables the complete construction of SPM (obtaining a CASE tool which provides complete support to the specified SPM). The specification of SPM focuses on its process part. To build the method model, the SPEM [17] and RAS [16] standards have been used. The method model is built in two phases, the method design where the method is described avoiding the specification of techniques or languages used in the process, and the method configuration, where the method design is completed with assets that determine specific techniques or languages for the elements of the method model. From the method model, a model transformation semi-automatically obtains the CASE tool that supports the SPM. This CASE tool is a MOSKitt reconfiguration that includes the necessary plugins to support the SPM. An important issue of this CASE tool is the process support included in it, which guides the software engineer during a project execution.

Regarding further work, we are working on the improvement of the set of tools that supports the methodological framework. In addition, we are concerning with one of the big challenges of ME [20], which takes into account the variability of the SPM both at modeling level and runtime. Variability appears as a relevant challenge in ME, since it is very common that context changes entailing SPM adaptation during the progress of a project. So, we are working on providing mechanisms to support this variability. At modeling level we propose the use of techniques based on fragment substitution to specify this variability. These techniques allow us to keep separately the common and variable parts of the SPM, which makes the models more legible and easier to specify and maintain. At implementation level, we propose the introduction in MOSKitt of a reconfiguration engine (for instance, MoRE [4]) to allow the CASE tool reconfiguration at runtime based on context changes.

References

[1] Brinkkemper, S.: Method Engineering: Engineering of Information Systems Development Methods and Tools. Information and Software Technology 38, 275–280 (1996)

[2] Brinkkemper, S., Saeki, M., Harmsen, F.: Meta-Modelling Based Assembly Techniques for Situational Method Engineering. Inf. Syst. 24, 209–228 (1999)

[3] Brinkkemper, S., Saeki, M., Harmsen, F.: A Method Engineering Language for the Description of Systems Development Methods. In: Dittrich, K.R., Geppert, A., Norrie, M.C. (eds.) CAiSE 2001. LNCS, vol. 2068, pp. 473–476. Springer, Heidelberg (2001)

[4] Cetina, C., Giner, P., Fons, J., Pelechano, V.: Autonomic Computing through Reuse of Variability Models at Runtime: The Case of Smart Homes, vol. 42, pp. 37–43. IEEE Computer Society Press, Los Alamitos (2009)

[5] Eclipse Modeling Framework Project, http://www.eclipse.org/modeling/emf/

[6] Eclipse Process Framework Project (EPF), http://www.eclipse.org/epf/

[7] Harmsen, F., Brinkkemper, S.: Design and Implementation of a Method Base Management System for a Situational CASE Environment. In: Asia-Pacific Software Engineering Conference, p. 430. IEEE Computer Society, Los Alamitos (1995)

[8] Henderson-Sellers, B.: Method engineering for OO systems development. Commun. ACM 46, 73–78 (2003)

[9] Ter Hofstede, A.H.M., Verhoef, T.F.: On the feasibility of situational method engineering. Inf. Syst. 22, 401–422 (1997)

[10] Kumar, K., Welke, R.J.: Methodology Engineering: A Proposal for Situation-Specific Methodology Construction. In: Challenges and Strategies for Research in Systems Development, pp. 257–269. John Wiley & Sons, Inc., Chichester (1992)

[11] Mirbel, I., Ralyté, J.: Situational method engineering: combining assembly-based and roadmap-driven approaches. Requir. Eng. 11, 58–78 (2005)

[12] MOdeling Software Kitt (MOSKitt), http://www.moskitt.org

[13] Niknafs, A., Ramsin, R.: Computer-Aided Method Engineering: An Analysis of Existing Environments. In: Bellahsène, Z., Léonard, M. (eds.) CAiSE 2008. LNCS, vol. 5074, pp. 525–540. Springer, Heidelberg (2008)

[14] Ralyté, J., Rolland, C.: An Assembly Process Model for Method Engineering. In: Dittrich, K.R., Geppert, A., Norrie, M.C. (eds.) CAiSE 2001. LNCS, vol. 2068, pp. 267–283. Springer, Heidelberg (2001)

[15] Ralyté, J., Rolland, C.: An Approach for Method Reengineering. In: Kunii, H.S., Jajodia, S., Sølvberg, A. (eds.) ER 2001. LNCS, vol. 2224, pp. 471–484. Springer, Heidelberg (2001)

[16] Reusable Asset Specification (RAS) OMG Available Specification version 2.2. OMG Document Number: formal/2005-11-02

[17] Software Process Engineering Meta-model (SPEM) OMG Available Specification version 2.0. OMG Document Number: formal/2008-04-01

[18] Torres, V.: A Ph.D. thesis entitled "A Web Engineering Approach for the Development of Business Process-Driven Web applications". Technical University of Valencia (2008), http://www.dsic.upv.es/mapa/ingles/desctesis.pl?tesis=etd-04112008-140714

[19] Xpand, http://www.eclipse.org/modeling/m2t/?project=xpand

[20] Armbrust, O., Katahira, M., Miyamoto, Y., Münch, J., Nakao, H., Ocampo, A.: Scoping Software Process Models - Initial Concepts and Experience from Defining Space Standards. In: Wang, Q., Pfahl, D., Raffo, D.M. (eds.) ICSP 2008. LNCS, vol. 5007, pp. 160–172. Springer, Heidelberg (2008)

Software Factories: Describing the Assembly Process

Maider Azanza[1], Oscar Díaz[1], and Salvador Trujillo[2]

[1] University of the Basque Country, San Sebastián, Spain
{maider.azanza,oscar.diaz}@ehu.es
[2] IKERLAN Research Centre, Mondragón, Spain
strujillo@ikerlan.es

Abstract. *Software Factories* pose a paradigm shift that promises to turn application assembly more cost effective through systematic reuse. These advances in software industrialization have however reduced the cost of coding applications at the expense of increasing assembling complexity, i.e., the process of coming up with the final end application. To alleviate this problem, we advocate for a new discipline inside the general software development process, i.e. *Assembly Plan Management*, that permits to face complexity in assembly processes. A non-trivial case study application is presented.

1 Introduction

The software industry remains reliant on the craftsmanship of skilled individuals engaged in labor intensive manual tasks. However, growing pressure to reduce cost and time to market, and to improve software quality, may catalyze a transition to more automated methods. In this environment, *Software Factories (SFs)* represent a paradigm shift with the promise to make application assembly more cost effective through systematic reuse. This fosters the raise of supply chains while opening the door to mass customization.

SFs capture the entire knowledge on how to produce the applications within a specific product family. SFs offer such knowlege in the form of assets like patterns, frameworks, models and tools. Those assets are then systematically used to automate the delivery of family members. This impacts significanly on reducing cost and time to market, while improving product quality over one-off development [9]. However, these advances in software industrialization reduce the cost of coding applications at the expense of increasing assembling complexity, i.e., the process of coming up with the final end product (hereafter referred to as the *Assembly Process*).

Advanced engineering paradigms to support SFs illustrate this point: *Model Driven Engineering (MDE)* and *Software Product Line Engineering (SPLE)*. MDE raises the level of abstraction, defining models that capture the specifics of the application at hand, which will then be transformed into the actual application code implementation. As for SPLE, it aims at building a set of related

J. Münch, Y. Yang, and W. Schäfer (Eds.): ICSP 2010, LNCS 6195, pp. 126–137, 2010.

products out of a common set of core assets. Unlike MDE, now the stress is not so much on the abstraction level at which software is specified, but on conceiving programs as pre-planned variations from core assets.

Both SPLE and MDE depart from one-off development to provide an infrastructure where different (though related) applications can be obtained. An *SPLE Assembly Process* starts with the core assets where variation points are gradually instantiated to establish the features which the end application will eventually exhibit. Here, the SF outputs applications that mainly differ on the extent they support a set of pre-planned functional options. By contrast, an *MDE Assembly Process* is conceived as a pipeline of models and model transformations from abstract to more concrete realizations of the end application in an specific platform. Here, the SF delivers applications that mainly differ on the underlying technological platform.

Both SPLE-based and MDE-based assembly processes are complex in their own right [13,16]. While, the complementary nature of SPLE and MDE has raised wide expectations among the community (e.g. variability can be more concisely described at model level rather than at code, transformations can also be subject to variability hence addressing non-functional requirements, etc) [12], the combined use of SPLE and MDE puts even more stringent demands on the assembly process. We have experienced this difficulty ourselves. In [15], we reported a combined use of SPLE and MDE where facing the assembly process resulted overall complex. Completing the assembling process for just an individual application of the family took itself four people/day.

Based on these observations, this work advocates for a new discipline inside the general software development process, i.e. the *Assembly Plan Management*. The activities, roles and phases of this discipline are described, and illustrated for a compound SPL/MDE-based application development. The concerns, roles or assets needed for assembling programs in such a setting are described for this application. Two common approaches to face complexity are abstraction and separation of concerns. Accordingly, more abstract assembling constructs are introduced, and distinct regards are decoupled among different activities. SPEM is used as a notation.

2 Background

The SEI Product Line Practice Framework. A *Software Product Line (SPL)* is defined as a set of software-intensive systems sharing a common, managed set of features that satisfy the specific needs of a particular market segment or mission, and that are developed from a common set of core assets in a prescribed way [4]. Unlike project-based approaches targeted to one-off development, SPLs can have quite a long life-cycle since they provide the framework to build distinct products along time. Therefore, SPL processes, and the associated organizational structure are more permanent in nature, leading to a fundamental paradigm shift compared to a project-based approach.

Table 1. Practice Areas in the SEI's PLP Framework

Software engineering practice areas	Technical management practice areas	Organizational management practice areas
1. Architecture Definition 2. Architecture Evaluation 3. Component Development 4. COTS Utilization 5. Mining Existing Assets 6. Requirements Engineering 7. Software System Integration 8. Testing 9. Understanding Relevant Domains	1. Configuration Management 2. Data Collection, Metrics, and Tracking 3. Make/Buy/Mine/Commission Analysis 4. Process Definition 5. Scoping 6. Technical Planning 7. Technical Risk Management 8. Tool Support	1. Building a Business Case 2. Customer Interface Management 3. Developing an Acquisition Strategy 4. Funding 5. Launching and Institutionalizing 6. Market Analysis 7. Operations 8. Organizational Planning 9. Organizational Risk Management 10. Structuring the Organization 11. Technology Forecasting 12. Training

A *Product Line Practice (PLP) Framework* was proposed by SEI in 2000. The PLP Framework is built around three essential activities: *Core Asset Development* (a.k.a Domain Engineering), *Product Development* (a.k.a. Application Engineering), and *Process Management*. *Core Asset Development* is mainly concerned with defining the product line scope and producing the core assets from which the products will be built. *Product Development* consists in turning these core assets into products, and *Process Management* oversees both these activities at the project and organizational level.

This framework includes 29 practice areas grouped along these three essential activities. Table 1 summarizes the Practice Areas in the framework. Unlike activity-based grouping (as in RUP), PLP aggregates practices based on the skills required to perform the activities of the practice areas. Notice *"Process Definition"* as part of Technical Management. Although *"Process Definition"* can include a broad range of tasks, the focus of this paper is on the *Assembly Plan Management*: the specification and documentation of the process used to generate products from the core assets while maintaining the architectural integrity of the product line. Specifically, we look at how the combined used of SPLE and MDE impacts this practice. Next we outline these two practices, highlighting their impact on product assembly.

Model Driven Engineering. MDE is a paradigm of software development where the primary software artifacts are models from which code and other artifacts are generated according to best practices [8]. Consequently, MDE focuses on the construction of models, specification of transformation patterns, and automatic generation of code. And, the *Assembly Process* is regarded as a pipeline of model transformations that eventually leads to an executable application. Hence, the *MDE Assembly Process* can be basically described as an equation where transformations are regarded as functions applied to models that deliver other models at a lower abstraction level. For instance, the equation $app = t_2 \bullet t_1 \bullet m_0$ indicates that the *app* application is obtained by successively transforming model m_0 into code by using transformation t_1 and t_2. Here, transformations are exogenous, i.e. the source and target models conform to different metamodels.

Feature Oriented Software Development. SPLE does not face a single product but a family of products where their similarities make reuse a certainty rather than a possibility. So, the attention is not focused any more on a product for a specific customer (e.g. building a website for Iberia) but on an specific application domain, (e.g. constructing a website for airlines). Hence, the challenge rests on establishing the scope of the SPL (a.k.a the domain), identifying the variations to support (through the feature model [10]), and developing the infrastructure that permits a product of the family to be developed in a cost-effective way while keeping high quality standards.

Feature Oriented Software Development (FOSD) is one of the techniques to realize SPLE. FOSD is a paradigm for creating software product lines where customized programs are obtained by composing features [2]. Hence, features not only describe increments in program functionality that serve to distinguish between members of the product family, but are the actual software building blocks. A product line in an FOSD includes a *base* that expresses the greatest common denominator of all SPL members, and a set of meaningful increments of functionality (hereafter referred to as *deltas*) that implement the features. The *SPLE Assembly Process* can then be described as an equation. For instance, the equation $app = d_2 \bullet d_1 \bullet base$ indicates that *app* is obtained by composing deltas d_1 and d_2 to the *base*. Unlike the MDE case, now delta transformations are endogenous, i.e. the source and target models conform to the same metamodel.

3 Motivation by Example

We outline our experience on a software factory: *PinkCreek*, which is a product line of portlets (building blocks of web portals) for the provision of flight reservation capabilities to travel-agency portals [6]. The challenges were two fold. First, both the diversity and unstability of Web platforms advice to abstract away from platform specificities into a platform-independent model. This grounds the use of MDE. On the other hand, flight reservation is very similar among companies but not exactly the same. Companies exhibit variations in how flight reservation is conducted. Such diversity is captured through *deltas* that end up being supported using SPLE techniques. This combined setting can be characterized by a *(deltas, transformations)* pair : *deltas* (i.e. features) stand for variations on flight reservation whereas *transformations* account for mappings between the distinct levels of abstraction at which flight booking is captured. Next paragraphs describe the distinct artifacts that arise from both the MDE and the SPLE perspectives (a more complete account can be found at [15]).

MDE perspective. An MDE practitioner would first strive to abstract from the different Web platforms that can realize *PinkCreek*. To this end, *State Charts* (*SC*) are introduced to model flight-reservation control flow in a platform-independent way. The application is described as sequence of states where each state represents an HTML fragment (i.e. a unit of delivery during user interaction). States are connected by transitions whose handlers either execute some action, render some view, or both. A *State Chart* is then mapped into a model for portlet controlers: the *Ctrl* metamodel. *Ctrl* models are in turn, mapped into *Act* and *View* models, that define the actions to be performed and the views to be rendered during the controller execution, respectively, in a platform-independent way. Finally, technical platforms include *Java/Jak* (i.e. a Java language for supporting *deltas* [2]) and *Java Server Pages (JSP)*.

Summing it up, *PinkCreek*'s metamodels include *SC, Ctrl, Act, View,* and *Java/Jak* and *JSP* as technological platforms. This implies the existence of transformations among distinct metamodels and the technological platforms, namely: *sc2ctrl, ctrl2act, ctrl2view, act2jak* and *view2jsp*. For instance, the equation $app = act2Jak \bullet ctrl2act \bullet sc2ctrl \bullet baseModelSC$ specifies a transformation chain from a *baseModel* statechart to its realization down to *Jak* code.

SPL Perspective. An SPL practitioner would first look at cases for variability. The variability on flight reservation includes the possibility of on-line checking or the alternatives to compensate travel agencies for their cooperation when inlaying this portlet into the agency's portal (e.g. click-through fees, where the carrier will pay the agency based on the number of users who access the portlet; bounties, where the carrier will pay the agency based on the number of users who actually sign up for the carrier services through the agency portal; and transaction fees, where the incomes of the ticket sales are split between the carrier and the agency). A one-size-fits-all flight-booking portlet is inappropriate. Rather, a base core can be leveraged along the required functionality. This is realized through deltas. PinkCreek's *deltas* include: *Reservation, ClickThroughFees, BountyFees* and *TransactionFees.*

Delta composition can then be regarded as function composition. For instance, the equation $app = bountyFees \bullet reservation \bullet baseModelSC$ increments the *baseModel* described as a statechart with the *reservation* functionality, and this in turn, with the *bountyFees* functionality. Notice that both deltas should be described at the same level of abstraction as the *baseModel*, i.e. statecharts.

Transformations and deltas define a two-dimensional space for application assembly (see Figure 1). Moving downwards implies adding more details about the technological platform: from platform-independent (e.g. statecharts) to platform-specific models (e.g. Java/Jak). On the other hand, moving along the horizontal axis adds deltas to the final product. The different values of this horizontal dimension should not be understood as a sequence but as a partial order. That is, the order in which deltas are composed depends on the potential dependencies among their feature counterparts. For instance, a requirement dependency can exists so that *reservation* must be applied before *bountyFees*. This is captured by the feature model [10].

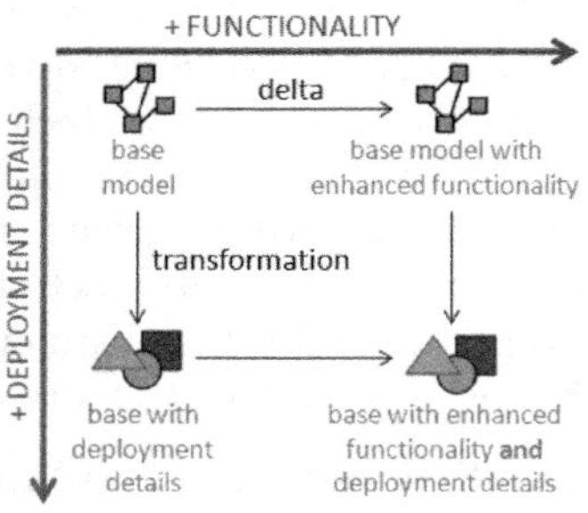

Fig. 1. The Assembly Space

Contrasting deltas with traditional vertical transformatios introduces the question of whether such operations are commutative. As Figure 1 suggests, the order (1. delta, 2. transformation) and (1. transformation, 2. delta) may not matter in some domains. From this perspective, ensuring commutativity can be regarded as an additional proof of the validity of transformations and deltas [1,15].

Assembly Process. An assembly process can then be described as a path along this assembly space. For instance, the equation $app = act2jak \bullet ctrl2act \bullet sc2ctrl \bullet bountyFees \bullet baseModelSC$ takes the *baseModelSC* as a start, enlarges its functionality by leveraging the *baseModelSC* with *bountyFees*, and finally, moves down to code by applying transformation *sc2ctrl*, *sc2act* and *act2Jak*. The outcome is a Java/Jak program that provides flight reservation with bounty fees as the payment mechanism.

At the time of *PinkCreek* development, we did not have a clear guideline that allowed for *declaratively* describing the assembly process as a delta-transformation high-level equation. As a result, we found ourselves programming intricate and compound scripts to achieve assembly. The insights gained that provide the grounds for this work, include,

1. *The Assembly Process is complex. PinkCreek* scripts, which realize the assembly process, accounted on average for 500 LOC of batch processes using 300 LOC of ANT makefiles and 2 KLOC of Java code.
2. *The Assembly Process needs to be designed.* We design because there are options and tradeoffs. Design is a way to handle complexity by abstracting away from the large number of details and focusing on the essentials. There is not a single way to application production. Distinct assembly alternatives may need to be contrasted and assembly counterpoints can arise.
3. *The Assembly Process becomes repetitive.* The paradox is that the assembly process is typically geared towards the reuse of source code, but its realization often lacks such reuse. This occurs in our case study where no reuse mechanism was initially in place. Specifically, defining alternative assembly processes involved a great deal of potential reuse but, puzzling enough in an MDPLE setting, the unique technique available for reuse was rudimentary *"clone&own"*. It did not take long to realize that this technique did not scale up.

Wrapping it up, a need was felt for a plan that manages how the assembly process is defined, allowing its design and capitalizing on reuse. The following section describes such plan.

4 Assembly Plan Management

Our claim is that the combined use of MDE and SPLE increases the burden of application development in general, and application assembly in particular. Therefore, additional effort should be dedicated to come up with an infrastructure (i.e. core assets) that facilitates application assembly during Application Engineering. The effort to build such infrastructure will payoff by streamlining the assembly process.

Our aim is to automate the process of constructing assembly process. Such automation is achieved though the so-called *Assembly Machine Tool*. In product manufacturing, a *Machine Tool* is a powered mechanical device, typically used to fabricate metal components of machines[1]. Machine tools that operate under automatic control are also known as computerized numerical control machines where the machine tool is fed with a program that dictates the process that constructs the desired item.

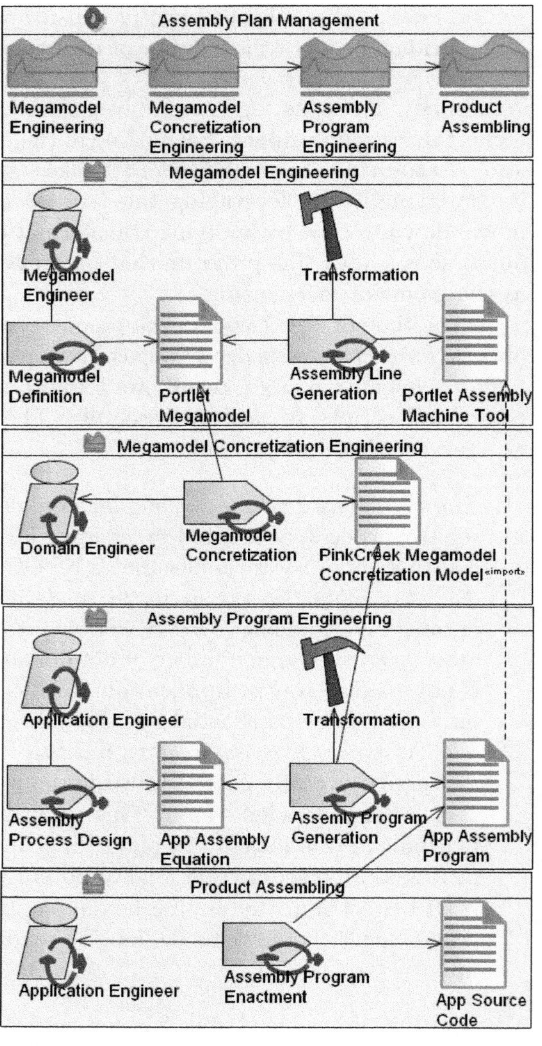

Fig. 2. SPEM Diagram of the Assembly Plan Management Discipline

This notion of numerical control machines is used here to describe the assembly infraestructure. The machine tool is realized through a library. The numerical control program is supported through an *Assembly Program*. This assembly program can, in turn, be defined by an *Assembly Equation*, which is a declarative specification that embodies a partially ordered set of transformations and delta compositions. Given an assembly equation, the assembly program will be automatically generated. Enacting this assembly program will deliver the *application* (i.e. the set of *code* artifacts) that exhibits the desired features.

To describe this process, we resort to *Software Process Engineering Metamodel (SPEM)* [11] an initiative of the *Object Management Group (OMG)* for software process modeling. It is a methodology-independent language based on UML. Hereafter, SPEM terminology is used to specify the tasks, artifacts and roles that produce an application.

[1] *http://en.wikipedia.org/wiki/Machine_tool*

According to SPEM a software development process is defined as a collaboration between abstract active entities called *process roles* that perform operations called *tasks* on concrete, tangible entities called *work products*. A *discipline* partitions tasks within a process according to a common theme. For example, in the Unified Process nine disciplines are described (e.g. Business Modeling, Requirement Management, Analysis and Design, Implementation, Test, etc). This work introduces a new discipline in the development of a software factory: the *Assembly Plan Management*, which splits along four phases: *Megamodel Engineering, Megamodel Concretization Engineering, Assembly Program Engineering* and *Product Assembling.* Figure 2 outlines the different roles, work products and tasks supporting this endeavour. Next, we delve into the details of each phase.

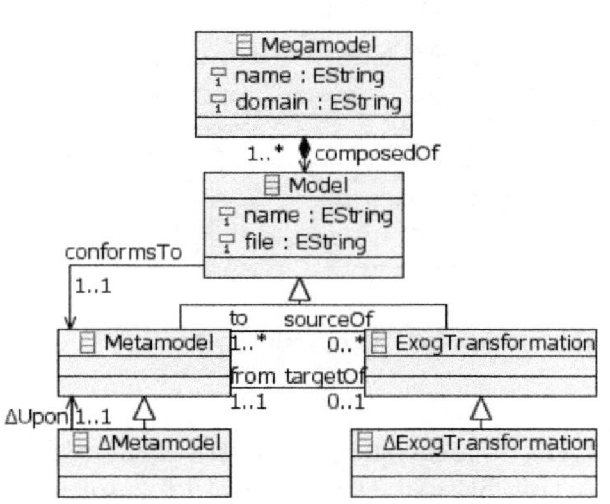

Fig. 3. Megamodel Metamodel

Megamodel Engineering Phase. This phase sets the *conceptual framework* to support the SF: which metamodels to use (e.g. statecharts vs. state-transition diagrams)?, how is variability supported (e.g. collaboration vs. aspects)? which transformation language is to be used (e.g. QVT vs. ATL)? which are the exogenous transformations that map between different metamodels?

`Megamodel` is the term chosen to capture this conceptual framework where models or metamodels are considered as a whole together with tools, transformations and other global entities that belong to the same domain [3]. In this way, a megamodel provides a model to classify the metamodels and transformations involved in the SPL. Figure 3 presents the metamodel for megamodels.

Based on this metamodel, the `Megamodel Engineer` decides the metamodels and transformations to be used to support the domain at hand. For our sample case, Figure 4 presents such megamodel. Note that *delta metamodels* and *delta exogenous transformations* are defined along with metamodels and exogenous transformations. In this case the figure is symmetrical, i.e. a delta metamodel and delta based transformation exist for every metamodel and every exogenous transformation.Nevertheless, this is not always the case. From our limited experience, delta transformations pose a significant engineering challenge, although the benefits they entail are also substantial [1,15].

This megamodel serves as a main input to obtain the `Portlet Assembly Machine Tool`. An *Assembly Machine Tool* is a library that collects a set of functions that realize model transformations. For our sample case, such library will contain functions for all the exogenous transformatios, namely, *sc2ctrl, ctrl2act, act2jak, ctrl2vw* and *vw2jsp* along with their corresponding delta transformations

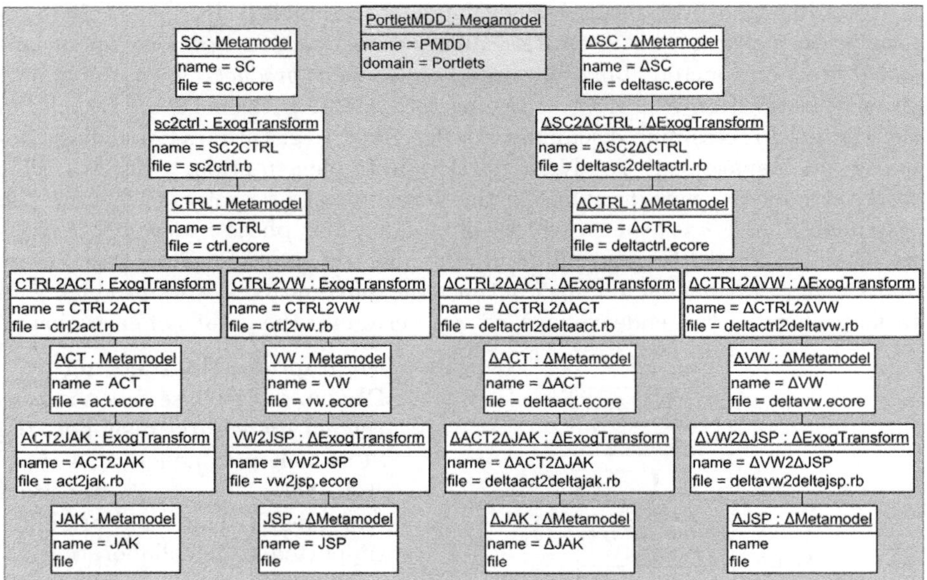

Fig. 4. Portlet MDD Assembly Megamodel

as stated in Figure 4. These functions will be later enacted by the *Assembly Program*. It is important to highlight that this library can be reused for any portlet SPL as long as the same metamodels are used to describe the artifacts, so this task has to be performed only once.

Megamodel Concretization Engineering Phase. A megamodel provides a common framework that can support different SPLs as long as they all use the same metamodels. For instance, the megamodel depicted in Figure 4 can describe not only *PinkCreek* but any SPL where `SC`, `Ctrl` and the other metamodels as well as deltas are the mechanisms used to capture domain specification and variability. Now, these metamodels and deltas are concretized for the domain at hand (e.g. *PinkCreek*). This basically means to define the *base* and the *deltas* for *PinkCreek*. The `PinkCreek Megamodel Concretization Model` behaves as a catalogue of these artifacts where information about the base and deltas are collected as well as their location in the project directory. In this way, the *Assembly Program* will be able to locate the deltas. This prevents the need to manually repeat this information every time an *Assembly Program* is to be enacted.

Assembly Program Engineering Phase. During this phase the *Application Engineer* declaratively describes the assembly process as an *Assembly Equation*. For instance, she decides to add the *bountyFees* feature to the *baseModel* and then, move down to code by applying transformation *sc2ctrl*, *sc2act* and *act2Jak*. The $app = act2jak \bullet ctrl2act \bullet sc2ctrl \bullet bountyFees \bullet baseModelSC$ reflects this decision. Equation operands include model transformations (e.g. *act2jak*) and deltas (e.g. *bountyFees*). The former are realized as functions of the `Assembly Machine Tool` obtained during *Megamodel Engineering*. As for deltas, they are obtained by referring to the `Megamodel Concretization Model` which is obtained during the *Megamodel Concretization Phase*.

Hence, an *Assembly Equation* is a declarative description of how a final application is to be assembled. This equation is then mapped to an executable *Assembly Program*, through a model-to-text transformation. The outcome is a Java/Jak *Assembly Program* that provides flight reservation with bounty fees as the payment mechanism.

Product Assembling. This phase is limited to enacting the `Assembly Program` which delivers the `Application Source`, i.e. a set of *code* artifacts that compile into the desired application binary.

5 Discussion

This work is based on some perceived liabilities on the what-is-to-come in application assembly, namely: complexity (i.e. assembly programs become larger), choiceful (i.e. assembly programs becomes fork-like), and *"clonefulness"* (i.e. some assembly tasks are repetitive which leads to code snippets being repeated) (see Section 3). The expected benefit of our approach would be the improvement of this situation. Next, we evaluate to which extent this aim is achieved.

Handling Complexity. Before this work, an average assembly program to create a single portlet in PinkCreek accounted for 500 LOC of batch processes using 300 LOC of ANT makefiles and 2 KLOC of Java code. More important, it took around 4 people/day to complete. Now, an assembly program to build a portlet with 5 features is specified with an equation of 15 LOC. This is providing that the *Megamodel Engineering Phase* and the *Megamodel Concretization Engineering Phase* have already been performed, where each took around one hour and were only carried out once for all programs. This is an improvement of at least one order of magnitude in the effort needed to develop the assembly program.

Handling Choices. Assembly programs are now specified at a higher abstraction level instead of being directly implemented. This allows the Application Engineer to concentrate on the design of the assembly process, pondering the advantages and trade-offs of each decision, without worrying about implementation details. Currently the only decision available is the order of the operations when assembling a product (in domains where the order is unimportant). However, the equation could be enriched with more decisions related to the assembly process . These choices in the *Assembly Process* can be captured as part of the variability of the production plan [5].

Handling *"Clonefulness"*. As assembly gets more complex, an increase in the number of clones, i.e. chunks of code that are repeated in distinct parts of the program, is observed. This is what we meant when we stated that assembly programs are cloneful. Such *"clonefulness"* calls for a reuse mechanism that departs from traditional *"clone&own"* practices. This is precisely what we achieved by abstracting away from code and moving to a higher level where clones are generated through transformations from the abstract model and where reuse is accomplished in a systematic manner using model driven techniques. Model transformations were only the first mechanism provided to foster reuse. We also introduced the notion of *Assembly Machine Tool*, a reusable library that provides operations for model transformation within the scope set by a megamodel, and which is reusable by every product family defined in such domain.

6 Related Work

Software Factories bring a perspective change in how software is developed where one of the changes is the importance of application assembly. Greenfield and Short state that in the near future most development will be component assembly, involving customization, adaptation and extension [9]. Having experienced this ourselves, we motivated the need for assembly processes to be designed and described the *Assembly Plan Management* as the means to fulfill that need.

Model management, of which application assembly is part, has been identified as one of the challenges that need to be addressed if MDE is to succeed [7]. In this line, megamodels establish and use global relationships on models, metamodels and transformations, ignoring the internal details of these global entities [3]. Megamodels, however, only reflect structural relationships. We believe this should be complemented with the corresponding processes in order to achieve the MDE vision. Lately, different tools have aimed at this problem.

As an example, UniTI is a model-based approach to reuse and compose transformations in a technology-independent fashion [16]. UniTI focuses on transformation execution to yield a single product, but it does not consider product families. Our work faces the complexity that arises when MDE and SPLE are combined. This shows up the increasing complexity of program assembling, and raises some issues that do not appear when MDE transformation are considered in isolation.

A preliminary work in extending assembly equations with model transformations was presented in [14]. This work develops those first steps by defining the assembly process as a central asset in software factories and the Assembly Plan Management as a new discipline inside the general software development process that yields the assembly process implementation.

7 Conclusions

Software Factories represent a paradigm shift that promises to make application assembly more cost effective through systematic reuse, enabling the formation of supply chains and opening the door to mass customization. Along these lines, this paper motivated the need for a new discipline in software development: the Assembly Plan Management. This discipline promotes the assembly process as a *first-class* citizen in the software development. Essentially, the Assembly Plan Management introduces a model driven approach to the generation of assembly programs in a software factory based on a model driven product line.

The main contribution of our work is that assembly processes are no longer implemented, but are modeled and thus designed, raising the abstraction level in assembly processes. This makes the reuse of assembly processes possible. We evaluated our ideas with a case study. Our future plans involve considering variability in the assembly process. According to our previous work, the production plan is subject to variability [5]. From this perspective, the assembly process may also have to cope with such variability.

Acknowledgments. This work was co-supported by the Spanish Ministry of Education, and the European Social Fund under contract MODELINE, TIN2008-06507-C02-01 and TIN2008-06507-C02-02.

References

1. Batory, D., Azanza, M., Saraiva, J.: The Objects and Arrows of Computational Design. In: Czarnecki, K., Ober, I., Bruel, J.-M., Uhl, A., Völter, M. (eds.) MODELS 2008. LNCS, vol. 5301, pp. 1–20. Springer, Heidelberg (2008)
2. Batory, D., Neal Sarvela, J., Rauschmayer, A.: Scaling Step-Wise Refinement. IEEE Transactions on Software Engineering, TSE (2004)
3. Bézivin, J., Jouault, F., Rosenthal, P., Valduriez, P.: Modeling in the Large and Modeling in the Small. In: MDAFA (2004)
4. Clements, P., Northrop, L.M.: Software Product Lines - Practices and Patterns. Addison-Wesley, Reading (2001)
5. Díaz, O., Trujillo, S., Anfurrutia, F.I.: Supporting Production Strategies as Refinements of the Production Process. In: Obbink, H., Pohl, K. (eds.) SPLC 2005. LNCS, vol. 3714, pp. 210–221. Springer, Heidelberg (2005)
6. Díaz, O., Trujillo, S., Perez, S.: Turning Portlets into Services: the Consumer Profile. In: WWW (2007)
7. France, R., Rumpe, B.: Model-driven development of complex software: A research roadmap. In: FOSE (2007)
8. Frankel, D.S.: Model Driven Architecture: Applying MDA to Enterprise Computing. Wiley, Chichester (2003)
9. Greenfield, J., Short, K.: Software Factories: Assembling Applications with Patterns, Models, Frameworks and Tools. In: OOPSLA Companion (2003)
10. Kang, K.C., Cohen, S.G., Hess, J.A., Novak, W.E., Peterson, A.S.: Feature Oriented Domain Analysis (foda) Feasability Study. Technical Report CMU/SEI-90-TR-21, Software Engineering Institute (November 1990)
11. OMG. Software Process Engineering Metamodel Specification. Formal Specification (April 2008), `http://www.omg.org/spec/SPEM/2.0/PDF`
12. AMPLE Project. Aspect-Oriented, Model-Driven Product Line Engineering (2009), `http://ample.holos.pt/`
13. Rivera, J.E., Ruiz-Gonzalez, D., Lopez-Romero, F., Bautista, J., Vallecillo, A.: Orchestrating ATL Model Transformations. In: MtATL (2009)
14. Trujillo, S., Azanza, M., Díaz, O.: Generative Metaprogramming. In: GPCE (2007)
15. Trujillo, S., Batory, D., Díaz, O.: Feature Oriented Model Driven Development: A Case Study for Portlets. In: ICSE (2007)
16. Vanhooff, B., Ayed, D., Van Baelen, S., Joosen, W., Berbers, Y.: UniTI: A Unified Transformation Infrastructure. In: Engels, G., Opdyke, B., Schmidt, D.C., Weil, F. (eds.) MODELS 2007. LNCS, vol. 4735, pp. 31–45. Springer, Heidelberg (2007)

How to Welcome Software Process Improvement and Avoid Resistance to Change

Daniela C.C. Peixoto[1], Vitor A. Batista[2], Rodolfo F. Resende[1], and Clarindo Isaías P.S. Pádua[2]

[1] Department of Computer Science – Federal University of Minas Gerais, Brazil
[2] Synergia, Department of Computer Science, Federal University of Minas Gerais, Brazil
{cascini,vitor,rodolfo,clarindo}@dcc.ufmg.br

Abstract. Pressures for more complex products, customer dissatisfaction and problems related to cost and schedule overruns increase the need for effective management response and for improvement of software development practices. In this context, cultural aspects can influence and interfere in a successful implementation of a software process improvement program. This paper explores cultural issues, discussing in a detailed way one de-motivator factor to implement successfully a software process improvement action. The analysis was carried out in a software development organization and provided some insights into how this organization would overcome it. We backed our studies conducting a process simulation. Our findings suggest that other than finance, technology and other issues, the cultural aspects should be among the first concerns to be taken into account when implementing a Software Process Improvement program. Our main contribution is to give evidences that a small change in the behavior of the software development team members can improve the quality of the product and reduce development rework.

Keywords: Software Process Improvement, Resistance, Cultural Aspects, Simulation.

1 Introduction

Implementing a successful Software Process Improvement (SPI) is a challenging issue that many software companies face today. Many organizations experience a successful start on their SPI initiative and after some phases of their improvement process they realize that the engagement to change weakens significantly after the initial excitement [1]. Previous studies show critical factors that can be sources for this problem e.g. resistance to change, previous negative experience, lack of the evidence of the benefits, imposition, resource constraints and commercial pressures to meet customer demands [2, 3].

Human, social and organizational factors play a decisive role for the success or failure of a process improvement initiative and cultural issues emerge as an important player of the changing workplace [4].

In this work, we study and evaluate the implications of one de-motivator factor for SPI, the resistance of practitioners to adopt a new practice. This problem occurs when

J. Münch, Y. Yang, and W. Schäfer (Eds.): ICSP 2010, LNCS 6195, pp. 138–149, 2010.

practitioners are not adequately encouraged to give up the old practices that they are familiar with and that they feel comfortable with [2]. As Humphrey observed [5] this is not a trivial problem "particularly because even intelligent people often will not do things that common logic, experience, and even hard evidence suggests that they should." We will also present the impact of this factor into organization's projects through the analysis of an improvement practice. In addition, we provide some evaluation of the benefits of this specific improvement practice, using process simulation.

The motivation of this work is to show that some barriers for SPI can be overcome with a simple modification of team behavior, which will impact considerably in the project results. More specifically, we will present one initiative, a simple modification of the quality procedure, which was implemented to reduce rework. Considering the successful results of this initiative, we believe that it can be easily incorporated in many industrial software development processes.

In the next section we present the relevant features of the organization under study, including a brief description of its software development process. In Section 3, we describe the organization improvement effort that was structured as a Defect Causal Analysis process. Section 4 provides an analysis of the results using process simulation. Section 5 concludes the work and suggests some directions for further research.

2 Organization Background

Here we describe a work that was performed as a collaborative study with Synergia. Synergia is a laboratory for software and systems engineering, hosted in the Computer Science Department at Federal University of Minas Gerais, Brazil. Synergia is internally organized as a commercial software development organization, but it also retains important academic characteristics [6]. Synergia maintains 85 people in its staff composed by undergraduate and graduate students and non-student graduated professionals, most with a Computer Science background.

Synergia uses a tailored version of the Praxis model-driven software development process [7] in its software and systems engineering projects, called Praxis-Synergia. Although the Praxis process has been designed and applied primarily for education and training in Software Engineering, it provides tailoring guidelines, which must be interpreted according to the current situation of the development organization. The Praxis material is available in a book and kept updated in the author's Web site[1].

One important characteristic of Praxis, which is maintained in the tailored version, is that it models the development of each product use case as a sequence of development states or control marks. The name of each state evokes how far the use case has advanced towards complete implementation and acceptance. Table 1 summarizes these states and a detailed discussion of them can be found in Pádua [6, 8]. Each state is associated with one or more quality control procedures such as inspections, tests and management reviews. During the execution of these activities each found defect is recorded.

---

[1] www.dcc.ufmg.br/~wilson/praxis/ (in Portuguese)

Table 1. Praxis use case development states (adapted from [6])

State	Output	Quality Procedure
Identified	Use-case diagrams (requirements view)	Management review
Detailed	Use-case descriptions; low fidelity prototype; interface and non-functional requirements (requirements view)	Requirements inspection
Analyzed	Use-case realizations; detailed class diagrams (analysis view)	Analysis inspection
Designed	Design use-case descriptions; concrete user interfaces diagrams and specifications; high fidelity prototype (external design view)	External design inspection
Specified	Test specifications (test design view)	Test design inspection
Realized	Design use case realizations (internal design view); source code and unit test scripts for lower architecture layers	Unit tests; implementation inspection
Implemented	Source code and test scripts for upper architecture layers; executable code	Integration tests; implementation and internal design inspection
Verified	Verified executable code; user documentation	System tests
Validated	Validated executable	User appraisal
Complete	Complete code and artifact baseline	Quality audit

3 The SPI Initiative

During 2007, Synergia managed its improvement effort by analyzing problems in a specific project. The work was organized as a Defect Causal Analysis (DCA) process [9]. The DCA process selects recurring problems with the aim of identifying their principal causes and propose some solutions to avoid (or reduce) new occurrences. According to Boehm & Basili [10] about 80% of rework comes from 20% of the defects. DCA selects problems from the organization database for periodic causal analysis meetings. Many of the recommendations resulting from causal analysis meetings are small changes that improve communications and processes in small ways. However, these small changes can have dramatic impacts over the long-term.

The meetings were conduct by the causal analysis teams (four teams), which consisted of the software developers who had greater knowledge about the product and process. Each team represented an area of the process where it was observed significant amount of defects: usability, test, design and implementation. Each team analyzed the problems considered the most relevant. The causal analysis meetings produced some recommendations (short-term and/or long-term) for the action team. The action team was in charge of prioritizing the actions proposals, allocating resources, monitoring the progress and communicating the status of each action to all stakeholders.

At that time, the largest running project, referred here as Project TBI (To-Be-Improved), was chosen to assure that the recommendations would be executed. Part of the people responsible for Project TBI participated in the causal analysis meetings. The causal analysis work was concluded on time with some reasonable results.

The problem discussed in this article was detected while performing the quality procedures of the **Implemented** state (see Table 1). Before delivering the executable code to the Test team, the developers themselves were required to execute a list of test procedures (a subset of the complete Manual Test Specification). The purpose of this verification was to identify errors made by the developers themselves with the aim of treating them before the execution of the test procedures by the Test team. For example, a nonoperational *save* command or in some cases whole inoperative use case could pass unnoticed. It is worth to mention, in previous projects (before Project TBI), when this verification practice was adopted, the number of critical defects detected by the testers dropped significantly. With these observations and some analysis by the Software Process team, the organization decided to incorporate this practice in its development process. Project TBI adopted it as a task required for advancing the use case from **Realized** to **Implemented** state (Figure 1).

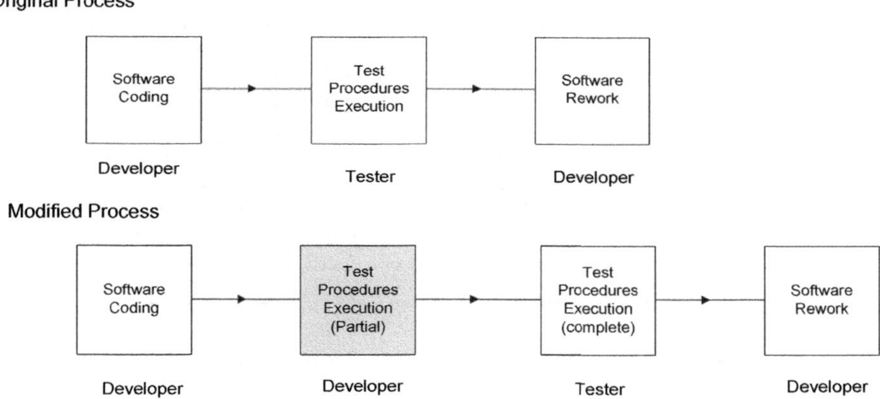

Fig. 1. Process Flow Chart for the Original and Modified Process

Although in Project TBI all developers were required to execute the list of test procedures, they did not execute it correctly or they did not execute it at all. In a broader evaluation, the non-execution of these test procedures could be a result of time pressure, project cost overrun, and lack of training or experience of the team. But at Project TBI, the developer had enough time to do their task and they knew or were trained in what they had to inspect. Trying to find one possible cause, the developers in a DCA meeting were asked about the reasons. It was not possible to identify one specific source of the problem. However, the interviews drew attention to a specific team behavior: they simply neglected this task. But, why this happened? Even if the project manager had required the developers to execute this procedure they did not execute them! One rationale behind this problem could be resistance to change, or in other words, the resistance to include this practice in the developers' list of 'daily' practices. Considering this hypothesis, one proposed solution was to force the developers to execute the test procedures using a specific tool, which records each step executed and the test result (whether it succeeded or failed). In this way, the developers would provide to the Test team an evidence, metaphorically like signing a document, that they had really executed the test procedures.

The action group monitored and evaluated the implementation of this action in Project TBI to see if it would produce some positive effect. Surprisingly, the result lived up the expectations, mainly because after 5 months the benefits of this unique action amounted to 217% of the investments in DCA meetings. Table 2 summarizes the problem.

Table 2. Problem addressed by the Implementation DCA Team

Problem	Many critical defects detected during the verification task of the executable code carried out by the testers.
Cause	Developers did not execute correctly the test procedures before delivering the use case to the Test team. Eventually, the developers did some corrections in the test procedures when the latter had some problems or were invalid or ambiguous.
Solution	The IBM Rational Manual Tester (RMT), a testing tool that forces the developer to record each step during the verification of the test procedures, was incorporated into the process. A log produced by the tool should be extensively evaluated by the Test team in order to ensure that the developer performed these manual tests properly, before the verification of the complete test procedures.
Benefits	After five months of implementation, the benefit of this action amounted to 217% of the investment in DCA meetings. At the end of Project TBI, there was an average reduction of 5.66 hours / use case (45%) of rework to fix and check for defects. A total saving of 796 h. The number of use cases without defects increased from 21% to 53%. The average number of defects reduced from 5.1 to 1.7 defects / use case and the number of critical defects reduced in 70%.

Trying to understand the resistance of the developers to change behavior, we found some studies discussing how cultural aspects can affect software process improvement programs [4, 11, 12]. Evaluating the data from the Hofstede's popular cultural dimensions [13], we observed that in Brazil the highest Hofstede's Dimension is Uncertainty of Avoidance with a score of 76. This suggests that the society has low level of tolerance for uncertainty, does not readily accept change, and is very risk adverse [13].

With this unexpected positive result, the organization plans to incorporate this practice into every inspection during the whole development process. In the next section we evaluate the benefits of this adoption using process simulation.

4 Simulation Execution and Analysis

Software process simulation is gaining increasing interest among academic researchers and practitioners alike as an approach for [14]: strategic management, planning, control and operational management, process improvement, technology adoption, understanding, training and learning.

Several studies have shown the use of Software Process Simulation for SPI. Christie [15] presented how a software process simulation can support CMM in all 5 levels. In a more recent work, Raffo & Wakeland [16] presented a detailed report about how Process Simulation Modeling has been implemented within industry and government organizations to improve their processes and achieve higher levels of process maturity. Via many examples, this work showed how process simulation supports CMMI Process Areas from maturity level 2 through level 5 and how some simulation results can be useful in determining financial performance measurements such as Return on Investment and Net Present Value. In another article, Raffo [17] showed that simulation can provide quantitative assessment of the risk and/or uncertainty associated with process change and support quantitative prediction of project level performance in terms of effort, staffing, schedule and quality.

In our work we use process simulation to forecast the impact of applying our specific process improvement practice before each inspection, as illustrated in Figure 2.

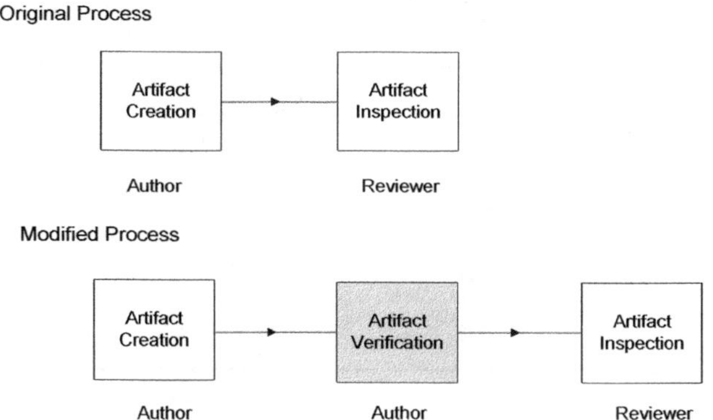

Fig. 2. Process Flow Chart for the Original and Modified Process

Specifically, using simulation we aimed to answer the following questions:

What is the amount of rework reduction with the adoption of the verification practice before each inspection?
What is the best configuration for the adoption of this practice?

The verification practice is also carried out using RMT. In this case, the check-list items are documented in this tool, allowing the author's verification before delivering the artifact for the inspection. The objective is the same, forcing the author to check these items. In our analysis, we observed that some items of the organization's check-list are subjective. For example, "A brief documentation of the use case is clear and accurately describes its purpose". These items can also be included in the RMT as a way to remind the author to check them. However, in this case, we believe that the detection of this type of error by the author may be difficult, mainly because he/she has written the documentation as clear and as accurately as possible in his/her point of view.

The model used in this study is a model of the Praxis-Synergia process as shown in Figure 3. The model has been calibrated with historical data from the organization and it has been validated against the performance data from one large-project (with the size of 585 thousand non-blank non-comment lines of code).

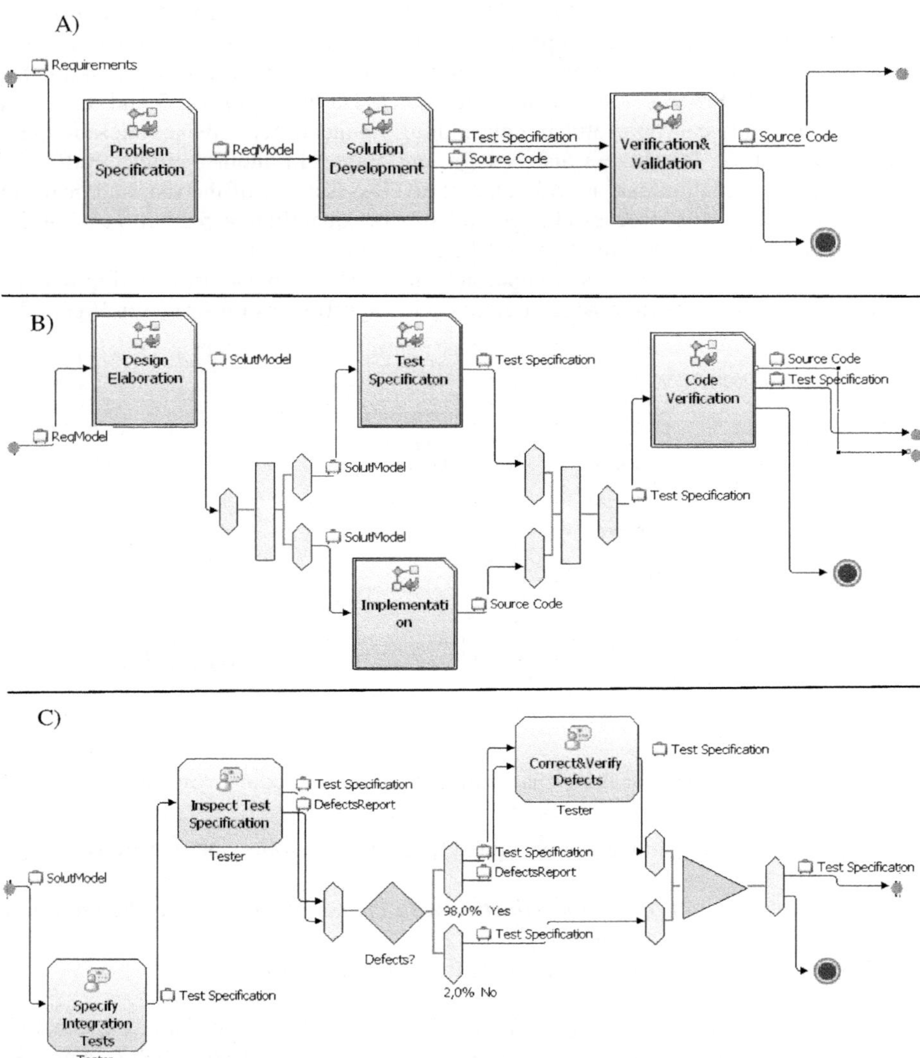

Fig. 3. Praxis-Synergia Process Simulation Model into 3 levels of abstraction. A) First level of abstraction of the software development process. B) Detailed model of the 'Solution Development' process. C) Detailed model of the 'Test Specification' Process.

The tool used to build the model was *IBM WebSphere Business Modeler (WBM) Advanced Edition*. This tool offers process modeling, simulation and analysis capabilities, with the aim of helping business users to understand, document, and deploy business processes for continuous improvement.

The following data were used to calibrate our model:

- Probability distribution of the effort of each task of the whole process. This information was collect from the organization database. We analyzed the effort distribution in previous projects and then used probabilistic distributions that best fitted the data.
- Average cost per hour of each team role.
- Percentage of use case that present defects during each inspection.

Note that some data presented in this article is marked to protect the organization confidentiality.

Some consolidated baseline data from the Praxis-Synergia Simulation Model in Figure 3 are shown in Table 3 and Table 4. Table 3 shows the effort in hours (work and rework) of each inspection. The numbers, after each inspection type, identify different inspections, with different perspectives, of the same artifact. Table 4 presents the effort, in hours, required for some process activities to produce the following artifacts: Problem Model (Requirement activities), Solution Model (Design activity), Test Specification (Test activity) and Source Code (Implementation activity).

Table 3. Baseline performance of the inspections for the AS-IS process

Effort (h) / Inspection type	Work		Rework	
	Mean	Std	Mean	Std
Requirement 1	3.25	2.08	3.52	3.98
Requirement 2	6.47	4.50	8.52	9.09
Design 1	4.44	3.16	7.66	8.11
Design 2	3.40	1.73	1.86	2.23
Design 3	5.75	4.54	6.00	6.98
Test	9.35	8.12	8.23	9.7
Implementation 1	2.99	2.50	6.01	10.73
Implementation 2	2.19	2.26	6.84	10.18
Implementation 3	9.49	8.80	12.58	14.4
Implementation 4	5.58	3.42	8.14	14.18

Table 4. Baseline performance of the activities for the AS-IS process

Effort (h) / Task	Work	
	Mean	Std
Requirement 1	19.64	16.43
Requirement 2	23.01	13.7
Design	43.18	32.5
Test	24.41	18.27
Implementation	137.2	145.6

In this study, we considered the following scenarios for the simulation:

- Scenario 1 – all inspections: reduction of 30 % of the rework, increase of 20% of the number of inspections without defects and increasing of 10% of the authors' work to verify the artifacts. All these values were derived using the available historical data and using expert judgment.

- Scenario 2 –groups of inspections: the inspections of three main Praxis-Synergia artifacts were grouped into (see Table 3): requirement inspections (Problem Model), design inspections (Solution Model) and implementation inspections (Source Code). Then, we changed their parameters accordingly to Scenario 1. The aim is to identify the best configuration for RMT adoption.

After running the simulation, the WBM tool aggregates the results by the expected probability of one path of the model to be followed. This value is expressed as a percentage. Figure 4 illustrates the probability distribution of the rework for the AS-IS process, considering 20 runs of the model.

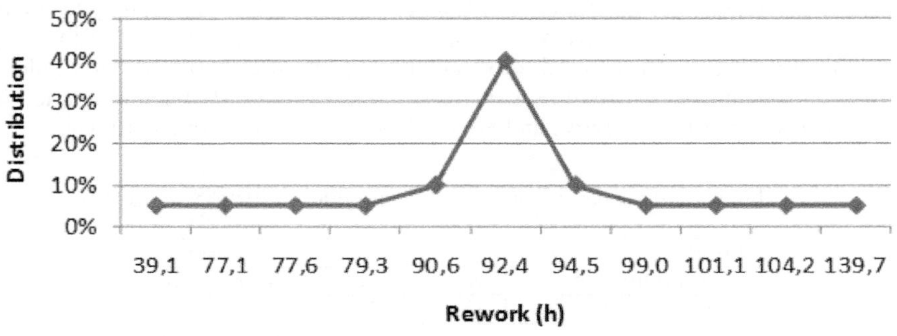

Fig. 4. Expected probability of each simulation execution of the AS-IS process

The average work for the AS-IS scenario is 325.34 hours and the average rework is 91.32 hours per use case.

4.1 Scenario 1: All Inspections

In this scenario, we made changes to represent the utilization of the RMT in each inspection of the software development process. The Praxis-Synergia development process has 10 inspections and the average duration and rework of each inspection was shown in Table 3.

We made changes into the model to represent this scenario, and then we ran the model for 20 runs. Figure 5 shows the distribution of the rework probabilities for this scenario. In this case, 10% of the process instances have a rework of 49.4 hours.

The average work for the TO-BE scenario is 410.77 hours and the average rework is 40.45 hours per use case. Despite the increase in the number of work hours, the rework reduced drastically (~56% of reduction). The work increased mainly because of the amount of author's effort required to verify the check-list items before delivering the artifact for inspection. The total effort of the AS-IS scenario, 416.66 hours, is less than the total effort of the TO-BE scenario, 451.22 hours. However, evaluating the cost we observed that the TO-BE scenario presents a reduction of 2.8% of the total cost comparing with the AS-IS scenario.

It is interesting to note that, in terms of effort, the reduction of the rework seems to not compensate the work of implementation of the RMT in each inspection. But we know that detecting and correcting errors in earlier stages of the process signify cost reductions [18]. In addition, the simulations have shown that will be worthwhile to use RMT when considering the cost parameter.

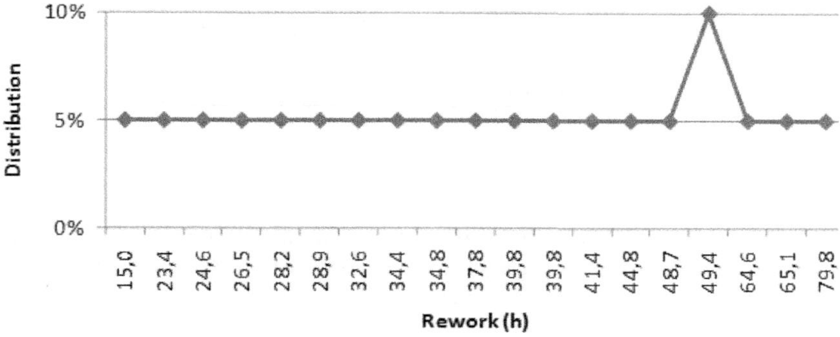

Fig. 5. Expected probability of each simulation execution of the TO-BE process

4.2 Scenario 2: Applying the RMT in Groups of Inspections

For this scenario, we examined the impact of implementing the verification practice in some specific group of inspections, including: a) requirement inspections; b) design inspections; and c) implementation inspections.

We made changes to the model to represent these alternative configurations, and then we ran each model for 20 runs. We compare the results of the AS-IS and the TO-BE processes. Table 5 summarizes the results.

Table 5. Effort performance of Scenario 2

Average Effort (h) / Inspection Group	AS-IS		TO-BE	
	Work	Rework	Work	Rework
Requirement	59.61	15.71	64.22	5.81
Design	53.45	16.35	56.84	10.35
Implementation	248.47	61.47	290.75	26.42

Similar to scenario 1, the rework reduced in some cases more than 50%. However the total work of using RMT for implementation inspections is higher than not using it. The reason for this is that one specific implementation activity (see Table 4), coding, is very time-consuming and, in some cases, it takes more than 50% of the total work to develop a use case from scratch. In this case, with an additional verification task, the artifact will take a longer time to be delivered for the inspections. However, at this stage the rework activities cost more.

In Table 6, we can observe that the cost of the TO-BE process is less than the cost of the AS-IS process for all groups of inspections. This result is similar to the first simulation result.

Although, in some cases the total effort increased, we believe, based on the positive results, that RMT can be used in all inspections of the whole development process.

Table 6. Cost performance of Scenario 2

Average Cost (R$) / Inspection Group	AS-IS	TO-BE
Requirement	1,561.38	1,472.58
Design	2,051.03	1,959.35
Implementation	6,137.18	5,978.05

5 Conclusion

Software development takes place within a rich cultural environment. To be successful, a software process initiative needs to recognize this aspect and make explicit the software practices as they are understood and applied by the software engineering team. In this context, our work discussed one specific cultural factor, the resistance to change, that affected a successful implementation of a software process improvement action in a specific organization. In addition, we also showed how this organization overcame this de-motivator factor through an adoption of a specific verification practice.

We used simulation to forecast what-if scenarios for adoption of this practice. For that, we created a model of the organization's software development process. Then we run the model for two scenarios: using this practice in the whole process and using it in specific phases of the software development process. In both cases, the results provided evidences of a considerable reduction in terms of rework and cost.

Through a real experience, we expect that the findings of this research not only help managers to understand the impact of cultural factors that may de-motivate practitioners from supporting some improvements but also assist them in designing and evaluating the effects of implementing improvement initiatives.

We also believe that similar work can be done in other organizations, more specifically the adoption of the verification practice in software development processes. After this study, the organization considered process simulation an important tool to evaluate the adoption of process changes and it plans to incorporate the verification practice in its next projects. The future results will permit us to contrast the previous simulations results with real ones.

Acknowledgements. We would like to thank IBM Rational for supporting this work, within the IBM Academic Initiative. We also would like to thank Capes Foundation (grant n. BEX 1893/09-2).

References

1. Börjesson, A., Mathiassen, L.: Making SPI Happen: The IDEAL Distribution of Effort. In: Proceedings of the 36th Annual Hawaii International Conference on System Sciences, HICSS 2003, January, 6–9, p. 328. IEEE Computer Society Press, Los Alamitos (2003)

2. Baddoo, N., Hall, T.: De-motivators for software process improvement: an analysis of practitioners' views. Journal of Systems and Software 66(1), 23–33 (2003)
3. Nasir, M.H.N., Ahmad, R., Hassan, N.H.: Resistance factors in the implementation of software process improvement project. Journal of Computer Science 4(3), 211–219 (2008)
4. Siakas, K.V.: What has Culture to do with SPI? In: Proceedings of the 28th Euromicro Conference, EUROMICRO 2002, Dortmund, Germany, September, 4–6, pp. 376–381. IEEE Computer Society Press, Los Alamitos (2002)
5. Humphrey, W.S.: Why don't they practice what we preach? Annals of Software Engineering 6(1/4), 201–222 (1998)
6. Pádua, C., Pimentel, B., Pádua, W., Machado, F.: Transitioning model-driven development from academia to real life. In: Proceedings of Educators' Symposium of the ACM / IEEE 9th International Conference on Model Driven Engineering Languages and Systems, Genova, Italy, October, 1–6, pp. 61–77 (2006)
7. Pádua, W.: A Software Process for Time-constrained Course Projects. In: Proceedings of the 28th International Conference on Software Engineering, ICSE 2006, Shanghai, China, May 20–28, pp. 707–710 (2006)
8. Pádua, W.: Quality Gates in Use-Case Driven Development. In: Proceedings of the Fourth Workshop on Software Quality, 28th International Conference on Software Engineering, WoSQ 2006, Shanghai, China, May 21, pp. 33–38 (2006)
9. Card, D.N.: Learning from Our Mistakes with Defect Causal Analysis. IEEE Software 15(1), 56–63 (1998)
10. Boehm, B., Basili, V.R.: Software Defect Reduction Top 10 List. IEEE Computer 34(1), 135–137 (2001)
11. Siakas, K.V., Balstrup, B.: A field-study of Cultural Influences on Software Process Improvement in a Global Organization. In: Proceedings of European Software Process Improvement Conference, EuroSPI 2000, Copenhagen, Denmark, November 7–9 (2000)
12. Wong, B., Hasa, S.: Cultural Influences and Differences in Software Process Improvement Programs. In: Proceedings of the 6th International Workshop on Software Quality, WoSQ 2008, Leipzig, Germany, May 10, pp. 3–10 (2008)
13. Hofstede, G., Hofstede, G.-J.: Cultures and Organizations: Software of the Mind, 2nd edn. McGraw-Hill, New York (2004)
14. Kellner, M.I., Madachy, R.J., Raffo, D.M.: Software process simulation modeling: Why? What? How? Journal of Systems and Software 46(2/3), 91–105 (1999)
15. Christie, A.M.: Simulation in support of CMM-based process improvement. Journal of Systems and Software 46(2/3), 107–112 (1999)
16. Raffo, D.M., Wakeland, W.: Moving Up the CMMI Capability and Maturity Levels Using Simulation. Technical Report CMU/SEI-2008-TR-002. Software Engineering Institute, Carnegie Mellon University, Pittsburgh, PA (2008)
17. Raffo, D.M., Vandeville, J.V., Martin, R.H.: Software process simulation to achieve higher CMM levels. Journal of Systems and Software 46(2/3), 163–172 (1999)
18. Madachy, R.J.: A software project dynamics model for process cost, schedule and risk assessment. Doctoral Thesis. Department of Industrial and Systems Engineering, University of Southern California, Los Angeles, CA (1994)

The Incremental Commitment Model Process Patterns for Rapid-Fielding Projects

Supannika Koolmanojwong and Barry Boehm

Center of Systems and Software Engineering
University of Souther California
Los Angeles, CA 90089-0781
{koolmano,boehm}@usc.edu

Abstract. To provide better services to customers and not to be left behind in a competitive business environment, a wide variety of ready-to-use software and technologies are available for one to grab and build up software systems at a very fast pace. Rapid fielding plays a major role in developing software systems to provide a quick response to the organization. This paper investigates the appropriateness of current software development processes and develops new software development process guidelines, focusing on four process patterns: Use single Non-Developmental Item (NDI), NDI-intensive, Services-intensive, and Architected Agile. Currently, there is no single software development process model that is applicable to all four process patterns, but the Incremental Commitment Model (ICM) can help a new project converge on a process that fits their process drivers. This paper also presents process decision criteria in terms of these drivers and relates them to the ICM Electronic Process Guide.

Keywords: Software Process Modeling and Representation, Software Process Guidelines, Non-Developmental Item (NDI), Net-Centric Services (NCS), Rapid Fielding, Rapid Applications.

1 Introduction

The growing diversity of software systems (requirements-driven, Non-Developmental-driven, services-driven, learning-driven, qualities-driven, systems of systems) has made it clear that there are no one-size-fits-all processes for the full range of software systems. Rapid Fielding is becoming an increasingly important software system objective. To fit into market windows and respond to competition, several possible process patterns can be used. Some process models are being developed that provide specific evidence-based and risk-based decision points. One of the most thoroughly elaborated of these models is the Incremental Commitment Model (ICM) [1]. To quickly select and follow the appropriate process pattern helps the development to finish the project faster and more efficiently. Overall characteristics of each process pattern and the ICM decision points have been defined on a general-experience basis [2] but process guidelines and process selection decision criteria are lacking on the ability to help produce a viable process decision early in the life cycle.

J. Münch, Y. Yang, and W. Schäfer (Eds.): ICSP 2010, LNCS 6195, pp. 150–162, 2010.

For rapid-fielding projects, current technologies like Net-Centric Services (NCS) and Non-Developmental Items (NDI) provide ready-to-use functionalities, which in turn speed up the software development process. In addition, agile process with agile-ready people can provide faster time to market [3]. NDI, such as COTS, open source software or free library, plays crucial roles in today's software development [4]. Considering the tendency toward net-centric services usage, reflected in USC's Software Engineering Class Projects [5], Fig. 1 shows an increasing trend in using net centric services in real-client software development projects. A similar trend is shown in the industry: 80% of the world economy provides services in various forms [6]. Based on programmableweb.com [7], there are at least 3 new mashups or web service extensions created and listed at this website every day. The users who are consuming these services need to know how to select the right service and utilize the service properly. The service-intensive or NDI-intensive application developers need to choose the appropriate process guidelines.

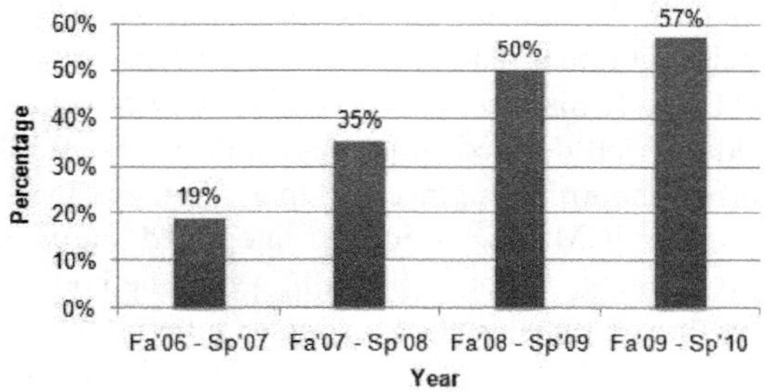

Fig. 1. Net Centric Services Usage in Software Development Projects in USC Software Engineering Class

This paper presents three new software development processes, for Architected Agile, Use single NDI, and Services-Intensive, and one updated software development process, NDI-intensive, which are extended from Yang and Boehm's COTS-Based Application Development guidelines (CBD) [8] by applying the risk-driven approach of the ICM and feedback from Bhuta's empirical analysis on COTS interoperability assessment [9]. This paper also reports the current rapid-fielding software development process investigation and analysis, the decision driver of process pattern selection, and the software development process guidelines for 4 process patterns which are implemented and represented in terms of the electronic process guide.

This paper is organized as followed: Section 2 contains background information of the ICM, the differences between NDI and NCS, and USC Software Engineering course. Section 3 provides information about the nature of rapid-fielding projects, process decision drivers, process selection graph, and the ICM EPG. Section 4 contains preliminary empirical project results on process selection and on the results of process usage. Section 5 provides conclusions and future work.

2 Background

2.1 The Incremental Commitment Model (ICM)

The ICM [2] is a new generation process model. ICM covers the full system development life cycle consisting of the Exploration phase, Valuation phase, Foundations phase, Development phase, and Operation phase. ICM has been evaluated to be a flexible but robust framework for system development [2]. The core concepts of the ICM include 1) commitment and accountability of system stakeholders, 2) success-critical stakeholder satisficing, 3) incremental growth of system definition and stakeholder commitment, 4) concurrent engineering, 5) iterative development cycles, and 6) risk-based activity levels and milestones. One of the main focuses of the ICM is feasibility analysis; evidence must be provided by the developer and validated by independent experts. The ICM combines the strengths of various current process models and limits their weaknesses. The ICM, like the V-Model [10], emphasizes early verification and validation, but allows for multiple-incremental interpretation and emphasizes concurrent rather than sequential engineering. Compared to the Spiral Model [11], the ICM also focuses on risk-driven activity prioritization, but offers an improvement by adding well-defined in-process milestones. While ICM, RUP, and MBASE [12] perform concurrent engineering that stabilizes the software process at anchor point milestones, ICM also supports integrated hardware-software-human factors oriented development. Comparing with Agile methods [3], ICM embraces adaptability to unexpected change and at the same time allows scalability. In [2], it shows how the ICM can be applied to a broad spectrum of software-intensive systems processes, which are categorized into 12 process patterns as follows: Use Single NDI, Agile, Architected Agile, Formal Methods, Hardware with embedded Software component, Indivisible Initial Operational Capability, NDI- intensive, Hybrid agile/ plan-driven system, Multi-owner system of systems, Family of systems, Brownfield, and Services-Intensive.

2.2 Process Patterns of Software Development Project

For the small e-services projects developed in our project course, four of the 12 process patterns of the ICM [15] predominate:

- Architected Agile - For less than 80 agile-ready-people team size and a fairly mature technology project, agile methods can be scaled up using an Architected Agile approach emphasizing early investment in a change-prescient architecture and all success-critical-stakeholders team building [2]. The Valuation phase and Foundations phases can be brief. A scrum of Scrums approach can be used in the Development phase. For example, a database application project that majority of the implementation tasks are building the right architecture and custom coding.
- Use Single NDI – When an appropriate NDI (COTS, open source, reuse library, customer-furnished package) solution is available, it is an option to either use the NDI or develop perhaps a better version by oneself or outsource such a

development which generally incurs more expense and takes longer to begin capitalizing on its benefits. On the other hand, an NDI may come with high volatility, complexity, or incompatibility. Major effort will then be spent on appraising the NDI. For example, an accounting system that could be totally satisfied by using a single ready-made accounting management software.

- NDI-Intensive –NDI-Intensive system is a system where 30 - 90% of end-user functionality is provided by NDI [4]. A great deal of attention goes into appraising the functionality and interoperability of NDI, effort spent on NDI tailoring and Integration, and NDI upgrade synchronization and evolution [14]. For example, a website development project that majority of the functionalities are provided by one or more read-made software, but needs additional custom coding, tailoring or glue coding.
- Services-Intensive –Net Centric Services support community service organizations in their online information processing services such as donation, communication or their special interest group activities such as discussion boards, file sharing, and cloud computing. Similar to NDI-Intensive, the focus goes to appraising the functionality of the available services and tailoring to meet needs. For example, a website development project that some functionalities are provided by other online services and may need additional custom coding, tailoring or glue coding.

The proposed four process patterns of software development processes in ICM are developed by combining strengths from several development processes. The Architected Agile case balances a plan-driven approach in building up the steady architecture and an agile-driven approach in iterative incremental and frequent delivery as practice in Scrum [16] or Agile Unified Process [3]. The Software Engineering Institute (SEI) CMMI-COTS [17] and USC-CSSE COTS-Based Development (CBD) Guidelines [8] provide strong foundations for Use Single NDI, NDI-Intensive or COTS-Based systems (CBS). Regarding Services-Intensive, most of the processes, including CMMI-SVC [6], cover only the process of how to develop and maintain web services. None of them are able to pick, choose and use available online services.

Although the Services-Intensive case is similar to the NDI-intensive case, we found that the differences between NDI and NCS shown in Table 1 below make the CBD guidelines an imperfect fit with a Services-Based development process.

Table 2 summarizes the overview characteristics of rapid fielding projects in each process pattern. As shown in Fig. 2, different risk patterns for each project yields different software processes. For example, in the second case, when in the Exploration phase, the developers spend a good amount of effort to explore and find a perfect NDI that satisfied all the win conditions, the development team could skip the Valuation and Foundations phase. In the third and the fourth case, if the development team found possible NDIs/NCSs in the Exploration phase, the team could spend more effort evaluating the NDIs/NCSs, prioritizing their win-conditions or constraints. On the other hand, since NDIs/NCSs will provide a majority of the end product features, the development team could spend less time in Foundations and Development-related efforts. But NDI and NCS have different risk patterns; hence they need different process to follow.

Table 1. Differences between NDI and Net-Centric Services

Category	Non-Developmental Item [includes open source, customer-furnished software]	Net-Centric Services
Payment	• Some tools have no monetary cost • Expensive initial costs, moderate recurring fee, training fee, licensing arrangement-dependent	• Free/ pay per transaction • Low initial costs, moderate marginal cost, duration depending license
Platform	• Specific/ limited to specific platform • Generally supported on a subset of platforms or multiple platforms but with different editions	• Platform and language independent; • Server /client can be on different platform • Machines Interaction over a network
Integration	• Generally more tightly coupled • Not very flexible on existing legacy systems when proprietary standard • Difficult when platform dependent and different technologies involved in it. • detailed documentation and on-site extensive support	• Generally more loosely coupled • Common web standards • Requires internet access • Support forums /API documentation • Integration could be done merely in code, without additional installation of external component
Changes	• Version freezable, under user control • Designed for specific use so costly for customization and change • Change on server side doesn't impact the client side • Major releases once in a while • Requires end user intervention to upgrade	• Out of developers/users' control • Not easy to predict change • End-user has the latest version Change on the server side can result in the client side • Minor releases frequently (through patching) • Does not require end user intervention
Extensions	• Only if source is provided and the license permits • Extension must be delivered to and performed at the end-user's site • Custom extensions may not be compatible with future releases	• Extension is limited to data provided by the web services • In-house extension such as wrapper or mashup • Little control over performance overhead
Evaluation Criteria	• Cost, size, extensibility, scalability, reliability, dependency, support, maintainability, upgrades, access to source, code-escrow considerations • Upfront costs opposed to subscription • Platform compatibility; Feature controllability	• Cost, reliability, speed, support availability, predicted longevity of the service provider, bandwidth • Recurring costs to use of the service and future functionality offered • Standards compatibility; Feature- data controllability
Support Services	• Support sometimes available for a fee • Help topics or FAQs would likely not be updated after installation • Upgrades/ data migration support • Can be customized for specific user • Upgrade through purchasing new releases, self-install	• Support generally not available • Help topics frequently updated; self-learning • Usually not customized • Patching on service provider's side; mostly not require installation on client side
Data	• Data often stored locally. • Backups: responsibility of the user • Data access is generally fast • Possible variety of proprietary formats • May be inflexible but more secure • Platform-dependent data format • Can process data offline	• Data stored on host's servers. • Backups by provider • Data access could be slower • Common XML standard • Data from different web services can be used by a single client program • Process data online

Table 2. Characteristics of the Rapid-Fielding Process Patterns

Process patterns	**Architected Agile**	**Use Single NDI**	**NDI- intensive**	**Services-intensive**
Example	Business data processing	Small accounting	Supply chain management	Community Services
Size, Complexity	Med		Med-High	Low-Med
Change Rate (%/Month)	1-10		0.3-3	0.3-3
Criticality	Med-High		Med-Very High	Low-Med
NDI Support	Good; most in place	Complete	NDI-driven architecture	Tailorable service elements
Organizational and Personnel Capability	Agile-ready Med-high		NDIexperienced; med-high	NDI- experienced
Time/Build; Time/Increment	2-4 wks; 2-6 months		SW:1-4 wks; Systems: 6-18 mos	<= 1 day; 6-12 months

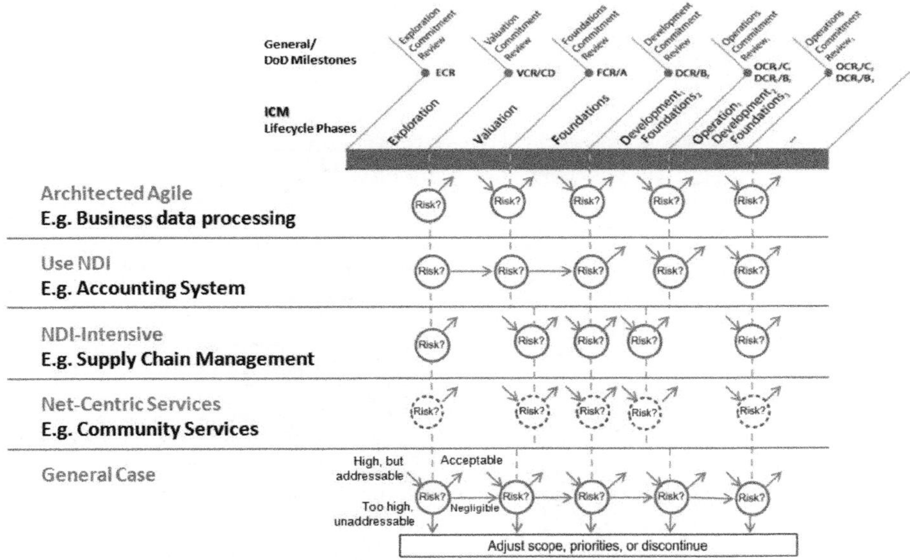

Fig. 2. Different Risk Patterns yield Different Processes

2.3 USC Software Engineering Course

In the keystone two-semester team project graduate software engineering course sequence CS577ab [5] at USC, students learn through experience how to use good software engineering practices to develop software systems from the Exploration Phase to the Operation Phase, all within a 24-week schedule. Six on-campus and two off-campus students team up to develop real-client software system products. All teams will follow the ICM Exploration Phase guidelines to determine their most appropriate process pattern. Most of the clients are neighborhood non-profit organizations, small businesses or USC departments. Because of the semester break between

Fall and Spring semester, for the Software Engineering class, we added a short Rebaselined Foundations phase to accommodate the possible changes.

3 Rapid-Fielding Process Guidelines

3.1 The Incremental Commitment Model for Rapid Fielding Projects

As shown in Fig. 4, a rapid fielding project starts by identifying the objectives, constraints and priorities (OC&P) and exploring all possible software development alternatives. If there is no relevant NCS or NDI that would satisfy the OC&Ps and OC&Ps cannot be adjusted, then this project will proceed to follow the Architected Agile process. The first three phases will be focused on building a change-prescient architecture and user/developer/customer team building. In the development phase and

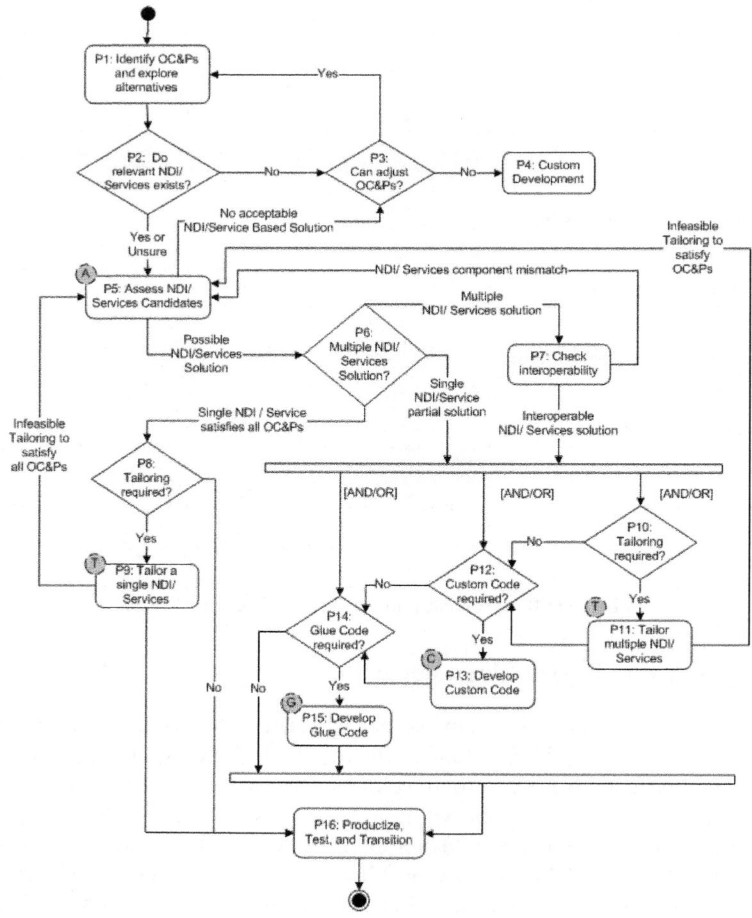

Fig. 3. Overall process for Rapid-Fielding Projects

operation phase, with the agile techniques, the developers welcome and manage change through a product backlog, planning capabilities for multiple future increments, based on stakeholder priorities.

On the other hand, if there are possible NDI/NCSs that satisfy the project's OC&Ps, the project will proceed with either Use Single NDI, Services-Intensive, or NDI-Intensive process pattern. In the Exploration and Valuation phase, spend a good amount of time in assessing NDI/NCS candidates. If multiple candidates are required, one needs to analyze their interoperability. When the selected NDI/NCS provides full or partial functionalities, the foundations phase could be skipped or shorten. In the development phase, perform custom coding, tailoring or glue coding as required.

For all rapid-fielding projects, synchronization and stabilization are required for each and between development cycles. Continuous verification and validation is also required for quality assessments.

3.2 The Incremental Commitment Model – Electronic Process Guide (ICM EPG)

Having properly-defined software process models is essential, but the ability to effectively communicate those models to the software engineers is also important. For Software Engineering class at USC, we have been using the IBM Rational Method Composer (RMC) to develop an Electronic Process Guide (EPG) for the ICM. The ICM EPG enables process users/ students to understand the overall process as well as specific areas of focus. The ICM EPG as shown in Fig. 4, describes the software development process by providing guidance in multiple-view representations, which are role-based representation, activity-based representation, chronological event-based representation, and artifact-based representation. Moreover, additional artifact templates and supplementary guides

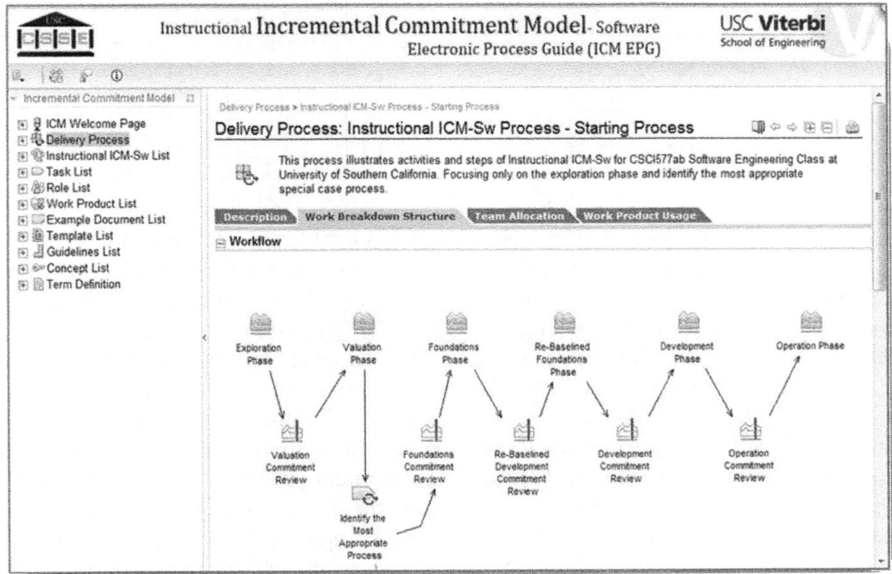

Fig. 4. An Example Screenshot of the ICM EPG

have been demonstrated to speed up the users' learning curve and support them in their development process [18,19].

3.3 Process Decision Drivers

In order to select the appropriate process pattern, the development team will use the 16 decision drivers presented in Table 3 to evaluate the project status and map it with the possible maximum-minimum boundary range of each possible process pattern. The "Importance" attribute, whose values are 1-Low, 2-Medium, 3-High, will act as a tie breaker to support decision making in selecting the best fit process pattern. The value of project status ranges from 0-Very Low to 4-Very High.

Table 3. Process Decision Drivers

Decision Criteria	Importance	Architected Agile	Use NDI	NDI-Intensive	Services-Intensive
Alternatives					
More than 30% of features available in NDI/NCS		0 – 1	2 – 3	3 – 4	3 – 4
Has a single NDI/NCS that satisfies a complete solution		0 – 1	4	2 – 3	2 – 3
Very unique/ inflexible business process		2 – 4	0 – 1	0 – 1	0 – 1
Life Cycle					
Need control over upgrade / maintenance		2 – 4	0 – 1	0 – 1	0 – 1
Rapid Deployment; Faster time to market		0 – 1	4	2 - 4	2 – 3
Architecture					
Critical on compatibility		2 – 4	3 – 4	1 – 3	2 – 4
Internet Connection Independence		0 – 4	0 – 4	0 – 4	0
Need high level of services / performance		0 – 4	0 – 3	0 – 3	0 – 2
Need high security		2 – 4	0 - 4	0 – 4	0 – 2
Asynchronous Communication		0 – 4	0 – 4	0 – 4	0
Access Data anywhere		0 – 4	0 – 4	0 – 4	4
Resources					
Critical mass schedule constraints		0 – 1	3 – 4	2 – 3	2 – 4
Lack of Personnel Capability		0 – 2	3 – 4	2 – 4	2 – 3
Little to no upfront costs (hardware and software)		0 – 2	2 – 4	2 – 4	3 – 4
Low total cost of ownership		0 – 1	0 – 3	0 – 3	2 – 4
Not-so-powerful local machines		1 – 4	1 – 3	0 – 4	3 – 4

Fig. 5 shows an example of a website development team. The team found a possible content management system NDI, but it does not satisfy all of the capability win conditions. The team rates the project status based on 16 decision drivers, the result is shown in the blue line. The background block diagram is the max-min boundary of NDI-Intensive project defined in Table 3. The red underline represents High Importance level, while green dashed underline represents Low Importance level.

When the blue point lies on gray box, it shows that the project status conform to the process pattern on that driver. As a result, the decision driver shows that this team could follow the NDI-intensive software development process. On the other hand, as shown in Fig. 6, if we plot the project status on the Architected Agile process pattern, 8 non-conforming points are found. As a result, comparing Fig. 5and Fig. 6, there are less non-conforming points on Fig. 5, so that means this project would fit more to the NDI-Intensive process pattern.

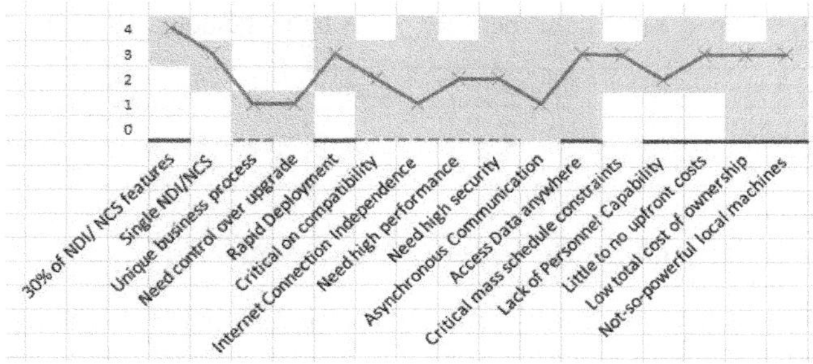

Fig. 5. An example of using decision drivers to map project status with the NDI-Intensive process pattern

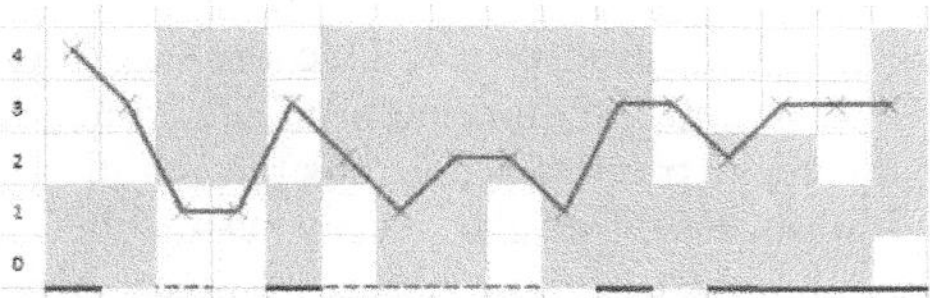

Fig. 6. An example of using decision drivers to map project status with the Architected Agile process pattern

4 Preliminary Results

In Fall 2009, Software Engineering students at USC have used the ICM EPG to guide their rapid-fielding software development projects. Once the students form their teams and select the projects, teams will follow the ICM Exploration phase process to determine their most appropriate process patterns. 28% of projects are able to deliver in one semester, instead of two semesters comparing to 12.5% from previous year. Clients are highly satisfied with the project results.

4.1 Preliminary Results on the ICM EPG

With the data from effort reporting system, Table 4 shows that with the ICM EPG, process users and developers spent less time in learning about the process and with the help of templates and supporting documents, they saved more than 20 hours per person in documentation effort.

The result of our experiment also shows that the EPG is very effective in terms of communicating the process model to the developers. With the role-oriented process information and rich set of notations such as process element icons and graphical representations, process users and developers found that it is easy for them to learn about their roles, responsibilities, activities, and functionalities. For the process engineers, IBM Rational Method Composer (RMC) supports process reuse, tailoring and configuration. The ICM EPG can be extended to support process management because RMC is fully interoperable with various project management tools.

Table 4. Comparison of effort between paper-based guidelines and the ICM EPG

Guidelines \ Average Effort (hours)	Learning	Documentation	Total Effort
Paper-based process guidelines	15.2	69.2	209.57
ICM EPG	11.9	46.6	175.8

4.2 Preliminary Results on the Process Decision Drivers

Comparing the result of the teams' process selection by using process decision drivers with the experts' opinion from the architecture review board, 8 out of 14 teams selected the right process pattern from beginning of the valuation phase. Three out of 14 teams selected wrong process pattern because of unclear project scope, but the teams followed the right process after further exploration, more prototyping or found available NCS/NDI. Two out of 14 teams faced the minor changes, so they have to change the process by the end of Valuation phase. One project followed the right process pattern but found that the client's requirement is infeasible within a defined budget and schedule, hence the team proposed the feasible solution and had to switch the process 3 times. In addition, based on the survey result, the process decision drivers help the teams to select the most suitable process pattern. Moreover, when the scope or status of the project changes, the development teams found it useful to reconfirm or to re-identify the process pattern with the process decision drivers.

4.3 Limitations

This section discusses possible validity threats and ways in which the threats could be reduced.

- Inconsistent Effort Reporting: It is possible that there might be inaccurate efforts reported, so 2 forms of effort reporting will be used.
- Non-representativeness of subjects: On-Campus students might not represent software engineers in the industry. However, the clients and off-campus students are full-time working professionals.
- Learning Curve: Providing tutorials and discussion sessions in order to build the foundations for all participants.
- Non-representativeness of projects: Although conforming to fixed semester schedules, this is to some degree representative of fixed-schedule industry projects. The projects are small e-services applications, but are developed for real clients, and used the same NDI/NCS. Moreover, the process guidelines and decision drivers are cross checked with experts in the field for enterprise-level compatibility.

5 Conclusions and Future Work

The growing diversity of software systems and the wide variety of current technologies provide us new opportunities for rapid-fielding strategy. The Incremental Commitment Model (ICM) is the most thoroughly elaborated process model with specific evidence-based and risk-based decision points. Architected Agile, Use Single NDI, NDI-intensive, and Services-intensive are four common ICM process patterns in rapid-fielding project. Four process guidelines are developed in the form of the ICM EPG. The result of the experiment shows that, at least for small, real-client e-services project, the EPG is very effective in terms of communicating and learning the process model and speeding up the development process. The process pattern decision drivers help the development teams produce a viable process decision very early in the life cycle process with faster time to market and high customer satisfaction. Continuing efforts are underway to evaluate the efficacy of the ICM by analyzing risk patterns, incidence of direction changes at reviews relative to outcomes and team performance based on team grading and compare to previous years data.

References

1. Pew, R.W., Mavor, A.S.: Human-System Integration in the System Development Process: A New Look. National Academy Press, Washington (2007)
2. Boehm, B., Lane, J., Koolmanojwong, S.: A Risk-Driven Process Decision Table to Guide System Development Rigor. In: Proceedings of the 19th International Conference on Systems Engineering, Singapore (July 2009)
3. Agile, Principles behind the agile manifesto, `http://agilemanifesto.org/principles.html`
4. Yang, Y.: Composable Risk-Driven Processes for Developing Software Systems from Commercial-Off-The-Shelf (COTS) Products: PhD Dissertation, Department of Computer Science, University of Southern California (December 2006)
5. USC CSCI577ab Software Engineering Course, `http://greenbay.usc.edu/csci577/fall2009/site/index.html`
6. CMMI for Services Version1.2, `ftp://ftp.sei.cmu.edu/pub/documents/09.reports/09tr001.doc`
7. ProgrammableWeb, `http://www.programmableweb.com/mashups` (accessed on 11/9/2009)
8. Yang, Y., Boehm, B.: COTS-Based Development Process guidelines, `http://greenbay.usc.edu/csci577/spring2007/site/guidelines/CBA-AssessmentIntensive.pdf` (accessed 08/24/07)
9. Bhuta, J.: A Framework for Intelligent Assessment and Resolution of Commercial-Off-The-Shelf Product Incompatibilities, PhD Dissertation, Department of Computer Science, University of Southern California (August 2007)
10. V-Model Lifecycle Process Model, `http://www.v-modell.iabg.de/kurzb/vm/k_vm_e.doc` (accessed on 10/9/2009)
11. Boehm, B.: A Spiral Model of Software Development and Enhancement. IEEE Computer 21(5), 61–72 (1988)
12. Boehm, B.: Anchoring the Software Process. IEEE Software 13(4), 73–82 (1996)
13. Boehm, B., Turner, R.: Balancing agility and discipline: a guide for the perplexed. Addison-Wesley, Boston (2004)
14. Li, J., Bjoernson, F.O., Conradi, R., Kampenes, V.B.: An empirical study of variations in COTS-Based Software Development Processes in Norwegian IT industry. Journal of Empirical Software Engineering 11(3), 433–461 (2006)
15. Boehm, B., Lane, J., Koolmanojwong, S.: A Risk-Driven Process Decision Table to Guide System Development Rigor. In: Proceedings of the 19th International Conference on Software Engineering, Singapore (July 2009)

16. Rising, L., Janoff, N.: The Scrum Software Development Process for Small Teams. IEEE Software (July/August 2000)
17. CMMI for COTS-based Systems, `http://www.sei.cmu.edu/publications/documents/03.reports/03tr022.html`
18. Koolmanojwong, S., et al.: Comparative Experiences with Software Process Modeling Tools for the Incremental Commitment Model, In: USC CSSE Technical Report 2007-824
19. Phongpaibul, M., Koolmanojwong, S., Lam, A., Boehm, B.: Comparative Experiences with Electronic Process Guide Generator Tools. In: Wang, Q., Pfahl, D., Raffo, D.M. (eds.) ICSP 2007. LNCS, vol. 4470, pp. 61–72. Springer, Heidelberg (2007)

A Repository of Agile Method Fragments

Hesam Chiniforooshan Esfahani[1] and Eric Yu[2]

[1] Department of Computer Science
[2] Faculty of Information
University of Toronto
hesam@cs.toronto.edu, yu@ischool.utoronto.ca

Abstract. Despite the prevalence of agile methods, few software companies adopt a prescribed agile process in its entirety. For many practitioners, agile software development is about picking up fragments from various agile methods, assembling them as a light-weight process, and deploying them in their software projects. Given the growing number of published empirical studies about using agile in different project situations, it is now possible to gain a more realistic view of what each agile method fragment can accomplish, and the necessary requisites for its successful deployment. With the aim of making this knowledge more accessible, this paper introduces a repository of agile method fragments, which organizes the evidential knowledge according to their objectives and requisites. The knowledge is gathered through systematic review of empirical studies which investigated the enactment of agile methods in various project situations. In addition, the paper proposes a modeling paradigm for visualizing the stored knowledge of method fragments, to facilitate the subsequent assembly task.

Keywords: Agile Methods, Evidence-Based Software Engineering, Software Process Engineering, Process Modeling, Goal-Oriented Analysis and Modeling.

1 Introduction

In recent years, agile methods for software development have seen widespread adoption and experimentation. Agile methods are appealing partly due to their inherent characteristics such as simplicity, and partly due to problems with traditional methods [1, 2]. The prevalence of agile methods has provided a suitable test-bed for software researchers, to run empirical studies, and analyze different aspects of agile methods in real trials. Every year, a considerable number of empirical studies emerge, each addressing specific concerns of deploying agile methods in various projects/organizations. These studies, which mostly take macro-process view to the research of agile processes [3], form a large body of knowledge about various fragments (constituent pieces) of agile methods. For instance, a simple title-based search in just the IEEE Explorer for "Pair Programming" returns over 50 results, mostly reporting on empirical studies.

Despite the abundance of empirical data for agile methods, there is no systematic support to take advantages of that knowledge, to make it more usable and accessible. This issue becomes more serious when we consider the way that software industry

J. Münch, Y. Yang, and W. Schäfer (Eds.): ICSP 2010, LNCS 6195, pp. 163–174, 2010.

deploys agile methods. For many project managers agile software development means to deploy a number of agile method fragments, and then try as hard as possible to get the works done. Based on a recent survey, around 60% of software companies do not follow any particular method, and just deploy some techniques and tools introduced by different methods [4]. This approach exposes a software company to the risk of adopting inappropriate development methods, which is a serious threat to the success of software projects [5]. Most likely, the complicated solutions of process (or method) engineering would not be acknowledged by many agile software companies. But, a promising solution can be a one that facilitates their access to the experience of other practitioners in using different agile method fragments, and helps them decide on the appropriateness of their own process.

This paper introduces a structured repository of agile method fragments (AMFs). For each AMF, the repository entry states the objectives that the AMF aims to contribute to, and a set of requisites that are needed for its success. The knowledge of this repository has been gathered through systematic review [6] of empirical studies on agile methods, i.e., the objectives and requisites of each AMF have been synthesized by reviewing results from experiments or reported experiences, not from the motivational description of an agile method. The repository is evidence-based, as it provides contextual evidences from empirical studies, which explain situations in which a particular objective or requisite of an AMF had been met or not. In addition, this repository offers a visualization of AMF data, using a goal-oriented notation.

Taking the evidence-based approach for populating this repository helped us to present some interesting results about the contextual aspects of AMFs. There exist numerous reports that studied the impact of different project contexts on the success or failure of AMFs. For instance, this repository contains project contexts in which Pair Programming (as a sample AMF) either helped or impeded a project to be on-time to market. The evidential knowledge of this repository can be useful for project managers, in order to come up with more appropriate sets of method fragments for their particular projects/organizations. It can also facilitate the introduction of a new agile method to an organization, and the reuse of its prior successful and unsuccessful experiences. The repository is being tested at a major telecom company in a software process improvement initiative.

2 Related Work

A number of process engineering frameworks include method repositories as components. For instance, the Open Process Framework (OPF) [7] is a process (method) engineering framework, which contains a repository of method fragments. Similarly, the Eclipse Process Framework (EPF) [8] is an Eclipse-based process engineering tool, which also provides a number of libraries for some well-known methodologies, e.g., RUP and Scrum. These repositories are mainly aimed at describing the constituting elements of a methodology by breaking it down to a number of fragments, and then describing each method fragment in terms of its type, functionality, needed skills, relevant roles, etc. However, these repositories are not concerned about presenting actual evidences about the success or failure of various method fragments under different project situations.

Evidence-Based Software Engineering (EBSE) has been introduced to take advantage of practitioners' experience with using different tools and techniques of software engineering [9]. One of basic approaches of EBSE is *Systematic Review*, whose goal is to gather results from different empirical studies, and through analysis and synthesis of extracted data, draw reasonable conclusions [6]. Given the growing number of empirical studies about agile software development methods, systematic review can be a proper approach for building a repository of agile method fragments including pragmatic evidences from experiences and experiments. This approach has been used for agile methods, e.g., in the Software Engineering Evidence Database (SEED) [10], although the presented knowledge was not systematically analyzed.

This paper follows the definition of method fragment as defined in [11], which considers an AMF as a piece of an agile software development method, and classifies method fragments into two categories: *Process Fragments* and *Product Fragments*. For instance, "Pair Programming" is an AMF of the XP methodology, which is a process fragment, while "Sprint Backlog" is a product fragment of Scrum.

3 Research Method

The research method of this study is the systematic review [6] of published literature on empirical studies of agile methods. First, to clarify the objective of systematic review, we specified our research questions. Then, we set up a review protocol that specified the criteria of study selection, the strategy of data extraction, and the approach of analyzing and aggregating the extracted data, and synthesizing the results. The final stage of systematic review is the reporting of results, which we publish in textual table format and as graphical models.

3.1 Research Questions

Systematic reviews should be targeted towards clear research questions [6, 9]. In this research we were looking for answers to the following questions:

1. What are the actual beneficial outcomes achieved by an agile method fragment? These will be treated as *objectives* in the repository entry so that fragments can be retrieved according to desired outcomes. The description of a method fragment typically comes with promises about its benefits, in terms of quality goals that it contributes to. For instance, "enhanced quality of communication" is one of the major promises of many agile method fragments. But, is that really the case? Is there any evidence for this claim? Do method fragments always contribute positively to their objectives, or can they produce adverse contributions under specific situations?
2. What unanticipated side-effects have been discovered when the method fragment was put to use under different conditions? These issues will be treated as objectives to which a method fragment negatively contributes. For instance, Pair Programming (PP) can result in the reduction of Lines-of-Code (LOC) per programmer per month. Thus, PP makes a negative contribution to the productivity of individuals (with respect to the LOC factor). In this research we are looking to identify such side-effects, as well as evidences for their appearance in empirical studies.

3. What are the necessary conditions for the method fragment to be used successfully? These will be treated as requisites in the repository entry of each AMF. The description of every method fragment typically suggests a number of requisites for its successful enactment. However, these requisites might not be attainable or necessary in all project situations. For instance, "equal engagement of pair in programming" is one of the requisites of "Pair Programming". But, is it always attainable? In what situations is this requisite most likely to be denied? Furthermore, empirical experience with an AMF may have revealed additional requisites.

Here, we stress the importance of finding actual evidences for the claimed objectives and requisites of AMFs. Such evidences will improve the reliability of the repository, provided that they correctly represent the situation of source evidences. Thus, we had to carefully consider those particular aspects of the reviewed empirical studies (project/organizational factors), which could impact the enactment of their AMFs. Following this approach, the final repository will contain a considerable amount of situational experiences of AMFs, which can be used in process improvement initiatives.

3.2 Study Selection

We started the research by selecting 20 agile method fragments for consideration. For each method fragment we looked up published empirical studies that explained the enactment of that method fragment in a particular project/organization. We searched the major collections of computer science publications, including IEEE Explorer, ScienceDirect, SpringerLink, and ACM Digital Library. We used search queries that contained the name of the method fragment, the name of the originating agile method, and some phrases for retrieving empirical studies, such as: Case study, Experiment Report, Ethnography, or Survey.

In addition to published empirical studies in academic journals and conferences, we also considered articles from agile web forums as complementary sources for our reviewed empirical studies. Every selected paper or article was then evaluated with respect to the following items: 1- reliability of reported data; 2- reproducibility of study; 3- relevance to the research questions; 4- quality of situation description (context for enacting AMF). Only publications that meet all of the above criteria are used as sources, and are listed as references.

3.3 Data Extraction

While reviewing the selected empirical studies, we were looking for either explicit or implicit answers to our research questions. For data extraction, we obtained answers for the following questions for every reviewed paper:

- What is the type of this empirical study? (Controlled Experiment, Survey, Interview, Experience report, Ethnography, Case Study)
- What agile method fragments have been investigated in this study?
- What are the distinguishing characteristics of the context of this study? (Human/organization factors, such as cultural issues, structure of development teams, and the distribution of expertise; project related factors, such as complexity and market pressure)

- Does the paper describe the benefits/side-effects of deploying an agile method fragment in terms of impacting some method objectives? If yes, what are those objectives? How are they impacted, i.e., did the method fragment help to attain those objectives, or had the opposite effect?
- Does the paper highlight any situational factor that particularly impacted the enactment of method fragment? If yes, what are those factors? How do they influence the enactment of method fragment (improving or impeding)?

We did not begin the systematic review with a preconceived list of objectives or requisites, since one of the purposes of the research was to identify the evidential objectives and requisites of AMFs. However, after reviewing and analyzing a number of publications for each AMF, such lists began to emerge. Afterwards, we were considering those lists while reviewing a paper, and also reread some of the initially reviewed papers.

3.4 Data Analysis and Aggregation

The extracted data from reviewed empirical studies were then analyzed and aggregated as units of knowledge for every method fragment. Data analysis was performed in order to:

- Clarify the contributions of method fragments to objectives. The contribution relations were represented qualitatively, using a five-value scale (--, -, ?, +, ++). Negative contributions represent the cases where a method fragment was reported to strongly deny (--) or somewhat deny (-) an objective; unaffecting contributions (?) represent cases where an study reported that an AMF does not have any significant contribution to a particular objective; and positive ones represent the cases where a method fragment was reported to strongly satisfy (++) or somewhat satisfy (+) a quality objective.
- Resolve the naming problems that were due to synonyms or homonyms. Empirical studies use different terms and taxonomies to describe process objectives. We analyzed the extracted data to harmonize the various terminologies of reviewed studies. Table 4 shows a subset of a harmonized taxonomy of AMF objectives.
- Classify the method objectives and requisites into two-level categories. The extracted objectives (or requisite) were classified either as major or minor categories. Minor categories are considered as subcategories of major ones, and represent more delicate aspects of a major quality objective (or requisite). Although the objectives and requisites of a method fragment can be detailed with further levels of refinement, for the sake of simplicity, we consider only two levels for the current design of the repository. **Table 2** and Table 3 show two examples of this categorization.

The analyzed data were then aggregated with what had been collected previously. The knowledge of each method fragment was aggregated in two tables, one for its objectives and the other for its requisites. Data aggregation for an AMF was either in the form of adding a new objective or requisite; or providing a new piece of evidence for an existing contribution relation. The final stage of data aggregation was to make generic snapshots, which are two dimensional tables that show the identified (and unidentified) relations of all method fragments to all objectives or requisites. Generic snapshots facilitate the comparison of method fragments, and provide insights for further empirical studies to uncover the potential relations between agile method fragments and process objectives or requisites. Table 4 shows a sample generic snapshot.

3.5 Data Visualization

An appropriate modeling paradigm for visualizing the collected data of this study should be capable of representing method objectives and requisites, also the contribution relations of AMFs to their objectives and their dependency relations to their requisites. These features have been well-addressed in Goal-Oriented Requirements Engineering (GORE), where goal models are used to express how domain objects (such as activities and resources) contribute to domain goals [12]. In this research we use the *i** goal-oriented modeling framework for visualizing the collected knowledge of AMFs. Table 1 describes a subset of *i** modeling elements, which are used for visualizing the objectives and requisites of method fragments. Fig. 1 shows an example of AMF visualization. Further description of our approach in modeling method fragments, and their application in process engineering are presented in [13].

Table 1. The use of *i** modeling notation for visualizing method fragments

i* Modeling Element	Description	*i** Graphical Notation
Task	Represents the enactment of an AMF	Deploy Pair Programming
Softgoal	Represents an AMF objective or a requisite	Increased Productivity
Contribution Relation	Visualizes the contribution relation of an AMF to its objectives	Some +
Decomposition Relation	Visualizes the dependency relation of an AMF to its requisites	

4 Results

As mentioned before, the results of data extraction and analysis for each agile method fragment are aggregated into an objectives table and a requisites table. Due to space limits, we cannot present the results of our study for all of the reviewed method fragments. As an example, this section presents a subset of the knowledge for two AMFs: "Pair Programming" and "Daily Scrum Meeting". The complete set of tables are publicly accessible at: http://www.cs.utoronto.ca/km/MFR/MF.htm.

4.1 Agile Method Fragments: Objectives

Table 2 shows a subset of the objectives of the agile method fragment "Pair Programming" (PP). It presents different types of contributions that PP might make to its objectives, along with references to the empirical studies which have investigated these issues. The situations in which the stated contributions had occurred are briefly described. For instance, it shows that Pair Programming, in general cases (represented as "In General"), contributes strongly and positively to the objective "Reduced Defects in Code". It also provides evidence from a controlled experiment, which qualifies this contribution with more specific situational information (complex system with junior developers).

Table 2. A subset of major and minor objectives of "Pair Programming", along with situational evidences for contributions that this AMF can make towards them

Major Objective	Minor Objective	Contribution	Study	Situation
Improved Effectiveness	Increased productivity (LOC/Month/developer)	+	[14, 15]	Pairs with heterogeneous personality profile
		--	[16, 17]	Pairing Professional Developers, or developers similar expertise
	Improved Design Quality	++	[18-20]	In General
	Improved Creativity	+	[20, 21]	In General
	Reduced Defects in Code (Better Correctness)	++	[16, 18-20]	In General
		++	[22]	Complex Systems, Junior Developers
	Faster Problem Solving	+	[18, 23, 24]	In General
		+	[22]	Simple Systems, intermediate or senior developers
	Be on-time to market	+	[23]	In General
		-	[23]	Large project, limited number of developers, market pressure

Objectives of a method fragment can be classified into two categories. The first category are those to which the method fragment makes situation-independent contributions, i.e., the change of context does not change the contribution type. For example, in all of the reviewed empirical studies, Pair Programming is reported to have a positive contribution to the objective "Faster Problem Solving". The second category is for objectives to which the contribution of method fragment is situation-dependent, i.e., a change in context can alter the type of contribution. For instance, the default contribution of "Pair Programming" to the objective "Be on-time to market" is positive, but [23] reports that Pair Programming in the context of a large project with limited number of developers and high market pressure can contribute negatively to that objective. It should be noted that Table 2 and 3 only list subsets of the empirical studies that we reviewed for the AMFs, for lack of space.

4.2 Agile Method Fragments: Requisites

As an example of evidential knowledge about requisites, Table 3 shows a subset of major and minor requisites of the agile method fragment "Daily Scrum Meeting".

For each requisite, the table presents a number of empirical studies which had reported the impact of that requisite on the success or failure of daily scrum meetings. This table briefly describes the significant situational factors of the referenced studies, and mentions the achievement (or denial) status of requisites in those situations. The achievement status of requisites is specified either as: Denied (D), Partly Denied (PD), Partly Satisfied (PS), or Satisfied (S).

Table 3. A subset of major and minor requisites of "Daily Scrum Meeting", and their achievement status in a number of referenced empirical studies

<table>
<tr><th>Major Req.</th><th>Minor Requisite</th><th>Achiev. Status</th><th>Study</th><th>Situation</th></tr>
<tr><td rowspan="7">Meeting Be effective</td><td>Skilled Leadership</td><td>PD</td><td>[25, 26]</td><td>Scrum Master failure in organizing meetings and running them quickly</td></tr>
<tr><td>Real time Information Passing</td><td>D</td><td>[27] [28]</td><td>Distributed Development : Different time zones</td></tr>
<tr><td>High quality of communication</td><td>PD</td><td>[27]</td><td>Distributed Development : Different Languages</td></tr>
<tr><td rowspan="3">High quality of collaboration</td><td>PD</td><td>[29, 30]</td><td>Managers/developers gap</td></tr>
<tr><td>PD</td><td>[29, 30]</td><td>Culture of Individual Working or Lack of team-ware attitude</td></tr>
<tr><td>PD</td><td>[30]</td><td>Tendency to waterfall development, formal meetings</td></tr>
<tr><td>everyone be committed to attend the meetings</td><td>PD</td><td>[5, 31]</td><td>Professional developers, meetings seem superficial</td></tr>
</table>

4.3 Agile Method Fragments: Visualization

Figure 1 shows a sample visualization of an agile method fragment. It depicts some of the objectives to which pair programming contributes. For instance, it shows that pair programming makes a positive (+) contribution to the objective "Better Time to Market". We used four types of contribution relations (adopted from i* framework), in order to represent the contribution of an AMF to its objectives: "+" representing positive contributions; "++" representing strong positive contributions; "-" representing negative contributions; and "--" representing strong negative contributions. Fig. 1 also shows the dependency of the AMF pair programming on some of its requisites, e.g., "Effective Collaboration of Pairs".

4.4 Agile Method Fragments: Generic Snapshots

One of the results of this study is a set of generic snapshots, which summarizes the relations of all (or several) AMFs to all (or several) of the identified objectives or requisites. These snapshots are called generic because they are not bound to any particular AMF, and typically represent a number of AMFs. For example, Table 4 shows

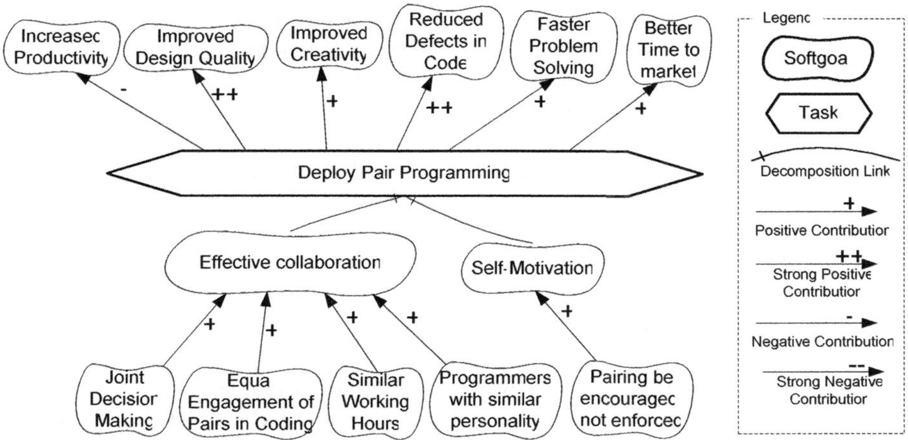

Fig. 1. Visualization of the agile method fragment "Pair Programming", for a subset of its objectives and requisites

Table 4. Generic snapshot: A list of minor objectives of five agile method fragments, all related to the major objective "Improved Efficiency", and the contributions of the AMFs to them

Major Objective	Minor Objective	Pair Prog.	Daily Scrum Meeting	Open Office Space	On-site Customer	Time-Boxing + MoSCoW
Improved Effectiveness	Increased productivity (LOC/Month/developer)	--				
	Reduced Development Cost	-, ?				
	Improved Design (product) Quality	++				-
	Improved Creativity Potential	+				
	Reduced Defects in Code	++, ?				
	Faster Problem Solving	+, ?		++		
	Be on-time to market	+, -				++
	Elimination of redundant tasks		++			
	Earlier Detection of Dev. issues		++			
	Reduced need for documentation			++	++, --	
	Be Focused on work			--		
	Balancing conflicts of customer needs and developer's expectations				++	
	Fast Resolving of requirement issues				++	
	Controlled Risks per Iteration					+

a list of minor objectives of five agile method fragments, all related to the major objective "Improved Efficiency". Due to space limits we could not present the contribution of other agile method fragments to these objectives, as well as other major objectives. The online version of the repository contains similar tables for other major objectives, e.g., "Improved Communication", "Improved Collaboration", "Higher Job Satisfaction", and so forth. Note that an empty cell in the table does not necessarily mean that there is no contribution relation between the corresponding agile method fragment and objective. Further investigations in the empirical studies of software processes might supply further contribution relations to the table.

5 Discussion and Future Work

So far the repository has been populated with the knowledge of 20 agile method fragments. The website for this repository is being regularly updated to reflect the latest findings of empirical software engineering about agile method fragments. The plan is to expand the repository to non-agile method fragments. Work has started to collect and analyze method fragments for requirements engineering, agile as well as non-agile.

We have planned to use the analyzed empirical data in the repository in different ways. In another work [13], we explained how to use the evidence-based repository in the context of method engineering. In that work we introduced a process evaluation technique, which takes the pre-constructed goal models and investigates the suitability of a set of AMFs for a particular project/organization. Once the repository is suitably populated, we plan to deploy its data in a number of industrial case studies, in order to first validate the evaluation algorithm proposed in [13], and explore a new approach of method engineering which is based on evidence from empirical research in software processes.

Another opportunity for using this repository is in software process improvement (SPI). In particular we are developing an Agile SPI technique, in which the structured knowledge of this repository about possible objectives of an AMF and its recommended requisites, along with pre-analyzed situational evidences, can facilitate the process of finding improvement points of an agile process in a given project/organization. We have started a trial of the Agile SPI technique in a large software organization, and hope to reach first results within the next few months.

The construction of this repository encountered a number of challenges. The first was the uneven availability of empirical results among AMFs. For instance, while there is plenty of empirical literature on "Pair Programming", there is little on "Domain Object Modeling", which is an AMF of Feature Driven Development (FDD). This issue has caused some of the studied AMFs to be weak in evidence support. The repository thus have the added benefit of revealing gaps in empirical research, prompting further studies to fill those gaps. The second problem was the correct codification of project situations. In some of the empirical studies the descriptions of project situation was not clear or too sketchy to be reliable for adding to the repository. In such cases we either disregarded the study, or tried to find the data that was directly related to the stated outcomes. Our third problem was the flip side of the first. For some AMFs there exists a huge number of empirical studies. We tried to cover as many as we could, and will add further data to the repository as more papers are reviewed.

Acknowledgements. Financial support from the Natural Sciences and Engineering Research Council of Canada is gratefully acknowledged.

References

1. Boehm, B., Turner, R.: Balancing Agility and Discipline, a Guide for the Perplexed. Addison-Wesley, Reading (2003)
2. Cohn, M., Ford, D.: Introducing an Agile Process to an Organization. Computer 36(6), 74–78 (2003)
3. Osterweil, L.: Unifying Microprocess and Macroprocess Research. In: Li, M., Boehm, B., Osterweil, L.J. (eds.) SPW 2005. LNCS, vol. 3840, pp. 68–74. Springer, Heidelberg (2006)
4. Bygstad, B., Ghinea, G., Brevik, E.: Software development methods and usability: Perspectives from a survey in the software industry in Norway. Interacting with Computers 20(3), 375–385 (2008)
5. Linda, R., Norman, S.J.: The Scrum Software Development Process for Small Teams. IEEE Softw. 17(4), 26–32 (2000)
6. Kitchenham, B.: Procedures for Performing Systematic Reviews, TR/SE-0401, Software Engineering Group, Department of Computer Science, Keele University (2004)
7. Firesmith, D.: Open Process Framework (OPF) (accessible via: date accessed: November 2009)
8. Epf. Eclipse Process Framework Project (EPF) (2006), `http://www.eclipse.org/epf/` (cited June 2009)
9. Kitchenham, B.A., Dyba, T., Jorgensen, M.: Evidence-Based Software Engineering. In: Proceedings of the 26th International Conference on Software Engineering. IEEE Computer Society, Los Alamitos (2004)
10. Janzen, D.: SEED: Software Engineering Evidence Database, accessible via: `http://evidencebasedse.com/` (date accessed: January 2010)
11. Brinkkemper, S.: Method engineering: engineering of information systems development methods and tools. Information and Software Technology 38(4), 275–280 (1996)
12. Yu, E.S.K.: Towards modelling and reasoning support for early-phase requirements engineering. In: Proceedings of the Third IEEE International Symposium on Requirements Engineering. IEEE Computer Society, Los Alamitos (1997)
13. Chiniforooshan Esfahani, H., Yu, E.: Situational Evaluation of Method Fragments: An Evidence-Based Goal-Oriented Approach. Submitted to Conference on Advanced Information Systems Engineering, CAiSE 2010 (2010)
14. Sfetsos, P., Stamelos, I., Angelis, L., Deligiannis, I.: An experimental investigation of personality types impact on pair effectiveness in pair programming. Empirical Software Engineering 14(2), 187–226 (2009)
15. Choi, K.S., Deek, F.P., Im, I.: Exploring the underlying aspects of pair programming: The impact of personality. Information and Software Technology 50(11), 1114–1126 (2008)
16. Pikkarainen, M., Haikara, J., Salo, O., Abrahamsson, P., Still, J.: The impact of agile practices on communication in software development. Empirical Software Engineering 13(3), 303–337 (2008)
17. O'donnell, M.J., Richardson, I.: Problems Encountered When Implementing Agile Methods in a Very Small Company. In: Software Process Improvement, pp. 13–24. Springer, Heidelberg (2008)
18. Cockburn, A.: Selecting a project's methodology. IEEE Software 17(4), 64–71 (2000)

19. Williams, L., Mcdowell, C., Nagappan, N., Fernald, J., Werner, L.: Building pair programming knowledge through a family of experiments. In: Proceedings of 2003 International Symposium on Empirical Software Engineering. IEEE Press, Los Alamitos (2003)
20. Williams, L.: Integrating pair programming into a software development process. In: Proceedings of 14th Conference on Software Engineering Education and Training Charlotte. IEEE Computer Society, USA (2001)
21. Mujeeb-U-Rehman, M., Xiaohu, Y., Jinxiang, D., Abdul Ghafoor, M.: Heterogeneous and homogenous pairs in pair programming: an empirical analysis. In: Canadian Conference on Electrical and Computer Engineering. IEEE Press, Los Alamitos (2005)
22. Arisholm, E., Gallis, H., Dyba, T., Sjoberg, D.I.K.: Evaluating Pair Programming with Respect to System Complexity and Programmer Expertise. IEEE Transactions on Software Engineering 33(2), 65–86 (2007)
23. Padberg, F., Muller, M.M.: Analyzing the cost and benefit of pair programming. In: Proceedings of Ninth International Software Metrics Symposium. IEEE Press, Los Alamitos (2003)
24. Charles, P., Jan Willem, H.: Using Extreme Programming in a Maintenance Environment. IEEE Softw. 18(6), 42–50 (2001)
25. Begel, A., Nagappan, N.: Usage and Perceptions of Agile Software Development in an Industrial Context: An Exploratory Study. In: First International Symposium on Empirical Software Engineering and Measurement, ESEM 2007 (2007)
26. Judy, K.H., Krumins-Beens, I.: Great Scrums Need Great Product Owners: Unbounded Collaboration and Collective Product Ownership. In: Proceedings of the 41st Annual Hawaii International Conference on System Sciences (2008)
27. Sutherland, J., Viktorov, A., Blount, J., Puntikov, N.: Distributed Scrum: Agile Project Management with Outsourced Development Teams. In: 40th Annual Hawaii International Conference on System Sciences (2007)
28. Berczuk, S.: Back to Basics: The Role of Agile Principles in Success with an Distributed Scrum Team. Agile (2007)
29. Larman, C., Vodde, B.: Top Ten Organizational Impediments (2009)
30. Fredrick, C.: How Douglas County, CO Cut A Project Timeline In Half. Agile Journal (2007)
31. Lewis, J., Neher, K.: Over the Waterfall in a Barrel - MSIT Adventures in Scrum. IEEE Publications, Agile (2007)

OAP: Toward a Process for an Open World

Yuanzhi Wang

Department of Computer Science
The Australian National University, Australia
derek.wang@anu.edu.au

Abstract. To deal with increasing complexity, volatility, and uncertainty, a process for engineering software-intensive systems in an open world, called Organic Aggregation Process (OAP), is proposed. It is based on a concept called "Organic Aggregation", and consists of a coherent and flexible aggregation of carefully-categorised, hierarchically organised, and inter-connected activities. It supports flexible process aggregations via a capacity reuse mechanism called *Epitome*. A model-driven method and a supporting tool environment are integrated into OAP, which enables efficient manipulation and utilisation of OAP models, and automatic generation of concrete systems. It supports, and promotes a focus on, high-level intellectual efforts such as perception of reality, rationalisation of problem situations, and derivation of "soft" desired ends. A proof-of-concept case study is briefly presented in this paper to illustrate the application of OAP approach in a real world setting.

Keywords: Process, Software Engineering, Software Process, MDE.

1 Introduction

The variety, complexity, and dynamic of software-intensive systems have been significantly increased because of advances in technologies and society in the open environments of present era. Owing to increasing complexities, volatility, and uncertainty involved in an open world, the well-known gap between computing capabilities and usage demands has reached a critical level that hinders successful engineering of complex systems in such an environment [1]. Therefore, it becomes pressingly necessary to assess the problems of current engineering approaches and to explore different ways to address such a great challenge.

In this paper, an engineering process called Organic Aggregation Process, or OAP for short, is proposed. It consists of a set of inter-connected activities that are organised in a coherent and flexible hierarchy. This structure aims to form a coherent linkage between human intellectual efforts and practical reality. That is, a path from human perception of complex problem situations to sensible desired engineering ends, and to practical engineering actions that eventually improve the situations. Such a linkage can be aggregated organically through a capacity reuse mechanism, in support of organic agility. Moreover, a model-driven method and some supporting tools are integrated into OAP, and facilitate management of its engineering activities in a dynamically complex environment.

J. Münch, Y. Yang, and W. Schäfer (Eds.): ICSP 2010, LNCS 6195, pp. 175–187, 2010.

Briefly, by synthesising a coherent and flexible conceptual structure, a model-driven methodology, and an integrated tool environment, OAP aims to: 1) promote a focus on higher-level intellectual efforts within a cognitive world of mind, especially perception of reality, rationalisation of problem situations, and derivation of "soft" desired ends; and 2) co-ordinate conduction of various activities in a coherent, flexible, and reusable means towards systematic generation of software systems that improve the perceived problematic situations.

The remainder of the paper is organised as follows: section 2 briefly analyses existing process models of engineering and problem-solving; section 3 presents the OAP process in terms of its coherent and flexible conceptual structure, modelling mechanism, and integrated tool environment; section 4,using a proof-of-concept case study, illustrates how OAP approach is applied in a real-world setting to meet its objectives ; section 5 analyses the positive results, contribution, and limitation of this work based on the case study; Finally, section 6 presents a summary of this paper and concludes some contributions of this work.

2 Background and Related Work

The origin of a notion of processes can be traced back to ancient Greek philosopher Heraclitus, who held that the essence of the world is not material substance of things but rather a continuous natural process, or "flux" in his term [2]. Whitehead's definition of a *process* is "a sequentially structured sequence of successive stages or phases" [3]. In the context of software engineering, Fuggetta defined a process as "the coherent set of policies, organisational structures, technologies, procedures, and artefacts that are needed to conceive, develop, deploy, and maintain a software product" [4]. These definitions all involve a concept of life-cycle, and some composing elements with a structure of certain shape or format.

Similarly, Royce's influential waterfall model [5] is a software process that consists of a sequence of activities such as requirements analysis, design, and implementation. This approach gradually evolved into more iterative, incremental, and evolutionary models, sometimes called Iterative and Incremental Development (IID) [6], such as spiral model, rapid prototyping, Rational Unified Process (RUP), and more recently, agile methodologies. John Boyd's *Observation, Orientation, Decision, and Action* (OODA) loop, as a decision-making process model, was designed to cope with highly dynamic and competitive environments by accelerating a person's own loop and weakening opponents' abilities to complete their loops at faster paces [7]. This model has been successfully adopted in critical and dynamic environments such as military battles and business competition.

This paper, however, argues that these approaches are inadequate to deal with great challenges of complexity, volatility, and uncertainty, which are commonly involved in open environments. For example, OODA model and its followers, in general, are too abstract and coarse-grained, and lack some fundamental elements in an engineering context, such as clearly defined activities at detail level, their boundaries and relationships, and supporting tools. It provides neither guidelines with regards to internal structures and content, nor representational formalisms for each phase, in a concrete sense. Application of such a process is hence not controllable in an engineering context.

More importantly, after decades of evolution, these process models are still fundamentally based on the same concept, that is, pre-defined decomposition and refinement of life-cycle at fixed levels and rigid activity dependencies, which is referred as rigid plan-driven processes in this paper. For example, most IID processes have the same pre-defined phases such as Analysis, Design, Implementation, Test, and Verification, although at different paces, or sometimes with feedback added to different phases in the loop [6]. Similarly, RUP comprises Inception, Elaboration, Construction and Transition. Whereas agile methodologies normally consist of Exploration, Planning, Iteration and Release[8]. So does OODA model and its followers.

These rigid plan-driven processes, although effective in some complex and safety-critical systems, lack flexibility and agility because they are often time-consuming to carry out in the first place, drawn in time or quickly become out of synchronisation, and are difficult to change over time [9]. Although agile methodologies aim to address this issue by using a lightweight process with shorter iterative development cycles and quick feedback, they lack order and cohesion in complex situations, and therefore are usually used only for small and medium sized projects [9].

3 OAP Process Model for Software-Intensive Systems Engineering

OAP approach is fundamentally based a concept called *Organic Aggregation* with an aim of addressing the grand challenges of an open world. An *aggregation* means a synthetic approach to look at the world that is aggregated by interrelated elements in a hierarchy [10]. Being *organic* means being coherent, ordered, sensible, and more importantly, being flexible enough to be able to continuously evolve towards a new favourable order from emerging chaos, at a pace faster than the changing rate of chaotic situation. *Organic Aggregation* therefore means creative synthesis of systems, such as objects, events, and processes, that is in a coherent order, and capable of coping with ever-changing chaotic environments.

Specifically, this concept is applied to not only the structure and interrelationships of process, but also its composing sub-processes, subordinate activities, and the products they produce. That is, a process is an *organic aggregations* of inter-related internal elements that are arranged in a coherent, efficient, and flexible way. In the meantime, capabilities to carry on sub-processes or internal activities, as well as the products they produce, such as various models and artefacts, also form *organic aggregations* that can be used, or reused, to aggregate other systems. These concepts are incorporated into the coherent structure of OAP and its mechanism to reuse knowledge and capacities, and are illustrated in the following sections.

3.1 The Coherent Structure of OAP

OAP is coherently organised as a coherent hierarchy that has multiple levels. Its structure at a fundamental level is depicted on the left-hand side of figure 1. The central thick line represents engineering experience that provides an interaction interface between the world of *Reality* and *Mind.* It helps to distinguish human intellectual efforts from externally observable reality. On the one hand, the world of *Mind* involves important intellectual and cognitive activities that are essential precondition of problem-solving in complex problematic or chaotic engineering situation. On the other hand, since activities within the world of *Reality* are closer to physical environments, and are better understood and controllable compared with mental activities, they can be reproduced, automated, or controlled in a relatively easy way.

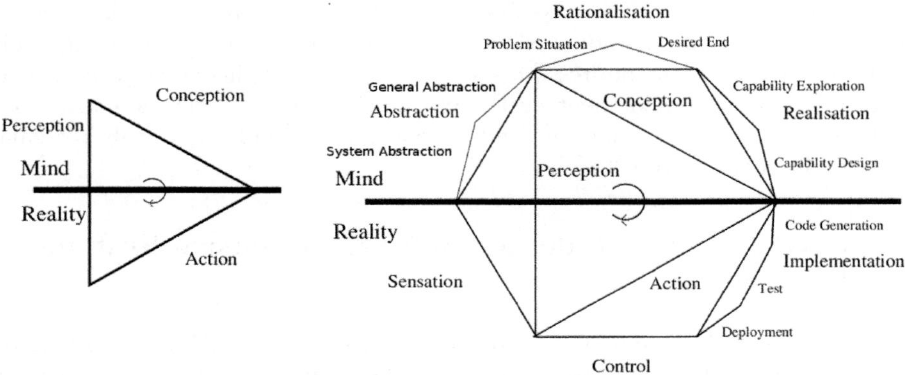

Fig. 1. A coherent conceptual structure of Organic Aggregation Process (OAP)

At this level, OAP consists of three interconnected activities, namely *Perception*, *Conception*, and *Action*, represented by straight lines with name beside them. These activities, collectively, connect the world of *Mind* with *Reality. Perception* is a set of activities that acquire information or knowledge about the *Reality*, and derive relevant representations in the world of *Mind*, which can be located, used, and reused by successive activities. *Conception* is human intellectual activities in the scope of *Mind*, which involve reasoning, rationalisation, decision-making, or plan-making sub-processes. *Action*, conducted in the world of *Reality*, deals with problematic situations by doing things, reacting to events, and other interactions with the outside worlds, according to outputs from *Perception* and *Conception*, such as knowledge of involved situations, desired ends, rules and laws, designs and plans. These activities are interconnected with each other and form continuous and iterative forward loops.

Moreover, activities at this level are composed of subordinate activities at more detailed levels, as depicted on the right-hand side of figure 1. *Perception* consists of *Sensation* and *Abstraction*. The former involves activities that directly collect required data from *Reality*, such as physical measurement of temperature and humidity, or real-time network performance monitoring. Whereas *Abstraction*, occurring in the world of *Mind*, is a type of activities that generalise or interpret the data or information collected by *Sensation*, and produce representations of relevant *Reality* in *Mind*. A collection, or repository, of *Abstraction* forms valuable aggregations of knowledge about the *Reality*.

Conception consists of *Rationalisation* and *Realisation*, both of which occur in the world of *Mind*, and are crucial intellectual efforts towards engineering problem-solving. *Rationalisation* is defined as activities to explore, understand, and represent sensible stimuli and desired intentions that explain or positively reinforce *Action*. It plays a significant, although not exclusive, role that binds *Mind* with *Action* and influences the way *Reality* is altered. Whereas *Realisation* is defined as activities that involve design, formation, and judgement of global plans and decisions that consist of low-level and fine-grain sequence of local activities and capabilities, which are justified, either empirically, or theoretically, in the sense that occuring behaviours in accordance with them can approximate the identified desired ends, and more importantly, improve problematic situations.

Action, involving activities in the world of *Reality*, consists of *Implementation* and *Control*. In contrast to thinking, reasoning, or designing activities in *Mind*, *Implementation* is about actually doing things or carrying out plans in *Reality* according to outputs of *Realisation*, and in pursuit of achieving identified desired ends from *Rationalisation*. *Control* provides run-time monitoring and management of systems during continuous interactions between systems and environments. *Action* is guided by *Conception* and influenced by *Perception*.

As shown in the figure, the above activities can have subordinate activities at more detailed levels. For example, *Abstraction* includes *System Abstraction* and *General Abstraction*; *Rationalisation* consists of *Problem Situation* and *Desired End*. Due to the space limitation, they are not discussed in this section, their meaning can be derived from their names and definitions of their superordinate activities, and can be understood through modelling context in section 3.2, and examples illustrated in section 4.

It is important to note that the hierarchical structure of OAP is not rigid. Although of activities at superordinate, or more fundamental, levels are less likely to change, the nature and inner structure of activities at subordinate, or more detailed, levels can be adjusted in different context, as long as their purposes and functions still conform to those of their superordinate activities. For example, depending on whether target systems are services or embedded systems, *Realisation* can consist of either capability discovery and capability design, or functional design and simulation. In certain sense, superordinate activities define stable interfaces and scope for their subordinates to conform to. While the content of the latter might differs in different situations.

More importantly, OAP provides a mechanism to reuse engineering capacities, which enables and supports flexible aggregation of process activities and agile engineering in a dynamic and uncertain environment. A concept called *Epitome* is designed for this purpose. An *Epitome* of engineering capacity is a typical means, being generalised from proven examples, to achieve the desired result for a type of activities. It encapsulates typical engineering capacities in the form of service. For instance, based on certain *Perception*, a particular activity of *Problem Situation* recognises and represents a problematic situation. Such capacity is encapsulated in an *Epitome* called "Epitome 1" as depicted in figure 2. It can be used to produce the same representation of problems under the same situation, for future reference or aggregations. Such an *epitome* is created by generalising a proven instance of example, which is a process called *Epitomisation*. A collection of *Epitomes* provides a *Horizontal Aggregation* of valuable engineering assets, just like a collection of *Abstraction* forms valuable aggregation of knowledge about the *Reality*.

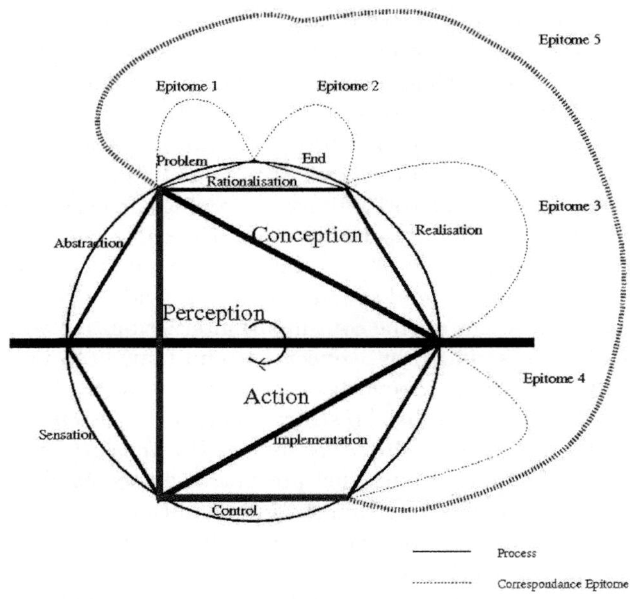

Fig. 2. An example of flexible aggregations of process using *Epitomes*

Moreover, *Epitome* can be aggregated hierarchically to form *Vertical Aggregation*, which can be used to create tight correspondence, or *Aggregation Linkage* between two process activities that would otherwise not directly relate to each other. Figure 2 depicts it. If a perceived situation has been improved through application of a series of *Epitomes*: from "Epitome 1" to "Epitome 4", which, respectively, encapsulates activity capacity for *Problem Situation*, *Desired End*, *Realisation*, and *implementation* at various levels, we can aggregate these *Epitomes* into a single one called "Epitome 5", as a typical means to generate specific ends, which creates a "strong correspondence" between a *Perception* of situation and desired improvements in *Reality*. The "strong correspondence" here means that the coherently interconnected capacities provide a typical, and proven way to make improvement to a particular type of problematic situations. Once justified by empirical experience, "Epitome 5" can be directly applied on a specific situation and makes desired improvement. Therefore, engineering activities can be directly aggregated together to achieve desired results without having to go through predefined subordinate or intermediate activities.

3.2 A Model-Driven Method and Supporting Tools

To facilitate process activities and their interactions, OAP integrates a model-driven method in a unified fashion, in the sense that everything is supported by models within a consistent infrastructure. That is, various models, either specially-designed ones such as Problem Situation Model (PSM) and Desired End Model (DEM) in *Rationalisation*, or general-purpose ones such as UML Activity Diagrams, are used as specific means to explore, represent, and utilise outcomes of various activities. All OAP models such PSM and DEM are manipulated in the same way within an integrated environment.

As an example, we briefly describe the meta-model of PSM as depicted in figure 3. It consists of a number of *Problems* that might violate specific higher-order, or subordinate, *Purposes*, or be caused by some *Facts* that are constrained by *Reality*, and cause, or be caused by, other problems.

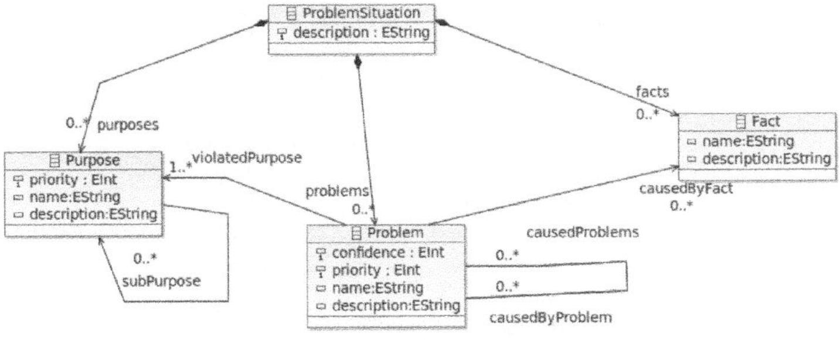

Fig. 3. The meta-model of *Problem Situation*

To facilitate application of OAP, a range of graphical tools have been developed, and are integrated in the Integrated Process Environment for OAP (IPEOAP). It is developed using Java programming language on top of Eclipse IDE and other Eclipse modelling Framework (EMF) supported modules. A range of graphical model editors are provided to view, create and modify models for different OAP activities, such as PSM and DEM. Example of these models and their manipulation in IPEOAP will be briefly presented in section 4. Moreover, IPEOAP also supports automatic transformation of models and systematic generation of desired artefacts. For example, PSM can be automatically transformed into documents that describe the problematic situations. Similarly, a UML activity diagram in *Realisation* is translated into lower-level run-time representations, such as BPEL artefacts or Java code.

4 A Case Study

In order to obtain insights about the effect and value of OAP by applying its concepts, methods, and tools in a real-world setting, a controlled case study is conducted in the context of the First Home Saver Accounts (FHSA), a scheme introduced by the Australian federal government that aims to help young residents to purchase their first homes, by providing subsidy of government contributions and tax benefits. The purpose is to implement a proof-of-concept, as opposed to proof-of-performance, to demonstrate that the process meets its objectives in general, that is, a process mechanism to deal with a problematic situation in a complex and dynamic environment. A proof-of-concept system is produced using IPEOAP toolkit. Apache Tomcat web server is used to host the generated web content. Apache Axis2 Web Service Engine and ODE are used to host generated Java web services and BPEL. JBoss provides application server that contains some Java business logic. Derby Database is used for database implementation.

The OAP process started with *Abstraction*, which includes modelling of current business domains such as structure and process of business. UML Class Diagrams are used to model static information structure such as Customer, Bank Account, Clerk. UML Activity Diagrams are used to model business behaviour and workflow such as managing FHSA account. These models are created and managed within IPEOAP using Eclipse UML2 tools.

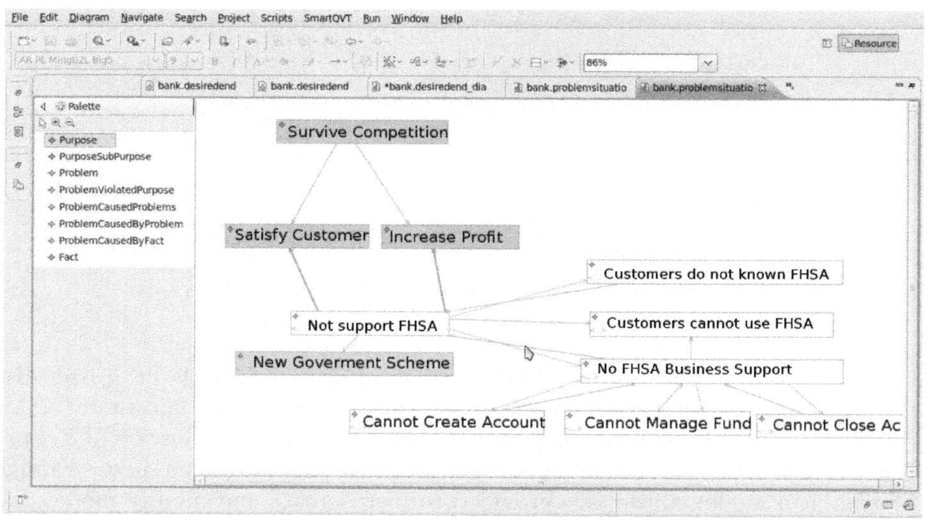

Fig. 4. An example of Problem Situation Model (PSM) in FHSA

To illustrate the concept and application of PSM in an IPEOAP environment, figure 4 shows a simple example of PSM for a financial institution that does not support FHSA scheme. It contains a higher order *Purpose*: namely "Survive competition" that has two subordinate *Purposes*: "Satisfy customer" and "Increase profit". It also has a high level *Problem*, "Not support FHSA", which violates the above *Purposes*. This problem is caused by a *Fact*: "New Goverment Scheme", that is, the government just officially released the consolidated version of policy recently and the organisation simply does not have the resources to react promptly in an uncertain market. This *Problem* is also caused by some other *Problems*. For example, many customers do not recognise the benefits of FHSA. Moreover, many of them are not eligible and the proportion of these customers remain unknown due to lack of information. Therefore, as a strategic management decision, no business support for FHSA was provided at the time of FHSA announcement. This directly leads to some subordinate *Problems*: "Existing customers cannot create their first FHSA account", "Cannot manage existing fund", and "Cannot terminate existing fund". This scenario exemplifies a typical complex problem situation that modern organisations are often involved in a dynamic marketing and legislation environment. As shown in the figure, IPEOAP provides a graphical editing tool that enables efficient creation and manipulation of PSM elements and their relationships. Moreover, using its transformation engine, the PSM is automatically transformed into HTML documents with informative details that describe the situation, which help business stakeholders to explore, understand, and communicate the problem situations.

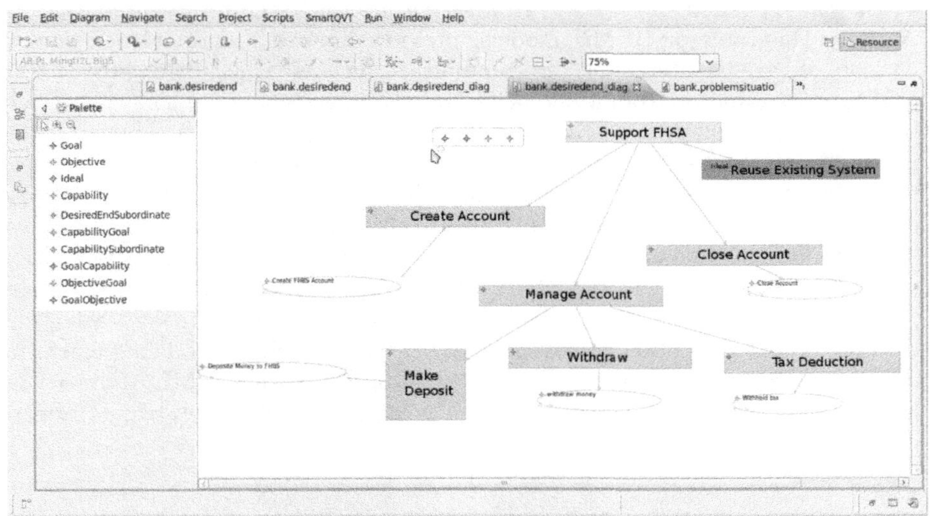

Fig. 5. An example of Desired End Model (DEM) in FHSA

The value of such a PSM lies in its function of facilitating not only discovery and communication of complex business situations and concerns at early stages of process life cycle, but also systematic derivation of relevant and sensible engineering artefacts during successive activities, such as DEM. It hence provides justification of and guidance for derivation of *Implementation* that alters the states of *reality* in the "right" way.

For instance, in accordance with every identified *Problem* in a PSM, specific DEMs are systematically derived with an aim of improving the situation. As an example, "A lack of business support for FHSA" is regarded as a critical problem in PSM from business operational point of view. A DEM is hence created as depicted by figure 5. It contains an *Ideal*: "Reuse existing account management system" and a more specific *Objective*, "Support FHSA", which has a number of concrete and operational *Goals*, such as "Create Account", "Close Account", and "Manage Account". The latter also contains some subordinate *Goals*, such as "Make Deposit", "Withdraw fund", and "Tax Deduction". Like PSM, creation and manipulation of DEM is also graphically supported by IPEOAP.

The value of DEM lies in the fact that it provides a mechanism to capture less-rigid intentions and desires that involve certain degree of uncertainty, such as ideals that are often impossible to achieve. Desired intentions are justified as long as they improve identified problematic situations at a desired level of satisfaction. Pragmatically, DEM has its value in facilitating derivation of conceptual planning and design in successive *Realisation* activities, which, in turn, guide, direct, or generate desired *Implementation* to change the *reality* as expected.

For example, in accordance with every *Goal* in above DEM, such as "Create a FHSA account", more specific *Realisation* models are systematically derived to satisfy these desired ends. These *Realisation* models, often represented as UML Activity Diagrams or BPMN models, provide detailed functional design that consists of various interconnected capabilities, such as "Check Eligibility", "Import user information from Tax office", and "Create account", which collectively satisfy the *Goal* of creating FHSA accounts for owners of FHSA scheme.

Finally, these abstract *Realisation* models, independent of specific implementation platform, are systematically, and almost automatically, translated into concrete *Implementation* artefacts, such as BPEL, software programs in Java programming language, or textual plan instructions, for specific implementation platform. The generated artefacts can be executed in run-time environment in *Reality* to satisfy the *Desired End* and improve identified *Problem Situation*. Because of advances of technologies in MDE, such as Eclipse modeling platform, transformations between abstract *Realisation* models such as UML Activity Diagrams and *Implementation* artefacts such as BPEL are relatively straightforward and are not presented in this paper.

5 An Analysis of OAP

The case study shows some positive results. Firstly, the modelling mechanism in OAP, such as PSM and DEM, provides an effective formalism to explore, reason about, and rationalise problematic situations, and to form rational desired ends to improve such situations. These important higher level intellectual efforts justify and foster engineering design decisions and design of plans. Exploration and clarification of problematic situation using PSM helps to identify higher level purposes and problems with high priority that were not initial recognised in a local problem scope. For example, a lack of FHSA business support is later confirmed as a strategic problem due to its violation with high level critical purposes. Secondly, the interrelationship between OAP activities are systematically supported by linkages between various higher level models, with aid of integrated tool environment that fosters and automates access to unified model repository and transformation engines. Thirdly, improvement to engineering productivity is observed although not formally measured against other approaches. The proof-of-concept implementation enables encapsulation of knowledge and engineering capacities, and allows automatic generation of concrete documentation and systems based on a series of interconnected OAP models. Therefore, the majority of engineering efforts is designing and managing new abstract models, such as PSM and DEM as illustrated in this section. With support from IPEOAP, these modelling and transformation tasks were achieved in a short period of time.

This approach is different from Boyd's OODA loop in the sense that it is more concrete, specific, clearly defined, and generally better supported in an engineering context. For example, the boundaries, content, relationships, and value of involved activities are defined or clarified in the context of software-intensive systems engineering. Various representational formalisms, either specially designed, or general purpose, modelling language, are provided for OAP activities, with support from integrated tools. Moreover, instead of simply accelerating the pace of process, this approach provides a mechanism to reuse knowledge and capabilities in support of system flexibility and agility, which enables formation of coherent aggregation of engineering knowledge and process.

Its *Rationalisation* approach in *Mind* differs from traditional requirement engineering in terms of scope, mechanism, and "softness". Traditional requirement elicitation, analysis and management usually takes a rigid and "hard" approach, which is based on an assumption that there are requirements, clearly-definable and stable, out there to be collected in all situations. However, we believe such an assumption is not always valid in an open environment, where situations are complex, volatile, and uncertain. The common concept of "requirement" does not involve or imply "soft" intentions and desires that involve certain degree of uncertainty in problematic situations, which, undeniably, also influence the way engineering plans and design are derived and carried out. On the contrary, our approach provides a specific means to enable and support discovery, understanding and utilisation of these aspects of engineering. That is, it incorporates the concept of *Desired End* in the context of identified problematic situations, and systematically provides sensible targets for *Realisation* such as engineering planning and design. Its aim is to improve problematic situation to a satisfied degree, as opposed to achieving a "we-must-do-THIS" type of "requirements".

The proof-of-concept also reveals some issues and limitations. Currently not all parts of the OAP conceptual model are supported, such as *Sensation*, *Test* and *Control*. They are not incorporated appropriately in OAP at this stage because of a lack of deep understanding of their nature and characteristics. Moreover, process monitor and debugging activities are not supported, which makes it hard to identify problems when things go wrong. Furthermore, there are no analysis tools applied to identify syntactic issues on abstract models, which makes it less efficient to find and remove problems before model transformations get started. More importantly, no process metrics are applied to quantitatively evaluate the effectiveness of this process, especially in comparison with other approaches. Further work on these issues have been considered.

6 Conclusion

Aiming at addressing engineering challenges in an open world, we propose a novel engineering process called Organic Aggregation Process (OAP). It consists of: 1) a coherent and flexible conceptual model that consists of various carefully-categorised, well-organised, and inter-connected activities at various levels; 2) a model-driven method that enables and supports various activities using various specially-designed, or general-purpose, modelling and model transformation mechanisms; and 3) an integrated supporting tools environment called IPEOAP that provides unified modelling features including graphical manipulation of OAP model, and enables systematic generation of concrete systems.

The contributions of this work include: 1) It provides a coherent and flexible conceptual framework for engineering process to deal with dynamically complex open world; 2) It supports , and promotes a focus on, higher-level intellectual efforts within the world of *Mind*. Specifically, it provides i) a *Problem Situation* modelling mechanism to explore, understand, and capture complex problem situations that involve certain degree of uncertainty; and ii) a *Desired End* modelling mechanism to derive and represent "soft" desired ends and intentions in the context of identified problematic situations; 3) It provides a mechanism to coherently and systematically link various engineering activities, which, collectively, aim to tackle problem situations using intellectual capacities of *Mind*, and to form sensible *actions* to achieve desired improvement in *Reality*; 4) It provides a mechanism to capture and reuse engineering capacities and knowledge that supports flexible process aggregations and organic engineering agility.

A proof-of-concept case study is also presented in this paper to demonstrates the concepts and application of the OAP. Evidence shows that this process model can be applied in real settings and achieves its design goals in general. It helps to manage engineering processes in a complex problem situations and improve engineering efficiency in both world of *Mind* and *Reality*. However, some important limitations are also revealed, which lead to some future work, including improvement, more comprehensive empirical assessment and evaluation.

References

1. Baresi, L.: Toward open-world software: Issue and challenges. Computer 39, 36–43 (2006)
2. Aurobindo, S.: Heraclitus. Arya Publishing House, Calcutta (1941)

3. Whitehead, A.: Process and reality: corrected edition. The Free Press, New York (1978)
4. Fuggetta, A.: Software process: a roadmap. In: Proceedings of the conference on the future of software engineering, pp. 25–34 (2000)
5. Royce, W.: Managing the development of large software systems. Proceedings of IEEE Wescon 26, 9 (1970)
6. Larman, C., Basili, V.: Iterative and incremental development: A brief history. Computer, 47–56 (2003)
7. Osinga, F.: Science, strategy and war: the strategic theory of John Boyd. Routledge Abingdon, UK (2007)
8. Beck, K., Andres, C.: Extreme programming explained: embrace change. Addison-Wesley Professional, Reading (2004)
9. Shapiro, S.: Splitting the difference: The historical necessity of synthesis in software engineering. IEEE Annals of the History of Computing, 20–54 (1997)
10. Checkland, P.: Systems thinking, systems practice. J. Wiley, New York (1981)

An Automatic Approach to Aid Process Integration within a Secure Software Processes Family

Jia-kuan Ma, Ya-sha Wang*, Lei Shi, and Hong Mei

Key Laboratory of High Confidence Software Technologies,
Ministry of Education School of Electronics Engineering and Computer Science,
Peking University, Beijing, 100871, China
{majk06,wangys,shilei07}@sei.pku.edu.cn, meih@pku.edu.cn

Abstract. Defining secure processes is an important means for assuring software security. A wealth of dedicated secure processes has emerged in these years. These processes are similar to some extent, while differ from one another in detail. Conceptually, they can be further regarded as a so called "Process Family". In order to integrate practices from different family members, and further improve efficiency and effectiveness compared to using a single process, in this paper we propose an automatic approach to implement the integration of the three forefront secure processes, namely, CLASP, SDL and Touchpoints. Moreover, we select a module from an e-government project in China, and conduct an exploratory experiment to compare our approach with cases when one single secure process is employed. The empirical result confirms the positive effects of our approach.

Keywords: Secure software process; Process family; Process integration.

1 Introduction

As software has been playing an ever-increasing role in many domains, security of software systems has attracted more and more interest [1, 2]. Within software engineering community, as an illustration, International Workshop on Software Engineering for Secure Systems (SESS) has been held annually from year 2005, in conjunction with International Conference on Software Engineering (ICSE). Furthermore, "how to define and support the process of building secure software" has served as a key and constant topic ever since, which indicates the important role processes play in assuring software security.

Over the years, several dedicated processes on security have been proposed, e.g. CLASP [3], SDL [4], Touchpoints [5], SQUARE [6] , SecureXP [7], etc. Three forefront and widely-used representatives are CLASP, SDL, Touchpoints [8], thus in this paper we concentrate our discussion on them. These processes each results from organizing a group of best practices on security insurance, and augments general process frameworks (e.g. Unified Process, Microsoft Process, etc.) by adding into new activities, artifacts, and roles. Take Touchpoints as an example. One of its seven touch

* Corresponding author.

J. Münch, Y. Yang, and W. Schäfer (Eds.): ICSP 2010, LNCS 6195, pp. 188–199, 2010.

points, namely Penetration Testing, proposes performing "Negative Test" in addition to traditional functional testing (which can be regarded as "Positive Testing"). In this way, security testers can better ensure the status of system when attacks arrive.

On one hand, each of these processes is designed under certain background and concerns, thus embodies its own characteristics and focuses. For example, according to a comparative study of CLASP, SDL, Touchpoints [8] , SDL is very thorough in architectural threat analysis, Touchpoints provides a systematic way of eliciting analysis-level threats and CLASP includes the best support for architectural design. On the other hand, processes oriented to the same domain are not totally different. There usually exist similarities among these processes, especially from a broader point of view. For example, [8] reveals that CLASP, SDL and Touchpoints all employ misuse cases to represent anti-requirements, and perform threat modeling during analysis and design time.

Conceptually, these processes can be further regarded as a so called "Process Family" [9, 10], which aims to integrate different processes to more closely match the special scenarios users might meet. Such integration, stated in [8] as "combining the strong points of all approaches in order to distill an improved, consolidated process", is proposed to be promising.

However, integration within a process family cannot be implemented by simply adding members together, since redundancy or conflicts can arise when composing units (we define 'unit' as one or a group of related activities in this paper) from different processes (detailed examples can be referred in section 2). Therefore, we proposed an approach which can aid the process integration by answering the following two questions:

Q1: how to decompose a holistic process into units with proper granularity?
Q2: how to establish the implicit relations among the divided units?

By decomposing member processes into units with proper granularity, users can choose basic units from different processes and compose them into larger units in a stepwise way, until a complete secure process suitable for the specific project context is created. Moreover, establishing the implicit relations among the divided units can provide necessary supports when users select and compose various units. For example, a user can browse "equivalent" units from different secure processes, and choose one that best meets characteristics of the project in hand. Moreover, "dependency" relations can prevent users from semantic conflicts or misses during integration.

Providing such answers via manual analysis tend to be very costly, for the amount of activities is large in scale and certain constrains should be followed when integrating activities from different processes. For example, activity A may require the outcome of activity B as its input. In this case, if users choose A, then B should also be incorporated. To avoid violating these constrains, restrict examinations have to be performed, which is also costly and error-prone if conducted manually. Based on these analyses, we implement our approach as an algorithm that can be automatically executed by computers, thus significantly save cost comparing with manual operations.

The rest of this paper is organized as follows. Section 2 enumerates several cases during integration, and provides each case with an intuitive analysis. Section 3 formalizes previous analysis and then presents the details of our approach. Section 4 describes an exploratory experiment for sake of evaluation. Finally, we survey related work in Section 5 and conclude in Section 6.

2 Analysis

As a starting point, let us consider the following motivating cases when integrating units from different secure processes. We set our range of study to be the three high-profile secure processes (i.e. CLASP, SDL and Touchponts) mentioned above. The original contents of these processes are published via website (CLASP) or books (SDL and Touchpoints), where typical process structures hide within massive text descriptions. Therefore, for sake of simplicity and authority, we borrow the activity matrix already established in [11] , which results from collecting all activities from the three processes investigated. Furthermore, these activities are organized into a tree structure after adding phases (e.g. Architecture Design) and brief titles for a group of activities (e.g. Security response planning). An excerpt of the matrix is shown in Figure 1.

Detailed Design	SDL	CLASP	Touchpoints
5.1. Assess the privacy impact rating of the project	✓	✗	✗
5.2. Software attack surface reduction			
5.2.1. Remove unimportant features	✓	✗	✗
5.2.2. Determine who needs access from where	✓	✗	✗
5.2.3. Reduce privileges	✓	✗	✗
5.2.4. Identify system entry points	✗	✓	✗
5.2.5. Map roles to entry points	✗	✓	✗
5.2.6. Map resources to entry points	✗	✓	✗
5.2.7. Scrub attack-surface	✓	✗	✗
5.3. Class design annotation			
5.3.1. Map data elements to resources and capabilities	✗	✓	✗
5.3.2. Annotate fields with policy information	✗	✓	✗
5.3.3. Annotate methods with policy data	✗	✓	✗
5.4. Database security configuration			
5.4.1. Identify candidate configuration	✗	✓	✗
5.4.2. Validate configuration	✗	✓	✗
5.5. Make your product updatable	✓	✗	✗

Fig. 1. An excerpt of the process structure in [11]

- Case A: Two activities from different processes have the same functionality, whereas differ in implementation details. In this case, we should choose either one from them, because having them both in the integrated process simultaneously will cause unnecessary function redundancy. For instance, both CLASP and Touchpoints have their own versions of activity "Identify & describe threat agents". Only one of them should appear in the integrated process.
- Case B: One activity in a process has the same functionality as a group of activities from another process. In this case, we should choose either one from them as well, because having them both in the integrated process simultaneously will cause unnecessary function redundancy. For instance, in order to inspect potential access control risk, SDL suggests "Determine who needs access from where", while CLASP employs two activities, namely "Identify system entry points" and "Map roles to entry points" as a solution. Thus, only one of them can appear in the integrated process.
- Case C: Units from different processes can perfectly connect. In this case, we can simply choose both of them and join them together, because the output

artifact of one unit can be passed as the input artifact of another unit. "Identify & describe threat agents" from CLASP and "Review & revise threat agents" from Touchpoints can be regarded as such an example.

- Case D: Units from different processes have conflicts. As an example, consider integrating "Review & revise threat agents" from Touchpoints with any unit from SDL. Since SDL provides no activity to create agents, it is impossible for "Review & revise threat agents" to work with the absence of the input artifact required. In this case, we cannot join them together.
- Case E: Units from different processes are mutually independent. In this case, they can coexist well with each other, because they neither overlap in function, nor require each other to produce the needed input artifact. Still consider "Identify & describe threat agents" from CLASP as an example, integrating it with SDL's "Make your product updatable" is feasible.

3 Approach

3.1 Formalization

In the cases listed in section 2, we judge the integration feasibility by intuition and common sense, which cannot be supported automatically. However, if we look into the input and output artifacts of units from case A to E, we can get several observations. To this end, we first make the following formal definitions:

For artifact a1 and a2, let a1 = a2 when a1 and a2 have the same semantics. Usually the concrete syntax of artifacts is indicated by the host process (or the organization employing this process). Therefore, when comparing artifacts from different processes, it's important to focus on their semantics (what's in them) instead of their forms (how they are written). In our approach, we merge artifacts with the same semantics into equal artifacts when extending activity matrix with artifact information. Moreover, as some artifacts in not explicitly introduced in these processes, we judge their semantics by the context information.

For unit u, let u.in = {a | a is an input artifact for u}, u.in = Φ when unit u receives no artifact; let u.out = {a | a is an output artifact for u}, u.out = Φ when unit u produces no artifact.

Based on artifact information, we can define several relations between two activities.

Definition: Equivalence Relation
If u1.in = u2.in and u1.out = u2.out, then u1 and u2 satisfy the equivalence relation. As a result, either u1 or u2 can appear in the integrated process. Case A and case B are such examples.

Definition: Dependency Relation
If u1.out = u2.in, then u1 and u2 satisfy the dependency relation. As a result, u1 and u2 can be integrated together. Case C is such an example.

If u1.in ≠ Φ && u2.out ≠ u1.in, or u2.in ≠ Φ && u1.out ≠ u2.in, then u1 and u2 cannot satisfy the dependency relation. As a result, u1 and u2 cannot be integrated together. Case D is such an example.

Definition: Independency Relation
If u1.in = Φ and u2.in = Φ, then u1 and u2 satisfy the independency relation. As a result, u1 and u2 can be integrated together. Case E is such an example.

An additional conclusion drawn from above is that the entire probability space has been covered by case A to case E, as shown in Figure 2.

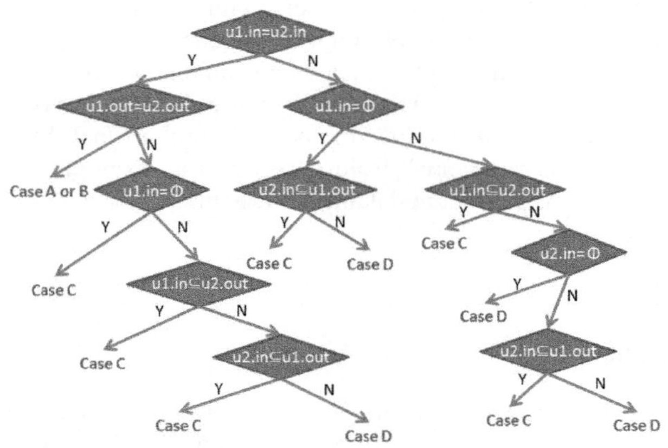

Fig. 2. A probability tree depicting the entire probability coverage by Case A to E

Therefore, our previous analysis for these cases is complete in concept and can be popularized to integrated processes containing various kinds of units.

Based on previous analysis, our basic idea can be summarized as follows.

1) For every process, take each of its activity as an initial unit;
2) Based on artifact information, establish equivalence, dependency and independency relations between units, according to the predicate expressions derived above.
3) Globally merge units into larger clusters according to relations among them.

3.2 Data Preparation

For the purpose of easy and clear comparison, [11] introduced activity matrix. To better support our approach, we extend the original activity matrix as follows:

1) Complement input and output artifact information for each activity. In case some activities do not involve any concrete artifact, we label "null" to represent such a condition.
2) Remove all the brief titles, which are manually added to represent semantic means for a group of activities. Since our approach take each atomic activity (i.e. the leaf node) as an initial unit, and leverage artifact information to deduce the function of a unit, these titles are somewhat redundant.

3.3 Algorithm

Implementing the above basic idea onto the extended activity matrix, we have a corresponding algorithm, as shown in Figure 3.

The main stream of the algorithm is to decompose processes into atomic units first (line 2 to 7); then continuously merge them into larger units, according to equivalence relation (line 10 to 17) and dependency relation (line 18 to 26) between any two of units. For each unit, we set its type attribute, where 'eq' stands for equivalence relation of its child units, 'dep' for dependency relation and 'reg' for the rest.

A notable point in the algorithm is the "late-deletion" when merging two dependent units into a larger one (line 25 and 26), whereas equivalent units get deleted once after merge (line 17). This is because compared with equivalence relation, dependency relation is not transitive. Formally, if (a, b) satisfies equivalence relation, and (b, c) satisfies equivalence relation, we can deduce that (a, c) satisfies equivalence relation as well. However, this is not the case for dependency relation. Therefore, using a larger unit to replace two equivalent units will not lose any other equivalent unit to be merged later; but the two dependent units have to be retained in case other dependency relations involving either of them can be built. In our solution, we leverage garbageList (line 25) to label dependency units in the first place and delete them after the iteration.

Let `Processes`: **List of source processes**
Let `pi.activities` : **List of activities in process** pi
Let `x.input` : **List of input artifacts of activity (unit)** x
Let `x.output` : **List of output artifacts of activity (unit)** x
Let `u.subUnits` : **List of internal contents of unit** u
Let `garbageList` : **List of to-delete units**

```
1   For each pi in Processes
2     For each ai of pi.activities
3       Create unit ui
4       ui.type = reg
5       ui.input = ai.input
6       ui.ouput = ai.output
7       Add ai to ui.subUnits
8   While True
9     Do repeat
10      For each u1,u2 in e
11        If u1.input == u2.input and u1.output == u2.output
12          Create unit u3
13          u3.type = eq
14          u3.input = u1.input
15          u3.ouput = u1.output
16          Copy u1 and u2 to u3.subUnits
17          Delete u1 and u2
18      For each u1,u2 in e
19        If u1.input != Φ and u1.input is subset of u2.output
20          Create unit u3
21          u3.type = dep
22          u3.input = u2.input23          u3.ouput = u1.output
24          Copy u1 and u2 to u3.subUnits
25          Add u1 and u2 to garbageList
26      Delete all units in garbageList
27    Until e does not change
```

Fig. 3. An algorithm to divide processes into a group of units with certain relations

The end loop criteria "Until e does not change (line 27)" stands for our continuous merge strategy. Each loop merges units into larger ones, which constitute new candidates for the next composition. Since each non-skipped loop reduces at least 1 unit (only merge two units), for input scale of n units, in the worst case the algorithm can take no more than n-1 steps (this is merely a theoretical coarse estimation) to stop. Therefore the algorithm is inherently convergent.

The output of algorithm is a group of units with certain relations, which constitute a unit library. A piece of result we gain on CLASP, SDL and Touchpoints is showed in Figure 4. Units in the same slashed rectangle (a single activity or a group of activities connected by solid arrows) have equivalence relations, and slashed arrow represents dependency relations between two units.

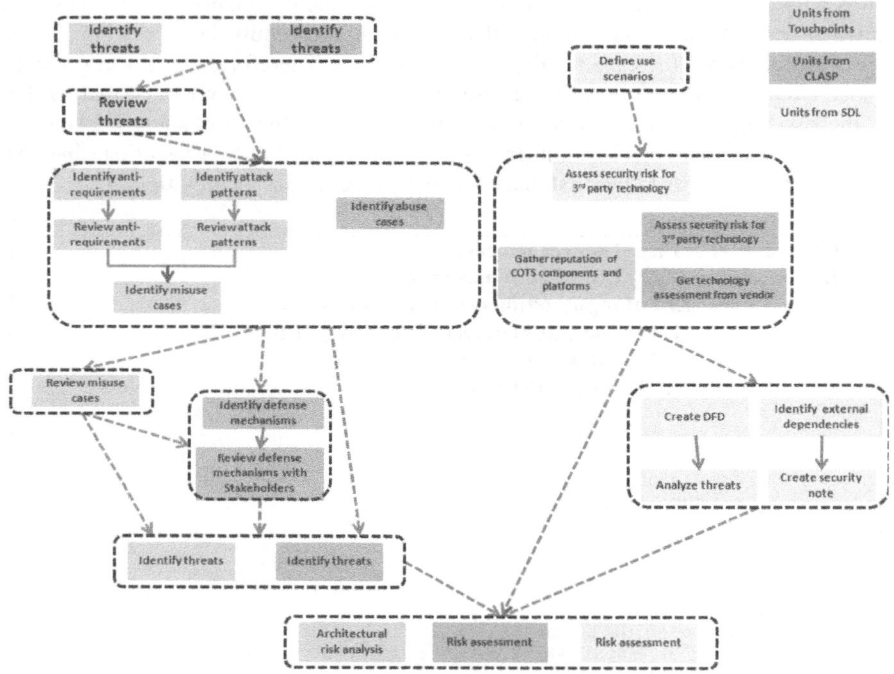

Fig. 4. An excerpt of the unit library we construct

4 An Exploratory Experiment

We conduct an exploratory experiment to study the practical effects of our approach. The major objective is to investigate whether the approach proposed by this paper can promote the efficiency and effectiveness of security support in software process. To this end, we first discuss experiment settings in section 4.1. Then, we describe the research method employed in this experiment in section 4.2. Finally, section 4.3 presents the result and corresponding analysis.

4.1 Experiment Setting

One fundamental assumption behind our approach is that by reorganizing secure process family into a group of units with certain relations, creation of a better integrated process comparing with any individual secure process can be supported within relatively low-effort. To evaluate this assumption, the most straightforward way is conducting a controlled experiment. That is to say, with other factors as stable as possible, compare a case where our approach is applied with cases where our approach is absent. Particularly, under ideal conditions we should find an ongoing software project in industry, then ask several groups of people (on close productivity level) to carry out this project simultaneously, where one group leverages our approach and others apply a certain dedicated secure process respectively. Finally, the costs (e.g. man-month spent on secure process) and benefits (security improvement of products) can be compared.

However, as it has been pointed out early in software engineering community, conducting such a controlled experiment in industrial environment is extremely difficult. Since actual project is mostly one-off (and faces constrains like budget, time), it is nearly impossible to perform multiple experiments on a single case. Moreover, factors such as people cannot be easily controlled in industrial setting as well. Therefore, we decide to get around these challenges by making certain tradeoffs.

Instead of selecting an ongoing project and real project participants, we choose a project with the following features:

F1. Product security is important for the project.
F2. The project did not leverage any dedicated secure process during development.
F3. The project has been finished and the final product has gone through security assessment, where the detected security issues are recorded.
F4. In-process artifacts of the project are complete and available.
F5. The size of project should be relatively small in scale.

Based on the decisions above, we choose a module from an e-government project. The project is to build a website for the government office of x city located in northern China. The module we choose is a "Problem and Feedback" platform, where citizens can leave their questions or suggestions. The administrator of this platform classifies these questions into several categories, and delivers them to corresponding officials. The feedback of officials will finally be published on the platform as well.

This module was written in Java and JSP, consisting of 953 lines of code (3rd party code is not counted). The whole project was developed following a customized Unified Process, where no specific secure process was employed. However, the website has taken a security assessment before delivering to customers, where amount of security issues were found. As a result, additional rework and testing were performed, and the delivery date was postpone for two weeks. For the module we choose, there are four threat issues identified:

T1: The module leverages a 3rd party forum component. According to the design, users can only login with the account registered from the government office website. However, the forum component's own user management function was not forbidden. As a result, a user can add this additional user management function's path after the module's original URL, and get around functions provided by the module to register, login and even create a post by an illegal accountant she/he created her/himself.

T2: According to the design, if a user login contiguously fails for three times, the system will prevent him from retrying in the next twenty-four hours. However, the module records the time count in the browser's cookie. By modifying this data from cookie, an attacker can try the password with no times limit.

T3: The module does not guard against SQL injection. An attacker can add SQL statements into the submitted form, then get or even modify confidential data in database.

T4: According to the design, only the administrator can add reply for a question. However, the module only judge a user's role by retrieving user type flag from cookie. In this case, an attacker can fake as the administrator by setting his cookie.

Moreover, we choose six volunteers from our lab to act as project participants. They are both master students majoring in software engineering.

4.2 Research Method

Our experiment is conducted in seven steps:

Step 1: Design and perform a two-week training for all the six volunteers. During the training, all the participants study the official books and documents for CLASP, SDL and Touchpoints. We also hold four seminars for face-to-face discussion so that consensus on these secure processes can be ensured.

Step 2: Invite the project's manager to give an orientation of the whole project. In this way the unrelated difficulties caused by participants' unfamiliar with the project can be eliminated.

Step 3: Randomly select three students (Let them be s1, s2, s3), assign CLASP to s1, SDL to s2, Touchpoints to s3, and ask them to execute their assigned process on the chosen project. Record results from their separate execution.

Step 4: Provide s1, s2 and s3 the unit library built by our approach. Ask each of them to customize his own secure process (Let these processes be p1, p2, p3).

Step 5: For the rest three students (Let them be s4, s5, s6), assign p1 to s4, p2 to s5, p3 to s6, and ask them to execute their assigned process on the chosen project. Record results from their separate execution.

Step 6: Interview each participant.

Step 7: Compare and analyze results from step 3, step 5 and step 6.

4.3 Results

The result of our experiment is summarized in Table 1.

Table 1. The result of our experiment

Participant	Process	Time Consumed					T1	T2	T3	T4
		Total	Analysis	Design	Implementation	Testing				
s1	CLASP	30h	13h	10h	4h	3h	Y	Y	Y	N
s2	SDL	41h	4h	25h	5h	7h	Y	N	N	Y
s3	Touchpoints	25h	9h	7h	2h	7h	Y	Y	N	N
s4	p1	29h	14h	9h	3h	3h	Y	Y	Y	N
s5	p2	32h	13h	12h	2h	5h	Y	Y	Y	N
s6	p3	31h	19h	7h	3h	3h	Y	Y	N	Y

For each participant, we record the time he takes when executing the assigned process. We also label the phase of execution along with the time records. Therefore, we have the total time in count as well as time spent on different phases (i.e. analysis, design, implementation and testing). The time information is regarded as the cost indicator for a secure process. For the benefit measurement, we compare the threat identified during each process's execution with the pre-recorded threat list (i.e. T1, T2, T3 and T4). The "Y" and "N" in the last four columns represents whether the given threat has been identified (Y) or not (N).

As the participants are students instead of professionals, the absolute number of time spent on each process may have systematic deviation (longer than real cases). However, the relative ratios among different time pieces still make sense (as participants hold a similar productivity level). For the total time, we can see SDL > p2 > p3 > CLASP > p1 > Touchpoints. In the three original secure processes, SDL seems to be the most heavyweight. Interview with s2 confirms this, mostly for SDL requires taking the STRIDE check for each element in the DFD. As a result, s2 substitute the intensive check activities with units from Touchpoints when customizing p2. Similar cases also happen between (CLASP, p1) and (Touchponts, p3), whereas s3 introduces more time-consuming units from other processes when customizing p3. For time spent in different phases, we can conclude that design and analysis take up large part of secure process. It seems that the conclusion on total time also holds in most phases: the customized process being more lightweight when its designer executes a heavyweight process, and vice versa.

For the identified threats, none of the cases cover the whole threats. T1 is identified by all the 6 processes, for dealing with 3rd party component is an important aspect for all the secure processes we study. T2, however, does not handled by SDL. According to our interview with s2, he did not consider such an abuse usage when executing SDL, and so as T3 (a typical attack pattern). SDL shows advantages when applying its STIDE model to identify T4, compared with CLASP and Touchpoints. After customized, the three new processes identify more threats (average 3) than the three original processes (average 2.3), which can be an evidence for the effectiveness of our approach.

As a final remark, we define Threats_Indentified / TotalTime_Consumed as a simple indicator for assessing secure processes. In this respect, we have: p1 > CLASP > p3 > p2 > Touchpoints > SDL. Generally, we can conclude that the three customized processes shows higher efficiency than single dedicated processes.

4.4 Threats to Validity

Broadly, there are questions about the extent to which the results gained by studying a small module would popularize, questions regarding the rationalization of our research method, and questions related to the chosen of p1 to p3 in our experiment.

We choose a small module on purpose (according to experiment setting F5), but this module is also security-critical (according to experiment setting F1). Considering most systems valuing trustworthiness commonly employ a well designed architecture composed of highly-coherent and loosely-coupled modules, we believe the conclusion gained from this module can be popularized to larger systems.

The rationalization of our research method is also an important point. The basic idea behind our experiment design is to simulate the case in industrial environment with afforded cost, as close as possible. Therefore, we require the project chosen should have complete in-process artifacts and make use of them when necessary, as if our secure team and other project participants work together at the same time. Admittedly, we have to abandon activities involving other stakeholders (e.g. customers, developers), which may influence the power of processes we study. Moreover, we train volunteers from our lab with the three secure processes as well as the chosen project's basic information, so that they can act like qualified secure team members. Besides these compromises, an additional benefit gained from our method is the acquisition of an easy, uniform and objective assessment basis for secure processes, which results from using a completed project with all its security issue recorded.

Last but not least, the three customized processes, namely p1, p2 and p3, are worthy of further discussion. The actual success of our approach highly depends on users' ability to customize a suitable process. In our experiment, we ask s1, s2 and s3 to customize their processes respectively, right after executing a certain dedicated secure process assigned to him. The main reason for this is we want to simulate real cases where processes are customized by knowledgeable managers based on their past experience with secure processes. Admittedly, the experiment can be further improved by letting participants experience more than one secure processes before perform customization, if resources permit.

5 Related Work

In [8], a systematic comprehension of three secure processes (CLASP, SDL and Touchpoints) is performed. One important conclusion of [8] is that the three processes compared are similar in many aspects, while have their own features. None of them is absolutely better than others, for each process has its advantages as well as disadvantages. Such a claim is close to the process family concept proposed by [9-10]. In [9-10], a board and general proposal for software process family is presented. However, how to implement the construction and application of process family is not mentioned in detail. Our work can be seen as a concrete step towards such a direction.

To our best knowledge, the idea of automatically integrating secure processes in the same family is new. There have been efforts on decomposing certain processes into more fine-grained units, and organizing them [12-14]. However, these approaches are highly manual. For example, OOSP [12] summarizes and organizes a group of patterns for object-oriented development. These patterns come from manual extraction of expert knowledge. Compared to them, we focus on providing automatic support, aiming to promote the usability and usefulness of the entire approach.

6 Conclusion

Supporting security is often an important requirement in many software projects. Over the years, a wealth of dedicated secure processes has emerged, forming a so called "Process Family". Conceptually, such a process family can take advantage of different security processes at a time. However, how to integrate secure processes within a process family should be answered first.

Therefore, we proposed an automatic approach to aid the integration of the three forefront secure processes, namely, CLASP, SDL and Touchpoints. Moreover, in order to evaluate our approach, we have conducted an exploratory experiment on a module from an e-government project. By comparing our approach with cases when one single secure process is employed, we find the result confirms the positive effects of our approach.

Our next step will be promoting our approach into industry. Currently, several Chinese software companies have expressed their great interest to try our approach in their projects. A concrete and substantial corporation plan is under discussion. We expect to gain more observations and insights in the near future.

Acknowledgement

This work is founded by the National Basic Research Program of China (973) under Grant No. 2009CB320703, the High-Tech Research and Development Program of China under Grant No. 2007AA010301 and the Science Fund for Creative Research Groups of China under Grant No. 60821003

References

[1] Taylor, D., McGraw, G.: Adopting a software security improvement program. IEEE Security & Privacy (2005)
[2] Byer, D., Shahmehri, N.: Design of a Process for Software Security. In: International Conference on Availability, Reliability and Security (2007)
[3] lightweight application security process, `http://www.owasp.org`
[4] Steve, L., Michael., H.: The Security Development Lifecycle (SDL): A Process for Developing Demonstrably More Secure Software. Microsoft Press, Redmond (2006)
[5] Gary, M.: Software Security: Building Security. Addison Wesley, Reading (2006)
[6] Mead, N.R., Houg, E.D., Stehney, T.R.: Security Quality Requirements Engineering (Square) Methodology. Software Eng. Inst., Carnegie Mellon Univ. (2005)
[7] Boström., G., et al.: Extending XP Practices to Support Security Requirements Engineering. In: International Workshop Software Eng. for Secure Systems, SESS (2006)
[8] Bart, R.S., Koen, D., Johan, B., Wouter, G.: On the secure software development process: CLASP, SDL and Touchpoints compared. Information and Software Technology, 1152–1171 (2008)
[9] Simidchieva, B.I., Clarke. L.A., Osterweil, L.J.: Representing Process Variation with a Process Family. In: International Conference on Software Process (2007)
[10] Sutton, S.M., Osterweil, L.J.: Product families and process families. In: Software Process Workshop (1996)
[11] Buyens, J.G.K., Win, B.D., Scandariato, R., Joosen, W.: Similarities and differences between CLASP, SDL, and Touchpoints: the activity-matrix, K.U. Leuven, Department of Computer Science (2007)
[12] Ambler, S.W.: Process Patterns: Building Large-Scale Systems using Object technology. SIGS Books/Cambridge University Press, New York (1998)
[13] Land, I.C.R., Larsson, S.: Process Patterns for Software Systems In-house Integration and Merge – Experiences from Industry. In: Software Engineering and Advanced Applications (2005)
[14] Wang, Y., Meng, X.-x., Shi, L., Wang, F.-j.: A Process Pattern Language for Agile Methods. In: Asia-Pacific Software Engineering Conference (2007)

Engineering Adaptive IT Service Support Processes Using Meta-modeling Technologies

Beijun Shen[1,2], Xin Huang[1], Kai Zhou[1], and Wenwei Tang[3]

[1] School of Software, Shanghai Jiaotong University, Shanghai 200240, China
{bjshen,hxin,zhoukai}@sjtu.edu.cn
[2] Key Laboratory of High Confidence Software Technologies (Peking University), Ministry of Education, Beijing, 100871, China
[3] IBM Corp., Shanghai 201203, China
wwtang@ibm.com

Abstract. IT service support is a process-oriented practice that strives to manage the efficient supply of IT services with guaranteed quality. Many organizations adopt best practices and tools in order to improve the maturity of IT service support processes. However, when existing solutions and methodologies are applied in various organizations, the customization efforts and costs are usually large. And also dynamic changes during IT service support process execution can't be supported by almost all of the existed tools. Furthermore, process model integration, reuse and exchange still remain challenges in IT service support process modeling area. In this context, an IT service support process metamodel is presented in this paper. The metamodel extends a generic business process definition metamodel – BPDM, through its domain characteristics. Based on the proposed metamodel, we develop a flexible IT service support process engineering platform, which integrates and automates IT service support processes including incident, problem, change, release and configuration management. In contrast to other IT service support tools, besides process modeling and enactment, it can evolve the metamodel, interchange process models with other tools through metamodel parsing adapter flexibly, and also support adaptive process management via metamodel-based ECA rules.

Keywords: IT service support, process engineering, Metamodel, MDA.

1 Introduction

With the rapid evolution of Information Technologies (IT), to many organizations, the importance of IT has been unceasingly increasing, more and more getting into the main business of an organization in depth. As a result of its increasing role in the organization, the focus of IT management has moved from device-oriented management to service-oriented management [1]. Many organizations have tried to adopt IT service support processes, techniques and tools to manage the efficient supply of IT services with guaranteed quality. Efforts have been taken to make a progress, but new challenges emerged: (1) When existing solutions are applied in various organizations, the customization costs are usually too large, small firms in particular [2]. (2) Dynamic changes during IT service support process execution can't be supported by almost all of the

J. Münch, Y. Yang, and W. Schäfer (Eds.): ICSP 2010, LNCS 6195, pp. 200–210, 2010.

existed tools. (3) Even with universal understanding of IT service support concepts, integration, reuse and exchange of process models in different process model languages still remain challenges.

In this paper, meta-modeling of IT service support process is provided to solve the above problems. Metamodel is an explicit model of the constructs and rules needed to build specific models within a domain of interest. We propose a metamodel of IT service support process, then develop a flexible IT service support process engineering platform based on it, where a process modeling tool is developed by model driven approach, and a set of flexible IT service support process rules are designed and implemented to support adaptive process management.

The rest of the paper is organized as follows: Section 2 introduces IT service support process metamodel. Section 3 briefly describes the architecture of IT service support process engineering platform. Section 4 explains the MDA approach applied in development of process modeling tool. Section 5 focuses on business rule design for adaptive process management. Section 6 presents related work, and finally section 7 concludes the paper.

2 Metamodel of IT Service Support Process

To be the base of IT service support process engineering, the proposed metamodel should satisfy the following requirements: (1) It should describe the core concepts of IT service support process clearly and systematically. (2) It should support metamodel-based process modeling and business rule design. (3) It should avail integration, exchange, reuse of metamodel-based process models in different modeling languages.

2.1 Meta-modeling Approach

There are many separate business process domains, such as software process, supply chain, workflow, manufacturing process and etc. IT service support process is business process too, which has five core sub-processes: incident management process, problem management process, configuration management process, change management process, and release management process [4]. While each domain has its own distinct metamodels, there exist some core similarities. It may thus be interesting to propose an IT service process metamodel inheriting a more generic business process metamodel, as shown in Figure 1. Expected benefits are reuse and facilities for process models translation from one metamodel to another.Using this process metamodel architecture, the IT service support process meta-modeling method consists of two steps:

Step1: Select an appropriate business process metamodel. We should first analyze IT service support domain and extract its abstract process concepts based on its best practices. Comparing these entities with concepts of existed business process metamodels, we can select the most appropriate one.

Step2: Extend generic process metamodel to build the IT service support process metamodel. It will be extended to include features and particular concepts of IT service support process domain, using the Meta-Object Facility (MOF) [5] technology.

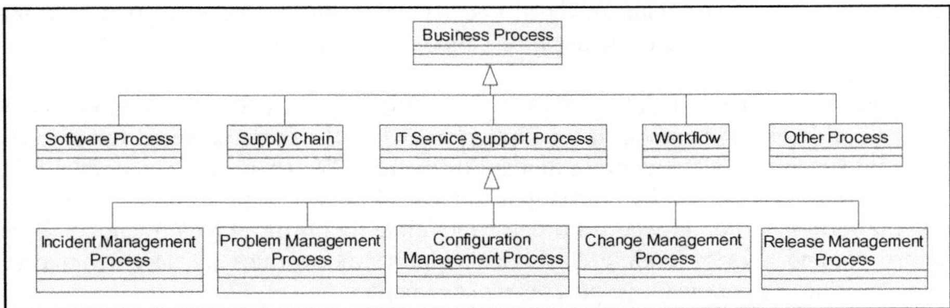

Fig. 1. Process metamodel architecture

In the following sub-sections, the above meta-modeling steps will be discussed in details.

2.2 Select an Appropriate Business Process Metamodel

IT Infrastructure Library (ITIL) [4] which was developed by the Central Computer and Telecommunications Agency of the UK government in the middle of 1980s, provides a comprehensive, consistent and coherent set of best practices for IT and is becoming the de facto standard for IT service support. So, we extract IT service support process concepts from ITIL specifications. From the process aspect, the key concepts of IT service support include process, activity, role, actor, resource and so on. Then we compare these concepts with core elements of four popular business process metamodels -- Simple Metamodel for Business Process (SMBP) [7], UML Activity Diagram (UML AD) [8], Event Process Chain (EPC) [9], Business Process Definition Metamodel (BPDM) [10], as shown in Table 1. Through the above analysis, we come to conclude that BPDM best supports modeling of IT service support process.

Table 1. Comparison of Core Elements of Metamodels for Business Processes

Core Element of IT Service Support	Core Element of SMBP	Core Element of EPC	Core Element of UML AD	Core Element of BPDM
Process	Process	Function	(not sepecified)	Process
Activity	Process	Function	Activity	Activity
Action	Activity	ElementaryFunction	Action	Simple Activity
Role	(not sepecified)	Organisation Role	Swimlane	Performer Role
Processor Role	(not sepecified)	(not sepecified)	(not sepecified)	Processor Role
Resource	Data	Information Object	LinkEndData	Holder

BPDM is proposed by OMG. It provides the capability to represent and model business processes independent of notation or methodology thus bringing these different approaches together into a cohesive capability through using metamodel. This metamodel captures the meaning behind the notations and technologies in a way that can help integrate them and leverage existing assets and new designs. The metamodel behind BPDM uses the OMG MOF standard to capture business processes in this very general way, and to provide XML syntax for storing and transferring business process models between tools and infrastructures. So, the BPDM metamodel is selected as a base for IT service support process metamodel. Fig. 2 shows the core of BPDM Metamodel.

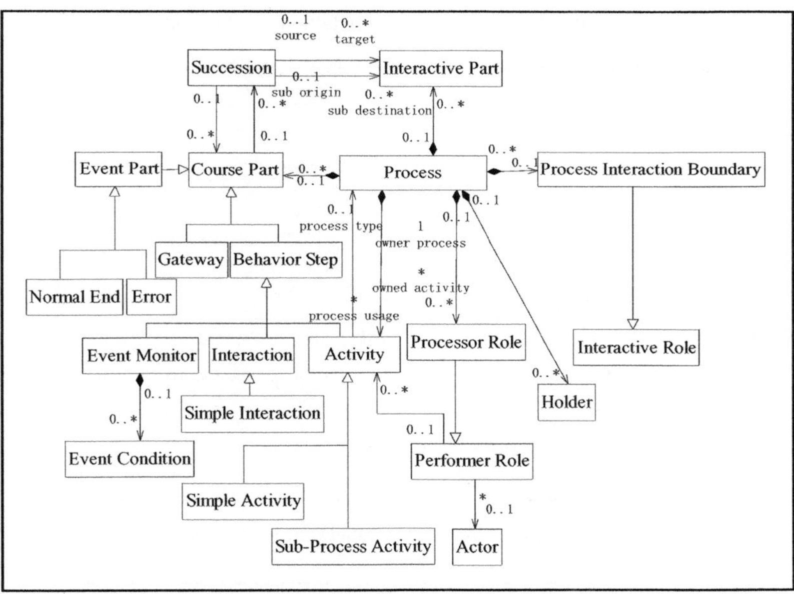

Fig. 2. BPDM core element metamodel

2.3 Build IT Service Support Process Metamodel

We extend BPDM for better reflecting the characteristics of IT service support process from three aspects: activity, resource, and interaction. The extension of BPDM is also in accordance with MOF. Fig. 3 shows an activity view of metamodel extension, where several simple activities/ actions (e.g. Email Message, Record, and Feedback) are defined. These activities form the atomic behavior of the process.

Fig. 4 shows a resource view of metamodel extension, where "Resource" extends "Holder" because resource is playing an important role in IT service support process. Like a Behavior Step indicates the state in process, the new added "State" class also makes the lifecycle of the resource accessible. Some kinds of resources are listed in the metamodel, such as "Incident Record" and "Problem Record".

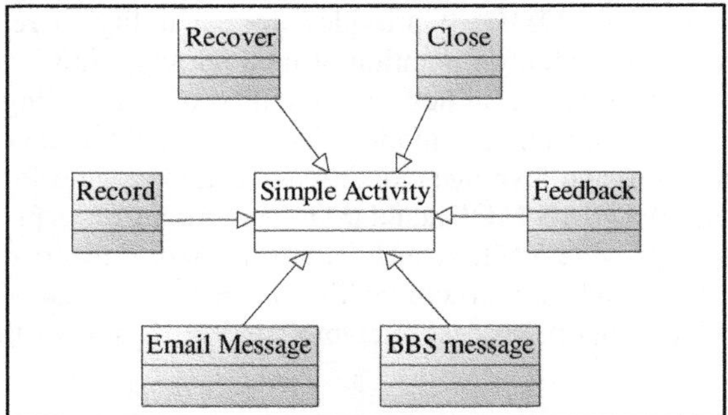

Fig. 3. Activity view of metamodel extension

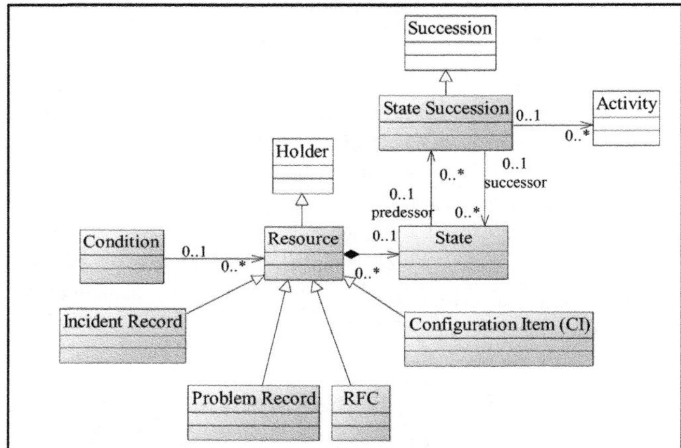

Fig. 4. Resource view of metamodel extension

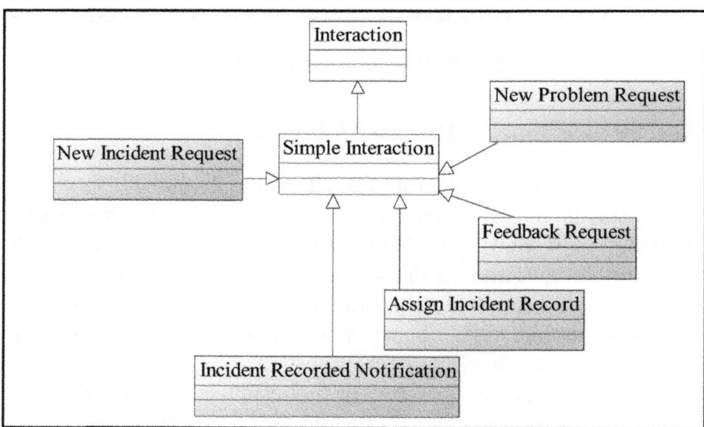

Fig. 5. Interaction view of metamodel extension

"State" can be changed by certain activity. Also "State" has its succession, namely "State Succession", which can connect to different "State" objects. The transition between states is inspired by activities.

Fig. 5 shows an interaction view of metamodel extension, where several kinds of simple interactions are listed, such as "New Incident Request" and "Incident Recorded Notification".

3 IT Service Support Process Engineering Platform

Based on the proposed IT service support process metamodel, we develop a flexible IT service support process engineering platform named ITSPP, to support the IT service support process modeling, business rule management and process enactment.

ITSSP consists of four main modules: IT Service Support Process Modeler, IT Service Support Process Engine, Business Rule Definer and Business Rule Engine, as shown in Fig. 6. IT Service Support Process Modeler provides graphic UI to define the process models based on Metamodel. IT service support Process Engine executes the defined processes. Business Rule Engine checks the Business Rules and runs them when events occur.

ITSSP is a J2EE application. Several frameworks are used for developing: ExtJS for designing friendly user interface, Struts+Spring+Hibernate for handling and accessing web request/response data. The Business Rule Engine is implemented using Spring AOP technology.

In the following sections, we will examine how ITSSP realizes IT service support process modeling and business rule based on metamodel.

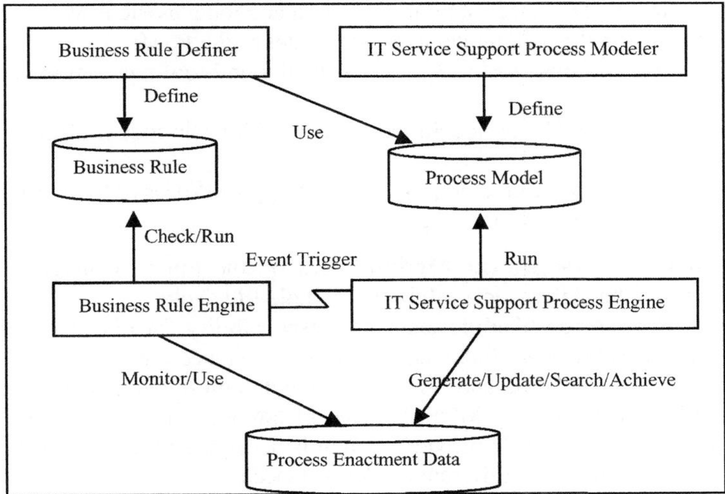

Fig. 6. Structure of IT service support process engineering platform

4 Model-Driven Development of IT Service Support Process Modeling Tool

We develop IT service support Process Modeler in ITSSP by Model Driven Architecture (MDA) development approach [3], which was brought forward by Object Management Group (OMG). In MDA methodology, the construction of applications focuses on the definition of platform-independent models (PIM) which are further used to generate platform-specific models (PSM) and later, code automatically.

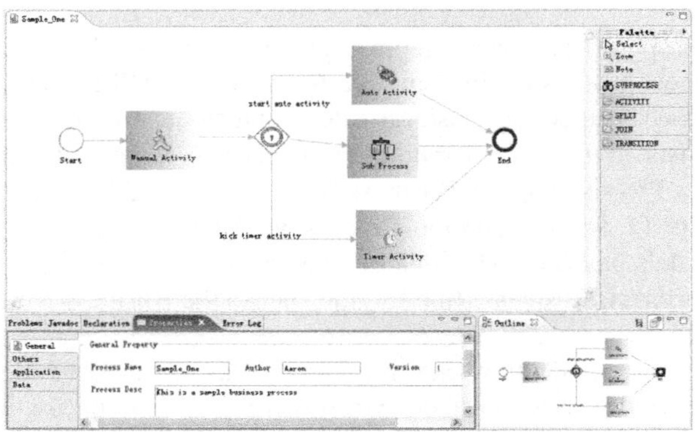

Fig. 7. GUI screenshot of IT service support process modeler

The development of IT Service Support Process Modeler consists of following steps, using GMF, an open-source framework under Eclipse:

Step 1, define the IT service support process metamodel as the PIM;

Step 2, transform the metamodel to Ecore model as the PSM;

Step 3, create assisting models (graphical model and tool panel model) needed by GMF;

Step 4, generate the IT Service Support Process Modeler code scaffold from above models.

Using model driven architecture, IT Service Support Process Modeler is composed of 5 logical modules, as shown in Fig. 8.

1) **Metamodel Management Module** takes on the job of managing model instances based on the metamodel, within their whole life cycle.

2) **Model Persistence Module** takes the responsibility for object serialization. It adopts XMI (XML Metadata Interchange) as its persistence mechanism, which is also a standard proposed by OMG and is chosen as the default implementation of serialization in GMF framework. Any MOF depicted metamodel can be serialized into XMI format. The key attribute is "xmi:type", which is configured for model type, thus, the entry point for adaptation of different model instances.

3) **Graphical Controlling Module** holds the mapping relationship between the graphical model instances and the underlying domain model objects. It visualizes the underlying model objects, and provides model verification functions from both syntactic and semantic aspects.

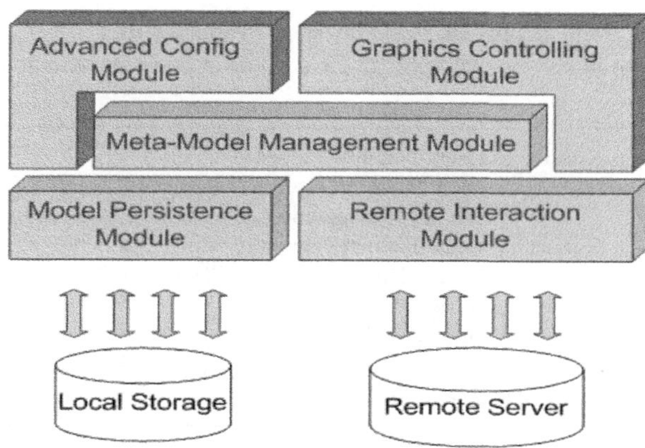

Fig. 8. Structure of IT service support process modeler

4) **Advanced Configuration Module** implements the detailed setting-up functionalities. On the basis of GMF, it offers the configuration functions in a consistent way, which is the "Property View" in eclipse platform. For instance, the assignment of "Role" in a process is just performed by this module.

5) **Remote Interaction Module** defines the interface of interaction with external system. "Remote Open", "Remote Save", "Deploy", "Search" and "Remote Delete" interfaces are implemented here. All of these are presented in terms of "Action" in eclipse platform.

Using an MDA approach in the construction of this tool allows it to be adjusted easily with respect to modifications in the metamodel. Also the transformation between IT service support process models and other business process models is supported through metamodel parsing adapters in this tool, which allows interchange process information with other tools.

5 Process Rule for Adaptive IT Service Process Management

IT Service Support Process Modeler allows users to define their personalized process models in a visual way. However, the defined process model is lack of adaptability, in that the process is predefined, static, and does not evolve because there is no support for dynamic process change in its specifications. The only method to accept change is to sequentially stop the currently running process, modify the process definition, and then redeploy it to the process engine [20]. So, it can't satisfy the agility feature of IT service support processes, which should quickly respond to changes.

In ITSSP, Event-Condition-Action rules are used as part of its process architecture, to realize such flexible process management. The implementation of rules cut across several activities of a process definition, which can be changed dynamically in run-time. From the view of modularity and adaptability, it is important to separate business rules from the core IT service support processes.

An ECA rule has the general syntax:

on event **if** condition **do** actions

When certain event occurs and condition is available, then action or application is executed. Fig. 9 shows some examples of ECA rules in an incident management process.

```
Rule1: On (NewIncidentRequest)
         If (equal (IncidentRecord.Emergency,"High")
         Do Email_Message.do (...)
Rule2: On (NewIncidentRequest)
      If (equal (IncidentRecord.Type,"Hardware")
         Do Assign.do(...)
Rule3: On (IncidentClosureRequest)
         If (equal (IncidentRecord.State,"Open")
         Do Transition.do(...)
```

Fig. 9. ECA rule examples for Incident Management Process

Rule1: when a new incident with high emergency happens, system will inform the staff with Email. Rule2: when a new incident typed hardware happens, system will dispatch it to a specific expert. Rule3: when the incident closed, the state of the incident is set closed.

In ITSSP, all parameters (event, condition and action) in ECA rules use the core elements in IT service support process metamodel. These rules can be defined and managed dynamically during process enactment by Business Rule Definer, and checked and run by Business Rule Engine. We use AOP technology to implement the Business Rule Engine.

6 Related Work

Related work can be presented from three aspects: IT service support process modeling, meta-modeling and tool.

1) IT service support process modeling
Process modeling is a hot topic and attracts global research and practice. Lots of process modeling languages are provided with suitable control flow features such as BPEL4WS [10], XPDL/BPMN [11], ebXML/BPSS [12], UML [8], and Event-Process-Chain (EPC) [9]. However, although these process modeling languages are capable of modeling process for IT service support, they generally lack expressiveness regarding the IT service support domain characteristics. To our best knowledge, there is no dedicated modeling language designed for IT service support process. Commercial organization ARIS is also working on this ITIL Reference Model, but its target is to clarify the ITIL concepts, and not to model related processes.

2) IT service support process metamodel
Metamodel is the base of model. So far, there are many publications and researches about process metamodel. These metamodels construct and refine the concepts in process domains such as software development [13], security [14], performance [15] and broader process framework [16] and so on. However, research work on IT service

support metamodel is quite limited. [17] presents an IT Service evaluation metamodel, and has different focus from our work. [18] gives a pioneer work on problem management process metamodel. Based on his work, [19] makes an improvement and proposes an ITIL Definition Metamodel. However, their work still stays very brief as the metamodel only covers problem management process and main concepts.

3) IT service support process engineering tool
There have been some commercial tools of IT service support process engineering such as IBM's Tivoli solution, HP Openview, BMC's Remedys solution, CA's ServicePlus Service Desk etc. All of these tools focus to provide services to large IT organizations, meeting their different requirements through offline configuration or offshore development. However, few of them support dynamic changes during process executions, and also the process models from these different tools can't be integrated, interchanged and reused easily.

Our work is developing an adaptive IT service process engineering platform using meta-modeling technology. This platform can not only help to model the IT service support process visually, but also support dynamic process changes via ECA rules, evolve metamodel, and interchange process models with other tools flexibly.

7 Conclusions

In this paper, we propose an ITIL-based IT service support metamodel through extending a generic business process metamodel by IT service support domain characteristics. Based on the proposed metamodel, we have developed a flexible IT service support process platform — ITSSP. The platform integrates and automates IT service support processes including incident, problem, change, release and configuration management. It not only supports process modeling and enactment, but also supports adaptive process management via ECA rules.

Using meta-modeling technology in IT service support processes engineering, has gained following benefits:

1) Supporting the changes of IT service support processes on demand, both at model level and at metamodel level.
2) Assisting model integration, exchange and reuse between IT service support process and other business processes.
3) Generating code scaffold of IT service support process modeling tool from metamodels, following MDA approach.
4) Facilitating the design of IT service support process rules with the core elements of metamodel, to support dynamic process logic changes.

Since March, 2009, ITSSP has been deployed in three companies: Shanghai Hardware Fasteners Co., Ltd, China Network Co., Ltd, YunHao Machine Electronic System Engineering Co., Ltd. All of these practices have shown that ITSSP provides flexible approaches to static process modeling and dynamic rule definition, and it helps them to build an IT service support system with process engineering technology, thus improves the quality and efficiency of their IT services.

Acknowledgements. This research is supported by the Opening Project of Shanghai Key Lab of Advanced Manufacturing Environment (No. KF200902), and the Opening Project of Key Laboratory of High Confidence Software Technologies (No. HCST201001).

References

1. Drago, R.B., et al.: A Proposed Web Tool for IT Environment Service Management. In: Proceedings of International Conference on Internet and Web Applications and Services (2006)
2. Aileen, C.S., Tan, W.G.: Implementation of IT Infrastructure Library (ITIL) in Australia: Progress and success factors. In: IT Governance International Conference, Auckland, NZ (2005)
3. Mi, P., Scacchi, W.: A Meta-Model for Formulating Knowledge-Based Models of Software Development. Special issue: Decision Support Systems 17(4) (1996)
4. The Stationery Office, Office of Government Commerce, United Kingdom: ITIL and IT Service Management (2010), http://www.itil.org.uk
5. OMG: Meta Object Facility (MOF) 2.0 Core Specification, OMG Adopted Specification ptc/03-10-04 (2003)
6. Mendling, J., van Dongen, B.F., van der Aalst, W.M.P.: Getting Rid of the OR-Join in Business Process Models. In: Enterprise Distributed Object Computing Conference (2007)
7. Curtis, B., Kellner, M., Over, J.: Process Modeling. Communication of the ACM 35(9) (1992)
8. OMG: Unified Modeling Language (UML) Specification: Superstructure, V2.0 (2005), http://www.omg.org/docs/formal/05-07-04.pdf
9. OMG: Business Process Definition Metamodel (BPDM). OMG Adopted Specification ptc/03-10-04 (2003)
10. OASIS: Web Services Business Process Execution Language. V2.0 (2007), http://docs.oasis-open.org/wsbpel/2.0/OS/wsbpel-v2.0-OS.html
11. OMG: BPMN Specification V2.0 (2009), http://www.bpmn.org/
12. OASIS: Business Process Specification Schema v1.01 (2001), http://www.ebxml.org/specs/
13. Florac, W.A., Carleton, A.D.: Measuring the Software Process: statistical process control for software process improvement. Addison-Wesley Professional, Boston (1999)
14. OMG: Enterprise Distributed Object Computing, OMG Adopted Specification ptc/03-10-04 (2003)
15. Bézivin, J.: On the unification power of models. Software and System Modeling 4, 2 (2005)
16. Firesmith, D.G., Henderson-Sellers: The OPEN Process Framework. The OPEN Series. Addison-Wesley, London (2002)
17. Goeken, M., Alter, S.: Representing IT Governance Frameworks as Metamodels. In: Proceedings of the 2008 International Conference on e-Learning, e-Business, Enterprise Information Systems, and e-Government (2008)
18. Jäntti, M., Eerola, A.: A Conceptual Model of IT Service Problem Management. In: Proceedings of the IEEE Conference on Service Systems and Service Management (ISSSM 2006). University of Technology of Troyes, France (2006)
19. Strahonja, V.: Definition Metamodel of ITIL. Information Systems Development Challenges in Practice, Theory, and Education, vol. 2 (2009)
20. Park, C., Choi, H., et al.: Knowledge-based AOP Framework for Business Rule Aspects in Business Process. ETRI Journal 29(4) (2007)

Modeling a Resource-Constrained Test-and-Fix Cycle and Test Phase Duration

Dan Houston and Man Lieu

The Aerospace Corporation, P.O. Box 92957, Los Angeles, California 90009
{daniel.x.houston,man.v.lieu}@aero.org

Abstract. Software process simulation has been proposed as a means of studying software development processes and answering specific questions about them, such as, "How feasible is a schedule?" This study looked at the question of schedule feasibility for a testing process constrained by availability of test facilities. Simulation models of the testing process were used to identify the significant factors affecting the test duration, estimate a likely completion time for the testing, and provide an empirical basis for re-planning the testing.

Keywords: Test and fix cycle, software rework cycles, test phase duration simulation, resource-constrained testing.

1 How Long Will Testing Take?

An old question in systems development asks, "How long will it take until the software is ready?" For many projects, this comes down to a test-and-fix cycle, often complicated by a number of factors such as schedule pressure, software quality, required software reliability, testing capability, and availability of test resources. The real difficulty lies, however, in understanding the dynamics of the rework process, a decidedly nonlinear process that defies linear attempts at estimation [1]. Lacking simulation tools and expertise, and faced with schedule pressure, an organization may succumb to the temptation of believing that a linear estimate—such as "30 hours per test case"—is adequate and, as they start to fall behind, that "we can make the schedule because testing will go faster as we get further along."

Initially motivated by a planning need [2] for having good estimates of test phase durations of real-time embedded software projects, we investigated this question of test schedule feasibility by modeling the software testing phase. We found that for real-time software, the real-time testing in dedicated facilities can be the bottleneck of the testing phase, so we focused particularly on the real-time test-and-fix cycle constrained by test facility availability. However, our modeling purpose has also included understanding and explaining [2] results in terms of the dynamics of the rework cycle. This need has been as important as planning because modeling lessons have been used to support data collection and process improvement decisions.

As the modeling scope is the test phase, the model flow is test cases and includes delays contributing to the test phase duration. We modeled the test phase duration across three stages: development of test cases, the software test-and-fix cycle (TaF),

J. Münch, Y. Yang, and W. Schäfer (Eds.): ICSP 2010, LNCS 6195, pp. 211–221, 2010.

and final testing (FT). In the first stage, each test case is developed and initially tested. When it is ready, it goes into the TaF stage with the target software for testing in a dedicated test facility. Once a test case runs fully in the real-time test facility without displaying anomalous behavior, it is ready for final test. The TaF stage may require multiple sessions in a test facility due to defects found, but the FT stage is expected to proceed without problems.

We used the models initially with designed experiments to learn about the factors driving a resource-constrained test-and-fix cycle. In subsequent work, we developed a procedure for applying the model to specific projects. The first part of the procedure is interviewing project personnel to learn the specifics of their resource-constrained testing phase so that models can be calibrated to adequately represent their testing phase. The other part of the procedure is obtaining and analyzing defect data from previous activities, such as peer reviews, as a basis for estimating the number of defects to be discovered. Later, the learning process continues as project performance data becomes available and that is used to improve the modeling so that it better represents the actual process.

This paper uses an example aggregated from the class of software development projects having a test-facility-constrained test phase. Test plans for these projects typically specify 100 to 200 test cases, so our example uses 150 test cases to illustrate common test completion behavior for this class of projects.

2 Related Work

Software process simulation models have long included defect detection and rework flows. To name a few, Abdel-Hamid and Madnick [3], Tvedt [4], and Zhang *et al.* [5] provide examples of software development simulation models that include defect detection and rework flows. However, the scope of these models is wider than the interest of this study. Also, these models do not use cyclic flows to model testing and fixing because, at their levels of abstraction, software was assumed to pass through once, usually with retesting included in the fixing activity.

The process described here includes a cyclic rework process, one in which software and test cases needed to pass through a test facility multiple times as defects were detected and fixed before the test case and software went back into the test facility for retesting. Modeling of rework cycles has been explored extensively by Cooper [6] and by Ford and Sterman [7], which both view product development as a rework process using a cyclic flow in a system dynamics model. In addition to the rework cycle, Cooper's model emphasizes the effects of various productivity-modifying factors such as staffing characteristics (hiring, experience, turnover, morale, and overtime), perceived progress, schedule pressure, and engineering revisions. In contrast, Ford's model supports representation of multiple phases using two rework loops, one for defects found in-phase and another for defects found downstream.

3 Models Employed

We had developed a versatile, multiphase system dynamics model of software development based on Ford's model. Our model was designed to represent a wide variety of hierarchically-organized software development projects using a matrix that specifies phase dependencies. Each phase is represented by an instance of the work/rework structure (Figure 1). Phases are related through three parameters: fraction of upstream defects found in the focal phase, fraction of released defects found downstream, and amount of work available based on work completed in the predecessor phase.

To apply the multiphase model to the testing process, we had to determine what constituted the primary flow and settled on test cases, which includes the software being tested, a significant execution thread through the software, and staff required to run the test. This definition allows us to avoid measuring the staff and productivity, concerning ourselves with only the time required for each operation in the process.

The multiphase model was configured such that the *producing work products* rate represented the first pass of work and *reworking work products* represented subsequent passes in each of the three stages. For the second stage, TaF, *producing work products* represented the first run using each test case with the software and *reworking work products* represented all subsequent test runs in this stage.

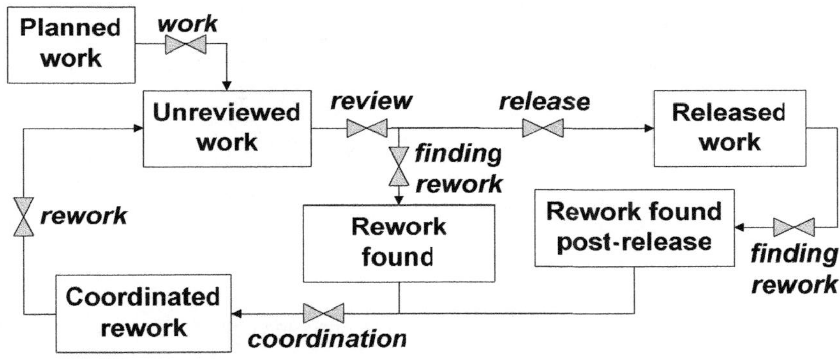

Fig. 1. Graphical View of the SDM Primary Workflow Loops

Discussions with project managers elicited five parameters of primary concern in the TaF stage: the incoming rate of test cases from the first stage, the availability of test facilities (*Test Facility Availability*), the time required to exercise each test case (*Test Run Duration*), the number of test runs required for each test case to ensure it runs without problems (*Runs per Test Case*), and the time to fix each problem found in testing (*Fix Time*).

In the course of configuring the multiphase model to the testing phase, we realized that it needed more detail to adequately represent the TaF stage of cycling each test case through testing and fixing. Specifically, a continuous model calculates a fraction of a flow to be reworked rather than circulating all work products for rework a number of times dependent on number of defects. We also needed to specify wait times for test cases and run experiments by varying the input parameters. These requirements are addressed better by modeling entities rather than continuous flow. Consequently, we produced a discrete event model for the TaF stage only and take the results back into the multiphase model.

The discrete event model (Figure 2) depicts arriving test cases receiving a value for the attribute, *Runs per Test Case*. Test cases are queued for a test facility and in the queue they are sorted by the number of runs that each has completed so far, giving preference of test facility usage to cases further along in the testing process. The test case at the front of the queue enters the first available facility, staying for the time required to perform the test case. After the test, the number of test sessions for the test case is incremented and checked: if it has reached its required number of runs, it is released for final testing, otherwise it is delayed while a problem is diagnosed and fixed. After the *Fix Time*, the test case is returned to the queue for another test run.

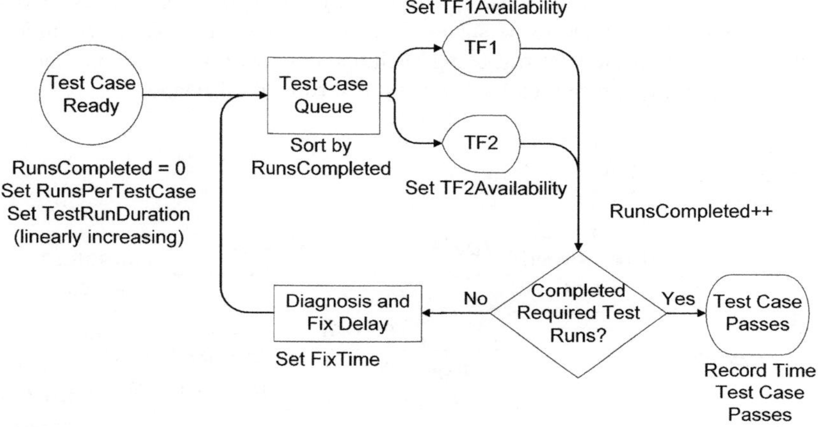

Fig. 2. Discrete Event Model of Software Testing Constrained by Test Facility Availability

4 Discovering Significant Factors and Behavior

The first experiment performed on the model was designed to determine the relative importance of the modeled input factors. The arrival rate of test cases is often a constant value, in this example, one new test case per day available for testing. For the remainder of the factors, a full factorial (2^4) experiment was run per Table 1.

Table 1. Factors and Values for Screening Experiment

Factor	Low Value	High Value
Test Facility Availability	60 hrs/ week	100 hrs/week
Runs per Test Case	2	8
Test Run Duration	2 hrs	5 hrs
Fix Time	24 hrs	96 hrs

Project personnel often expect that *Test Facility Availability* is the dominant factor in the test-and-fix cycle. However, experiments have shown that *Runs per Test Case* is the dominant factor in software test duration, in this example solely contributing to 54% of TaF duration variation and contributing to another 22% through interactions with other factors. In particular, this factor interacts strongly with *Test Run Duration.*

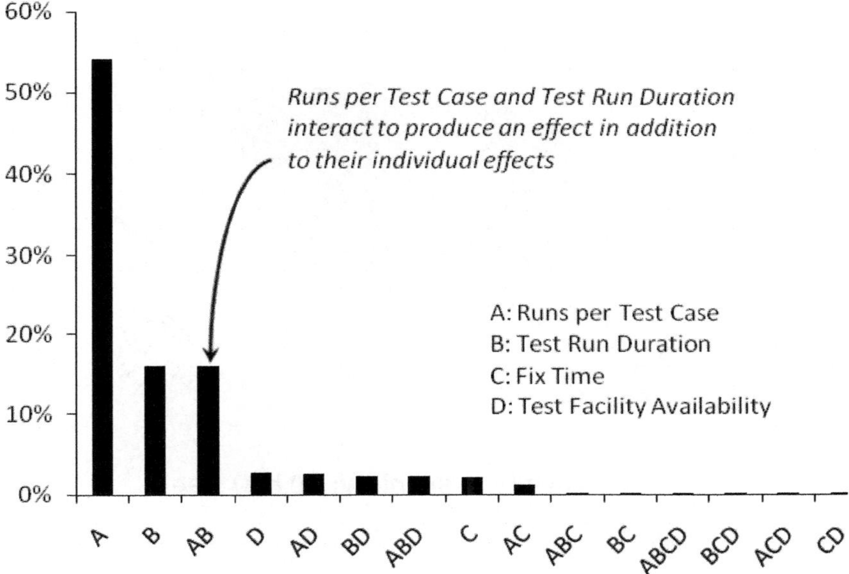

Fig. 3. Percent contribution to variation in software test-and-fix cycle duration

In a follow-up experiment, additional points were added to the experimental design (Table 2) in order to obtain response surfaces and a better understanding of the constrained test-and-fix cycle behavior. This experiment considered *Test Facility Availability* at two levels, 60 and 100 hours per week.

Table 2. Factors and Values for a Response Surface

Factor	Values
Test Facility Availability	60 and 100 hrs/week
Runs per Test Case	2, 4, 6, 8
Test Run Duration	2, 3, 4, 5 hrs
Fix Time	7 days

Response surfaces produced by this experiment show two regions distinguished by a threshold (Figure 4). On one side of the threshold is a planar surface; on the other, a steeply ascending surface rising to the point of the highest values of *Test Run Duration* and *Runs per Test Case*.

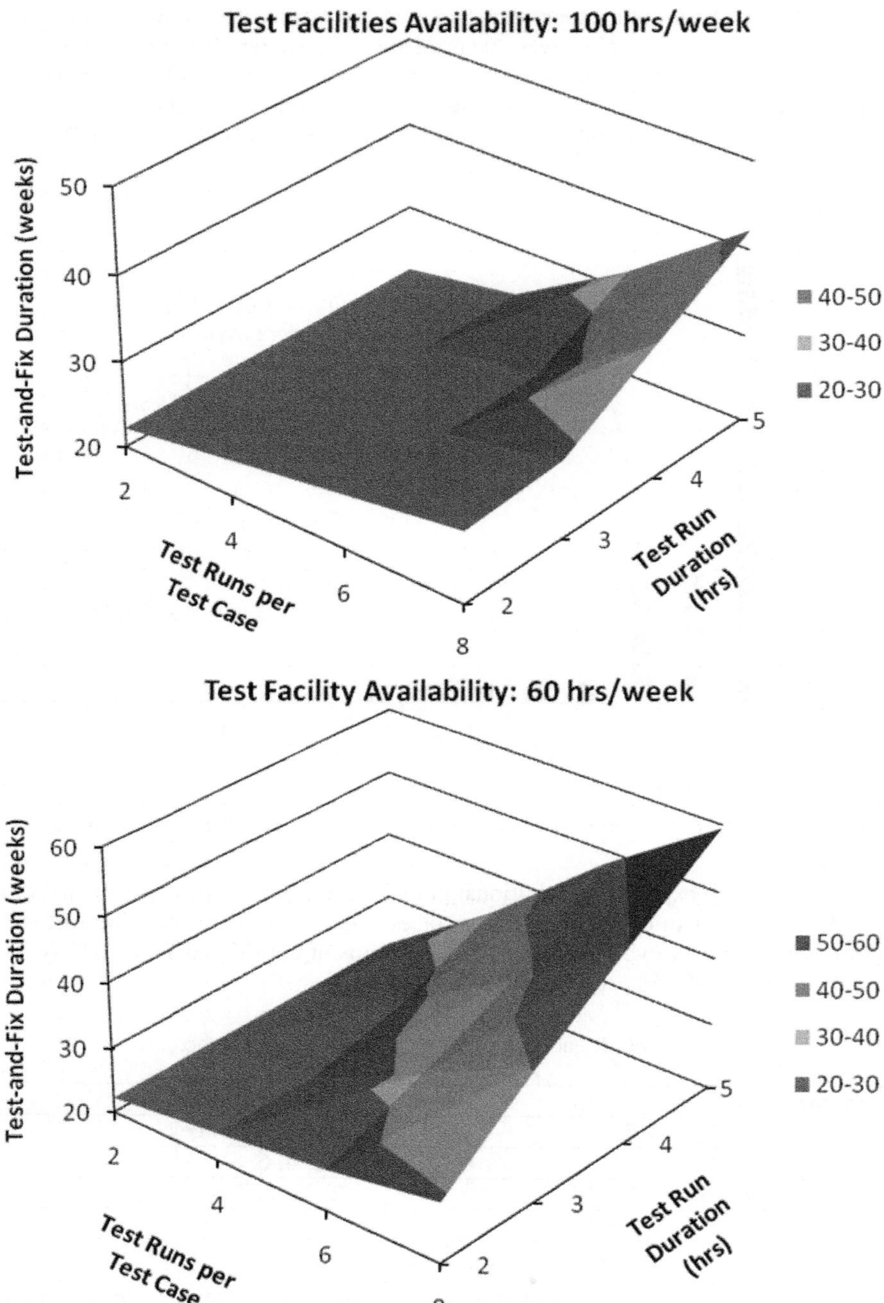

Fig. 4. Response surfaces showing interaction at full test facility utilization

The influence of *Runs per Test Case* is evident in both regions. The planar region reflects almost no increased duration due to *Test Run Duration*, but a slowly rising duration due to *Runs per Test Case*. In the steeply ascending region, *Runs per Test Case* interacts strongly with *Test Run Duration*.

The threshold represents the points at which the test facilities are fully utilized. When all other factors are constant, the full utilization threshold is a function of test facility availability. Thus, as *Test Facility Availability* decreases, shown in the contrast of the two Figure 4 graphs, the threshold moves out across the planar region, adding more area to the steeply ascending region and causing it to rise to a higher point. In practical terms, this means that the tighter constraint on test facility availability produces full utilization sooner and the accompanying interaction between *Test Run Duration* and *Runs per Test Case* lengthens the TaF duration.

It became clear from Figures 3 and 4 that test facility availability, though not the dominant factor in duration of the constrained test-and-fix cycle, is active as a facilitator of the dominance and interaction of other factors.

5 Modeling Likely Scenario and Alternatives

The next experiment used likely inputs to estimate the duration of the test-and-fix cycle (Table 3). In this example, the project plans to use each test facility 40 hours per week. The number of runs per test case can vary widely depending on staff experience, process maturity, and so forth, but our experience suggested a discrete distribution in which some cases require only 2 runs, a few might require as many as 8, and the most likely number of runs per test case was 4. The time required to run individual test cases, including the amount of test facility time required for setup and documentation, was modeled as a continuous triangular distribution between 2 and 5 hours with a mode of 3.5. Experience in previous projects showed that fixes normally required between one and two weeks, so *Fix Time* was modeled as a uniform discrete distribution for this period. Table 3 lists the distributions and how they were sampled.

Table 3. Inputs for estimating test-and-fix cycle duration

Factor	Values	Sample
Test Facility Availability	Both test facilities at 40 hrs/week each	Constant for all simulation runs
Runs per Test Case	(2, .1), (3, .1), (4, .3) (5, .2), (6, .1) (7, .05), (8,.05)	Randomly for each test case in each simulation run
Test Run Duration	Triangular(2, 3.5, 5) hrs	Randomly for each test case in each simulation run
Fix Time	(7, .125), (8, .125), (9, .125), (10, .125), (11, .125), (12, .125), (13, .125), (14, .125) days	Randomly for each test cycle of each test case in each simulation run

Figure 5 shows the results of 15 simulation runs, enough to exhibit both the variation and the pattern of test case completions. Despite the input variations, the completion time curves for 150 test cases produced a clear pattern comprised of two sections:

the curved tails and the straight middle. The length of the tails was found to be dependent on the *Fix Time* values: as the *Fix Time* distribution increases, it takes longer to initially complete test cases, as well as to clear the last test cases out of the cycle. The straight middle region occurs with full utilization of the test facilities. The slope of this linear region is largely determined by test facility availability, with a limit due to the incoming rate of test cases.

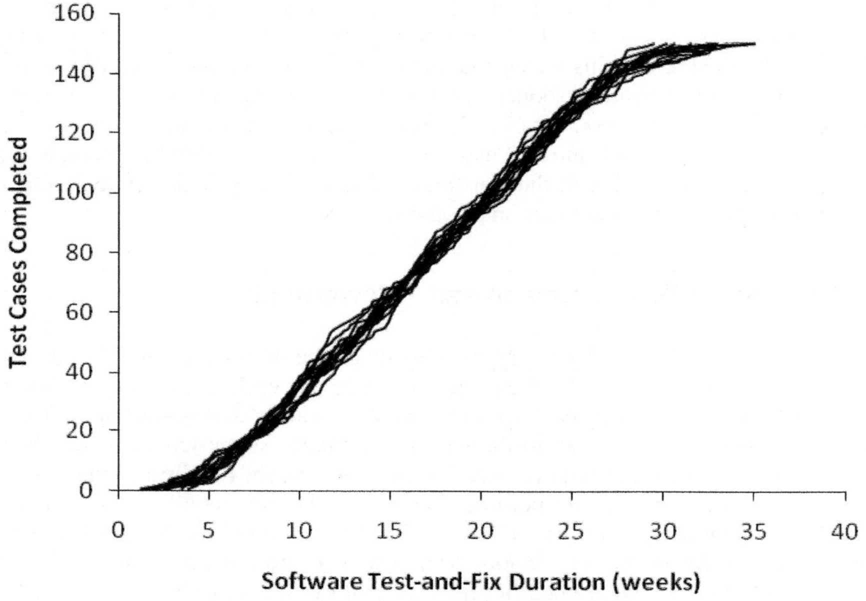

Fig. 5. Test case completion times for 15 simulation model runs

Confidence and prediction intervals are calculated for estimation purposes. For this example, the 95% confidence interval on the mean duration is 32 to 34 weeks (error estimate = .43), and the 95% prediction interval on duration is 29 to 36 weeks.

Project personnel often want to look at ways to reduce the test phase duration, so a number of questions about alternatives have been posed and studied using the model. For example, two questions were asked about increasing test facility availability, either through taking time late in the test phase from another test facility, or by constructing a new test facility. Neither of these options significantly reduced TaF duration because the additional testing capacity came too late in the TaF stage.

Sometimes project personnel question the initial assumptions behind their inputs and ask for simulation results using more optimistic assumptions. To illustrate, more optimistic distributions for *Runs per Test Case* and for *Fix Time* were tried in this example and they produced better results: improved *Fix Time* alone resulted in a 12% duration reduction, improved *Runs per Test Case* alone produced a 26% improvement, and improved *Fix Time* and *Runs per Test Case* together produced a 43% improvement. Achieving these results in practice is considered unlikely but they can demonstrate what is required to achieve a proposed test schedule.

6 Multiphase Model

The results of the constrained test-and-fix cycle model were taken back into the multiphase continuous model by calibrating the multiphase model to reproduce a 33 week TaF stage. The multiphase model had been configured to reproduce an incoming rate of one test case per day from the test case development stage. The final step in configuring the multiphase model was setting the concurrency and productivity for the final test (FT) stage.

Two cases were modeled based on resource contention. If the TaF runs are given priority over FT runs for test facility usage, then test cases completing TaF (thick, long dashes) proceed smoothly and FT completions (thick, short dashes) follow, more slowly at first but then rapidly as TaF is completed. On the other hand, if management chose to show test phase completion as soon as possible for some test cases, FT testing preempts TaF testing: TaF completes more slowly (thin dashes) while FT completion is accelerated (thin dotted line). Regardless of TaF or FT priority, FT completes very soon after TaF. However, the simulation results suggest that giving FT priority over TaF could delay the overall completion of testing, by about 2 weeks in this example (magnified showing that the thin dashed/dotted lines converge on 150 after the thick dashed lines).

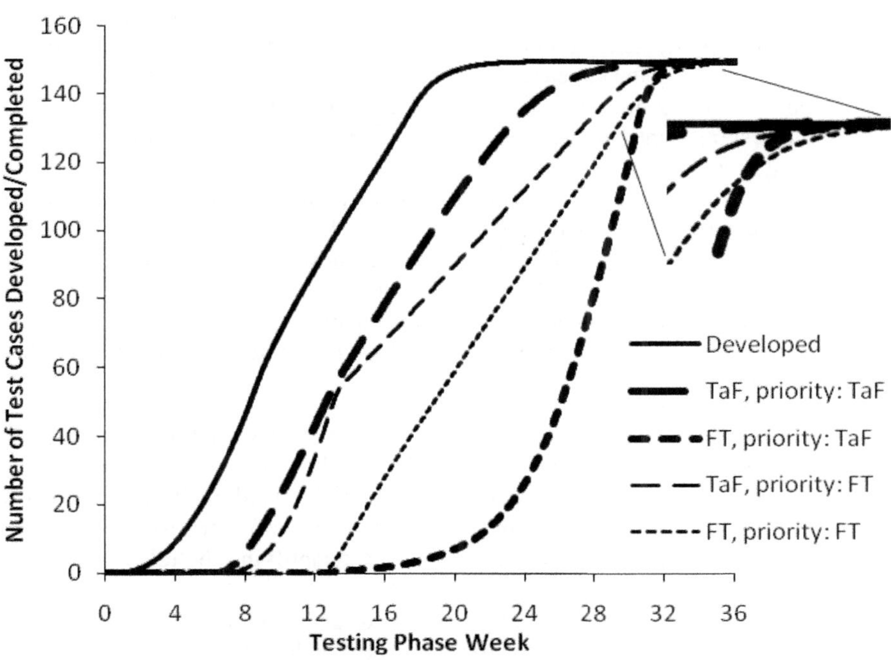

Fig. 6. Multiphase model results for completing development and use of test cases

7 Conclusions and Recommendations

This modeling project allowed us to identify the number of test runs per test case, rather than test facility availability, as the dominant factor in test phase duration. Though test facilities certainly enabled earlier completion of the test phase, the more important factor is reducing the number of test runs per test case because limited test resource availability greatly magnifies the effect of this factor once the test facilities become fully utilized. This factor is almost entirely dependent on the quality of the inputs to the testing phase, most importantly the software under test but also the test cases and the test facility.

Furthermore, we have found that the effects of delays and factor interactions are generally not understood and therefore not taken into account when estimating test duration.

Understanding the TaF cycle dynamics, we have been able to recommend a set of guidelines for reducing the duration of this cycle, ordering the first four based on the relative influence of factors.

- Conduct well-performed quality-inducing activities—for example, peer reviews, unit testing, and defect causal analysis—prior to employing the test facilities. The modeling provided case-based, quantitative support for this quality cost principle.
- Reduce the number of test sessions. If a test case fails, continue running it as far as possible in order to find further anomalies. Reduce diagnostic time through good anomaly documentation. This trade-off in favor of reducing the number of test runs comes at the expense of the less important factor, test run duration.
- Reduce the fixed time of test runs (setup, recordkeeping, saving files). Automation can significantly reduce time in a test facility, as well as facilitating good documentation of anomalies.
- Reduce the learning time of testers through training and regular communication. The efficiency of a test team can be undermined by individuals optimizing.
- Complete TaF before FT. This suggests that showing progress early may carry a cost in the form of a longer overall duration.
- As the end of TaF approaches, focus on reducing the time to provide fixes. As fewer test cases are left in the test-and-fix cycle, fix delays can dominate the cycle duration.

Though these guidelines may seem obvious to those well-versed in the economics of software quality, many development groups have only a vague notion of quality costs and, working under cost and schedule pressures, are inclined to choose poorly. Using a simulation model to demonstrate the dynamics of a specific process can make a very persuasive argument for good choices, as well as quantifying the relative importance of factors.

In addition to general guidelines produced for projects, specific modeling results have also been beneficial. In at least one case, modeling and simulation demonstrated that a proposed schedule was unrealistically optimistic. In that case, our recommendations to the test team helped them to mitigate some of the risks to the testing schedule.

8 Further Research

This modeling project has been very helpful in providing better planning information to project personnel. It is currently being used to track actual results and improve test phase forecasting. In addition, we plan to re-implement the models in a hybrid model.

References

1. Dörner, D.: The Logic of Failure: Recognizing and Avoiding Error in Complex Situations. Perseus Publishing, Cambridge (1996)
2. Kellner, M., Madachy, R., Raffo, D.: Software Process Simulation Modeling: Why? What? How? Journal of Systems and Software 46(2/3), 91–105 (1991)
3. Abdel-Hamid, T.K., Madnick, S.E.: Software Project Dynamics. Prentice Hall, Englewoord Cliffs (1991)
4. Tvedt, J.D.: An Extensible Model for Evaluating the Impact of Process Improvements of Software Development Time. PhD dissertation. Arizona State University (1996)
5. Zhang, H., Jeffrey, R., Zhu, L.: Hybrid Modeling of Test-and-Fix Processes in Incremental Development. In: Wang, Q., Pfahl, D., Raffo, D.M. (eds.) ICSP 2008. LNCS, vol. 5007, pp. 333–344. Springer, Heidelberg (2008)
6. Cooper, K.G., Mullen, T.W.: Swords and plowshares: The rework cycle of defense and commercial software development projects. American Programmer 6(5), 41–51 (1993)
7. Ford, D.N., Sterman, J.D.: Dynamic Modeling of Product Development Processes. System Dynamics Review 14(1), 31–68 (1998)

Visual Patterns in Issue Tracking Data

Patrick Knab[1], Martin Pinzger[2], and Harald C. Gall[1]

[1] Department of Informatics, University of Zurich, Switzerland
knab@ifi.uzh.ch, gall@ifi.uzh.ch
[2] Department of Software Technology, Delft University of Technology, The Netherlands
m.pinzger@tudelft.nl

Abstract. Software development teams gather valuable data about features and bugs in issue tracking systems. This information can be used to measure and improve the efficiency and effectiveness of the development process. In this paper we present an approach that harnesses the extraordinary capability of the human brain to detect visual patterns. We specify generic visual process patterns that can be found in issue tracking data. With these patterns we can analyze information about effort estimation, and the length, and sequence of problem resolution activities. In an industrial case study we apply our interactive tool to identify instances of these patterns and discuss our observations. Our approach was validated through extensive discussions with multiple project managers and developers, as well as feedback from the project review board.

1 Introduction

Most software development organizations have issue tracking systems in place where various information about the software development process is stored. Also with all the information requirements from CMMI and ISO certifications, there is a huge amount of data available for investigation. Applied correctly, the insights from such an investigation help to improve the development process.

However the data gathered from software projects have some properties that makes it hard to get meaningful results from traditional statistical analyses. The same properties are also deterrent to more advanced data mining approaches.

One of the biggest problem for statistical approaches is the severe right skewed distribution of the data gathered from software projects: Using problem reports (PRs) as a starting point we usually see a huge amount of problems that are fixed in a short amount of time, take only little effort, and affect only a small amount of source code modules. Calculating averages, comparing distributions, etc. does not yield the required insights. In the end, what does it mean if we can improve the average resolution time from 1 hour to 50 minutes, or even lower. It is very unlikely that the accuracy of the entered measures, *e.g.*, resolution time or effort, was that accurate to begin with. But on the other hand, finding the reasons why certain problems took more than 100 hours to be resolved, and present common patterns for these outliers, can help a manager to significantly improve the process.

J. Münch, Y. Yang, and W. Schäfer (Eds.): ICSP 2010, LNCS 6195, pp. 222–233, 2010.

Another problem with all the data gathered in software project repositories is quality. If the data is not used and discussed on a regular basis inside the project team, the accuracy of the human entered data is at best questionable. Entering accurate information is time consuming and does not yield direct results, *i.e.*, no new features get implemented. It is therefore difficult to motivate developers to dedicate enough time to this administrative tasks.

Given the difficulties stated above, we developed a visual approach that is strong in outlier detection, supports the discovery of common patterns, and helps in promoting discussions among the participating stakeholders regarding process development metrics. It also provides facilities to detect flaws in the entered data. The approach is based on the Micro/Macro Reading idea [1] and provides a combination of Overview and Details-on-demand where the big picture as well as detailed problem report (PR) information are displayed at the same time. This is a very important property of our approach and helpful for visual pattern detection.

In [2] we already presented the interactive features for data exploration. In this paper we present and discuss generic visual patterns found in effort measurement and problem life-cycle data. We also apply our visualization technique to an industrial case study conducted in the EUREKA/ITEA[1] project SERIOUS[2].

Discussing the results of our analysis with a group of project managers from our industrial partner, managers and researchers from the other partners, as well as the ITEA review board, which also consist of members from the industry, we have strong anecdotal evidence that our approach stimulates discussion, is easy to understand, and provides valuable insights into the data buried in software project repositories.

The remainder of this paper is organized as follows: in the next section we describe the data of our case study. In Section 3 we show the relevant elements of our visualization approach. In Section 4 we present typical patterns found in project data, and in Section 5 we present our case study and discuss the detected patterns. In Section 6 we present related work and then conclude in Section 7.

2 Industrial Data Set

In this section, we describe the data from our case study in more detail and establish the background for the next section where we present our visualization building blocks.

Out of the many attributes associated with a problem report we focus mainly on the following four:

- *estimatedEffort*: The estimated total effort in person hours to fix the problem
- *actualEffort*: The actual total effort in person hours
- *analyzer*: The person responsible to analyze the problem and estimate the effort
- *priority*: The priority assigned to the problem, possible values are: low, medium, high, and top

[1] http://www.itea2.org/

[2] Software Evolution, Refactoring, Improvement of Operational & Usable Systems.

The *estimatedEffort* is an estimate done by the *analyzer* who can be either a specially assigned person or the problem report owner herself. The *actualEffort* is the total effort actually used to fix the problem. It includes the analysis, the resolution, as well as the evaluation effort.

These attributes are relevant to improve the planning and resource allocation. If we know which PR needs the most effort, we can allocate more resources to the resolution of this PR. Here *estimatedEffort* comes into play, and also the difference between estimated and actual effort, because the quality of the estimates decides how well the effort prediction works. Based on priority more or less resources might be allocated to certain PRs.

In addition to the problem report attributes, we also extracted life-cycle data from the log files. The log files contain all changes to all the PR fields including status changes, *e.g.*, a PR is changed from *submitted* to *in_analysis*. All the PR (problem report) life-cycle states are shown in Figure 1. The states connected by thick solid arrows constitute the regular path a problem report travels from submitted to concluded. The other states (gray in the figure) are possible but less frequent. States can also be skipped or reached repeatedly, indicated by the dashed arrows.

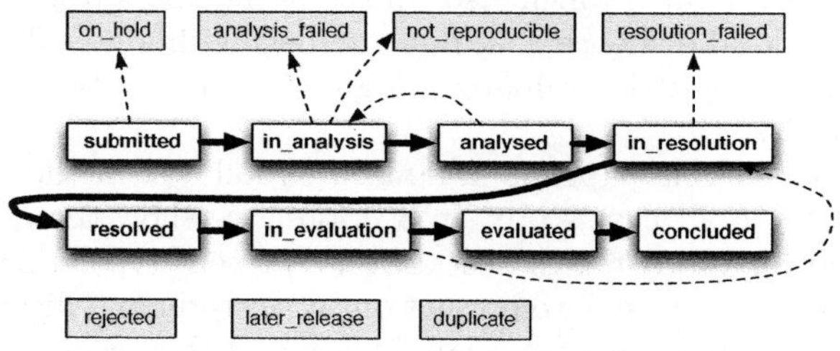

Fig. 1. Life-cycle States of Problem Reports

In an analysis, the transitions and the durations in the life-cylce of a PR allows to answer various questions concerning the relation of effort and time spent in the various phases, *e.g.*, *in_analysis* or *in_resolution*. Also the relation between priority and, for example, the duration of the *submitted* phase can give us interesting insights. In the case of a high priority PR we would expect a short *submitted* phase, since work was started as soon as possible.

3 Visualization Building Blocks

We present three relevant views of our visualization approach and the generic patterns that can be observed.

For the visualization of effort measures, we use **Polymetric Views** [3]. In Figure 2 the basic concepts of our visualization are shown: the width of the boxes

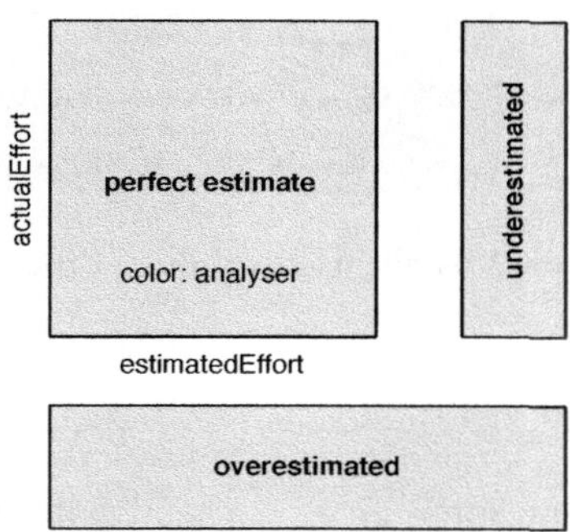

Fig. 2. Polymetric Effort Shape Patterns

is determined by the value of the *estimatedEffort* and the height by the value of the *actualEffort*. The effort measure is the sum of all efforts that were exerted to resolve the issue described by the problem report.

With this mapping we can get a quick and effective overview over the quality of estimates: balanced estimates (square boxes) constitute problems that were estimated accurately with respect to the actual resolution effort needed; underestimated (boxes that are thin and tall), and overestimated (boxes that are short and broad) PRs can also be spotted easily.

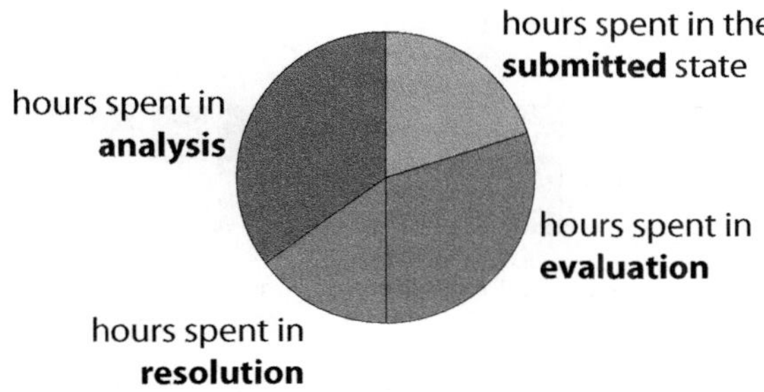

Fig. 3. Pie Chart Visualization Showing Process Step Lengths

To visualize the relative duration of process steps we use a **Pie Chart Visualization**. In Figure 3 we show a single pie with the mapping to the four process steps: *submitted, in_analysis, in_resolution, in_evaluation*. The size (*i.e.*, the area) of the pie is mapped to the total time from the creation of the PR until it was closed.

Finally our **Phase View Visualization** in Figure 4 is concerned with the process life-cycle sequence. This view depicts the sequence of the process steps, and allows an investigator to spot cycles and other exceptional situations.

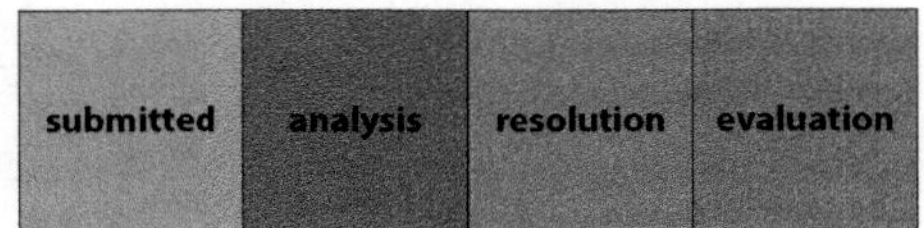

Fig. 4. Phase View Visualization to Show Process Step Sequences

4 Visual Patterns

In this section we present some generic visual patterns that we found in the course of our investigations. In the next section we will then show the actual instances of these patterns in the data of our industrial case study. The first part of this section presents the patterns for the **Polymetric Views**, followed by the patterns for our **Pie Chart View**, as well as our **Phase View** in the second part.

4.1 Effort Estimation Patterns

For all effort estimation patterns that we present in this paper, we mapped the color of the boxes to the analyzer. With this mapping we can assess the behavior of individual analyzers.

Fig. 5. Perfect Effort Estimates

In Figure 5 we see the pattern that we strive for. All the estimates of the four analyzers are perfect squares, *i.e.*, estimated and actual effort are the same. The problem with such a pattern, should it occur in actual data, is, that it is, most certainly, to good to be true. Therefore if one sees only or mostly squares this would be a strong indication that something with the data entry is wrong. If the picture looks like in Figure 6 the perfect estimates of the analyzer that was mapped to the blue boxes stand out. A manager should investigate the reason for this unlikely pattern.

Another pattern that indicates a flaw in the data entry is shown in Figure 7. In picture d) *always the same*, all the boxes have the same width which means, that the entered estimate was always the same. This is again a strong indication that the effort estimation was not done carefully or something else went wrong.

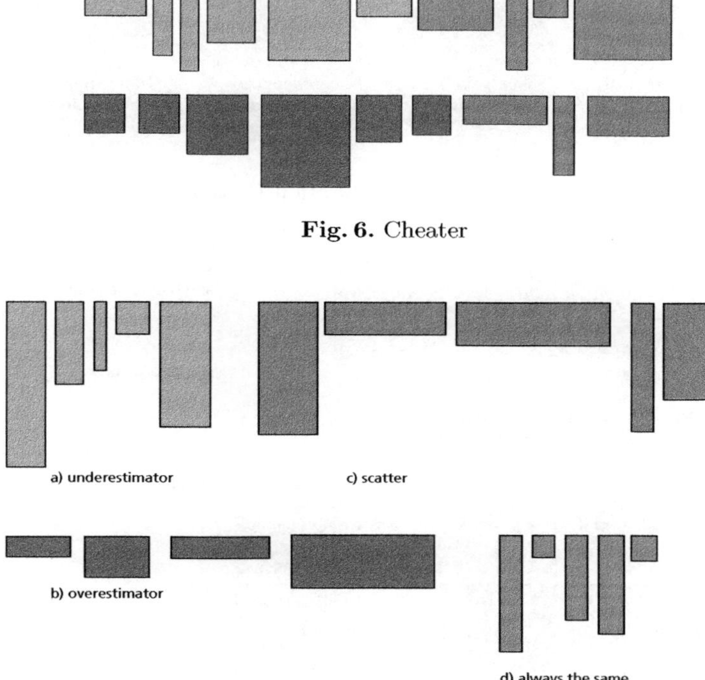

Fig. 6. Cheater

Fig. 7. Visual Effort Estimation Patterns

Again, the manager responsible for the estimation process should talk to the analyzer and improve the situation.

The patterns a) *underestimator* and b) *overestimator* provide probably the best information to improve the performance of certain analyzers. These analyzers show a strong tendency either towards underestimation or towards overestimation. With such a clear tendency it should be easy to correct their estimation behavior and improve the quality of the estimates. The pattern c) *scatter* shows a problem that is harder to correct since the effort estimations deviate in both directions, without a strong tendency that can easily be corrected. Therefore the only way to improve the quality of the estimates is to train the analyzer. Another explanation for the inaccurate estimates could also be that this particular analyzer just got the problems which are the hardest to analyze.

Similar considerations apply also to the patterns a) *underestimator* and b) *overestimator*. There are always multiple possible explanations for a weak estimation performance and it is necessary to investigate further, and especially discuss the initial findings with the affected engineers.

The primary goal of our visualization approach is not to asses the performance of analyzers but to help improve the software development process and find unwanted patterns that can then be corrected. If a correction is not possible

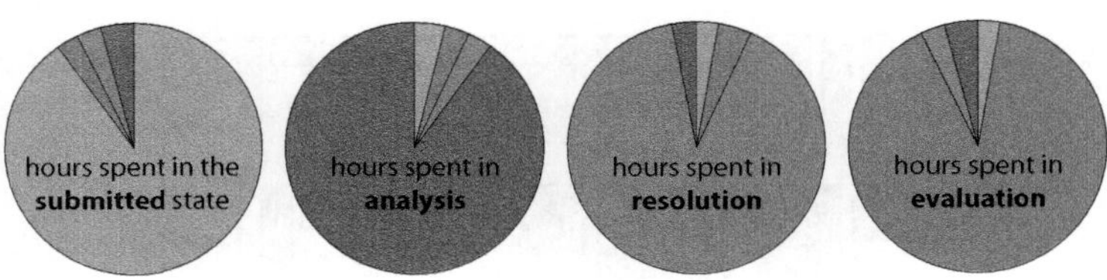

Fig. 8. Life-Cycle Duration Patterns

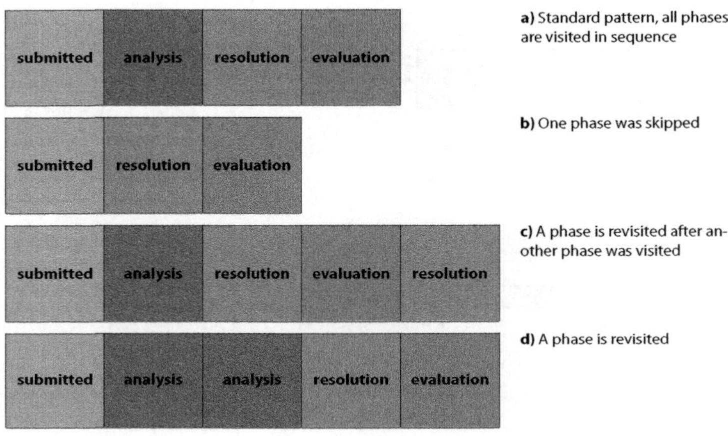

Fig. 9. Life-Cycle Sequence Patterns

then at least more knowledge about dependencies in the software process can be gained, which should than lead to improvements in future projects.

4.2 Process Life-Cycle Patterns

We present two visualizations for life-cycle patterns. One, the **Pie View** is mainly concerned with dominating process phases, *i.e.*, process phases, such as evaluation, that dominate the overall problem handling duration. In Figure 8 we depicted the possible domination patterns. The **Phase View** is then concerned with life-cycle step sequences. In Figure 9 we see the basic sequence patterns.

In combination with priority measures, the patterns provide information to improve the process and speed up the handling of high priority items. This can also be seen in the discussion of our case study in the next section.

5 Case Study

The case study is based on a five year multisite project in the consumer electronics domain. The issue tracking repository contains approx. 20'000 problem reports (PRs) that were handled by 368 distinct *analyzers*.

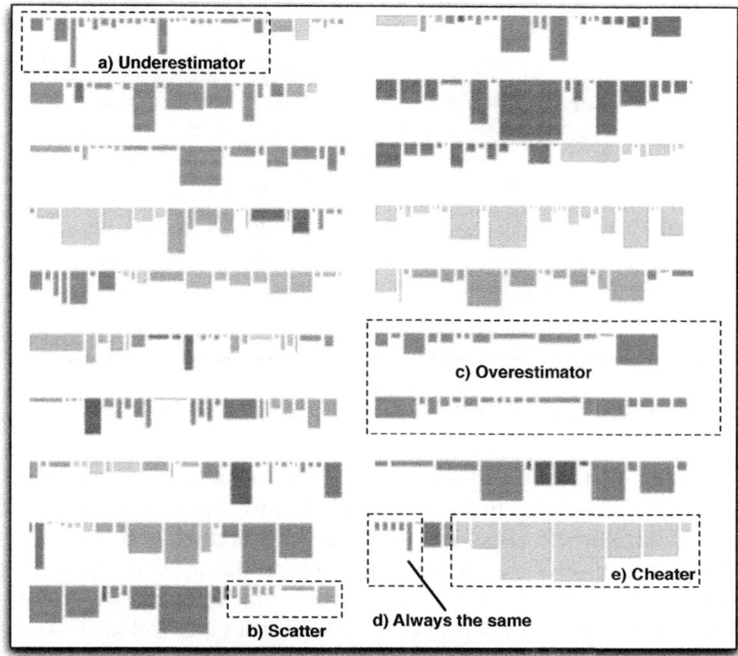

Fig. 10. Effort View on PRs Grouped and Colored According to the Analyzer

In Figure 10 we configured a view that groups and colorizes PRs according to the analyzer that did the estimation. Looking for patterns, we can see that there is a mix of estimation errors as well as some fairly well estimated PRs. There are instances of all the presented effort estimation patterns. We have highlighted an example for every pattern in Figure 10, but one can easily spot other occurrences for other analyzers.

Discussing the highlighted cases we see a), b), and c) where the main concern is to improve the quality of the estimates, but we have also the cases d) *always the same* and e) *cheater*. For d) and e) it might be advisable for a manager to talk to the corresponding analyzers and maybe also take the estimation performance from other projects into consideration. Since for d) the average actual effort is not that big, the impact on the overall project efficiency might be neglected. But for e) not only the perfect estimates are suspicious, but the actual effort measures are among the biggest in this display, and therefore the impact on the overall estimation quality is significant.

In Figure 11 we show the pie view for all top and high priority problems. In this view one of the main advantages of our visualization approach is very obvious. By presenting the complete context, *i.e.*, all the problem reports for the selected priority we automatically focus on problems with the most impact, *i.e.*, the biggest ones. Considering that we are looking at high priority items,

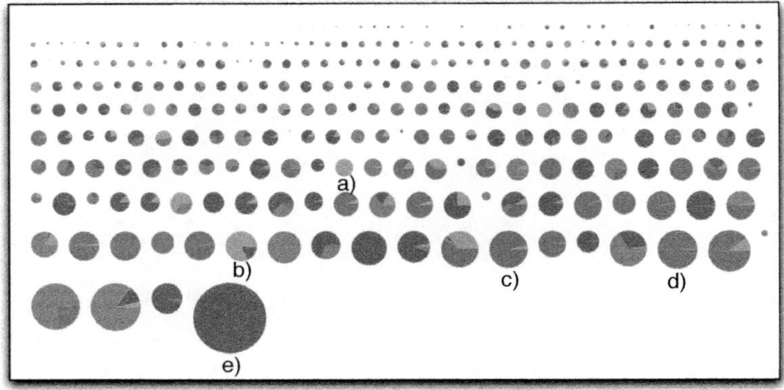

Fig. 11. Pie View for Top and High Priority Problems

the problems labeled a) and b) stand out, because they stayed most of the time in the submitted state. Again looking at their surrounding, almost no other pie displays a similar pattern. It might therefore be worthwhile to take a closer look at a) and b). We selected c) and d) to represent the most dominant pattern in this visualization. There are a lot of problems that spent most of their time in evaluation, and therefore took a long time until they were closed. And finally e) stands out in two ways, it is the biggest pie and it is also totally blue. Consulting the detailed log file for this problem we see that after an initial analysis that yielded a "not repeatable" verdict, the report was not touched for a long time until it finally was rejected. This is rather surprising, since one would expect that, for high priority bugs, there is pressure to close problems as fast as possible.

In Figure 12, we select the biggest pies from Figure 11 and further analyze them in our Phase View visualization. We selected the problems labeled a), b), and c) because they look the most interesting. In the handling of problem a) a lot of shuffling between different analyzers has happened. From the log file we

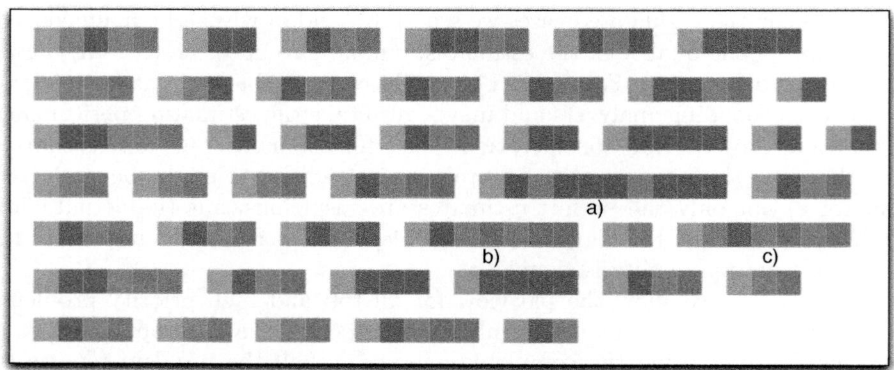

Fig. 12. Phase View for Top and High Priority Problems

can extract that every blue block represents a change in the analyzer. There were in total seven analyzers involved and in the end the problem report was marked as a duplicate. The first resolution attempt for the problem labeled b) did not succeed and a second attempt was necessary. And for c) there were three attempts necessary. Another interesting fact that we can spot by looking at c) is, that the first resolution phase was not preceded by an analysis. This might be acceptable behavior or something that should be corrected. Looking at the other problems we can spot quite a few that are missing an initial analysis phase.

We can see from these examples, that by using this easy to understand visualizations, we have already gained insights into potential points for improvement. It is important to keep in mind, that one of the main goals of our approach is to improve awareness for hidden problems and stimulate discussion, and not so much to provide ready made action plans.

6 Related Work

D'Ambros *et al.* used data from a release history database (RHDB) [4] to visualize the life-cycle of bugs [5]. With the System Radiography and the Bug Watch View, they provided a tool to focus on time, activity and severity/priority aspects of bugs. The advantage of such a visualization is the possibility to switch easily between an overview picture and a detailed inspection of an individual bug.

Halverson *et al.* [6] devised a visualization that focuses on the social aspects of change requests and problem reports. Similar to our approach, they also visualize state changes and reveal problematic patterns such as multiple resolve/reopen cycles.

The main differences between these related approaches and ours is that the state changes or the bug activity, in our approach, is only one of many possibilities to look at the data. Also the relatively simple process model underlying Bugzilla, and the missing effort measures, result in a different kind of analysis.

In [7] Weiss *et al.* predict the effort a problem requires to get fixed by analyzing the problem description and search for similar problem reports. The average effort it took these similar problems is than used as a prediction. This relates to our approach in the way, that it uses only the attributes of the problem report without relying on additional information such as source code changes.

Other approaches, such as the one from Ko *et al.* [8] analyze the linguistic characteristics of problem report descriptions to improve the quality of these reports by providing better tool support for problem report entry. Focusing especially on the quality of bug reports, Hooimeijer *et al.* [9] assume that higher quality bug reports are adressed more quickly than those with lower quality. Based on this assumption they use various bug report attributes, *e.g.*, severity, readability, submitter reputation, etc., and predict if a bug report is adressed in a given amount of time.

Who should fix this bug [10] by Anvik *et al.* uses data mining techniques to suggest suitable developers to whom a bug should be assigned. The same authors describe in [11] the problems that arise when using open bug repositories, *e.g.*, duplicates and irrelevant reports. From our experience with an inhouse commercial bug repository we can generally observe similar problems, but less frequently, since the process of bug submission and handling is controlled more tightly.

Most of the presented additional information that researchers are extracting from SCM systems could be integrated in a future version of our approach by simple adding additional possibilities for coloring the polymetric views or adding new sort orders.

7 Conclusions

In this paper we presented an interactive approach to detect visual patterns in issue tracking data. Our approach allows us to detect outliers, flaws in the data entry process, and interesting properties of individual data points.

The visual nature of the approach enhances the awareness for the buried information and promotes discussion between the various stakeholders.

In an industrial case study, we applied our interactive tool to detect instances of the presented generic effort estimation, process step length, and process step sequence patterns. We demonstrated how one can detect relevant information in our easy to understand visualizations.

Discussion with project managers and other software development professionals provided strong anecdotal evidence that our approach is indeed capable to improve certain aspects of the software development process in the companies that participated in this innovation project. In all discussions the participants were especially impressed by the straightforward interpretation of the visualizations. This is a key point to promote the adaption of such a tool in the companies of the industrial partners.

Acknowledgments

This work was sponsored in part by the Eureka 2023 Programme under grants of the ITEA project if04032. It was also supported by the Swiss National Science Foundation under grants of the Project DiCoSA - Distributed Collaborative Software Analysis (SNF Project No. 118063).

References

1. Tufte, E.R.: Envisioning Information. Graphics Press (May 1990)
2. Knab, P., Pinzger, M., Fluri, B., Gall, H.C.: Interactive Views for Analyzing Problem Reports. In: ICSM 2009 Proceedings of the 25th International Conference on Software Maintenance, pp. 527–530 (2009)
3. Lanza, M., Ducasse, S.: Polymetric views — a lightweight visual approach to reverse engineering. IEEE Transactions on Software Engineering 29(9), 782–795 (2003)

4. Fischer, M., Pinzger, M., Gall, H.: Populating a release history database from version control and bug tracking systems. In: Proceedings of the International Conference on Software Maintenance, Amsterdam, Netherlands, pp. 23–32. IEEE Computer Society Press, Los Alamitos (2003)
5. D'Ambros, M., Lanza, M., Pinzger, M.: "a bug's life" - visualizing a bug database. In: Proceedings of VISSOFT 2007 (4th IEEE International Workshop on Visualizing Software For Understanding and Analysis), June 2007, pp. 113–120. IEEE CS Press, Los Alamitos (2007)
6. Halverson, C.A., Ellis, J.B., Danis, C., Kellogg, W.A.: Designing task visualizations to support the coordination of work in software development. In: CSCW 2006: Proceedings of the 2006 20th anniversary conference on Computer supported cooperative work, pp. 39–48. ACM, New York (2006)
7. Weiss, C., Premraj, R., Zimmermann, T., Zeller, A.: How long will it take to fix this bug? In: MSR 2007: Proceedings of the Fourth International Workshop on Mining Software Repositories, Washington, DC, USA, p. 1. IEEE Computer Society, Los Alamitos (2007)
8. Ko, A.J., Myers, B.A., Chau, D.H.: A linguistic analysis of how people describe software problems. In: VLHCC 2006: Proceedings of the Visual Languages and Human-Centric Computing, Washington, DC, USA, pp. 127–134. IEEE Computer Society Press, Los Alamitos (2006)
9. Hooimeijer, P., Weimer, W.: Modeling bug report quality. In: ASE 2007: Proceedings of the twenty-second IEEE/ACM international conference on Automated software engineering, pp. 34–43. ACM, New York (2007)
10. Anvik, J., Hiew, L., Murphy, G.C.: Who should fix this bug? In: ICSE 2006: Proceedings of the 28th international conference on Software engineering, pp. 361–370. ACM, New York (2006)
11. Anvik, J., Hiew, L., Murphy, G.C.: Coping with an open bug repository. In: eclipse 2005: Proceedings of the 2005 OOPSLA workshop on Eclipse technology eXchange, pp. 35–39. ACM, New York (2005)

Disruption-Driven Resource Rescheduling in Software Development Processes

Junchao Xiao[1,2], Leon J. Osterweil[2], Qing Wang[1], and Mingshu Li[1,3]

[1] Laboratory for Internet Software Technologies, Institute of Software, Chinese Academy of Sciences, Beijing 100190, China
[2] Department of Computer Science University of Massachusetts, Amherst, MA 01003-9264 USA
[3] Key Laboratory for Computer Science, Institute of Software, Chinese Academy of Sciences, Beijing 100190, China

Abstract. Real world systems can be thought of as structures of activities that require resources in order to execute. Careful allocation of resources can improve system performance by enabling more efficient use of resources. Resource allocation decisions can be facilitated when process flow and estimates of time and resource requirements are statically determinable. But this information is difficult to be sure of in disruption prone systems, where unexpected events can necessitate process changes and make it difficult or impossible to be sure of time and resource requirements. This paper approaches the problems posed by such disruptions by using a Time Window based INcremental resource Scheduling method (TWINS). We show how to use TWINS to respond to disruptions by doing reactive rescheduling over a relatively small set of activities. This approach uses a genetic algorithm. It is evaluated by using it to schedule resources dynamically during the simulation of some example software development processes. Results indicate that this dynamic approach produces good results obtained at affordable costs.

Keywords: Incremental resource scheduling, time window, reactive rescheduling, proactive rescheduling.

1 Introduction

Complex systems are typically comprised of a group of activities, each of whose executions requires different resources that have various capabilities and availabilities. Careful resource scheduling can reduce resource contention, thereby reducing delays and inefficiencies, and in doing so, can increase the value of the system [1-3].

A lot of work has investigated different approaches to determining optimal schedules of assignment of resources to system activities. One approach is static resource scheduling [1, 2, 4-7], in which a complete schedule of resource assignment is computed in advance based on advance knowledge of the sequence of activities to be performed and the size and duration of all these activities [8, 9].

However, in disruption prone systems like those used in software development and healthcare, activity estimates may unreliable, and uncertainties such as the sudden

J. Münch, Y. Yang, and W. Schäfer (Eds.): ICSP 2010, LNCS 6195, pp. 234–247, 2010.

arrival of rush orders, unexpectedly slow activity performance, inaccurate estimates, and unexpected lack of resources [10] are numerous. These uncertainties dynamically change the execution environment and create the potential for consequent schedule disruptions [11, 12], thus making scheduling results unreliable and uncertain. In response to such uncertainties, researchers have studied different kinds of dynamic resource scheduling approaches [11], such as robust scheduling [13-16] and reactive scheduling [17, 18]. Though these methods seem effective in addressing some uncertainties, they have the following problems:

- Robust scheduling is most effective when there are limited and predictable disruptions in process executions. If exceptions exceed the scope that a robust approach can deal with, rescheduling is needed, and this becomes a reactive scheduling approach.
- Reactive scheduling addresses unexpected events and other uncertainties by responding with a rescheduling. But each rescheduling covers all possible future activities. Thus it can be expected that the rescheduling results will encompass a lot of uncertainties that will probably cause future disruptions that will necessitate further reschedulings.

These issues seem particularly troublesome in fast changing environments such as software development, where process execution plans may need to change continually. To tackle this sort of problem, we have suggested (in [19]) the use of planning incremental rescheduling, where rescheduling was expected to happen frequently, and over only a modest-sized scope. In [19] we assumed that accurate estimates for the execution times of tasks, and precise definitions of software process steps are available to guide such incremental rescheduling activities. In that work, reschedulings were undertaken proactively, and unexpected disruptions such as process delay and future activity changes, were not taken into account. But in actual practice, such events are common and should indeed be used to trigger reschedulings. Thus, in this work, we address the need to deal with such disruptive events.

In this work we present an approach that supports both proactive incremental rescheduling of resources, and reactive rescheduling of resources in response to the occurrence of unexpected disruptive events. This paper extends the dynamic resource rescheduling method presented in [19] and proposes a ***T**ime **W**indow based **IN**cremental resource **S**cheduling method* (**TWINS**). The method decomposes the overall resource scheduling problem into a series of dynamic reschedulings continuously happening either proactively or reactively and covering only selected subsets of activities. A genetic algorithm (GA) [20] is used as the basis for our scheduling approach. In addition to its speed, another advantage of GA is that it can readily incorporate many types of constraints into the definition and solution of the scheduling problem.

We have implemented TWINS and evaluated its effectiveness using different time windows and different disruptions to generate different resource allocation schedules. The results obtained show that TWINS is effective in dealing with the needs for both short-range schedules that can be quite accurate because they have fewer uncertainties to deal with, and long-range schedules that must deal with greater uncertainties, yet still be highly accurate.

The paper is organized as follows. Section 2 presents the TWINS framework. Section 3 presents some details of the components and technologies used in our TWINS implementation. Section 4 describes a simulation of a software development process and reports on some case studies aimed at evaluating this approach. Section 5 presents conclusions and suggests future work.

2 Time-Window Based INcremental Scheduling (TWINS)

TWINS decomposes a large end-to-end resource scheduling problem into a series of dynamic reschedulings. The rescheduling in TWINS can be triggered either 1) reactively, when events occur that are beyond the scope of what we have been able to anticipate, or preferably, 2) proactively, at time points that may be dictated by recognition of upcoming uncertainties derived from analysis of precise and detailed system definitions. Each incremental rescheduling activity covers only the tasks that will occur within a specified time window.

The time window can be a given time interval or a specified number of activities. It is important to select the right size for this window. If the window is too small, more frequent reschedulings may be needed, but they may produce more accurate results. If the window is large, scheduling may cover more activities, but scheduling cost may be high, and more disruptions that require new rescheduling are likely to be encountered during execution of steps that have been included in the scheduling window. Indeed it may be the case that the size of the scheduling window may have to be estimated differently depending upon whether the rescheduling was undertaken proactive or reactively. The TWINS method shown in Fig 1 has also been presented in [19]. We summarize it here for completeness. The method consists of the following major components:

- **Scheduling activity set constructor.** This component selects activities from a process system and assembles the rescheduling problem, which consists principally of a specification of the activities that may possibly be executed in the near future (within the time window). The scheduling activity set constructor relies upon a specification of the system.
- **Scheduler** component, which uses the output of the scheduling activity set constructor and a Genetic Algorithm (GA) to identify the specific resources to be used to support the execution of each activity. A repository of specifications of available resources is also used to support this scheduling.
- **Rescheduling indicator** component, which determines when rescheduling should be done. Rescheduling is triggered when the rescheduling indicator determines that activities outside the window needed to be executed. This component could also be used to identify when certain types of unexpected events make rescheduling desirable or necessary.
- **System execution** component, which provides execution events needed to update the system execution state upon which the rescheduling indicator and the scheduler rely.

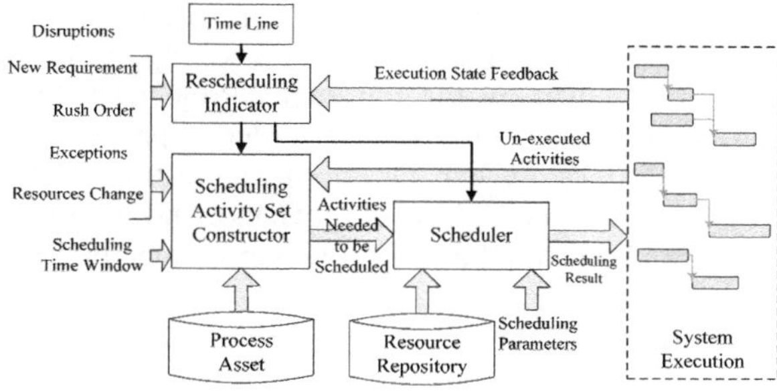

Fig. 1. The TWINS Method

3 TWINS Implementation

3.1 Process Activity Definition

A complete, precise, and detailed system definition can improve the quality of the resource scheduling need to support execution of the processes in that system. As in [19], we also choose Little-JIL [21, 22] to define the system for which we will do our scheduling. A Little-JIL process definition consists of a specification of three components, an artifact collection (not described here due to space constraints), an activity specification, and a resource repository. A Little-JIL activity specification is defined as a hierarchy of steps, each of which represents an activity to be performed by an assigned resource (referred to as its agent). Each step has a name and a set of badges to represent control flow among its sub-steps, its interface, the exceptions it handles, etc. A leaf step (one with no sub-steps) represents an activity to be performed by an agent, without any guidance from the process. Each step specification also contains a collection of resource requests. Each request in the collection is described by the following definition.

Definition 1. $Req = (ResName, Capability_1, SkillLevel_1, ..., Capability_r, SkillLevel_r)$, **where,**

- *ResName* is the type of the resource being requested, (e.g. requirement analyst, coder, tester), which indicates the kinds of capabilities that this resource has.
- $Capability_i$ is a capability that is being requested.
- $SkillLevel_i$ is the minimum level of skill in $Capability_i$ that is being requested.

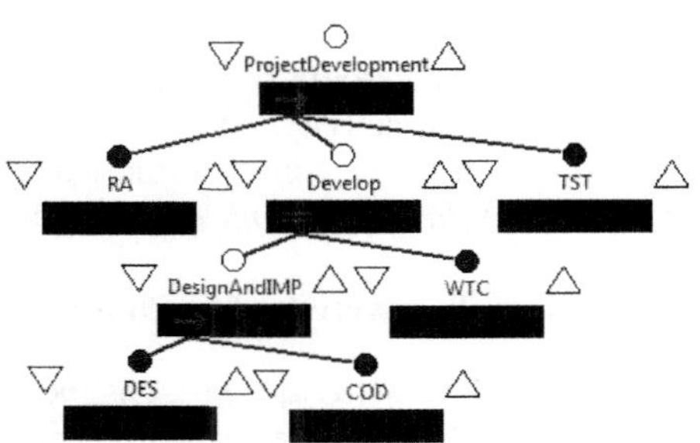

Fig. 2. Module development process

Fig 2 shows a Little-JIL activity definition that defines a software development process. Note that a different instance of this process is instantiated for every new project, and thus the work of a typical development organization is represented by the concurrent execution of several instances of this process. Each process needs the same types of resources, which must be provided by one central resource repository. This sets up resource contention. Each process instance is represented by the top step, "ProjectDevelopment". The right arrow in this step specifies that, in sequential order, a project is developed by requirement analysis (RA), development (Develop), and testing (TST). Development is further decomposed into design (DES), coding (COD), and writing test cases (WTC). WTC is executed in parallel with DES and COD (represented by "=" sign).

3.2 Resource Repository

The resource repository is the second key component of a Little-JIL process definition. It contains a set of resource instances that are available for assignment to the tasks specified in the Little-JIL activity diagram.

Thus, $ResourceRepositiory = \{Res_1, Res_2, ..., Res_l\}$, where each element of this set has certain capabilities and availabilities. A resource is defined as follows:

Definition 2. $Res = (ID, ResName, Attributes, SchedulableTimeTable, Capability_1, SkillLevel_1, Productivity_1, Capability_2, SkillLevel_2, Productivity_2, ...)$

where,

- *ID* is a prose identification of the resource.
- *ResName* is the type of the resource, which indicates the kinds of capabilities that this resource has, such as software analyst and designer.
- *Attributes* is a set of (*name*, *value*) pairs that describe the resource. Some example attribute names might be *Age*, *Experience_Level*, and *Salary_Rate*.
- *SchedulableTimeTable* is a representation of the times when a resource is available to be assigned to an activity. This consists of a set of schedulable time intervals, defined by a start time (*st*) and end time (*et*). The resource can be assigned to an activity during any of the specified time intervals. Thus,

  $$SchedulableTimeTable = \{[st_1, et_1], [st_2, et_2], ..., [st_s, et_s]\}$$
- $Capability_i$ (i = 1, 2 ...) is the ith kind of capability that the resource has to offer. For example, a coder has the capability of using JAVA for coding.
- $SkillLevel_i$ (i = 1, 2 ...) is the level of quality at which the resource is able to perform $Capability_i$.
- $Productivity_i$ (i = 1, 2 ...) is the average productivity that the resource is able to achieve in performing $Capability_i$.

Assume that an activity specifies that *S* is the quantity of $Capability_i$ required in order to complete the activity. Then $S/Productivity_i$, is the amount of time that resource *R* requires in order to complete the activity. Only if this amount of time is contained within R's *SchedulableTimeTable* attribute, can *R* be assigned that activity.

3.3 Scheduling Activity Set Constructor

The Scheduling Activity Set Constructor assembles all of the information needed in order to make scheduling decisions. This function determines which upcoming activities fall within the scheduling time window (whose size has been previously determined), and assembles the activities into a graph called the Dynamic Flow Graph (DFG). The DFG is derived from an analysis of another graph called the resource utilization flow graph (RUFG). Space limitations prevent a full discussion of how these graphs are built and used, and so we summarize descriptions of them. Details describing the DFG and RUFG are provided in [23]

The RUFG is a directed graph, derived from a Little-JIL activity diagram, which represents all the possible execution sequences of the process. Each node in the RUFG represents a step in the Little-JIL process definition and is annotated with precise and detailed information about the resource needs of the step. Thus, the RUFG is a representation of the static structure of the process.

Our rescheduling approach, however, uses dynamic process state information to take dynamic constraints and uncertainties into account. Thus when a rescheduling is needed we use the static RUFG and dynamic state information to generate a dynamic flow graph (DFG) that is then used as the basis for the rescheduling. The DFG incorporates both the RUFG's static information and runtime state information such as which activities are currently executing in parallel, which resources are allocated to them, and the priority level assigned to each activity.

The size and shape of the DFG is determined by a specification of the time window, which dictates how many of the future execution possibilities are to be considered in the rescheduling. At present we define the size of a time window by an integer that represents the length of the longest sequence of possible future activities that make resource requests. Thus, specifically, if L is the integer used to define time window W and $CURRACT$ is the set of activities that are currently being performed,

$$CURRACT = \{activity_1, activity_2, ..., activity_n\},$$

then node $NODE$ is included in W if and only if $NODE$ requires the allocation of resources, and, for some i, $1 \leq i \leq n$, there is a path, P, in the RUFG

$$P = (activity_i, n_1, n_2, ..., n_k, NODE)$$

such that the number of nodes n_j, $1 \leq j \leq k$ that make resource requests is less than L-1.

Further details about the definition of the RUFG and DFG are omitted due to space constraints. In addition, note that other approaches may be used to define the scheduling window, and the one just defined is used here as an example.

3.4 Using a GA to Do Resource Scheduling

By being careful to keep time windows small we can assure that our scheduling problems remain relatively tractable. We nevertheless expect that our windows may still be large enough to contain quantities of activities and resources that are sufficiently large to require considerable scheduling computation. Thus in this work we have extended the GA designed in [19] as the basis for each rescheduling.

3.4.1 Encoding and Decoding

We used the binary representation of integers to help encode the rescheduling problem as a chromosome. Note that because the set of DFG nodes waiting to be scheduled changes during process execution, new chromosomes must be built for each rescheduling. For each DFG node, N, in a time window (i.e. each node waiting for the assignment of resources), we establish a set of resource genes and a set of priority genes. Suppose N requires m resources. Then each of the m resource requests that have B_m candidate resources is encoded as a set of binary genes (i.e. genes whose value can be only 0 or 1), where the size of the set is the smallest integer greater than or equal to $\log_2 B_m$. The binary values of these $\log_2 B_m$ genes are used to represent the decimal number of a candidate resource, namely one that could be selected to satisfy the corresponding request. Similarly, the priority level of the node is represented by a set of g binary priority genes. When two or more DFG nodes contend for the same resource, the node whose priority genes specify the highest priority is assigned to the resource. The structure of such a chromosome is shown in Fig 3.

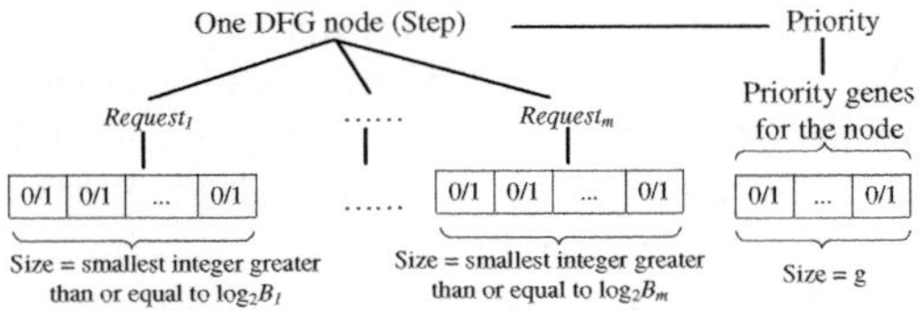

Fig. 3. Chromosome structure

Each chromosome encoded by the above method can, subject to the application of constraints, be decoded as a scheduling scheme, namely the assignment of a specific resource to each of the requests made by each of the activities in the time window. Decoding is done by reversing the encoding process.

3.4.2 Fitness Function

The role of the fitness function is to evaluate the relative desirability of each of the chromosomes as a solution to the resource rescheduling problem. The fitness function to be used must be designed to meet the needs of each individual scheduling problem. The fitness function used in evaluation in this paper was first presented in [19]. It was created to address resource allocation in the domain of software development. As this is the domain of evaluation in this paper too, we reuse this fitness function in this paper too. Note that this fitness function does not attempt to increase the value for all steps of all projects, only the value for the steps that are involved in the time window.

3.5 Rescheduling Indicator

The rescheduling indicator determines the circumstances under which a rescheduling should be carried out based on such runtime state information as the activities currently being executed, the resources being used, resource capacity that is available, and different kinds of uncertainty-causing events. Research is needed to determine the rescheduling criteria that should be used for each of the many different kinds of resource allocation problems. And, indeed, different criteria may trigger reschedulings based upon time windows of different sizes, and rescheduling decisions may be made differently under different execution circumstances. What follows are examples of events that could be used in dynamically determining whether a rescheduling should be performed:

- **Delay of currently executing activity:** if the currently executing activity is delayed, and it causes other activities that use the same resources to be unable to obtain the resources that they need at their starting time, a rescheduling should be carried out.

- **Identifying changes to a future activity:** a future activity is an activity that has not yet been executed. If during execution of one activity it is determined that changes will cause a future activity to have insufficient resources allocated to it, then a rescheduling should be carried out.
- **Arrival of new requirement:** as soon as the need to meet a new requirement is realized, a rescheduling to allocate resources to this new requirement must be carried out.
- **Un-assigned allocation of successive activities:** once an activity has completed, if any of its successor activities has not been allocated resources, a rescheduling should be carried out.

Note that the first two of these items characterize unexpected runtime situations that are necessitate relatively more disruptive reactive scheduling. The last two items characterize predictable situations that trigger proactive rescheduling. This proactive rescheduling is more desirable as its results should be expected to be less disruptive and more accurate.

4 Evaluation

To support the analysis of the effectiveness of our approach, we used it to allocate resources during the running of simulations of processes that define how software project developments perform their activities and utilize their resources.

4.1 The Simulation Setting

4.1.1 Process, Projects, and Resources

The process that was used as the principal basis for the case study presented here is the Little-JIL process shown in Fig 2. Note that non-leaf steps are used essentially to create scopes, and "real work" is done only by leaf steps. Thus, the resource requests are shown in Table 1 only for each leaf step in this process. And each step only needs one resource.

We assume that there nine projects named P1 to P9 that are executing simultaneously in this case study and each project is executing a different instance of the same process. Assume the scale of these projects are all 8KLOC, the cost constraint for each project is $50,000, the benefit of finishing ahead of deadline is $400/day, and the deadline delay penalty is $800/day. Projects P1 to P3 can start on 2009-01-01, and must finish by 2009-06-30. Projects P4 to P6 can start on 2009-04-01, and must finish by 2009-09-30. Projects P7 to P9 can start on 2009-07-01 and must finish by 2009-12-30.

Table 1. Resource requests of leaf step

Step	Request (ResName, Capability, SkillLevel)
RA	(Analyst, OOA, 3)
DEC	(Designer, OOD, 3)
COD	(Coder, JAVA, 3)
WTC	(Tester, WTC, 3)
TST	(Tester, TST, 3)

The different kinds of resources available in the case study include analyst, designer, coder, and tester. They are described in Table 2. We use dates for *SchedulableTimeTable* entries, and in each weekday, the available workload is eight person-hours, while on Saturday and Sunday, the available workload is zero.

Table 2. Available resource descriptions

ID	Name	Human Name	Schedulable Time Table	(Capability, Skill Level, Productivity)	Salary-Rate ($/hour)
1	Analyst	HR1	[2009-01-01, 2011-12-31]	(OOA, 4, 0.06)	70
2	Analyst	HR2	[2009-01-01, 2011-12-31]	(OOA, 4, 0.04)	45
3	Designer	HR3	[2009-01-01, 2011-12-31]	(OOD, 4, 0.06)	60
4	Designer	HR4	[2009-01-01, 2011-12-31]	(OOD, 4, 0.05)	60
5	Coder	HR5	[2009-01-01, 2011-12-31]	(JAVA, 4, 0.04)	45
6	Coder	HR6	[2009-01-01, 2011-12-31]	(JAVA, 3, 0.03)	35
7	Tester	HR7	[2009-01-01, 2011-12-31]	(WTC, 4, 0.05), (TST, 4, 0.05)	45
8	Tester	HR8	[2009-01-01, 2011-12-31]	(WTC, 4, 0.03) , (TST, 4, 0.04)	40

4.1.2 Resource Contention and Different Kinds of Events

For our case study, we assumed that all projects could be pursued simultaneously, but that only limited resources were available and each resource could perform only one step at the same time, thereby creating significant resource contention.

TWINS constructed its scheduling problems by assembling in its time window all activities for all the projects that fall within the time window specification. For this case study we hypothesized three "*arrival of new requirement*" events, thus causing three predictable reschedulings. But we did not hypothesize any "*un-assigned allocation of successive activities*" events that would have triggered predictable reschedulings. On the other hand, we hypothesized the following unpredictable events in the simulation, using as an example the disruption caused by a 20% increase in execution time.

- **Delay of currently executing activity**:
  - o When COD of P1, P2, and P3 is executing, the time for executing it increases by 20% over the initial plan;
  - o When TST of P4, P5, and P6 is executing, the time for executing it increases by 20% over the initial plan;
  - o When DEC of P7, P8, and P9 is executing, the time for executing it increases by 20% over the initial plan;

- **Identifying changes to a future activity (only workload increases for future activities are used in this simulation, changes may also include the need to deal with new events such as the insertion of new requirements)**:
  - o RA of P1, P2, and P3 causes DEC of the same project to increase by 20%;
  - o RA of P4, P5, and P6 causes COD of the same project to increase by 20%;
  - o RA of P7, P8, and P9 causes TST of the same project to increase by 20%;

The trigger times of these events are the completion dates of RA. If the corresponding changed activities have allocated resources at the trigger time, a new rescheduling needs to be carried out.

The trigger times for these events are the planned end times of the activities.

4.2 Simulation Experiment

GA-based scheduling uses a population of chromosomes to define and solve the scheduling problem. A chromosome evolution process that includes fitness computation for each chromosome, selection, crossover, and mutation can typically be expected to provide near optimal scheduling results. For TWINS, we set the chromosome population to 100, the crossover rate to 0.8, the mutation rate to 0.02, and generation number to 500.

TWINS uses an appropriate incremental scheduling time window to reduce uncertainties in scheduling results. We used the following simulation scenarios to evaluate the effects of using TWINS:

- Change the time window size and analyze the numbers of reschedulings caused by different kinds of events. Use these results to demonstrate the stability, accuracy, and uncertainty of scheduling results generated from different time window sizes.
- Change the number of events and compare the rescheduling number results obtained from running simulations by using different window sizes. Use these results to demonstrate the circumstances when TWINS is relatively more effective.

4.2.1 Scheduling Cost Variation with Changing Window Size

One key issue in using TWINS is how to determine the size of the window to be used in a rescheduling. The window size affects the number of different kinds of reschedulings that will be necessitated, as well as the costs of the reschedulings. Thus one major goal of our experimentation is to provide gain insight into the question of what window size should be selected in order to provide a good compromise between the accuracy and scheduling stability that is obtained from more frequent reschedulings using smaller windows vs. the reduced costs of less frequent reschedulings over larger window sizes that nevertheless lead to greater uncertainty.

Fig 4 shows the influence of different window sizes on the number of reschedulings and the total time of a simulation run. Note that when the size of the time window increases, more events are included in the window, and the following results are obtained:

- The number of "*arrival of new requirement*" events is always 3 because all projects arrive at times when those three events are scheduled to occur.
- The number of "*delay of currently executing activity*" reschedulings seems to increase as the time window sizes increases. If the time window size increases, more activities will be included in the window and will affect each other, thus increasing the probability that "delay of current executing activity" events will affect the scheduled result of other activities. That seems to explain why reschedulings caused by this event tend to increase.
- The number of "*identifying changes to a future activity*" reschedulings also seems to increase with increases in window size. If time window size increases, the currently

executing activities and the future activities that are changed by these events are more likely to be in the same window. Thus reschedulings caused by "identify the changes of a future activity" increase as time window size increases.

- The number of "*un-assigned allocation of successive activities*" reschedulings seems to decrease with increases in time window size. If the time window size increases, before the start of execution of activities for which resources are not yet allocated, there is a higher probability that new reschedulings caused by other kinds of events may occur causing these future activities to lose their allocated resources.

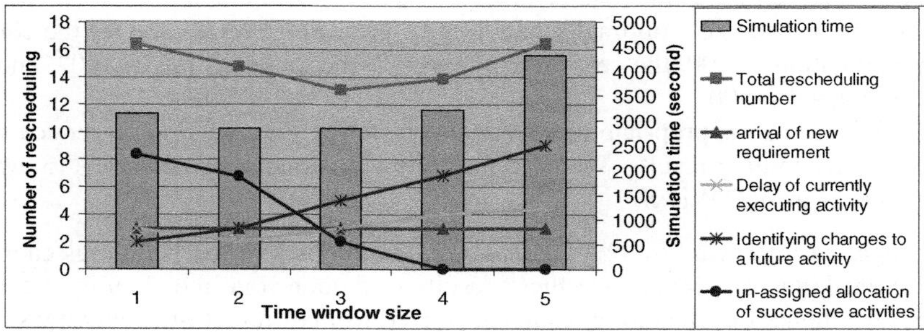

Fig. 4. Number of different kinds of reschedulings and the total rescheduling time (results are averages of 20 different simulations)

The above analysis shows that a small time window causes a lower number of reactive reschedulings, but a larger number of proactive reschedulings. An appropriately chosen time window size (3 in this example) causes a minimum number of reschedulings. Our research is still quite preliminary, but it suggests that this optimal window size may be context dependent and that more research is needed to understand better what features and state information should be used (and how) to help predict optimal window size.

4.2.2 Scheduling Cost Variation with Different Number of Disruptions

Another of the advantages that we believe are derived from the TWINS approach is that it can be particularly useful in increasing the stability of environments that must deal with a lot of disruptions.

To evaluate this hypothesis, we have compared the results obtained from running simulations by using different window sizes and total number of "*delay of currently executing activity*", "*identifying changes to a future activity*", and "*un-assigned allocation of successive activities*" disruptions. We set window size as 2 and 5 respectively. We then compared the results obtained when have to deal with all these disruptions; disruptions to only 6 projects: P1, P2, P4, P5, P7, and P8; having to deal with disruptions to only 3 projects: P1, P4, and P7; and having to deal with no disruptions at all.

Fig 5 shows that if there are a large number of disruptions, a small window size can reduce the number of reschedulings needed. But as the number of disruptive events decreases, the system becomes more stable and larger window sizes can be used, which reduces the number of needed reschedulings. This case study shows that relatively small time windows are likely to be most effective when there are a large number of disruptions in systems, while large time windows are effective when a system is less prone to disruptions.

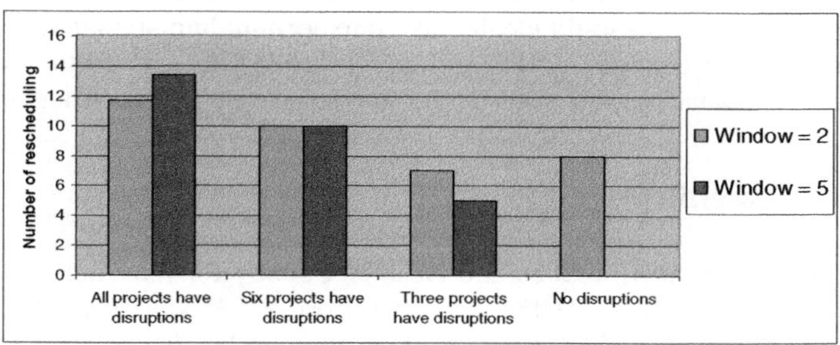

Fig. 5. Comparisons of the effects of different number of disruptions (results are averages of 20 different simulations)

5 Summary and Future Work

This paper has presented a Time Window based INcremental resource Scheduling method (TWINS) that uses a genetic algorithm. We used this method to develop a scheduling tool that was integrated with an existing discrete event simulation system in order to study the effectiveness of the approach in creating good resource allocation schedules in affordable time. We used this system to support a variety of simulations of software development processes. These initial case studies suggest that this approach can be effective. In order to gain more confidence in the approach further research is needed, however.

Future work

Determining optimal window size: As noted in the previous section research is needed in order to determine what window size should be used in rescheduling. In addition, we will also explore how to dynamically change time window size based on consideration of the appropriate runtime state and parameter information.

Analysis of different processes and domains: This paper mainly focuses on changing window size when attempting to address how to deal with disruptions that are caused by four different kinds of events in the software development process domain. Different processes from different domains should be studied as well.

More kinds of events: There are additional kinds of disruptive events in software development that could also be studied. For example, the execution of one activity may introduce the need for adding more detailed step specifications to another activity or may even create the need for an entirely new activity. Future work should address the issues of how to deal with these disruptions.

Evaluation in real software organizations: This paper only uses simulation to evaluate TWINS. Real applications and experiences with the method in actual software development are needed to further evaluate the TWINS approach.

Complex factors related to human resources: The scheduling of human resources in software development should ideally take into account human motivations, learning ability, productivity changes, and the effects of collaboration. Future work should take these complex factors into consideration to improve our models and methods.

Acknowledgments

We would like to thank Bin Chen and Heather Conboy for their help with the transformation from Little-JIL to RUFG, and Prof. Lori A. Clarke, Dr. M. S. Raunak, and Sandy Wise for their valuable feedback about this work. This paper is supported by the National Natural Science Foundation of China under grant Nos. 90718042, 60903051, the Hi-Tech Research and Development Program (863 Program) of China under grant No. 2007AA010303, as well as the National Basic Research Program (973 program) under grant No. 2007CB310802. This work was also supported by the National Science Foundation under Awards No. CCR-0205575, CCR-0427071, CCF-0820198, and IIS-0705772. Any opinions, findings, and conclusions or recommendations expressed in this publication are those of the author(s) and do not necessarily reflect the views of the National Science Foundation.

References

[1] Alba, E., Chicano, J.F.: Software Project Management with GAs. Journal of Information Sciences 177, 2380–2401 (2007)

[2] Xiao, J., Wang, Q., Li, M., Yang, Q., Xie, L., Liu, D.: Value-based Multiple Software Projects Scheduling with Genetic Algorithm. In: Wang, Q., Garousi, V., Madachy, R., Pfahl, D. (eds.) ICSP 2009. LNCS, vol. 5543, pp. 50–62. Springer, Heidelberg (2009)

[3] Biffl, S., Aurum, A., Boehm, B., Erdogmus, H., Grünbacher, P.: Value-Based Software Engineering. Springer, Heidelberg (2005)

[4] Barreto, A., Barros, M.d.O., Werner, C.M.L.: Staffing a software project: A constraint satisfaction and optimization-based approach. Computer & Operations Research 35, 3073–3089 (2008)

[5] Pham, D.-N., Klinkert, A.: Surgical case scheduling as a generalized job shop scheduling problem. European Journal of Operational Research 185, 1011–1025 (2008)

[6] Goncalves, J.F., Mendes, J.J.M., Resende, M.G.C.: A Genetic Algorithm for the Resource Constrained Multi-project Scheduling Problem. European Journal of Operational Research 189, 1171–1190 (2008)

[7] Peteghem, V.V., Vanhoucke, M.: A genetic algorithm for the preemptive and non-preemptive multi-mode resource-constrained project scheduling problem. European Journal of Operational Research (2009)

[8] Fowler, J.W., Monch, L., Rose, O.: Scheduling and Simulation. In: Herrmann, J.W. (ed.) Handbook of Production Scheduling, pp. 109–133. Springer, US (2006)

[9] Pfeiffer, A.s., Kadar, B., Monostori, L.s.: Stability-oriented evaluation of rescheduling strategies, by using simulation. Computers in Industry 58, 630–643 (2007)

[10] Herrmann, J.W.: Rescheduling Startegies, Policies, and Methods. In: Handbook of Production Scheduling, pp. 135–148
[11] Herroelen, W., Leus, R.: Project Scheduling under Uncertainty: Survey and Research Potentials. European Journal of Operational Research 165, 289–306 (2005)
[12] Antoniol, G., Penta, M.D., Harman, M.: A Robust Search–Based Approach to Project Management in the Presence of Abandonment, Rework, Error and Uncertainty. In: Proceedings of the 10th International Symposium on Software Metrics, pp. 172–183 (2004)
[13] Li, Z., Ierapetritou, M.G.: Robust Optimization for Process Scheduling Under Uncertainty. Industrial and Engineering Chemistry Research 47, 4148–4157 (2008)
[14] Al-Fawzan, M.A., Haouari, M.: A bi-objective model for robust resource-constrained project scheduling. International Journal of Production Economics 96, 175–187 (2005)
[15] Wang, J.: A fuzzy robust scheduling approach for product development projects. European Journal of Operational Research 152, 180–194 (2004)
[16] Ghezail, F., Pierreval, H., Hajri-Gabouj, S.: Analysis of robustness in proactive scheduling: A graphical approach. Computers & Industrial Engineering (2009)
[17] Rangsaritratsamee, R., Ferrell Jr., W.G., Kurz, M.B.: Dynamic rescheduling that simultaneously considers efficiency and stability. Computers & Industrial Engineering 46, 1–15 (2004)
[18] Yang, B.: Single Machine Rescheduling with New Jobs Arrivals and Processing Time Compression. International Journal of Advanced Manufacturing Technology 34, 378–384 (2007)
[19] Xiao, J., Osterweil, L.J., Wang, Q., Li, M.: Dynamic Resource Scheduling in Disruption-Prone Software Development Environments. Department of Computer Science, University of Massachusetts, Amherst, MA 01003 UM-CS-2009-050 (2009)
[20] Holland, J.H.: Adaptation in natural and artificial systems. MIT Press, Cambridge (1992)
[21] Cass, A.G., Lerner, B.S., McCall, E.K., Osterweil, L.J., Stanley, J., Sutton, M., Wise, A.: Little-JIL/Juliette: A Process Definition Language and Interpreter. In: Proceedings of the 22nd International Conference on Software Engineering, Limerick, Ireland, pp. 754–757 (2000)
[22] Wise, A.: Little-JIL 1.5 Language Report, Department of Computer Science, University of Massachusetts, Amherst UM-CS-2006-51 (2006)
[23] Xiao, J., Osterweil, L.J., Wang, Q., Li, M.: Dynamic Scheduling in Systems with Complex Resource Allocation Requirements. Department of Computer Science at the University of Massachusetts Amherst. Technical report: UM-CS-2009-049 (2009)

MODAL: A SPEM Extension to Improve Co-design Process Models

Ali Koudri and Joel Champeau

ENSIETA
2 rue Francois Verny, 29806 Brest cedex, France
firstname.lastname@ensieta.fr

Abstract. Process engineering has been applied for several years in software developments, with more or less success thanks to the use of process languages easing analysis, improvement and even execution of software processes. In this paper, we present a SPEM derived metamodel that takes advantages of Model Based Engineering and innovative approaches of process engineering. Through this work, we try to clarify the definition of process components in order to be able to construct and execute MBE processes "On-Demand".

Keywords: MBE, Intention, Strategy, Process Component.

1 Introduction

System and software processes are generally compared to transformation chain transforming a product (customer requirements) into another one (delivered system). Involved stakeholders use domain relative languages and tools. Thus, implied interactions can be at the source of several errors, possibly catastrophic [1]. In this context, the goal of process engineering is to formally describe processes, execute them and collect data from their observation in order to improve their definition [2].

Besides, Model Based Engineering (MBE) has been successfully applied in software development. MBE is a paradigm based on intensive use of models. A model is an abstraction of another entity, either physical or logical, easing its design and analysis. Indeed, a process can also be modeled and analyzed if related concepts are well reified. Based on this idea, several process modeling languages (meta-processes) have been proposed. Among the main ones, we can cite SPEM [3] which stands for System and Software Process Engineering Modeling language and has been standardized by the Object Management Group (OMG).

In this paper, we point out the lacks of current process modeling languages to achieve integration of MBE into system and software process models. We propose an extension of SPEM called MODAL (Model Oriented Development Application Language) which intends to fill the shortcomings of SPEM 2.0. This extension introduces additional concepts enabling "Model Based Process" definition and elicitation. This work contributes to reinforce the semantics of process

J. Münch, Y. Yang, and W. Schäfer (Eds.): ICSP 2010, LNCS 6195, pp. 248–259, 2010.

models through: separation of intentions of processes from their realization, alignment of work product definition to model, formalization of constraints related to business or standard rules and clarification of process component definition.

The remainder of this paper is organized as follows: in the second part, we give a brief overview of the related works followed by the motivations of our works; in the third section, we present the main concepts introduced in the MODAL metamodel, illustrated by excerpts from an industrial case study; in the fourth section, we discuss the relevancy of our works compared to existing approaches. Finally, the conclusion presents open issues and future works.

2 Related Works and Motivations

Process engineering relies on formal representations of processes highlighting their relevant characteristics and allowing thus: a better control of intellectual processes of design and analysis thanks to clear identification of activities, input/output artifacts as well as responsibilities [4]; relevant evaluations of process enactment [5]; the insurance of adequacy between process improvement goals and quality of delivered products [6]; and a better control of complexity and scaling.

Processes formalization requires process representations using well-adapted notations having clear semantics [7]. Surveys and comparisons of numerous formalisms can be found in [8]. For instance, SPEM is well suited to the representation of system and software processes because, in addition to generic process concepts (role, activity, product, etc.), it provides an extension mechanism allowing modeling and documentation of a wide range of processes. Tools supporting SPEM are numerous. Among them, we can cite the EPF project [1].

Even if current meta-processes allow a finer representation of processes, none of studied formalisms addresses the modeling of process models causality. Indeed, according to [9], their comprehension would be a great help to processes improvement. To this purpose, the authors propose an intellectual framework called the "Four-Worlds Framework" allowing a better comprehension of the complexity of processes both in their elaboration and in their observation. The concepts of intention and strategy introduced in this work are clearly essential to the comprehension and the improvement of processes, but they are definitely missing from SPEM.

Besides, in the scope of continuous maturation of processes, several works point out the lacks of SPEM regarding executability or data management. For instance, in [10], the authors highlight issues of the SPEM specification regarding controlled enactment through executability. This feature is of first importance to insure adequacy between process life cycle and its definition. To this end, the authors propose to add an operational semantics through an extension called xSPEM (Executable SPEM). Then, execution of process models produce traces that can be re-injected in order to improve their definition. In this approach, such re-injection can only be performed manually because SPEM lacks concepts enabling such feature. To this end, in [11], the authors propose an extension of

[1] http://www.eclipse.org/epf/

SPEM that handle data management and retro-annotation issues. This extension allows iterative improvement of processes through automatic collect and exploitation of process data.

Beyond continuous maturation, capitalization and reuse of process knowledge is a key issue addressed by process engineering communities. Several works have shown the relevancy to adapt software components to system and software processes. The notion of process component have been introduced in the SPEM 2.0 specification. But according to [12], this definition is too basic and the author proposes a clearer definition of process component that integrates some of the major concerns of the MBE (model analysis, model transformations, etc.). In [13], the authors discuss the specification of "MDA Tool Components" which is a process component characterized by the services they provide to the external world.

This paper intends to make converge Process Engineering and MBE techniques taking benefits of both communities. We suggest introducing notions of intention and strategy into the SPEM metamodel through our MODAL extension. Besides, we will see that introduction of these concepts allows refinement of process components definition which encapsulates all or any of the process activities as well as definitions of related artifacts and constraints. We think adopting a full MBE approach can help to automate part or possibly the whole process through the clear identification of all design and analysis activities of the process, including (meta-) models and transformation rules. Then, advantages of MBE become clear as process models allow establishing: traceability between requirements and system functions, critical path, relationships between models, management of complexity through mastered transformations, etc. Furthermore, an MBE approach can improve consistency of data exchanged between involved domains through model transformations. Consequently, consistency between process development plan and its execution becomes implicit.

3 Introduced Concepts

In this section, we present the main concepts introduced to improve the definition of the SPEM 2.0 metamodel and we illustrate them with excerpts taken from a co-design process model targeting re-programmable platforms presented in [14].

Intention. Processes are the essence of the realization of a product. Depending on the process community (Information System, Workflow, etc.), process definition can be centered on products, activities or organization. In the context of MBE, processes are centered on models. The notion of reason which guides our choices is introduced under the concept of intention. Two domains are actually interested in the concept of intention: the artificial intelligence domain (multi-agents systems) [15,16] and the information system domain [17].

The artificial intelligence is interested in the realization of programs by being inspired by rational agents. An agent is said rational if he chooses to realize actions based on what he knows about the world or his faiths [16]. In [15], author proposes the BDI model (Belief, Desire and Intention) which advances the process of reasoning which we use every day: Belief is what the agent knows of its environment; Desire represents possible states it tries to reach; Intention is a goal (final or intermediate) it intends to bring to a successful conclusion.

Besides, information system community in [17] defines the notion of intention as "a goal, an objective that the application engineer has in mind at a given point of time". Authors of this definition implement an entity containing a panel of prescriptive processes, a map made of intentions connected by strategies. Since several strategies are possible to reach an intention, a process can be dynamically reconfigurable. Intentions allow, among others, a better understanding and a better reasoning leading to the final product. But contrary to authors of this definition, we think intentions do not build the process, they accompany it.

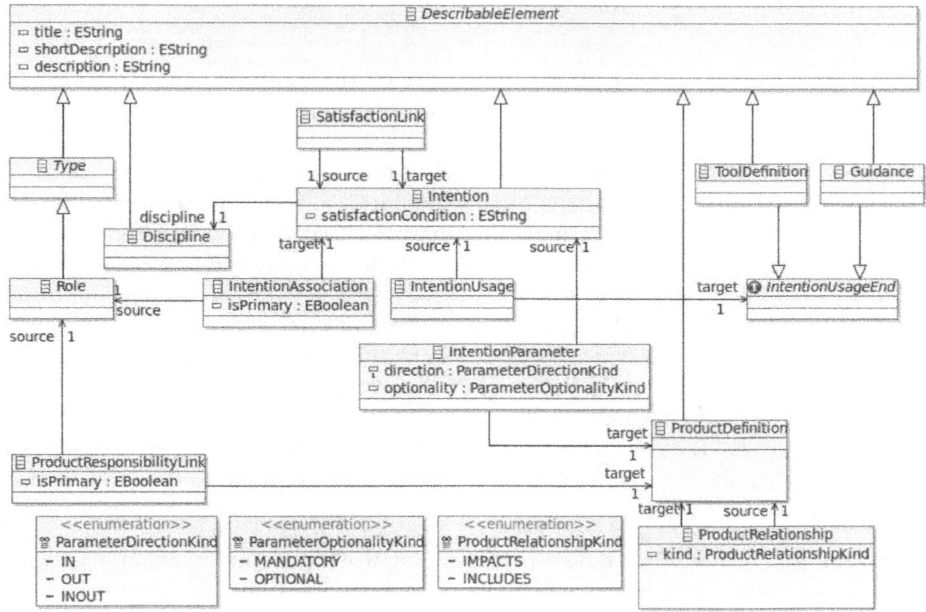

Fig. 1. Abstract Syntax of Intention and Strategy

Figure 1 gives an overview of the abstract syntax of intention and strategy (presented below). An intention defines a methodological objective set by various stakeholders. It uses definition of generic tools as well as generic business rules, related to standards or to the organization. Intentions are linked through satisfaction links which define a map of intentions.

Figure 2 extracted from our reference model shows a simplified view of an intention diagram in which we can see that the system architect and the tester share two common intentions which are "Design coarse grain architecture" and "Design fine grain architecture". The satisfaction of the second intention depends on the satisfaction of the first one which leads to the definition of a computation independent model.

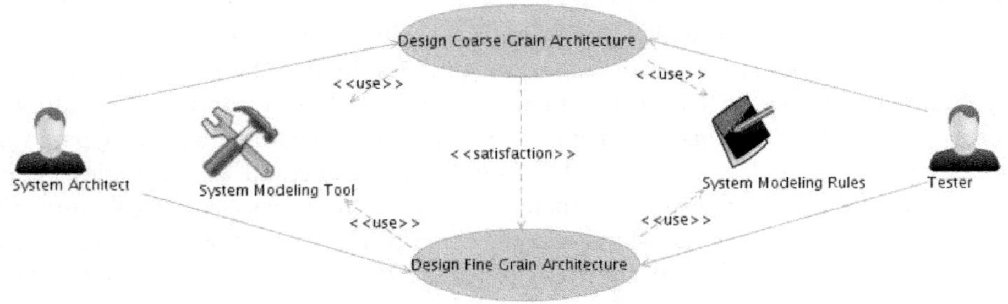

Fig. 2. Example of Intention Satisfaction Map

Strategy. Definition of a strategy starts with the analysis of the intention it tends to satisfy. It mainly consists in establishing a consensus between the various stakeholders implied in the satisfaction of the considered intention and lead to elaboration of an initial plan, which is a synopsis representing a map of interconnected resources or activities. Meanwhile intentions set an intellectual framework to processes using generic definitions (tools, rules, etc.), strategies realize them thanks to the definition of mappings between generic definitions and specific technological spaces. Indeed, a strategy sets a gateway between informal and formal worlds through "Technological Resolutions".

For instance, table 1 shows some of the technological resolutions we made in the context of the MoPCoM SoC / SoPC process.

The strategy map presented in figure 3 represents the counterpart of the intention map presented above along with process constraints expressed in KerMeta syntax. In this diagram, strategies make use of skills, tools as well as constrained activities.

Models as Work Products. In SPEM, a work product is an artifact that can be produced, consumed or transformed by an activity. We think that, in the context of MBE, the notion of work product should be refined to the definition of model. Also, for a better definition of strategies and a finer control of processes, we associate a life cycle with models produced or consumed during process execution. Figure 4 shows the abstract syntax of our definition of work product in the context of MBE. For each used meta-class, we associate a life cycle that defines the possible state in which any conformant artifact can be.

Table 1. Example of Technological Resolutions

Intention Artifact	Technological Resolution
System Modeling Tool	Papyrus
Metamodeling Tool	Eclipse + KerMeta
Methodological Rule	OCL Constraint
System Modeling Language	SysML
Platform Modeling Language	MARTE

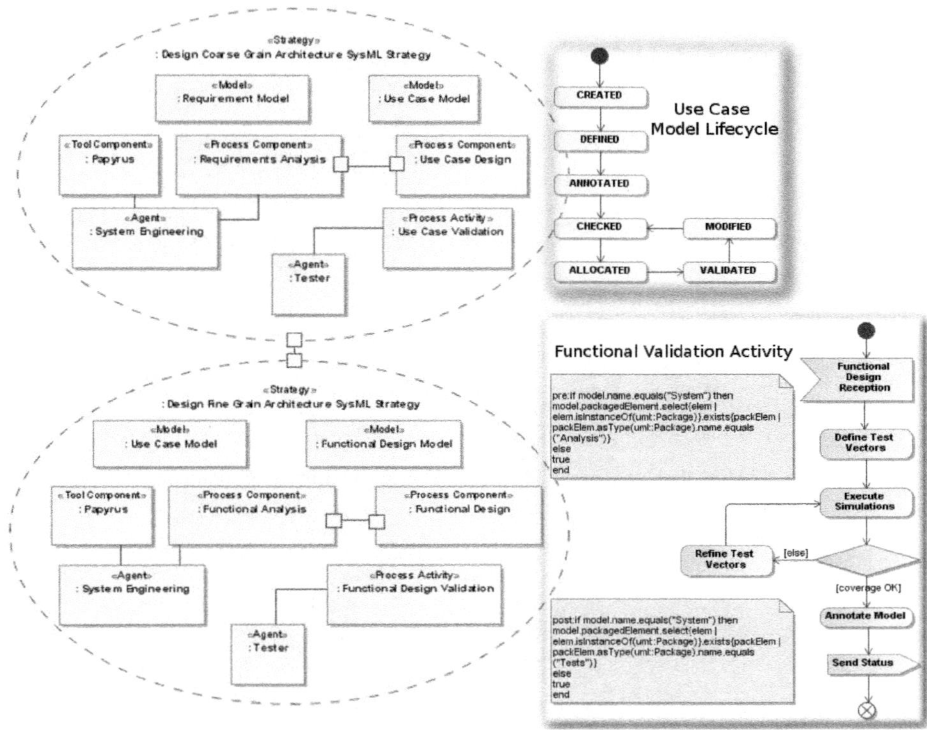

Fig. 3. Example of Strategy Map

Then, constraints that guard execution of activities can use information related to the state of the incoming artifact for a finer control. For instance, in figure 3, we can see a use case model used in a process activity along with its lifecycle.

Constraints. Associated to strategies and process activities, a particular care to definition of constraints is required. Expression of constraints targets process breakdowns including products, and without a clear definition of all those elements, expression of such constraints can be done only thanks to the use of natural language. Indeed, constraints can help to insure the consistency of the process regarding applied standards or any business rules.

Thanks to our work product definition refinement, execution of process activities can now be guarded by more formal constraints insuring a finer grained causality in the definition of processes. This approach is of great importance in the context of MBE processes where wide scope languages are used. Typical example is UML that can be used to cover a very large part of the process activities. It is then essential to identify which subset of the language is useful for any of those activities. Figure 5 shows the abstract syntax of process constraints. Although process constraints allow a better control of process activities, we think

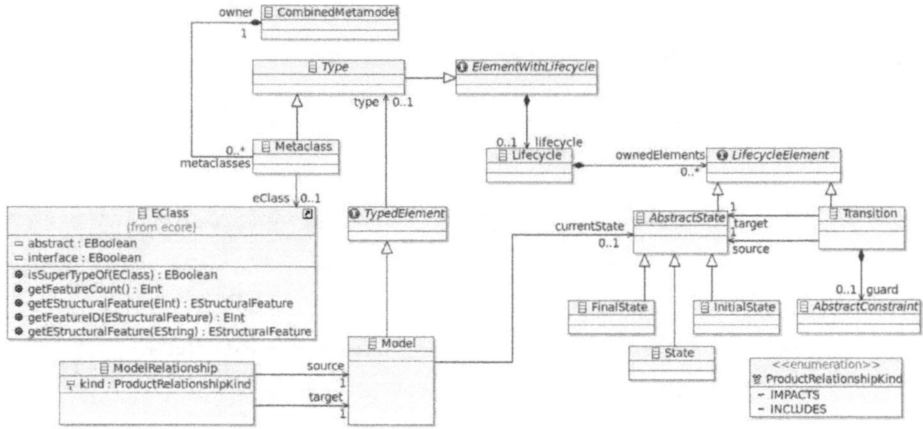

Fig. 4. Excerpt of MODAL Work Product Definition

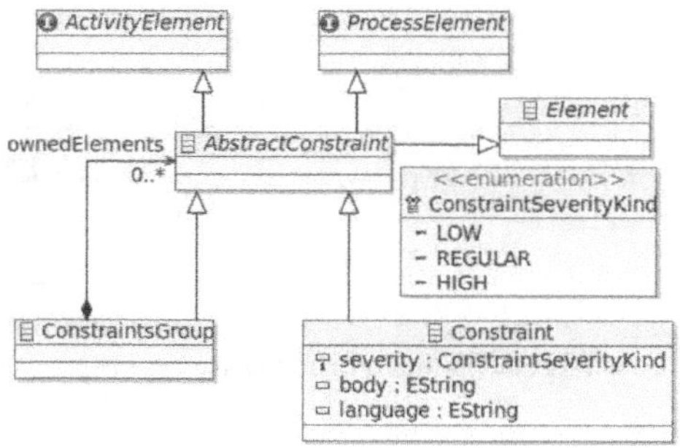

Fig. 5. Abstract Syntax of Process Constraints

that their application could be relaxed to take into account specific business needs. To this purpose, we associate a level of severity to constraints because in some occasion, violation of a constraint can be accepted. Figure 3 shows strategies that are guarded by several constraints expressed in KerMeta syntax and the table 2 shows examples of such constraints.

Process Components. We have seen in section 2 that process components offer several advantages to encapsulation and reuse of process knowledge. Unfortunately, the SPEM metamodel does not give a precise definition of process components. Then, our idea is to take benefits from propositions presented above to clarify the definition of process components. Figure 6 presents the abstract syntax of the process component in our extension. A process component is a concurrent entity communicating through connectors implementing high level services. It is mainly characterized by its public and private parts. Whereas its public part exposes all the services it offers to the outside world, its private part

Table 2. Constraints Formalization

Source	Constraint	Context	Formalization	Severity
Referential	A platform should at least owns one clock	HW_Resource	self.ownedElements.exists(e|e.isInstance(Property) and e.type.stereotypes. contains("HW_Clock"))	REGULAR
DO-258	Operations body should not be empty	Operation	self.body <> null	HIGH

deals with the realization of these services, even by delegation (use of services provided by internal parts) or through activation of internal behaviors. More precisely, its private part encapsulate definition of activities related to some abstraction level, languages and associated tools in order to realize published services. The use of models implies for the component the knowledge related to corresponding metamodels.

Figure 7 shows the top level of the MoPCoM SoC / SoPC process component which gathers the definition of the whole process through interconnected parts. Those parts encapsulate definition of activities, constraints, models and so on. For instance, the *Abstract Modeling Level* process component provides the description of the expected level of concurrency and pipeline of the input application model through the mapping of functional blocks onto an abstract platform. The *Execution Modeling Level* process component provides the topology of the execution platform of the application defined in terms of execution, communication or storage nodes in order to proceed to coarse grain analysis.

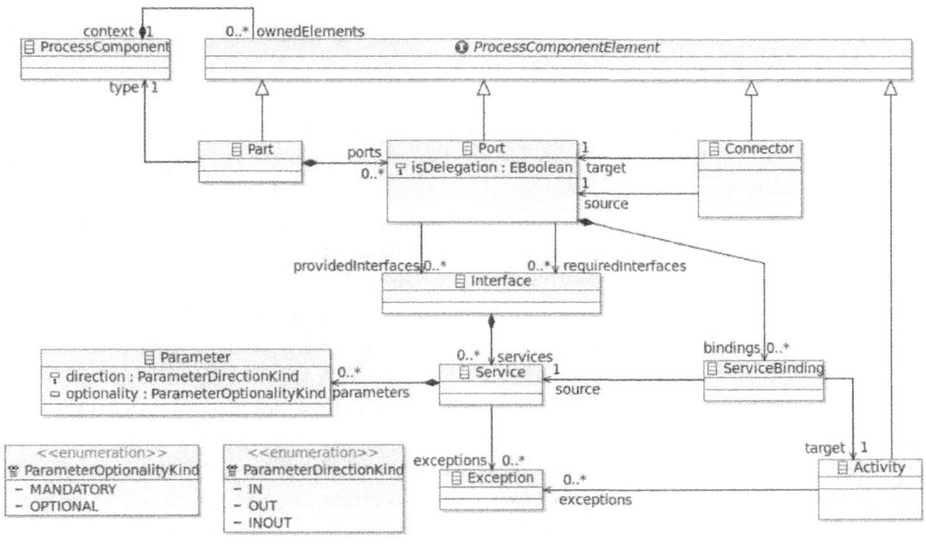

Fig. 6. Excerpt of MODAL Process Component Definition

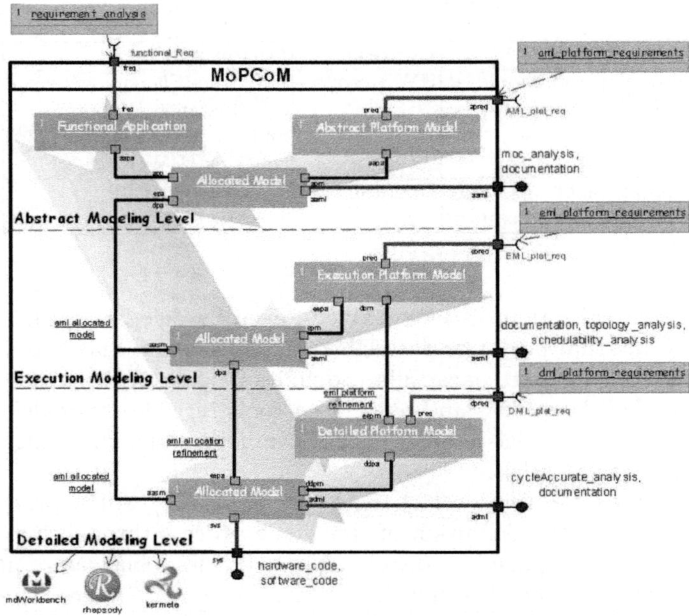

Fig. 7. MoPCoM SoC/SoPC Process Overview

The *Detailed Modeling Level* process component provides a detailed description of the execution platform of the application in order to proceed to fine grained analysis.

4 Discussion

Using SPEM fits well to system or software process representation when captured models are contemplative. For instance, the reference process implementation in the EPF project is OpenUP (Open Unified Process). This model is considered precise only because of the great number of provided details. Still, this model stay informal and its strict application remains subject to interpretation. We have to face the limits of SPEM when we try to achieve process enactment through execution. Especially, we are not able to take advantages of MBE techniques to automate processes, even partially. Of course, several propositions overcome the shortcomings of SPEM (see section 2) but those solutions are local. Then, we propose a more global approach that integrates those local solutions into large processes.

Even if more experimentation is needed to validate our propositions, we can yet make some interesting assessments. For instance, building large process models requires clear viewpoints facilitating process analysis. Such viewpoints in SPEM can be achieved only thanks to a coarse decomposition of process activities. This approach does not facilitate analysis because an activity definition is yet a proposition of a solution. Indeed, we need to make a clear separation between processes needs and their solutions. The notions of intention and strategy contributes to provide such feature.

The choice of particular solutions thanks to technological resolutions can contribute to the establishment of executable processes only if all aspects of the solutions are "machine readable". For instance, in SPEM, activities can be decomposed thanks to the use of dedicated action language. Unfortunately, artifacts produced, consumed or transformed by those activities are actually black boxes. Since SPEM has been clearly defined in the context of MBE, it should be coherent to consider that a work product can be described using models. Making this assumption, we can make a good trade-off between description and execution. Also, without the refinement of the definition of work products, expression of actions or constraints can only be informal. Then, our extension contributes to executability of actions and allows expression of constraints that can be automatically checked. Moreover, regarding application of constraints, the notion of severity introduced in MODAL brings more flexibility compared to SPEM.

Finally, process components defined in SPEM can only encapsulates informal knowledge. Thanks to the clarification proposed in the previous section, we can now turn process components from informal to executable. Beyond executability, those features contribute to more unambiguous knowledge capture. Table below sums up contributions of MODAL compared to SPEM.

Table 3. SPEM vs MODAL Comparison

	SPEM	**MODAL**
Need Formalization	?	Intention
Solution Formalization	Activity	Strategy
Work Product Usability	No	Yes
Constraint Usability	No	Yes
Activity Executability	No	Yes
Process Component Executability	No	Yes

The proposed approach contributes to create tool chains on-demand, which constitutes a challenge to handle obsolescence of technologies. We are still working on generation of executable process components deployed in a distributed environment. We have used Eclipse[2] and related technologies (EMF, CNF, GMF, KerMeta) in order to tool our extension.

5 Conclusion and Future Works

In this paper, we have presented an extension of the SPEM metamodel called MODAL. This extension introduces concepts of intention and strategies and

[2] http://www.eclipse.org

align the definition of work product to model. This allows refinement of process contraint and process component definition. MODAL models highlight the strong correlation between processes, work products, languages and tools. This extension contributes then to reinforce the semantics of process models. Propositions of the extension have been experimented on an industrial co-design project in Thales Company, developing embedded systems. Our experiment shows that SPEM, complemented by our proposition, can fit to processes involving several heterogeneous businesses (system, software, platform, signals).

Future works will have to make effective the implementation of process components in order to manage definition of tools chain which seems to be the only way to manage the growing complexity of future development. Besides, the proposed metamodel will have to provide mechanisms allowing customization of existing process components to manage product lines.

Acknowledgements. This work is part of the MoPCoM SoC/SoPC project. More information is available in `http://www.mopcom.fr`.

References

1. standishgroup: Standish group chaos report (2006)
2. Baldassarre, M.T., Boffoli, N., Bruno, G., Caivano, D.: Statistically based process monitoring: Lessons from the trench. In: Wang, Q., Garousi, V., Madachy, R., Pfahl, D. (eds.) ICSP 2009. LNCS, vol. 5543, pp. 11–23. Springer, Heidelberg (2009)
3. OMG: SPEM 2.0. Technical Report ptc/05-01-06, Object Management Group (2008)
4. Scacchi, W.: Process models in software engineering. Encyclopedia of Software Engineering 13, 31–39 (2001)
5. Zhang, H., Kitchenham, B., Jeffery, R.: Qualitative vs. quantitative software process simulation modeling: Conversion and comparison. In: ASWEC 2009: Proceedings of the 2009 Australian Software Engineering Conference, Washington, DC, USA, pp. 345–354. IEEE Computer Society, Los Alamitos (2009)
6. Jung, H.W., Goldenson, D.R.: Evaluating the relationship between process improvement and schedule deviation in software maintenance. Inf. Softw. Technol. 51(2), 351–361 (2009)
7. Osterweil, L.J.: Formalisms to support the definition of processes. J. Comput. Sci. Technol. 24(2), 198–211 (2009)
8. Bendraou, R.: UML4SPM: Un Langage De Modélisation De Procédés De Développement Logiciel Exécutable Et Orienté Modèle. PhD thesis, Université Pierre et Marie Curie (2007)
9. Rolland, C.: A comprehensive view of process engineering. In: Pernici, B., Thanos, C. (eds.) CAiSE 1998. LNCS, vol. 1413, pp. 1–24. Springer, Heidelberg (1998)
10. Bendraou, R., Combemale, B., Cregut, X., Gervais, M.P.: Definition of an executable spem 2.0. In: APSEC 2007: Proceedings of the 14th Asia-Pacific Software Engineering Conference (APSEC 2007), Washington, DC, USA, pp. 390–397. IEEE Computer Society, Los Alamitos (2007)
11. Larrucea, X., Bozheva, T.: Towards an agile process pattern modeling framework. In: SE 2007: Proceedings of the 25th conference on IASTED International Multi-Conference, Anaheim, CA, USA, pp. 61–65. ACTA Press (2007)

12. Mekerke, F.: Structuration des modèles orientés métiers pour les systèmes embarqués. PhD thesis, Lisyc (2008)
13. Bézivin, J., Gérard, S., Muller, P.A., Rioux, L.: Mda components: Challenges and opportunities. In: Workshop on Metamodelling for MDA, York, England, pp. 23–41 (2003)
14. Koudri, A., Champeau, J., Aulagnier, D., Soulard, P.: Mopcom/marte process applied to a cognitive radio system design and analysis. In: Paige, R.F., Hartman, A., Rensink, A. (eds.) ECMDA-FA 2009. LNCS, vol. 5562, pp. 277–288. Springer, Heidelberg (2009)
15. Bratman, M.E.: Intention, Plans, and Practical Reason. Harvard University Press, Cambridge (1987)
16. Wooldridge, M.J.: Reasoning about Rational Agents. The MIT Press, Cambridge (2000)
17. Rolland, C., Prakash, N., Benjamen, A.: A multi-model of process modelling. Requirement Engineering 4, 169–187 (1999)

Application of Re-estimation in Re-planning of Software Product Releases

Ahmed Al-Emran[1], Anas Jadallah[1], Elham Paikari[1], Dietmar Pfahl[1,3], and Günther Ruhe[1,2,4]

[1] Department of Electrical & Computer Engineering, Schulich School of Engineering, University of Calgary
[2] Department of Computer Science, University of Calgary
[3] Department of Informatics, University of Oslo
[4] Expert Decisions Inc., Calgary
{aalemran,agjadall,epaikari,dpfahl,ruhe}@ucalgary.ca

Context: Re-planning of product releases is a very dynamic endeavor and new research methods or improvements of existing methods are still required. This paper explores the role of re-estimation in the re-planning process of product releases.

Objective: The purpose of this study is to analyze effects of defect and effort re-estimation in the process of release re-planning. In particular, two questions are answered: Question 1: In the absence of re-estimation, does conducting re-planning have any advantages over not conducting re-planning? Question 2: In the case of re-planning, does conducting re-estimation have any advantages over not conducting re-estimation?

Method: The proposed method H2W-Pred extends the existing H2W re-planning method by accommodating dynamic updates on defect and effort estimates whenever re-planning takes place. Based on the updates, effort for development of new functionality needs to be re-adjusted and balanced against the additional effort necessary to ensure quality early. The proposed approach is illustrated by case examples with simulated data.

Results: The simulation results show that conducting re-planning yields better release value in terms of functionality than not conducting re-planning. Furthermore, performing re-estimation when doing re-planning generates a portfolio of solutions that help balance trade-offs between several aspects of release value, e.g., between functionality and quality.

Conclusion: If the development of a product release requires balancing between potentially conflictive aspects, such as quality vs. functionality, then re-estimation in the re-planning process is beneficial.

Keywords: Release planning, Re-planning process, H2W method, Decision support, Effort estimation, and Defect estimation.

1 Introduction and Motivation

Planning of product releases addresses the problem of assigning features to a sequence of releases such that the technical, resources, risk, and budget constraints are met [1].

J. Münch, Y. Yang, and W. Schäfer (Eds.): ICSP 2010, LNCS 6195, pp. 260–272, 2010.

A product feature is a set of logically related requirements that provide a capability to the user and enable the satisfaction of business objectives [2]. But planning is not a onetime effort. Due to the dynamic change in the planning parameters, plans need to be adjusted to new priorities, budgets, time lines and new arriving features. Following that pathway, release planning becomes an ongoing effort to accommodate all these changes in a best possible way. However, this process currently is far from being well controlled. A survey over 8000 projects undertaken by 350 US companies revealed that one third of the projects were never completed and one half succeeded only partially. The third major source of the failure (11%) was changing requirements [3].

The focus of this work is on a method for systematic re-planning of product releases exploiting re-estimation. We propose and initially evaluate a new decision support method called H2W-Pred. The new method is an extension of the former re-planning method H2W [4]. As for H2W, the method answers the questions of "How?", "When?", and "What?" related to the process of product release re-planning. However, the new method emphasized the need of re-estimation and shows that re-planning based on re-estimation provides better results.

In the rest of the paper, Section 2 formalizes the re-planning problem whereas Section 3 gives a description of the actual re-planning method called H2W-Pred. The method is illustrated in Section 4 by an illustrative case study. As part of an empirical evaluation of the method, in Section 5, we conduct a simulation experiment to compare the case of not allowing re-planning and with the two cases of allowing re-planning with and without re-estimation. The emphasis here is not on the re-estimation method, but on the impact of planning with updated information. Section 6 discusses related work, the study results and associated validity threats. The paper concluded with a summary and an outlook on future research in Section 7.

2 Formalization of Re-planning

Re-planning of software product releases being in progress of implementation is based on different types of information related to the existing plan, the change requests, and the capacities and time interval of the release under investigation.

2.1 Release Information

The re-planning process happens in a given release period denoted by [T1,T2]. The implementation process of the planned release starts at t = T1. The planned release date is t = T2. Each feature has some estimated effort for its implementation and each release has a limited effort capacity CAP. The capacity limits the number of features that can be implemented in the proposed plan.

2.2 Existing Plan

At the beginning of the re-planning process, we assume a set F = {f(1)... f(N)} of features. The actual plan is described by the set of features selected from F for implementation in the given release. We describe the plan by a Boolean vector x with

$$x(n) = 1 \text{ iff feature } f(n) \text{ is selected from } F \text{ for implementation} \quad (1)$$

This plan can be determined by any of the existing methods mentioned above. We will later see that our greedy re-planning method can be used as well to determine an initial plan.

Each feature f(n) for n = 1..N is characterized by a set of attributes. If attribute effort(n) describes the (estimated) effort for implementation of feature f(n), then we have

$$\Sigma_{n=1..N}\ x(n)\ \text{effort}(n) \leq \text{CAP} \tag{2}$$

In addition to effort, other attributes that we consider are risk(n) and value(n) that represent a risk and a benefit value of the feature, respectively.

2.3 Change Requests

In the process of implementation of a once agreed upon plan, change request might occur. A change request relates to changing an already accepted feature (some of the data of its related attributes) or requesting a new feature. The set of change request is dynamically changing, so we need to describe them in dependence of time.

We define by CR(t) the set of all change requests from the beginning of the release period (t = T1) until point in time t $\in$ (T1, T2]. The change requests themselves are denoted by f(N+1), f(N+2), ... f(N_t) where N_t denotes the number of change requests until point in time t. Each change request f(n), n = N+1 … N_t is characterized by four attributes called risk(n), value(n), time(n) and effort(n).

Both risk and the feature's value (from a stakeholder viewpoint) are classified on a nine-point scale with values ranging from 1 (extremely low) to 9 (extremely high). A change request f(n) is arriving at point in time t denoted by t = time(n) and is estimated to consume effort in the amount of effort(n). Both the risk and the value estimation are assumed to be the result of stakeholder (and expert) evaluation as described in [5]. Experts can estimate the level of risk for features from previous project history. For estimation of effort, a variety of known methods and techniques can potentially be applied. A method for estimation in consideration of change was studied in [6].

3 Re-planning Method H2W-PRED

The proposed H2W-Pred method is an extension of H2W re-planning method (1 and [4]). H2W addresses the questions "When?", "What?" and "How?" in the context of re-planning for product releases. In H2W-Pred, we accommodate re-estimation of effort and the number of defects. The three main steps of the method are described below using a template explaining the purpose, roles involved, as well as input and output artifacts. The whole H2W-Pred method is illustrated in Section 4 by an illustrative case study example.

3.1 Step 1: When to Re-plan?

The "when to re-plan?" decides when to initiate re-planning. For simplicity, we use fixed intervals for re-planning (i.e., re-planning is initiated at fixed points in time), to study and analyze the impact of the frequency of re-planning for different scenarios.

Table 1. Key parameters for Step 1

Purpose	Specify fixed interval for re-planning
Roles	Project manager
Description: The idea is to specify the points in time where re-planning is triggered depending on the frequency of re-planning required.	
Input	Release planning period [T1,T2]
Output	Re-planning times t ∈ (T1, T2]

For more flexible re-planning strategies we refer to Chapter 7 in [1]. The key parameters for Step 1 are summarized in Table 4.

3.2 Step 2: What to Re-plan?

The "what to re-plan?" determines what to include in the re-planning process. Since re-planning tries to produce up-to-date release plans by accommodating change requests, the features planned but not yet implemented as well as change requests are included in the re-planning process.

In addition to that, predictive models are applied at re-planning iterations for re-estimating effort and defects as follows:

1. Effort re-estimation: since implementation of new features in previous iterations update the system as well as the data repository, re-estimations in the following iterations may perform better and converge towards the actual effort, which increases release plans quality.
2. Defect re-estimation: since early defect detection before system test and operations is a cost-effective strategy for software quality improvement 7, we apply defect prediction model at re-planning iterations to capture and remove defects rather than waiting for all functional implementation to be finished.

The key parameters for Step 2 are summarized in Table 5.

Table 2. Key parameters for Step 2

Purpose	Determine what to include in the re-planning process
Roles	Project manager and software architect
Description: The Project manager selects change requests and unimplemented features in the baseline release plan, while the software architect uses effort and defect prediction models to predict defects and re-estimate effort needed to implementing selected features based on the new updates	
Input	The set of features F, change requests CR(t)
Output	The set of features F1 ⊆ (F U CR(t)) for re-planning as well as their updated effort estimates and number of predicted defects

3.3 Step 3: How to Re-plan?

The "how to re-plan?" describes the actual process of producing up-to-date release plans. Candidate features and change requests are ranked based on their distance to the ideal point [8] in a space compromising three dimensions; value in terms of stakeholders' satisfaction, cost in terms of persons-hours, and risk in terms of stakeholders acceptance. This ideal point represents the best theoretical point having extremely low cost, extremely low risk and extremely high value. After that, greedy optimization [9] is applied adding the most attractive features to the capacities remaining. The key parameters for Step 3 are summarized in Table 6.

Table 3. Key parameters for Step 3

Purpose	Producing up-to-date release plan by accommodating change requests as well as new effort and defects estimates.
Roles	Project manager and stakeholders.
Description: Candidate features are updated by new effort estimates while stakeholders vote for change requests. The resulting set of features and change requests are prioritized according to their distance to the ideal point. Greedy optimization is applied to add most attractive features to the capacities remaining after compromising between additional effort needed for QA activates and effort need to implement these features.	
Input	The set of features F1 selected for re-planning as well as their updated effort estimates and number of predicted defects
Output	The set of features F2 ⊆ F1 representing the new up-to-date release plan as well as resources allocated for fixing predicted defects.

4 Illustrative Case Study

To illustrate the working principle of our method, we present a simple case example where the considered feature set is taken from real-world data. Both features and their effort estimates were taken from the product release planning of the decision support tool ReleasePlanner™ [10]. All the other data of this case example were generated using synthetically.

Table 4. Initial feature set

f(n)	effort(n)	value(n)	risk(n)	f(n)	effort(n)	value(n)	risk(n)	f(n)	effort(n)	value(n)	risk(n)	f(n)	effort(n)	value(n)	risk(n)
1	16	5	9	14	45	1	5	27	27	4	7	40	90	7	4
2	16	2	3	15	45	3	2	28	95	6	1	41	10	5	6
3	17	2	8	16	17	7	6	29	70	2	9	42	10	9	1
4	30	6	6	17	40	6	2	30	55	1	7	43	36	1	2
5	29	6	3	18	85	1	4	31	41	9	6	44	34	9	6
6	23	3	8	19	22	2	1	32	10	9	4	45	45	9	8
7	4	7	4	20	83	9	4	33	5	9	3	46	29	2	4
8	65	9	2	21	31	6	7	34	80	1	2	47	40	3	3
9	9	9	5	22	28	3	4	35	60	9	9	48	75	7	1
10	31	3	9	23	38	7	1	36	45	5	7	49	55	9	7
11	75	6	7	24	20	4	3	37	50	7	5	50	6	9	8
12	45	1	4	25	80	1	4	38	10	2	3				
13	60	6	4	26	75	9	6	39	100	3	7				

4.1 Release Information and Baseline Plan

The case example includes:

- A set of 50 initial features, F = {f(1), f(2), ..., f(50)} with their corresponding attributes as shown in Table 4
- Effort capacity, CAP = 700
- Release start time, T1 = 0
- Release end time, T2 = 100
- Two re-planning iterations called I1 and I2 and considered. The first iteration I1 ends at time 50, and the second iteration I2 ends at time 100.

4.2 Baseline Planning

Table 5 provides the details of the baseline release planning (serving as a reference point for subsequent re-planning). First, features are prioritized (c.f., Table 5(a)) based on the distance to the ideal point as discussed in [4]. In addition to features' value and risk, the distance calculation (i.e., Dist(n)) is relying on their effort normalized in 9-point scale (denoted by normEff(n)).

Afterwards, greedy optimization is applied that takes top-ranked features one by one from the priority list (until T2) to determine baseline solution (c.f., Table 5(b)). In this case, 24 features could be accommodated in the baseline plan that totals a functional value of 156. This value is computed by adding up value(n) for all 24 features that could be accommodated in the release. First half of the baseline plan i.e., until implementation of feature f(44) has been scheduled in iteration I1 and rest of the baseline plan has been scheduled in iteration I2.

Table 5. Baseline planning

Prioritization of Features based on Distance to Ideal Point								
f(n)	normEff(n)	Dist(n)	f(n)	normEff(n)	Dist(n)	f(n)	normEff(n)	Dist(n)
42	1	0.00	13	6	6.56	43	4	8.60
33	1	2.00	21	3	7.00	40	9	8.78
32	1	3.00	22	3	7.00	1	2	9.00
7	1	3.61	47	4	7.00	11	7	9.00
23	4	3.61	50	1	7.00	6	3	9.43
9	1	4.00	19	2	7.07	12	5	9.43
5	3	4.12	49	5	7.21	35	6	9.43
17	4	4.36	15	5	7.28	14	5	9.80
8	6	5.10	38	1	7.28	3	2	9.95
16	2	5.48	2	2	7.35	10	3	10.20
24	2	5.48	20	8	7.62	34	8	10.68
31	4	5.83	26	7	7.81	30	5	10.77
44	4	5.83	46	3	7.87	18	8	11.05
37	5	6.00	27	3	8.06	25	8	11.05
4	3	6.16	45	5	8.06	39	9	11.66
48	7	6.32	36	5	8.25	29	7	12.21
41	1	6.40	28	9	8.54			

(a)

Baseline Plan (I1)			Baseline Plan (I2)		
f(n)	start(n)	end(n)	f(n)	start(n)	end(n)
42	0.00	1.43	37	46.00	53.14
33	1.43	2.14	4	53.14	57.43
32	2.14	3.57	48	57.43	68.14
7	3.57	4.14	41	68.14	69.57
23	4.14	9.57	13	69.57	78.14
9	9.57	10.86	21	78.14	82.57
5	10.86	15.00	22	82.57	86.57
17	15.00	20.71	47	86.57	92.29
8	20.71	30.00	50	92.29	93.14
16	30.00	32.43	19	93.14	96.29
24	32.43	35.29	38	96.29	97.71
31	35.29	41.14	Functional value: 156		
44	41.14	46.00			

(b)

4.3 Effort and Defect Re-estimation

We apply two analogy based method for effort and defect re-estimation that uses latest information on already developed features in the previous iterations. For effort re-estimation, we apply the method AQUA [11] using estimation by analogy and learning. For defect re-estimation, we apply a case-based reasoning technique [12]. The re-estimation based re-planning approach of the paper is applicable to alternative techniques as well.

Table 6 shows the evolution of effort estimates in iterations I1 and I2. Note that, some of the estimation values are missing. This is due to the fact that either features have been realized already before further re-estimation or they have never been realized. For example, initial effort estimation of f(5) for iteration I1 was 29pd (i.e, person-days), however, it took 39.88pd (which is actual effort or AE). Since f(5) is implemented within I1, it was required to re-estimated its effort for I2. On the other hand, f(1) has never been implemented. That is why AE could never be known and effort was estimated/re-estimated in each iteration. Effort of F(50) was estimated as 6pd for I1, then re-estimated as 4.44pd for I2, and finally implemented in I2 with 4.62pd.

Table 6. Effort re-estimation of initial set of features

f(n)	I1	I2	AE	f(n)	I1	I2	AE	f(n)	I1	I2	AE	f(n)	I1	I2	AE	f(n)	I1	I2	AE
1	16	12.46		11	75	61.80		21	31	28.70		31	41		45.92	41	10	13.96	
2	16	22.26		12	45	76.27		22	28			32	10		12.35	42	10		13.15
3	17	16.42		13	60	96.00		23	38		38.19	33	5		6.38	43	36	51.95	
4	30		24.30	14	45	62.75		24	20		18.40	34	80	97.97		44	34		40.63
5	29		39.88	15	45	61.13		25	80	93.61		35	60	55.27		45	45	65.34	
6	23	23.39		16	17		21.93	26	75	97.00		36	45	61.55		46	29	29.07	
7	4		5.36	17	40		37.60	27	27	33.38		37	50	48.91		47	40	45.13	
8	65		66.62	18	85	95.00		28	95	99.47		38	10	9.67		48	75	89.94	
9	9		8.91	19	22			29	70	78.70		39	100	97.00		49	55	81.00	
10	31	42.90		20	83	99.89		30	55	92.98		40	90	98.33		50	6	4.44	4.62

4.4 Change Requests/Newly Arrive Features

We simulate the random occurrence of change requests by the customer i.e., arrival of new features at different points in time within the release duration (T1, T2). In this illustrative case, they are: f(51), f(52), ..., f(63). The corresponding attribute values are also randomly generated and the value ranges for their attributes are the same as the features in the initial feature set (e.g., 9 point scale). The arrival time of change request, time(n), is equally distributed over the period (T1, T2]. Table 7(a) provides all information about the simulated data for the newly arrived features as well as their effort evolution over iterations.

4.5 Iterations and Re-Planning Scenario

The development of the release follows the realization of features in the same order as they are in the baseline plan (c.f., Table 5 (b)). After the first iteration i.e., I1 is completed, 13 features have been implemented as shown in Table 7(b). By comparing completed iteration I1 with the baseline iteration I1 (c.f., Table 5(b)), we can see that the same features are implemented that were planned in the baseline since neither re-planning took place nor re-estimation is conducted. The only differences lie on the development times of the features i.e., in start(n) and end(n). This is because, actual efforts (i.e., AE of Table 7(a)) are used since actual efforts are now known as these features are already realized.

At the end of the first iteration, two predictive models are applied to re-estimate feature efforts for the next iteration and unknown defects generated from previously implemented iterations. Afterwards, re-planning event takes place for allocating available efforts to rest of the release based on all project updates. These updates include adjustment of feature effort (by effort prediction model), additional QA effort for detected defects (by defect prediction model) to be removed, and newly arrived features that have been arrived until end of iteration I1 (c.f., shaded portion of Table 7(a)). Upper part of Table 7(c) provides the updated plan for iteration I2 – first, additional QA activity is scheduled, and then three features are planned based on distance to ideal point and available effort. The re-planning event accommodates two of the newly arrived features (i.e., f(58) and f(52)). f(4) is the only feature from the baseline plan that could be included in second (also last) iteration I2. Lower part of Table 7(c) shows completed iteration I2 where f(50) could also be accommodated due to overestimation of some features' efforts.

Table 7. Summary of release progress in two iterations

Change Requests and their Effort Re-estimations							
f(n)	effort(n)	value(n)	risk(n)	time(n)	I1	I2	AE
51	89.97	6	4	11	89.97	62.08	
52	45.19	9	6	15	45.19		37.98
53	48.16	7	6	19	48.16	67.65	
54	95.00	4	7	22	95.00	94.40	
55	89.26	3	5	31	89.26	98.00	
56	95.00	7	9	34	95.00	98.00	
57	96.00	2	8	41	96.00	89.23	
58	47.25	9	4	43	47.25		37.80
59	95.25	9	9	61	95.25	95.00	
60	56.80	3	8	79	56.80	90.72	
61	14.05	8	7	83	14.05	12.84	
62	28.75	4	3	84	28.75	21.67	
63	20.67	4	4	88	20.67	27.60	

(a)

Completed Iteration I1		
f(n)	start(n)	end(n)
42	0.00	1.88
33	1.88	2.79
32	2.79	4.55
7	4.55	5.32
23	5.32	10.78
9	10.78	12.05
5	12.05	17.74
17	17.74	23.12
8	23.12	32.63
16	32.63	35.77
24	35.77	38.40
31	38.40	44.96
44	44.96	50.76

(b)

Re-planned Iteration I2		
f(n)	start(n)	end(n)
Add. QA	50.76	83.76
58	83.76	90.51
4	90.51	93.25
52	93.25	99.71
Completed Iteration I2		
f(n)	start(n)	end(n)
Add. QA	50.76	83.76
58	83.76	89.16
4	89.16	92.63
52	92.63	98.06
50	98.06	98.69

(c)

4.6 Case Example Summary

The case example summary compares the final results with the baseline plan to report what we have gained and what we have loose as shown in Table 8.

In this particular case, 33 unknown defects could be discovered and removed early. However, with a cost of 231 person-days effort dedicated towards additional QA activities (other than regular QA activities like testing after functional development). Since the total effort capacity is fixed (700 person-days), the development effort is reduced by the same amount as the increase in QA effort. This reduction of development effort results in seven[1] baseline features to be discarded from the release which in turn reduces functional value.

[1] Two other baseline features are discarded in exchange of two new feature inclusions.

Table 8. Baseline plan vs. revised plan

Profile for Baseline Plan Before Development Starts						
Iteration Duration	Functional Value	# of Features Discarded	# of Features Implemented	Development Effort	Additional QA Effort	# of Defects Removed
50	156	0	24	700	0	0
Profile for Application of Predictive Models and Release Re-planning After Development Ends						
Iteration Duration	Functional Value	# of Features Discarded	# of Features Implemented	Development Effort	Additional QA Effort	# of Defects Removed
50	133	9	17	469	231	33

5 Simulation Experiment

In this section, we perform an analysis based on simulated data for the same project as studied in Section 4. We performed 1000 simulation runs for different iteration durations with randomly generated data in order to explore the impact of re-estimation. For each simulation run, 50 initial features were generated with risk and value attributes in a 9-point scale and with effort attribute up to 100 person-days. In each simulation run, a total of 7 developers and a maximum of 700 efforts capacity (person-days), and 100 days of make-spans are considered. Some of the features from the original set with the shortest distance to the ideal point are selected for the baseline plan.

Without loss of generality, the numbers of new incoming features is assumed to be one quarter of the number of initial features, and the new features can arrive at anytime during the release development applying distribution UNIFORM(0, 100). As part of the analysis, three cases (scenarios) were studied for the varying data:

CASE A: No re-planning and no re-estimation.

CASE B: Allows re-planning of features without re-estimation.

CASE C: Allows re-planning of features with re-estimation.

Based on these cases, two key questions were analyzed:

Question 1: In the absence of re-estimation, does conducting re-planning have any advantages over not conducting re-planning?

Question 2: In the case of re-planning, does conducting re-estimation have any advantages over not conducting re-estimation.

Answering Question 1 requires comparison between CASE A and CASE B whereas answering Question 2 requires comparison between CASE B and CASE C.

Table 9 provides simulation results where each row represents summary of 1000 simulation runs. The first two columns are used for classification purpose whereas the subsequent columns report average simulation outcomes. The very first column groups simulation results corresponding to CASE A (i.e., first data row), CASE B (i.e., middle three data rows), and CASE C (i.e., last three data rows). CASE A has only one data row since no re-planning is considered and features are realized within single iteration. "Number of Iterations" specifies number of equal length iteration in the release. "Functional Value" is the (average) sum over "value(n)" attributes of the implemented features in the release. The last three columns represent effort (in person-days) required for feature implementation, effort (in person-days) for additional quality assurance activities if unknown defect needs to be located and removed, and number of defects removed, respectively.

Table 9. Simulation results: CASE A vs. CASE B vs. CASE C

CASE	Number of Iterations	Average Functional Value	Average Development Effort	Average Additional QA Effort	Average # of Removed Defects
A	1	148.19	700.00	0.00	0.00
B	2	153.96	700.00	0.00	0.00
	5	157.00	700.00	0.00	0.00
	10	156.86	700.00	0.00	0.00
C	2	125.65	475.52	224.48	32.07
	5	103.37	337.73	362.27	55.75
	10	89.14	258.71	441.29	73.04

5.1 Answer to Question 1

Three data rows of CASE B are compared here with one data row of CASE A in Table 9. CASE B consists of three scenarios with 2, 5, and 10 iterations equally divided within release duration (i.e., 100 working days). Re-planning event takes place at the end of all iterations except the last one. Therefore, first, second, and third scenarios consist 1, 4, 9 re-planning events, respectively.

By comparing CASE A with CASE B in Table 9, CASE B appears to be better in terms of functional value. The reason behind such result is that re-planning permits exchange of features i.e., replacing once declared features by some of the newly arriving features that are comparatively more attractive in terms of "distance to ideal point".

5.2 Answer to Question 2

Three scenarios of CASE C (where re-planning is conducted along with re-estimation) are compared with three scenarios of CASE B (where re-planning is not allowed) and three scenarios of CASE C in Table 9. We can make the following observations from this comparison:

1. CASE C is worse than CASE B in terms of functional value offered.
2. CASE C is better than CASE B in terms of quality value (defects detected early).
3. With an increasing number of re-planning iterations (and thus with an increasing number of re-estimations), there is a stronger emphasis on early defect detection, and consequently a decrease of functional value offered.

In order to remove the discovered defects early during functional development, additional quality assurance (QA) effort is required. This compensates the available effort capacity for regular implementation effort. This results in some features being discarded from baseline plan, less features to be implemented, and hence, less functional value being offered.

The earlier defects are detected and removed, the less the cost relatively to the total project effort [7]. Results of CASE C support making trade-off decisions. In dependence of the relative value of new functionality and quality (reduced number of defects), the product manager can suggest the most appropriate compromise decision.

6 Related Work and Discussion

Several methods and techniques have been proposed for product release planning (see for example [13], [14], [15]). None of these methods addresses the issue of dynamically changing feature requests. Changing features can involve the arrival of new features or the change of existing features. Needs for having a change management process in place that handles the re-planning of release plans are discussed in [1] and [16]. The estimated impact of uncertainties related to the effort and arrival time of features well as the availability and productivity of developers has been studied in [17].

Models for release re-planning without re-estimation have proven relevant in various practical applications [18]. As a "proof-of-concept", the applicability of our new method combining release re-planning with re-estimation models has been demonstrated by a case example. Even though we performed analyses by varying data in 1000 simulation runs, a practical evaluation of the proposed method is outstanding. There is no claim of its external validity at this point in time.

There are also limitations regarding internal validity of our simulation experiments. This is due to simplifications made about the underlying assumptions. Firstly, we just consider "effort" as the only attribute characterizing the amount of implementation needed to create the feature. However, effort in reality is composed of different types of resources. In a more fine-grained model, different types of resources would need to be considered. A second assumption is related to completeness of feature implementation. In case of any re-planning, we need information about which features are already finished, which ones are in progress, and which one are not yet started. Consequently, some form of operational planning needs to be in place to track this. We also have made the simplifying assumption that the features are pursued in the order of priority (highest rated feature comes first) with all effort spent on the feature in progress. In other words, we have the model of serial implementation of all the features. This again is a simplification which allows re-planning in a reasonable amount of time and with a reasonable amount of computational effort.

In general, we consider the method practically applicable whenever some form of effort and defect prediction is available with the data currently collected. Although the results of re-planning will become more reliable with more reliable data and re-estimations, our main focus is on a comparison with the situation where no re-planning is done and the case that no re-estimation is conducted.

7 Summary and Future Research

We propose a new method for re-planning of product releases with emphasis on re-estimation at the beginning of each re-planning iteration. While there is a range of methods potentially applicable for these purposes, we demonstrate the principal benefit of re-planning in general and of re-planning exploiting re-estimation in particular. Currently, no product release re-planning method is known for the same purpose.

The effectiveness of the method was tested for a re-planning problem with data generated synthetically. Under the assumptions made, it was shown that re-planning improves functional value of a product. In addition, it was shown that application of re-estimation is more beneficial since this balances the total effort available between creating new functionality and ensuring a high quality (lower number of remaining defects) type of product. In dependence of the product quality demands and the impact of delivering faulty products to the customers, the product manager can make an informed trade-off decision between functionality and fewer defects (based on higher effort spent on quality assurance).

The results of this paper are considered part of an ongoing effort to offer decision support in the context of software release planning [1]. Although the preliminary results are promising, there is outstanding future research to be done. First of all, we look for a real-world project able to provide data for both effort and defect prediction in an incremental development project. Second, we need to fully integrate specific prediction methods into H2W-Pred. Third, the quality of the proposed solutions could be improved by replacing the current greedy optimization with better, but more complex optimization procedures.

Acknowledgement

Part of the work presented was financially supported by the Natural Sciences and Engineering Research Council (NSERC) of Canada under Discovery Grant no. 250343-07. Ahmed Al-Emran would like to thank iCORE, NSERC, and the Killam Trust for their Postgraduate/pre-doctoral scholarships and to ExtendSim for supporting implementation of the research prototype.

References

1. Ruhe, G.: Product Release Planning – Methods, Tools and Applications. CRC Press, Boca Raton (appear in 2010)
2. Wiegers, K.: Software Requirements. Microsoft Press (2003)
3. Lamsweerde, V.A.: Requirements engineering in the year 00: a research perspective. In: 22nd International Conference on Software Engineering, ACM Press, New York (2000)
4. Jadallah, A., Al-Emran, A., Moussavi, M., Ruhe, G.: The How? When? and What? for the Process of Re-Planning for Product Releases. In: Wang, Q., Garousi, V., Madachy, R., Pfahl, D. (eds.) ICSP 2009. LNCS, vol. 5543, pp. 24–37. Springer, Heidelberg (2009)
5. Ngo-The, A., Ruhe, G.: Optimized Resource Allocation for Software Release Planning. IEEE Transactions on Software Engineering 35, 109–123 (2009)
6. Ramil, J.F.: Continual Resource Estimation for Evolving Software. In: International Conference on Software Maintenance 2003, pp. 289–292. IEEE Press, Washington DC (2003)
7. Khoshgoftaar, T.M., Ganesan, K., Allen, E.B., Ross, F.D., Munikoti, R., Goel, N., Nandi, A.: Predicting fault-prone modules with case-based reasoning. In: 8th International Symposium on Software Reliability Engineering, pp. 27–35. IEEE Press, Los Alamitos (1997)

8. Steuer, R.E.: Multiple Criteria Optimization: Theory, Computation, and Application. John Wiley, New York (1986)
9. Cormen, T.H., Leiserson, C.E., Rivest, R.L., Stein, C.: Introduction to Algorithms. The MIT Press, Cambridge (2007)
10. ReleasePlanner™, Expert Decisions Inc., `http://www.releaseplanner.com`
11. Li, J., Ruhe, G., Al-Emran, A., Richter, M.M.: A Flexible Method for Effort Estimation by Analogy. Journal Empirical Software Engineering 12(1), 65–106 (2007)
12. Paikari, E.: Analogy based Defect Prediction Model. Technical Report, Software Engineering Decision Support Laboratory, University of Calgary, SEDS-TR-086/2009
13. Bagnall, A.J., Rayward-Smith, V.J., Whittley, I.M.: The Next Release Problem. Information and Software Technology 43, 883–890 (2001)
14. Jung, H.W.: Optimizing value and cost in requirements analysis. IEEE Software 15, 74–78 (1998)
15. Van den Akker, M., Brinkkemper, S., Diepen, G., Versendaal, J.: Software product release planning through optimization and what-if analysis. Information and Software Technology 50, 101–111 (2008)
16. Stark, G., Skillicorn, A., Ameele, R.: An Examination of the Effects of Requirements Changes on Software Maintenance Releases. Journal of Software Maintenance: Research and Practice 11, 293–309 (1999)
17. Al-Emran, A., Kapur, P., Pfahl, D., Ruhe, G.: Studying the Impact of Uncertainty in Operational Release Planning - an Integrated Method and its Initial Evaluation. Information and Software Technology 52, 446–461 (2010)
18. AlBourae, T., Ruhe, G., Moussavi, M.: Lightweight Re-planning of Software Product Releases. In: 14th IEEE International Requirements Engineering Conference, pp. 27–34. IEEE Press, Washington DC (2006)

Software Process Model Blueprints*

Julio Ariel Hurtado Alegría[1,2], Alejandro Lagos[1], Alexandre Bergel[1], and María Cecilia Bastarrica[1]

[1] Computer Science Department, Universidad de Chile, Chile
[2] IDIS Research Group, University of Cauca, Colombia
{jhurtado,alagos,abergel,cecilia}@dcc.uchile.cl

Abstract. Explicitly defining a software process model is widely recognized as a good software engineering practice. However, having a defined process does not necessarily mean that this process is good, sound and/or useful. There have been several approaches for software process evaluation including testing, simulation and metrics; the first one requires software process enactment, i.e., an expensive, risky and long process, and the others require high expertise for correctly interpreting their meaning. In this paper we propose a visual approach for software process model evaluation based on three architectural view types, each one focusing on basic process elements: Role Blueprint, Task Blueprint and Work Product Blueprint. They enable visual evaluation of different perspectives of a software process, each being relevant for a particular stakeholder. We illustrate the proposed approach by applying it to the software process defined for a real world company that develops software for retail. We show how design errors were identified.

1 Introduction

There is a generalized agreement among software practitioners about the relevance of counting on a well defined process model for systematizing development. There have been several efforts in aiding organizations toward this goal: maturity models and standards that describe which elements should be part of a software process, notations that allow rigorous specification, and tools that support these notations. However, having a well defined software process does not necessarily mean having a good process.

It is not apparent how to determine if a software process is good, or if it can be improved in any sense before it is enacted [16]. The software process metamodel SPEM 2.0 [15] proposes wellformedness rules for software process definition but their scope is limited. For example, SPEM 2.0 does not determine if for a given process some of the roles are overloaded, if there are work products that are bottlenecks, or if there is no clear termination condition for a task cycle. What is even more difficult about these issues is that they do not always constitute errors, but they are indicators that something may not be right [10]. Even though there are some metrics defined for measuring software processes [2], they provide

* The work of Julio Hurtado Alegría has been partly funded by NIC Chile.

J. Münch, Y. Yang, and W. Schäfer (Eds.): ICSP 2010, LNCS 6195, pp. 273–284, 2010.

little intuition about what may be wrong, where the error is, and how to find opportunities for improvement when there is no apparent error. How can we present a rich software process on mere flat diagrams? Software processes should represent a complex, dynamic and multidimensional world. Moreover, available tools are usually intended only for software process visual specification, and not for evaluation, let alone visual evaluation.

The convenience of specifying the software architecture with multiple views has been agreed upon [3]. Different stakeholders require different information for evaluations, thus it seems natural to deal with multiple process architectural views [11]. We specify our process models using the SPEM 2.0 standard. Process architectural views are built following an architectural recovery approach such that they allow us to evaluate different process characteristics. We propose three process architectural view types: ROLE BLUEPRINT, TASK BLUEPRINT and WORK PRODUCT BLUEPRINT. These blueprints are process views that make use of metrics computed from a process model for easing understanding and evaluating different aspects not available in SPEM 2.0 and its associated tools. These visualizations have been implemented in the ProcessModel tool[1] based on Moose technology and the Mondrian tool. Visualization aids in data analysis and problem detection [14]. Using different concerns about process models in a graphical manner, we make use of the human visual capacity for interpreting the process in context and to evaluate its coherence and suitability [13].

We have applied our approach to the process model specification of DTS, a real world small company that develops software for retail. We have been able to identify several problems in the process and the company's stakeholders agreed that they were actual problems. The process has been redefined and the changes are currently being applied.

2 Related Work

Software quality is a key issue in software engineering, and it highly depends on the process used for developing it [8]. Software process quality assurance can be addressed in different ways: metrics, testing, simulation, or formal reviews.

Canfora et. al. [2] define some ratio metrics for measuring overall software processes, but based on this general data it is hard to know what is wrong, where the error is located, and how to find opportunities for improvement when there is no apparent error. However, these metrics are a key starting point. We use them as a basis over which we build a visual layer to evaluate more specific aspects of different process model elements. We define a evaluation approach based on visualization whereas Canfora et. al. propose and validate some general metrics. Our approach is based on the evidence about the visualization aids in data analysis and problem detection [14]. Further we visualize different concerns about process models using the human visual capacity for interpreting the process in context and to evaluate its coherence and suitability [13].

[1] Freely available at `http://www.moosetechnology.org/tools/ProcessModel`

In Process Model Testing, process models are checked against their specifications [16]. An example of process testing is a software process assessment, where a process and its corresponding model are evaluated based on a capability maturity framework. This approach is present in CMMI [19] and ISO/IEC15504 [9]. This kind of testing activities can only be carried out once the process model has already been implemented, tailored and enacted. It checks for adherence to a standard but it does not evaluate the appropriateness of the process for the organizational or project needs. Process testing requires very long time cycles. Gruhn [7] has proposed a verification technique based on simulation results and execution trace evaluation. Simulation has a shorter cycle, but it still requires enactment data. This is an appropriate verification technique if the process model is known to be suitable for the environment, but if the model is incomplete, underspecified or it is not suitable for the organization, the process model simulation will not yield the expected results.

Cook and Wolf [4] present a formal verification and validation technique for identifying and measuring the discrepancies between process models and actual executions. They do not address suitability, completeness or consistency of the process model. Pérez et al. [17] suggest to evaluate the congruence between the process model and a given environment based on past data. However, obtaining these measurements is hard and the results are not precise. Formal specifications and checking based on Petri Nets in a multi-view approach are presented in [5], but formal checking has semantic limitations. Our process model blueprints use SPEM 2.0 models to recover and visualize them independently using some basic metrics, and the evaluation can be delegated to process designers in an informal but structured and practical way.

Software inspections, walkthroughs, and technical reviews, are widely used to improve software quality, so they are promising techniques for software processes too. The key idea is that a group of experienced software engineers, meeting together to review a software product, can improve its quality by detecting defects that the product designer or developer could have overseen. Our proposal consists of a tool that supports the software process model review based on visual mechanisms. According to [18], the review process has three main tasks: defect discovery, defect collection, and defect discrimination. The defect discovery is the one that demands the highest expertise. The approach and tool presented in this paper is intended to facilitate the process model defect discovery in a visual way inside a planned verification and validation context. Also, the specific solution presented in this paper can be useful for a process designer to gain some insights about the process model design and potentially find some problems.

3 Problems in Software Process Model Evaluation

Defining a software development process is an effort to systematize and improve software development. However, defining a software process does not necessarily imply that the process is complete, sound and/or well defined.

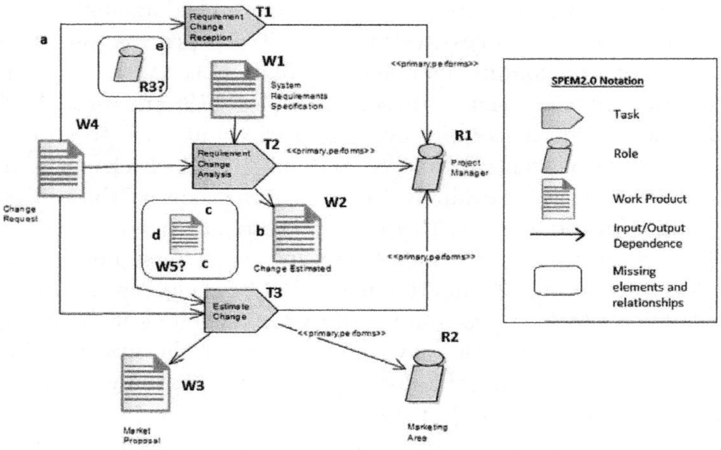

Fig. 1. SPEM Model Fragment for Requirements Change Management

SPEM is a specific standard language used to define software process models. Enterprise Architect (EA)[2] and Eclipse Process Framework (EPF)[3] are two popular integrated development environments (IDE) used to describe and visualize SPEM processes. We argue that the representations provided by these tools are not enough for easily assessing model quality. As an illustration, we will use the process model used in DTS, a small software company.

The software process model used by DTS is written in SPEM and it is composed of 57 tasks, 66 work products and 9 roles. We consider the complete process, including project management, testing, requirements management and technical development. Figure 1 is a screenshot of a piece of the DTS process model visualized using EA. This model excerpt focuses on part of the requirements change management area and represents the main dependencies between tasks and their related roles and work products. The process model adopted at DTS received a careful attention in its conception by dedicated engineers. However, a number of problems were recently detected but not easily identified.

Incorrect relationships (a,b): W4 (Change Request) should be an output of T1 (Requirement Change Reception) instead of being an input, and W2 (Change Estimated) should be an output of T3 (Estimate Change) instead of T2 (Requirement Change Analysis). The change request is received by task *Requirement Change Reception* and is used by all other tasks. The *Change Estimated* work product is the result of the *Estimate Change* task.

Missing elements (d,e): W5 (Requirement Change Analysis) is required as output of T2 (Requirement Change Analysis) and input of T3 (Estimate Change). A new role R3 (*Client*) is required because it is involved in T1 and T2

[2] `http://www.sparxsystems.com.au`

[3] `http://www.eclipse.org/epf`

(Requirements Change Reception and Analysis). W5 and R3 are missing because the process has been inadequately designed.

Missing relationships (c): control links from work product W5 (Requirement Change Analysis) to task T2 (Requirement Change Analysis) as output and to task T3 (Estimate Change) as input are missing. Without W5 between T2 and T3, the information flow remains underspecified.

These anomalies in the DTS process were not easily identified mainly due to scalability, complexity and availability issues. Figure 1 depicts only a small portion of the complete process. The complete process is multi screen which makes it difficult to analyze. Many different sources of information are gathered in the picture obtained from EA. As a consequence, checking the validity of the model is often perceived as a tedious activity. A global picture can be obtained through a simple composition within the environment, but this composition is not automatically built in a global fashion by SPEM modeling tools.

Although we conducted our analysis on EA and EPF, the same actions could have been made in other tools (including SPEM as UML Profile). To tackle these issues, we propose to complement the process designer's activities with a number of extra visualizations. Simulation is not a practical option because SPEM 2.0 neither provides concepts nor formalisms for executing process models [1].

4 Multiple Software Process Model Blueprints

There is no unique perfect view to visually render a software process model [10]. As for most engineering activities, defining a robust, efficient and multi-view software process is a non-trivial activity that requires flexible and expressive tools. As a complement to software process design tools, we propose a visual approach to evaluate some quality criteria. We introduce the notion of blueprint as a partial but focused graphical representation of a software process model.

4.1 Process Model Blueprints in a Nutshell

Process model blueprints are graphical representations meant to help software process designers to (i) assess the quality of software process models and (ii) identify anomalies in a model and provide hints on how to fix them. The essence of these blueprints is to facilitate the comparison between elements for a given selected domain using a graph metaphor, composed of nodes and edges.

The size of a node or an edge tells us about their relative importance. In the case that a node is "much larger" than others, this should draw the attention of the process designer because it may reveal an anomaly or a misconception. We identified three blueprints that help identifying opportunities for improving software process models. Each of them focuses on a particular domain, namely *roles*, *tasks* and *work products*. Table 1 summarizes the meaning of boxes, edges and dimensions for each of these blueprints.

The visualizations we propose are based on *polymetric views* [12]. A *polymetric view* is a lightweight software visualization technique enriched with software

Table 1. Blueprints Details

	Role Blueprint	*Task Blueprint*	*Work Product Blueprint*
Layout	Circle layout	Tree ordered layout	Tree ordered layout
Node	Role	Task	Work product
Edge	Role collaboration	Task order dependence	Work product production dependence
Scope	Full Process Model	Full Process Model	Full Process Model
Node color	Associated guidances	Associated roles	Associated guidances
Node height	Required and produced work products	Required work products	Tasks where it is an input
Node width	Tasks where it participates	Produced work products	Tasks where the it is an output

metrics information. It has been successfully used to provide "software maps" intended to help comprehension and visualization.

Given two-dimensional nodes representing entities we follow the intuitive notion that the wider and the higher the node is, the bigger the measurements its size is telling. The color interval between white and black may render another measurement. The convention that is usually adopted [6] is that the higher the measurement the darker the node is. Thus light gray represents a smaller metric measurement than dark gray. An edge between two nodes n and m may be directed representing asymmetry. Direction is usually graphically represented with an arrow. We are not making use of other edge measurements.

4.2 Role Blueprint

Description and Specification: this blueprint shows a role-oriented perspective of a process model. A role (called *Role Definition* in SPEM 2.0) defines a set of skills, competences and responsibilities required for performing it. A role is responsible of some tasks and could participate in others; also a role is responsible of some work products. In general, the more associated to tasks, work products and guidances a role is, the heavier the load the role will have. In this blueprint a role is represented as a node. The width represents the quantity of tasks and the height the quantity of work products this role is in charge of. An edge between two roles represents the collaboration between them, i.e., they work on the same task. Collaboration is not explicit in a SPEM 2.0 model, but it can be deduced.

Example: the Role Blueprint of DTS is presented in Fig. 2. It shows collaboration between roles, so we can see that the *Client* appears isolated. This situation suggests that this role is either not involved in the process (and it is a possible conceptual problem), or that the process has been badly specified. On the other hand, the *Analyst* role should have been related to *Engineer Manager* and it is not, so this is an underspecification of the process model. In this blueprint two roles are much larger than the others: they have more work products assigned and they participate in more tasks. Also the role *Client* is small, and this issue suggests that it is not an active participant in the software process.

Interpretation: this blueprint allows us to evaluate if the assigned responsibility is suitable for process requirements. We can also discover overloaded roles

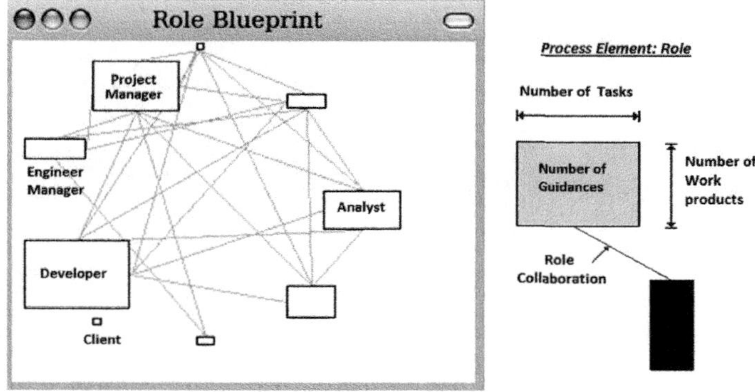

Fig. 2. Role Blueprint of the DTS Process Model

when lightweight roles are expected or vice versa, an isolated role when collaboration is required, and roles without training material when it is necessary for a good performance. Therefore, a complex role could be decomposed, simple roles could be integrated, training material could be added, collaborative techniques and enactment constraints could be added.

4.3 Task Blueprint

Description and Specification: this blueprint shows a task-oriented perspective of the process model. A task (*Task Definition* in SPEM 2.0) is the basic element for defining a process. It defines a work unit assignable to roles. A task is associated to input and output work products. A task has a clear purpose: it provides a complete explanation step by step of the associated work. In this blueprint a node is a task. The width and hight of a task node represent the quantity of work products that are required and produced, respectively, and the color represents the number of roles involved. A directed edge between two tasks states an dependency between them: T1 depends on T2 if T1 uses work products produced by T2. The organization of the tasks uses a TreeOrderLayout, so they are placed in a top-down fashion to reflect the dependency order. As a natural and intuitive good practice, each task should be connected to a previous and a next task, except for the first and the last.

Example: the TASK BLUEPRINT of DTS is presented in Fig. 3. Node size shows their complexity. In the example, the *Requirements Review* task is more complex than all others, so decomposition may be needed, e.g. *Requirements Review* could be decomposed into *Software Requirements Review* and *User Requirements Review*. Color shows participant roles, so *User Requirements Definition* does not have associated roles. This is a specification error unless the task is automatic. Other problems may be identified in the model such as the existence of many initial and final tasks: tasks without a possible next or previous task. Another problem arises due to the multiple links between tasks of different process

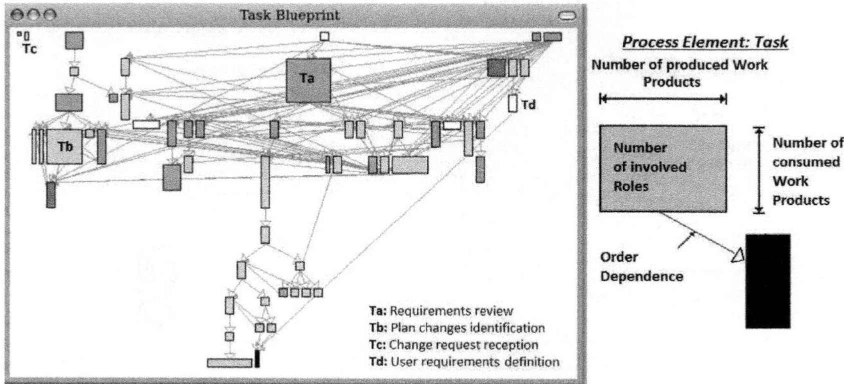

Fig. 3. Task Blueprint of the DTS Process Model

areas, indicating a high coupling between main process components. The tasks on the upper left represent the management process area, those on the upper right correspond to engineering process area and those on the bottom belong to testing. These process areas, interpreted as process components, should be connected with as few dependencies as possible using process ports as SPEM2.0 suggests; they can be used with composed work products and reports generated from other work products between main or facade tasks inside each process component. Related small tasks can be redefined as steps of a larger task.

Interpretation: this blueprint allows us to evaluate if task granularity is appropriate for process requirements. It enables the discovery of a complex task, or a disconnected task or task sub graph. A complex task could be decomposed and simple tasks could be integrated. Similarly, this blueprint can be used to find SPI opportunities and misspecifications such as high coupling, final or initial tasks with next or previous tasks, and tasks without assigned roles.

4.4 WorkProduct Blueprint

Description and Specification: this blueprint shows a work product-oriented perspective of the process model. A work product (*Work Product Definition* in SPEM 2.0) is used, modified or produced by tasks. Roles use work products to perform tasks and produce other work products. Roles are responsible for work products, so they aid in identifying skills required for producing them. In this blueprint each node is a work product. The width and height of the node represent the quantity of tasks where the work product is an input or an output, respectively. The color refers to the quantity of associated guidances. An edge between two work products designates a dependency: W1 depends on W2, if W1 is an output of a task where W2 is input. Any work product should be connected to previous and next work products except for the first and the last.

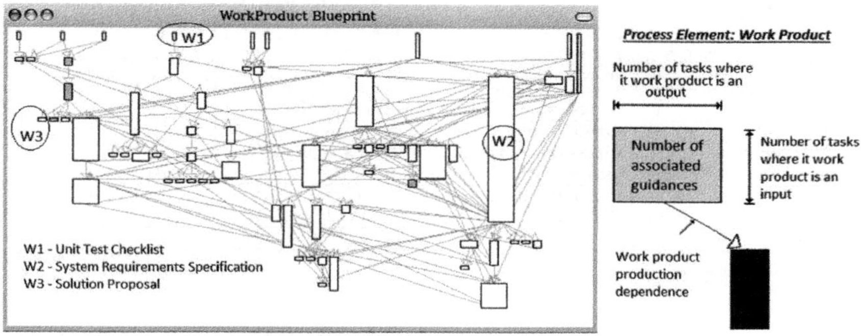

Fig. 4. Work Product Blueprint of the DTS Process Model

Example: the WORK PRODUCT BLUEPRINT of DTS is presented in Fig. 4. This blueprint shows a process with small work products except for a few of them. *System Requirements Specification* is big and it can probably be divided into simpler work products. Very few work products appear colored, so this process has not defined a homogeneous guidance for executing the defined process, i.e. the process may not be repeatable because each performer may choose a different the representation. The work product *Unit Test Checklist* is produced during the development, but it is not represented in the model, so it is incorrectly modeled as an initial work product. The same situation occurs with *Solution Proposal* because even if it is not a final product, no task consumes it. It is either a waste work product, so process grease can be eliminated (process improvement), or it was wrongly specified (process model specification improvement).

Interpretation: this blueprint allows us to evaluate if a work product is a bottleneck risk, to discover a disconnected work product, or to identify isolated descriptions in the process model. It can also be used to find SPI opportunities such as complex, bottleneck or waste work products. Guidances are very important in this blueprint because the more formal a process model is the more reference material it needs, so the darker the nodes will be. For example, Unified Process defines templates for each work product, whereas Extreme Programming does not. Similar to tasks, work products must be separated by process areas; connections between them are first candidates to be component ports.

5 Process Model Blueprints Application: A Study Case

DTS's development process has been defined as a SPEM 2.0 model and implemented in EPF. Even though some evaluations such as CMMI appraisals were included, there is still no information about the quality of the process model itself or the adequacy with the company's goals. As part of its SPI project DTS wants to assess the quality of its process, so they used the Process Model Blueprints. The problems found were used as input for the following improvement cycle.

Table 2. Process Model Problems Identified with PMBlueprints

Blueprint	*Identified Problems*	*Quantity*	*Improvements*
WorkProduct Blueprint	Few guidelines, some are very long, some are disconnected, many initial and final artifacts	31	23
Task Blueprint	Tasks without roles, disconnected tasks, many initial tasks, many final tasks, many relationships big tasks, deformed tasks	22	19
Role Blueprint	Roles with light load, roles with weight load, roles isolated, there are few guidelines	7	5
Total		60	47

The evaluation process was carried out by two process engineers, one from DTS and another one from the University of Chile, and two software engineers for process definition. The steps followed were:

(1) Visualization: the process engineers imported the model from EPF and they realized a short review. Some errors in the tool were identified and some aspects were tuned. A first visualization of the blueprints was generated.

(2) Potential problem identification: for each blueprint problems were identified. Each problem was recorded and a trivial analysis was realized in this step.

(3) Problem analysis: each blueprint was used to find a symptom of a problem and the related elements. For example, *Analysis* was not related to *Client* and *Chief Engineer* roles, so it is possible that some tasks where these roles participated were not adequately specified. Some problems required more analysis and discussion with users of the software process.

(4) Data collection: the potential and actual problems were collected, and also some solutions were proposed.

(5) Data analysis: the data collected in this study case was analyzed and the main results are presented below.

Table 2 summarizes the main problems found during the evaluation. For a total of 132 process elements, 47 actual problems were found (false positives have been discarded). So, the process model error rate was of 0.356 errors per model element. In general, the review found that there were few guidances associated to model elements. This situation suggests low formality in software process specification. Disconnected elements cause modeling problems: some connections were omitted at modeling time and others caused serious conceptual problems in the software process. For example, the isolated *Client* role was a symptom of a problem, and actually a big problem: the client was not involved in many tasks where his/her participation is required, specially in requirements tasks. We suggest two kinds of improvements:

Software Process Improvements: the main suggested improvements are: increase guidance for roles (guide of work) and for work products (templates, examples and concepts); task re-design for getting tasks of medium size (neither too large nor too small), such as *Requirements Review*; big work products decomposition such as *System Requirements Specification*; decrease coupling between

Table 3. Improvements suggested with PMBlueprints

Blueprint	*Improvements to Specification*	*Improvements to Process*
WorkProduct Blueprint	19	4
Task Blueprint	16	3
Role Blueprint	2	3
Total	37	10

process areas, with few relationships between work products and tasks; increase the *client* participation and improve the collaboration required between the *Analyst* and *Engineer Manager* roles. The bottleneck risks identified on the *System Requirement Specification*, *Alpha Component* and *Alpha System Cycle n* work products are normal bottlenecks because of the incremental nature of the software process, so these work products are completed and refined in each cycle of the software process. However, the *Architecture* work product and its associated tasks are not suitable to this incremental development.

Software Process Model Specification Improvement: the main improvements to software model specification are about missing nodes, edges and guidances. Several problems were identified directly, others required more analysis as collaboration between specific roles, and others were generally due to conceptual problems of the software process.

6 Conclusion and Further Work

As a complement to process model design, it is also necessary to evaluate software processes. This paper presents a mechanism for recovering software process architectural views based on blueprint visualization. Many process model blueprints can be defined, but three essential ones have been described here: Task Blueprint, Role Blueprint and Work Product Blueprint. The approach has been complemented with ProcessModel, the visualization tool we built (all screenshot used in this paper were obtained from ProcessModel), based on Mondrian and Moose. This tool imports process models defined in SPEM 2.0 from EPF, and automatically produces the blueprints described in this paper. These blueprints are used to find errors and problems in the specification and improvement phases of software process model. The paper presents an experience with a process being implemented in a small company using EPF. The assessment we conducted identified a number of important problems. This experience lets us conclude that our approach is useful for the evaluation of software process models within a SPI project. However, more experience is required for more conclusive results; metrics and blueprints should also be extended, formalized and validated. Some limitations of our approach occur because different visualizations can be obtained from different metrics, so there is no unique way of measuring and the interpretation must be put in context. The approach can be extended using goal oriented metrics. Currently, the approach is been used for evaluating the open source process models defined in the EPF website, and it is being applied in other small companies in Chile. Also the tool is being improved, and other blueprints can be defined based on other concepts and elements defined in SPEM 2.0, or based on other metrics.

References

1. Bendraou, R., Jezéquél, J.-M., Fleurey, F.: Combining Aspect and Model-Driven Engineering Approaches for Software Process Modeling and Execution. In: Wang, Q., Garousi, V., Madachy, R., Pfahl, D. (eds.) ICSP 2009. LNCS, vol. 5543, pp. 148–160. Springer, Heidelberg (2009)
2. Canfora, G., García, F., Piattini, M., Ruiz, F., Visaggio, C.A.: A family of experiments to validate metrics for software process models. Journal of Systems and Software 77(2), 113–129 (2005)
3. Clements, P., Bachmann, F., Bass, L., Garlan, D., Ivers, J., Little, R., Nord, R., Stafford, J.: Documenting Software Architectures. Addison-Wesley, Reading (2002)
4. Cook, J.E., Wolf, A.L.: Software process validation: quantitatively measuring the correspondence of a process to a model. ACM TOSEM 8(2), 147–176 (1999)
5. Ge, J., Hu, H., Gu, Q., Lu, J.: Modeling Multi-View Software Process with Object Petri Nets. In: ICSEA 2006, p. 41 (2006)
6. Gîrba, T., Lanza, M.: Visualizing and characterizing the evolution of class hierarchies. In: WOOR 2004 - 5th ECOOP (2004)
7. Gruhn, V.: Validation and verification of software process models. In: Proc. of the Software development environments and CASE technology, pp. 271–286 (1991)
8. Humphrey, W.S.: Managing the Software Process. Addison-Wesley, Reading (1989)
9. ISO./IEC 15504 : Information technology - software process assessment and improvement. Technical report, Int. Organization for Standardization (1998)
10. Jacobs, D., Marlin, C.: Multiple view software process support using the Multi-View architecture. In: ISAW-2 and Viewpoints 1996, pp. 217–221. ACM, New York (1996)
11. Jacobs, D., Marlin, C.D.: Software process representation to support multiple views. IJSEKE 1995 5(4), 585–597 (1995)
12. Lanza, M., Ducasse, S.: Polymetric Views-A Lightweight Visual Approach to Reverse Engineering. TSE 2003 29(9), 782–795 (2003)
13. Larkin, J.H., Simon, H.A.: Why a Diagram is (Sometimes) Worth Ten Thousand Words. Cognitive Science 11(1), 65–100 (1987)
14. Lee, M.D., Butavicius, M.A., Reilly, R.E.: An Empirical Evaluation of Chernoff Faces, Star Glyphs, and Spatial Visualizations for Binary Data. In: APVis 2003, pp. 1–10. Australian Computer Society Inc. (2003)
15. OMG. Software Process Engineering Metamodel SPEM 2.0 OMG. Technical Report ptc/08-04-01, Object Managemente Group (2008)
16. Osterweil, L.: Software processes are software too. In: ICSE 1987, Los Alamitos, CA, USA, pp. 2–13. IEEE Computer Society Press, Los Alamitos (1987)
17. Perez, G., El Emam, K., Madhavji, N.H.: Evaluating the congruence of a software process model in a given environment. In: ICSP 1996, p. 49 (1996)
18. Sauer, C., Jeffery, D.R., Land, L., Yetton, P.: The effectiveness of software development technical reviews: a behaviorally motivated program of research. IEEE Transactions on Software Engineering 26(1), 1–14 (2000)
19. SEI. CMMI for Development, Version 1.2. Technical Report CMU/SEI-2006-TR-008, Software Engineering Institute (2006)

Measurement and Analysis of Process Audit: A Case Study

Fengdi Shu[1], Qi Li[2], Qing Wang[1], and Haopeng Zhang[1,3]

[1] Lab for Internet Software Technologies, Institute of Software, Chinese Academy of Sciences, China
[2] University of Southern California, USA
[3] Graduate University of Chinese Academy of Sciences, China
fdshu@itechs.iscas.ac.cn, qli1@usc.edu, {wq,zhanghaopeng}@itechs.iscas.ac.cn

Abstract. Process audit is one of the popular quality assurance activities. It helps individual projects to be in conformity with the process definition, standard, etc. and provide insights for process improvement. However, to the best of our knowledge, little quantitative analysis of process audit has been reported so far. The paper introduces a case study of quantitatively analyzing process audit based on the practice of a Chinese software research and development organization, CSRD. It presents a measurement schema for evaluating the effectiveness and efficiency of process audit from various facets. The study shows that the auditing process in CSRD has contributed to the process management and improvement and brought value to the organization. The presented measurement and analysis methods and empirical results can provide reference for other organizations within similar context.

Keywords: process audit, measurement, GQM.

1 Introduction

Process audit, or conformance audit [1] with checklists, is a widely used software quality assurance activity for organizations conducting process management and improvement. The goal of process audit is to assess the conformance of the process execution against the process definition or standards with the direct results of Not Compatible (NC) items. It may help individual projects in compliance with the defined process and standards and provide insight for process improvement. Process audit has two active modes of operation: appraisal and analysis [2]. As for the appraisal mode, auditors use checklists to evaluate the implementation of a process to make sure it in compliance with the process description, standards, and procedures, reflecting the visibility of the project process in time. In the analysis mode, auditors question the process definition, standard, etc, which are used in support of the processes.

The assessment of effectiveness and efficiency is one of the key issues for mature and successful process audit. However, there have been few researches or reports about the assessment of process quality assurance or assessment related processes [1, 3, 4, 6]. J.M. Gasston et al. [3] presented a conceptual model for the assessment of the effectiveness of software processes and reported an empirical case study; while

J. Münch, Y. Yang, and W. Schäfer (Eds.): ICSP 2010, LNCS 6195, pp. 285–296, 2010.

they didn't use quantitative measurement and the case study is about the configuration management process. Timo Makinen et al. [4] introduced a project of establishing a software process improvement network, during which the assessment process was assessed and 20 propositions to improve the assessment process came out. R. Craig Smith [6] introduced the experiences of using IEEE Std 1028 [5] as the basic standard for developing the audit program and focused on the challenges and lessons learned by using this IEEE Std., CMM, and the IS0 9001 standard from a process assurance perspective. Alain April et al. [1] presented a perspective on measuring process assurance and lessons learned from the assessment of the individual conformance of projects to the Corporate Software Development Process of an organization aiming at CMM level 2. The reasons associated with some major deviations were analyzed but without quantitative analysis reported.

In the paper, we introduce the measurement and analysis of the process audit practice of a Chinese software development organization, CSRD. To the best of our knowledge, it is the first empirical report about the quantitative assessment of the process audit in an industrial context with the process maturity of CMMI level 3.

The paper is organized as follows. Section 2 introduces the context; section 3 presents the measurement schema of process audit; section 4 illustrates the measurement and analysis of process audit; section 5 discusses the treats to validity and lessons learned; and section 6 concludes the paper and introduces our future work.

2 Context

CSRD began to audit process from year 2005 when moving towards CMMI ML3 and passed the appraisal the same year. It has an independent quality assurance group and takes process compliance as an important management goal. The core products of CSRD are the series of SoftPM, a toolkit designed for software process management and process improvement [7]. CSRD itself uses SoftPM to define its processes, maintain process assets, monitor and control projects, and collect and analyze process data for continuous process improvement, etc.

The current checklists set of CSRD covers processes classified as four categories in accordance with CMMI v1.2 [8]. For a project, its process audit should be planned at the planning phase, including the processes to be audited and corresponding audit criteria and timing. A project consists of multiple processes and each process may be audited for several times.

The execution of the audit of a specific process of a project includes following steps. First, the auditor pinpoints detailed checking items, evaluates the expected completion of outputs, and arranges the interviews. Second, the auditor conducts the interviews and checks the work products of the process according to each selected checking item. Subsequently, besides the summarized information of the audit execution, the auditor reports the detailed attributes of each NC, such as the description and severity; and then these NCs are verified through the communication with the project team. Once verified, the NC becomes a problem and corresponding corrective actions should be defined. The verification and correction of the NC are called as the disposal of the NC and the results should also be recorded. Track records of all NCs should be kept and the auditor closes the report when the disposal of all NCs is cleared and let involved people know that the items are closed.

3 Measurement Schema of Process Audit

We define the measurement schema according to the GQM (Goal-Question-Metrics) method [9]. The goal, questions, and corresponding metrics (CMetrics for short) are listed as follows and the definitions of metrics are listed in Table 1. Except M2 and M3 are nominal, all the others are numerical.

Goal: Assessing the effectiveness and efficiency of the process audit and exploring whether there are differences in the effectiveness and efficiency of the process audit in terms of the auditors and audited processes and projects respectively.

Questions and corresponding metrics:

Q1: who conduct the process audit? (CMetrics: M0);

Q2: what are the NCs due to the implementation of process? (CMetrics: M1)

Q3: what are the NCs due to the process definitions and standards? (CMetrics: M2);

Q4: how about the quantity of the audit results? (CMetrics: M3, M4, M5, and M6);

Q5: how about the precision of the process audit? (CMetrics: M7);

Q6: how about the cost and efficiency of NC detection and disposal? (CMetrics: M8, M9, M10, M11, and M12);

Q7: are there significant differences in the effectiveness and efficiency of process audit in terms of the auditors and audited processes and projects? (CMetrics: M0, M3, M4, M5, M6, M7, M8, M9, M10, M11, and M12)

Q8: is the process auditing process is stable? (CMetrics: M3, M4, M5, M6, M7, M8, M9, M10, M11, and M12)

Table 1. Metrics for the Measurement of effectiveness and efficiency of process audit

Applicable levels	ID	Name	Meanings
Auditor	M0	ExpAud	the auditor's experience in process audit in terms of the number of half a year
audit execution	M1	ProbPE	problems about the process implementation
	M2	ProbPD	problems due to process definitions, standards, etc.
Audit execution, process of a project, process (such as CM), and project	M3	NcNum	the number of NCs
	M4	ProbNum	the number of NCs confirmed as problems
	M5	SerNcNum	the number of NCs with degree larger than 2
	M6	SerNcProp	the ratio of SerNcNum to NcNum; 1, if NcNum is 0
	M7	ProbProp	the ratio of ProbNum to NcNum; 1, if NcNum is 0
	M8	AuditEffort	the workload of the audit;
	M9	ProbDetCost	the ratio of AuditEffort to ProbNum; null, if ProbNum is 0
	M10	ProbDetEff	the ratio of ProbNum to AuditEffort
NC verified as problem	M11	NcToProb	the time for the verification of the NC, i.e. from the time the NC is submitted to the time it is confirmed as a problem
Problem	M12	ProbDur	the duration of the problem, i.e. the time from the problem is submitted to the time it is closed

4 Illustration of Quantitative Analysis of Process Audit

We sampled 8 of the 15 versions of SoftPM, which were developed as 15 complete projects, and analyzed the audit of 7 processes which were audited for all projects: CM (Configuration Management), PDL (Project Development Lifecycle Standard Process), PMC (Project Monitoring and Control), PP (Project Planning), REQM (Requirements Management), REV (Review), and TEST (Software Testing). The sizes of these versions are from 4.5 to 31 KLOC and the main development languages and tools include JBuilder, Tomcat, MySQL, Eclipse, etc. Six auditors finished the audit. The most skilled one had more than 4 years experiences in process audit and the least skilled one with less than one year experience when they conducted the audit.

The analysis is performed in following steps:

(1) Extracting raw data from the database of SoftPM and related documents, such as audit reports, NCs lists, related task reports and project reports.

(2) Consolidating the original information and checking and resolving the inconsistency between them.

(3) Analyzing data, presenting results, and performing causal analysis and discussion.

In all we studied records of 275 process audit executions consisting of 686 NC and 475 problem records. SPSS Statistical Product and Service Solutions [10] was used for helping with statistical analysis. Due to the limited space, only following three parts of the analysis will be reported in details. Subsequently, questions defined will be answered and discussed.

4.1 Typical NCs

Table 2 lists the top 3 most often NCs of each process, and problems due to the process definitions and standards include:

N1: The configuration items IDs are in chaos due to no formal naming standard.

N2: There is no user requirements validation process for customization projects.

N3: Task planning documents are inconsistent with the Gantt Graphs split on SoftPM.

N4: The practical efficiency of the unit testing standard is poor.

N5: The coding standard is infeasible.

N6: The requirements of the unit testing standard are beyond the capability of the tester and impractical for tight schedule.

N7: It is not required that the changes of requirements must be confirmed and its impact should be analyzed before they are approved.

N8: There is no configuration management process for periphery developing tools.

4.2 Comparison of Metrics with Respect to the Auditors and Audited Processes and Projects

The comparisons are conducted on two sets of metrics. One consists of the metrics from M3 to M10 at the levels of audit execution and process of a project; the other includes the metrics about NCs and problems, M11 and M12.

Table 2. Top 3 most typical NCs of each process

Process	Top 3 most often NCs
CM	The content of the baseline is incomplete. The changes of related baselines are inconsistent. The baseline has not been set in accordance with the project plan.
PDL	The requirements information is incomplete. The project closing doesn't follow the defined procedure. The execution of the design process does not comply with the definition.
PP	Reasonable milestone checking points have not been defined. The WBS has not fully identified the expected activities and products. The project process tailoring is not reasonable.
PMC	The personal report or task report is incomplete. The planned effort is not full load. The problem list has not been updated in time.
REQM	The requirements tracking information has not been updated in time. The requirements tracking information is incomplete, especially information from testers and designers. The changing records of the requirements baselines are incomplete.
REV	The review report is incomplete. The status of defects has not been updated in time. Independent review results have not been submitted.
TEST	The execution records of test use cases are incomplete. Test cases haven't been updated in time. Not all requirements use cases are covered by test cases

First, we applied descriptive statistics on the data, such as Measures of central tendency and dispersion, Histogram, Q-Q plot, Scatterplot, and Box plot. Due to the limited space, only three of the results presented here.

As for the level of process, Fig. 1 shows the proportion of each process with respect to the number of audit executions, NCs, problems, and serious NCs. It tells, for example, PMC is the process that have been audited most often and with most NCs and problems and PP is the process with most serious NCs.

Fig. 2 shows some comparison information of the audit executions of each process. For instance, it tells that the mean value of the number of NCs, problems, and serious NCs and Problem detection efficiency of the audit executions of PP is the largest and the mean values of ProbPorp of the audit executions of each process are similar.

Figure 3 is the Box plot of ProbDur of each process. It also presents some comparison information about the duration of problems of each process, such as the average value and scope of the problem duration of each process.

Subsequently, we carried out statistical hypothesis test on these data. Due to the heterogeneity of variance and abnormal distribution of all the data, we conducted Friedman Test [11], a kind of non-parametric test.

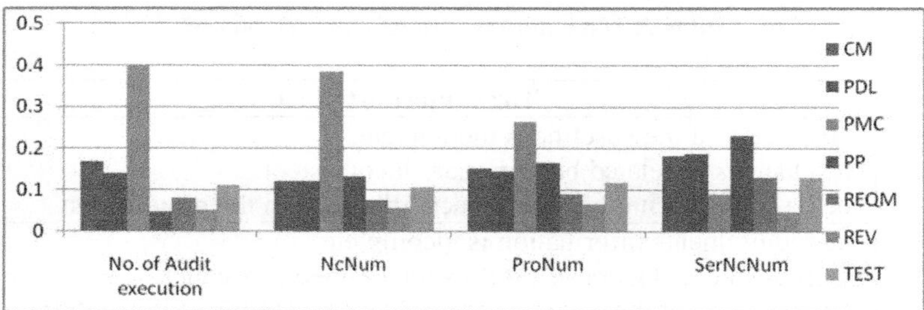

Fig. 1. Prop. of the number of audit executions, NCs, problems, and serious NCs of each process

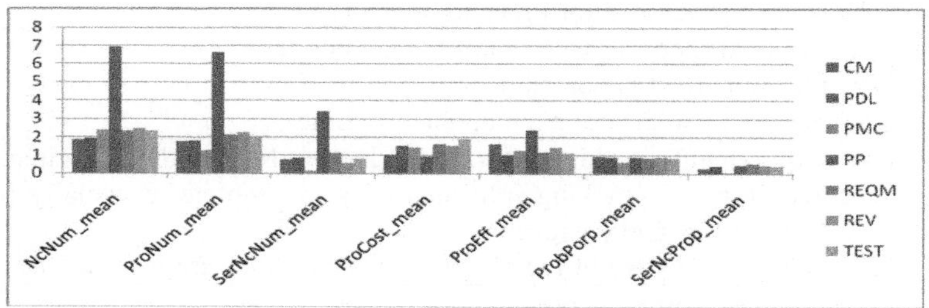

Fig. 2. The mean value of the number of NCs, problems, serious NCs and the mean value of ProCost, ProEff, ProbPorp, and SerNcProp of the audit executions of each process

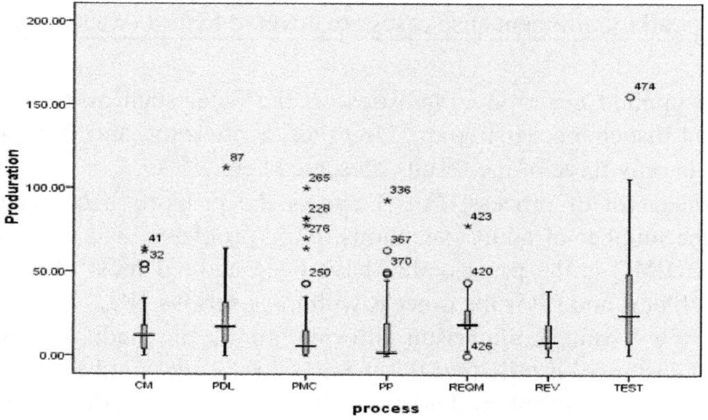

Fig. 3. Box plot of ProbDur of each process

As for the first metrics set, with the significance level of 0.05, we found that there are no significant differences among these processes and projects respectively with respect to AuditEffort and ProbDetCost, while there are for the other cases. Subsequently, we calculated the Spearman's rank correlation coefficient between the experiences of auditors and the rank values set of the metrics of metrics set One resulted from above Friedman tests. From Table 3, we can see that ProbNum, SerNcProp, and ProbDetEff have significant positive correlation with the experiences of the auditors.

Table 3. Spearman's rank correlation coefficient between the experiences of the auditors and the rank values set of metrics of the first metrics set resulted from the Friedman tests

		Nc-Num	Pro-Num	SerNc-Num	Audit-Effort	Prob-Porp	SerNc-Prop	Prob-Det-Cost	Prob-Det-Eff
ExpAud	Correlation Coefficient	0.714	1.000**	0.754	-0.371	0.657	.886*	-0.714	1.000**
	Sig. (2-tailed)	0.111	.	0.084	0.468	0.156	0.019	0.111	.

* Correlation is significant at the 0.05 level (2-tailed).
** Correlation is significant at the 0.01 level (2-tailed).

As for metrics M11 and M12, based on the correlation analysis and further records reading and interviews, we got following findings:

(1) ProbDur has no significant correlation with the experiences of the problem solvers and testers.
(2) NCs and problems submitted later had relatively shorter time to be verified and disposed.
(3) The more serious the NC is, the more quickly it was verified.
(4) Problems with higher serious degree took more time to deal with.

4.3 Process Auditing Process Analysis Using Statistical Process Control

Statistical process control (SPC) is the application of statistical methods to the monitoring and control of a process to ensure that it operates at its full potential to produce conforming product [12]. We used SPC to analyze the process auditing process based on data of all numerical metrics except M0 at the level of audit execution. Due to the abnormal distribution of data, we only used control charts to analyze the stability of process audit with following control policies: RR1: above +3 sigma, below -3 sigma; RR2: 6 in a row trending up, 6 in a row trending down; and RR3: 14 in a row alternating.

For example, as Fig. 4, the Individual (X) and moving range (mR) chart of Prob-DetCost shows, there are 4 abnormal points that all are above the upper limit. The efforts of these executions are 5, 5.5, 8, and 8 man-hours and the number of detected problems is 1, 0, 1, and 1 respectively. Compared with the mean audit effort of 2.65 man-hours and mean number of problems of 1.87, the rather heavy effort and few detected problems may explain these abnormalities. Furthermore, we found that these audit executions all belong to two major versions and were conducted at the end of the projects, so there would be many activities and products to check and some existing problems have been detected and corrected by former audit executions.

All studied metrics failed at and only at run rule RR1, which means as an "early" alarm indicator that must stimulate looking for possible assignable causes [13]. Subsequently, we disaggregated the data into sub-data sets according to the auditor and audited process and project respectively and drew control charts on these sub-data sets. We wanted to explore whether the process type, projects characteristics, and experience of auditor are assignable causes; while for more than 85 percent disaggregated data sets, RR1 still fails.

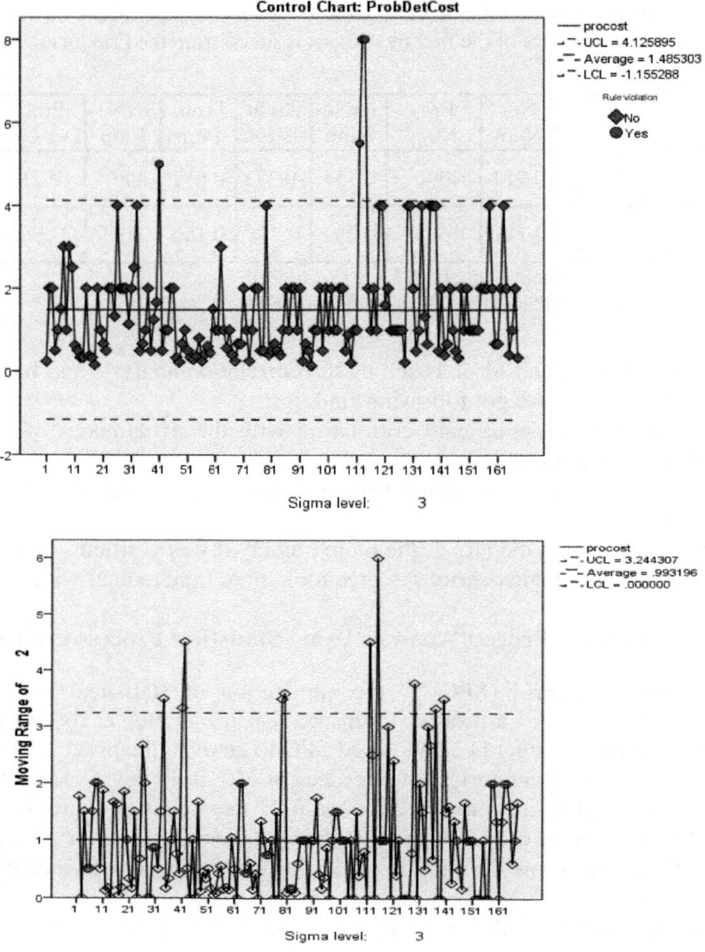

Fig. 4. XmR charts on all the ProbDetCost data points

4.4 Answers to Defined Questions

Question Q1 is answered directly by the value of M0. As for Q4, Q5, Q6, we applied descriptive statistics on related metrics, which is omitted due to limited space. As for Q8, Section 4.3 tells that the process auditing process is out of control and presents an "early" alarm indicating possible assignable causes should be looking for. Answers to Q2, Q3 and Q7 will be discussed in more details as follows.

Q2, Q3: What are the NCs and why there are deviations?

Based on the NCs presented in Section 4.1, we studied why these NCs occurred and what they would lead to and investigated the corresponding corrective actions. Due to the limited space, only some examples are listed as follows.

For the NCs due to the process definitions and standards, the related organizational process definitions and standards have been modified or enhanced accordingly except N3. For N3, the latest version of SoftPM is going to generate planning documents automatically from the defined Gantt graph since it is tedious to manually keep the consistency between the planning documents and the Gantt Graphs split on SoftPM.

As for the NCs of missing personal task reports, through interviews, we found that there are three main reasons: forgetting to, being too busy to fill in, and taking the reporting as trivial. For CSRD, an organization emphasizing process management and improvement, these reports are important for the measurement and analysis of processes and for managers to control the projects, and may provide information for process improvement. Therefore, CSRD took several measures to eliminate such NCs, such as emphasizing the importance of process management and reporting, adding a functionality of automatically sending email reminders of filling the reports every reporting day, and improving the feasibility of the reporting functionality of SoftPM.

The tracking of requirements is an important but a strenuous task and most NCs of REQM are about it. The latest version of SoftPM will provide some new requirements management functionalities, such as checking the completeness of requirements related information, automatically generating some information in the requirements tracking matrix, e.g. some from the users' requirements to the code and test cases.

In summary, the process audit in CSRD has the expected appraisal and analysis modes of operation, and tools could not guarantee the quality of process but may aid in decreasing some kinds of NCs.

Q7: Comparisons of process audit in terms of the auditors and audited processes and projects

Based on the comparison analysis presented in Section 4.2, we performed further analysis and some examples are listed as follows.

As for the differences between auditors with different experiences, we summarized two main characteristics of the audit of auditors with little experiences:

(1) They seldom identified those checking items that were not suitable for a specific project due to their unfamiliarity with the process definition and project's characteristics.

(2) Many NCs detected by them are superficial or bureaucratic NCs.

As for the duration of problems, we analyzed the top 3 reasons of those problems with abnormal long duration: being due to the problems of process definition, heavy workload, and little concerns about the NCs.

As for these various processes, there are multiple reasons that may lead to the differences between the process audits of them. For example, the checking and correction of NCs of various processes may cost differently, such as most NCs of PMC are about reporting, which can be detected and recovered more easily compared with some NCs of PP, such as the unreasonable milestone checking points or process tailoring. The checking frequency of various processes is different. For example, usually, PMC is audited once a week while PP audited once or twice during the whole project. Besides, the different execution time points may lead to different number of products and activities to be checked, which may have something to do with the effort and results of the audit.

As for the studied projects, though they all are releases of SoftPM, some of them are major versions while the others are minor versions or customized versions. Therefore, even for the same process, the checking items to examine and the amount of the products and activities to check of these projects may also be different. Besides, the difference in schedule tightness may lead to the difference in the process executions of various projects.

In summary, there are differences in process audits at multiple levels with respect to the auditors and audited processes and projects. The experiences of auditors, the type of process, and the characteristics of projects all may affect the process audit.

5 Discussion

5.1 Treats to Validity

The measurement schema is the kernel of our work. We designed it using the GQM method based on our knowledge about process and measurement [14] and consulting the conceptual model presented in [3]. Some of the metrics are obvious, such as the number of problems detected in an audit execution; others are defined referring some well-know metrics, such as the problem detection cost and efficiency.

The quality of data is fundamental to the quality of our analysis. We collected data from multiple sources, including audit reports, NCs lists, related task reports, project reports, etc., and then verified the raw data, such as NC lists manually, consolidated the original information, checked and resolved the inconsistency between related sources. Through these ways, we try to assurance the quality of studied data.

Multiple analysis methods were used carefully to implement and support each other. We applied descriptive statistics as well as statistical hypothesis test and correlation analysis to explore the differences in metrics data. We paid much attention to the usage assumptions of the statistical analysis techniques that are used in our case study. Especially for SPC, it is still a controversial issue that whether SPC can be used for estimating parameters for some probability model [15]. However, SPC used in our analysis is to characterize the process behavior rather than estimating parameters. In this sense, SPC works fine for our study, while we admit that there is still a long way to systematically apply SPC to monitor and control the process auditing process. Furthermore, we carried causal analysis on the statistical analysis results according to the characteristics of the processes, projects, and auditors.

The application of the measurement system in CSRD illustrates its practicality and usage in the specific context. Since we just sampled 8 projects from the 15 versions of SoftPM, a small size population of one organization, we cannot proclaim the results are of statistical significance nor they definitely hold in any other circumstances. Whereas, our work, including the measurement and analysis methods and the study results can give some references for other organizations within similar context, such as taking process compliance as an important management quality goal, having some organizational capability of quantitative analysis, and so on.

5.2 Lessons Learned

The effectiveness and performance of process audit consist of multiple dimensions and factors, so does the measurement for it. For example, for an audit execution, besides the number of the detected NCs, the proportion of NCs that are confirmed as problems should also be taken into account. Besides the process type, the experiences of auditors and characteristics of projects all may affect the execution of process audit.

As for the data analysis, process data usually has some characteristics which are not ideal for statistical analysis and even make some analysis techniques unavailable, such as small sample, abnormal distribution, and heterogeneity of variance. For example, we thought the interaction of process type, project feature, and auditor experiences have correlations with defined effectiveness and efficiency metrics. Due to the abnormal distribution and heterogeneity of variance of the data, we cannot apply ANOVA (Analysis of variance). Then we set new attributes to denote the interaction of these factors, but failed to test the correlations due to too few samples. In some cases, the violation of usage assumption will lead to unacceptably misleading results; while in others, such as the full capability of the technique is not needed or the precision of the result is not required heavily, it is possible that the violation of assumptions does not hurt the intended studies. Therefore, we should choose the analysis techniques comprehensively according to the study goal and characteristics of data as well as the usage conditions of the analysis techniques.

6 Conclusion and Future Work

Process audit is a quality assurance activity to help individual projects keep pace with the defined process and provide insight for process improvement. However, to the best of our knowledge, little quantitative analysis of process audit has been reported. The paper introduces a case study of quantitatively analyzing process audit based on the practice of CSRD. It presents a measurement schema for evaluating the effectiveness and efficiency of process audit from various facets. The study shows that the auditing process in CSRD has contributed to the process management and improvement. The presented measurement and analysis methods and empirical results can provide references for other organizations within similar context.

It is our research goal to seek more evidences about the relationship between the quality of project process and the success of project. So in the future, we will collect more data and explore the relationship between the effectiveness and efficiency of process audit and the quality, cost, and schedule of the project. Besides, we will apply the presented research methods to some kind of software development method.

Acknowledgements

This work is supported by the National Natural Science Foundation of China under Grant Nos. 90718042, 60873072, and 60903050; the National Hi-Tech R&D Plan of China under Grant Nos. 2007AA010303; the National Basic Research Program under Grant No. 2007CB310802.

References

1. April, A., Abran, A., Merlo, E.: Process assurance audits: lessons learned. In: 20th ICSE 1998, pp. 482–485. IEEE Computer Society, Kyoto (1998)
2. Baysinger, S.M.: The Complete Guide to the CQA. Quality Publishing Inc., Tucson (1997)
3. Gasston, J.L., Rout, T.P.: Can the effectiveness of software processes be assessed? Software Quality Journal 3, 153–166 (1994)
4. Makinen, T., Varkoi, T., Jaakkola, H.: Assessment of a software process assessment process. Management of Engineering and Technology 1, 437 (2001)
5. IEEE Computer Society: IEEE Standard for Software Reviews and Audits, IEEE Std 1028-1993, IEEE, New York
6. Smith, R.C.: Software development process standards: Challenges for process assurance. In: 3rd ISESS, pp. 180–186. IEEE Computer Society, Los Alamitos (1997)
7. Wang, Q., Li, M.: Measuring and improving software process in China. In: 2005 International Symposium on Empirical Software Engineering, pp. 183–192 (2005)
8. CMMI Product Team: CMMI® for Development, Version 1.2. Pittsburgh, PA, Carnegie Mellon Software Engineering Insitute (2006)
9. Basili, V.R., Caldiera, G., Rombach, H.D.: The goal question metric approach. Encyclopedia of software engineering, pp. 528–532 (1994)
10. SPSS: http://www.spss.com
11. Wu, X.: Statistics: From data to conclusions. China Statistics Press, Beijing (2004)
12. Florac, W.A., Carleton, A.D.: Measuring the software process: statistical process control for software process improvement. Addison-Wesley Longman Publishing Co., Inc, Amsterdam (1999)
13. Baldassarre, M.T., Boffoli, N., Bruno, G., Caivano, D.: Statistically based process monitoring: lessons from the trench. In: Wang, Q., Garousi, V., Madachy, R., Pfahl, D. (eds.) ICSP 2009. LNCS, vol. 5543, pp. 11–23. Springer, Heidelberg (2009)
14. Munson, J.C.: Software engineering measurement. Auerbach (2003)
15. Weller, E., Card, D.: Applying SPC to Software Development: Where and Why. IEEE Software 25, 48–51 (2008)

A Fuzzy-Based Method for Evaluating the Trustworthiness of Software Processes

Haopeng Zhang[1,2], Fengdi Shu[1], Ye Yang[1], Xu Wang[1,3], and Qing Wang[1]

[1] Lab for Internet Software Technologies, Institute of Software Chinese Academy of Sciences
[2] Graduate University of Chinese Academy of Sciences
[3] Department of Software Engineering, Software College of NanKai University
{zhanghaopeng,fdshu,ye,wangxu,wq}@itechs.iscas.ac.cn

Abstract. Software trustworthiness is built in its development and maintenance processes. Effective software measurement system can help to assess and predict the trustworthiness of end products in early software lifecycles in order to plan for proper corrective actions to meet trustworthiness objectives. However, it is a challenging task to aggregate individual metric data and derive a single, overall trustworthiness indicator given the hierarchies in software measurement system as well as heterogeneity within a mix of metric data. In addition, very few metric data can be collected precisely and without subjective judgment inherent in data reporters or collecting tools. In this paper, based on the theory of fuzzy set and the AHP method, we propose an evaluation method supporting fuzzy data and multiple types of values, for evaluating process trustworthiness in the form of user-customized levels. A case study is also presented to illustrate the application of our method.

Keywords: software process trustworthiness, process evaluation, fuzzy set, Analytic Hierarchy Process.

1 Introduction

Based on the long-term experience and theoretical analyses in software engineering, it is generally accepted that software processes to a large extent determine the corresponding software products.

In our previous work [1], we proposed the concept of Process Trustworthiness as a capability indicator to measure the relative degree of confidence for certain software processes to deliver trustworthy software. Furthermore, we developed the software process trustworthiness model and the corresponding trustworthiness measurement system [2]. These models form the groundwork for evaluating the trustworthiness of software processes with respect to metric data collected at process execution time. Based on investigation of existing evaluation methods, we think a good process evaluation method should:

- base on quantitative data to minimize subjectivity related to qualitative data;
- take consideration of the uncertainty situation since for some metrics it is difficult to get accurate values;

J. Münch, Y. Yang, and W. Schäfer (Eds.): ICSP 2010, LNCS 6195, pp. 297–308, 2010.

- be general with respect to different processes trustworthiness objectives;
- could not only be used to evaluate completed projects, but also a process or a phase of a process.

Based on the requirements above, we propose a Fuzzy-Based Method for Evaluating the Trustworthiness of Software Processes (FETP). FETP is a flexible method which can be tailored according to different trustworthiness objectives, and could be used either after a complete project or in the process of a project. Within FETP, Analytic Hierarchy Process (AHP) method [3] is adopted to determine the weights of the metrics. Meanwhile, a new fuzzy calculating procedure is developed which supports multiple types of value including qualitative and quantitative data, outputting user-customized trustworthiness levels and the membership degree of each level as the result. The case study section will give an example where FETP is applied to a certain scenario.

The paper is organized as follows: section 2 discusses related and previous work; section 3 elaborates our method; section 4 is a case study of the method, and section 5 is the conclusion.

2 Related and Previous Work

The method we propose is based on our previous work of a process trustworthiness measurement system [2]. Meanwhile, we adopt Analytic Hierarchy Process (AHP) as the method to determine the weights of the metrics, and the evaluation method we propose is improved from the conventional Fuzzy Comprehensive Evaluation Method. This section will give a brief introduction to the related work.

2.1 Software Process Trustworthiness Measurement System

Trusted Software Methodology (TSM) [4][5]was a methodology developed and evolved by US National Security Agency and three other organizations, to define a note for software trustworthiness and provide a means for assessing and improving it. It provided 44 generally-accepted trust principles and practical process guidance in examining and evaluating trustworthiness threats during the development process. We matched these trust principles with relevant Process Areas (PA) defined in CMMI [6][7], and each identified PA was attached with a relevant set of trust principles and extended into a corresponding Trustworthy Process Area (TPA). Moreover, the software process trustworthiness measurement system is developed to provide a series of measures for each TPA based on the general and special practices in the area, from three dimensions including process entity, process behavior, and process product [2][8], as summarized in Table 1.

Table 1. Summary of Trustworthiness Measures

Dimensions	Quality	Cost	Schedule
Process Entity	8	25	0
Process Behavior	33	25	12
Process Product	37	14	0

2.2 Analytic Hierarchy Process (AHP)

Our trustworthiness measurement system is established as a hierarchy, where the metrics in the same level may have different significance. Meanwhile, we expect to take full advantage of qualitative information such as subjective comparisons, and thereby obtain relative quantitative results. For these reasons, we choose the Analytic Hierarchy Process (AHP) method to determine the weights of the metrics. The procedure for using the AHP can be summarized as follows: first, the problem should be modeled as a hierarchy, which is to explore the aspects of the problem at levels from general to detailed, and then express it in the multileveled way; second, a series of judgment matrixes should be established by making a series of judgments based on pairwise comparisons of the elements in the same level; third, the consistency of each judgment matrix should be checked, and if the consistency is unacceptable, we should adjust the judgments of the matrix; fourth, for each judgment matrix, when the absolute value of eigenvalue λ gets to the maximum value, the normalized values of the solution W to the equation $AW= \lambda_{max}W$ are the weights of the elements; finally, the weights of each level should be synthesized, and then we could get the absolute weight of each element and further determine the priority of each element, which can be used to make the final decision.

2.3 Conventional Comprehensive Fuzzy Evaluation Method

Considering of the metrics whose accurate values are difficult to get, we expect a method with fuzzy-related theories. Fuzzy set [9][10] was a theory used in a wide range of domains in which information was incomplete or imprecise, based on which a comprehensive fuzzy evaluation method was provided, in order to evaluate the object with uncertainty.

The procedure of the comprehensive fuzzy evaluation method can be summarized as follows: first, an index set should be determined, whose elements are the characteristics of the object being evaluated; second, the number of estimation scales should be defined, which cannot be changed in the same evaluation process; third, a membership degree of each scale should be assigned for each element in the index set, which forms an evaluation matrix R

$$R=(r_{ij})_{m\times n}=\begin{bmatrix} r_{11} & \cdots & r_{1n} \\ \vdots & \ddots & \vdots \\ r_{m1} & \cdots & r_{mn} \end{bmatrix} \tag{1}$$

where m is the number of the elements, n is the numbers of the evaluation scales, and r_{ij} means the membership degree of the j th scale for the i th element; finally, a fuzzy subset that consists of the weights of all the elements should be determined, and then we synthesize the evaluation matrix and the fuzzy subset, and the result is a decision set with the same number of scales as each element. The decision set is the result of the evaluation process, each element of which means the membership degree of the corresponding scale.

3 The FETP Method

This section will describe our Fuzzy-Based Method for Evaluating the Trustworthiness of Software Processes (FETP) in detail. The framework of the method is shown in Fig. 1. As the requirements are not the same for different software organizations, our method is proposed for the evaluation of different levels of software process, including a complete software development process, a certain phase or an iteration in a process. Therefore, the FETP method includes tailoring the measurement system and determining the weight of each metric in the tailored system according to the application context. In order to compute data with various types, we propose a normalizing method based on historical data, and further unify the normalized data in the same type. Furthermore, we make improvement on the conventional comprehensive fuzzy evaluation method, and propose a new method in which each metric could have different number of scales. The evaluating result could be represented as the form of "trustworthiness level + the membership degree of each level", where the number of the levels could be customized by users.

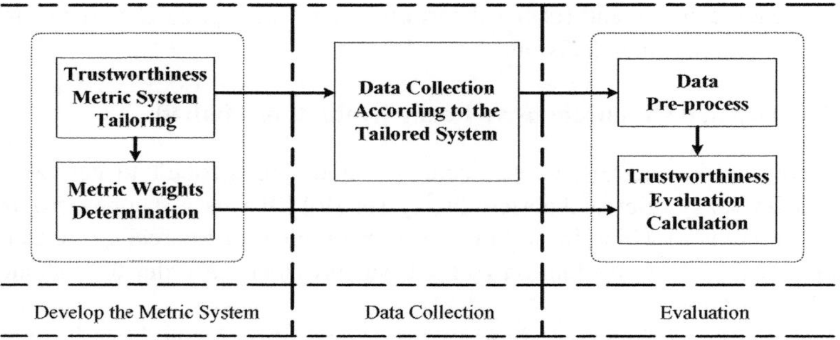

Fig. 1. Framework of the FETP method

In this section we will further describe the following parts of our method in detail: data type definitions, trustworthiness measurement system tailoring, metric weight determination, data pre-process, evaluation calculation, and the historical database support.

3.1 Data Type Definitions

The FETP method supports various types of data, thus we could choose the most appropriate forms to describe the metrics in order that each metric could contain as much information as possible. In our preliminary work of the process trustworthiness metric system, we defined three types for data: Boolean type, Level type and Numerical type. These types cannot fully reflect the characteristics of the metrics in some cases, and thus we introduce the concept of membership degree from the fuzzy set theory, and use numerical interval to further describe the data. Table 2 shows the four types after the extension to our early work.

Table 2. Four types of data supported by FETP method

Metric Type	Metric Representation	Example
Boolean	YES / NO	*Whether have use case specification* = YES
Numerical	Any certain value	*Efficiency of reviewing and testing* = 0.714
Levels + Membership Degrees	{$Class_1(p_1\%)$, $Class_2(p_2\%)$,…, $Class_n(p_n\%)$}	*Coverage of testing cases*= {Poor(10%), Good(37%), Excellent(53%)}
Numerical Intervals + Membership Degrees	{[$Interval_1$](p1%), [$Interval_2$](p2%),…, [$Interval_n$](pn%)}	*Scale deviation between delivered product and the requirement* = {[0, 0.33](0%), [0.33, 0.67](16.7%), [0.67, 1.00](83.3%)}

The definitions of the four types are as follows:

1) **Boolean Type.** It is a common metric type which could directly shows whether an object is satisfied. When one metric has only two opposite states, it can be considered as Boolean type, and we assign the value such as YES or NO to the metric.

2) **Numerical Type.** This type of metric is used to indicate a certain numeric value. When the value collected is certain, we assign it to this type of metric. If there are some uncertainties when collecting data, we tend to describe it with the following two types.

3) **Levels + Membership Degrees.** In practice, we used to describe an object with a certain level or several levels, but actually it could to some extent belong to one level, and to some extent belong to other levels. Based on this consideration we introduce the concept on membership degree from the fuzzy set theory, and propose a new metric type that consists of two parts: the levels and the membership degrees for the levels. We use the form of percentage to indicate a membership degree, which could be considered as the possibility that one object might belong to the corresponding level.

4) **Numerical Intervals + Membership Degrees.** Similar to Type 3), we propose a new type for quantitative data, which consists of two parts: the numerical intervals that one object might belong to, and the membership degrees attached to the intervals. The interval may be a discrete value.

3.2 Trustworthiness Measurement System Tailoring

As mentioned above, the trustworthiness measurement system we proposed involved various aspects and levels of software process. Therefore, we need tailor the measurement system before evaluation according to the concrete scenarios using certain rules, for example, the Trust Principles in TSM.

3.3 Metric Weight Determination Based on AHP

In this section we will further elaborate the application of AHP in the context of our trustworthiness measurement system.

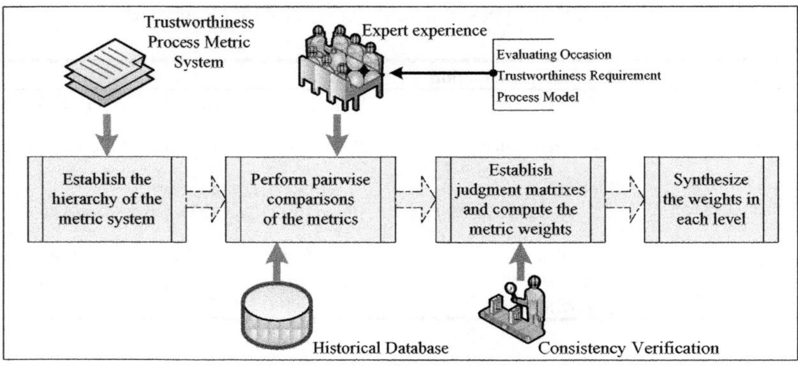

Fig. 2. Procedures of the weight determination with AHP

As shows in Fig. 2, based on our previous work [1] we first establish the hierarchy according to the tailored trustworthiness measurement system. We regard the software process trustworthiness as the overall objective, and then divide the metrics into different levels. For example, we could first group the TPAs by the definitions of TAPA, TMPA and TEPA [1] as the level under the overall objective, and the next level are the TPAs in each of the three groups, under which are the metrics of each TPA. Afterwards a tree structure is established, where every leaf is a metric.

Next we need to establish the judgment matrixes top-down with pairwise comparisons of the metrics in each level. The basis of the comparisons is from two aspects: expert experience and the historical data. On one hand, a group of domain experts give their results for every comparison respectively, and the final comparison results are the composite opinions of the experts. On the other hand, we could also refer to the historical data during the comparison process, which will be described later in 3.6. The two aspects complement each other, and each importance could be adjusted according to actual conditions, thus ensuring both the flexibility and objectivity of the results.

Several judgment matrixes are established after the comparisons of all the levels. When the consistency of each matrix is acceptable, we could obtain the relative weights of the metrics. After the synthesis of the metric weights in each level, we finally get the absolute weights of all the metrics.

3.4 Data Pre-processing

Since we have defined four types of metrics, it is necessary to perform pre-processing of the data before the evaluation calculation. The pre-processing consists of two steps: the first is data normalization, and then is the data unification.

The purpose of the data normalization is to convert all the data to the same interval, for which we use the method of Min-Max Normalization [11], and normalize all the quantitative data to [0, 1] based on the historical data. Assume the maximum value of a metric in the historical database is e_{max}, the minimum value is e_{min}, and the actual value we collected is e. If the direction of e is positive, which means bigger value is better, the value after normalization is $(e-e_{min})/(e_{max}-e_{min})$; and if the direction of e is negative, which means smaller value is better, the value after normalization is $(e_{max}-e)/(e_{max}-e_{min})$. For the data in the form of intervals, we could also use the procedures, consider the endpoint of the interval as the value e, and perform the normalization accordingly. Such procedures will ensure all the quantitative data have values in the interval [0, 1], and have the consistency directions.

After the normalization of the data, we adopt the following steps to unify the form of metric data:

1) For a metric of Boolean type, we assign 1 to the positive value, and 0 to the negative value, and then it becomes a Numerical data, for which we assign 100% as the membership degree to the original value. As mentioned above, the "discrete values + membership degrees" form could also be considered as the "Numerical Intervals + Membership Degrees". For example, the value of a metric is {A(a%), B(b%), C(c%)}, and after unification it should be {[A,A](a%), [B,B](b%), [C,C](c%)}.

2) For a metric of the type "Levels + Membership Degrees", we also unify it to the type of "Numerical Intervals + Membership Degrees". Assume that a metric consists of N levels, p_k means the membership degree of the k th level, and the type could be represented as

$$\{Class_1(p_1), Class_2(p_2), \ldots, Class_N(p_N)\}$$

Then we divide [0, 1] to N equal intervals, and convert the original $Class_k(p_k)(k=1,2,\ldots,N)$ to $[(k-1)/N, k/N)(p_k)$ $(k=1,2,\ldots,N)$, after which the metric should be

$$\{[0, 1/N)(p_1), [1/N, 2/N)(p_2), \ldots, [(N-1)/N, 1](p_N)\}$$

So far, we have unified all the types to the "Numerical Intervals + Membership Degrees" type.

3.5 Trustworthiness Evaluation Calculation

After the preparations above, the weights of the metrics have been determined, and the values of the metrics have been unified to the "Numerical Intervals + Membership Degrees" type, based on which this section will give a description on the calculating procedures of the trustworthiness evaluation, with the final result in the form of "user-customized trustworthiness level + the membership degree of each level".

At first we give some definitions to the variables and operations:

Definition 1. $X=\{x_1, x_2, \ldots, x_m\}$ is an evaluation set consisting of m metrics.

Definition 2. $W=\{w_1, w_2, \ldots, w_m\}$ is a set of m metric weights, each corresponding to the metric in X.

Definition 3. The metric x_i consists of n_i elements. An element contains two parts: an interval $[a_{ij},b_{ij}]$ $(i=1, \ldots, m, j=1, \ldots, n_{i-1})$, and the membership degree $p_{ij}(i=1, \ldots, m, j=1, \ldots, n_i)$. Therefore,

$$x_i=\{[a_{i1},b_{i1}](p_{i1}), [a_{i2},b_{i2}](p_{i2}), \ldots, [a_{i,ni},b_{i,ni}](p_{i,ni})\} . \quad (2)$$

then weight x_i, that is

$$w_ix_i=\{w_i[a_{i1}, b_{i1}](p_{i1}), w_i[a_{i2}, b_{i2}](p_{i2}), \ldots, w_i[a_{i,ni}, b_{i,ni}](p_{i,ni})\} . \quad (3)$$

we denote $w_i[a_{i1}, b_{i1})(p_{i1})$ as u_{i1}, and then

$$w_i x_i = \{u_{i1}, u_{i2}, \ldots, u_{i,ni}\} . \tag{4}$$

Definition 4. We define × as the operation among different elements. When x_i's *f*th element u_{if} does the operation × with x_k's *g* th element u_{kg}, that is

$$u_{if} \times u_{kg} = w_i[a_{if}, b_{if}](p_{if}) \times w_k[a_{kg}, b_{kg}](p_{kg}) = [w_i a_{if} + w_k a_{kg}, w_i b_{if} + w_k b_{kg}](p_{if}\, p_{kg}) . \tag{5}$$

The operation among three elements can be represented as

$$u_{if} \times u_{kg} \times u_{jh} = w_i[a_{if}, b_{if}](p_{if}) \times w_k[a_{kg}, b_{kg}](p_{kg}) \times w_j[a_{jh}, b_{jh}](p_{jh}) = [w_i a_{if} + w_k a_{kg} + w_j a_{jh}, w_i b_{if} + w_k b_{kg} + w_j b_{jh}](p_{if}\, p_{kg} p_{jh}) . \tag{6}$$

and it is the similar in the situation with more than three elements.

Definition 5. We define $\frown$ as the operation among different metrics, which means the evaluation using these metrics. $x_i \frown x_k$ means an operation similar to Cartesian Product, and the result is

$$x_i \frown x_k = \{u_{im} \times u_{kn} \mid u_{im} \in w_i x_i, u_{kn} \in w_k x_k\} . \tag{7}$$

The operation among three metrics can be represented as

$$x_i \frown x_k \frown x_j = \{u_{im} \times u_{kn} \times u_{jl} \mid u_{im} \in w_i x_i, u_{kn} \in w_k x_k, u_{jl} \in w_j x_j\} . \tag{8}$$

and it is the similar in the situation with more than three metrics.

Based on the definitions above, we could easily calculate the intermediate result Y, which is the product of the operation $\frown$ among all the metrics, that is

$$Y = x_1 \frown x_2 \frown x_3 \frown \ldots \frown x_m . \tag{9}$$

As mentioned above, the metric x_i consists of n_i elements and the number of metrics is *m*, and thus the number of elements in the intermediate result Y is

$$N = n_1 n_2 \cdots n_m = \prod_{k=1}^{m} n_k \tag{10}$$

so the intermediate result Y can be represented as

$$Y = \{[c_1, d_1](q_1), [c_2, d_2](q_2), \ldots, [c_N, d_N](q_N)\} . \tag{11}$$

in which $q_k (k=1, 2, \ldots, N)$ is the membership degree of the interval $[c_k, d_k]$ $(k=1, 2, \ldots, N)$.

There might be overlap among the intervals of the elements in Y, so the result is not explicit enough, thus needs further calculation to convert it to several connected but not intersect intervals.

Since the intervals of the elements in the metrics are in [0, 1] after normalization, it can be proved that the intervals of the elements in Y are also in [0, 1] after the calculating procedures above. We partition [0, 1] into T equal subintervals, each of which can be represented as $[(s-1)/T, s/T] (s=1, 2, \ldots, T)$, denoted as $[t_{s-1}, t_s]$ for short. In order to map the overlapping intervals of Y to the T equal subintervals, we need to introduce a quantity considering both the lengths of the intervals and the membership degrees, which we define as membership degree density. The definition is as follows:

Definition 6. For the k th (k=1, 2… N) element in the intermediate result Y, when $c_k \neq d_k$, we define the membership degree density μ_k as

$$\mu_k = \frac{q_k}{d_k - c_k}(c_k \neq d_k) \tag{12}$$

Based on the definition, we further denote l_{ks} as the overlapping length between $[c_k,d_k]$ (k=1, 2, …, N) and the s th (s=1, 2, …, T) interval $[t_{s-1},t_s]$ of [0,1], and we calculate l_{ks} from the formula

$$l_{ks} = \begin{cases} 0 & (c_k > t_s \quad or \quad d_k < t_{s-1}) \\ d_k - c_k & (c_k > t_{s-1} \quad and \quad d_k < t_s) \\ t_s - t_{s-1} & (c_k < t_{s-1} \quad and \quad d_k > t_s) \\ t_s - c_k & (t_s > c_k > t_{s-1} \quad and \quad d_k > t_s) \\ d_k - t_{s-1} & (t_s > d_k > t_{s-1} \quad and \quad c_k < t_{s-1}) \end{cases} \tag{13}$$

We define the membership degree in $[t_{s-1},t_s]$ of the k th element as b_{ks}, and when $c_k \neq d_k$, $b_{ks}=l_{ks}\mu_k$. If $c_k=d_k$ and the membership of $[c_k,d_k]$ is q_k, when $c_k \in [t_{s-1},t_s]$, $b_{ks}=q_k$; and when $c_k \notin [t_{s-1},t_s]$, $b_{ks}=0$. Therefore, the membership degree of the s th interval $[t_{s-1},t_s]$ is

$$r_s = \sum_{k=1}^{N} b_{ks} \tag{14}$$

and the final result Z could be represented as

$$Z = \{[t_0, t_1)(r_1), [t_1,t_2)(r_2), \ldots, [t_{T-1},t_T](r_T)\} . \tag{15}$$

The value of the intervals reflects the extent of trustworthiness, so we could consider the intervals of the element as the levels of trustworthiness, where higher level means more trustworthy. Since the value of T is determined during the calculation, users could assign different value to it, which means the method could provide the result with various levels of trustworthiness. Therefore, compared with the Conventional Comprehensive Fuzzy Evaluation Method, our method is not restricted by the fixed numbers of the intervals and the single form of the values, both for the input and output, and thus it is more flexible and applicable.

3.6 Historical Database Support

The historical database is an essential component in our method. The content of the database is mainly from the data accumulated in the evaluation process. Besides, the organization could also add data to the database by other means. In the process of trustworthiness evaluation, there are two procedures that need the support of the database. On the one hand, when we make the pairwise comparisons of the metrics, the database should provide historical data as the reference basis; on the other hand, in the procedure of data pre-processing, the historical data used to perform the Min-Max Normalization is from the historical database. Meanwhile, the intermediate and the final results contain rich information, which are important experience for the software organizations.

4 Case Study

In this section, we take the example of eight versions of SoftPM [12], which is the lead product of a software organization rated at CMMI maturity level 3 in China. We apply the FETP method to a certain process of these eight versions of SoftPM, and then discuss the results with statistical analyses.

4.1 Application

We implemented trustworthiness evaluation for the Review and Test Processes of the eight versions. According to the trustworthiness requirements and the evaluation occasion, we tailor our trustworthiness measurement system and select nine metrics for the Review and Test Processes, as shown in Table 2.

Table 2. Metrics for the Review and Test Processes

Metric	Meaning	Value Type
M01	Whether the review is planned in advance.	Boolean [Yes/No]
M02	Proportion of the review defects whose severities are recorded.	Levels[No, Vague, Clear] + Membership Degrees
M03	Completeness of the review summary report.	Levels[Poor, Good, Excellent] + Membership Degrees
M04	Average number of days for fixing one review defect.	Numerical
M05	Average number of days for fixing one bug.	Numerical
M06	Proportion of review and test work load.	Numerical
M07	Efficiency of review and test.	Numerical
M08	Coverage of test cases.	Levels[Poor, Good, Excellent] + Membership Degrees
M09	Proportion of the remaining testing bugs.	Numerical

Table 3. AHP Judgment Matrix of the Metrics for the Review and Test Processes

	M01	M02	M03	M04	M05	M06	M07	M08	M09
M01	1	3	1/5	1/3	1/3	1/5	1/5	1/5	1/5
M02	1/3	1	1/3	1	1/3	1/5	1/5	1/5	1/5
M03	5	3	1	3	3	1/3	1/3	1/3	1/3
M04	3	1	1/3	1	3	1/5	1/5	1/5	1/5
M05	3	3	1/3	1/3	1	1/5	1/5	1/5	1/3
M06	5	5	3	5	5	1	1	1	1/3
M07	5	5	3	5	5	1	1	1/3	1
M08	5	5	3	5	5	1	3	1	1/3
M09	5	5	3	5	3	3	1	3	1
CR=0.089	0.030	0.028	0.088	0.046	0.043	0.170	0.170	0.192	0.232

Afterwards, we determine the weights of the metrics based on the AHP method described in 3.2. We combine the expert experience and the historical data to make the pairwise comparisons of the metrics, and establish the judgment matrix. We further solve the matrix and get the weights of the metrics, as shown in Table 3.

We calculate the trustworthiness of the process with the weights and collected metric values, with the historical data in the database of the software organization. We define 5 levels of trustworthiness, and get the results shown in Table 4.

Table 4. Membership Degrees at Each Trustworthiness Level of the 8 Versions

Ver.	Membership Degrees of Each Level (%)					Ver.	Membership Degrees of Each Level (%)				
	1	2	3	4	5		1	2	3	4	5
V1	72.5	27.5	0	0	0	V5	0	0	100.0	0	0
V2	0	0	100.0	0	0	V6	0	0	95.9	4.10	0
V3	0	100.0	0	0	0	V7	0	0	100	0	0
V4	0	13.5	86.5	0	0	V8	0	0	0	100	0

4.2 Analysis and Discussion

We define a value as Trustworthiness Median Value, where the membership degrees at the two sides of the value are equal for each evaluation result. We calculate the eight Trustworthiness Median Values, and show them on the same chart with the values of the Defect Density at Release Time, which could to some extent reflect the trustworthiness of the processes. The chart is shown in Fig. 3.

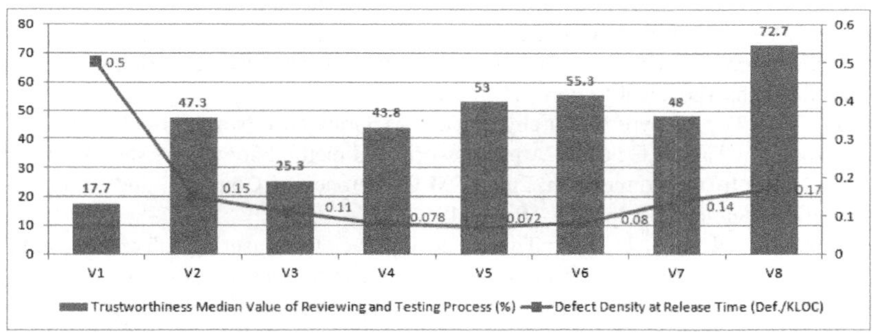

Fig. 3. Trustworthiness Median Values and Defect Density at Release Time

Based on the data, we further carry on a correlation analysis between the Trustworthiness Median Values and the Defect Density Values at Release Time, and the Pearson's Correlation Coefficient is *-0.559*, which reflects the negative correlation between them at a certain degree. The result is consistent with the real situation, where process with higher trustworthiness leads to lower defect density of software product.

5 Conclusions

This paper proposed an evaluation method of software process trustworthiness which supports various evaluation occasions and multiple data types. The AHP method was used to compute the weight of metrics and the theory of fuzzy set was introduced thus made the method applicable to the situations with uncertainty, based on which we developed a procedure to perform the calculation with the values and the weights of metrics, outputting the result of trustworthiness in the form of user-customized trustworthiness levels and the membership degree of each level. We applied the method in the real case of process trustworthiness evaluation, and the initial application of the method shows encouraging results in practical application. A tool prototype is under development at this stage, and our future work is to integrate this tool with SoftPM [12][13] to consume large amount of metric data reported in SoftPM and provide evaluation results of process trustworthiness, as well as continuing to refine our methods based on application feedbacks.

Acknowledgements

This work is supported by the National Natural Science Foundation of China under Grant Nos. 90718042, 60873072, and 60903050; the National Hi-Tech R&D Plan of China under Grant Nos. 2007AA010303; the National Basic Research Program under Grant No. 2007CB310802.

References

1. Yang, Y., Wang, Q., Li, M.: Proceedings of the International Conference on Software Process, Vancouver, B.C., Canada (2009)
2. Shu, F., Jiang, N., Gou, L.: Technical Report: A Trustworthiness Measurement Model. ISCAS/iTechs Technical Report #106 (2008)
3. Saaty, T.L.: The Analytic Hierarchy Process. McGraw-Hill, New York (1990)
4. Amoroso, E., Taylor, C., et al.: A process-oriented methodology for assessing and improving software trustworthiness. In: 2nd ACM Conference on Computer and communications security, Virginia, USA, pp. 39–50 (1994)
5. Amoroso, E., Nguyen, T., et al.: Toward an approach to measuring software trust. In: IEEE Computer Society Symposium on Research in Security and Privacy (1991)
6. CMMI Product Team. CMMI® for Development, Version 1.2. Pittsburgh, PA, Carnegie Mellon Software Engineering Insitute (2006)
7. Chrissis, M.B., Konrad, M., Shrum, S.: CMMI®: Guidelines for Process Integration and Product Improvement. Addison-Wesley Publishing Company, Boston (2006)
8. Wang, Q., Yang, Y.: Technical Report: A Process-Centric Methodology to Software Trustworthiness Assurance. ISCAS/iTechs Technical Report #105 (2008)
9. Zadeh, L.A.: Fuzzy Sets. Information Control, 338–353 (1965)
10. Klir, G.J., Yuan, B.: Fuzzy Sets and Fuzzy Logic. Theory and Applications. Prentice Hall, New Jersey (1995)
11. Han, J., Kamber, M.: Data Mining: Concepts and Techniques. Morgan Kaufmann, San Francisco (2006)
12. Wang, Q., Li, M.: Software Process Management: Practices in China. In: Software Process Workshop, Beijing (2005)
13. Wang, Q., Li, M.: Measuring and improving software process in China. In: International Symposium on Empirical Software Engineering (2005)
14. Tan, T., He, M., et al.: An Analysis to Understand Software Trustworthiness. In: The 9th International Conference for Young Computer Scientists (2008)
15. Du, J., Tan, T., He, M., et al.: Technical Report: A Process-Centric Approach to Assure Software Trustworthiness. ISCAS/iTechs Technical Report #106 (2008)

Software Process Simulation Modeling: An Extended Systematic Review

He Zhang[1], Barbara Kitchenham[2], and Dietmar Pfahl[3]

[1] National ICT Australia
University of New South Wales, Australia
he.zhang@nicta.com.au
[2] School of Computer Science and Mathematics, Keele University, UK
barbara@cs.keele.ac.uk
[3] University of Oslo, Norway
University of Calgary, Canada
dietmarp@ifi.uio.no, dpfahl@ucalgary.ca

Abstract. Software Process Simulation Modeling (SPSM) research has increased in the past two decades, especially since the first ProSim Workshop held in 1998. Our research aims to systematically assess how SPSM has evolved during the past 10 years in particular whether the purposes for SPSM, the simulation paradigms, tools, research topics, and the model scopes and outputs have changed. We performed a systematic literature review of the SPSM research in two subsequent stages, and identified 156 relevant studies in four categories. This paper reports the review process of the second stage and the preliminary results by aggregating studies from the two stages. Although the load of SPSM studies was dominated in ProSim/ICSP community, the outside research presented more diversity in some aspects. We also perceived an immediate need for refining and updating the reasons and the classification scheme for SPSM introduced by Kellner, Madachy and Raffo (KMR).

1 Introduction

Software Process Simulation Modeling (SPSM) research has increased in the past two decades, especially since the first ProSim[1] Workshop held in 1998 and Kellner, Madachy and Raffo's (KMR) paper addressed the fundamental "*why, what and how*" questions of process simulation in software engineering. After 10 years (1998-2007) progress, there is a need for a timely review of the research done in SPSM, to update the current state-of-the-art, to summarize the experiences and lessons, and to portray a full overview of SPSM research.

In ICSP 2008, we reported the first stage of our Systematic Literature Review (SLR) on SPSM [1], which focused on the research published through ProSim/ICSP channels over the decade (1998-2007). Nevertheless, a broader view of SPSM research in software engineering will make this systematic literature review more valuable to the software process community, which is the

[1] International Workshop on Software Process Simulation Modeling.

J. Münch, Y. Yang, and W. Schäfer (Eds.): ICSP 2010, LNCS 6195, pp. 309–320, 2010.

motivation for the second stage of this review. During this review stage, another relevant SLR [2] on the role of SPSM in software risk management was conducted and reported, which focused a special use of SPSM based on the 27 studies from a sub-scope of our review.

This paper reports the process and the preliminary results of the second stage SLR, which searched and aggregated evidence from the publication channels outside ProSim/ICSP to address our original research questions. As the continuous work of our former stage, the results derived from this stage also serves as a validation of the '*facts*', '*trends*', and '*directions*' identified in our first stage [3], as well as the latest update and enhancement to the topics discussed in KMR's paper [4]. Additionally, our staged SLR enables a comparison of the research characteristics and preferences within and outside ProSim/ICSP community.

2 Method: The Extended Systematic Review

The Stage 2 of this systematic review continuously followed Kitchenham's guidelines [5]. As the method and process of Stage 1 of this SLR was reported in [1], this paper instead only reports the difference between the two stages.

In order to maintain the consistency, integrity and comparability between the two stages of SLR, there were no significant change to the original six research questions [1]. Thus, the second stage of this systematic review also addresses the following research questions:

Q1. *What were the purposes or motivations for SPSM in the last decade?*
Q2. *Which simulation paradigms have been applied in the last decade, and how popular were they in SPSM?*
Q3. *Which simulation tools are available for SPSM and have been in use in the last decade?*
Q4. *On model level, what were research topics and model scopes focused by process simulation models?*
Q5. *On parameter level, what were the output variables of interest when developing process simulation models?*
Q6. *Which simulation paradigm is the most appropriate for a specific SPSM purpose and scope?*

The three researchers involved in the first stage continued to work in their roles during the second stage. In addition, one more researcher was invited to join in the expert panel to ensure the review quality.

2.1 Search Strategy

In the first stage review, we employed manual search on ProSim/ICSP related publication channels only. The search scope was extended in the Stage 2 by including more conference (workshop) proceedings and journals that are relevant to software process research and empirical software engineering. In addition, the automated search method [5] was employed in this stage as a complement to the

Table 1. Search sources for Stage 2 of the SLR

Source	Period	Method
Conference proceedings		
Proceedings of ICSE (incl. Workshops, excl. ProSim)	'98-'07	Manual
Proceedings of PROFES Conference	'99-'07	Manual
Proceedings of ISESE/METRICS/ESEM conference	'02-'07	Manual
Proceedings of SEKE conference	'98-'07	Manual
Journals		
IEEE Transactions on Software Engineering (TSE)	'98-'07	Manual
ACM Transactions on Software Engineering & Methodology (TOSEM)	'98-'07	Manual
Journal of Systems & Software (JSS)	'98-'07	Manual
Journal of Software Process: Improvement & Practice (SPIP)	'98-'07	Manual
Journal of information and software technology (IST)	'98-'07	Manual
International Journal of Software Engineering and Knowledge Engineering (IJSEKE)	'98-'07	Manual
Digital Libraries		
IEEE Xplore	'98-'07	Automated
ACM difital library	'98-'07	Automated
ScienceDirect	'98-'07	Automated
SpringerLink	'98-'07	Automated

manual search in order to identify as many SPSM studies as possible. Table 1 summarizes the sources searched in Stage 2.

By following the systematic literature search process suggested in [6], the search terms for automated search were elicited based on observation of the studies found by the manual search in the both stages. Then we combined the terms to form the following search string, which was further coded into the equivalent forms to match the search syntax of different digital libraries. The string was searched in the fields of *title-abstract-keyword*. Note that 'system dynamics' was explicitly designated in the search string because 'simulation' does not appear in the search fields of some relevant studies using SD.

```
((software process) OR (software project) OR (software product)
OR (software evolution)) AND (simulation OR simulator OR simulate
OR (dynamic model) OR (system dynamics))
```

2.2 Study Selection

The studies retrieved through the literature search were further screened and selected. The entire selection process was performed by the principal researcher. The initial selection (after literature search) applied the same criteria in [1] to identify and exclude the irrelevant studies. The *title-abstract-keyword* and *conclusion* of each paper were read as the evidence for inclusion/exclusion. Any selection difficulties were escalated to the expert panel for final decision.

When the full-text of each paper was read in data extraction, more duplicate publications and irrelevant studies were identified and excluded (see Section 3).

2.3 Study Classification

The first stage SLR identified four categories of SPSM study [1]. These four types of studies focus on different aspects of software process simulation research, and may give answers to the research questions from different points of view. Category B studies introduce and provide effective paradigms, methods and tools for constructing process simulation models or simulators (Category A studies). These simulation models can be further adopted for different purposes in industrial context by following the practical solutions or guidelines (Category C studies). The experience (Category D studies) collected from modeling and adoption can be used as feedback to iteratively improve SPSM research [3].

A. Software process simulation models or simulators;
B. Process simulation modeling paradigms, methodologies, and environments;
C. Applications, guidelines, frameworks, and solutions for adopting process simulation in software engineering practice;
D. Experience reports and empirical studies of SPSM research and practice.

Due to some minor disagreements experienced between the principal and the secondary researchers in the classification on a small number of studies (between Category B and C), we further specified a set of concrete criteria (questions) to facilitate the effective identification of each study's category (in Table 2). If a '*yes*' answer applies to any question related to one study type, this study was allocated the corresponding (one or more) category.

Table 2. Questions for study classification

Category	Question
A	- Was a new process simulation model or simulator presented in the study? - Was a process simulation model or simulator applied in a new SE domain or a new practical context?
B	- Compared with previous studies, was a new simulation modeling paradigm introduced into SPSM? - Was a new process simulation environment or tool developed and described? - Was a methodology or framework proposed or developed for improving SPSM? - Were any factors associated to SPSM discussed in the study?
C	- Was a new application of SPSM introduced to SE domain? - Was a guideline or framework of directing SPSM solution to one specific problem or context proposed or developed?
D	- Did the study report any experience (qualitative or quantitative) of applying SPSM in industry? - Did the study report how a process simulation model or simulator has been built or calibrated with empirical data? - Did the study report an empirical study related to SPSM?

2.4 Data Extraction and Quality Assessment

Data extraction and quality assessment were performed by the principal and the secondary reviewer independently. The former was responsible for reviewing all primary studies, extracting data, and assessing study quality. The other selected and reviewed approximately 15% studies for validation of the extraction and assessment. When there were disagreements could not be resolved, the final decision was made by the principal researcher.

The study attributes for *data extraction* and questions for *quality assessment* can be found in [1]. Due to the abovementioned considerations, we did not propose any changes in these activities in Stage 2.

3 Results

3.1 Primary Studies

After literature search and initial study selection, 79 relevant studies were uploaded into the online system (`http://systematicreviews.org`) for more careful selection and data extraction. By reading the full-text, 19 studies were further excluded because they are *1*) duplicate publications; *2*) not simulation studies on *software process* (e.g., simulation of software systems); or *3*) research proposals without implementation.

Finally, the second stage included 60 relevant studies in addition to those found by the first stage review. In total, 156 (S1:96/S2:60) primary studies[2] on SPSM research were identified from 1998 to 2007. They form a comprehensive body of research of software process simulation.

Table 3 shows the number of SPSM studies published during the decade, which are grouped by two review stages. The number of published studies per year was between 15 and 19 after Y2K, and stabilized at 18 or 19 after 2004. This stability applies to all papers during the period, irrespective of whether or not they were ProSim related papers. The overall number of conference publications (77) is very close to the journal publications (79) over the period.

Table 3. Identified as primary studies in the staged SLR

	1998	1999	2000	2001	2002	2003	2004	2005	2006	2007	**Sum**
Stage One											
- ProSim/ICSP	2	0	2	n/a	n/a	11	6	7	4	8	**40**
- JSS/SPIP special issues	0	11	9	12	7	0	5	4	6	2	**56**
Stage Two											
- Conference/workshop	2	3	2	3	6	1	3	7	3	7	**37**
- Journal	0	0	4	3	2	3	4	1	5	1	**23**
Total	4	14	17	18	15	15	18	19	18	18	**156**

Table 3 also shows that the number of SPSM studies significantly increased after the first ProSim workshop (ProSim'98), which demonstrates the positive effect of ProSim series workshops to software process simulation research.

Table 4 lists the top conferences and journals where the researchers published their SPSM studies in the decade. Apart from ProSim/ICSP venues (including SPIP and JSS), IST and PROFES also have dominated outside publications.

It is worth noticing that most primary studies cited either [7] or [4], which are the seminal work and landmark paper on SPSM.

3.2 Classification

The second stage review confirmed the classification from Stage 1 is appropriate. Each included primary study was classified into one or more of the four categories. Figure 1 shows the distribution of study categories over the decade. It is clear that Category A studies (simulation models) were dominant in every single year during the period.

[2] The full study list will be online for public access at `http://systematicreviews.org`

Table 4. Top conferences & journals publishing SPSM studies

Rank	Journal	#Studies(S1/S2)	Rank	Conference	#Studies(S1/S2)
1	SPIP	36(33/3)	1	ProSim	32(32/0)
2	JSS	25(23/2)	2	ICSP	8(8/0)
3	IST	6(0/6)	3	PROFES	5(0/5)
4	IJSEKE	4(0/4)	4	ICSE/EWSPT/ASWEC	3(0/3)

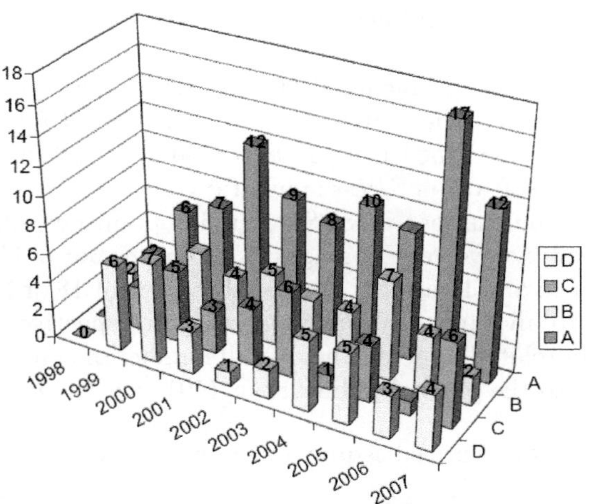

Fig. 1. Study category distribution over years

In total, 92 Category A studies (59%) describing software process simulation models (simulators) were found from literature, 56 from Stage 1 and 36 from Stage 2. Most studies of Category B discussed methods of constructing process simulation model more correctly, effectively and efficiently. Some papers introduced either novel simulation paradigms or simulation environments. The classification found 37 (24%) studies falling into two categories, and 5 studies that were identified as combinations of three categories.

3.3 Quality Assessment

The quality of the included studies was assessed using the checklist in [1]. Fig. 2 shows the average quality score after normalization. Fig. 2-a depicts the varying study quality from both stages per paper type over the decade. The overall study quality was not stable till 2003. Since then, the quality of the journal articles has been better than the conference/workshop papers.

Fig. 2-b compares the average study quality from each stage. From 2002, the quality of studies published in ProSim/ICSP (from Stage 1) was better than the studies published in other venues (in Stage 2) in most cases by paper type, particularly journal publications. This was probably because ProSim/ICSP encouraged more researchers to publish their quality research on SPSM.

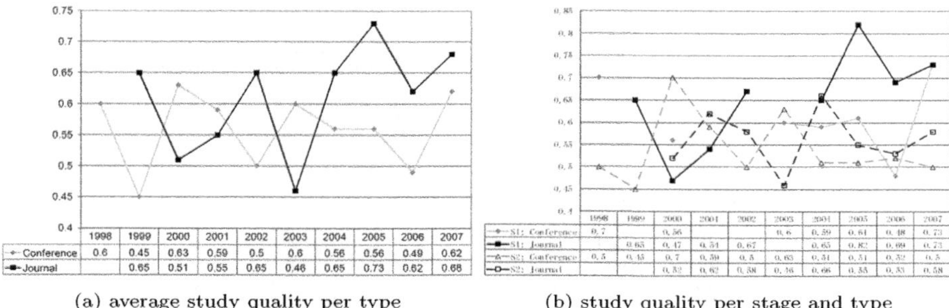

(a) average study quality per type

(b) study quality per stage and type

Fig. 2. Study quality assessment over years

4 Discussion

Following up our discussion in [1], this section focuses on the preliminary answers to the first five research questions (Q1-Q5), but provides a broader view by synthesizing the results from the both stages.

4.1 Research Purposes (Q1)

In the first ProSim Workshop (1998), KMR presented a wide variety of reasons for undertaking simulations of software process models [4]. Primarily, process simulation is an aid to decision making. They identified six specific purposes for SPSM. Our first stage SLR extended and restructured them to be ten purposes [1] based on the observation of SPSM studies.

The second stage SLR confirmed that these ten purposes for SPSM research identified in Stage 1. After minor refinements, these research purposes were grouped in three levels (i.e. *cognitive level, tactical level, strategic level*). Table 5 reports the categories and relationships.

4.2 Modeling Paradigms (Q2)

The diversity and complexity of software processes and the richness of research questions (concluded into simulation purposes in Table 5) determine the different capabilities of simulation paradigms needed.

Overall, 15 simulation modeling paradigms were found in our two-staged SLR. Table 6 shows the paradigms used by more than one applied study. The rightmost column indicates the number of studies (not limited to Category A) using or addressing the corresponding paradigm (the leftmost column). The first number in the bracket denotes the study number from Stage 1 (S1), and it is followed by the number from Stage 2 (S2) for comparison.

System Dynamics (SD, 47%) and Discrete-Event Simulation (DES, 31%) are the most popular technologies in SPSM. Other paradigms include State-Based Simulation (SBS), Qualitative (or semi-quantitative) Simulation (QSIM),

Table 5. SPSM purposes, levels, and model scopes

Purposes	Cognitive	Tactical	Strategic
Understanding	✓		
Communication	✓		
Process investigation	✓		
Education (training & learning)	✓		
Prediction & planning		✓	✓
Control & operational management		✓	✓
Risk management		✓	✓
Process improvement		✓	✓
Technology adoption		✓	✓
Tradeoff analysis & optimising		✓	✓

Role-Playing Game (RPG), Agent-Based Simulation (ABS), Discrete-Time Simulation (DTS), Knowledge-Based Simulation (KBS), Markov Process (MP), Cognitive Map (CM). These paradigms provide modelers with a number of options for modeling software processes at different abstraction levels, and enrich the modeling technologies (SD, DES, SBS and KBS) discussed by KMR [4].

Our first stage review identified 10 simulation paradigms for SPSM research. Compared to Stage 1, however, more paradigms (12) were employed by the fewer studies from the second stage, 5 of which are new to ProSim community. They are MP, CM, Specification and Description Language (SDL), Dynamic System Theory (DST), and Self-Organized Criticality (SOC). Most of these are not the conventional simulation paradigms.

Table 6. Modeling paradigms and simulation tools

Rank	Paradigm	Simulation tool or package	#Studies(S1/S2)
1	SD	Vensim(12/4), iThink(3/3), PowerSim(0/1)	74(47/27)
2	DES	Extend(11/4), DSOL(1/0), QNAP2(1/1), DEVSim++(1/0), DEVSJava(1/0), MicroSaint(0/1), SimJava(0/1)	48(30/18)
3	SBS		9(6/3)
4	QSIM	QSIM(2/1)	6(5/1)
5	RPG	SESAM(1/0)	6(3/3)
6	ABS	NetLogo(1/0), RePast(1/0)	5(3/2)
7	DTS		5(2/3)
8	KBS	PML(1/0)	4(4/0)
9	MP		2(0/2)
10	CM		2(0/2)

4.3 Simulation Tools (Q3)

Simulation toolkits and packages provide computer-aided environments (compilers, engines, or workbenches), with which modelers can develop and execute their simulation models. Our staged SLR found 15 tools or packages explicitly specified in Category A studies. Table 6 shows them and their application frequencies (in bracket). Considering the number of Category A studies, however, this information was difficult to extract because in many cases that the authors did not mention the tools they used in their papers. Some of them programmed their simulators from scratch.

Compared to the other paradigms, it seems that DES offers more tool options for its modelers in SPSM. Note that though Extend provides both *continuous* and *discrete* simulation capabilities, it was seldom used for *continuous* simulation alone in SPSM studies.

It is interesting that although Vensim and Extend are two popular simulation tools in ProSim community, their dominance was not found outside that community. Our review shows that most studies using them but published outside are also from the active researchers in ProSim/ICSP community. Instead, the researchers outside the ProSim/ICSP community seemed to prefer programming their models themselves.

4.4 Research Topics and Model Scopes (Q4)

Research Topic identifies the topics (problems) in software engineering that researchers choose investigate. It also determines the model's structure, input parameters, and output variables. In both stages of our SLR, we found 21 different research topics from Category A studies (as shown in Table 7), of which '*software maintenance*' and '*COTS-based development*' were added after analysis of the studies from Stage 2. 'Project', again, was the most studied model scope, particularly for 'generic development' (e.g., waterfall process model).

Model Scope specifies the boundary of a simulation model in two dimensions: time span and organisational breadth. To more properly differentiate and classify the model scopes of the published simulation models, their scopes were extended from 5 (defined by KMR [4]) to 7.

- **single phase** (e.g. some or all of design or testing phase)
- **multi-phase** (more than one single phase in project life cycle)
- **project** (single software project life cycle)
- **multi-project** (program life cycle, including multiple, successive or concurrent projects)
- **product** (software product life cycle, including development, deployment, and maintenance.)
- **evolution** (long-term product evolution, including successive releases of software product, i.e. software product line)
- **long-term organisation** (strategic considerations or planning spanning releases of multiple products over a substantial time span)

4.5 Simulation Outputs (Q5)

By carefully examining the simulation models described in Category A studies from the both stages, 15 output variables were identified (shown in Table 8), 12 of them from Stage 1 and 13 from Stage 2. The third column indicates the number of studies including the leftmost output variable, and the rightmost column shows their corresponding percentage in Category A studies (divided by

Table 7. Process simulation research topics vs. model scopes

Topic	single phase	multi-phase	project	multi-project	product	evolution	long-term	unknown	Sum (S1/S2)
generic development			9/10					1/2	**22(10/12)**
software evolution			1/0			7/1			**9(8/1)**
software process improvement	1/0	1/0					1/0	3/1	**7(6/1)**
requirements engineering	2/0		1/1		0/1	1/0		1/0	**7(5/2)**
incremental & concurrent development	1/0	2/0	1/2					1/0	**7(5/2)**
inspection & testing	1/2	0/2	0/1		0/1				**7(1/6)**
open-source development	1/0		0/1	1/0		2/0			**5(4/1)**
global development			1/0			3/0			**4(4/0)**
agile development			1/2					1/0	**4(2/2)**
software maintenance	0/1				0/3				**4(0/4)**
software economics	1/0		1/1		1/0				**4(3/1)**
acquisition & outsourcing		1/0	0/1					1/0	**3(2/1)**
software product-line					1/0		1/0		**2(2/0)**
quality assurance		1/0						1/0	**2(2/0)**
COTS-based development		0/1	0/1						**2(0/2)**
software engineering education			2/0						**2(2/0)**
software design	1/0								**1(1/0)**
software services					1/0				**1(1/0)**
risk management			1/0						**1(1/0)**
productivity analysis			1/0						**1(1/0)**
software reliability								1/0	**1(1/0)**
Total	7/3	4/3	19/20	1/0	2/5	8/1	2/0	9/3	**92(56/36)**

Table 8. Summary of simulation outputs

Output	Description	#Studies(S1/S2)	Percent
time	project schedule or elapsed time	44(20/24)	47.8%
effort	effort or cost	29(16/13)	31.5%
quality	product quality or defect level	23(11/12)	25%
size	requirement size or functionality	15(11/4)	16.3%
resource	resource utilization or staffing level	12(7/5)	13%
productivity	team or personal development productivity/competency	6(1/5)	6.5%
ROI or revenue	return on investment or cost/benefit analysis	4(2/2)	4.3%
plan	project or development plan (e.g. task allocation)	4(3/1)	4.3%
progress	project progress to completion by percent	4(0/4)	4.3%
market share	product market share	2(1/1)	2.2%
behavior	behavior patterns	2(1/2)	1.1%
index	nominal index	1(1/0)	1.1%
flow	process/work flow	1(1/0)	1.1%
change requests	requested changes to product	1(0/1)	1.1%
human exhaustion	level of people or team's exhaustion	1(0/1)	1.1%

92 - the number of Category A studies). Note that there are many simulation studies (models) with multiple outputs of interest.

In terms of Table 8, it is evident that *time*, *effort*, *quality*, *size* are the most common drivers for simulation studies of software process. There are 71% studies (65 out of 92) including either one of them or their combination as model outputs. This finding confirms that SPSM research focuses mainly on factors of interest to software project managers.

5 Conclusion

We conducted a two-staged systematic literature review of software process simulation modeling by systematically searching and aggregating studies published within and outside the ProSim/ICSP community from 1998 to 2007. The results and in-depth findings from the first stage were reported in [1] and [3]. As a continuation of previous research, this paper presents the process and the updated results of our second stage review. To be specific, this research contributes to software process research in the following aspects.

- A two-staged SLR which identified most SPSM studies and classified them into four categories builds a basis for future secondary studies in SPSM.
- A broad state-of-the-art of SPSM research is portrayed from diverse aspects: purposes, paradigms, topics, scopes, outputs, and so on.
- Updates to KMR's landmark paper based on the evolution over the decade since ProSim'98.
- An initial comparison between the SPSM related research reported within and outside the ProSim/ICSP community.

Some limitations still exist in the current study and need further improvements: *1)* the study categorization was mainly determined by the principal reviewer's final judgment, which may need further examination; *2)* the impact of study quality needs to be considered in data analysis, particularly for the inclusion of low quality studies.

As our SLR is also a kind of mapping study, which provides groups of studies in this domain, it can be used as a precursor to future more detailed secondary research. In particular, this work will be enhanced by including a more detailed analysis of the studies of Categories B, C and D.

Acknowledgment

NICTA is funded by the Australian Government as represented by the Department of Broadband, Communications and the Digital Economy and the Australian Research Council through the ICT Centre of Excellence program.

This work was also supported, in part, by Science Foundation Ireland grant 03/CE2/I303 1 to Lero - the Irish Software Engineering Research Centre (`www.lero.ie`).

References

1. Zhang, H., Kitchenham, B., Pfahl, D.: Reflections on 10 years of software process simulation modelling: A systematic review. In: Wang, Q., Pfahl, D., Raffo, D.M. (eds.) ICSP 2008. LNCS, vol. 5007, pp. 345–365. Springer, Heidelberg (2008)
2. Liu, D., Wang, Q., Xiao, J.: The role of software process simulation modeling in software risk management: A systematic review. In: Proceedings of the 3rd International Symposium on Empirical Software Engineering and Measurement (ESEM 2009), Lask Buena Vista, FL, October 2009, pp. 302–311. IEEE Computer Society, Los Alamitos (2009)

3. Zhang, H., Kitchenham, B., Pfahl, D.: Software process simulation modeling: Facts, trends, and directions. In: Proceedings of 15th Asia-Pacific Software Engineering Conference (APSEC 2008), Beijing, China, December 2008, pp. 59–66. IEEE Computer Society, Los Alamitos (2008)
4. Kellner, M.I., Madachy, R.J., Raffo, D.M.: Software process simulation modeling: Why? what? how? Journal of Systems and Software 46(2/3), 91–105 (1999)
5. Kitchenham, B., Charters, S.: Guidelines for performing systematic literature reviews in software engineering (version 2.3). Technical Report EBSE-2007-01, Software Engineering Group, School of Computer Science and Mathematics, Keele University, and Department of Computer Science, University of Durham (April 2007)
6. Zhang, H., Babar, M.A.: On searching relevant studies in software engineering. In: Proceedings of 14th International Conference on Evaluation and Assessment in Software Engineering (EASE'10), Keele, England, BCS (April 2010)
7. Abdel-Hamid, T.K., Madnick, S.E.: Software Project Dynamics: An Integrated Approach. Prentice Hall, Englewood Cliffs (1991)

SimSWE – A Library of Reusable Components for Software Process Simulation

Thomas Birkhölzer[1], Ray Madachy[2], Dietmar Pfahl[3,4], Dan Port[5], Harry Beitinger[1], Michael Schuster[1], and Alexey Olkov[5]

[1] University of Applied Sciences Konstanz, Konstanz, Germany
[2] Naval Postgraduate School, Monterey, USA
[3] University of Oslo, Oslo, Norway
[4] University of Calgary, Calgary, Canada
[5] University of Hawaii, USA

Abstract. SimSWE is a library of components for modeling and simulation of software engineering processes. It consists of a generic, implementation independent description of the components and a reference implementation using the MATLAB® / Simulink® environment. By providing ready-to-use building blocks for typical functionality, the library should facilitate and ease the use of simulation to analyze software engineering issues. The goals are to provide a collection of reusable components within an open and evolvable framework to help practitioners develop simulation models faster and enable researchers to implement complex modeling and simulation tasks. Currently, the library contains more than thirty components. It can be used under the LPGL license. The paper presents the current status of SimSWE to encourage its use and participation within the research community.

1 Introduction

Software engineering processes often form complex dynamic systems whose characteristics and behaviors are not easily analyzed by a simple static view. Quantitative process modeling and simulation have proven to be a valuable support in this situation. From early studies [1], software process simulation has advanced in various directions and many aspects of software engineering issues and processes have been modeled and analyzed using simulation methodologies. See [5] [8] [14] for an overview of this field and further references.

Based on the accomplished maturity of the domain, the time seems ripe to consolidate existing modeling and simulation knowledge into a library of reusable simulation components as a supporting platform for next generation software process models. The goal is to help practitioners to develop models easily [2] and enable researchers approach more complex modeling and simulation scenarios by providing encapsulated building blocks for commonplace functionality. There has been some work in this direction previously [7] [12], but these have not produced an openly available simulation library. The SimSWE library also partly originates from ideas presented in [9] [10].

J. Münch, Y. Yang, and W. Schäfer (Eds.): ICSP 2010, LNCS 6195, pp. 321–332, 2010.

The development of the SimSWE library relies on four factors which are considered of prime importance for its success:

- **Open source**
  The development of a comprehensive library requires cooperation, contributions, improvements as well critical reviews from as many participants as possible. The SimSWE library has been started by the authors as a joint initiative and will be shared under the GNU Lesser Public General License (LPGL) [6], see Section 5. All are invited to participate in this project.
- **Incorporation of different simulation types**
  The SimSWE library contains continuous time as well as discrete event components enabling model developers to choose the view that fits best to the problem at hand or even a hybrid approach (see Section 2.1).
- **Generic description and reference implementation**
  The generic description (see Section 2.3) enables the realization of the SimSWE components in various simulation environments. The reference implementation (see Section 2.4) provides proof of concept as well as plug-and-play usability.
- **Evolutionary design approach**
  Components require interfaces, generic abstractions and common definitions (see Section 2.2). Ideally, these are designed and corrected before any implementation. Realistically, however, this architecture will evolve with the scope and maturity of the library. Therefore, design and implementation of the SimSWE library is seen and planned as an iterative, evolutionary approach.

Section 2 elaborates these concepts. Section 3 provides an overview of the components already available and Section 4 demonstrates the use by example models. The paper concludes with an invitation for participation in Section 5, and a summary in Section 6.

2 Library Concepts

2.1 Simulation Types

In research and practice, two main approaches are used for software engineering process simulation: continuous time simulation (system dynamics) and discrete event simulation [15]. However, there is no inherent separation between these approaches. Continuous time models can be be recast into discrete event models, and similarly, discrete event simulation engines (tools) can approximate continuous time simulation. From a modeler's perspective, both approaches have their benefits and appropriate application, often even within the same model and thus can be combined yielding a hybrid model.

Therefore, the SimSWE library encompasses continuous time as well discrete event components (in some cases even for similar process elements). See for example the components *WorkTestRework* and *WorkTestReworkD* in Section 3. The choice is left to the user which approach suits best in a given context. It is planned for SimSWE to incorporate hybrid components as well as "glue"-utilities to interface between continuous time and discrete event parts in the future.

2.2 Component Development

Most of the SimSWE components have been extracted from existing simulation models, e.g., from [3] [4] [8] [11].

However, the design and development of an *encapsulated, reusable* component poses additional requirements beyond the transfer of equations and descriptions.

Inputs, outputs, and parameters must be identified. Unfortunately there is no clear-cut generic distinction to classify a factor as input (factors which are expected to depend dynamically on other parts) or as parameter (factors which are expected to be constant during a simulation). Dynamics and flows must be enabled for repeating cycles, e.g., multiple task or project cycles. Therefore, appropriate reset or restart functionality has to be added.

Component behavior must be (fault-)tolerant and robust to handle unusual or unintended parameters or input values, e.g., a decrease in task size during development. This often requires additional provisions, e.g., limiters, guards, assertion checks, etc. Moreover, abstractions and generic measures are introduced to enable reuse in various contexts. The most important abstractions in the SimSWE library are:

- Generic time measure without a specific unit. Depending on the context, one unit of time can be an hour, a day, a month, etc.
- Generic size measure without a specific unit. Depending on the context, one unit of size can be a function point, a source line of code, a module, a test case, etc. Moreover, the input and output signals are designed in most cases as size rates, e.g., changes of size. This facilitates piped interfacing.
- Generic productivity. The unit of productivity depends on the size and time units chosen for the respective component.

2.3 Generic Description

Each component is defined and specified by a tool independent generic description. This description should enable an assessment of the component without access to a specific tool and the transfer and implementation of the component in any (appropriate) environment.

Logic, formulas, and continuous time dynamics are specified using standard mathematical notations, e.g., differential or difference equations. Discrete event flows or operations are most often described by graphical representations, e.g., UML state machine diagrams.

The generic description of the currently implemented components and example simulations are available at [13].

2.4 Reference Implementation

For the reference implementation of the SimSWE library, the MATLAB / Simulink environment has been chosen as tool basis. It is based on a continuous time simulation engine but encompasses discrete event extensions as well. MATLAB / Simulink is a well established tool in many engineering disciplines. It contains an extensive set of predefined functions and building blocks for logic, mathematical evaluations, descriptions of dynamic systems, and signal generation, display, and analysis. Based on that, new components and component libraries can be easily defined and incorporated. Therefore, MATLAB / Simulink offers all the functionalities necessary to implement the SimSWE components and provides a comprehensive and mature development environment for model developers to build upon.

There are other tools with similar capabilities. A detailed tool evaluation, however, is beyond the scope of this paper. Instead, other reference implementations are encouraged to gain a more in depth understanding of the (sometimes subtle) distinctions, advantages and disadvantages - all based on the common grounding of the generic descriptions.

2.5 Structure of the Library

The SimSWE library is partitioned into two sets in order to account for different simulation paradigms as well different prerequisites for the reference implementation:

1. **SimSWE (basic)**
   This set contains continuous time based components only. The reference implementation of these components uses only the basic MATLAB / Simulink configuration without add-ons.
2. **SimSWE (extended)**
   This set contains components that also use discrete event blocks or models. The reference implementation of these components requires Simulink add-ons (at present Stateflow® and SimEvent®).

Each set is currently divided into six sub-collections representing different types of model components: Generators, Estimators, Generic Activities, Generic Processes, Management Components, and Utilities (see Section 3).

3 Component Overview

This section provides a basic overview of the status and the direction of SimSWE development. All components listed below are already implemented. However, the list of components as well as their systematics are expected to grow and evolve in the future. A documentation of each component can be found at [13].

3.1 SimSWE (Basic)

Generators

- *RequirementsGenerator* generates requirements for a project as a set of number-cost-value tuples. The value of all requirements and the cost of unimplemented requirements are randomly updated during simulation according to volatility parameters. The output requirements can be prioritized according to information such as cost, value, or cost-benefit (value per cost). The component is based on [11].

– *FunctionPointGenerator* generates function points for a project based on a set of characterising parameters.

Estimators

– *COCOMOIIEarlyDesign* estimates a project's cost and duration before the entire architecture is determined. It uses 7 Cost Driver and 5 Scale Factors. The component is based on COCOMO II [3].
– *COCOMOIIPostArchitecture* estimates a project's cost and duration based on detailed architecture parameters. It uses 17 Cost Driver and 5 Scale Factors. The component is based on COCOMO II [3].
– *SLOCEstimatorBasedOnFunctionPoints* estimates a project's source lines of code (SLOC) based on unadjusted function points using programming language conversion factors. The component is based on COCOMO II [3].
– *PerceivedQuality* models the asymmetric dynamic of the perception of quality changes: In case of a decrease of quality, the perceived quality follows this change very fast. In case of an increase, the build-up in perceived quality is much slower. The component is based on [8].

Generic Activities

– *Work* models the work on a given task or artifact (e.g., development) based on task size and productivity. The component is based on concepts of [8] and [4].
– *WorkWithCommunicationOverhead* models the work on a given task or artifact (e.g., development) based on task size considering communication overhead for adjusting the effective productivity. The component is based on concepts of [8] and [4].
– *WorkWithExperience* models the work on a given task or artifact (e.g., development) based on task size considering experience for adjusting the effective productivity. The component is based on concepts of [8] and [4].
– *VerificationAndValidation* models a verification and validation (V&V) activity.
– *WorkBreakdown* splits a task into pieces (smaller tasks).

Generic Processes

– *WorkTestRework* is a generic model of the production of an artifact followed by an associated V&V step. If the artifact does not yet meet the specified quality criterion, it is scheduled for rework. Rework and verification are cyclically traversed until the quality criterion is fulfilled. The model is based on [4].
– *SCRUM* is a generic model of an iterative process (SCRUM). Incoming tasks are split into assignments with a fixed time length (sprints). At the start of each assignment (sprint), the overall amount is broken down into tasks. Each task is performed as a Work-Test-Rework cycle. Unfinished tasks are rescheduled for the next assignment.

Management Components

- *HumanResourceChain* models recruitment and training of new staff using three levels of experience. The dynamics of a level depend on the promotion time and the quitting rate. The model is based on [8].
- *DelayBasedResourceAllocation* models allocation of additional resources in case of a pending delay of a project's end date.
- *BacklogBasedResourceDistribution* distributes available resources among a set of tasks such that each task will be finished at the same time (ideally). The model is based on [8].
- *CommunicationOverhead* models the communication overhead, which increases with the number of persons involved. The model is based on [8].
- *KnowledgeAcquisition* models the dynamics of learning and aging of knowledge and their influence on productivity in software development projects. The model is based on [8].
- *ExperienceAcquistion* models the influence of experience from actual or similar projects in the past on the current productivity. The productivity value grows log-linear with the actual experience value. The model is based on [8].
- *Training* models the assimilation process, when new personnel is added to a project. Adding new people to a project leads to a decrease of the productivity, because experienced developers are needed for training. The model is based on [8].

Utilities

- *LevelVariable* and *LevelVariableResetable* model a level variable with input and output rates.
- *AsymmetricDelay* allows to define different time constants for growth and attrition.
- *RateConversation* synchronizes two rates.
- *Size2Rate* converts a size into a rate.

3.2 SimSWE (Extended)

Generators

- *TaskGeneratorD* creates objects of type *Task* in random time intervals for discrete event processing.
- *MultiSizeTaskGeneratorD* creates large projects and smaller tasks in random time intervals for discrete event processing.

Generic Activities

- *ProductionD* models the work on a given task (e.g., development) based on a productivity. While the productivity is a continuous signal, a task is represented by a discrete object.
- *VerificationD* models the verification process on a given artifact or result. The artifact or result is represented by an discrete object of type *Task* with the attributes *Size* and *Quality*.

Generic Activities

– *WorkTestReworkD* is a generic model of the production of an artifact followed by an associated verification step using a discrete event object flow approach (instead of a time continuous representation, see *WorkTestRework*).

Management Components

– *KnowledgeAcquisitionExtended* demonstrates the dynamics of learning and aging of new learned knowledge. The extended version includes an knowledge level control to hold values in an specified range.

4 Examples

It is beyond the scope of this paper to present and discuss complete models and simulation examples, only the use of the SimSWE components are illustrated in this section. In the models shown below, the library components are drawn with a grey background. The other components are Simulink blocks providing glue logic, signal generation, and graphical display.

4.1 Prioritization Strategies

As a first example, the model presented in [11] is chosen. It simulates results of different requirements prioritization strategies with respect to cost effort or value in the presence of volatility. The core algorithm – randomized requirement generation and subsequent prioritizations – is represented by the *Requirements-Generator* component, which generates requirement sets which are subsequently prioritized according to some strategy (e.g. highest to lowest cost-benefit).

In order to complete a simulation model, i.e., to compute an actual throughput, a component resembling the actual development is needed. In [11], this has been emulated by a time delay proportional to the cost, i.e., a very simple development with constant productivity. The SimSWE model for this is presented in Figure 1.

In the context of the SimSWE library, this can easily be refined. As an example, the *WorkWithExperience* component is chosen, which incorporates a model for the increase of productivity during the course of a task due to familiarization and gained experience. This represents task-switching more realistically than a constant productivity devaluating requirements with small costs (short development time) to a certain amount, because their realization could not leverage the full productivity.

The refined model is depicted in Figure 2. The parameters were chosen to represent a moderate requirement volatility, a prioritization strategy with respect to *cost-benefit*, i.e., the highest *Value/Cost* requirements first, and an iterative re-prioritization during development according to the work performed as specified by *WorkWithExperience*.

A simulation run is shown in Figure 3. As expected, the cost-benefit at each step decreases during the course of the simulation because due to the prioritization, the requirements with the highest cost-benefit are implemented at the beginning.

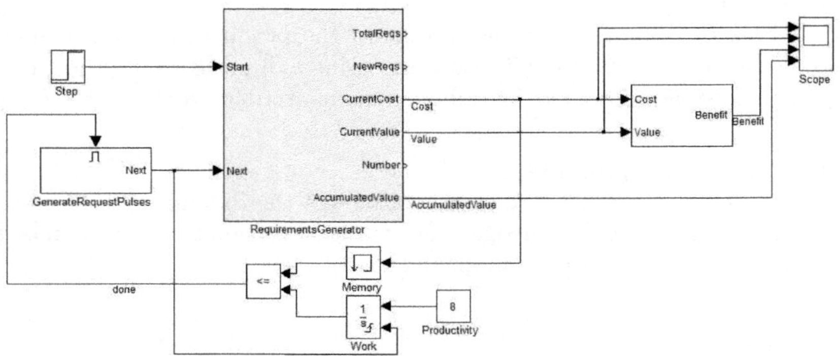

Fig. 1. Model for requirement prioritization analysis following [11]

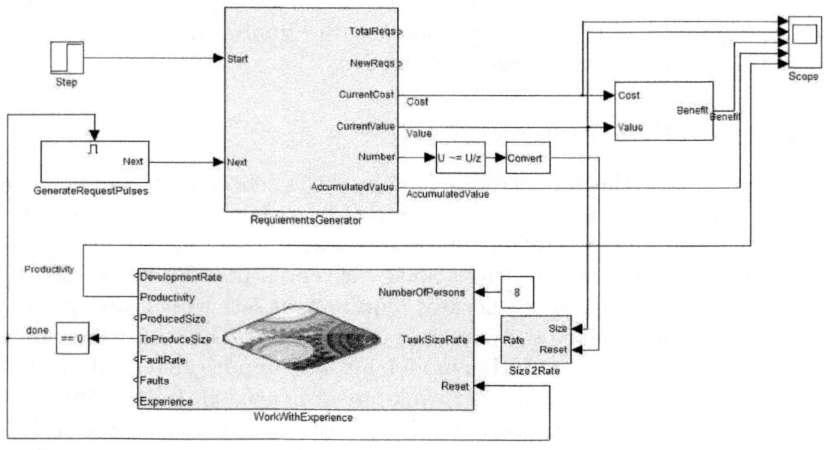

Fig. 2. Refined model for requirement prioritization analysis

However, this decrease is not monotonic due to the requirement volatility simulated as randomized changes of value and cost. The last plot in Figure 3 shows the changes of productivity due to familiarization with the respective requirements, development environment, and increased development skill.

This example demonstrates how the SimSWE framework and component library eases model development and enables the exploration of more complex simulations through reuse and extension.

4.2 Resource Allocation

As a second example, a dynamic resource allocation strategy taken from [8] is explored. The strategy has the goal to divide resources between different tasks such

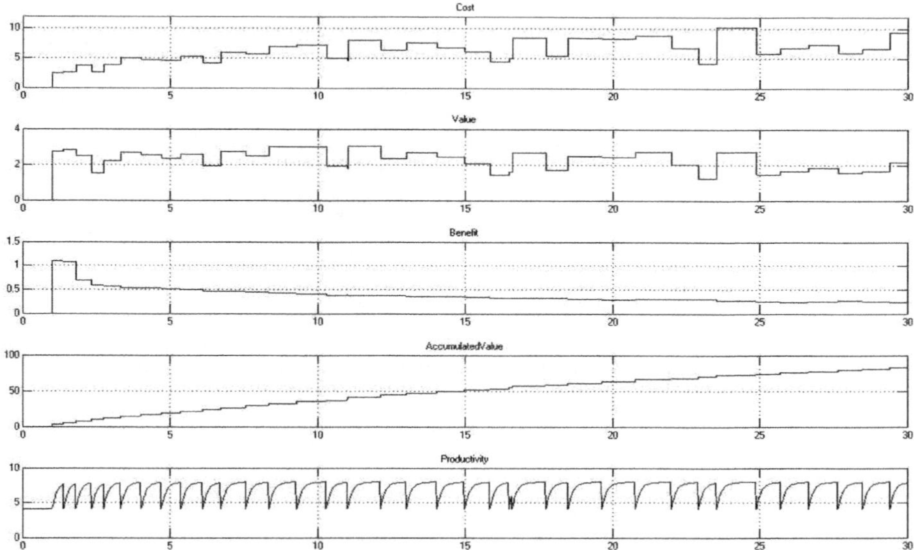

Fig. 3. Results of a simulation run of the model depicted in Figure 2

that all task are finished at the same time. This would be an optimal strategy in terms of a conjoint duration (e.g., if the tasks are work packages within a project). The strategy allocates the resources according to the estimated productivities for the respective task and the ratio of the respective task backlogs such that tasks with a larger expected workload get proportionally more resources. This strategy is implemented in the SimSWE component *BacklogBasedResourceDistribution*.

In the case of known, constant task sizes and productivities, the resource allocation would be constant as well. However, in the case of changing, unknown task sizes and productivities, a continuously adaptation would be necessary. But this is not a realistic project setting. Even in an agile management environment, resource reassignments will occur only within finite time steps. Therefore, the component calls for a fixed time interval between reassignments.

The model of Figure 4 is designed to test this strategy and to analyse the effects of various lengths of such reassignment intervals in the presence of "perturbances" like changing task sizes and time varying productivities (e.g., due to knowledge build-up). In this model, three SimSWE components are used: *BacklogBasedResourceDistribution*, *KnowledgeAcquistion*, and *Work*. Note, that many Simulink components (including *KnowledgeAcquistion* and *Work*) are able to process vectorized inputs concurrently, which is equivalent to placing instances of the component in parallel. By this means, the model of Figure 4 processes two tasks in parallel.

The *KnowledgeAcquistion* component is used to represent a knowledge build-up for each task. It is parametrized such that task T1 starts with a relative

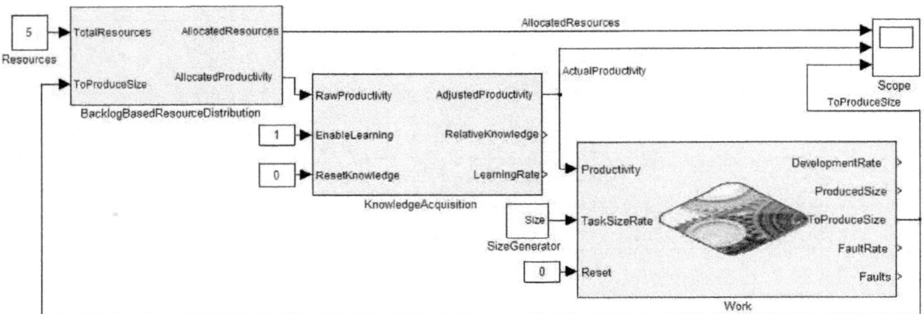

Fig. 4. Model for dynamic resource allocation under perturbances

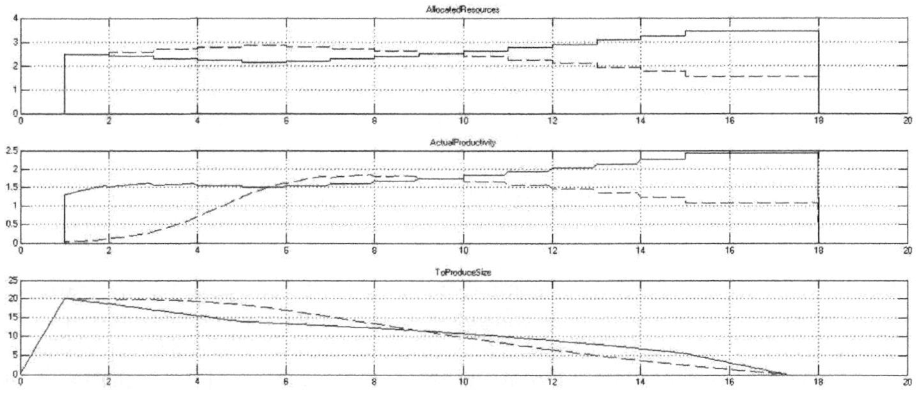

Fig. 5. Results of a simulation run of the model depicted in Figure 4. The values for task T1 are drawn as solid line, the values for task T2 as dashed line.

knowledge level of 50% while task T2 starts with a level of 0%. At the beginning, both task are defined with the same size. Between time $t = 5$ and time $t = 15$, task T1 is gradually increased by 50%.

Both effects are not taken into account in the resource allocation strategy in the first place. Nevertheless, the dynamic adaption is able to adjust to these perturbances as shown by the simulation, see Figure 5: The chart at the top shows the allocated resources. At the beginning, both tasks get equal resources due to their equal size. However, task T2 has initially a smaller effective productivity due to the lower initial knowledge level causing a smaller reduction in the backlog (the variable *ToProduceSize* as shown in the bottom chart). Therefore, task T2 get more resources assigned in the next assignment step. After about half of the simulation time has elapsed, the balance of resource assignments turns around, because the knowledge build-up (note the effect of the logistic learning curve in left half the chart *ActualProductivity*) saturates and the size of task T1 increases.

Such a model of an optimal resource allocation can also be used as a benchmark for other strategies.

5 Use and Participation

As stated in Section 1, the SimSWE library is developed and shared as Open Source. The license mode LPGL [6] was chosen because it permits the use of components in a proprietary context which might be desired or required for certain applications e.g. for security or competitive advantages. The latest version of the documentation including the generic descriptions is publicly available at [13]. Currently, the reference implementation is not published on the Web but available by request.

Of course, it is important to understand that the library and all components are still under development. Not all scenarios have been fully tested and it is realistic to assume that there are undetected errors and issues. Therefore, no guarantees can be granted. However, the source code is freely available for review and criticism.

The SimSWE venture to develop a comprehensive and trustworthy library can only succeed as a shared effort. Therefore, anyone is invited to participate and contribute to this development in any form. Some suggested ways to participate include:

- using the library components and contributing an example simulation,
- critically reviewing the descriptions and implementations (and reporting any error or issue detected),
- suggesting components,
- sharing of descriptions or models, which can be realized as a component, or
- describing and implementing components.

Any such contribution is welcome and appreciated!

6 Summary

SimSWE is a library of components for modeling software engineering tasks and processes. It consists of a generic description of the underlying models and a reference implementation as a Simulink library. At the current status, the library already contains more than thirty components. It is available (and further developed) as Open Source with our example simulations.

The advantages of such a library seem to be obvious: simulation models can be developed faster by using available building blocks and more realistic, and thus also more complex models can be build using predesigned, pretested parts encapsulating complexity. Indeed, the library has already proven useful in quickly replicating and refining previous simulations that were cumbersome to develop and extend and exemplified in Section 5.

Furthermore, a library of generally recognized relations and dynamics of software engineering related issues might also be used in the context of education and training: the generic descriptions can serve as a basis for discussions while their implications can visually be demonstrated by simulation runs. Up to now, there was no comparable library available for software process modeling and simulation. SimSWE should help to fill this gap and encourage stimulating and fruitful simulation based software process research.

References

1. Abdel-Hamid, T., Madnick, S.E.: Software project dynamics: an integrated approach. Prentice-Hall, Inc., Upper Saddle River (1991)
2. Angkasaputra, N., Pfahl, D.: Making software process simulation modeling agile and pattern-based. In: Proceedings of the 5th International Workshop on Software Process Simulation Modeling (ProSim 2004), pp. 222–227 (2004)
3. Boehm, B., Abts, C., Winsor, A., Chulani, S., Clark, B.K., Horowitz, E., Madachy, R., Reifer, D., Steece, B.: Software Cost Estimation with Cocomo II. Prentice Hall International, Englewood Cliffs (2000)
4. Garousi, V., Khosrovian, K., Pfahl, D.: A customizable pattern-based software process simulation model: design, calibration and application. Software Process: Improvement and Practice 14(3), 165–180 (2009)
5. Kellner, M.I., Madachy, R.J., Raffo, D.: Software process simulation modeling: Why? what? how? Journal of Systems and Software 46(2-3), 91–105 (1999)
6. GNU: lesser general public license, `http://www.gnu.org/copyleft/lesser.html` (last accessed on 2010-01-05)
7. Madachy, R.J.: Reusable model structures and behaviors for software processes. In: Wang, Q., Pfahl, D., Raffo, D.M., Wernick, P. (eds.) SPW 2006 and ProSim 2006. LNCS, vol. 3966, pp. 222–233. Springer, Heidelberg (2006)
8. Madachy, R.J.: Software Process Dynamics. John Wiley & Sons, Chichester (2008)
9. Pfahl, D.: Simkit – a software process simulation model construction kit in support of empirical research. In: Proceedings of the 5th ACM-IEEE International Symposium on Empirical Software Engineering (Volume II: Short Papers and Posters), ISESE 2006, pp. 3–5 (2006)
10. Pfahl, D.: Software process simulation frameworks in support of packaging and transferring empirical evidence. In: Basili, V.R., Rombach, H.D., Schneider, K., Kitchenham, B., Pfahl, D., Selby, R.W. (eds.) Empirical Software Engineering Issues. LNCS, vol. 4336, p. 133. Springer, Heidelberg (2007)
11. Port, D., Olkov, A., Menzies, T.: Using simulation to investigate requirements prioritization strategies. In: ASE, pp. 268–277. IEEE, Los Alamitos (2008)
12. Raffo, D., Nayak, U., Wakeland, W.: Implementing generalized process simulation models. In: Pfahl, D., Raffo, D., Rus, I., Wernick, P. (eds.) Proceedings of the 6th International Workshop on Software Process Simulation Modeling (ProSim 2005), Fraunhofer IRB, St. Louis (2005)
13. SimSWE-Wiki, `http://simswe.ei.htwg-konstanz.de/wiki_simswe/index.php/Main_Page` (last accessed on 2010-04-10)
14. Zhang, H., Kitchenham, B., Pfahl, D.: Software process simulation modeling: Facts, trends and directions. In: APSEC, pp. 59–66. IEEE Comp. Society, Los Alamitos (2008)
15. Zhang, H., Kitchenham, B., Pfahl, D.: Software process simulation over the past decade: trends discovery from a systematic review. In: Rombach, H.D., Elbaum, S.G., Münch, J. (eds.) ESEM, pp. 345–347. ACM, New York (2008)

Applications of a Generic Work-Test-Rework Component for Software Process Simulation

Thomas Birkhölzer[1], Dietmar Pfahl[2,3], and Michael Schuster[1]

[1] University of Applied Sciences Konstanz, Konstanz, Germany
[2] University of Oslo, Oslo, Norway
[3] University of Calgary, Calgary, Canada

Abstract. Software process simulation can be a valuable support for process analysis and improvement provided the respective model development can focus on the issues at hand without spending effort on basically modeling everything from scratch. Rather, the modeling groundwork should readily be available as building blocks for (re)use. In the domain of software engineering, the work-test-rework cycle is one of the most important reoccurring patterns – at the level of a individual tasks as well as at the level of process phases or projects in general. Therefore, a generic reusable simulation component, which captures and represents this pattern, has been realized as part of the SimSWE library. This *WorkTestRework* component is designed such that it provides comprehensive adaptability and flexibility to be used in different simulation scenarios and process contexts. This paper introduces the component and substantiates this claim by modeling typical, but very different process scenarios based on this component.

1 Introduction

During the last years, quantitative process modeling and simulation has been used to analyze various questions and issues in the domain of software engineering, see, e.g., [6] and [13] and the references therein for an overview of this field. At the beginning [1], models had to be designed from scratch developing and implementing every part of the model by oneself. However, this is obviously not reasonable in the long run. Therefore, research has been conducted in the last years to develop reusable patterns [2] [5], structures [8], or models [9]. In [5], a generic work-test-rework cycle was identified as one of the most important reoccurring activity patterns. For a formal analysis and description of rework activities see also [3].

Building on these results, this work goes one step further by introducing an *encapsulated* work-test-rework simulation component called *WorkTestRework* as a generic *ready-to-use* building block suitable for a wide range of simulation applications. This will help to develop models faster and to approach more complex modeling and simulation scenarios by reusing commonplace functionality. Thus,

J. Münch, Y. Yang, and W. Schäfer (Eds.): ICSP 2010, LNCS 6195, pp. 333–344, 2010.

the main contribution of this work is to improve reusability of simulation applications, not the discussion of structural details of the work-test-rework pattern or of a single application scenario. Therefore, this paper demonstrates the use of the *WorkTestRework* component in different modeling contexts (without elaborating them in detail) in order to substantiate the claim of generic nature and broad applicability. As a first context, sequential process models are discussed in Section 3. The second context is an iterative process model presented in Section 4. Before that, the component is introduced in Section 2. The paper concludes with a summarizing discussion in Section 5.

2 *WorkTestRework* Component

The *WorkTestRework* component is based on [5]. It models the production of an artifact followed by associated verification and validation (V&V) steps. If the artifact does not yet meet the specified quality criterion, it is scheduled for rework. Rework and V&V are cyclically traversed until the quality criterion is fulfilled. In this case, the artifact is released. Typical artifacts are requirement specifications, designs, code, user stories, test cases, etc. However, any other task, which requires effort and results in a revisable delivery, e.g., a make-or-buy evaluation, could be modeled by this pattern as well.

The component is part of SimSWE, a library of components for modeling and simulation of software engineering processes [12]. SimSWE provides a generic, implementation independent description of each component and a reference implementation as Simulink® library. Therefore, the *WorkTestRework* component can either be directly used as a Simulink component or realized in another simulation environment using the generic description. The SimSWE library is available under the GNU Lesser General Public License [7] at request. A description of the component (and the models presented in Section 3 and 4) can be found in the documentation at [12].

The outline of the component is shown in Figure 1. It has 8 inputs (values depending dynamically an other parts of the model), 4 parameters (values which are constant during an simulation), and 6 outputs. The parameters are not shown in Figure 1, because in Simulink they are entered using a mask.

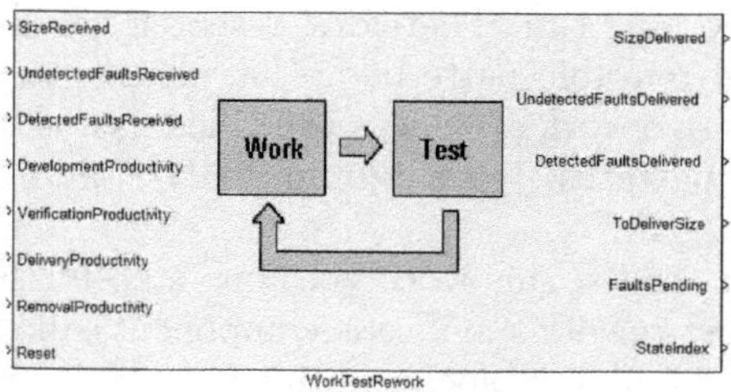

Fig. 1. *WorkTestRework* component

Inputs:
- *SizeReceived*: Rate of the designated size of the artifact.
- *UndetectedFaultsReceived*: Rate of the undetected faults in the designated artifact caused by undetected faults in the input.
- *DetectedFaultsReceived*: Rate of the known faults detected or caused by preceding activities.
- *DevelopmentProductivity*: Productivity of the initial work phase (development).
- *VerificationProductivity*: Productivity of the V&V step.
- *DeliveryProductivity*: Productivity of the delivery step.
- *RemovalProductivity*: Productivity of the rework step.
- *Reset*: Reset of the component to zero levels and idle state.

Parameters:
- *AverageVerEffectiveness*: Effectiveness of the V&V step as percentage of faults detected.
- *QualityLimit*: Release threshold with respect to the number of faults pending divided by the size of the artifact.
- *AverageFaultInjectionPerSizeUnit*: Number of faults injected during the initial development step.
- *AverageFaultInjectionPerFaultRemoval*: Number of faults injected during the rework step.

Outputs:
- *SizeDelivered*: Rate of the size of the artifact delivered. The artifact is delivered when the specified quality limit has been achieved.
- *UndetectedFaultsDelivered*: Rate of the undetected faults in the artifact delivered.
- *DetectedFaultsDelivered*: Rate of the known faults in the artifact delivered.
- *ToDeliverSize*: Designated[1] size of the artifact.
- *FaultsPending*: Current number of faults pending.
- *StateIndex*: Variable indicating the internal state of the artifact development: 0: idle (no activity); 1: the work step is active; 2: the rework step is active; 3: the V&V step is active; 4: the delivery step is active.

The first three inputs and the first three outputs are designed to connect *WorkTestRework*-components in a piped, sequential chain handing on artifacts, see Section 3 for examples. Designing these interfaces as rates simplifies the piped operation without additional handshake signals: an input, is interpreted as new assignment, if it is received before or after a release (*StateIndex* 0 or 4), or as changing size (e.g., caused by late requirements), if it is received during a ongoing development (*StateIndex* 1, 2, or 3).

The productivity inputs can be used to model dynamic resource allocation, e.g., due to resource build-up or competing assignments, as well as time varying productivity per resource, e.g., biased by training, experience, or motivation. In the SimSWE library, there are components available modeling these effects.

---

[1] In distinction to *SizeDelivered*, this output provides information about the (expected) size of the artifact prior to delivery, which might be useful in certain modeling contexts.

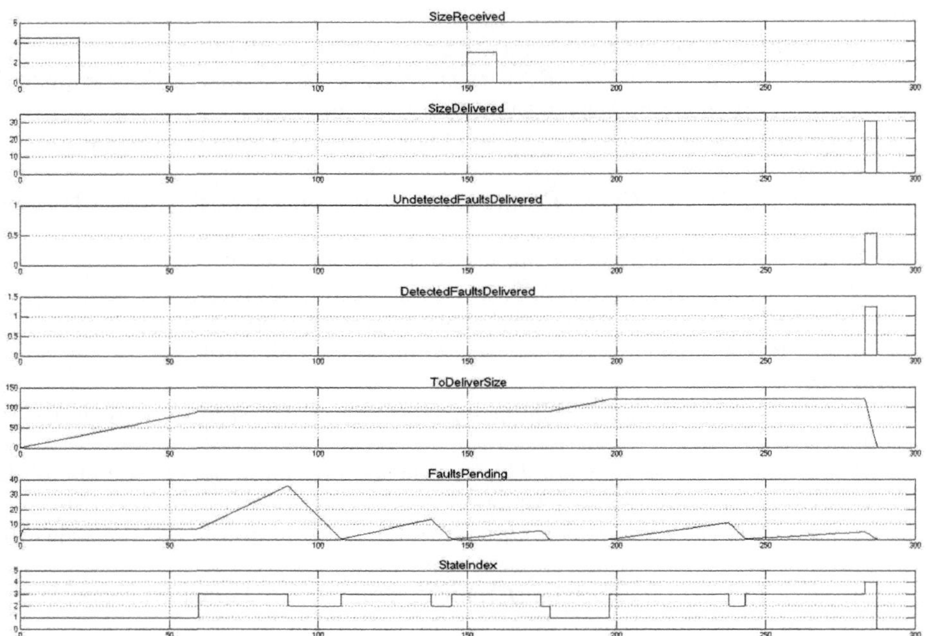

Fig. 2. Simulation run of an assignment with a late size increment

The interpretation of units is left to the user, e.g., depending on the context, one unit of time can be an hour, a day, a month, or one unit of size can be a function point, a source line of code, a module, a test case, etc. The units of productivity obviously depend on the size and time units chosen.

All inputs, parameters, and outputs (except *StateIndex*) are continuous variables assuming real values. If natural numbers are desired (e.g., for the number of faults), the real values could easily be rounded externally. However, a real value is maintained as output to allow to interpret 0.2 faults, e.g., as "probability of 20 percent to get one error" instead of rounding this to zero faults automatically.

Figure 2 shows a simulation demonstrating the typical behavior of the component. At the beginning, an assignment is received. At time 150, the assignment is enlarged by a late add-on. The areas under the rate signals (*SizeReceived*, *SizeDelivered*, *UndetectedFaultsDelivered*, *DetectedFaultsDelivered*) represent the actual sizes and fault counts. The *StateIndex* chart shows the cyclic traversal through the states work, V&V, and rework until the quality limit is reached and the artifact is delivered.

Note, that any work-test-rework activity delivers detected as well as undetected faults. To avoid the delivery of undetected faults, V&V effectiveness would have to be 100%. To avoid the delivery of detected faults, the fault injection during removal would have to be zero (because each V&V step is always followed by a rework step). Both are unrealistic values.

3 Sequential Processes

As a first exemplary context for the *WorkTestRework* component, sequential processes similar to a waterfall process, e.g. like the German “V-Modell” [4], are discussed. Such processes are divided into distinct, sequential phases. A subsequent phase starts only, if the release criteria of the preceding phase is met.

It could be argued that each phase follows structurally a work-test-rework pattern despite the differences and specialities, e.g., a requirement analysis phase focuses on requirement engineering (“work”), but has a review (“test”) and rework at the end as well. On the other hand, a test phase requires also a (short) test-setup (“work”). Therefore, a sequential process as a whole can be modeled as a sequence of work-test-rework activities. Figure 3 shows a model using six *WorkTestRework* components representing the phases (1) requirement analysis, (2) design, (3) implementation, (4) module test, (5) integration test, and (6) system test. The artifacts to be developed or worked on in each phase are the sets of deliverables of the respective phase, e.g., the requirement specification or tested modules.

The different characteristics of each phase (e.g., different importance and duration of work, V&V, and rework steps, different levels of effectiveness of the respective V&V practices) can be expressed using the productivity inputs and the parameters *AverageVerEffectiveness* and *QualityLimit*.

The flow of artifacts in such a process is straightforward: a delivered artifact is handed on to the next phase, i.e. the output *SizeDelivered* is just connected to the “next” input *SizeReceived*. Different size units in the different phases, e.g., size measured in function points in the requirement analysis phase and in source lines of code (SLOC) in the implementation phase, can be accounted for by a multiplication with an appropriate scaling factor. For the sake of simplicity, this is omitted in the model of Figure 3. A decomposition, e.g., into modules implemented in parallel, can be modeled as well by a split of the respective size. To this end, the *WorkTestRework* component can either be duplicated or used with vectorized signals (actually, the inputs, parameters, and outputs of the

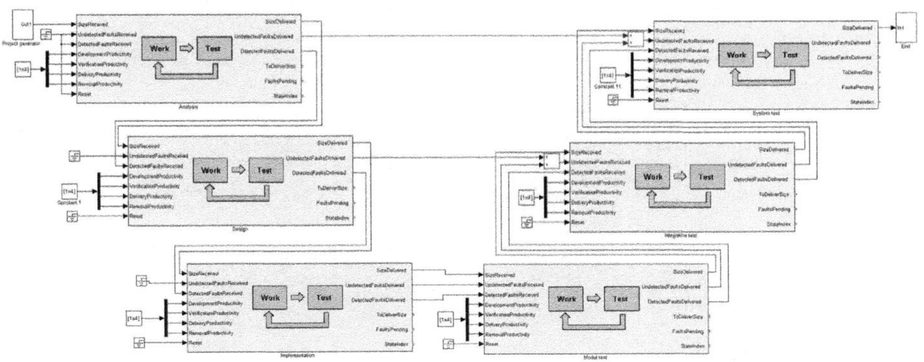

Fig. 3. Model of a sequential process with simplified fault flow

component can defined as arrays such that each index into the arrays effectively represents an independent processing channel).

An important issue is the flow of faults within such a sequential process. The model of Figure 3 represents a simple approach (suitable for small projects or organizations): First, the detected faults of a phase, which are below the quality limit (i.e. which are not reworked but delivered), are handled in the next phase as leftovers. To model this practice, the outputs *DetectedFaultsDelivered* are connected to the "next" input *DetectedFaultsReceived.* Second, a simplified categorization of the different test phases of the V-Modell assumes that the deliverable of the implementation phase is tested in the module test, the deliverable of the design phase in the integration test, and the deliverable of the requirement analysis in the system test. Therefore, undetected faults of the implementation phase are most likely to be found in the module test, undetected faults of the design phase in the integration test, and undetected faults of the requirement analysis phase in the system test. The undetected fault rates are connected accordingly in the model of Figure 3. Third, faults detected during a test phase, i.e., during module, integration, or system test are corrected within the respective test phase as rework without returning to a previous phase. Figure 3 represents this approach because there is no feedback from the test phases into earlier process phases.

However, the process of Figure 3 can be refined to represent more sophisticated fault handling procedures. For example, in many processes faults detected during a test phase are reposted as a change request into the respective upstream process phase, i.e., detected faults within a test phase trigger the development of a new artifact (change request deliverable) in the respective upstream phase. Subsequently, this artifact (e.g., a design change) follows the normal path, i.e, runs through the other process phases (implementation, module test, integration test, system test). Figure 4 includes such an extension as feedback from the test

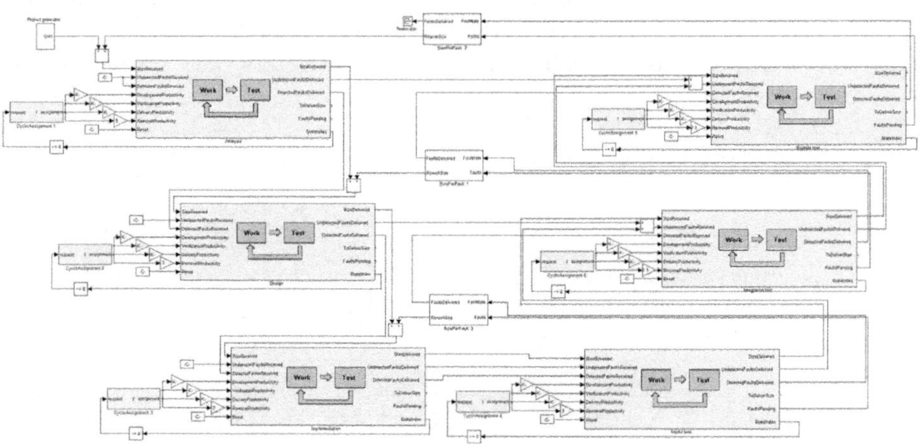

Fig. 4. Model of a sequential process with reposting of fault corrections into upstream process phases

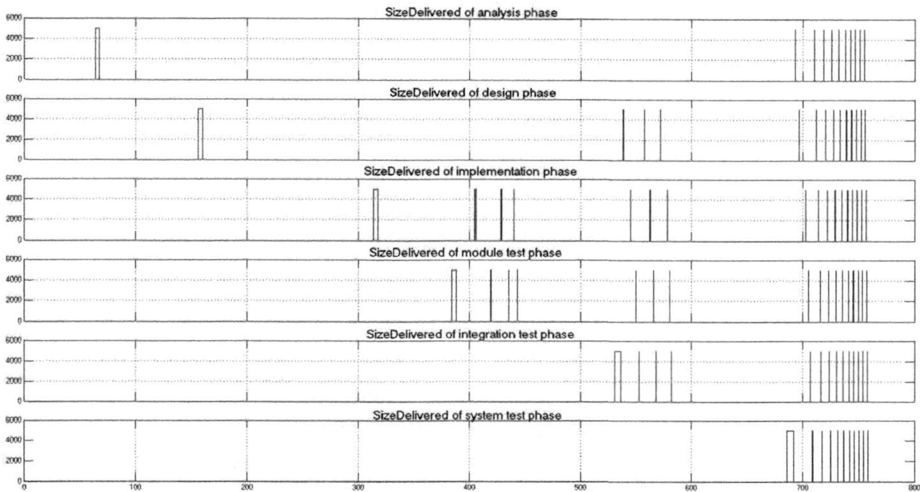

Fig. 5. Simulation of a sequential process with reposting of fault corrections into upstream process phases

phases into the respective upstream phases (each test phase has a feedback into only one upstream phase again just for simplicity).

Figure 5 shows a simulation of such an extended process. In the charts, only the deliverable rates of the different phases are shown, the wider the peak, the larger the deliverable. The reposting of the correction assignments (change requests) and their traversing through the other process phases are the series of small peaks following the main deliverable (wide peak). Note that due to their small size, these change requests are processed very fast (almost appearing as parallelism in the diagram).

Judging from the outcomes of Figure 5 only, the delay of a project due to the re-traversing of the upstream phases seems reasonable because the change requests traverse very fast through the process. However, this is only true, if the required resources are always immediately available, which is not a realistic assumption. Therefore, the model of Figure 4 contains a second set of extensions to represent an organization in which each process phase belongs to different organizational sub-units with own resources, but each sub-unit deals with only one task at a time. This means, a request of a project gets all the resources of a phase, but only on a first come first serve basis. Requests of projects arriving after the resources are claimed, are postponed until the preceding request is completely finished. The resulting queue is ordered according to the project number, which reflects the project start, i.e., older projects get priority.

To model such a scenario, the execution of multiple projects can be simulated in the model of Figure 4 using vectorized signals as mentioned above. The dimension of the vectors, i.e., the number of the projects, can be defined just by a parameter. The competing, mutually exclusive resource allocation is realized by the

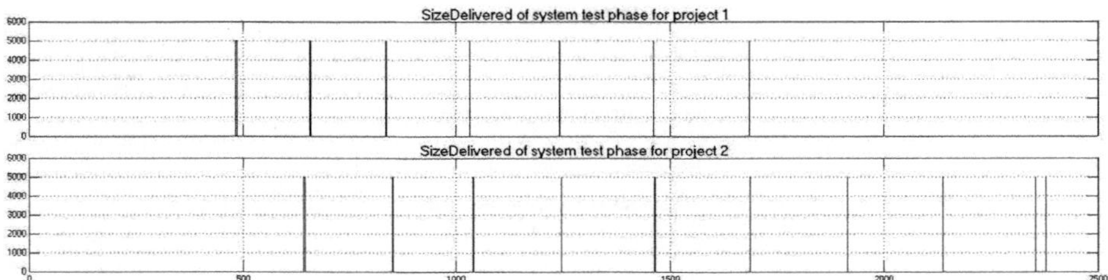

Fig. 6. Multi-project simulation of a sequential process with reposting of fault corrections into upstream process phases

component *CyclicAssignment* that basically switches the respective productivities on and off (a waiting task gets productivity zero).

Figure 6 shows the result of such a multi-project simulation displaying only the deliverable rates of the system test phase. The simulation demonstrates a drastic increase of project duration (arrival of the last deliverable after about 1700 time units in Figure 6 instead of about 760 time units in Figure 5) because the change request tasks – although small by themselves – are delayed by the other projects. This immediately suggests that more sophisticated resource allocation strategies should be devised, which could than again be tested using the simulation model.

4 Iterative Processes

As second context using a work-test-rework pattern, an iterative process model is presented modeling the Scrum framework [10] [11]. In a Scrum process, the project is divided into small tasks called user stories which are grouped into sprints. Nevertheless, these user stories are iteratively analyzed, designed, implemented ("work"), verified and validated ("test"), and corrected ("rework"). Therefore, the work-test-rework-cycle forms the core of an iterative process as well however processing singular pieces (user stories) instead of deliverables for a whole project as in Section 3.

For an iteration, the implementation of the user stories (tasks) are grouped into time-boxed sprints with a defined length, typically about 30 days. At the start of a sprint, the content of the sprint is fixed in the sprint planning meeting as sprint backlog. During the sprint, this backlog is worked off piecewise. Figure 7 shows the respective model of a sprint. The core element is the *WorkTestRework* component, which processes the single tasks (user stories).

The subsystem *ResourceManagement*, see Figure 8, contains the block modeling the sprint backlog (component named SprintBacklog). This block is a *WorkBreakdown* component, which is also part of the SimSWE library. The basic functionality of this component is a randomized break down of a larger artifact or task (sprint backlog) into smaller pieces (user stories). The characteristics of this decomposition can be configured by parameters. Finished artifacts (realizations of the user stories including code, test cases, documentation, etc.) are

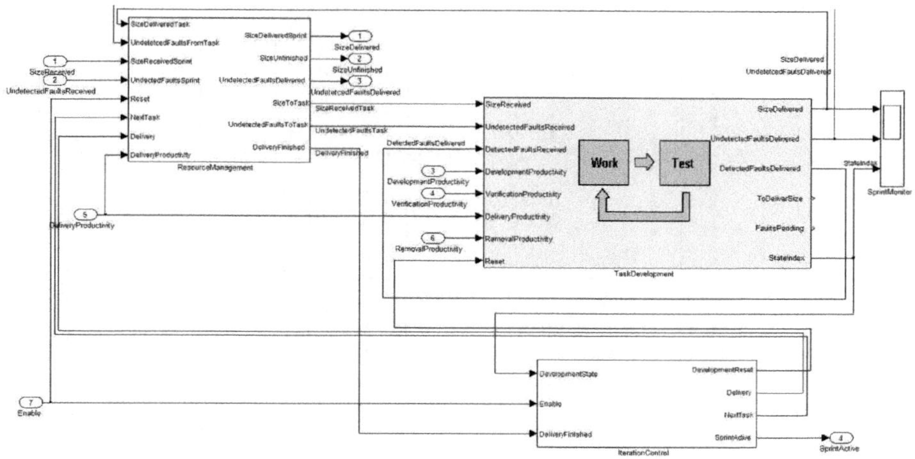

Fig. 7. Model of the subsystem *Sprint* of a Scrum process

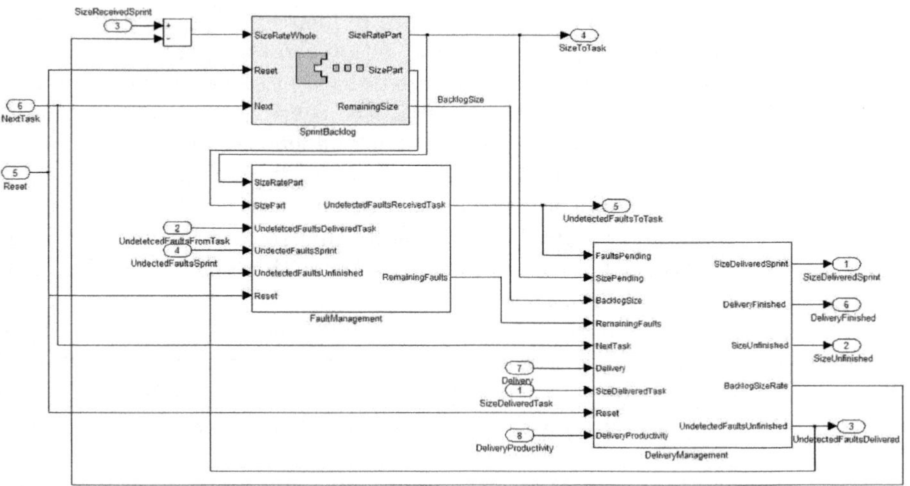

Fig. 8. Subsystem *ResourceManagement* of a sprint of a Scrum process

collected in the subsystem *DeliveryManagement* and delivered at the end of a sprint.

Beside the artifacts, faults must be handled as well. The fault handling in a Scrum process is less well defined. For the model it is assumed, that detected faults are corrected as soon as possible. Therefore, delivered faults from the *WorkTestRework* component are directly fed back as inputs to be corrected within the context of the next task.

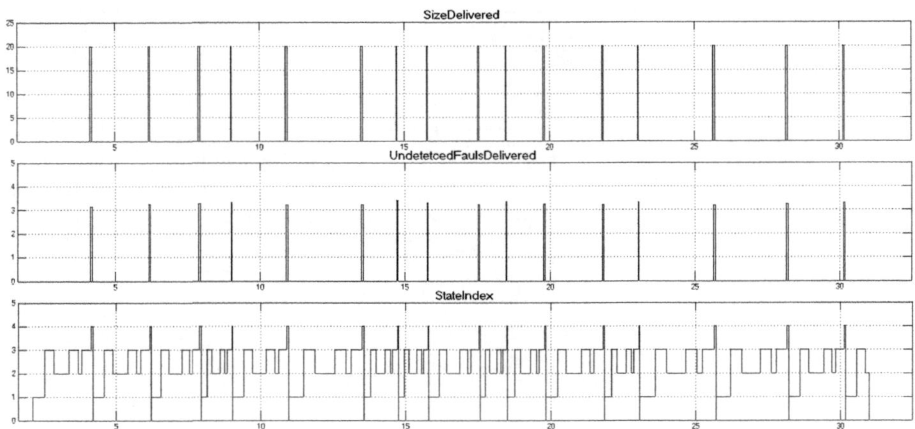

Fig. 9. Simulation of a single sprint in the context of a Scrum process

Undetected faults, on the other hand, are hidden in the delivered artifacts and need to be detected before any removal action can take place. However, the V&V effectiveness of faults within the context of a user story will be different to the V&V effectiveness of undetected faults in the context of another user story. Therefore, it is not appropriate to just feed back undetected errors into the next cycle. Instead, they are accumulated within the subsystem *FaultManagement*. A fraction of the resulting fault level (representing the accumulated hidden faults in the project) is routed to any new task according to a parameter specifying the effectiveness of the V&V steps of a user story with respect to faults in the deliverables of another user story.

Figure 9 shows a simulation run of a single sprint. The two top-level charts depict the delivery of the single tasks, the lower chart displays the cycling through the work-test-rework states for each task. Note, that the last task is canceled and not delivered (state 4 is not reached), because a sprint has a fixed, predefined duration.

A Scrum process consists of an iteration of such sprints as described above, the respective model is shown in Figure 10 containing the subsystem *Sprint*. The assignment for each sprint is taken from a product backlog (block named *ProductBacklog*, which is iteratively worked off similar to the sprint backlog. It is also be modeled using the *WorkBreakdown* component. Unfinished parts of the sprint backlog are (re)added to the product backlog at the end of a sprint.

Undetected faults of a sprint are accumulated as well. Again, a parameterizable fraction of these undetected faults are fed back into the next sprint iteration representing the faults, which might be detected in the next sprint representing the cross-sprint V&V coverage as described above.

Figure 11 shows a simulation of the complete Scrum process. The upper chart demonstrates the iterative project completion by the deliverables of the sprints.

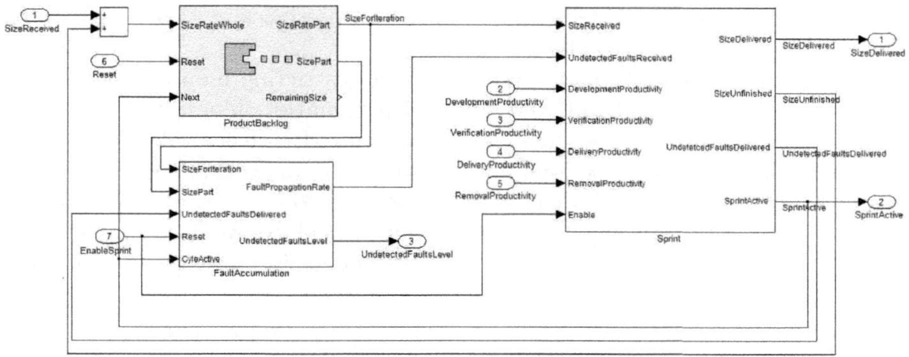

Fig. 10. Model of of a Scrum process consisting of an iteration of sprints

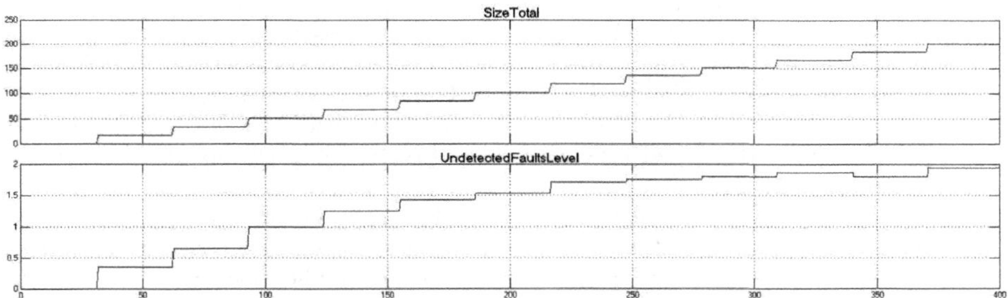

Fig. 11. Simulation of project developed with a Scrum process

The lower chart indicates that the number of undetected faults increases at the beginning, but approaches an approximately stable level in the second half of the simulation time. This is due to the modeling of a fixed V&V coverage across user stories or sprints respectively as described above. It might be an interesting issue for further research to assess, whether this model reflects real world observations, and to devise more appropriate models otherwise.

The model of the Scrum process as shown in Figure 10 is in turn encapsulated as a *Scrum* component as part of the SimSWE library. A complete description of the component can be found in the related documentation at [12].

5 Discussion

The examples above demonstrate that the *WorkTestRework* component can be used in different contexts representing different work types and artifacts (requirement analysis, coding, test) as well as different scopes (project, task) just by appropriate interfacing and parametrization. Based on this, effects of different process settings, e.g., verification and validation intensities at various phases, can be analyzed just by different parameter settings. Moreover, extensions could easily be added to the model using the generic interfaces as demonstrated for fault handling and resource allocation.

By providing essential functionality without restricting adaptability or flexibility, even complex modeling and simulation scenarios (like the multi-project simulation or the iteration workflow) can be realized with feasible effort. Thus, the generic *WorkTestRework* component could be an important support for process developers and modelers enabling to focus on the issues at hand by alleviating the need to (re)implement generic parts. Such reusable components are considered an important groundwork for next generation process modeling and simulation.

References

1. Abdel-Hamid, T., Madnick, S.E.: Software project dynamics: an integrated approach. Prentice-Hall, Inc., Upper Saddle River (1991)
2. Angkasaputra, N., Pfahl, D.: Making software process simulation modeling agile and pattern-based. In: Proceedings of the 5th International Workshop on Software Process Simulation Modeling (ProSim 2004), pp. 222–227 (2004)
3. Cass, A.G., Sutton Jr., S.M., Osterweil, L.J.: Formalizing rework in software processes. In: Oquendo, F. (ed.) EWSPT 2003. LNCS, vol. 2786, pp. 16–31. Springer, Heidelberg (2003)
4. Das V-Modell, `http://v-modell.iabg.de` (last accessed on 2010-01-05)
5. Garousi, V., Khosrovian, K., Pfahl, D.: A customizable pattern-based software process simulation model: design, calibration and application. Software Process: Improvement and Practice 14(3), 165–180 (2009)
6. Kellner, M.I., Madachy, R.J., Raffo, D.: Software process simulation modeling: Why? what? how? Journal of Systems and Software 46(2-3), 91–105 (1999)
7. GNU lesser general public license, `http://www.gnu.org/copyleft/lesser.html` (last accessed on 2010-01-05)
8. Madachy, R.J.: Reusable model structures and behaviors for software processes. In: Wang, Q., Pfahl, D., Raffo, D.M., Wernick, P. (eds.) SPW 2006 and ProSim 2006. LNCS, vol. 3966, pp. 222–233. Springer, Heidelberg (2006)
9. Raffo, D., Nayak, U., Wakeland, W.: Implementing generalized process simulation models. In: Pfahl, D., Raffo, D., Rus, I., Wernick, P. (eds.) Proceedings of the 6th International Workshop on Software Process Simulation Modeling (ProSim 2005), Fraunhofer IRB, St. Louis (2005)
10. Schwaber, K.: Scrum development process. In: Proceedings of the Conference on Object-Oriented Programing Systems, Languages, and Applications (OOPSLA 1995) Workshop on Business Object Design and Implementation (1995)
11. ScrumAlliance, `http://www.scrumalliance.org` (last accessed on 2010-01-05)
12. SimSWE-Wiki, `http://simswe.ei.htwg-konstanz.de/wiki_simswe/index.php/Main_Page` (last accessed on 2010-04-10)
13. Zhang, H., Kitchenham, B., Pfahl, D.: Software process simulation modeling: Facts, trends and directions. In: APSEC, pp. 59–66. IEEE Comp. Society, Los Alamitos (2008)

An Empirical Study of Lead-Times in Incremental and Agile Software Development

Kai Petersen

Blekinge Institute of Technology Box 520,
SE-37225 Ronneby, Sweden
Ericsson AB,
Sweden

Abstract. Short lead-times are essential in order to have a first-move advantages and to be able to react on changes on a fast-paced market. Agile software development is a development paradigm that aims at being able to respond quickly to changes in customer needs. So far, to the best of our knowledge no empirical study has investigated lead-times with regard to different aspects (distribution between phases, difference of lead-time with regard to architecture dependencies, and size). However, in order to improve lead-times it is important to understand the behavior of lead-times. In this study the lead-times of a large-scale company employing incremental and agile practices are analyzed. The analysis focuses on 12 systems at Ericsson AB, Sweden.

1 Introduction

Lead-time (also referred to as cycle-times) is the time it takes to process an order from the request till the delivery [1]. An analysis and improvement of lead-time is highly relevant. Not being able to deliver in short lead-times leads to a number of disadvantages on the market, identified in the study of Bratthall et al. [2]: (1) The risk of market lock-out is reduced [3]. Bratthall et al. [2] provided a concrete example for that where one of the interviewees reported that they had to stall the introduction of a new product because the competitor was introducing a similar product one week earlier; (2) An early enrollment of a new product increase probability of market dominance [4]. One of the participants in the study of Bratthall et al. [2] reported that due to introducing a product three months after a competitor the company is holding 30 % less of the world market in comparison to the market leader; (3) Another benefit of being early on the market is that the product conforms more to the expectations of the market [5]. This is due to the market dynamics. Petersen et al. [6] found that a large portion (26 %) of gathered requirements are already discarded during development. Furthermore, the long lead-time provides a time-window for change requests and rework.

The review of literature revealed that, to the best of our knowledge, an empirical analysis of lead-times in incremental and agile development has not been conducted so far. However, as there is an increasing number of companies employing incremental and agile practices it is important to understand lead-time

J. Münch, Y. Yang, and W. Schäfer (Eds.): ICSP 2010, LNCS 6195, pp. 345–356, 2010.

behavior. The studied company intended to determine target levels for lead-times. The open question at the company was whether requirements should have different target levels depending on the following factors:

1. The distribution of lead-times between different phases.
2. The impact a requirement has on the systems. The impact is measured in terms of number of affected systems. Here we distinguish between single-system requirements (a requirement only affects one system) and multi-system requirements (a requirement affects at least two systems).
3. The size of the requirements.

This study investigated the effect of the three factors on lead-time. It is important to stress that existing work indicates what outcomes can be expected for the different factors, the expected results being presented in the related work. However, the outcome to be expected was not clear to the practitioners in the studied company. Hence, this study sets out with formulating a set of hypotheses related to the factors without assuming a specific outcome of the hypotheses prior to analyzing them.

The research method used was an industrial case study of a company developing large-scale systems in the telecommunication domain. The quantitative data was collected from a company proprietary system keeping track of the requirements flow throughout the software development lifecycle.

The remainder of the paper is structured as follows. Section 2 presents related work. The research method is explained in Section 3. The results of the study are shown in Section 4. Section 5 discusses the results. Section 6 concludes the paper.

2 Related Work

Petersen et al. [6] present lead-times for waterfall development, showing that the majority of the time (41 %) is spent on requirements engineering activities. The remaining time was distributed as follows: 17 % in design and implementation, 19 % on verification, and 23 % on the release project. As in agile software development the main activitis should be coding and testing [7] the literature would suggest that those are the most time consuming activities.

Petersen and Wohlin [8] investigated issues hindering the performance of incremental and agile development. When scaling agile the main issues are (1) complex decision making in the requirements phase; (2) dependencies of complex systems are not discovered early on; and (3) agile does not scale well as complex architecture requires up-front planning. Given this qualitative result the literature indicates that with increase of requirements impact the lead-time should increase. For example, if a requirement can only be deliverable when parts of it are implemented across several systems a delay in one system would lead to prolonged lead-times for this requirement.

Harter et al. [9] identified that lines of code (size) is a predictor for cycle time. This was confirmed by [10] who found that size was the only predictor for lead-time. Hence, from the related work point of view an increase of size should lead to an increase of lead-time.

Collier [11] summarizes a number of issues in cycle time reduction and states: (1) size prolongs lead-time, and (2) dependencies influence lead-time.

Carmel [12] investigated key success factors for achieving short lead-times. The finding shows that team factors (small team size, cross-functional teams, motivation) are critical. Furthermore, an awareness of lead-times is important to choose actions specifically targeted towards lead-time reduction. However, it is important to take quality into consideration when taking actions towards lead-time reduction.

None of the lead-time studies focuses on agile development, and hence raising the need for empirical studies on lead-time in an incremental and agile development context.

3 Research Method

The research method used was a quantitative case study, the case being the telecommunication company Ericsson AB. The systems studied were developed in Sweden and India.

3.1 Research Context

The research context is important to describe in order to know to what degree the results of the study can be generalized [13]. Table 1 shows the context elements for this study. The analysis focused on in total 12 systems of which 3 systems are independent. The remaining nine systems belong to a very large communication system and are highly dependent on each other. Thus, all requirements belonging to the independent systems are treated as single-system requirements. The same applies to requirements only affecting one of the nine dependent systems.

The process of the company is shown in Figure 1. Requirements from the market are prioritized and described as high level requirements (HLR) in form

Table 1. Context Elements

Element	Description
Maturity	All systems older than 5 years
Size	Large-scale system with more than 5,000,000 LOC
Number of systems	9 dependent systems (indexed as A to I) and 3 independent (indexed as J to K)
Domain	Telecommunication
Market	Highly dynamic and customized market
Process	On the principle level incremental process with agile practices in development teams
Certification	ISO 9001:2000
Practices	Continuous integration; Internal and external releases; Time-boxing with sprints; Face-to-face interaction (stand-up meetings, co-located teams); Requirements prioritization with metaphors and Detailed requirements (Digital Product Backlog); Refactoring and system improvements

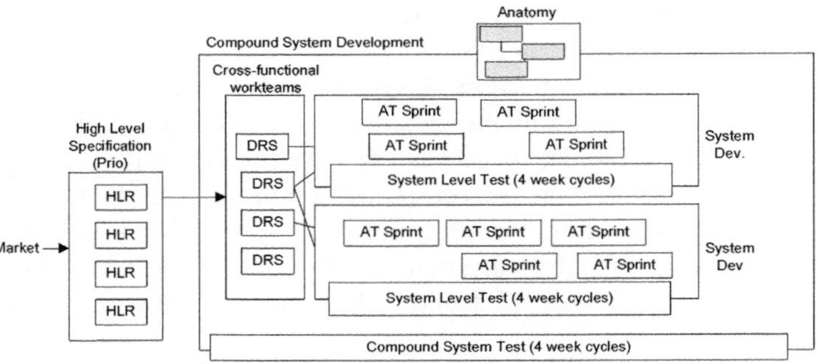

Fig. 1. Development Process

of metaphors. These are further detailed by cross-functional work teams (people knowing the market and people knowing the technology) to detailed requirements specifications (DRS). The anatomy of the system is used to identify the impact of the HLR on the system. The impact determines how many systems are affected by the requirement. A requirement affecting one system is referred to as single-system requirement, while a requirement affecting multiple system is referred to as a multi-system requirement. Within system development agile teams (ATs) implement and unit test the requirements within four week sprints. The teams deliver the requirements to the system level test to continuously verify the integration on system level every four weeks. Furthermore, the system development delivers their increments to the compound system test, which is also integrating in four week cycles. Requirements having passed the test are handed over to the release projects to be packaged for the market.

3.2 Hypotheses

The hypotheses are related to differences between multi- and single-system requirements, the distribution of the lead-time between phases, and the difference between sizes of requirements. As mentioned earlier the goal is not to reject the null hypotheses, but to determine whether the different factors lead to differences in lead-time. In the case of not rejecting the null-hypotheses the factors do not affect the lead-time, while the rejection of the null-hypotheses implies that the factors effect lead-time. The following hypotheses were made:

- *Phases:* There is no difference in lead-time between phases ($H_{0,phaswe}$) opposed to there is a is a difference ($H_{a,phase}$).
- *Multi vs. Single:* There is no difference between multi- and single-system requirements ($H_{0,mult}$) opposed to there is a difference ($H_{a,mult}$).
- *Size:* There is no difference between sizes ($H_{0,size}$) opposed to there is a difference ($H_{a,size}$).

3.3 Data Collection

The lead-time is determined by keeping track of the duration the high level requirements reside in different states. When a certain activity related to the high-level requirement is executed (e.g. specification of the requirement) then the requirement is put into that state. For the tracking of lead-times a time-stamp was captured whenever a requirement enters a state, and leaves a state.

The lead-time data was collected from an electronic Kanban solution where the requirements can be moved between phases to change their state. The system can be edited over the web, showing the lists of the requirements and in which phase they are. Whenever a person is moving a requirement from one phase to another, a date is entered for this movement. The requirements go through the following states:

- *State Detailed Requirements Specification:* The state starts with the decision to hand over requirement to the cross-functional work-team for specification, and ends with the hand-over to the development organization.
- *State Implementation and Unit Test:* The state starts with the hand-over of the requirement to the development organization and ends with the delivery to the system test.
- *State Node/System Test:* The state starts with the hand-over of the requirement to the system/node test and ends with the successful completion of the compound system test. The time includes maintenance for fixing discovered defects.
- *State Ready for Release:* The state starts when the requirement has successfully completed the compound system test and thus is ready for release to the customer.

From the duration the requirements stay in the states the following lead-times were calculated:

- LT_a: Lead-time of a specific activity a based on the duration a requirement resided in the state related to the activity.
- LT_{n-a}: Lead-time starting with an activity a and ending with an activity n. In order to calculate this lead-time, the sum of the durations of all activities to work on a specific high-level requirement were calculated.

Waiting times are included in the lead-times. The accuracy of the measures is high as the data was under regular review due to that the electronic Kanban solution was used in daily work, and the data was subject to a monthly analysis and review.

3.4 Data Analysis

The descriptive statistics used were box-plots illustrating the spread of the data. The hypotheses were analyzed by identifying whether there is a relationship between the variable lead-time and the variables phases ($H_{0,phase}$) and system impact ($H_{0,mult}$). For the relationship between lead-time and system impact the Pearson correlation was used to determine whether there is a linear relationship, and the Spearman correlation to test whether there is a non-linear relationship. For the relationship between lead-time and phase ($H_{0,phase}$) no correlation was used as phase is a categorical variable. In order to capture whether phase leads to variance in lead-time we test whether specific phases lead to variance in lead-time, this is done by using stepwise regression analysis. Thereby, for each category a dummy variable is introduced.

If there is a relationship between the variables (e.g. between system impact and lead-time) this would mean that the system impact would be a variable explaining some of the variance in the lead-time. The hypotheses for size ($H_{0,size}$) was only evaluated using descriptive statistics due to the limited number of data points.

3.5 Threats to Validity

Four types of threats to validity are distinguished, namely conclusion validity (ability to draw conclusions about relationships based on statistical inference), internal validity (ability to isolate and identify factors affecting the studied variables without the researchers knowledge), construct validity (ability to measure the object being studied), and external validity (ability to generalize the results) [14].

Conclusion Validity: The statistical inferences that could be made from this study to a population are limited as this study investigates one particular case. In consequence, no inference statistics for comparing sample means and medians with regard to statistical significance are used. Instead correlation analysis was used, correlation analysis being much more common for observational studies such as case studies. For the test of hypotheses $H_{0,phase}$ we used stepwise regression analysis, regression analysis being a tool of statistical inference. Hence, the interpretation of regression analysis in observational studies has to be done with great care as for a single case study no random sampling with regard to a population has been conducted. The main purpose of the regression was to investigate whether the category leads to variance in lead-time at the specific company. That is, companies with similar contexts might make similar observations, but an inference to the population of companies using incremental and agile methods based on the regression would be misleading.

Internal Validity: One threat to internal validity is the objectivity of measurements, affected by the interpretation of the researcher. To reduce the risk the researcher presented the lead-time data during one meeting and discussed it with peers at the company.

Construct Validity: Reactive bias is a threat where the presence of the researcher influences the outcome of the study. The risk is low due that the researcher is employed at the company, and has been working with the company for a couple of years. Correct data is another threat to validity (in this case whether the lead-time data is accurately entered and up-to-date). As the system and the data entered support the practitioners in their daily work the data is continuously updated. Furthermore, the system provides an overview of missing values, aiding in keeping the data complete which reduces the risk.

External Validity: One risk to external validity is the focus on one company and thus the limitation in generalizing the result. To reduce the risk multiple systems were studied. Furthermore, the context of the case was described as this makes explicit to what degree the results are generalizable. In this case the results apply to large-scale software development with parallel system development and incremental deliveries to system testing. Agile practices were applied on team-level.

4 Results

4.1 Time Distribution Phases

Figure 2 shows the box-plots for lead-times between phases P1 (requirements specification), P2 (implementation and unit test), P3 (node and system test), and P4 (release projects). The box-plots do not provide a clear indication of the differences of lead-time distribution between phases as the box-plots show high overlaps between the phases.

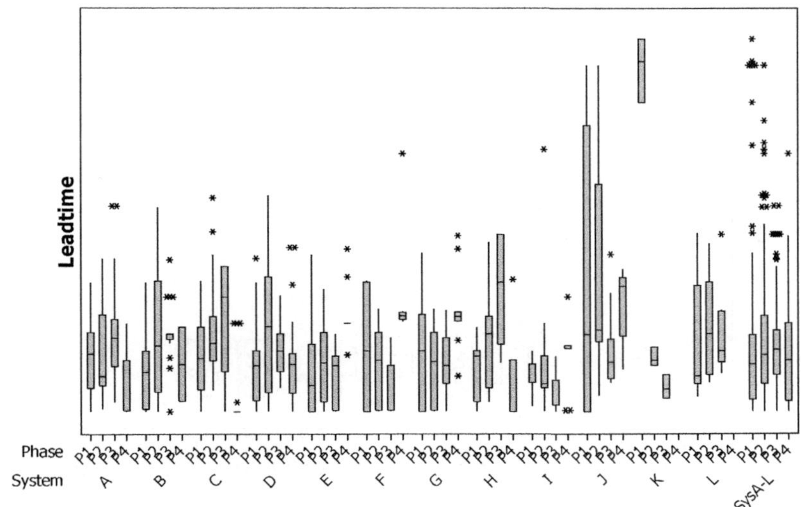

Fig. 2. Comparison of Lead-Times between Phases

Table 2 provides an overview of the statistical results of the correlations between phase and lead-time across systems. The stepwise regression shows that Dummy 4 was highly significant in the regression. Though, the overall explanatory power (which was slightly increased by the introduction of the Dummy 1) is still very low and accounts for 1.14 % of the variance in lead-time (R^2). Hence, $H_{0,phase}$ cannot be rejected with respect to this particular case.

Table 2. Results for Distribution of Lead-Time Phases, N=823

Step	One	Two
Constant	49.91	52.03
Dummy 4 (P4)	-8.9	-11.0
t-value	-2.5	-2.94
p-value	0.013	0.003
Dummy 1 (P1)	-	-6.4
t-value	-	-1.79
p-value	-	0.074
Expl. power R^2	0.0075	0.0114

4.2 Multi-System vs. Single-System Requirements

Figure 3 shows single system requirements (labeled as 0) in comparison to multi-system requirements (labeled as 1) for all phases and for the total lead-time. The box-plots indicate that there is no difference between single and multi-system requirements. In fact, it is clearly visible that the boxes and the median values are on the same level.

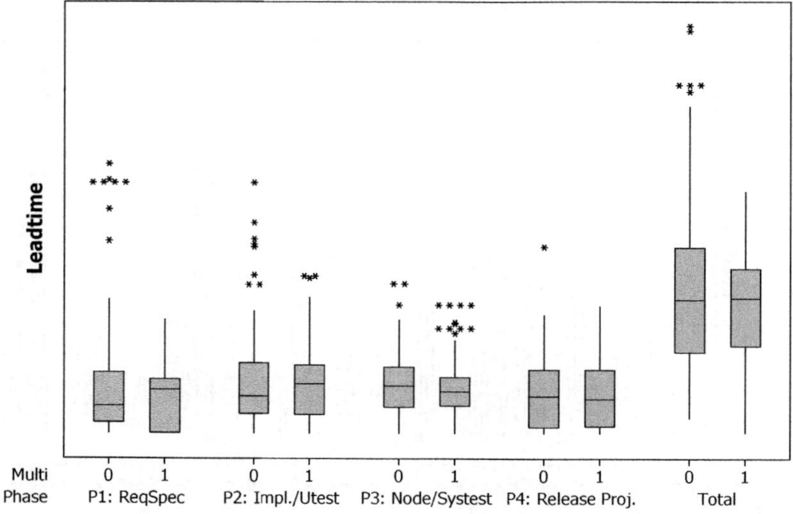

Fig. 3. Single-System (label=0) vs. Multi-System Requirements (label=1)

As there is no observable difference between system impacts we investigated whether the number of systems a requirement is dependent on has an influence on lead-time. As shown in the box-plots in Figure 4 the lead-time does not increase with a higher number of affected systems. On the single system side even more outliers to the top of the box-plot can be found for all phases.

The correlation analysis between system impact and lead-time across systems is shown in Table 3. The table shows that the correlations are neither close to

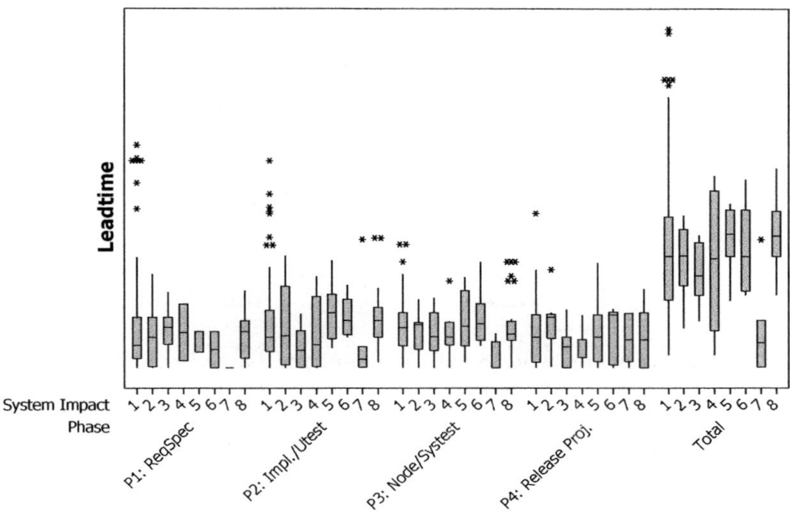

Fig. 4. Difference for System Impact (Number of systems a requirement is affecting, ranging from 1-8)

Table 3. Test Results for $H_{0,multi}$, N=823

Statistic	Value	p
Pearson (φ)	-0.029	0.41
Spearman (ρ)	0.074	0.57
Expl. power (R^2)	0.001	

$+/-1$, and are not significant. Hence, this indicates that the two variables do not seem to be related in the case of this company, leading to a rejection of $H_{0,multi}$.

4.3 Difference between Small / Medium / Large

Figure 5 shows the difference of lead-time between phases grouped by size, the size being an expert estimate by requirements and system analysts. The sizes are defined as intervals in person days, where $Small(S) := [0; 300]$, $Medium(M) := [301; 699]$, and $Large(L) := [700; \infty]$. No correlation analysis was used for analyzing this data as three groups only have two values, namely P2-Large, P3-Medium, and P3-Large. The reason for the limitation was that only recently the requirements were attributed with the size.

However, the data already shows that the difference for size seems to be small in the phases requirements specification and node as well as compound system testing. However, the size of requirements in the design phase shows a trend of increased lead-time with increased size.

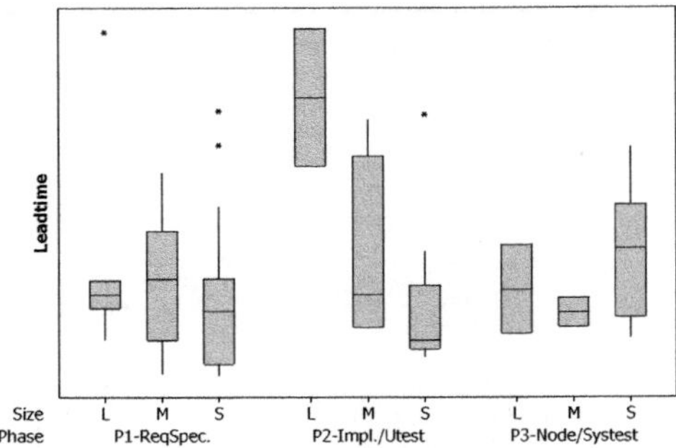

Fig. 5. Difference for Small, Medium, and Large Requirements

5 Discussion

This section presents the practical and research implications. Furthermore, the reasons for the results seen in the hypotheses tests are provided. The explanations have been discussed within an analysis team at the studied companies and the team agreed on the explanations given.

5.1 Practical Implications

No Difference in Lead-Times Between Phases: One explanation for the similarities of lead-times between phases is that large-scale system requires more specification and testing, and that system integration is more challenging when having systems of very large scale. Thus, systems documentation and management activities should only be removed with care in this context as otherwise there is a risk of breaking the consistency of the large system. Furthermore, there is no single phase that requires a specific focus on shortening the lead-time due to that there is no particularly time-consuming activity. Hence, in the studied context the result contradicts what would be expected from the assumptions made in literature. A consequence for practice is that one should investigate which are the value-adding activities in the development life-cycle, and reduce the non-value adding activities. An approach for that is lean software development [15].

No difference in Multi vs. Single System Requirements: The number of dependencies a requirement has does not increase the lead-time. An explanation is that with requirements affected by multiple systems the systems drive each other to be fast as they can only deliver value together. The same driving force is not found on single system requirements. However, we can hypothesize that single system lead-time can be shortened more easily, the reason being that waiting due to dependencies in a compound system requires the resolution of these dependencies to reduce the lead-time. On the other hand, no technical dependencies have to be resolved to remove lead-time in single systems.

Difference in Size: No major difference can be observed between small, medium and large requirements, except for large requirements in implementation and unit test. That is, at a specific size the lead-time for implementation and test increases drastically. In consequence, there seems to be a limit that the size should have to avoid longer lead-times. This result is well in line with the findings presented in literature (cf [9,10]).

5.2 Research Implications

The study investigated a very large system, hence research should focus on investigating time consumption for different contexts (e.g. small systems). This helps to understand the scalability of agile in relation to lead-times and with that the ability to respond quickly to market needs. Furthermore, the impact of size on lead-time is interesting to understand in order to right-size requirements.

In this study we have shown the absence of explanatory power for the variance in lead-time for phases and system impact. As time is such an important outcome variable research should focus on investigating the impact of other variables (e.g. experience, schedule pressure, team and organizational size, distribution, etc.) in a broader scale. Broader scale means that a sample of projects should be selected, e.g. by using publicly available repository with project data.

6 Conclusion

This paper evaluates software development lead-time in the context of a large-scale organization using incremental and agile practices. The following observations were made regarding lead-time:

- Phases do not explain much of the variance in lead-time. From literature one would expect that implementation and testing are the most time-consuming activities in agile development. However, due to the context (large-scale) other phases are equally time-consuming.
- There is no difference in lead-time for singe-system and multi-system requirements. This finding also contradicts literature. An explanation is that if a requirement has impact on multiple systems these systems drive each other in implementing the requirements quickly.
- With increasing size the lead-time within the implementation phase increases. This finding is in agreement with the related work.

In future work lead-times should be investigated in different contexts to provide further understanding of the behavior of lead-times in incremental and agile development.

References

1. Carreira, B.: Lean manufacturing that works: powerful tools for dramatically reducing waste and maximizing profits. American Management Association, New York (2005)

2. Bratthall, L., Runeson, P., Adelswärd, K., Eriksson, W.: A survey of lead-time challenges in the development and evolution of distributed real-time systems. Information & Software Technology 42(13), 947–958 (2000)
3. Schilling, M.A.: Technological lockout: an integrative model of the economic and strategic factors driving technology success and failure. Academy of Management Review 23(2), 267–284 (1998)
4. Urban, G.L., Carter, T., Gaskin, S., Mucha, Z.: Market share rewards to pioneering brands: an empirical analysis and strategic implications. Management Science 32(6), 645–659 (1986)
5. Stalk, G.: Time - the next source of competitive advantage. Harvard Business Review 66(4) (1988)
6. Petersen, K., Wohlin, C., Baca, D.: The waterfall model in large-scale development. In: Proceedings of the 10th International Conference on Product-Focused Software Process Improvement (PROFES 2009), pp. 386–400 (2009)
7. Beck, K.: Embracing change with extreme programming. IEEE Computer 32(10), 70–77 (1999)
8. Petersen, K., Wohlin, C.: A comparison of issues and advantages in agile and incremental development between state of the art and an industrial case. Journal of Systems and Software 82(9) (2009)
9. Harter, D.E., Krishnan, M.S., Slaughter, S.A.: Effects of process maturity on quality, cycle time, and effort in software product development. Management Science 46(4) (2000)
10. Agrawal, M., Chari, K.: Software effort, quality, and cycle time: A study of cmm level 5 projects. IEEE Trans. Software Eng. 33(3), 145–156 (2007)
11. Aoyama, M.: Issues in software cycle time reduction. In: Proceedings of the 1995 IEEE Fourteenth Annual International Phoenix Conference on Computers and Communications, pp. 302–309 (1995)
12. Carmel, E.: Cycle time in packaged software firms. Journal of Product Innovation Management 12(2), 110–123 (1995)
13. Petersen, K., Wohlin, C.: Context in industrial software engineering research. In: Proceedings of the 3rd International Symposium on Empirical Software Engineering and Measurement, pp. 401–404 (2010)
14. Wohlin, C., Runeson, P., Höst, M., Ohlsson, M.C., Regnell, B., Wesslen, A.: Experimentation in Software Engineering: An Introduction (International Series in Software Engineering). Springer, Heidelberg (2000)
15. Poppendieck, M., Poppendieck, T.: Lean software development: an agile toolkit. Addison-Wesley, Boston (2003)

Improving the ROI of Software Quality Assurance Activities: An Empirical Study

Qi Li[1], Fengdi Shu[2], Barry Boehm[1], and Qing Wang[2]

[1] University of Southern California,
941 w. 37th Place Los Angeles, CA 90089-0781
[2] Laboratory for Internet Software Technologies, Institute of Software,
The Chinese Academy of Sciences, Beijing 100080, China
{qli1,bohem}@usc.edu, {fdshu,wq}@itechs.iscas.ac.cn

Abstract. Review, process audit, and testing are three main Quality Assurance activities during the software development life cycle. They complement each other to examine work products for defects and improvement opportunities to the largest extent. Understanding the effort distribution and inter-correlation among them will facilitate software organization project planning, improve the software quality within the budget and schedule and make continuous process improvement. This paper reports some empirical findings of effort distribution pattern of the three types of QA activities from a series of incremental projects in China. The result of the study gives us some implications on how to identify which type of QA activity is insufficient while others might be overdone, how to balance the effort allocation and planning for future projects, how to improve the weak part of each QA activity and finally improve the Return On Investment (ROI) of QA activities and the whole process effectiveness under the specific organization context.

Keywords: Quality Assurance, Review, Testing, Process Audit.

1 Introduction

For a successful project, acceptable quality must be achieved within an acceptable cost and a reasonable schedule. Generally, if a high-quality product is required, more effort would be put on quality assurance activities to achieve the required quality goal. IEEE's definition of Software Quality Assurance is: "A planned and systematic pattern of all actions necessary to provide adequate confidence that an item or product conforms to established technical requirements and a set of activities designed to evaluate the process by which the products are developed or manufactured"[1]. Review, process audit and testing are three popular quality assurance activities during the software life cycle. Review, often referred to requirements review, formal design reviews, peer reviews (inspection and walkthrough), is usually considered to be the most effective quality assurance activity and the best industry practice according to many research findings[2-5]. The maximum benefits come from review would prevent defects and save fixing time in future work [6]. However, some studies show that one should not expect to replace testing with reviews [6, 7]. Although the two quality assurance activities are

J. Münch, Y. Yang, and W. Schäfer (Eds.): ICSP 2010, LNCS 6195, pp. 357–368, 2010.

overlapping in finding some common types of defects, e.g. simple programming blunders and logic defects, they are fairly complementary in capturing different types of defects. Defects of specification, missing portions, developer blind spots are easier to be found by review, however, defects of numerical approximations and program dynamics are harder to be found by review because reviewers can't tell how fast and reliable the system will be, how user-friendly the system is by just reviewing and deducing from the abstract requirement, design documents or codes. Testing serves as a hands-on experience of the actual and operational system that review can't achieve by imaging. It is good at finding numerical approximations and program dynamics defects but harder to find defects of specification, missing portions, and developer blind spots [6, 7]. Although process audit has an indirect impact on the software product, it has been widely accepted that [8] process audit can help developing team to work on the right direction, adopt and tailor the most effective method that comes from the best industrial practices to the specific context of the project, improve the process effectiveness and finally improve the software quality.

Because the three types of quality assurance activities are complementary and can't be replaced by one another, how to balance the effort allocation among them to improve resource allocation efficiency and maximize the Return On Investment (ROI) of the entire quality assurance if we consider them as investments to the software development life cycle is still an important yet challenging issue for project planning. In this paper, based on the data from a Chinese software organization, we do an effort distribution pattern analysis of three types of software quality assurance activities and propose a diagnostic model to identify which type of QA activity is insufficient while others might be overdone. This will give process implication on how to balance QA effort allocation for future quality management plan, how to improve the weak part of QA activities and finally improve the whole QA activities' effectiveness under the specific organization context.

The remainder of the paper is structured as follows: section 2 will introduce related work, section 3 will introduce the background and data source of the study; section 4 will discuss the objective, methodology, major results of data analysis and process implication; section 5 will discuss about the threats of validity; section 6 is the conclusion.

2 Related Work

The efficiency of review and testing are compared in [11]. To determine the Defect Removal Fraction (DRFs) associated with each of the six levels (i.e., Very Low, Low, Nominal, High, Very High, Extra High) of the three profiles (i.e., automated analysis, people reviews, execution testing and tools) for each of three types of defect artifacts (i.e., requirement defects, design defects, and code defects), it conducted a two-round Delphi. This study found that people review is the most efficient on removing requirement and design defects, and testing is the most efficient on removing code defects.

In [12], Capers Jones lists Defect Removal Efficiency of 16 combinations of 4 defect removal methods: design inspections, code inspections, quality assurance (corresponds to process audit in our study), and testing [12]. These results show that, on one side, no single defect removal method is adequate, on the other side, implies that removal efficiency from better to worse would be design inspections, code inspections, testing and process audit.

However, both the results are generally from expert Delphi estimation and lack quantitative verification. Second, both of them are based on the assumption that all these defect removal strategies have been done sufficiently, but in practice, they might be done insufficiently due to inappropriate project planning, time constraints or market pressure. Meanwhile, from the economic aspect, the ROI might be negative if they have been done sufficiently enough without consideration of cost. So both of the related work doesn't give any clue on optimal QA effort allocation guidelines to maximize the ROI of QA activities. Although iDAVE [13] gives the decision support of how much QA is enough, but it doesn't address how much reviewing, process auditing, and testing is enough respectively.

3 Background and Data Source of the Study

The empirical study is based on the process data from developing a series of incremental R&D software projects within a medium-sized software organization in China. The lead product is the software quality management platform (SoftPM) platform, targeting to facilitate the process improvement initiatives in many small and medium software organizations in China. The quality management group is responsible for implementing the three types of QA activities during the whole project life cycle. Every incremental version of this project shares the same quality goal before releasing: that is the rate of requirements coverage by test cases is 100%, all planned test cases executed and passed; no non-trivial defects are detected during at least one day of continuous testing, and satisfy the quality goal of 0.2defects/KLOC when it is released.

We extract raw data from related plans, records and reports, consolidate the original information, resolve the inconsistency and finally get QA data from five incremental versions as shown in Appendix from Table 6 to Table 9. The meanings of data items are also explained in the italic words below the tables.

4 Objective, Methodology, Result and Process Implication

The work performed in this study aims to supplement the sparse work on empirical assessment of effort distribution patterns of quality assurance activities, develop understanding to the effectiveness of different types of quality assurance activities during software life cycle, and provide guidelines and process implication for quality managers in planning and balancing the effort distribution to maximize the ROI of QA activities. This empirical study follows the Goal/Question/Metric (GQM) methodology [14], the GQM model used in this study is shown as follows:

- Goal: Improve the ROI of QA activities
  - Question 1(Q1): What is the baseline of QA activities effort allocation under the specific organization context?

- ✓ Metric1(M1):Statistic description: Mean, Median, Standard Deviation of Effort Distribution Percentage
- o Question 2(Q2): How to identify which QA activities might be insufficient while others might be overdone?
  - ✓ Metric2(M2):Regression Diagnostic Model
  - ✓ Metric3(M3):Cost of Finding and Removing Defects in Each Phase
  - ✓ Metric4(M4):Distribution of Types of Defects Found by Testing
- o Question 3(Q3): How to improve reviewing if it is insufficient?
  - ✓ Metric3(M5): Filter Effectiveness
- o Question 4(Q4): How to improve process audit if it is insufficient?
  - ✓ Metric4(M6): NCs (Not Compatibles) Distribution
- o Question 5(Q5): How to improve testing if it is insufficient?
  - ✓ Metric5(M7):Value-based Software Testing: Feature Prioritization [10]

To improve the ROI of QA activities in this Chinese software organization, understanding the current state of QA activities effort distribution serves as the first step for improvement, M1 measures the current state based on history data and provides the baseline for further improvement. M2 works as a diagnostics model to identify which QA activities might be done insufficiently while others might be overdone in order to input more effort on the more cost-effective activities to improve the ROI of QA activities. M3, M4 supports and verifies M2. M5, M6 and M7 answer the question that how to improve reviewing, process auditing and testing process respectively if they are insufficient from M2's diagnostics and process implication.

4.1 Question 1 and Metric 1

We could see in Table 1 that if we want to keep the current process maturity and also achieve the same quality goal of 0.2defects/KLOC when it is released, the Chinese software organization should put total around 40.13% effort on the QA activities: review effort 4.30%, testing effort 34.47% and process audit effort 1.70% respectively. The statistic description of QA effort distribution gives a baseline of required QA effort percentage for required quality goals.

Table 1. Statistic Description of distributions of three types of QA activities

	E_Re%	E_Test%	E_PA%	E_QA%
V2.5	4.90%	31.58%	1.78%	38.27%
V2.6	4.74%	21.61%	2.51%	28.85%
V3.0	0.38%	48.81%	1.49%	50.68%
V3.1	3.74%	48.03%	1.00%	52.76%
V3.1.1	7.76%	22.33%	NA	30.09%
Mean	*4.30%*	*34.47%*	*1.70%*	*40.13%*
Median	*4.74%*	*31.58%*	*1.64%*	*38.27%*
Stdev	*2.66%*	*13.33%*	*0.63%*	*11.21%*

4.2 Question 2 and Metric 2, 3, 4

Metric 2: Regression Diagnostic Model

Based on the data in Table 6 in Appendix, Pearson correlation coefficients between the effort percentages of the three quality assurance activities are shown in Table 2. We can see in that the effort percentage of testing is inversely proportional to that of both review and process audit with a highly negative correlation coefficient -0.73 and -0.92 respectively which means and is directly reflected in Figure 1 that as the review and process audit effort percentages tends to increase, the percentage of testing tends to decrease. These results might imply that if the organization put more effort on review and process audit, they could save effort in testing to achieve the same quality goal.

Table 2. Correlation between Effort Percentages

	E_Re%	E_PA%	E_Test%
E_Re%	1.00		
E_PA%	0.40	1.00	
E_Test%	-0.73	-0.92	1.00

To further investigate how much testing effort could save if adding more effort on review and process audit, we do a multivariable linear regression analysis using Equation 1: E_Test% as the dependent variable, E_Re% and E_PA% as the independent variables, A is the regression constant, B and C are the regression coefficients of E_Re% and E_PA% respectively.

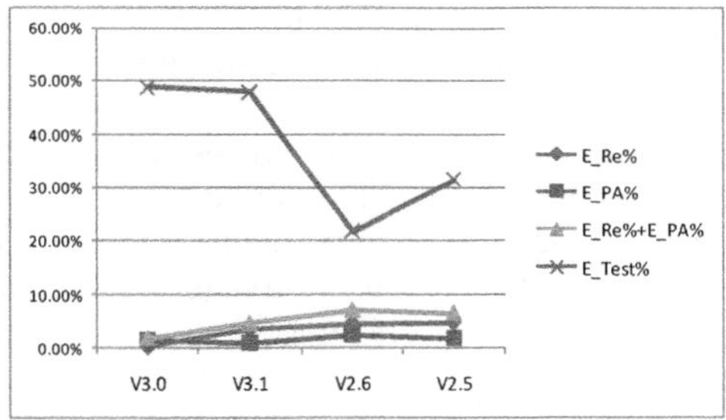

Fig. 1. Correlation between Effort Percentages

$$E\_Test\% = A + B * E\_Re\% + C * E\_PA\% \qquad \textit{Equation 1}$$

Table 3 below shows the regression model result for this organization based on the date from Table 6 in Appendix. To determine the statistical significance of multivariable regression equation, F test is usually adopted. As shown in Table 3, the Significance F value (0.036) of this regression equation is below 0.05, so the regression equation is significant. All other coefficients are statistically significant except the P-value of E_Re% is a little bit above 0.05.

Table 3. Multivariable Regression Analysis

E_Test%=	*0.73*	*-2.69*E_Re%*	*-15.73*E_PA%*
t Stat	53.82	-10.96	-19.24
P-value	0.012	0.057	0.0333
F (Significance F)	393.11(0.036)		

From this equation, assuming that other factors are the same, if review effort is increased by 1%, testing effort is saved by 2.69%. The same analysis for process audit is that if process audit effort is increased by 1%, testing effort is going to be saved by

15.73%. The ROI of putting more effort on the review and process audit would be (2.69%-1%)/1%=1.69 and (15.73%-1%)/1%=14.73 respectively.

Further considerations about this linear equation would be: First, under the extreme condition that E_Re% and E_PA% are both set to 0, which means the organization doesn't have any activities related to review and process audit, the testing would take up as high as 73% of the total engineering effort to satisfy the required quality goal. This percentage of testing is far beyond the benchmark from industry at the same level of quality which implies that the unreasonable QA effort allocation leads to a huge waste of resources and effort. Second, if the coefficient of E_Re% or E_PA% stands in the range from -1 to 0, which means if you add 1% more effort to review or process audit, it will save less than 1% testing effort, so the ROI of adding more effort on review or process audit will be negative. In such cases, you should reconsider about reducing the effort put on review and process audit, and put more on testing. In sum, this equation gives quality managers some insights about how to balance the effort put on testing, process audit, and review based on history project data.

Process Implication: For this case study, testing is the most labor-intensive activities of the QA activities and the effort put on review and process audit is insufficient, this might give the quality manager some process improvement implication that putting more effort on review and process audit to save the testing time, and finally shorten the schedule and save the whole cost. Also, since the ROI of adding more effort on process audit is larger than that of adding more effort on review, it also gives some implications that for this software organization, improving the process audit activity might be more cost-effective.

Metric 3: Cost of Finding and Removing Defects

In order to compare cost of finding and removing defects at each phase, we use Equation 2 below based on the data from Table 6, Table 7 and Table 8. Cost of finding and removing Non-Conformances (NCs) by process audit could be calculated from Table 9. We lack some data of reviewing effort and defects in coding phase, so we compare the requirement, design and testing phase's cost of finding and removing defects here, and the cost of finding and removing NCs as shown in Table 4.

Cost of finding and removing defects= Hours spent on reviewing or testing in the phase/ numbers of defects found and removed in the phase *Equation 2*

We can see that the hours spent on finding and removing per defect is increasing from requirement to testing, this means that the cost of finding and removing defects is increasing as the project goes on. This finding from this Chinese organization is also similar to other surveys carried out by IBM, TRW, GTE and summarized by Boehm [6]. The hours spent on finding and removing per NC by process audit is also much smaller than those spent on finding and removing per defect by testing.

Process Implication: These findings from this analysis continue to support that process audit and reviewing are more effective and efficient to detect defects than testing. Adding more effort on early review, defects finding and process audit is more cost-effective.

Table 4. Hours per defect spent on finding and removing defects in each phase

(Hours/defect)	Hrs/Def_Req	Hrs/Def_Des	Hrs/Def_Test	Hrs/NC_PA
V2.5	0.97	1.94	3.90	NA
V2.6	1.33	1.42	1.02	NA
V3.0	0.57	2.72	6.23	2.32
V3.1	1.81	2.17	14.32	0.59
V3.1.1	0.58	2.06	4.51	NA
Mean	***1.05***	***2.06***	***5.99***	***1.45***
Median	***0.97***	***2.06***	***4.51***	***1.45***
Stdev	***0.53***	***0.47***	***5.02***	***1.22***

Hrs/Def_Req: Hours spent on finding and removing per defect in requirement phase by reviewing
Hrs/Def_Des: Hours spent on finding and removing per defect in design phase by reviewing
Hrs/Def_Test: Hours spent on finding and removing per defect by testing
Hrs/NC_PA: Hours spent on finding and removing per NC by process audit

Metric 4: Distribution of Types of Defects Found by Testing

On the other side, from collecting the defects found in testing from V3.0, V3.1 and V3.1.1, we classify the defects according to their types (F-Function, G-Algorithm, U-User Interface, P-Performance) in Figure 2. We find that defects related to function takes the most part and this might imply that the insufficient effort on early review especially insufficient code walkthrough before testing. Defects related to user interface and performance are hard to be detected by review but can be more easily detected by testing, so this would verify again that testing activity serves to complement review activity.

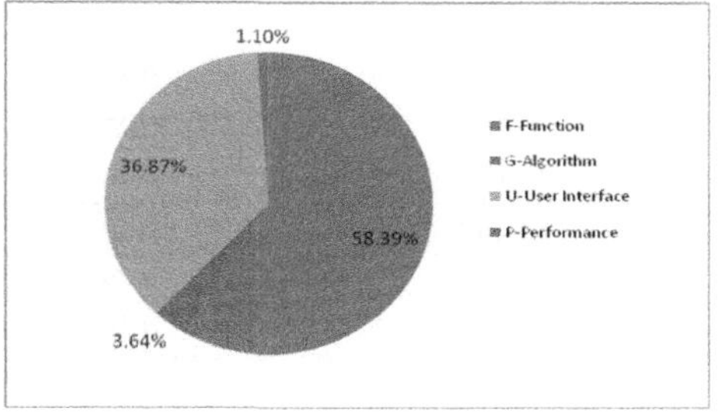

Fig. 2. Distribution of Types of Defects Found by Testing

4.3 Question 3 and Metric 5

From the analysis above, we see that it would be better to put more effort on early review. The next question is shall we put equal effort on the requirement review, design review and code walkthrough? A straight answer would be put the extra effort on the weakest part would be more cost-effective. The next analysis will help quality managers to identify which review is the weakest according to the context of the organization.

Review serves as filters, removing a percentage of the defects and let the left to enter to the next phases, the definition the Filter Effectiveness (FE) of each phase:

Filter Effectiveness=defects found in this phase/defects introduced in this phase
Equation 3

For simplicity, in our case, we define the Filter Effectiveness as follows:

Filter Effectiveness= defects found in this phase/ (defects found in this phase+ defects introduced in this phase and found by testing)

Equation 4

Process Implication: Based on the data from Table 7 and Table 8, we get the Filter Effectiveness of each phase by reviewing in Table 5. We could see that the Filter Effectiveness decreases as the project goes on, especially in coding phase, as low as 0.01 in V3.0. The process implication here might be that the development team relies highly on the testing group. They should put more effort on code walkthrough and unit testing before they release codes to the testing team.

Table 5. Filter Effectiveness of Each Phase by Reviewing

Percentage	FE_Re_Req	FE_Re_Des	FE_Re_Cod
V2.5	0.76	0.41	NA
V2.6	0.32	0.27	NA
V3.0	0.44	0.09	0.01
V3.1	0.97	0.50	0.19
V3.1.1	0.98	0.84	0.10
Mean	***0.69***	***0.42***	***0.10***
Median	***0.76***	***0.41***	***0.10***
Stdev	***0.30***	***0.28***	***0.09***

4.4 Question 4 and Metric 6

From the analysis in section 4.2, it would be beneficial if we put more effort on process audit too and this might even be more effective than review. The independent auditors check the process with a set of checklists for the Process Areas that refer to CMMI v1.2 [9]. The NCs found for Process Areas are shown in Table 9. We find that Project Monitoring and Control (PMC) and Project Planning (PP) take most part of the NCs.

To get the further information from these NCs, we find that the main problem for PMC is that developers often neglect submitting their periodical reports in time. Main items of these reports include task completion ratio, planned and actual effort, problems or risks they encounter. These reports are usually used by project manager to monitor developers' task progress, identify risks and issues. However, missing these reports would blindfold eyes of the project manager, some critical risks or issues might be delayed to solve. By investigating the NCs related to PP, the most common problem is that planned and actual effort displays a huge gap. Overestimating the task effort might lead to project delay, shorten the time for testing and lead to low quality product, while underestimates might lead to resource waste. The large proportion of NCs related to PP shows the weakness of the effort estimation for project planning. Further improvement would include creating guidelines for project effort estimation, adopting more systematic and professional effort estimation methods or tools, such as COCOMO tool to bridge the gap.

Process Implication: Although this organization has already passed CMMI level 4, but for this project, it is observable that it is operating at much lower CMMI levels (e.g. lack of reporting and cost estimation). This analysis serves as a caution for this organization to maintain their process maturity on a higher level and keep continuous process improvement by putting more effort on process audit and improving the process of Project Planning and Project Monitoring and Control in the future would benefit the process improvement and achieve a higher ROI.

5 Threats to Validity

• **Oversimplified assumptions of Regression Model:** In this paper, we use a linear regression Equation 1 to simply identify that further improvement in review and process audit activities would save effort for testing. The assumption of this regression equation is that the utility function of each QA activity is linear. However, the utility function of QA activities is not simply linear in real life, usually it comes out as an "S" shape production function. Basically, initial effort is put on preparation for review, process audit and testing, such as making plans for each activity, developing review checklists, process audit checklists, and test cases, scripts etc. with little return at the Investment phase. Then, when these QA activities are performed, it goes to the High-payoff phase, in which most obvious defects are found by reviewing and testing, most NCs are indentified by process audit. Later, as more effort is put on QA activities, it becomes harder to find more defects or identify more NCs when it comes to the Diminishing Return phase. The linear regression here helps quality managers to identify whether the current effort distribution of the three QA activities is reasonable or not, if not, which one should be improved. Future work would include finding out what the optimal composite strategy is to maximize the ROI of QA activities. We plan to use Indifference Curves and Budget Constraints analysis from Microeconomics Utility theory to build the model to solve this problem. The best combination is the point where the indifference curve and the budget line are tangent.

• **Data Acquisition for other organizations:** Another assumption of building the regression diagnostic model is under the organizational context of a series of projects of the same organization with the same process maturity and quality goal. In this case study, we do this analysis based on a series of maintenance and evolution projects with the same process maturity level and quality goals. This assumption limits its adoption by only those organizations that collect and have the required process data.

• **Data Quantity and Soundness of Statistical Analysis:** In this case study, the data is very limited with missing data. Usually, for parametric statistics, e.g. the Pearson correlation analysis and Ordinary Least Squares Regression we use in this case study, they have strict assumptions, e.g. the data used should be of Normal (Gaussian) distribution. It is quite difficult to check this assumption with so few data points in this case study, and this is a threat to our analysis's validity. Besides, we simply assume that all releases are the same without normalization against the different size and complexity of different releases. In reality, different releases may involve work of different nature, requiring different types of QA activities, and different effort distribution patterns. In the future, we plan to continue collecting the updated data to check representativeness of data and modeling assumptions in order to refine the model.

• **Data Variance Analysis:** In this case study, overall we deal with averages without further analysis for its variance, e.g. baseline of required QA effort percentage in Table 1, Cost of Finding and Removing Defects in Table 4 and Filter Effectiveness of Each Phase by Reviewing in Table 5. We plan to revisit the raw data in the future to do deeper root-cause analysis for variance, especially the large ones.

6 Conclusion and Future Work

In order to identify the most effective effort distribution pattern of QA activities to finally improve the whole process effectiveness, in this study, we do a series of empirical analysis based on the history project data from a Chinese software organization. The results from this study further support that early review is more effective than late testing; process audit, at least in this study, might be even more effective to prevent the defect introduction; these three types of QA activities complement each other to achieve the required quality goal.

The procedure of these analysis would help quality managers to identify which type of QA activity is insufficient while others might be overdone, how to identify and improve the weakest part of QA activities, how to balance the effort allocation and planning for future projects and finally improve the whole process effectiveness under the specific organization context.

We regard this empirical study as the first step towards a more comprehensive quantitative empirical study, where the nature of the quantitative functional forms of the optimal QA effort distribution pattern could be estimated. The empirical study also implies that testing is the most labor-intensive and might be the least cost-effective, however, serves as an irreplaceable role in the software life cycle. Future work would include adopting value-based principles to each QA activity to improve its effectiveness respectively, e.g. [10], and expand the basis of this approach to find a way to balance the effort distribution of QA activities to maximize its ROI. This would involve more data and analysis of the relative cost-effectiveness of the various techniques across various classes of defects [6], as being investigated in [15] via Orthogonal Defect Classification.

Acknowledgement

This work is cooperatively supported by the National Natural Science Foundation of China under Grant Nos. 90718042, 60873072, and 60903050; the National Hi-Tech R&D Plan of China under Grant Nos. 2007AA010303, 2007AA01Z186 and 2007AA01Z179; the National Basic Research Program under Grant No. 2007CB310802.

References

1. IEEE, IEEE Std 610.12-1990-IEEE Standard Glossary of Software Engineering Terminology, Corrected Edition, in IEEE Software Engineering Standards Collection, The Institute of Electrical and Electronics Engineers, New York (February 1991)
2. Gilb, Tom, Graham, D.: Software Inspection. Addison-Wesley, Wokingham (1993)

3. Grady, R.B., Van Slack, T.: Key Lessons in Achieving Widespread Inspection Use. IEEE Software 11(4), 46–57 (1994)
4. Holland, D.: Document Inspection as an Agent of Change. Software Quality Professional 2(1), 22–33 (1999)
5. Humphrey, W.S.: Managing the Software Process. Addison-Wesley, Reading (1989)
6. Boehm, B.W.: Software Engineering Economics. Prentice Hall, Englewood Cliffs (1981)
7. Wiegers, K.E.: Seven Truths about Peer Reviews. Cutter IT Journal (July 2002)
8. April, A., et al.: Process Assurance Audits: Lessons Learned. In: Proceedings of ICSE 1998, pp. 482–485 (1998)
9. CMMI Product Team. CMMI for Development, Version 1.2. Technical Report CMU/SEI-2006-TR-008 (2006)
10. Li, Q., et al.: Bridge the Gap between Software Test Process and Business Value: a Case Study. In: Wang, Q., Garousi, V., Madachy, R., Pfahl, D. (eds.) ICSP 2009. LNCS, vol. 5543, pp. 212–223. Springer, Heidelberg (2009)
11. Boehm, B.W., et al.: Software Cost Estimation with COCOMO II, ch. 5, Table 5.37. Prentice Hall, NY (2000)
12. Jones, C.: Applied Software Measurement: Global Analysis of Productivity and Quality, 3rd edn. McGraw-Hill, New York (2008)
13. Boehm, B.W., Huang, L., Jain, A., Madachy, R.J.: The ROI of Software Dependability: The iDAVE Model. IEEE Software 21(3), 54–61 (2004)
14. Basili, V., Caldiera, G., Rombach, H.D.: The Goal Question Metric Approach, Encyclopedia of Software Engineering. John Wiley & Sons, Inc., Chichester (1994)
15. Madachy, R.J., Boehm, B.W.: Assessing Quality Processes with ODC COQUALMO. In: Wang, Q., Pfahl, D., Raffo, D.M. (eds.) ICSP 2008. LNCS, vol. 5007, pp. 198–209. Springer, Heidelberg (2008)

Appendix

Table 6. Effort (Man-Hours) and its Percentages of Each QA Activity

	E_Re_Req	E_Re_Des	E_Re_Cod	E_Re
V2.5	269.7(3.29%)	132(1.61%)	NA	401.7(4.90%)
V2.6	24(2.77%)	17(1.96%)	NA	41(4.74%)
V3.0	41.5(0.13%)	79(0.25%)	NA	120.5(0.38%)
V3.1	458(2.82%)	13(0.08%)	135(0.83%)	606(3.74%)
V3.1.1	35(2.14%)	74(4.52%)	18(1.10%)	127(7.76%)
	E_PA	**E_Test**	**E_Total**	
V2.5	146(1.78%)	2587(31.58%)	8192	
V2.6	21.7(2.51%)	187(21.61%)	865.5	
V3.0	472.65(1.49%)	15466(48.81%)	31684.5	
V3.1	162(1.00%)	7787.6(48.03%)	16215.1	
V3.1.1	NA	365.5(22.33%)	1636.5	

E_Re_Req: Review effort in Requirement Phase; E_Re_Des: Review effort in Design Phase; E_Re_Cod: Review effort in Coding Phase
E_Re: Review effort; E_PA: Process Audit effort; E_Test: Testing effort
E_Total: Total effort for the project

Table 7. Defects found in Review Activities

	Def_Re_Req	Def_Re_Des	Def_Re_Cod	Def_Re_Total
V2.5	277	68	NA	345
V2.6	18	12	NA	30
V3.0	73	29	18	120
V3.1	253	6	121	380
V3.1.1	60	36	8	104

Def_Re_Req: Defects found in requirement phase by reviewing. Def_Re_Des: Defects found in design phase by reviewing. Def_Re_Cod: Defects found in coding phase by reviewing. De_Re_Total: Total defects found by reviewing

Table 8. Defects found in Testing Activities

	Def_Intro_Req	Def_Intro_Des	Def_Intro_Cod	Def_Test_Total
V2.5	88	97	478	663
V2.6	38	32	114	184
V3.0	93	296	2095	2484
V3.1	8	6	530	544
V3.1.1	1	7	73	81

Def_Intro_Req: Defects introduced in requirement phase and found by testing
Def_Intro_Des: Defects introduced in design phase and found by testing
Def_Intro_Cod: Defects introduced in coding phase and found by testing
Def_Test_Total: Total defects found by testing

Table 9. NCs Distribution

	NC	PP	PMC	CM	TEST	REV	PM	PDL	RD	OT	REQM
V3.0	194	47	90	8	4		2				43
V3.1	257	26	81	29	59	24	9	0	3	0	26
V3.1.1	44	18	4	7	2	1		3	8	1	

NC: Total NC number for each incremental version. Project Planning (PP), Project Monitoring and Control (PMC), Requirements Management (REQM), Configuration Management (CM), Requirements Development (RD), Organizational Training (OT), Software Testing (TEST), Review (REV), Project Development Lifecycle Standard Process (PDL)

Benchmarking the Customer Configuration Updating Process of the International Product Software Industry

Slinger Jansen[1], Wouter Buts[1], Sjaak Brinkkemper[1], and André van der Hoek[2]

[1] Department of Information and Computing Sciences, Utrecht University, Utrecht, The Netherlands
{s.jansen,wftbuts,s.brinkkemper}@cs.uu.nl
[2] Department of Informatics, University of California, Irvine, CA, USA
andre@ics.uci.edu

Abstract. Product software vendors have trouble defining their customer configuration updating process; release, delivery and deployment are generally underrated and thus less attention is paid to them. This paper presents an international benchmark survey providing statistical evidence that product software vendors who invest in the customer configuration updating process perceive that they are more successful than those who do not. Furthermore, the benchmark survey provides a vivid picture of the customer configuration updating practices of product software vendors and that customer configuration updating is an underdeveloped process.

1 Introduction

Software engineering research has always focused on improving methods and processes that have an end-goal of producing a working system. This focus generally does not include the processes around release, delivery, deployment, and run-time monitoring of a system. Only few theoretical studies regarding the CCU process have been conducted, such as Carzaniga's software deployment characterization framework [1] and Hall, Heimbigner, and Wolf's development of tools for software deployment [2] and Jansen et al.'s evaluation of deployment tools [3]. Empirically, CCU has received little scientific attention. The survey presented in this paper attempts to fill that niche.

Product software is defined as a packaged configuration of software components or a software-based service, with auxiliary materials, which is released for and traded in a specific market [4]. Customer configuration updating (CCU) is defined as the combination of the vendor side release process, the product or update delivery process, the customer side deployment process and the usage process [5]. The CCU model, created by Jansen and Brinkkemper, was used to create a survey among several Dutch product software vendors, to establish how mature Dutch product software vendors are in regards to CCU [6]. In this paper the survey is extended and repeated in an international setting. The survey was conducted from the University of California, Irvine. Seventy-eight companies,

J. Münch, Y. Yang, and W. Schäfer (Eds.): ICSP 2010, LNCS 6195, pp. 369–380, 2010.

from twenty-six countries, participated in the survey. The respondents are product managers. The participating companies received a custom-made benchmark report in which their CCU process is compared to the total respondent base and competitors in the same industry.

The contribution of this research is threefold. First, the state of the practice of the CCU process of international product software vendors is investigated and reported. Second, a benchmark is created for international product software vendors, which gives them a clear insight in their CCU process. Third, three hypotheses are investigated. Section 2 presents the CCU model. Based on this model, CCU processes and practices are defined. In Section 3, the research design is presented, consisting of the hypotheses and research approach. The research approach includes the creation of the survey that is designed to measure the processes and practices defined in Section 2. In Section 4, the raw survey results are presented, including the data for each CCU process. This data enables us to report on the state of the practice of CCU. Section 5 presents our in-depth analysis of the hypotheses and section 6 touches upon validity constraints. Finally, in Section 7 the conclusions are presented and possibilities for future research are discussed.

2 Customer Configuration Updating

The survey presented in this paper, is based on Jansen and Brinkkemper's CCU model, displayed in Figure 1. The CCU model consists of a state diagram of the customer on the right side and the supporting vendor functions on the left. A specific concern for product software vendors is that every vendor has to release, deliver and deploy its product(s) on a wide range of systems, in many variations, and for a wide range of customers [7]. Each of the CCU processes represents several practices. The practices consist of one or more capabilities. A vendors CCU maturity is measured by one question per capability in the survey.

The processes and their practices used in the benchmark survey are defined using the SPICE model for process assessment [8] [6]. The SPICE model defines a process as "a statement of purpose and an essential set of practices that address that purpose". SPICE was used as a tool to help shape the survey and enabled the researchers to take the CCU model and derive practices and capabilities from the processes in a structured matter. The processes are defined as follows:

Release - The release process is made up of four practices. The first practice is release frequency. The capabilities falling under the frequency practice are that a vendor must frequently release major, minor, and bug fix releases and that a vendor must synchronize these releases with customer convenience and demand. The second practice is explicit release planning, which constitutes how releases are planned within the organization. The third practice concerns release scenarios and touches upon aspects such as scenario management and particular policies involved. The final practice is management of (external) components and dependencies. All dependencies between components, be they products that have been built by the vendor or purchased externally, must be managed by creating explicit dependencies between these products and components.

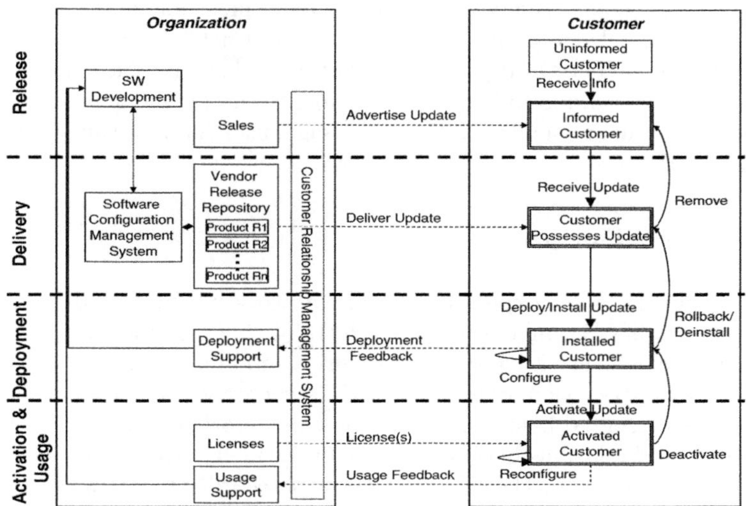

Fig. 1. CCU Model

Delivery - With regards to the delivery process there are two practices to be defined. The first practice prescribes that vendors must use every possible channel for the distribution of products and updates [3]. A vendor conforms to this practice when the product is (for instance) not only available through the commercial website but through physical media as well, such as for instance USB sticks. The more channels the vendor uses to eliminate manual intervention for product and update delivery, the higher its scores are. The second practice states that every possible method for delivery must be applied for knowledge delivery. The knowledge, such as product updates, product news, and customer feedback, should, for instance, be delivered through (semi-) automatic push and pull delivery.

Deployment - There are four practices defined for the deployment process. To begin with, a product must be removable without leaving any remnants of data on a system. Secondly, dependency management should be implemented, consisting of making dependencies explicit, and checking the customer's configuration before product deployment, to foresee and prevent errors. The third deployment practice is that updates and installations must be able to deal with customizations made by customers or third parties. A vendor supports the customization practice when a software architecture is in place that enables customizations. The fourth practice is deployment reliability, which is ensured by capabilities such as validity checks, feedback reports, and externalization of customer specific changes and data [9].

Usage - A vendors usage process is based on three practices. The first is license usage. A vendor must (semi) automatically handle all license requests and distribute licenses. A vendor supports the license practice once customers can explicitly manage their licenses and once licenses are generated automatically when a sales contract is signed. Secondly, vendors must make use of feedback to gain as much knowledge about the product in the field as possible (use usage- and error reports). The third practice is that a vendor must be aware of its payment methods. A vendor sufficiently implements the payment practice when it incorporates payment calculation through usage, user (name), time unit, floating user, lump sum etc.

3 Research Design

In the area of CCU some explorative empirical work has been undertaken in the form of case studies [5] and design research [10] [11] [2]. As the research area matures, surveys can be used to generalize theories and findings from the explorative work. During the execution of the Dutch CCU survey comparable hypotheses were addressed, as presented below [6]. Based on the hypothesis in the Dutch survey, researchers found relations between change in the CCU process and success. Furthermore, vendor views on the CCU process were recorded through the use of open questions. In this research we repeat some of these questions in order to find out if they hold on an international scale. We address the following hypotheses:

H1: Recent changes to the CCU process make the software product more successful. When a software vendor changes its CCU process, it is likely to improve customer experience and reduce the cost of updating per customer. Research shows that Dutch companies *experience* increased product success after adjusting the CCU process [6].

H2: The priority that the vendor gives to the CCU process has significant impact on the success of the software product. It is hypothesized that software vendors who highly prioritize the CCU process dedicate more resources to the CCU process, which should result in a more successful product.

H3: In their estimations for the future with regard to the state of the practice of CCU, product software vendors are looking for update tools that automate the CCU process and are customizable as well. Based on Hall et al. [2], it is hypothesized that the CCU process will evolve towards a more automated and customizable CCU process. At this point update tools are available, but most of them are not generic enough to be adopted by software vendors. Building tools (internally) from scratch, on the other hand, is an expensive and time-consuming process. It is hypothesized that product managers are looking for a tool combining the best of both worlds.

Respondents - Respondents organizational roles and functions matched the following profile: the respondent is a product manager (or someone with a related function who has more than average knowledge of the CCU process) at a product software company and completes the survey with regard to one product in the vendor's portfolio. Furthermore, the product is a software product that is delivered to customers and runs at the customer site. The respondent's derived profile was explained in the invitation letter regarding the survey as well as at the front page of the survey website. Respondents were approached direct, indirect and through domain specific discussion groups. The respondents that were targeted directly were approached through University of California industry connections. These contacts consisted of business partners, alumni, and external student advisors. From these leads, a list of people matching the profile was generated. Potential respondents were invited by email twice. The survey was sent out to over 200 e-mail adresses that were gathered from websites. Also, the survey was posted on a well-visited forum. No questions concerned the way in which the respondent heard about the survey.

Survey tool - The research question and hypotheses stated above are investigated by conducting an online benchmark survey and the analysis of the data resulting from this survey. The survey consists of fifteen sections with four to fourteen questions per section, adding up to a total of ninety-four questions. The survey contained open, yes/no and multiple-choice questions[1].

An online survey tool was chosen because a large number of questions had to be answered. We aimed for more than fifty respondents, which makes interviews and paper surveys inefficient tools to use. The survey was accessible through a website of the University of California, Irvine. After considering a final selection of tools, Net Questionnaires was selected. Net Questionnaires offers the same functions as a lot of other online survey tools but in addition offers support for multiple types of questions and extensive SPSS export functionality. The tool also allows respondents to pause the survey to continue at a later point in time. The ability to pause the survey is convenient for such a lengthy survey. The respondents are also able to browse back and forth through different survey sections to confirm and change earlier answers. The survey was pre-tested by two product software mangers during think aloud sessions, which led to minor changes in use of language and terms. The majority of the questions contained mouse over events that provided the respondents with explanations and examples to clarify question goals. The survey's underlying concepts were tested in five expert interviews. A thinking aloud session with two potential respondents going over the questionnaire resulted in small changes.

4 Results

The results can be downloaded[2]. The majority of the respondents' job functions are closely related to the CCU process (developer, development manager, chief executive or chief operating officer). Most of the participating companies are relatively small: the smaller participant companies are startups or small businesses (one to ten employees). The current market is constantly bombarded with new entrants and these companies are more eager to share their information in an effort to improve their organization. A comparable amount of respondents can be found in the range of fifty up to five hundred employees. The majority

[1] The survey can be downloaded (in pdf format) from the following website: `http://www.ccubenchmark.com`, verified on 15/10/'09.

[2] `http://www.softwareecosystems.org/SCR-2008-051.pdf`, verified on 15/10/'09.

of the respondents produce products that are released in more than one market. Furthermore, most commonly the respondents build products for business productivity or system management.

To date, C++ is the main development technology for the survey respondents. Next to C++, C, Java, Basic and C# are frequently used technologies. 66.7% of the respondents has their headquarters in the United States. The dataset contains companies from 26 different countries. 95% of these companies release their product in the US, compared to 73% in Europe and around 50% in both central and southern America as well as Asia. Moreover, 73% of the companies build their product in the US. Europe and Asia coming (respectively 28 and 14 percent) are also favorable building locations. The US leads with 74%, Europe comes in second place with 24% in regards to the region where intellectual property is registered. The product sizes range from 200 to 2000 KLOC. About half (53%) of the respondents indicate that their products architecture is based on the client-server principle. Almost the same can be said for the products following the stand-alone architecture (49%). Many companies introduce parts of their products as web-based components (33%). To complete the general data overview: 18% of the respondents indicate they use open source components, where 78% do not. This leaves 4% of the company products to be completely open source.

Release - Generally, major product releases are published on a yearly basis. In addition to these yearly major releases, minor releases are made available to the market every three to ten months. Bug fix releases show a different pattern. Some respondents publish these releases (almost) daily, others choose to adapt to a reoccurring monthly schedule. Nine respondents do not use any form of pilot testing before releasing the product or update. The rest use between one and one hundred fifty pilot testers, with a mean of fourteen. Slightly more than half of the product software vendors take customer convenience into account with regard to release time (57%). Less than half of the tested companies use a formalized release planning that contains specific dates for upcoming major, minor and bug fix releases (45%). Of the respondents that actually perform release planning, the largest part publishes its release planning in such a way that all internal and product stakeholders can access the planning at all times (83%). Also, with regard to responding vendors that indicate to use a release planning, more than half of them use a formal publication policy concerning the release planning document, which specifies policy decisions for a specific release (57%). Just more than half of the respondents use a formalized release scenario that describes what happens step by step on a release day (56%). 70% of the companies use tools to support the CCU process. Another aspect related to explicit management of tools is dependency management on third-party components. 69% of the software vendors show that they explicitly manage relations between the products they are selling and the external components that are needed to deliver an executable package. Finally only 38% uses components-of-the-shelf. Half of the vendors release their product when it is most convenient to the customer. More than two thirds of the respondents explicitly manage these relations.

Delivery - When one is dealing with the delivery process in a product software company, choices have to be made regarding the information flows to customers. As it turns out, the majority of companies informs their customers through a website with all relevant information (84%). Sending individual emails is a popular tool as well (81%). Interesting to note here is that only a small portion of the software vendors uses unconventional methods to approach their existing and new customers. Possibilities such as informing the customer through the product (17%), newsletters (9%), general announcement lists (10%) and automatic push of updates and information (8%) are used less frequently. Other approaches are the use of skilled account/sales managers, blogs and user forums. 69% of the software vendors inform their customer between once a week and once every three months. Most of the respondents initiate contact on a monthly basis. The majority of respondents use e-mail as a way for customers to contact them and convey their problems (81%). Almost half of that same group indicates to offer an online bug system for their customers to report problems (46%). 72 companies let their customers manually pull the releases from the vendor servers. 23 let users automatically pull releases from their servers. 18 respondents manually push the product to the customer, where only 10 do the push automatically. 30% of the responding companies use an update tool that updates the product on the customer side. Respondents estimate that, on average, 7.9% of their product installations fail at first attempt.

Deployment - For major releases, respondents indicate that 86% of their customers install the product between one day and three to six months after receiving news of an update. For minor releases, the same conclusion can be drawn. Bugfix releases are generally deployed sooner. 85% of bugfix releases are installed between one day and one month with the highest answer density towards one day. The use of USB sticks is attractive (20%) for software delivery. Another frequently used method is the file transfer protocol (FTP, 30%). In 56% of these software vendors the update tool is able to update the program at runtime. All except one of the companies using an update tool are sure that their tool is still able to deploy the product if the customer implements customizations, extensions and/or customer specific solutions. 56% manage the relations between proprietary and external products. Only 56% separates all data produced by the user (documents, preferences) form the product data (components). Only thirty percent of respondents use an update tool to deploy its product at the customer side, even though on average eight percent of the product installations fail.

Usage - The respondents prefer payment per user (name): 46% of the respondents use this licensing method. Other frequently used methods are pay per usage (35%), lump sum (19%), pay for services (12%) and open source/no payment (12%). Of the companies providing licenses, 17 out of 57 allow the customer to renew, extend or expand the license without action or intervention from the product software vendor side. Exactly half of the respondents offer their customers licenses that expire. In 65 percent of the software vendors the responding company is aware of the way that their customers customize products. 27 of the 78 participating companies send automatic error reports when errors occur during product usage by the customer. From those 27, one does not actually analyze the data fed back through the error reporting system. 31 companies indicate that their products generate usage reports, 25 of them actually analyze these generated results. License management is generally automated.

Other results - Respondents indicate to have made small changes to their CCU process over the last two years (49%). 23% indicates not to have changed anything, 22% has made large changes and 6% has completely re-designed the CCU process. The reasons given most frequently for improving the CCU process, are to serve customers more cost effectively, serve more customers, reduce the number of installation problems and shorten the release cycle. Respondents indicate to have other goals as well, such as simplifying the CCU process, increasing stability of the product, better personal customer service and product quality improvement. The respondents were asked how their product's success had changed over the last two years. Finally, 34 respondents see the CCU process as a (very) high priority process, 35 are indifferent thinking CCU is neither a high or low priority process and 9 respondents think it is a low priority process. The following was derived from some of the open questions:

Deployment failure - According to submitters, future deployment failure will be reduced by introducing testing procedures during the development phase, user acceptance testing, and in depth pre-release code reviews. Submitters agree that more planning, a controlled release process, auto updates, a more robust setup process, and dependency checks should be used.

Custom made and commercially purchased tools - 50% of the respondents see proprietary tools as being adequate. A small group says they would rather have bought a solid commercial build tool to avoid a big part of current problems and have access to support. The problem that is mentioned most often is that of license management. A large group of submitters would like to be able to implement a CRM module accessible by clients.

Evolving CCU process - Most experts believe that better organized firms will make CCU a more central part of their infrastructure and procedures. The only way to make it a more central part is to automate a significant part of the CCU process, which will also involve support automation. Managers think that more commercial tools will become available to support customer release management. Integration between aspects of customer release management such as installation tools, product delivery and customer registration and bug tracking is needed. Others think that there is no magic bullet and no significant changes, since large corporations tend to more tightly control software deployment. These problems will remain issues for as long as tools/environments/systems change. When asking for the best possible solution for CCU the experts indicate that they are looking for a customizable, stable, fully automated updating product with sophisticated configuration options, robust logging and reporting. But, managers are not sure if there is a 'best' solution that is perfect for every single case.

5 Results Analysis

H1: Recent change in the CCU process has significant impact on the *percieved* success of the software product. In order to investigate H1 two specific questions were asked in the survey, being "Please indicate how your CCU process evolved over the last two years" and "Please indicate how your product developed over the last two years". To the first question the respondent could answer on a four point scale ranging from minor changes to a complete process redesign and to the second question the respondent's answer could range from much less successful to much more successful. A cross-tab analysis was conducted with a chi-square test between the variables of change and success (Pearson Chi-Square = 37.7, $p < 0.01$). Figure 2 shows the cross-tab analysis results. The horizontal axis shows the dependent *success* variable and the vertical axis shows the *change* variable. The category: "the product is much less successful" was omitted in the analysis because no respondents chose it. The figure shows increasing percentages towards larger changes in the CCU process combined with the respondents belief of a more successful product as the line in Figure 2 indicates. The software vendors are divided in four main groups in Figure 1. Groups two and three support the hypothesis. Group two contains the software vendors with small to no changes in the CCU process and are "less successful" as well "as as successful as two years ago". Group three contains the software vendors with large and complete redesign changes in the CCU process whose products success increased. The relationships are in line with the hypothesis. Groups one and four do not support the hypothesis. By creating a group division one is able to create a three dimensional table. In addition to these questions, an extra question was asked that explicitly linked the change and success variables. Group two and three were expected to show a higher percentage towards a strong relation between success and changes because these groups implemented large changes that resulted in more success or implemented small or no changes, which resulted in no or less success. The opposite goes for group one and four. *H1 holds,*

3. 4.

			Please indicate how your product developed over the last two years				Total
			The product is much more succesfull than two years ago	The product is more succesfull than two years ago	The product is about as succesfull than two years ago	The product is less succesfull than two years ago	
Please indicate how your CCU process has evolved over the last two years	No Changes	Count	2	4	6	6	18
		Percentage	11,10%	22,20%	33,30%	33,30%	100,00%
	Small improvements (new CM system etc.)	Count	9	12	16	1	38
		Percentage	23,70%	31,60%	42,10%	2,60%	100,00%
	Large improvements (automatic license gen.)	Count	9	7	1	0	17
		Percentage	52,90%	41,20%	5,90%	0,00%	100,00%
	Complete process re-design	Count	5	0	0	0	5
		Percentage	100,00%	0,00%	0,00%	0,00%	100,00%
Total		Count	25	23	23	7	78
		Percentage	32,05%	29,49%	29,49%	8,97%	100,00%

1. 2.

Fig. 2. CCU process change / product success crosstab

with a minor proviso. For this survey, product sales, revenues, and profit were not taken into account due to the diverse nature of respondents. As such, the relationship is a perceived relationship and can not be validated fully.

H2: The priority that the vendor gives to the CCU process has significant impact on the success of the software product. In this hypothesis the relation between the vendor's CCU process priority and its effect on product success is investigated. The same approach as in H1 is adopted. Two question variables, being product success and CCU process priority, were compared in a cross-tab analysis. The chi-square test was conducted (Pearson Chi-Square: 44.5, $p < 0.01$), which proves that there is a relation. Looking at these results it can be concluded that when product software vendors regard their CCU process to be of a (very) high priority, their product success is significantly higher. *H2 holds*, though be it with the same proviso as for *H1*.

H3: In their estimations for the future with regard to the state of the practice of CCU, product software vendors are looking for customizable update tools that automate the CCU process. Based on the results from the open questions we accept the hypothesis. The respondents see automation as the way to further reduce cost per customer. An interesting addition is the mention of web-based solutions by some of the respondents. Where possible, some of the vendors hope to soon release a web based version of their product, such that customers no longer have to bother with deploying a product themselves. *H3 holds.*

Table 1. Relation (success) development and changes in CCU

	Group 1	Group 2	Group 3	Group 4
Success strongly influenced by changes	26%	10%	81%	0%
Success partially influenced by changes	33%	76%	19%	0%
Success not influenced by changes	41%	14%	0%	100%

There are several differences between the Dutch and international respondents. For instance, the number of employees is 120 times bigger on average for international respondents, ten times more end users are served, and products consist of more KLOC. Surprising results are that the number of used programming languages is smaller for international vendors and that Dutch vendors work more efficient with a 1:4 (employee/customer) ratio, over a 1:1.5 ratio for international companies. The Dutch outperform their international colleagues in some areas, such as pre-installation configuration checks.

6 Threats to Validity

The **construct validity** of the research is safeguarded in different ways. The questions in the survey are based upon scientific constructs derived from literature. Respondents were asked to provide data from an existing product. To counteract guessing behavior, each question included the "I don't know" option. Survey heuristics developed by Fowler were applied in detail [12]. Possible problems with regard to understanding the questions were checked through expert interviews and think-aloud sessions.

In regards to **internal validity** The survey respondents were treated anonymously, with regard to each other and could not see input of other participants. Such a participant approach improves the truthfulness and reliability of answers. Furthermore, the respondents were promised to receive an extensive benchmark report including customized advice as incentive to participate in the research. An important threat to H1 is the possible bias of providing social desirable answers. In other words: when a respondent indicates to have made (major) changes to its CCU process over the last two years, it might be more tempted to say that its product was (a lot) more successful after this. There are vendors that indicate to have a product that is less successful even though changes in the CCU process might have been made. These results strengthen our belief that the possible bias is of low risk to the research outcomes.

The challenge of getting respondents to participate in the research was addressed by offering them a customized benchmark report. Commercial resources and contacts through industry and university networks were used to advertise the survey amongst the target audience to gain a large data set to improve **external validity**. After excluding incomplete- and non targeted respondent software vendors from the dataset, seventy-eight software vendors remained.

	International	Dutch
avg # employees	3124	26
avg # customers	1001-5000	51-100
avg # end users	5001 -10000	501-1000
avg # KLOC	501-1000	121-200
avg # programming languages used	1,59	2,57
avg # non english translations	3,68	2,85
avg # developers (FTE)	8,17	7,29
avg product age (years)	7,6	9,8
avg # pilot testers	13,54	5,08

Fig. 3. Dutch/International Comparison

7 Discussion and Conclusions

This paper presents the results of survey research amongst seventy-eight international products software vendors. The survey is based on the CCU model [3]. The survey allows us to compare research results to data from earlier research [6] and generalize conclusions. Results from specific hypotheses show that changes in the CCU process as well as prioritization of the CCU process have a significant positive effect on product success.

The benchmark survey results show that CCU is an underdeveloped area. More attention and better tooling is needed. Investments in the CCU process improve the *perceived* product success, customer service and update and deployment reliability. The realization that almost every CCU process is barely covered and the fact that the majority of the respondents suggest the use of a tool that is currently unavailable to counteract these problems show that CCU is still developing. The significant relation between CCU improvement and product success proves that CCU is a worthy area for further research.

References

1. Carzaniga, A., Fuggetta, A., Hall, R., van der Hoek, A., Heimbigner, D., Wolf, A.: A characterization framework for software deployment technologies (1998)
2. Hall, R.S., Heimbigner, D., Wolf, A.L.: A cooperative approach to support software deployment using the software dock. In: Proceedings of the International Conference on Software Engineering, pp. 174–183 (1999)
3. Jansen, S., Brinkkemper, S., Ballintijn, G.: A process framework and typology for software product updaters. In: Ninth Eur. Conf. on Software Maintenance and Reengineering, pp. 265–274. IEEE, Los Angeles (2005)
4. Brinkkemper, S., Xu, L.: Concepts for product software. European Journal of Information Systems 16, 531–541
5. Jansen, S., Ballintijn, G., Brinkkemper, S., van Nieuwland, A.: Integrated development and maintenance for the release, delivery, deployment, and customization of product software: a case study in mass-market ERP software. Journal of Software Maintenance and Evolution: Research and Practice 18, 133–151 (2006)
6. Jansen, S., Brinkkemper, S., Helms, R.: Benchmarking the Customer Configuration Updating Practices of Product Software Vendors, 82–91 (2008)
7. van der Schuur, H., Jansen, S., Brinkkemper, S.: Becoming Responsive to Service Usage and Performance Changes by Applying Service Feedback Metrics to Software Maintenance. In: Proceedings of the 4th Intl. ERCIM Workshop on Software Evolution and Evolvability, pp. 53–62 (2008)
8. Joint Technical Subcommittee between ISO (International Organization for Standardization) and IEC (International Electrotechnical Commission), Iso/iec 15504, a.k.a. spice (software process improvement and capability determination)
9. Dolstra, E.: Integrating software construction and software deployment. In: Westfechtel, B., van der Hoek, A. (eds.) SCM 2001 and SCM 2003. LNCS, vol. 2649, pp. 102–117. Springer, Heidelberg (2003)
10. Dolstra, E., Visser, E., de Jonge, M.: Imposing a memory management discipline on software deployment. In: Proceedings of the International Conference on Software Engineering. IEEE, Los Alamitos (2004)
11. Jansen, S.: Pheme: An infrastructure to enable any type of communication between a software vendor and an end-user . In: Proceedings of the International Conference on Software Maintenance 2007, tool demonstration (2007)
12. Fowler, J.F.J.: Improving survey questions: Design and evaluation. Sage, Thousand Oaks (1995)

Author Index

GPSR Compliance

The European Union's (EU) General Product Safety Regulation (GPSR) is a set of rules that requires consumer products to be safe and our obligations to ensure this.

If you have any concerns about our products, you can contact us on ProductSafety@springernature.com

In case Publisher is established outside the EU, the EU authorized representative is:

Springer Nature Customer Service Center GmbH
Europaplatz 3
69115 Heidelberg, Germany

Batch number: 09478804

Printed by Printforce, the Netherlands